T0304362

'nother great textbook by Paul Burns. The revised ⸻ the 'namic world of entrepreneurial behaviour, with well thought-out contemporary case ⸻udies and pedagogy alongside a progressive structure throughout. The text is cleverly ⸻ositioned for both undergraduates and postgraduates, offering a broad appeal to all.'
—**Kevin Blanchard,** *University of Lincoln, UK*

'⸻aul Burns gracefully connects the deep theoretical foundations of corporate entrepreneur-⸻hip with the existential yet clear and present challenges that corporations face every day. Lively ⸻iscussions of contemporary issues in the domain are supported by relevant and high value-⸻dded figures, tables, lists, and, perhaps most importantly, case insights that help crystallize the ⸻pics discussed. Overall, the book is both robust and fresh. I am genuinely excited about using ⸻is textbook in both my undergraduate and graduate corporate entrepreneurship courses.'
—**Nesij Huvaj,** *Suffolk University, USA*

'⸻m a real advocate of this textbook and am delighted that there is a new edition! I have ⸻egularly used the previous version with Executive MBA and final year undergraduate ⸻ntrepreneurship and innovation students. The case studies and group discussions are par-⸻icularly helpful for bringing theoretical frameworks alive. The jewel in the crown, for me, ⸻s the Corporate Entrepreneurship Audit tool!'
—**Karen Bill,** *University of Worcester, UK*

'⸻ up-to-date textbook that helps lecturers flip their classrooms into action-oriented ⸻aunchpads for experiential innovations. The exciting way in which Professor Burns inte-⸻rates organizational, strategic, cultural and corporate governance theories with cases, ⸻eflections and activities from around the world makes this book a dynamic and effective ⸻esource for lecturers and students of corporate entrepreneurship.'
—**Mayank Kumar Golpelwar,**
City University of Applied Sciences (Bremen), Germany

'The new edition of *Corporate Entrepreneurship and Innovation* builds upon an already solid textbook and takes it to the next level. Professor Burns' textbook teaches the hows and whys of corporate entrepreneurship at a level undergraduate students can understand. The updated case studies about companies worldwide not only highlight important concepts using an international lens but will engage my students in lively classroom discussions. Kudos to Professor Burns for giving students an edge as they become corporate entrepreneurs.'
—**Jay Azriel,** *York College of Pennsylvania, USA*

'*Corporate Entrepreneurship and Innovation* is a thorough guide to business development and innovation in contemporary business. Indispensable for entrepreneurship students and practi-tioners in developing their knowledge in this field, it is also a vital tool for educators in providing a structured approach to learning about contemporary matters in entrepreneurship.'
—**Robert Bowen,** *Swansea University, UK*

'This book provides distinct insights into the development of the entrepreneurial mindset. The use of various learning resources provides an effective balance between knowing how and knowing why. I applaud the author especially for the case insights which cover a broad range of sectors and countries, both developed and developing. I recommend this book to both undergraduates and postgraduates.'
—**Juliet Puchert,** *University of Fort Hare, South Africa*

'This is a detailed, in-depth, accessible and wide ranging book that deserves to hold pride of place in any comprehensive library of entrepreneurship theory and practice. Burns' latest edition is carefully organized to take the reader effortlessly and elegantly from "knowing how" to "knowing-why". The wide range of varied but seamlessly integrated elements provides inspiration, provokes curiosity, and involves both group and individual opportunities for deep and effective learning. Burns robustly answers the challenge of how to create entrepreneurial transformation in larger organizations.'

—Joanna Berry, *Durham University, UK*

'*Corporate Entrepreneurship and Innovation* is a very comprehensive textbook with updated cases from both developed and emerging economies, and from both traditional and new industries. It can also serve as a nice reference book for practitioners and researchers.'

—Xufei Ma, *City University of Hong Kong, Hong Kong*

'Detailed textbooks on corporate entrepreneurship and innovation are hard to find. Professor Burns presents a thorough treatise in this new edition that is comprehensive, informative and accessible. The latest edition of this well-established book should benefit anyone interested in making organizations more entrepreneurial and innovative.'

—Mathew Hughes, *Loughborough University, UK*

'One of my favourite aspects of Paul Burns' new edition of *Corporate Entrepreneurship and Innovation* is the "Index of case insights", which not only offers a big picture about real world corporate entrepreneurship and innovation but also organizes various topics, sectors and countries in a unique way.'

—Vincent Chang, *China Europe International Business School, China*

'This textbook covers not only the latest insights into corporate entrepreneurship but also draws on case studies from organizations all over the globe in order to develop a cross-cultural understanding of entrepreneurship. Links to psychometric testing and practical information are an added bonus. This new edition is the best yet. Paul Burns has created a must-read textbook for the entrepreneurs and intrapreneurs of the future.'

—Bert Meeuwsen, *Wittenborg University of Applied Sciences, the Netherlands*

'This new edition has a greater focus on innovation and enhanced coverage of corporate entrepreneurship. Featuring case studies of high-profile companies from around the globe, this book provides excellent insights into contemporary theory and practice in corporate entrepreneurship and innovation.'

—Catherine Wang, *Brunel University London, UK*

'Paul Burns' *Corporate Entrepreneurship and Innovation* is one of the best textbooks to help students comprehend the fundamental pillars of contemporary entrepreneurialism from the eyes of corporations. The book actively facilitates the learning process by encouraging students to connect theory to practice by dint of a great deal of lively case insights from well-known enterprises in all parts of the world.'

—Celal Cahit Agar, *University of St Andrews, UK*

PAUL BURNS

CORPORATE ENTREPRENEURSHIP AND INNOVATION

fourth edition

BLOOMSBURY ACADEMIC
LONDON • NEW YORK • OXFORD • NEW DELHI • SYDNEY

BLOOMSBURY ACADEMIC
Bloomsbury Publishing Plc
50 Bedford Square, London, WC1B 3DP, UK
1385 Broadway, New York, NY 10018, USA
29 Earlsfort Terrace, Dublin 2, Ireland

BLOOMSBURY, BLOOMSBURY ACADEMIC and the Diana logo
are trademarks of Bloomsbury Publishing Plc

This edition published in 2020 by RED GLOBE PRESS
Previous editions printed under the imprint PALGRAVE
Reprinted by Bloomsbury Academic, 2022, 2024

Bloomsbury Publishing Plc does not have any control over, or responsibility for,
any third-party websites referred to or in this book. All internet addresses given
in this book were correct at the time of going to press. The author and publisher
regret any inconvenience caused if addresses have changed or sites have
ceased to exist, but can accept no responsibility for any such changes.

A catalogue record for this book is available from the British Library.

A catalogue record for this book is available from the Library of Congress.

ISBN: PB: 978-1-3520-0879-1
ePDF: 978-1-3520-0880-7
ePub: 978-1-3503-0488-8

Printed and bound in Great Britain

To find out more about our authors and books visit
www.bloomsbury.com and sign up for our newsletters.

To Jean - my love and inspiration
And my boys: Alex, Ben and Oli - my hope for the future

Brief contents

Brief contents

Contents

Contents

7. Managing the entrepreneurial organization   175

8. Managing risk in the entrepreneurial organization   203

Part III: Encouraging the entrepreneurial mindset   227

Contents

List of Figures and Tables

LIST OF FIGURES

LIST OF TABLES

ndex of case insights

About the Author

Paul Burns is Emeritus Professor of Entrepreneurship at the University of Bedfordshire Business School, UK. He has been Pro Vice Chancellor and for 10 years was Dean of the Business School, stepping down in 2011. Over his 40-year career he has been an academic, an accountant and an entrepreneur – giving him unrivalled academic and practical insight into the entrepreneurial process. As well as launching and running his own business, he has helped develop hundreds of business plans and has worked with entrepreneurs, small firms and their advisors, helping launch successful businesses.

For ten years, he was Professor of Small Business Development at Cranfield School of Management, UK, where, in 1983, he launched the Graduate Enterprise Programme in England, which was offered at dozens of universities. He started his academic career at Warwick University Business School, UK, where he set up their first Small Business Unit. For eight years he was Director of 3i European Enterprise Research Centre researching small firms and entrepreneurs across Europe. He has been a Visiting Fellow at Harvard Business School, USA and for three years was Visiting Professor at the Open University Business School, UK, where he developed the multimedia Small Business Programme which was screened on BBC2. He is a Fellow and a former President of the Institute for Small Business and Entrepreneurship (ISBE).

Paul qualified as a Chartered Accountant with Arthur Andersen & Co., where he worked with many growing businesses. He launched and ran his own business, Design for Learning Ltd., advising and training on entrepreneurship and growing firms where he worked with organizations such as the accounting firms Grant Thornton and BDO Stoy Hayward, venture capitalists 3i, and banks such as the Royal Bank of Scotland, Barclays and Lloyds. He has advised and consulted at various levels of government in the United Kingdom and overseas, and Margaret Thatcher wrote the foreword to one of his books, *Entrepreneur: Eight British success stories of the eighties* (MacMillan, 1988). He has authored dozens of books and hundreds of journal articles and research reports.

Also written by the same author and published by Red Globe Press:
Entrepreneurship and Small Business: Start-up, Growth and Maturity, 4th edn, 2016 (new edition coming in 2021!)

This textbook was first published in 2001. The third edition became the market-leading entrepreneurship textbook in the United Kingdom, praised for its 'authoritative blend of theory and practice', described as a 'joy to read' and as 'indispensable for any student of entrepreneurship'. The fourth edition features case studies from around the world, from Oman to Australia, as well as a range of multimedia content, including video case studies. It is described as 'one of the most comprehensive books in the area of entrepreneurship' – a 'masterpiece', 'highly engaging' and 'an exceptional treatise'. A new edition is due to be published in 2022.

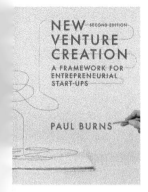

New Venture Creation: A Framework for Entrepreneurial Start-ups, **2nd edn, 2018**
This textbook was first published in 2014. Based on its own *New Venture Creation Framework* including a comprehensive set of online, interactive learning aids, it helps students through the whole process of new venture creation, including finding a business idea, developing a value proposition for customers and refining a business model that can be developed into a professional business plan. The first edition was praised as 'the go-to-guide when it comes to new venture creation' that is 'bound to ensure that this book becomes a core text for new venture creation modules'. The book is described as 'covering all the parts of the venture creation process without resorting to shortcuts' and a '*tour de force*' as well as being 'another gem from Paul Burns'.

Preface to the fourth edition

WHAT THE BOOK AIMS TO DO AND HOW IT HAS CHANGED

Large companies are waking up to the challenge of the increasing pace of change in market and the competitive challenge of small, entrepreneurial firms. Entrepreneurship and innovation are at the core of wealth creation and continuous innovation – both incremental and radical – is increasingly seen as essential to maintain competitive advantage both for companies and for nations as a whole. Innovation may be risky, but no innovation is riskier still And there are still lessons to be learned from the entrepreneurial approach, which can spot commercial opportunity, create innovation and bring it to the market quickly and effectively with minimal risk.

When the first edition of this book was published in 2005, large businesses were losing the battle against their smaller, more nimble adversaries. When published, this was one of only three books on the topic; indeed, when I started writing it three years earlier there were none. So there was no blueprint for how to approach the challenge of creating entrepreneurial transformation in larger organizations. But the approach I adopted then – analysing how entrepreneurs operate, what makes them tick and trying to systematically replicate that within an organizational framework – carries through into this fourth edition. I am pleased to say that there is now more research based on this approach. In this edition I have tried to take this approach a step further by looking at cognitive theory and how that might explain how the entrepreneurial mindset is developed and how it differs from that of other people – influencing their approach to creativity, decision-making, risk and management more generally.

What has changed over time is that the techniques employed by entrepreneurs to explore innovative opportunities have become more systematized with the development of a whole raft of 'lean start-up' methodologies. The realization that strategies must quickly change to suit changing circumstances has led to the acceptance of the concept of continuous 'strategizing' and less formal approaches to business model development throughout the concept development stage of innovations. My approach to the issue of managing the risk associated with innovation has changed. The more quantitative approach appropriate for incremental innovations is now contrasted to a more nuanced, knowledge-based and incremental approach for radical innovations. And the importance of risk management, in terms of creating sustainable shareholder value, is given more emphasis. The techniques and approaches outlined in the book are now increasingly being practised by the most innovative companies. This edition has more examples of good practice – and increasingly not just from the United States. Of the 70 Case insights, only 29 are from the United States. The rest are from around the world, from China to India, the UK to Denmark, the UAE to Oman.

WHO THE BOOK IS AIMED AT

The book is aimed at undergraduate and postgraduate courses in corporate entrepreneurship and/or innovation. Because of the Corporate Entrepreneurship Audit tool available on the companion website, it is particularly valuable to students with work experience or on part-time programmes (such as MBAs), who can apply many of the theories and techniques in the workplace. The book takes an organizational design approach to the challenge of innovation, bringing together entrepreneurial techniques and looking at their implementation within the context of a large organization. Whilst entrepreneurship is about self-development, corporate entrepreneurship is about organizational development.

Other books by the same author include:

New Venture Creation: A Framework for Entrepreneurial Start-ups (2nd edition, 2018)
Entrepreneurship and Small Business: Start-up, Growth and Maturity (4th edition, 2016)

LEARNING STYLE

Each chapter starts with clear learning outcomes that identify the key concepts to be covered and the key knowledge and skills that are gained by reading the chapter and undertaking the activities. At the end of each chapter there is a summary that provides an overview of the main points covered.

There are a number of learning resources in the book and its companion website (www.macmillanihe.com/Burns-CEI) that are designed to help students navigate the wheel of learning, as shown in Figure A, (explained in Chapter 2), taking them from 'knowing-how' to 'knowing-why'. During half of the cycle students test and experiment with the theories and concepts that they are introduced to and observe what happens through concrete experience – learning 'know-how'. In the second half of the cycle, they reflect on the observations and concepts, perhaps challenging them or forming new concepts of their own – learning 'know-why'. This is often called 'double-loop learning' – the best sort of learning which links knowing how with knowing why,

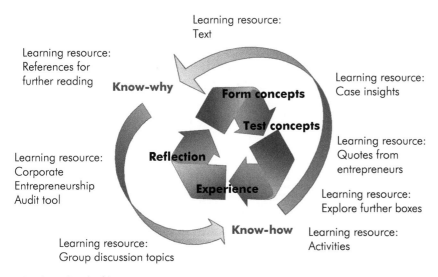

Figure A The wheel of learning

linking theory with practice. So effective learning involves forming concepts, testing concepts, experience and reflection. Arguably, traditional education has focused too much on the teaching of concepts and theories – and it is difficult to break away from this in a textbook – however, the book has additional learning resources that allow students to navigate the wheel of learning. These are in the book itself and on the companion website, with additional resources being signposted throughout both.

Case insights

Embedded in the chapters are 70 Case insights that highlight good and bad practice, each with questions, designed to make students think about and apply the concepts being explained and discussed in that chapter. This is the testing stage of the wheel of learning. Many case studies have links to related videos that can be accessed via the companion website. Case notes are available in the Instructor's Manual on the password-protected part of the companion website.

Quotes from entrepreneurs

Spread throughout this book are quotes from entrepreneurs around the world. They are designed to illustrate and reinforce the theoretical points being made in the text with practical opinions from the real world – there is nothing like an endorsement from an entrepreneur. This is the experience element of the wheel of learning.

Explore further boxes

These boxes direct students to various online resources, including assessment tools and psychometric tests, that will help them better understand the material discussed in the text.

Activities

Activities involve doing something, often further research or web-based tests or activities. This is the testing and experimenting phase of the cycle.

Group discussion topics

Each chapter has topics for group discussion or essay writing. These can be used as a basis for tutorials. They are designed to make students think about and reflect on the text material and develop their critical and reflective understanding of it and what it means in the real world. The summary and discussion topics help students discriminate between main and supporting points and provide mechanisms for self-teaching.

References for further reading

Each chapter has full journal and book references to encourage reflection on the topics in the text.

Corporate Entrepreneurship Audit tool

The final chapter outlines a Corporate Entrepreneurship Audit tool – a questionnaire that allows students to assess the entrepreneurial orientation of an organization and the 'fit' with the commercial environment it faces. This can be used to get students to apply the theories and concepts in the book to a real company. In using the tool, students must exercise their dgement and this should help them better understand the complexity of the concepts. For art-time students, it can be applied to the organization where they work. With appropriate uidance, the Audit can be used by the instructor as an assessment for the course. Both a aper version and an interactive version can be downloaded from the companion website.

COMPANION WEBSITE

ww.macmillanihe.com/Burns-CEI

Student resources on the companion website

tudents who purchase this book have access to a range of additional learning resources, ncluding:

➡ Video commentaries by the author in addition to *Case insight* video links, *Theory explored* video links and *Examples of practice* video links.
➡ Corporate Entrepreneurship Audit tool – paper and interactive versions of the tool that matches the entrepreneurial orientation of an organization against the commercial environment that it faces.
➡ Leadership Style Questionnaire – a self-assessment questionnaire that allows students to assess their own leadership style.
➡ Interactive chapter quizzes.
➡ Links to psychometric and other tests online.
➡ New Venture Creation Framework.
➡ Flashcard glossary.

Instructor resources on the companion website

As an instructor who has adopted this book for your course you have access to a password-protected Instructor's Manual to help plan and deliver your teaching. This contains chapter-by-chapter:

➡ Powerpoint slides;
➡ Teaching notes;
➡ Case insight notes;
➡ Web links to videos and other resources;
➡ Additional cases.

LEARNING OUTCOMES

On completing the course based on this book a student should be able to:

➡ Research and critically evaluate the entrepreneurial architecture of an organization and analyze how any deficiencies might be addressed;
➡ Describe the nature of entrepreneurship in individuals – character traits and approaches to business and management – and reflect their own entrepreneurial qualities;
➡ Describe the process of creativity and innovation, critically evaluate and reflect on their own aptitude to be creative and innovative and explain how creativity might be encouraged in others and in themselves;

➡ Critically analyze what is required to be an effective leader in different contexts;
➡ Critically analyze the culture and organizational structure of an organization in different contexts;
➡ Be able to develop entrepreneurial strategies that encourage growth and innovation in different contexts.

Students should also have developed cognitive skills in the following areas:

➡ Data and information interpretation, critical analysis and evaluation;
➡ Problem identification and solving skills;
➡ ICT skills, in particular the use of the internet;
➡ The ability to use research and link theory with practice;
➡ Independent and/or team-working skills;
➡ Writing and presentation skills.

The ability to work independently and entrepreneurially are key employability skills. On completing a course based on this book, students should have enhanced these skills. Entrepreneurship involves being creative and innovative and being able to spot commercial opportunities. A course based on this book shows how these skills can be operationalized within a larger organization.

Acknowledgements

I would like to thank all those who have helped me with this book, including students and staff who inspired me to write it. Particular thanks go to Isabelle Cheng and Peter Atkinson at Red Globe Press and the anonymous reviewers from around the world for their pertinent comments and suggestions. My thanks to Dr. Tahseen Arshi at the American University of Ras Al Khaimah (AURAK), UAE for the insight into this topic that he has provided over the years and permission to use his Case insight, Suhail Bhawan Group. Thanks to Crispin Reed for the anonymized data he provided that allowed me to construct Figure 13.2. I would also like to thank my wife, Dr. Jean Burns, who helps me with all my books, providing inspiration and insights but also for permission to use her Case insight, The London School. She always insists that I write in plain English and avoid jargon as much as possible.

Guided tour of the book

Learning outcomes

Every chapter begins with a number of learning outcomes, which highlight some of the key insights you should take away from reading each chapter.

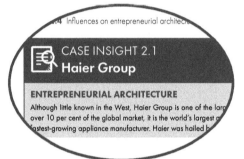

Case insights

The case studies in every chapter highlight good and bad examples of corporate entrepreneurship, and are all followed by questions designed to make you think about and apply the concepts being explained and discussed in that chapter.

Quotes

Spread throughout the book are quotes from entrepreneurs from around the world. They are designed to illustrate and reinforce the theoretical points being made in the text with practical opinions from the real world.

Explore further

These boxes direct you to various online resources, including assessment tools and psychometric tests, that will help you better understand the material discussed in the text.

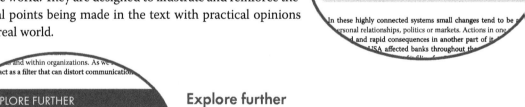

On-page glossary

An in-margin glossary provides succinct definitions of key terms, which are also highlighted in blue in the main body of text. A full glossary is also included at the back of the book.

hapter summaries

ey themes from each chapter are summarized at the end and can be
sed as a checklist to ensure that you have taken away the main
ssons in the text.

SUMMARY
- Innovation can take different forms: product; process and/or market inn
  is about doing things differently. Although scale of innovation is importan
  equally be gained by frequent, incremental innovations – a strategy that is
  majority of commercially significant innovations have come. Scale and fre
  with speed to market to produce competitive advantage.
- Invention is the extreme and riskiest form of innovation. Much early-sta
  public sector. But inventors and governments are not necessarily entre
  help of an entrepreneur or an entrepreneurial organisation to link th
  they, in turn, need the backing of financial institutions.
- Business model innovation is about developing innovative pla
  break from the dominant logic of a sector. This can lead t
  one existed before.

resources and markets is important. Sm
roducing radical, disruptive innovations. They seem to
although they tend to do this in sectors where resources are les

GROUP DISCUSSION QUESTIONS
1. What does innovation mean? Give some examples.
2. How can innovation be measured? Explain how it might be undertaken.
3. **What are the differences between creativity, invention and innovation? Wh**
   concepts and entrepreneurship?
4. Which countries are most associated with innovation? Why do you think t
5. Is there a 'best' type of innovation?
6. How do you evaluate the commercial potential of a radical innovation?
7. How do you evaluate the commercial potential of a project that invol
   models that work well?
8. What are the risks associated with innovation?
   What are the risks associated with market paradigm shif

Group discussion topics

At the end of each chapter is a list of topics for group discussion or
essay writing. These are designed to make you think about and
reflect on the text and develop your critical and reflective understanding of it and what it means for the real world.

Activities

Suggested activities at the end of each chapter encourage you to
do further research related to the content of the chapter, or to take
web-based tests or activities that will help develop your knowledge and skills further.

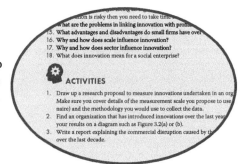

tion is risky then you need to take time
What are the problems in linking innovation with profi
15. **What advantages and disadvantages do small firms have over**
16. **Why and how does scale influence innovation?**
17. **Why and how does sector influence innovation?**
18. What does innovation mean for a social enterprise?

ACTIVITIES
1. Draw up a research proposal to measure innovations undertaken in an org
   Make sure you cover details of the measurement scale you propose to use
   naire) and the methodology you would use to collect the data.
2. Find an organization that has introduced innovations over the last year
   your results on a diagram such as Figure 3.2(a) or (b).
3. Write a report explaining the commercial disruption caused by th
   over the last decade.

are very price-competitive.
here is heavy expenditure on marketing within the in
20. There are many mergers and takeovers in the industry.
21. New markets are emerging continually.
22. The product/service portfolio is unbalanced.
23. Suppliers exert a great deal of power.
24. Good managers and staff are difficult to attract.
25. Developments in the industry depend very much on knowledge and inf

CORPORATE ENTREPRENEURSHIP AUDIT

The Corporate Entrepreneurship Audit (CEA) offers a structured, research
to assessing the entrepreneurial orientation of organizational architec
tool can be applied to any level of organization – the organizatio

Corporate Entrepreneurship Audit

The final chapter provides a Corporate Entrepreneurship Audit
tool – a questionnaire that allows you to assess the entrepreneurial
orientation of an organization and the 'fit' with the commercial
environment it faces. This will enable you to apply the theories and
concepts in the book to a real company. A paper and an interactive
version of the Audit are available on the companion website.

Tables and Figures

Tables and Figures throughout provide visual support to topics
covered in the body of the text and help to elucidate key concepts
and ideas.

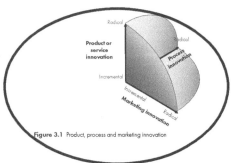

Figure 3.1 Product, process and marketing innovation

1 Introduction: Entrepreneurship – thriving in chaos

CONTENTS

- The new age of change and uncertainty
- The challenge of entrepreneurship
- Can big companies survive?
- Implications for big companies
- The entrepreneurial mindset
- Complexity theory and managing in chaos
- Summary
- Group discussion topics
- Activities
- References

CASE INSIGHTS

1.1   Jack Ma and Alibaba
1.2   Kiran Mazumdar-Shaw and Biocon
1.3   Jim Ratcliffe and Ineos
1.4   Steve Jobs and Apple (1)

Learning outcomes

When you have read this chapter and undertaken the related activities you will be able to:

➥ Critically analyze the impact of the rapidly changing environment and global connectivity on larger companies;

➥ Explain the role and importance of entrepreneurship in modern society and, in particular, its link with innovation;

- Critically analyze the problems large firms have in coping with this and the advantages enjoyed by small, more entrepreneurial firms;
- Explain why firms become more bureaucratic as they become old and larger and the implications for management and shareholder value;
- Understand the character traits and managerial characteristics of an entrepreneur and explain their importance in helping an organization manage in a changing, uncertain environment;
- Understand the relevance of complexity theory to this.

THE NEW AGE OF CHANGE AND UNCERTAINTY

Change – continuous and unpredictable, often turbulent and disruptive – has so far characterized the twenty-first century. Furthermore, the pace of change has accelerated, making it increasingly difficult to predict and manage. The idea that change has become endemic continuous and, above all, unpredictable, sometimes resulting in discontinuous or revolutionary shifts that can create chaos, has powerful implications for us all, but it is nothing new. The ancient Chinese saw change as endless and an essential feature of our universe – a pattern of cyclical coming and going, growth and decay, winter and summer, the yin of night and yang of day. Somehow the West had forgotten this, believing instead that we could create stability and certainty, that change was a series of discrete events that moved us from one stable state to another. Economists based theories on it. And economists, politicians and managers focused on the ways that change could be controlled and managed in a systematic way, turning to rational techniques of long-term planning and tight control systems.

> **"** As Darwin well understood, it is the species most responsive to change that is the best equipped for survival. **"**
>
> Luke Johnson, Chairman Risk Capital Partners, *The Sunday Times*, 21 May 2017

But where has this got us? The twenty-first century has seen the world in political turmoil. The US economy seems to have lost its dynamism, with current start-up activity half that of the previous generation and in sustained decline for the last 40 years (Economic Innovation Group, 2017). In contrast, China is experiencing unprecedented growth in non-state-owned (but often still state-linked) enterprise, with government calling for 'mass entrepreneurship and innovation'. It is moving from a dependence on the innovativeness of others to driving innovation itself. Economic power has shifted from West to East, in particular from the USA to China – and trade wars have started. Real wars have also flared across the Middle East and military tensions are high. Uncontrollable migration has characterized much of the turbulence and there has been a political backlash. Right-wing political parties have become more popular across the world and in 2016 both the UK vote to leave the European Union and the election of Donald Trump in the USA demonstrated a mistrust of the established order and echoed a cry to 'take back control', although, even if this is possible, by whom, from whom and to what purpose is less clear. The global banking crisis of 2008 saw the failure of a number of banks such as Lehman Brothers and Citigroup in the USA and the Royal Bank of Scotland (RBS) in the United Kingdom. It plunged the Western world into recession, robbing millions of their jobs, savings and homes. It caused disposable income in many countries to shrink, particularly amongst the poorest and most vulnerable, leading to greater income and wealth inequality and causing even more political unrest. By 2015, the world's richest 1 per cent owned more wealth than all the other 99 per cent put together (Hardoon et al., 2016).

Alongside this, we have seen unprecedented volatility in just about every market, from commodities to exchange rates, from stock markets to bond markets. Corporate scandals have dominated the headlines. Many internet giants stand accused of avoiding or at least evading tax and using tax havens to hoard cash. Companies like Alphabet (owners of Google and YouTube), Apple, Facebook and Amazon have been accused of stifling competition and wielding excessive monopoly power because they are able to dominate markets. The European Commission fined Google €2.4 billion in 2017 for abusing its market dominance as a search engine by giving illegal advantage to its own comparison shopping service, Google Shopping, whilst demoting the results of rival sites.

More worrying still is the question of how these internet companies use the data they have on customers for commercial and political purposes. Facebook has used the data they harvest to good effect to target precise customer segments with particular demographics. Facebook sells this targeting advertising facility to anybody who is willing to buy it and 99 per cent of its $10.3 billion turnover is derived from advertising. It can also deliver advertisements via a process of online auctions, which happen in real time whenever you click on a website. This is possible because just about every website you visit now plants a cookie on your web browser, meaning that when you go to a new website an instantaneous auction for the ads you see takes place. But these data can also be used for political rather than commercial purposes and, whilst in the USA attention has focused on Facebook, in China, where the internet is dominated by three giants – Alibaba, Baidu and Tencent – all three have close links to government and already accept state intervention and control. Indeed, China's sweeping new cybersecurity laws require all internet cloud services operating in China, such as those offered by Apple, to hold their data and encryption codes inside China's borders, making them accessible to the Chinese government.

Corporate scandals have a long history, affecting most advanced industrialized economies: for example, Enron (2001), WorldCom (2002), Freddie Mac (2003) and Bernie Madoff (2008) in the USA, Parmalat in Italy (2004), Saytam in India (2009), and Olympus in Japan (2013). You can add to these scandals those involving environmental issues such as BP and Deep Water Horizon (2010) and Volkswagen in Germany (2016). Companies fail all the time, but large corporate crashes have led to spectacular losses for creditors; for example, Eastman Kodak (2012) and Dynergy (2012) in the USA, OW Bunker A/S in Denmark (2014), British Home Stores (2016) and Carillion (2018) in the UK. And yet at the same time the salaries of the CEOs of the world's largest corporations continue to increase at rates well beyond those of other employees – symptomatic of increasing income inequality in most Western countries. The pay ratio between the CEO and the salary for the average employee in the largest 350 US companies rose from 10:1 between 1965 and 1978 to 240:1 between 1978 and 2016. In 2015, for example, Apple's CEO Tim Cook enjoyed pay of $9.2 million – a ratio of over 250:1. All these issues lead people to question corporate ethics.

monopoly The exclusive possession or control of the supply of or trade in a commodity or service by a company or group of companies

customers Those people who buy your product/service

> *We now stand on the threshold of a new age – the age of revolution. In our minds, we know the new age has already arrived: in our bellies, we're not sure we like it. For we know it is going to be an age of upheaval, of tumult, of fortunes made and unmade at head-snapping speed. For change has changed. No longer is it additive. No longer does it move in a straight line. In the twenty first century, change is discontinuous, abrupt, seditious.*
>
> Gary Hamel, 'Bringing Silicon Valley Inside', *Harvard Business Review*, September 2000

Underpinning this volatility is the development of globalization and global connectivity an increasingly complex world full of interconnections formed by a truly global marketplace linked by new technologies that allow instant communication with almost anywhere. We all know what others are doing – instantly. Social media is replacing mass media as the most effective means of communication. Media like Twitter and Facebook are providing 'echo chambers' for people with like-minded views, reinforcing both their political and commercial perceptions of the world to the point where commentators question whether we are now living in a 'post-truth' society with 'fake news' read by more people than 'real news'. It has been estimated that up to 70 per cent of people in the USA now get their 'news' exclusively from these sources and nobody really knows whether they can be trusted. Little wonder that the boundaries between 'truth' and 'lie', 'fact' and 'fiction' are becoming increasingly blurred.

social networks and media
Communication hosted on the internet or on smartphones, such as texting, tweeting or blogging, includes social networking sites such as Facebook, Twitter and YouTube

echo chambers
A metaphor describing a situation where beliefs are amplified or reinforced by communication and repetition inside a closed system such as news or social media

> We're living through the most profound transformation in our information environment since Johannes Guttenberg's invention of the printing press in circa 1439. And the problem with living through a revolution is that it is impossible to take the long view of what's happening. **"**
>
> John Naughton, *The Observer: The New Review*, 20 January 2019

In these highly connected systems small changes tend to be amplified – whether in interpersonal relationships, politics or markets. Actions in one part of the world can have unexpected and rapid consequences in another part of it. The 2008 collapse of Lehman Brothers in the USA affected banks throughout the world and triggered a major global financial crisis within hours of it filing for Chapter 11 bankruptcy. Little wonder, again, that control and use of these connections and these data can yield political or market dominance. These are issues that affect both democracy and markets. They go to the fundamentals of a free society and a free market. Knowledge and information may be power, but when distorted that power can be used for nefarious purposes. The internet giants, once lauded for their innovation and openness, are now being criticized for their aggressive use of monopoly and oligopoly power – to distort markets, magnify their profits, avoid taxes and even influence politics.

bankruptcy When you are unable to pay your debts and a court order is obtained by creditors to have your affairs placed in the hands of an official receiver

oligopoly A market or industry dominated by a small number of large sellers

This new globalization has meant that no business is safe from the chill winds of competition, a wind that is unforgiving of frailty and no respecter of past reputations. Commercial opportunities remain, but competition is now as much about survival as growth. There may be ample opportunities but they only go to those who can spot them first, are swift to adapt and are open and willing to change. Sometimes these opportunities break down established industry barriers and create new and unexpected sources of competition. The internet has caused disruption, generating as many threats as opportunities. It has led to an enormous growth in home shopping and deliveries and caused many high street retailers to radically reappraise their customer offerings. It will probably lead to high streets looking very different in the future. It has caused the music, video and print media industries to reappraise how their products are distributed.

To add to these problems, many sectors of the global economy are facing profound structural change. Take the oil and gas sector, where companies continue to invest some

700 billion a year in extracting and refining fossil fuels, with 40 per cent of it going to fuel vehicles. Oil exploration has a 25 year or longer investment horizon, but how will vehicles be powered in 25 years' time? The vehicle industry itself is changing, with the advent of electric cars and autonomous driving systems. Will demand still exist in 25 years' time or will autonomous driving electric taxis or hire vehicles have taken over?

Many established big-company sectors are seeing increasing concentration and consolidation as there is a focus on short-term profit generation by creating monopolies or oligopolies for their existing products and services rather than seeking to innovate. Uncertainty makes companies risk-averse and can lead to investment paralysis. Despite this, as global competition continues to increase, sources of real **competitive advantage** are proving increasingly difficult to sustain over any period of time. So much so that it is the ability to create new sources of competitive advantage quickly, again and again, that is proving to be the only really sustainable source of competitive advantage. At the same time as seeking new sources of competitive advantage, companies must continue to manage existing businesses. They must find ways of managing to achieve cost efficiencies whilst at the same time differentiating themselves from the competition. They must find ways to innovate at the same time as managing products at the mature stage of their **life-cycle**. Multinationals must find ways of understanding and reconciling customer needs in different countries, of reconciling global integration with local differentiation. And, despite their size, they must respond to changes in these needs quickly, just as they must react quickly to the actions of competitors. All these pressures and paradoxes have caused large firms to reconsider how they are structured and how they manage their diverse operations.

Just as global capitalism has raised many people out of poverty in the East, in recent years it has also fuelled increasing income inequality in the West. The 'collateral damage' caused by these winds of change can be huge, destroying whole communities and industries as jobs move to where resources are cheapest in the world. Only the so-called 'liberal elite' – the global 'establishment' – are seen as benefiting. Little wonder that ordinary people feel insecure and not in control. The old order may be changing but nobody really knows what the new order might look like. The public backlash against this unprecedented period of change has been resentment against 'the establishment' and, in particular, large, global corporations, especially banks. The old political orthodoxy of global neo-liberalism seems to be in decline and populist right-wing political parties in the ascendancy.

Where is all this leading? The advances in artificial intelligence and the trend towards more and more automation could lead to mass unemployment and wage stagnation. How will established, larger businesses respond? In the early part of the twentieth century they brought about wealth and prosperity for all, pioneering mass production and mass markets but have they lost their way in the twenty-first century? They seem not to be responding well to the needs of either the market or society, catering instead to the idea of ever-increasing shareholder value – and many question whether they are doing this effectively. And there are warnings here. As the *New Statesman* (4–10 May, 2018) said: 'In the age of the **'gig economy'**, Marx's analysis of capitalism – its tendency to create monopolies within markets, its maldistribution of wealth so as to fuel inequality and its separation and alienation of workers from those that own the means of production – can appear startlingly prescient and it demands a meaningful response.'

competitive advantage The advantage a firm has over its competitors, allowing it to generate higher sales or profit margins and/or retain more customers than its competitors

life-cycle Stages of life – can refer to a product, market or industry

gig economy Workers seeking temporary, short-term work 'gigs' or projects

THE CHALLENGE OF ENTREPRENEURSHIP

One response to these winds of change is a realization that security of employment is a thing of the past. Increasing numbers of people see self-employment as one way of regaining control of their lives – and there is no shortage of entrepreneurial role models. But whilst the chances of success on a global basis have probably never been higher and the costs of start-up low, most start-ups struggle to provide even a living wage for the founder. Many of the mushrooming number of 'gig workers', legally defined (in most countries) as self-employed, are tied to one larger firm. They are employed in low-earning jobs, sometimes earning below the statutory minimum wage and usually without any form of employment rights or protection. Based more on hope than realistic expectation, the reality is that most start-ups are born to stagnate and die, rather than to become the large corporations of the future.

Nevertheless some start-ups do succeed and grow and, in doing so, make their founders into millionaires. These young high-growth businesses – often called '**gazelles**' and '**unicorns**' – have a disproportionately large impact on a country's economic well-being. They are usually extremely innovative, shaking up and disrupting markets and industries. They create jobs and wealth. Over the last 30 years or so, **entrepreneurs** establishing new ventures have done more to create wealth than firms at any time before them – ever! For example, 95 per cent of the wealth of the USA has been created since 1980. In the UK, 'gazelles' and 'unicorns' have been estimated to represent only 2–4 per cent of firms but are responsible for the majority of employment growth (BERR, 2008). In the USA it has been estimated that the top performing 1 per cent of all firms generate about 40 per cent of new jobs (Strangler, 2010). Small, growing firms generally create jobs from which the rest of society benefits. They have outstripped large firms in terms of job generation, year on year. At times when larger firms have retrenched, smaller firms continue to offer job opportunities. It has been estimated that in the USA small firms generate half of GDP and over half of exports come from firms employing fewer than 20 people. In the UK middle-sized firms represent just 1 per cent of business but generate 30 per cent of GDP (GE Capital, 2012). No wonder our governments and media are so fascinated by them and their role is now so lauded by society.

Entrepreneurs have finally been recognized as a vital part of economic wealth generation. They have become the heroes of the business world, embodying ephemeral qualities that are envied by many people – freedom of spirit, creativity, vision and zeal. They have the courage, self-belief and commitment to turn dreams into realities. They are seen as catalysts for economic, and sometimes social, change. They disrupt industries through increased competition and change the way we are through innovation. Start-ups and entrepreneurial innovation also remain fundamental to the economic well-being of existing businesses. Many are bought out by yesterday's start-ups seeking to grow by expanding into new geographic areas or to extend or defend their market dominance in particular markets by restricting competition. They might also be seeking innovations that they are unable to produce themselves so as to enhance their product/market offering. But where entrepreneurs might thrive, big companies often struggle with these challenges – and seem not to be winning. They cut budgets, close plants, 'downsize', 'rightsize', 'deconstruct' – and go out of business.

gazelles Young, high-growth firms

unicorn A high-growth private company valued at over $1 billion

entrepreneur A person who creates and/or exploits change for profit, by innovating, accepting risk and moving resources to areas of higher return

CASE INSIGHT 1.1
Jack Ma and Alibaba

China

MILLIONAIRE ENTREPRENEUR

Alibaba Chairman Jack Ma, speaking in Shanghai in 2018. © Getty Images/Lintao Zhang

In 2018 Jack Ma, co-founder of Alibaba Group, announced that he would step down as chairman in 2019, handing over that position to Daniel Zhang, so he could focus on philanthropy. Ma had already stepped down as chief executive in 2013. Ma will remain a life-time member of the Alibaba Partnership, a group of 36 senior staff who appoint a majority of board seats and therefore effectively control the company.

Ma started as an English-language teacher. He first heard about the internet in 1994 and, when on a visit to the USA in 1995, used it to try to find out about China, discovering that there was very little information available. As a result, with the help of friends in the USA, he set up a business that created websites for Chinese companies called 'China Pages'. He then worked for a company set up by the Chinese government until 1999 when he left to launch Alibaba with 18 friends, based in his small apartment in Hangzhou, China.

As the Chinese economy grew and the use of the internet in China exploded, Alibaba thrived and expanded rapidly, thanks in part to Chinese government restrictions on foreign competition. Ma's membership of the Communist Party of China meant he was well connected. Now with operations in over 200 countries, Alibaba Group has become the world's largest retailer (online sales and profits have exceeded those of all US retailers combined since 2015), as well as one of the largest internet and artificial intelligence (AI) companies, venture capital firms and investment corporations. It is a multinational internet conglomerate, specializing in e-commerce, retail, the internet, AI and technology and is one of the ten most valuable companies in the world by market capitalization (second in Asia only to Tencent). Its US IPO in 2014 was the world's highest in history.

Alibaba Group's main areas of business (and subsidiary companies) include business-to-business (the original Alibaba), consumer-to-consumer and business-to-consumer sales services (Taobao Mall and Tmall) via web portals (UCWeb, AliOS), as well as retail sites (AliExpress – similar to eBay, and Juhuasuan – a group shopping site), electronic payment services (Alipay and Ant Financial – which handle more than half of China's vast mobile payments market), shopping comparison search engines (eTao) and cloud computing services (Alibaba Cloud).

Jack Ma's net worth is estimated to be some $35 billion (Forbes.com, 11 December 2018).

Question:

Can China produce another Jack Ma or has the commercial and political environment changed too much?

CASE INSIGHT 1.2
Kiran Mazumdar-Shaw and Biocon

India

MILLIONAIRE ENTREPRENEUR

Born in 1953 in Bangalore, India, Kiran Mazumdar-Shaw is one of the richest women in India. She is the founder of Biocon, a biotech company and India's largest producer of insulin. With a degree in zoology, she went on to take a postgraduate course and trained as a brewer in Australia, ahead of returning to India hoping to follow in her father's footsteps as a brew-master. Despite working in the brewing industry in India for a couple of years, she never achieved her ambition, finding her career blocked by sexism. Instead, in 1978, she was persuaded to set up a joint venture making enzymes in India.

Kiran Mazumdar-Shaw started Biocon India with Irishman Les Auchincloss in 1978 in the garage of her rented house in Bangalore with seed capital of only Rs 10,000 (about $150). It was a joint venture with Biocon Biochemicals, Ireland. Eventually she found a banker prepared to loan the company $45,000 and, from a facility in Bangalore making enzymes for the brewing industry, started to diversify. It became the first Indian company to manufacture and export enzymes to the USA and Europe. This gave her a flow of cash that she used to fund research and to start producing pharmaceutical drugs. The early years were hard.

> I was young, I was twenty five years old . . . banks were very nervous about lending to young entrepreneurs because they felt we didn't have the business experience . . . and then I had . . . this strange business called biotechnology which no one understood . . . Banks were very fearful of lending to a woman because I was considered high risk. (BBC News Business 11 April 2011)

In 1989, Kiran met the chairman of ICICI Bank, which had just launched a venture fund. The fund took a 20 per cent stake in the company and helped finance its move into biopharmaceuticals. Shortly after this Unilever took over Biocon Biochemicals, and bought ICICI's stake in Biocon India, at the same time increasing it to 50 per cent. In 1996 it entered the bio-pharmaceuticals and statins markets. One year later Unilever sold its share in Biocon Biochemicals, and Mazumdar-Shaw bought out Unilever and was able to start preparing Biocon India to float on the stock market, which it did in 2004, with a market value of $1.1bn.

Today Biocon has Asia's largest insulin and statin production facilities and its largest perfusion-based antibody production facility. It produces drugs for cancer, diabetes and auto-immune diseases and is developing the world's first oral insulin, currently undergoing Phase III clinical trials. It employs over 8000 people across its 10 subsidiaries and has a turnover in excess of Rs 26,000. It is listed on the Bombay and New York Stock Exchanges.

Kiran Mazumdar-Shaw has enjoyed many awards and honours. In 2010 *Time* magazine included her in their 100 most powerful people in the world; in 2016 *Forbes* magazine featured her on the Asia 50 Power Businesswomen list. She has featured in 'The Worldview 100 List' of the most influential visionaries (*Scientific American* magazine), in the '100 Leading Global Thinkers' (*Foreign Policy* magazine) and was ranked second in Global 'Medicine Maker Power List' (*The Medicine Maker* magazine). Passionate about providing affordable health care in India, she has funded the 1400-bed Mazumdar-Shaw Cancer Centre, a free cancer hospital in Bangalore. Every year, she donates $2 million to support health insurance coverage for some 100,000 Indian villagers.

Kiran Mazumdar-Shaw's net worth is estimated to be some $3.2 billion (Forbes.com, 11 December 2018).

Question:

How typical is this story? What are the chances of becoming a millionaire by starting your own business?

CAN BIG COMPANIES SURVIVE?

Big companies increasingly find it difficult to deal with this new age of uncertainty and super-competition. Start-ups and smaller ventures seem to find opportunities in the changes that these larger, more established firms find threatening. They react by innovating to better meet customer needs. By way of contrast, larger companies often react by down-sizing, concentrating on their core activities and subcontracting many of their other activities to smaller firms. And many go out of business. De Geus (1997) quoted a Dutch survey showing that the average corporate life expectancy in Japan and Europe was only 12.5 years, and that the average life expectancy of a multinational company – the Fortune 500 or equivalent – as being only between 40 and 50 years, with wide variations in life expectancy and many 'dying' much earlier than others. Daepp et al. (2015) cited a major study of US publicly traded companies that found that their half-life (the time needed for their share price to fall to half its initial value) was only ten years. Another study of US publicly traded companies by Reeves et al. (2016) found that they have a one-in-three chance of being delisted within five years and that their life expectancy had dropped to 31 years. This may not necessarily mean that they fail, but that they are taken over by another company. But corporate failures are also increasing. In 2016, public bankruptcies in the USA rose by more than 25 per cent, a quarter of which were large corporations with assets in excess of $1 billion and over 40 per cent in energy-related businesses. So does some fundamental law underpin the life expectancy of a commercial business?

Geoffrey West is a physicist and biologist who, with other researchers (Daepp et al., 2015), found a remarkable mathematical consistency to explain plant and animal life, growth and death – a set of rules that have been applied to cities and, more recently, corporations. The metabolic rate of most animals has been found to scale to the three-fourths power of an animal's mass. This means that if you double the mass of an animal it only requires 75 per cent more energy to stay alive. Put another way, when the number of cells doubles, the number of capillaries feeding them blood rises only 75 per cent (i.e., under 100 per cent). This is called 'sublinear' scaling and is shown in Figure 1.1(a). As animals get older and grow bigger, the flow of blood therefore fails to keep up with the growth in cells. Growth eventually stops and the animal eventually dies (line n in Figure 1.1(a)). Based on this theory and blood flow rates, the researchers produced mathematical models that accurately predicted the growth and life span of most animals – from the couple of years for a mouse, over 70 years for a human to over 200 years for a whale.

However, when the researchers turned their attention to cities they observed that the scaling laws applied differently. 'Sublinear' scaling applied to infrastructure, like petrol stations, where the scaling rate was 85 per cent (a result that held in the USA and Europe). As the city grew, it needed proportionately fewer things like petrol stations – a 15 per cent saving or economy of scale. However, the researchers also found the opposite relationship with the output of cities, indicated by a whole range of socio-economic measures associated with the interaction of humans such as wages, number of patents, restaurants, even the incidence of violent crimes. These measures of output *increased* at the rate of 115 per cent (i.e., over 100 per cent). This is called 'super-linear' scaling and is shown as the J curve in Figure 1.1(b) – a curve often seen when projecting the sales growth of a company. However, mathematically 'super-linear' scaling cannot continue forever (point t). It cannot grow to infinity and eventually it must collapse – typically as resources run out. And yet

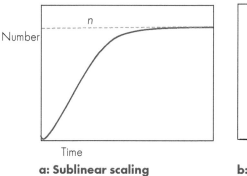
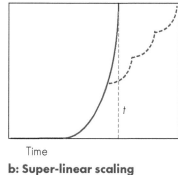

a: Sublinear scaling   **b: Super-linear scaling**

Figure 1.1 Scaling laws

economies of
scale The cost
advantages obtained
due to the scale of
operation, where cost
per unit of output
decreases with
increasing scale

initial public
offerings The stock
market launch of a
company, where shares
are sold to institutional
and usually also retail
investors

cities continue to grow. The researchers explained this by cycles of innovation that extended the resources and opportunities that cities are able to exploit – shown by the dotted extensions to the J curve. They explained the continuing growth of the city by the continuing inflow of people attracted by job vacancies, higher wages, more entertainment, cultural events etc., fuelled by the **economies of scale**, and underpinned by cycles of innovation that change everything. Cities just keep on growing – until they run out of resources which is another issue.

The researchers next turned their attention to corporations. They studied some 30,000 US public companies across many sectors from 1950 to 2009 and found that 'sublinear scaling laws applied, similar to those for animals. In other words, they became less efficient as they got bigger. The larger companies became, the lower the revenues per employee and the lower the profits as a percentage of sales. For companies that survive long enough to go public, the researchers found there was a period of rapid initial growth – represented by the classic 'hockey stick' graph often used by entrepreneurs for their **initial public offerings** (IPOs) and similar to the J curve of super-linear scaling (Figure 1.1b). However, after a period it then stabilized and stayed roughly the same, until the company eventually ceased to exist (specifically these companies stopped reporting financial results, but this could, for example, be because they have been taken over or acquired by another business): 'Then all of them turn over and stabilize at roughly the same value, if they survive. Their growth curve looks like yours and mine. Then, like you and me, they eventually die. This is quite different to the growth curve of a city, which is open ended' (West, 2015).

West speculated that this is because the success of large companies forces them to focus on the parts of the business that generate the biggest profit, emphasizing efficiency, and neglecting the newer parts and potential innovations. The companies become more bureaucratic, dominated by notions of economies of scale: 'It is no accident that when you become a massive company your R&D [research and development] is a tiny part of the enterprise. The life-cycle of the company then tends to follow, ironically, much more that of an organism, growing quickly at the beginning and then turning over and becoming static . . . dominated by economies of scale . . . Cities live for ever but all companies will die . . . Cities tolerate crazy people – companies don't' (West, 2015).

De Geus (1997) had reached similar conclusions about why some companies fail whilst others survive for longer: 'Companies die because their managers focus exclusively on producing goods and services and forget that the organization is a community of human beings at is in business – any business – to stay alive … The long-lived companies in our study tolerated activities in the margin: experiments and eccentricities that stretched their understanding.'

So, the notion that firms become less entrepreneurial and more bureaucratic as they grow is far from new. Greiner (1972) popularized the idea with his model of growth stages. In the model, each phase of growth is followed by a crisis that necessitates a change in the way the founder manages the business. If the crisis cannot be overcome, then the business risks failure. The length of time it takes to go through each phase depends on the industry in which the company operates. In fast-growing industries, the growth periods are relatively short; in slower growth industries, they tend to be longer. Each evolutionary phase requires a particular management style or emphasis to achieve growth. Greiner's model predicts four crises: leadership, autonomy, control and finally bureaucracy. Figure 1.2 shows these crises together with the changes in the emphasis needed by the founder; from operational skills to managerial and strategic skills.

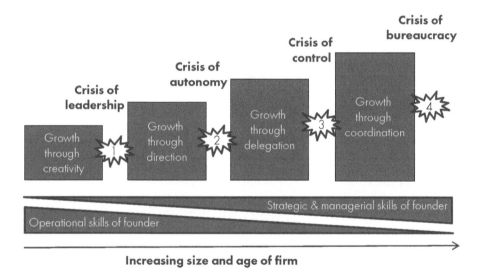

Figure 1.2 Growth stages of a firm

Whilst few experts would dispute the need to avoid too much bureaucracy and the importance of continuing innovation, it is worth noting two things. Firstly, the same degree of bureaucracy (or lack of it) may not be appropriate for all firms – indeed, even for the divisions and departments within them. At the same time not all firms (or the divisions and departments within them) may require or be able to innovate to the same extent. The issue is how to organize and manage to achieve the differences – a topic we shall return to later. Secondly, whilst accepting that companies, like animals, might have a natural life span, they may also, like animals, have spawned new offspring during that time – new ventures that have spun out of the old, all part of the never-ending cycle of birth and death. This is also an important issue that we shall return to later. So, to answer the question that was asked earlier, big companies can certainly extend their lives – but only by innovation. And whilst many will die – going into administration or, more likely, being taken over by another big company – the most successful will probably morph into some other form.

What is more, it has been suggested that the real contribution entrepreneurs make to innovation can be overestimated. Krippendorff (2019) looked at the 30 innovations that experts thought to have most transformed the world in the last three decades – big innovations like the portable computer, the internet, mobile phone and magnetic resonance imaging (MRI), etc. He claimed that most were the result of a more collaborative effort: 22 of the 30 had been conceived by employees and 23 of them had been developed when a larger community (including the public sector) formed around the idea. In addition, 28 of these transformative innovations were scaled and 16 were commercialized by competitors rather than the original innovators: 'We owe much of the modern world to the efforts and passions of internal innovators. To tell the true story of innovation, we would have to say that employees conceive of innovations, communities composed of corporations and institutions build them, and then the competition takes over to scale them' (Krippendorff, 2019) Innovation and its journey to the market is clearly a complex, collaborative process and one in which large organizations still have an important part to play.

IMPLICATIONS FOR BIG COMPANIES

The winds of change have caused a reappraisal of how shareholder value is maximized. The ability to innovate is highly valued and the speed of response to changing market needs is seen as essential. Alongside this realization, the focus has shifted from existing and past value to future value. Existing market share is valuable, but future market share, particularly of a new or emergent market, can be of more value – just look at the valuations put on some of the IPOs (initial public offerings) of internet businesses with little or no current revenue. We have moved from an industrial economy to a knowledge economy, driven by new digital technologies. There has been an accompanying shift in sources of shareholder value – from being vested in physical assets that can be purchased and restrict flexibility, to virtual assets that can be built up and can increase flexibility. Data and information on customers have become as valuable as the customers themselves – something that can not only be sold, but also used to create competitive advantage. Western companies like Facebook, Alphabet, Amazon, Apple, WhatsApp, Messenger and Instagram control enormous amounts of data on their users: 'Once we searched Google, but now Google searches us. Once we thought of digital services as free, but now surveillance capitalists think of us as free' (*The Observer: The New Review*, 20 January 2019). Eastern counterparts like Alibaba, Tencent and Baidu control just as much data but have far closer links with the Chinese government and are already using it to incentivise citizens to 'do good' using tradable credits.

> *Surveillance capitalism unilaterally claims human experience as free raw material for translation into behavioural data. [They are] fed into advanced manufacturing processes known as 'machine intelligence' and fabricated into prediction products that anticipate what you will do now, soon, and later. [They are] traded in a new kind of marketplace that I call behavioural futures markets. Surveillance capitalists have grown immensely wealthy from these trading operations, for many companies are willing to lay bets on our future behaviour.*
>
> Shoshana Zuboff, *The Age of Surveillance Capitalism: The Fight for the Future at the New Frontier of Power*, New York: Public Affairs, 2019

There is an increased focus on risk minimization and a realization that companies need to maximize their flexibility if they are to survive in this new, unpredictable age. Flexibility increases shareholder value. **Strategic options** are valuable when you face either an unexpected downturn or upturn, even at the expense of short-term profits. And high liquidity and good cash flow are needed to make the most of these options. These issues all have implications, not only for how strategy is developed, but also for deciding which sectors are attractive. They underline the need to continually question the basis for a firm's sustainable competitive advantage. As we have seen, in the modern economy, data can be more valuable than sales. In a super-competitive, global market **economies of scope** (when less of a resource is used because it is spread over multiple activities) can be more valuable than economies of scale, particularly when linked to a well-known brand, such as Apple or Virgin, that can be extended over a range of products or services.

Finally, issues of **corporate social responsibility** (CSR) and environmental sustainability have also increasingly come to influence shareholder value – for both ethical and commercial reasons. Just as they have become increasingly the focus for governments, they have also moved into the mainstream of strategy development for companies. CSR stock market indices have been developed and there is increasing pressure from customers, shareholders and governments for business leaders to develop and implement CSR and environmental policies. Brands can be damaged by unethical actions or a lack of social responsibility, as we saw earlier with BP (2010) and Volkswagen (2015), and many studies now link CSR to good financial performance (e.g. Carroll and Shabana, 2010; Margolis and Walsh, 2003; Orlitzy et al., 2003).

> **strategic options**
> Actions you might undertake if risks or opportunities materialize

> **economies of scope** (also called synergy) The term used when less of a resource is used because it is spread across multiple activities. Often referred to as '1 + 1 = 3'

> **corporate social responsibility** The combination of business ethics, social responsibility and environmental sustainability

> " Today's businesses, especially the large ones, simply will not survive in this period of rapid change and innovation unless they acquire entrepreneurial competence "
>
> Peter Drucker, *Innovation and Entrepreneurship: Practice and Principles,*
> London: Heinemann, 1985

This new age of uncertainty has powerful implications for all organizations and their managers and leaders. Planning for super-competition becomes problematic if you cannot predict the future and strategic management faces completely new challenges as the linear planning models used for decades, based on knowledge and information of the past, seem increasingly unrealistic. As Grant (2010) observed:

> *Not only is it impossible to forecast the business environment but managers cannot predict with any certainty what the outcome of their actions will be. The concept of the CEO as the peak decision maker and strategy architect is not only unrealistic – it is undesirable.*

Centralized control seems unable to cope with the scale and pace of change and the uncertainty, complexity and ambiguity associated with it – despite technology's improvements in communication. What is needed is a new approach that can handle complexity and uncertainty, one that 'learns by doing', combining speed of reaction with knowledge gathering and rapid learning from mistakes.

leadership This
is concerned with
setting direction,
communicating and
motivating staff

Traditional views of **leadership** as a command and control function seem increasingly to be obsolete as people show they also have power. Despite cultural diversity, these days 'nudge and influence' seems to be a far more effective form of leadership, at least in the West. In an increasingly affluent society, people are no longer motivated just by money. They are also more willing to question why they are undertaking certain tasks. Indeed, this is no bad thing in a commercial environment where creativity and innovation are such valuable resources. The questioning just needs to be channelled in the right directions.

Stock markets have typically adopted a short-term approach to profit generation and this has mitigated against investment in both innovation and CSR. Recently, however, public companies have become accountable to a wider range of stakeholders than ever before – shareholders, customers, employees, pressure groups and governments, often across national boundaries. Larger companies increasingly have to prove themselves, not just to financial markets, but also to ethical and environmental stakeholders. They have to navigate the politics of international markets. And there are signs that some are adopting new structures that allow them to invest in innovation without endangering their core business. For example, Google restructured in 2015 creating a new holding company called Alphabet with subsidiaries that focus on different types of activities. Google remained its core business and revenue earner whilst other subsidiaries focused on developing future revenue streams (Case insight 5.4). Alphabet does not intend to die young if it can help it.

Above all, managers have to embrace these winds of change and find ways of channeling them to the advantage of all stakeholders – no easy task. McMillan (2004) characterized what she called the 'traditional, classical, mechanistic' view of change as abnormal, potentially calamitous, an incremental linear event that is disruptive that can be controlled. She contrasted this to what she called the 'new, modern dynamic' view of change – one we would call the entrepreneurial view – as normal, continuous, turbulent, both revolutionary and incremental, uncontrollable and non-linear but full of opportunities. She went on to question our traditional approaches to leadership and strategy development and cast the net wide in searching for ideas about how to deal with change by saying that we need to look at quantum physics and complexity theory (a topic we shall return to later in this chapter).

> **“** We need to nurture future business leaders . . . to shape the vision of the world to come . . . It is like describing the shape of a large cloud in the sky, blown off by a strong wind. We know its shape and where it is because we see it and sense it. Although it is not entirely possible to describe it in a static way, a world-class entrepreneur can describe it and even capture a large chunk of it, converting it into raindrops or profit. **”**
>
> Kenichi Ohmae *The Next Global Stage: Challenges and Opportunities in our Borderless World*, New Jersey: Pearson Education, 2005

THE ENTREPRENEURIAL MINDSET

Entrepreneurial character traits

It is this entrepreneurial view of change that managers in large companies need to embrace and in doing so there are some lessons to be learned from entrepreneurs and how they approach the task of **management**. Underpinning how entrepreneurs approach business is their mindset – their character traits and their approach to making decisions in a risky, uncertain environment. In a one-person business it is a dominant influence. Research into the character traits of entrepreneurs is substantial and goes back over forty years. Numerous studies have consistently found robust linkages between entrepreneurship and psychological models of personality, even the more general ones. Harvested from numerous research studies (Burns, 2016), the character traits summarized in Figure 1.3 have been shown to incline an individual towards setting up their own business and help them navigate through the uncertainties of entrepreneurship. Entrepreneurs may be born with some of these traits, but they are also formed through their life experiences – family background, education, job experience, culture etc. This is important, as it shows that these traits can be influenced through the work environment. Each trait is a necessary but not a sufficient trait. The result is more than a simple sum of the traits. What is needed is the combination of all of them to be present.

management This is concerned with handling complexity in organizational processes and the execution of work

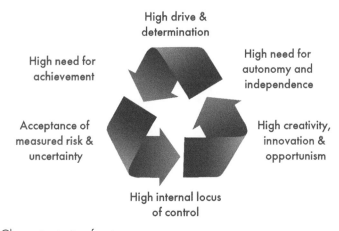

Figure 1.3 Character traits of entrepreneurs

Source (with references): P. Burns, *Entrepreneurship and Small Business: Start-up, Growth and Maturity*, London: Red Globe Press, 2016

Need for autonomy and independence

Entrepreneurs have a high need for autonomy and independence – a characteristic you may initially think is incompatible for a manager in a large firm. But you would be wrong. Independence means different things to different people: doing things differently, being in a situation where you can fulfil your potential or control your own destiny. And, whilst this may not seem to be a character trait that is easily transitioned into an organizational characteristic, autonomy of action can be a strong motivator when combined with other management tools.

Need for achievement

Entrepreneurs have a high need for achievement. However, people measure their achievement in different ways, depending on the type of person they are: for example, the satisfaction of producing a beautiful work of art, employing their hundredth person or making the magic $1 million dollars. For many entrepreneurs, money is just a badge of success, validating their achievement. What they are satisfying is their underlying need for achievement – recognition of their success. And while they may have a 'need' for achievement that does not

necessarily mean that they are actually high achievers, only that this 'need' creates a driv
within them. If they have a high need but achieve little, then they can be profoundly unhapp

Internal locus of control

Entrepreneurs have a high internal locus of control – a belief that they control their ow
destiny. They may believe in luck, but not fate. They believe that they can create their ow
destiny. This is underpinned by a high level of 'self-efficacy' – self-confidence (possibl
unfounded) in their ability to complete a task successfully – which can lead to over-opti
mism in decision-making. In extremis, a high internal locus of control can also manifes
itself in a desire to control everything and everyone around you. This can lead to a preoc
cupation with detail, overwork and stress, particularly if you feel you cannot trust thos
around you to complete the tasks delegated to them.

Drive and determination

Entrepreneurs have enormous drive and determination, motivated by their need fo
achievement and underpinned by internal locus of control, which gives them self-confi
dence in their ability to complete the task successfully. These three personality dimension
appear prominently in the academic literature. Because of their drive, entrepreneurs are
proactive rather than reactive and appear more decisive. They act quickly.

Creativity, innovation and opportunism

The ability to be creative and innovative is an important attribute of entrepreneurs, par
ticularly in growth businesses. But creativity can mean different things in different con
texts. For entrepreneurs, creativity is focused on commercial opportunities. They spot
an opportunity and then use creativity and innovation to exploit it. They tend to do
things differently. It is this trait – a willingness to search out or create new economic
opportunities – that distinguishes innovative entrepreneurs from the larger population
of self-employed (Wennekers and Thurik, 1999).

Acceptance of risk and uncertainty

Entrepreneurs are willing to take risks and live with uncertainty – things that can be very
stressful for most people. However, this does not mean entrepreneurs are gamblers. They
do not like risk and they will try to avoid or mitigate the risks they face and insure against
them using distinctive approaches that we shall outline in the next section. Most impor
tantly, they are willing to make decisions based upon incomplete information – a charac
teristic based upon their faith that they can influence the outcome (real or otherwise)
because of their high self-efficacy and internal locus of control.

Steve Jobs, co-founder of Apple, is an example of an entrepreneur with these character
traits. He clearly was a creative and opportunistic risk-taker. However, he was not an inven
tor. He 'borrowed' technology from others and made it attractive to customers, creating the
bridge between these innovations and the marketplace, allowing for successful commercial
exploitation. Jobs only ever worked for himself. He was certainly driven and controlling,
being notoriously difficult to work for, wanting 'impossible' things done within 'impossible'
time frames. He was labelled a 'control freak' and was accused by many of being rude and
abusive, and even bullying, in order to get his own way. He always believed he knew best
and wanted things done his way – quickly (see Case insight 1.4 and 6.2).

There are psychometric tests to assess personal entrepreneurial tendency and we shall
return to the topic when we look at the role of **intrapreneurs** in Chapter 13. One psychological

intrapreneur
Someone developing
new products or
businesses and
operating within a
company that is not
owned by them

model widely used to describe and structure personality traits generally is called the Big Five model, which measures:

- Openness – the tendency to favour creativity, new experiences, change and diversity – an important element of entrepreneurship.
- Extraversion – the tendency to favour an outgoing, talkative and energetic style of social interaction.
- Conscientiousness – the tendency to be self-regulating, self-disciplined with a high achievement orientation.
- Agreeableness – the tendency towards harmony and altruism in social interactions, showing greater trust and modesty, rather than being competitive.
- Neuroticism – the tendency towards negative feelings such as fear, guilt or worry, all of which creates stress – a tendency that makes people less likely to engage in activities involving risk or uncertainty.

Research indicates that individual entrepreneurs can be defined as high in Openness, Extraversion and Consciousness and low in Agreeableness and Neuroticism (Larson et al., 2002; Obschonka et al., 2013; Schmitt-Rodermund, 2004). Openness is the trait that shows the strongest positive effect on creativity and innovation (Ma, 2009), but low Agreeableness is also important (Ekehhammar et al., 2004). This is because people with low Agreeableness are those most likely to avoid the group-think or 'dominant logic' of a group or an organization – a topic we shall return to in the next chapter – and therefore more likely to generate radical new ideas (Kerr and Tindale, 2004).

dominant logic
Paradigms or conventions that establish a status quo that is rarely questioned

CASE INSIGHT 1.3
Jim Ratcliffe and Ineos

UK

MILLIONAIRE ENTREPRENEUR

The Ineos Group was founded in 1998 when Jim Ratcliffe, aged 45, led a £91 million management buyout of Inspec's chemicals division from BP. Ineos remains a private company. Born in 1952, Ratcliffe is a chemical engineer and a qualified accountant with a MBA who had previously worked for the US private equity house Advent – a job that gave him the deal expertise he needed for the buy-out. Since then, he has built Ineos into one of the three largest petrochemical companies in the world, employing over 18,500 people at 181 sites across 22 countries, generating a turnover of some £45 billion and profits of £5.15 billion. He owns 60 per cent of the company.

Ineos produces products for industries such as fuels and lubricants, packaging and food and construction – selling mainly to the USA, the UK, Germany, France and Benelux. Although not a household name, its products are used in many industrial processes: to clean water, manufacture antibiotics, make toothpaste, insulate homes, package food etc. Ineos is also involved in renewable energy and is one of the world's leading pioneers in the development of generating sustainable energy from waste material. Ratcliffe built up the group by buying subsidiaries that other petrochemical giants did not want, mainly at auction using debt finance.

We'd look at anything that came along – we were optimistic. We'd look at businesses that were unfashionable or unsexy, facilities owned by large corporations where you'd know they would be sloppy with fixed costs. We'd run them a bit better, reduce the costs, make them busy, and over the cycle they were very profitable. (The Sunday Times, 13 May 2018).

Ineos is made up of 20 stand-alone business units, headed by Ineos Capital, which is run by Ratcliffe and his two business partners, Andy Currie and John Reece. Ineos believes its strengths lie in its:

➡ High-quality, low-cost production facilities – Keeping costs to a minimum is a key operational imperative. The company has been accused of buying assets then cutting costs through the introduction of new working practices, lower wages etc. In 2008 and again in 2013 it was at the centre of major industrial relations disputes with the Unite Union over its decision to close the final salary pension scheme at its Grangemouth refinery in the UK. The union only accepted the closure of the scheme when Ineos announced that it would close the plant (this decision was then reversed).
➡ Well-located, well-invested, large plants that allow it to benefit from economies of scale – again keeping costs as low as possible.
➡ Leading market positions that allow it to be the supplier of choice for many large customers – large volume sales are essential for the economies of scale to be achieved.
➡ Experienced management – Ineos runs operations with minimal on-site management, using what it calls 'work teams', cutting out middle management. It claims this model is better suited to handling day-to-day workflows.
➡ Operating diversity in products, customers, geographic regions, applications and end-user markets.

In 2018 Jim Ratcliffe became the richest man in the UK with an estimate net worth of some £21 billion ($27 billion) (*The Sunday Times Rich List*, 13 May 2018).
Visit the Ineos website: **www.ineos.com.**

Questions:

1. Does Jim Ratcliffe show entrepreneurial character traits?
2. Is Ineos an entrepreneurial company? Explain.
3. Is there a difference between an entrepreneurial character and an entrepreneurial company? Explain.

Entrepreneurial management and leadership

There is strong empirical support for the view that strong competitive advantage and above-average financial performance stem from high levels of entrepreneurship (e.g., Fuentes and Gomez-Gras, 2011; Lee and Chu, 2011). So what can we learn from how entrepreneurs manage their businesses, in particular how they manage risk and develop strategy? Entrepreneurs are often seen as being intuitive, almost whimsical, in their decision-making. True, economists find it difficult to understand and to model their approach. It certainly does not fit well into 'logical' economic models such as discounted cash flow. The reason lies at the heart of any entrepreneurial venture – the greater degree of risk and uncertainty it faces. The result is a different approach to managing, developing strategy and making decisions that is just as logical but little understood.

The first thing to realize is that entrepreneurs may not use the jargon or established frameworks of strategy. Many do not produce **business plans**. Nevertheless, entrepreneurs instinctively arrive at the right decision. There is nothing wrong with this. The words and frameworks we might use in strategic analysis merely give meaning and logic to what they do. Many excellent musicians or athletes were not taught. They picked up the skills

business plan A formal document setting out the business model for an organization

nstinctively – although they developed through training and exercise. The second point is that entrepreneurs often claim to have achieved their success through luck rather than strategy. Never underestimate luck. We all need it and it plays a part, but remember that entrepreneurs have a strong internal locus of control which means that, whilst they may believe in luck, they do not believe in fate. They believe they can, and will, shape their own destinies and that may mean working to create more opportunities than most people. By creating more strategic options and opportunities they improve their chances of success-fully pursuing at least one. Make no mistake; entrepreneurs to a large extent create their own luck. Further proof of this was provided in an experiment by Wiseman (2003). He asked two groups of people – one that considered themselves lucky, the other that felt unlucky – to count the number of photographs in a newspaper. On the second page was a very large headline statement: 'Stop looking – there are 43 photographs in this newspaper'. Those who considered themselves unlucky tended to miss this and, on average, took two minutes to count the photographs compared to the few seconds for those who considered themselves lucky. He concluded that 'lucky people generate their own good fortune via four basic principles. They are skilled at creating and noticing chance opportunities, make lucky decisions by listening to their intuition, create self-fulfilling prophesies via positive expec-tations, and adopt a resilient attitude that transforms bad luck into good.' Make no mistake; to a large extent we all make our own luck.

> **❝** If you're not making mistakes, you're not trying hard enough. **❞**
>
> Andy Alderson, founder Vanarama, *The Sunday Times*, 17 June 2018

The management style of entrepreneurs is typically based upon informal personal rela-tionships rather than authority. And that means that formal lines of authority can be blurred, with a typical organizational structure resembling a spider's web with the entre-preneur at the centre receiving information and making decisions (Figure 1.4) – a structure that works well but, as we shall see in Chapter 5, only up to a certain size. At its best, these

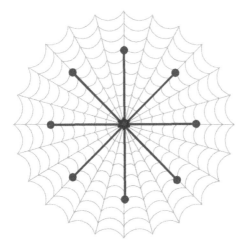

Figure 1.4 Spider's web organizational structure

strong internal relationships create a heightened sense of identity, loyalty and solidarity within the firm – a sense of an 'in-group' working together for a common purpose. And this emphasis on personal relationships permeates customer and supplier interactions, encouraging a sense of loyalty. They build into an invaluable network of contacts and goodwill that can be used whenever the firm needs to change or do something just a little more risky than the average firm. And the entrepreneur uses these networks of relationships to gain information and knowledge, which can mitigate the risks they face and help identify new commercial opportunities. They have 'inside information' – real or imagined – that reduces the risk and uncertainty in their minds.

Alongside a heightened sense of identity, successful entrepreneurs develop a strong **vision** for what they want to achieve. This is part of the fabric of their self-motivation. However, the path to achieving this vision is not always clear. Whilst big company executives might set goals and seek to achieve them sequentially and logically, entrepreneurs' goals are broad and evolve over time based on whatever personal strengths and resources they have, creatively reacting to contingencies as they occur (Sarasvathy, 2001). Trying to reconcile this lack of fit between aspirations and resources – where entrepreneurial firms are and where they might want to be – Hamel and Prahalad (1994) studied businesses that had successfully challenged established big companies in a range of industries. They found that these companies develop a strong **'strategic intent'**. This necessitates developing a common vision about the future, aligning staff behaviour with a common purpose and delegating and decentralizing decision-making – all recurrent themes in how entrepreneurs manage. They argued that 'the challengers had succeeded in creating entirely new forms of competitive advantage and dramatically rewriting the rules of engagement.' They were daring to be different. Managers in these firms imagined new products, services and even entire industries that did not exist and then went on to create them. They were not just benchmarking and analyzing competition, they were creating new marketplaces that they could dominate because it was a marketplace of their own making. But whilst these managers may be revolutionaries their feet were firmly on the ground because they understood their firm's **core competences** – the skills, resources and technologies that enabled them to provide benefits to customers.

And developing strategies that show them the path to take is never straightforward. Sarasvathy (2001) observed that entrepreneurs do not like formal research and planning. Whilst strategy can be developed in a systematic, almost mechanistic, manner many entrepreneurs often develop strategy instinctively and intuitively – they call it 'gut feel'. For them, strategies evolve on a step-by-step basis as one road-block after another is dismantled. If one step works then the second is taken. In this way decision-making is often seen as incremental and short-term (Burns and Whitehouse, 1995a, 1995b). Entrepreneurs do not wait for perfect knowledge or perfect opportunity. They learn by doing. They also appear to make extensive use of **cognitive heuristics** – simplifying strategies – based upon their past experiences (Delmar, 2000). These decision-making tools help make quick decisions in a fast-moving and uncertain world and, as we shall explore in Chapter 7, can sometimes lead to better decisions than exact calculations. However, given the inherent character traits of entrepreneurs, they can lead to over-optimism and underline the need for realistic risk assessment processes. Entrepreneurial decisions are therefore based upon these heuristics, past experiences, and the information entrepreneurs are receiving through their network of relationships as well as the opportunistic circumstances at the time. Improve any of these

vision What the business might become

strategic intent A strong underlying vision of what a company might become

core competences The skills, multiple resources and technologies that enable a company to provide benefits to customers and distinguish them in the marketplace

cognitive heuristics Simplifying strategies or approaches to decision-making, often based upon past experiences. Not guaranteed to be optimal

elements, for example by improving information flows inside and from outside an organization and by improving risk management, and you improve decision-making.

This 'gut feel' has also been described as 'muddling through' – a science that is as old as strategy itself (Lindblom, 1959). The implications of this approach for strategy development were explained by Mintzberg (1978), who contrasted what he called **emergent strategy** development with the text-book approach, which he called 'deliberate'. As he put it, with emergent strategy 'the strategy-making process is characterized by reactive solutions to existing problems ... The adaptive organization makes its decisions in incremental, serial steps'. Emergent strategy can only be developed through a process of continual **strategizing** – a process that involves evaluating strategic options. Because outcomes are uncertain, the more options available to an organization the better. These are all approaches that we shall return to later.

However, emergent and deliberate strategy development are not mutually exclusive. In a study of growing firms, McCarthy and Leavy (2000) showed that strategy development was *both* deliberate and emergent; changing from emergent to deliberate as the firm went through recurrent crises followed by periods of consolidation (Greiner's model in Figure 1.2). These crises force entrepreneurs to change their preconceptions and 'unlearn' bad habits or routines ahead of learning new ones (Cope, 2005). Therefore, rather than having only one style of strategy development, entrepreneurs would seem to adopt both, depending on circumstances. In this way the well-documented process of growth to crisis to consolidation parallels a process of emergent to deliberate and back to emergent strategy formulation, shown in Figure 1.5.

emergent strategy
Strategy development that is characterized by reactive solutions to existing problems

strategizing
Continuous assessment of the options about how to make the most of opportunities or avoid risks as they arise

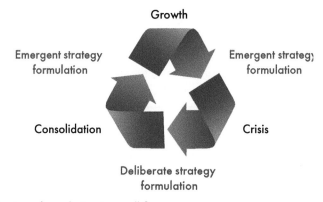

Figure 1.5 Strategy formulation in small firms

Ohmae (2005) used the Japanese word kosoryoku to describe what is needed to develop entrepreneurial strategy in an uncertain environment. He explained that it meant something that combined 'vision' with the notion of 'concept' and 'imagination'. Unlike imagination, however, it has no sense of daydreaming rather than an ability to see what is invisible and shape the future so that the vision succeeds: 'It is the product of imagination based on realistic understanding of what the shape of the oncoming world is and, pragmatically, the areas of business that you can capture successfully because you have the means of realizing the vision.'

Entrepreneurs also employ some specific strategies to minimize and manage the risks they face. For example, successful entrepreneurs tend to keep fixed costs as low as possible, for example by subcontracting activities or entering into partnerships. They tend to commit costs based upon what they judge to be their affordable loss – the maximum amount they can afford to lose in the event of failure (Sarasvathy, 2001) – a technique we shall return to in Chapter 11. Only after the opportunity has proved to be commercially viable will they invest more, which may be prudent and reflect their resource limits but then run the risk of losing **first-mover advantage** in a new market – a difficult judgement call. Frequently, therefore, they will experiment with a 'limited launch' into the market and learn from this – something now called a '**lean start-up**' (Ries, 2011), which we shall return to later. Successful entrepreneurs find ways of reconciling these issues – ways of developing strategy without overcommitting to one course of action and ways of minimizing their investment in resources.

And here we recognize reflections of how entrepreneurs, in their spider's web of influence, approach decision-making in a risky, uncertain and rapidly changing environment – through intuition, judgement, wisdom, experience and insight with holistic knowledge of operations and a strong vision of what they want to achieve. And there is nothing wrong with strategy that is emergent, incremental and adaptive. Indeed, as we shall see in the next section, it is an approach that resonates in complexity theory. However, that does not mean that strategy cannot be analyzed, managed and controlled. Strategic frameworks can help do that. These frameworks can help with strategizing – thinking about the future and analyzing options.

COMPLEXITY THEORY AND MANAGING IN CHAOS

Complexity theory seeks to explain how complex systems work. Complex adaptive systems are the result of multiple independent actions. They are unpredictable and small actions at one level that can have large-scale unexpected consequences elsewhere. Complexity theory hints that there is no stable equilibria in these situations – change can become continuous and unpredictable, which is what we see today. However, complexity theory also shows how truly adaptive systems cope with this environment. Complex systems therefore mirror today's increasingly interconnected global marketplace and the volatile, uncertain, complex and ambiguous environment it generates. This is why the theory is relevant. To succeed, entrepreneurial organizations need to harness change and make it work for their own advantage.

The first thing to observe is that the theory provides intellectual support to the 'emergent' school of strategy development, in contrast to the 'deliberate' school with its linearity of approach and centralized decision-making. It favours decentralization, the 'pushing down' of decision-making – empowering staff to make the 'right' decisions for the organization. Lots of small independent actions, if properly marshalled, are more likely to react appropriately and, just as importantly, less likely to make a big mistake. And, as we observe in our everyday life, complex social systems have a capacity to self-organize at the individual level, reacting and changing to create new systems and structures without being directed to do so.

It is this capacity to self-organize, to create new structures and systems, to make appropriate independent decisions rapidly that can give direction to the changes and create competitive advantage. The question therefore is how to create an environment that encourages

---

first-mover advantage The competitive advantage gained by being the first into a market

lean start-up The launch of a minimum viable product then using customer feedback in an iterative fashion to tailor it further to the specific needs of customers

elf-organization, with systems, structures and leadership that facilitate it. Complexity neory shows that there are three requirements to create effective self-organization:

➤ A common identity and purpose: There must be a clear understanding of and belief in the 'common good' (head and heart) that permits a common sense-making process within the organization;
➤ A free flow of knowledge and information: The organization as a whole must work on the same information in order to provide the possibility of synchronized behaviour;
➤ Strong personal relationships: These relationships are the pathways through which information is transmitted and then transformed into intelligent, coordinated action.

Complexity theory also gives us an intellectual basis for the apparent dilemma of whether o encourage incremental or radical change within an entrepreneurial organization. The theory tells us that the two are not mutually exclusive and shows that systems most likely o thrive in a turbulent environment are those that have the capability of making *both* mall-scale adaptations as well as large-scale revolutions. These systems exist at the 'edge of .haos', adapting all the time but able to make the occasional radical leap.

Now we start to see the keys to building an organization able to harness change to its advantage – one based on relationships with all stakeholders; one that harvests and uses knowledge and information to seek out opportunities and mitigate risks; one with a strong dentity that provides strategic intent and vision from which 'right' decisions might be made. Couple this with the character traits and approach to management of the entrepreneur and we have the blueprint of what an entrepreneurial organization might look like.

CASE INSIGHT 1.4
Steve Jobs and Apple (1)

USA

ENTREPRENEURIAL CHARACTER

Steve Jobs died on 5 October 2011, aged 56, of pancreatic cancer. He was the epitome of an entrepreneurial leader. He revolutionized three industries – computing, music sales and cinema animations. With Steve Wozniak, he co-founded Apple in 1976. Apple revolutionized the computer industry through its easy-to-use, innovative designs: the Mac with its computer mouse, the iPod with its click wheel and the iPhone with its 'user interface'. It revolutionized how digital content, in particular music, could be sold. Through Jobs' animation studio, Pixar, films such as *Toy Story* (1995) changed our ideas about the use of computer-generated animations. And yet Steve Jobs was not an inventor. He was the bridge between innovations and the marketplace – an entrepreneur – recognizing their commercial potential. Most of the technologies used by Apple originally came from the US government. Mazzucato (2018) listed 12; from microprocessors and CPUs to hard-drives, from LCDs to touch-screens, from lithium-based batteries to the internet itself. Apple's success lay in its ability to marry these complex technologies into user-friendly and attractive devices supplemented with powerful software mediums. It marketed its products brilliantly and developed dominant market positions. Not only did Jobs start up Apple; he was also the architect of its later growth. By the time of his death in 2011, Jobs had created the second most valuable company in the world, measured by market capitalization, with a cash mountain of $80 billion.

Born to a Syrian father and an American mother, Jobs was put up for adoption and was brought up by a blue-collar couple in San Francisco – something that left a deep scar. Whilst at high school, he met Steve Wozniak. After high school, he went to a liberal arts college but he dropped out after one term. Jobs grew his hair and did the sort of things that drop-outs at the time did. His engagement with Zen Buddhism, with a focus on stark, minimalist aesthetics and a belief in intuition, became ingrained in his personality; however, he never achieved the inner peace associated with it, rather he became driven by the particular challenges facing him at any time.

It was Wozniak who had the talent for electronics and designing circuits with the minimum number of chips. He built the first Apple computer. At the time Wozniak was working for Hewlett-Packard and Jobs for Atari. Apple I was a hobbyist machine assembled in Jobs' home and housed in a wooden box. The pair sold many of their personal possessions to get started. Jobs took on the role of businessman – the marketer who persuaded a local store to order 50, and then persuaded another local electrical store to give him 30 days' credit on the parts to build the computers. Jobs also persuaded Mike Markkula, a former Intel employee, to invest in the company and become its first chief executive. What followed was the classic Apple II with its simple design, full operating manual, built-in colour graphics, easily accessible expansion slots and ability to connect to a television It was an instant success. Apple went public in 1980 and had achieved a market valuation of $1.8 billion only four years after being launched.

Wozniak retired from Apple in 1981, following a serious plane accident. Jobs took over the development of Apple II's successor, the Apple Macintosh. The Mac was intended to be the first mass-market, closed-box computer using a mouse and graphic user interface. These ideas were not new. They had been developed by Xerox Palo Alto Research Centre (PARC) and had been tried out in high-priced computers (Xerox Star and Apple Lisa), without any commercial success. The Mac's launch was the start of what became the signature Jobs product launch. He appeared on stage with Bill Gates promising Mac versions of Word, Excel and PowerPoint. There were 20 full-page advertisements in major US magazines and a TV commercial that was shown in the USA during the 1984 Super Bowl, associating IBM with George Orwell's *1984* Big Brother. Nevertheless, the Mac failed to sell in the expected volumes and, in 1985, Apple closed three of its six factories, laying off 1200 employees. In the same year, Jobs was fired from Apple. In 1987, the Mac II was launched as a conventional three-piece computer system.

Jobs resented being fired, particularly by someone he had recruited two years earlier to the job of Chief Executive Officer – John Sculley, formerly president of PepsiCo. He took several Apple employees with him and set up another company (NeXT) to produce a powerful Unix workstation targeted at business and universities. It was very expensive and flopped, so the company switched to selling the operating systems, again without much initial success.

In 1986 Jobs bought the company that became Pixar. Initially, it produced the Pixar Image Computer, primarily selling to government and the medical market, but this was never a popular product. The company struggled selling off its hardware operations and, in an effort to demonstrate its software capabilities, began producing computer-animated commercials. This led to a deal in 1991 with the Walt Disney Corporation to produce three computer animated films, the first being the ground-breaking *Toy Story*. Released in 1995, this was an outstanding success, which was just as well because, as late as 1994, Jobs had considered selling off Pixar. After producing a series of highly successful, award-winning films Disney bought Pixar in 2006 at a valuation of $7.4 billion, making Jobs the largest shareholder in Disney.

Meanwhile the PC market had been transformed in 1995 by the launch of Microsoft Windows 95 which really popularized the mouse and graphic user interface. However, Apple was struggling to survive and the new Mac OS software was not working. At this time Apple was being managed by committees and it had lost its innovative flair. It knew it needed to buy-in a new operating system quickly, so it turned to Jobs and paid a much inflated price for NeXT. This turned out to be a reverse takeover and Jobs took over as Apple's 'interim CEO' in 1997.

Jobs ruthlessly killed off weak products and simplified product lines. He adapted NeXT's operating system to become the Mac OS X. He also started the process of creating the distinctive Apple designs with the teardrop-shaped iMac, followed by the portable iBook. Jobs explained his approach at the 1997 meeting of the Apple Worldwide Developers Association: 'Focusing is about saying no ... and the result of that focus is going to be some really great products where the total is much greater than the sum of the parts ... One of the things I've always found is that you've got to start with the customer experience and work backwards to the technology and try to figure out where you are going to try to sell it.'

Apple's fortunes were transformed when Jobs changed directions and launched the iPod in 2001. This was followed by the iTunes music store in 2003, which allowed music to be easily downloaded, albeit at a price. Until this innovation the music industry had been facing a decline in CD sales as more and more music was pirated through online sites. This started Apple on a growth path, which was reinforced in 2007 by the iPhone – a clever but expensive combination of cell phone, iPod and internet device – followed in 2010 by the iPad – a tablet computer without a physical keyboard. By 2011, Apple was selling more iPads than Macs.

Jobs was, of course, in the right place at the right time to capitalize on developments in computing. But he also shaped these developments to appeal to customers. The distinctive feature about Apple products was never the technological innovation – that normally came from elsewhere – but rather the application of an innovation to make the product easier and simpler to use, whether it be the physical product design or applications such as iTunes. Apple products were never cheap, but they had distinctive, eye-catching designs and were supported by massive marketing campaigns. Jobs, dressed in black turtle neck, jeans and trainers, used to launch products himself with carefully choreographed, pseudo-religious stage presentations. They attracted adoring fans who gave Jobs the status of a rock star and received worldwide press coverage.

We shall look at Jobs' leadership qualities in Case insight 6.2.

Questions:

1. What entrepreneurial qualities or characteristics did Jobs exhibit?
2. Why was he so successful? How much of this success was just good luck?

SUMMARY

- ➡ We are living in an age of uncertainty characterized by continuing, unpredictable and rapid change – change that is both incremental, radical and discontinuous. It is an increasingly complex world full of interconnections formed by a global marketplace linked by technology allowing instant communication and amplifying much of the volatility in it. And commercial power is shifting from West to East.

- ➡ Many larger firms are unable to cope with this volatility and increased competition. At the same time, those that are have been accused of exploiting their dominant market position to stifle competition; some have been accused of avoiding tax; others of using customer data unscrupulously. Many are accused of not doing enough to ensure environmental sustainability. These are issues that raise questions about their commitment to CSR.

- ➡ Whilst large firms flounder, small, entrepreneurial firms have thrived and, whilst their contribution to economic prosperity has become recognized, many entrepreneurs have become millionaires. The key to this success has been the ability of entrepreneurs to work with change to recognize unmet market needs and create commercial opportunities.

➡ The entrepreneurial character has six traits: a high need for autonomy and independence; a high need for achievement; a high internal locus of control; a high level of drive and determination; high creativity and innovation; and a willingness to work in uncertain environments and take measured risks.

➡ Entrepreneurial management is characterized as being a social activity that has a different approach to dealing with risk and uncertainty. Successful entrepreneurs generate strong relationships with all their stakeholders. They create a strong group identity and sense of purpose. They exert 'soft' influence with loose control structures. They mitigate risk through the knowledge and information they obtain through their network of relationships. These are important qualities that help deal with unpredictable environments the importance of which are underlined by complexity theory. Entrepreneurs go on to develop strategy differently, creating strategic intent but maintaining a loose, flexible strategy and continuously strategizing, creating as many strategic options as possible.

➡ As firms grow, they become more complex to manage and more bureaucratic. They tend to become more risk-averse and less innovative, defending their major income streams rather than trying to find new ones – a characteristic that can lead to their decline and closure. Large firms need to change their approach to leadership and management and find ways of becoming more entrepreneurial, encouraging innovation at all levels.

 GROUP DISCUSSION TOPICS

1. What do you understand by the term 'age of uncertainty'? Does it accurately describe the environment of today?
2. What are the implications of increasing global connectivity for society and companies?
3. Why are there so many corporate scandals? Are they inevitable? Are they a sign of anything else?
4. What has been the effect in your country of the 2008 banking crisis?
5. How important has technology been in influencing changes in society and commerce over the last 50 years?
6. How important is the issue of environmental sustainability? How responsive to it are large firms? How might this be increased?
7. When will Google 'die'? How is it likely to 'die'? How might it be able to sustain itself?
8. In the context of corporate life-cycles, is history bound to repeat itself?
9. Have small entrepreneurial firms responded better to the changing commercial environment than large firms?
10. What benefits does entrepreneurship bring to society?
11. Why do you think small firms have prospered rather than large firms over the last 50 years?
12. How does the management of a small, entrepreneurial firm differ from the management of a large one?
13. In a turbulent, changing environment, what advantages/disadvantages do *small* firms have?
14. In a turbulent, changing environment, what advantages/disadvantages do *large* firms have?
15. What is an entrepreneurial mindset?
16. Can large firms also be entrepreneurial? Is it in their interests to be so? What pressures are there for them not to be entrepreneurial?
17. If large firms were more entrepreneurial what would be the individual, economic and societal advantages?
18. How is complexity theory relevant to managing in a changing and uncertain environment?

ACTIVITIES

1. Critically analyze the political, economic, societal, technological, environmental and legal (PESTEL) trends that you predict over the next 10 years. Discuss with the class which will have the biggest effect on you and which will have the biggest effect on companies. Discuss with the class which pose the biggest threats and opportunities to companies.
2. List the pros and cons for a company of following a policy of environmental sustainability and critically analyze their effect on the firm's profitability. Discuss with the class.
3. Critically analyze Geoffrey West's hypothesis about corporate life expectancy. Discuss with the class whether it is likely to prove to be true.
4. Identify two large organizations that you would describe as entrepreneurial and explain why you would describe them this way. Are they commercially successful? Analyze the reasons for this.

REFERENCES

BERR (2008) 'High Growth Firms in the UK: Lessons from an Analysis of Comparative UK Performance', *Business, Enterprise and Regional Reform (BERR) Economics Paper 3*, November.

Burns, P. (2016) 4th edn., London: Red Globe Press.

Burns, P. and Whitehouse, O. (1995a) *Investment Criteria in Europe*, 3i European Enterprise Centre, Report 16, July.

Burns, P. and Whitehouse, O. (1995b) *Financing Enterprise in Europe* 2, 3i European Enterprise Centre, Report 17, October.

Carroll, A.B. and Shabana, K.M. (2010) 'The Business Case for Corporate Social Responsibility: A Review of Concepts, Research and Practise', *International Journal of Management Reviews*, http://academia.edu.

Cope, J. (2005) 'Toward a Dynamic Learning Perspective of Entrepreneurship', *Entrepreneurship Theory and Practice*, 29(4).

Daepp, M.I.G., Hamilton, M.J., West, G.B. and Bettencourt, L.M.A. (2015) 'The Mortality of Companies', *Royal Society Interface*, on: 10.1098/rsif.2015.0120.

de Geus, A. (1997) 'The Living Company', *Harvard Business Review*, March/April.

Delmar, F. (2000) 'The Psychology of the Entrepreneur' in S. Carter and D. Jones-Evans (eds) *Enterprise and Small Business: Principles, Practice and Policy* (1st edn.), London: Prentice Hall.

Economic Innovation Group (2017) *Dynamism in Retreat: Consequences for Regions, Markets and Workers*, February. Available at http://eig.org/wp-content/uploads/2017/07/Dynamism-in-Retreat-A.pdf.

Ekehhammar, B., Akrami, N. Gylie, M. and Zakrisson, I. (2004) 'What Matters Most to Prejudice: Big Five Personality, Social Dominance Orientation, or Right-Wing Authoritarianism?', *European Journal of Personality*, 18(6).

Fuentes, A.M. and Gomez-Gras, J.M. (2011) 'Radical and Incremental Entrepreneurial Orientation', *Journal of Management and Organization*, 17.

GE Capital (2012) *Leading from the Middle: The Untold Story of British Business*, London: GE Capital.

Grant, R.M. (2010) *Contemporary Strategic Analysis* (7th edn.), Chichester: Wiley.

Greiner, L.E. (1972) 'Evolution and Revolution as Organizations Grow', *Harvard Business Review*, July/August.

Hamel, G. and Prahalad, C.K. (1994) *Competing for the Future: Breakthrough Strategies for Seizing Control of Your Industry and Creating the Markets of Tomorrow*, Boston, MA: Harvard Business School Press.

Hardoon, D., Fuentes. R. and Ayeles, S. (2016) 'An Economy for the 1%: How Privilege and Power in the Economy Drive Extreme Inequality and How It Can Be Stopped', *Oxfam Briefing Paper 210*, Oxford: Oxfam International.

Kerr, N. and Tindale, S.R. (2004) 'Group Performance and Decision Making', *Annual Review of Psychology*, 55.

Krippendorff, K. (2019) *Driving Innovation from Within: A Guide for Internal Entrepreneurs*, New York, NY: Columbia University Press.

Larson, L.M., Rottinghaus, P.J. and Borgen, F.H (2002) 'Meta-analysis of Big-Six Interests and Big-Five Personality Factors', *Journal of Vocational Behaviour*, 61(2).

Lee, T.K. and Chu, W. (2011) 'Entrepreneurial Orientation and Competitive Advantage: The Mediation of Resource Value and Rareness', *African Journal of Business Management*, 5(33).

Lindblom, L.E. (1959) 'The Science of Muddling Through', *Public Administration Review*, 19, Spring.

Ma, H.H. (2009) 'The Effect Size of Variables Associated with Creativity: A Meta-Analysis', *Creativity Research Journal*, 21(1).

Margolis, J.D. and Walsh, J.P. (2003) 'Misery Loves Companies: Social Initiatives by Business', *Administrative Science Quarterly*, 48.

Mazzucato, M. (2018) *The Entrepreneurial State: Debunking Public vs Private Sector Myths*, London: Penguin Books.

McCarthy, B. and Leavy, B. (2000) 'Strategy Formation in Irish SMEs: A Phase Model of Process', *British Academy of Management Annual Conference*, Edinburgh.

McMillan, E. (2004) *Complexity, Organizations and Change*, London: Routledge.

Mintzberg, H. (1978) 'Patterns in Strategy Formation', *Management Science*, May 24, on: 10.1287/mnsc.24.9.934

Obschonka, M., Schmitt-Rodermund, E., Silbereisen, R.K., Gosling, S.D. and Potter, J. (2013) 'The Regional Distribution and Correlates of an Entrepreneurship-Prone Personality Profile in the United States, Germany and the United Kingdom: A Socioecological Perspective', *Journal of Personality and Social Psychology*, 105(1).

Orlitzy, M., Schmidt, F.L. and Rynes, S.L. (2003) 'Corporate Social Performance: A Meta-Analysis', *Organization Studies*, 24.

Reeves, M., Levin, S. and Ueda, D. (2016) 'The Biology of Corporate Survival', *Harvard Business Review*, January-February.

Ries, E. (2011) *The Lean Startup: How Today's Entrepreneurs Use Continuous Innovation to Create Radically Successful Businesses*, New York, NY: Crown Publishing.

Sarasvathy, S.D. (2001) 'Causation and Effectuation: Toward a Theoretical Shift from Economic Inevitability to Entrepreneurial Contingency', *The Academy of Management Review*, 26(2).

Schmitt-Rodermund, E. (2004) 'Pathways to Successful Entrepreneurship: Parenting, Personality, Early Entrepreneurial Competence and Interests', *Journal of Vocational Behaviour*, 65(3).

Strangler, D. (2010) 'High-Growth Firms and the Future of the American Economy', *Kauffman Foundation Research Series: Firm Growth and Economic Growth*, March. https://www.kauffman.org/~/media/kauffman_org/research%20 reports%20and%20covers/2010/04/highgrowthfirmsstudy.pdf

Wennekers, S. and Thurik, R. (1999) 'Linking Entrepreneurship and Economic Growth', *Small Business Economics*, 13(1).

West, G. (2015) *Strategy + Business*, Issue 81, Winter.

Wiseman, R. (2003) 'The Luck Factor', *The Skeptical Inquirer: The Magazine For Science And Reason*, 27(3).

 ONLINE RESOURCES AVAILABLE For further resources relating to this chapter see the companion website at **www.macmillanihe.com/Burns-CEI**

PART I

ENTREPRENEURSHIP AND INNOVATION

Having highlighted the entrepreneurial deficiencies in larger organizations, this section explains the themes of this book and sets the scene for subsequent chapters. Chapter 2 explains the concept of corporate entrepreneurship. It develops a framework for crafting an entrepreneurial organization using the concept of organizational architecture created through its culture, structure, leadership (and management) and strategies. It draws on learning organization literature to develop an understanding of the role of knowledge and learning in larger organizations. Chapter 3 explores the meaning of innovation and the different forms it can take. It looks at the relationship innovation has with risk, profitability and growth and the most innovative companies by size and sector.

Making an enduring company is far harder and more important than making a great product.

(Steve Jobs, founder Apple Corporation)

2 Corporate entrepreneurship

CONTENTS

- Entrepreneurial intensity
- Defining corporate entrepreneurship
- Entrepreneurial orientation
- Entrepreneurial architecture
- Architecture, relationships and organizational knowledge
- Architecture and organizational learning
- Matching architecture with environment
- Building entrepreneurial architecture
- Summary
- Group discussion topics
- Activities
- References

Learning outcomes

When you have read this chapter and undertaken the related activities you will be able to:

➥ Explain what is meant by the term 'corporate entrepreneurship' and critically analyze the terminology used around it;

➥ Explain what is meant by the term 'organizational architecture' and how it might be shaped through leadership and management, culture, structure and strategies so as to make an organization more entrepreneurial;

➥ Explain what is meant by the term 'learning organization' and how organizational learning and knowledge underpins an entrepreneurial architecture;

➥ Understand how context and environment should determine the appropriate architecture for an organization.

ENTREPRENEURIAL INTENSITY

entrepreneurial
intensity An
increase in both the
degree (or scale)
and the frequency
of entrepreneurial
activity within an
organization

Corporate entrepreneurship is the broad term used to describe entrepreneurial behaviour in an established, larger organization. The objective is to encourage greater **entrepreneurial intensity** within the organization by increasing both the degree, or scale and the frequency of entrepreneurial activity at all levels within it – at corporate, division, business unit, functional and/or project team levels. As shown in Figure 2.1, the degree (or scale) of the entrepreneurial activity can range from low/incremental to high/radical. Its frequency can also range from low/infrequent to high/frequent. Entrepreneurial activity might be evidenced by innovations in products, processes and marketing – a topic we shall return to in the next chapter. Entrepreneurial firms are constantly trying to extend this envelope of entrepreneurial intensity. Corporate entrepreneurship is the overarching term used to describe the mechanisms and processes they use to achieve this and the behavioural characteristics that underpin them.

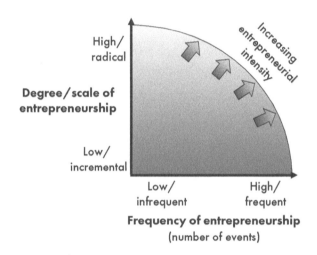

Figure 2.1 Entrepreneurial intensity

culture In an
organization this
is about the web of
unspoken, prevalent
norms, basic beliefs
and assumptions
about the 'right' way
to behave. Sometimes
simply described as
'how it is around here'

By increasing the **entrepreneurial intensity** it is believed that an organization will be better able to cope with change, better able to innovate and therefore better able to gain competitive advantage. The premise behind this approach to corporate entrepreneurship is that large firms need to adapt to an ever-changing environment if they are to survive, and to do so they need to adapt their strategies, structures and **cultures** so as to encourage entrepreneurial activity in individual employees (Peters and Waterman, 1982; Kanter, 1989; Sharma and Chrisman, 1999; Tushman and O'Reilly, 1996; Ghoshal and Bartlett, 1997). The key is the ability to initiate and manage rapid change in organisations, markets and industries – to initiate and manage innovation on a continuous basis. Ultimately, it is about maintaining and/or increasing competitive advantage and therefore profitability, but for more bureaucratic organizations it may be about survival.

> **❝** *Corporations have to dismantle bureaucracies to survive. Economies of scale are giving way to economies of scope, finding the right size for synergy, market flexibility and, above all, speed.* **❞**
>
> John Naisbitt (1994) *Global Paradox: The Bigger the World Economy, the More Powerful its Smallest Players,* London: BCA

Big companies ought to be good at innovation. After all, they have more resources, more knowledge and experience – more of everything to throw at the challenge. But the reality is that it is often newer, smaller businesses that come up with innovations, particularly radical ones. And, as the pace of change accelerates, they seem more able to cope. The core of the problem is that traditional management focuses on efficiency and effectiveness rather than creativity and innovation – control rather than empowerment. Foster and Kaplan (2001) argued that control processes can deaden the company to the vital and constant need for change. They wanted to abandon outdated, in-grown structures and rules and adopt new decision-making processes, control systems and mental models:

> *Managing for survival, even among the best and most revered corporations, does not guarantee strong, long-term performance. In fact quite the opposite is true... Unless companies open up their decision-making processes, relax conventional notions of control, and change at the pace and scale of the market, their performances will be drawn into an entropic slide to mediocrity.*

These are issues we shall develop in later chapters.

Big companies tend to look for cost savings through scale efficiencies rather than differentiation through economies of scope (**synergy**). They look for uniformity rather than diversity and stress discipline rather than motivation. They discourage what they see as the risk-taking associated with a market opportunity without the information to evaluate it, by which time the opportunity may have been seized by a small firm. All of this is understandable. After all, the core business, which probably generates the greatest profitability and represents the greatest corporate value, needs to be run efficiently and safeguarded. However, you disregard the future, and how markets and industries might change, at your peril.

synergy See economies of scope

In dealing with change and innovation, larger companies ought to have some significant advantages over small ones – for example, greater financial resources, credibility with stakeholders, established routes to market, trusted brands and, most valuable of all, large workforces. Indeed up to the middle of the last century large companies were thought of as the way mass economic needs would finally be met. The challenge is to find ways of transforming them so that they can bring their resources to bear on the challenges of the twenty-first century. Corporate entrepreneurship is now seen as a vital part of the strategies needed to rejuvenate these larger companies, maintaining their ability to innovate quickly through entrepreneurial activities (Antoncic, 2006; Burns, 2005; Brizek, 2014; Kuratko et al., 2013).

> *There is a real need for corporate entrepreneurs at the moment. For too long the prevailing consensus has been if it ain't broke, don't fix it but entrepreneurs recognize that action and change are crucial for maximizing potential and taking advantage of opportunities. You have to be tough and outgoing and not afraid of leaving calm waters to ride the waves of a storm.*
>
> Dianne Thompson, Chief Executive Camelot, *The Sunday Times*, 17 March 2002

DEFINING CORPORATE ENTREPRENEURSHIP

Although there is a large literature on the general phenomenon, stretching back over three decades, even as late as the 1980s some academics still believed it was difficult, if not impossible, for entrepreneurial activity to take place in larger organizations (Morse, 1986). Indeed, there was no real consensus on what the term 'corporate entrepreneurship' meant, which resulted in the topic being studied under a number of different headings. Figure 2.2 shows a hierarchy of the often-confusing terminology used in corporate entrepreneurship, each of which we shall explain. Entrepreneurial transformation, strategic renewal and strategic entrepreneurship are all terms used to describe entrepreneurial activities within larger organizations. They are evidenced by, and result from, an entrepreneurial orientation within the organization – a behavioural characteristic. This is achieved through an entrepreneurial architecture – a strategic alignment of corporate resources so as to encourage entrepreneurship and innovation on a sustainable basis. Both internal and external corporate venturing mechanisms are simply tools or techniques that are used within this architecture.

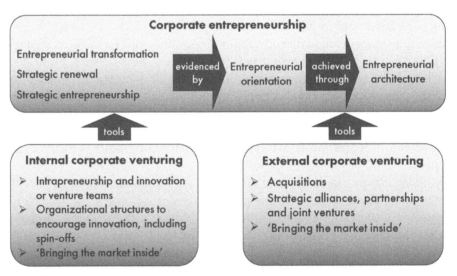

Figure 2.2 Hierarchy of terminology used in corporate entrepreneurship

strategic renewal
Changing the strategic direction of the organization so as to better cope with change and innovation. Often linked to a company attempting a turnaround

Much of the early literature is associated with corporate strategy rather than entrepreneurship. Sharma and Chrisman (1999) identified a number of terms used to describe entrepreneurial efforts within organizations, mainly under the headings of **strategic renewal** and corporate venturing. In the words of Zahra (1996): 'Corporate entrepreneurship is seen as the sum of a company's innovation, strategic renewal and venturing efforts.' Strategic enewal is about changing the strategic direction of the organization, usually implying that becomes more customer- and market-focused, more entrepreneurial (Sharma and Chrisman, 1999). Often linked to companies attempting to reverse continuing decline, it as also been called entrepreneurial transformation (Birkinshaw, 2003), whilst the processes and strategies adopted have more recently been called strategic entrepreneurship Morris et al., 2008; Kuratko and Audretko, 2009).

In fact, corporate venturing can be viewed simply as a series of tools or techniques that an help bring about or maintain strategic renewal (or any of these other terms) and encourage innovation. Some of these approaches relate to how the organization structures tself internally whilst others relate to how it structures itself externally. **Internal corporate venturing** is concerned with the organizational structures needed to encourage new usinesses to develop internally whilst aligning them with the company's existing activities (Burgelman, 1983; Drucker, 1985; Galbraith, 1982). It is particularly concerned with how companies can manage radical entrepreneurship and/or **disruptive innovation** Christensen, 1997). A significant strand of the literature in its own right is concerned vith intrapreneurs and **innovation** or **venture teams** – individuals and teams that develop new products or businesses. We return to this in chapters 9–13. **External corporate venturing** is concerned with how the organization structures itself externally. This may be hrough partnerships, strategic alliances and joint ventures (Chapter 5). It may also be hrough investments and acquisitions in strategically important smaller firms and the corporate venturing units needed to undertake this role (Chesbrough, 2002), which we return to in chapters 14–15. Another strand of the literature in both internal and external corporate venturing might be called 'bringing the market inside' (Birkinshaw, 2003). This focuses mainly on the structural changes needed to encourage entrepreneurial behaviour within an organization, in particular adopting market-based approaches to internal resource allocation such as spin-offs (Chapter 13) and venture funds (Chapter 14) (Foster and Kaplan, 2001; Hamel, 1999).

Organizations involved in these processes have been said to exhibit a sustained pattern of entrepreneurial behaviour over time. This has been called an **entrepreneurial orientation** and has attracted much attention in the literature on corporate entrepreneurship. However, its meaning is not always clear, particularly with regard to identifying how its dimensions are measured and therefore how entrepreneurship might be facilitated. We shall cover entrepreneurial orientation in more detail in the next section.

> *Entrepreneurship in large firms is, unequivocally, a precursor to innovation. In other words, the more entrepreneurial a large company is, the more innovative it will be in aligning its product or service offering with the demands of its intended market.*
>
> Mischa Kaplan, CEO of Cardinal Research Group, *Ottawa Business Journal*,
> 9 October 2018

Organizational architecture is a term that was first coined by Nadler et al. (1992). It is a metaphor used to describe the infrastructure an organization needs in order to build business processes that deliver its vision. Organizational architecture comprises the four pillars shown in Figure 2.3: leadership (and management), culture, structure (including systems) and strategies. These are the generalized building blocks from which any organizational 'climate' can be

internal corporate venturing Organizational structures needed to encourage new businesses to develop internally whilst aligning them with the company's existing activities

disruptive innovation Introducing radically new products or services into existing markets

innovation or venture teams A group developing new products or businesses and operating within a company that is not owned by them

external corporate venturing Strategic partnerships, alliances, etc. and the investment and acquisition by large companies in strategically important smaller firms

entrepreneurial orientation Organizations involved in processes to encourage entrepreneurship and that have exhibited a sustained pattern of entrepreneurial behaviour over time

organizational architecture The infrastructure needed to build processes that deliver an organization's vision. It comprises: leadership and management, culture; structure including systems; and strategies

entrepreneurial architecture
Organizational architecture that encourages entrepreneurship and innovation on a sustainable basis

constructed – including entrepreneurial orientation. **Entrepreneurial architecture** is a term used in the first edition of this book in 2005 to show how the organizational architecture might be structured so as to encourage entrepreneurship and innovation on a sustainable basis by embodying within it the DNA of the entrepreneur and how they manage. It is comprised of the same four elements: leadership, culture, structures and strategies. These are the tools that can create an entrepreneurial organization and encourage entrepreneurial orientation. We shall return to this after looking at entrepreneurial orientation in more detail.

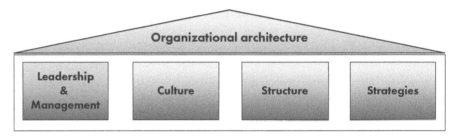

Figure 2.3 Four pillars of organizational architecture

ENTREPRENEURIAL ORIENTATION

Entrepreneurial orientation is probably the most widely used term to describe the entrepreneurial climate and strategy development process in larger firms and is probably the most widely used construct of corporate entrepreneurship (Covin et al., 2006; Wales et al., 2013). However, there is some debate about how patterns of entrepreneurial orientation behaviour might be defined (Covin and Wales, 2012) and it is often less than clear how they were derived. Lumpkin and Dess (1996) defined it as 'involving the intentions and actions of key players functioning in a dynamic generative process aimed at new venture creation', whilst focusing on processes, practices and decision-making. But it has been pointed out that over 19 different labels, involving over a dozen different frameworks, have been used for entrepreneurial orientation (Cogliser et al., 2008). Notwithstanding, most conceptualizations include three broad dimensions of 'organizational climate' (e.g. Lumpkin and Dess, 1996; Miller and Friesen, 1977; Rauch et al., 2009; Wales et al., 2013):

Innovativeness – This relates to the firm's encouragement of innovation through its systems, structures and strategies.
Risk-taking – This relates to the willingness of the firm to engage in what might be seen as risky strategies in pursuit of growth.
Pro-activeness – This relates to the firm's pro-active and speedy pursuit of new opportunities for growth through research, information search, etc.

A further two dimensions that broadened the scope of entrepreneurial orientation have also been shown to have validity (Lumpkin and Dess, 1996; Covin and Wales, 2012):

Competitive aggressiveness – This relates to how a firm engages with competitors in an aggressive way through its marketing strategies.
Internal autonomy – This relates to the ability of individuals or teams to bring forward new ideas.

Entrepreneurial orientation has been linked not only to new venture creation but also to improved financial performance (Miller, 2011). In a meta-analysis of 134 studies by Rauch et al. (2009), it was shown to be a strong predictor of firm performance. This study also showed that the most frequently used method of measuring entrepreneurial orientation was a simple nine-item psychometric scale developed by Covin and Slevin (1989) covering the original three dimensions of entrepreneurial orientation (innovativeness, risk-taking and pro-activeness), although it produced similar results to other variants. Indeed a later study by Wales et al. (2013) observed that roughly 80 per cent of prior studies adopted this conceptualization.

 EXPLORE FURTHER

Covin and Slevin (1989) developed a nine-item instrument to measure entrepreneurial orientation covering innovativeness, risk-taking and pro-activeness. Each dimension was covered by three questions with responses measured on a seven-point Likert scale.

It is available on www.entrepreneurialorientation.com/measures.html.

However, whilst there is some debate about the dimensions of entrepreneurial orientation and how it is conceptualized, there is even greater debate about how these dimensions might be measured. Measurement of entrepreneurial orientation raises a number of issues, not least the possibility of mixing cause (input) and effect (output). Conceptually, input (causal) measures – representing the organizational climate within a firm – ought to be used to measure entrepreneurial orientation. Output measures should reflect the effect entrepreneurial orientation has on entrepreneurial intensity – the scale and frequency of entrepreneurial events in Figure 2.1. One element of entrepreneurial orientation – innovativeness – is generally considered to be the most important and statistically influential (Lumpkin and Dess, 1996) and yet researchers have repeatedly confused input and output measures of this dimension (e.g. Covin and Slevin, 2012; Forsman, 2011). For example, Covin and Slevin's scale for innovativeness includes the question:

> How many new lines of products or services has your firm marketed in the past five years (or since its establishment)?

Respondents to this question are asked to rate firstly the number of innovations (low/high) and secondly their scale (minor/dramatic), providing data on only two out of nine questions. However, both these measures of innovation are output measures of entrepreneurial orientation (the effect), rather than behavioural input measures (the cause). Any relationship between entrepreneurial orientation and the improved financial performance observed by Rauch is therefore, at least in part, attributable to the volume and frequency of innovation, and the fact that innovation is linked to improved financial performance is not in doubt. The real question is which organizational climate, systems, strategies and capabilities encourage innovation.

In an attempt to clarify this dimension, some scholars have retitled the innovativeness dimension 'innovation orientation'. Siguaw et al. (2006) defined this as 'composed of learning philosophy, strategic direction and transformational beliefs that, in turn, guide and direct all organizational strategies and actions . . . to promote innovative thinking and facilitate successful development, evolution and execution of innovation'. Arshi and Burns (2018) broadened it even further to include innovation-building capabilities. These included organizational culture, structures, strategies and leadership and management – part of an entrepreneurial architecture – which they then then linked to the four elements of entrepreneurial orientation (risk-taking, pro-activeness, competitive aggressiveness and autonomy). Based upon an empirical study, they go on to show that this entrepreneurial orientation is an antecedent or precursor to innovation, influencing both in scale and frequency of innovation, and asserted that the broader entrepreneurial architecture framework can be used to structure and encourage innovation in larger firms. These measures 'weave a framework of supporting and collaborating acts of entrepreneurial behaviour resulting in enhanced innovation outputs'.

ENTREPRENEURIAL ARCHITECTURE

Entrepreneurial architecture seeks to embed entrepreneurial characteristics in the organization through the four pillars of organizational architecture: leadership (and management), culture, structure (including systems) and strategies. These characteristics are modelled from the entrepreneur themselves – their personal character traits and how they manage and make business decisions.

The generalized approach of looking at organizational architecture as a whole and then isolating those elements within it that might cause an organization to have a greater entrepreneurial orientation provides a more structured approach to the search for how to encourage entrepreneurship and provides a framework for understanding how these element arise – an approach that is missing in most of the literature. Whilst entrepreneurial orientation might focus on a few elements or dimensions of behaviour, entrepreneurial architecture looks at the whole organizational picture ensuring consistency between the four pillars. Not all firms are the same, producing different types of products/services in different industries for different markets. Entrepreneurial architecture can be adapted to different environments where different components become more or less important (Arshi and Burns, 2019). The importance of this environmental context is discussed later in this chapter.

Organizational architecture can be both internal and external. Internal architecture focuses on employees, generating a distinctive culture, a strong sense of collectivism, or being part of a team or an 'in-group', as we saw in Chapter 1. This collectivism comes from shared objectives and commonly accepted strategies. Strong internal architecture tends to attract like-minded people and this can be either a strength or, if it creates inflexibility, a weakness. External architecture focuses on other stakeholders such as customers, partners suppliers or subcontractors. It is often built on trusting relationships and shows itself in the sharing of information or other resources. For example, in the UK there is a cluster of small firms in South Wales which manufacture sofas. Around them is a skilled workforce and the infrastructure needed to support them. Italy has developed these clusters in numerous industries from knitwear and ties to tiles, all based in different geographic clusters.

Leadership and management styles, organizational cultures and structures are all linked - one reinforces the other. If one is inappropriate for the other two then the organization will not function as it should. What is more, certain styles are appropriate for different types of task, for different groups of people and for different situations and environments. And, as we saw in Chapter 1, complexity theory tells us that, when it comes to managing unpredictable change, the critical challenge is how to create an environment within an organization that encourages self-organization by creating systems, structures and leadership that facilitate it.

The tools that shape entrepreneurial architecture are shown in Figure 2.4. The elements are interrelated, each affecting the other, hence the direction of arrows. However, the leader's role is crucial. They have prime responsibility for shaping an organization's structure, culture and the strategies it develops, and hence its architecture. Having said that, how this is transmitted through the organization by its management and how managerial tasks are undertaken is also very important. This architecture needs to be responsive to the external environment the organization faces. Whilst central to the organization's strategy is the creation of entrepreneurial architecture, other strategies will be the product of it – strategy need not always come from the leader. The interplay of the factors in Figure 2.4 should determine strategy. In these circumstances strategy development becomes part of entrepreneurial architecture, creating an organization that is better able to respond to unpredictable change and opportunity in the way the entrepreneur does, making it better suited to survive in the age of uncertainty. And strategy development, like all aspects of entrepreneurial architecture, is difficult to copy because it is constantly evolving and adapting to the changing marketplace. Entrepreneurial architecture is a very real and valuable asset in its own right as it creates competitive advantage and is sustainable.

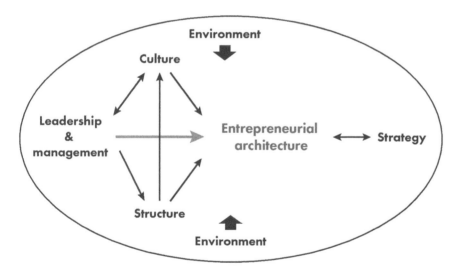

Figure 2.4 Influences on entrepreneurial architecture

CASE INSIGHT 2.1
Haier Group

China

ENTREPRENEURIAL ARCHITECTURE

Although little known in the West, Haier Group is one of the largest non-state-owned enterprises in China. With over 10 per cent of the global market, it is the world's largest manufacturer of 'white goods'. It is also the world's fastest-growing appliance manufacturer. Haier was hailed by *Strategy + Business* as a 'high-performing and truly entrepreneurial global business' (Issue 77, Winter 2014). Its CEO, Zhang Ruimin, was invited to give the keynote address at the 2013 annual meeting of the Academy of Management and was lauded by the journal for 'organizing the company around a conceptual framework that has guided its development for years – in Haier's case, practically since its founding'. In this framework you will recognise all the characteristics of corporate entrepreneurship.

As soon as a company grows large, its employees learn to work in accordance with the company's rules. As regulations multiply and companies control their employees more tightly, everyone becomes really good at following orders. Their sensitivity to the market decreases accordingly . . . Lack of entrepreneurial spirit is a major reason for the decreasing competitiveness – and even the eventual collapse – of big enterprises. It is an extremely difficult problem for Chinese companies in particular . . . An enterprise must evolve into a system that stands on its own, and does not depend on the whim and fancy of its current leader.

Haier started its life as a manufacturing firm that was partly owned by the city of Qingdao, one of China's first enterprise zones. It was not successful and many of their products had to be repaired before they could be used. Zhang, who was at this time an assistant administrator in the city, was instructed to find a managing director who could turn the business around. He failed and so in 1984, at the age of 25 and with little or no business experience, he took the job himself. It took time, but Zhang eventually succeeded.

Today Haier manufactures a wide range of appliances, including refrigerators, washers, dryers, entertainment electronics and air and water conditioners. It is an international company with manufacturing facilities in China, across Asia, the Middle East, Africa, South America and the USA (it bought GE Appliances in 2017). It has differentiated itself by targeting the needs of market niches. For example, it manufactures large washing machines for Pakistani robes, small ones for Chinese delicate fabrics and durable ones with large hoses for washing vegetables on Chinese farms. It has water purifiers that remove specific pollutants from each of 220,000 communities across China (it jointly holds some 20 water purification patents). In 2015, it launched the world's first 'pocket' washing machine, the CODO, which was the size of an electric shaver and weighing just 200g.

Haier is also repositioning itself from being a manufacturer to being a 'provider of solutions to consumers' problems', selling both home appliances and services such as water safety information. Part of this repositioning involves dealing with customers more directly, online and through social media, involving them in product selection (for example, by offering different configuration of products – colour and design), testing or reviews (sharing feedback) and even product development. The CODO idea came from an engineer in the company's washing machine R&D department and was developed by Haier's central R&D department in Japan. Once the project team had developed an early prototype, the project leader placed the concept onto the internet to get consumers' views which ranged from suggestions about the product, through to its name, colour and packaging.

We have a culture of self-questioning. Everyone is always challenging their own ideas and continuously surpassing themselves . . . Those inside Haier, especially managers, understand that it's crucial that we adapt to the evolving needs of users and the changing environment.

Haier's success hinges on four key capabilities:

➡ Customer-responsive innovation – The ability to tailor products or services to local needs;
➡ Operational excellence – The ability to produce high-quality products at very low prices through a commitment to continuous improvement, a zero-defect policy and internal competition;

➡ **Management of local distribution networks** – An ability developed in China's decentralized value chain and applied to emerging markets;

➡ **On-demand production and delivery** – Combining a customer-pull distribution chain and a zero-inventory logistics system to deliver high variety at very low cost.

Key to achieving this success was the move towards a flat organization structure with decentralized, participative management and autonomous but accountable work teams and platforms (topics we return to in later chapters). Every part of the company is an autonomous, platform-based profit centre or micro-enterprise. They can make their own decisions about target customers, employees and who they partner with – including other parts of the company. R&D projects embrace open innovation and can involve collaborative working with outside designers, academics – even competitors – through its own ecosystem of partners called HOPE (Haier Open Partnership Ecosystem). For example, the Air Box is a smartphone-controlled intelligent controller for monitoring and managing the climate in a building – linking heating, air conditioning and air filtration. The concept was developed with significant customer input, but the product was developed in partnership with Samsung and Apple so that it can control any climate control system, not just those manufactured by Haier. The company has so many innovations being developed that it now has its own in-house intellectual property team of some 40 specialists.

We used to have a pyramid style [organization] structure for our sales in China. The people in charge of sales had to manage business at the national, provincial, and city level. After the arrival of the internet age, we realized that under this triangular hierarchical structure, people had a difficult time adapting to the requirement of the times. So we reorganised ourselves as an entrepreneurial platform. We flattened everything out, taking out all the middle management. We decentralized the structure to one with more than 2,800 counties. Each county organization has seven people or fewer. (Zhang Ruimin, CEO, Haier Group, Strategy + Business, Issue 77, Winter 2014)

Haier is starting to expand its product/market offerings by developing a comprehensive series of 'smart solutions' for the home – the living room, kitchen, laundry room and bathroom. These network-enabled products use an open ecosystem-based platform called Haier U+ Smart Life Platform, which allows a wide range of products to be controlled remotely.

Visit the website: **www.haier.com**.

Questions:

1. Is Haier an entrepreneurial organization? If so, how does it achieve this? Is this part of an entrepreneurial architecture?
2. How would you go about the task of creating an entrepreneurial architecture? How difficult is it?

ARCHITECTURE, RELATIONSHIPS AND ORGANIZATIONAL KNOWLEDGE

A strong architecture creates a community, a sense of belonging with an almost familial bond – a sense of corporate identity. It is built upon strong, long-term *relationships* between all the stakeholders. Kay (1995) called them **relational contracts**, although they are not necessarily legal contracts. These are tacit contracts which are only partly specified and

relational contracts The strong, long-term relationships between stakeholders. Based on trust, despite being unwritten, they form tacit contracts concerning how to behave

only really enforced by the need of the parties to work together. Like all relationships, they are based upon mutual trust, underpinned by mutual self-interest and demonstrated by reciprocity (Dubini and Aldrich, 1991; Larson, 1992). This means that individuals understand that in exchange for their effort and commitment they will be paid a fair wage and the company will look after their interests and develop their potential. Reciprocal obligations are decisive for human well-being, underpinning family relationships. They instil ideas of fairness and generate loyalty. The nature of this relationship discourages one party from acting in some way at the expense of the other because it is important that they continue to work together. It also encourages each party to do the 'right thing' by the other because it further cements the relationship and is likely to result in some sort of reciprocity. In Chapter 1, we stressed the importance of relationships in the way entrepreneurs do business – they build into an invaluable network of contacts and goodwill. Developing a strong architecture therefore fits nicely into their style of management.

Just as entrepreneurs use networks of relationships to help them operate in a way that allows them to seize opportunities quickly, architecture allows the entrepreneurial firm to respond quickly and effectively to change and opportunity. Developing organizational architecture is a systematic exploitation of one of the main distinctive capabilities of entrepreneurs. It builds on dynamic capabilities that are difficult to copy. It does so by creating within the organization the knowledge and routines that enable this to happen smoothly and unhindered. Entrepreneurial architecture therefore creates an entrepreneurial organization. Staff are motivated or empowered to make this happen, knowing it is good for the organization. These relationships become institutionalized and can then create competitive advantage and barriers to market entry.

Using examples of small and large organizations, Kay emphasizes that architecture comprises patterns of long-term relationships which are 'complex, subtle and hard to define precisely or to replicate' and he observes that it is easier to sustain than to create and even more difficult to create in an organization that does not have it in the first place. Individuals participate in these relationships voluntarily because of a strong personal feeling that it is in their interests because they are participating in a 'repeated game' in which they share the rewards of collective achievement. These relationships solve problems of co-operation, co-ordination and commitment. They set the rules of the game and if you cheat you would find it difficult to play the game again with the same players. Trust can take time to build but is easily lost. These relationships are characterized as having a high, but structured degree of informality, something that can be mistaken as haphazard, chaotic or just lucky:

> *This informality is sometimes mistaken for disorganization – in popular discussion of chaos, entrepreneurship, or adhocracy as conditions of innovation – but truly chaotic organizations rarely perform well, and a system of relational contracts substitutes an extensive set of unwritten rules and expectations of behavior for the formal obligations of the classical contract. (Kay, 1995)*

Strong organizational architecture is difficult to copy because it is informal in nature, not based on legal contracts and not written down anywhere. Instead it relies on the complex network of personal relationships throughout the organization. Any one individual only knows or understands a small part of the overall structure. And just as entrepreneurs use

heir network of relationships to gain information and knowledge so as to mitigate risk, so
oo a strong architecture can create valuable *organizational knowledge*:

> *If there is a single central lesson . . . it is that the stability of relationships and the capacity
> to respond to change are mutually supportive, not mutually exclusive, requirements. It is
> within the context of long-term relationships . . . that the development of organizational
> knowledge, the free exchange of information, and a readiness to respond quickly and flex-
> ibly can be sustained . . . The value of architecture lies in the capacity of organizations
> which establish it to create organizational knowledge and routines, to respond flexibly to
> changing circumstances, and to achieve easy and open exchanges of information. Each is
> capable of creating an asset for the firm – organizational knowledge which is more than
> the sum of individual knowledge, flexibility, and responsiveness which extends to the insti-
> tution as well as to its members. (Kay, 1995).*

With this description we again glimpse reflections of the start-up entrepreneur in the middle of the spider's web of informal, personal relationships, recognizing opportunity everywhere, trying to innovate and trying to replicate success, using networks, relying on
personal relationships with customers, staff and suppliers. Entrepreneurs prefer influence
and informal relationships to formal contracts. They use these to secure repeat sales at the
expense of competitors and to secure resources or competitive advantage that they might
not otherwise have. Close partnerships with suppliers where information and knowledge is
shared can lead to significant advantages in lowering costs, lead times and inventories. All
these relationships are based on trust – 'my word is my bond' – and most involve a degree
of self-interest. The challenge in a larger organization is to replicate these relationships
across the whole organization and develop an entrepreneurial architecture.

ARCHITECTURE AND ORGANIZATIONAL LEARNING

As we commented in Chapter 1, entrepreneurs learn by doing – so-called experiential
learning – and they learn quickly not to repeat mistakes but to capitalize on success.
Because they are one person, knowledge and information is translated into learning continuously, quickly and without barriers. As the organization grows, the challenge is for this
process to be replicated across an entire organization. Strong architecture creates valuable
organizational information and knowledge, but how does this translate into organizational
learning? Real knowledge is about more than just information sharing. It is about learning
from each other and from outside the organization. It is about getting a better understanding of inter-relationships, complexities and causalities – the causes rather than just the
symptoms of a problem – and then translating this into future decision-making. Constant
learning by organizations requires the acquisition of new information, knowledge and skills
but also crucially the willingness to apply them to decision-making (Miller, 1996). It
includes the unlearning of old routines (Markoczy, 1994) so that the range of potential
behaviour is altered (Wilpert, 1995). This is at the heart of what a learning organization is
about and there are some lessons to be learned from how it goes about doing so.

A learning organization may be defined as one that 'facilitates the learning of all its
members and continuously transforms itself . . . adapting, changing, developing and transforming themselves in response to the needs, wishes and aspirations of people, inside and

outside' (Pedler et al., 1991). Writings on the learning organization stress how it is flexible, adaptable and better equipped to thrive in a turbulent environment. It facilitates learning for all its members and continually transforms itself:

➡ Encouraging systematic problem-solving.
➡ Encouraging experimentation and new approaches.
➡ Learning from past experience and history.
➡ Learning from best practice and outside experience.
➡ Being skilled at transferring knowledge in the organization.

Experiential learning is probably the most powerful form of learning. We learn most things in life – eating, crawling, walking and communicating – through trial and error; action, consequence, reflection and then remedial action. Building on Kolb's (1984) experiential learning cycle, Kim (1993) suggested that effective learning can be considered to be a revolving wheel – the wheel of learning in Figure 2.5: forming concepts, testing concepts, learning from this experience and then reflecting how the concept might be inappropriate, changed or improved. During half the cycle, you form and then test existing concepts and observe what happens through experience – learning 'know-how'. In the second half of the cycle, you are reflecting on the observations and forming new concepts – learning 'know-

double-loop learning
A learning cycle that moves from 'knowing-how' to 'knowing-why'. Often called the wheel of learning

why' – often called **double-loop learning** (Argyris and Schön, 1978). It is this second sort of learning that is of particular value to entrepreneurs because it is at this point that root causes of problems are diagnosed and systematic solutions put in place. This is when you question your dominant logic mental models – the assumptions and theories about the world upon which your learning is based. Dominant logic is the mindset with which an organization or industry collectively sees itself and the world it inhabits – its position with customers, competitors and other stakeholders. It filters the information, subconsciously interpreting environmental data in a certain way and influences behaviour. If you start asking 'why?', 'why not?' and questioning industry's dominant logic you start to reframe your thinking and become more creative and innovative, able to spot opportunities for new

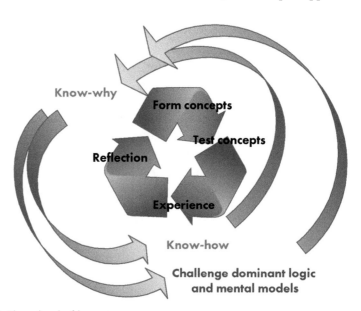

Figure 2.5 The wheel of learning

products or markets that others have failed to see. Real learning is about application, continuous problem-solving, and understanding the root cause of problems rather than being distracted by the symptoms.

Since dominant logic is a social construct it can be influenced and changed by the organizational architecture, albeit over time. By embedding double-loop learning within the organization you can change the dominant logic of managers and get them to reframe the way they approach business to become more creative. It is a vital skill for an entrepreneurial organization.

It is the constant turning of the wheel of learning, sharing knowledge of 'know-how' and 'know-why', that embeds double-loop learning within an organization. Dominant logic is challenged constantly. Over the years this generates organizational learning, and becomes part of the collective 'memory' of the organization. Although this accumulated knowledge is tacit (i.e. embedded in minds and activities, rather than written down) as well as being shadowy and fragile, it is unique to the organization and difficult to copy. It is therefore a valuable part of the architecture that underpins the organization's competitive advantage. Merx-Chermin and Nijhof (2005) argue that organizations must become truly learning organizations if they are to acquire new knowledge and capabilities in this way and that knowledge sharing and trust must be created for this to happen.

The literature on learning organizations also has things to say about how they should be led and managed. Senge (1992) observed that learning organizations can only be built by leaders with fire and passion: 'Learning organizations can be built only by individuals who put their life spirit into the task.' The similarity to the entrepreneur is striking. Indeed, the similarities can also be seen from the literature on entrepreneurs. For example, Timmons (1999) observed that successful entrepreneurs were: 'patient leaders, capable of instilling tangible visions and managing for the long haul. The entrepreneur is at once a learner and a teacher, a doer and a visionary.' Being a learner and a teacher are two of the prime tasks for a leader in a learning organization. And the parallels go further.

This approach to management and leadership requires a more collectivist culture – a belief that the interests of the organization and the individual are the same, with shared **values** and a sense of being part of a team or an 'in-group', an approach typically cultivated by the entrepreneurs. The atmosphere is cooperative within the 'in-group', although it may be competitive with 'out-groups'. As a result, staff feel empowered to influence the direction of the organization and believe that continually developing, learning and acquiring new knowledge is the way to do this. Truly entrepreneurial organizations, therefore, are also learning organizations. This goes to the heart of their architecture.

values Core beliefs

MATCHING ARCHITECTURE WITH ENVIRONMENT

Developing strong entrepreneurial architecture creates competitive advantage in certain types of environment. It is designed to facilitate change and encourage creativity and innovation. However, this may not be appropriate for all organizations. Entrepreneurial architecture is probably not appropriate for a benign, unchanging environment in which simple tasks are undertaken with a view to achieving maximum efficiency, for example for companies adopting a low-cost/low-price **business model**. Constructing an entrepreneurial architecture may involve extra costs compared with a more conventional architecture. It may also encourage behaviours that are considered 'inappropriate' in these circumstances. However, such companies need to beware of changes in the environment, for example

business model A plan for how a business competes, uses its resources, structures its relationships, communicates with customers, creates value and generates profits

45

when disruptive shifts in the market take place, meaning that their business model is no longer attractive to customers.

If an organization's architecture does not 'fit' with its commercial environment, the organization will not prosper. As explained in Chapter 1, entrepreneurial firms thrive in environments of change, chaos, complexity, competition, uncertainty and even contradiction where innovation is essential. These are highly competitive and rapidly changing markets facing pressures for greater corporate social responsibility and problems in attracting suitable staff. The exact form an organization's architecture should take also depends on the economic, technological and societal environment in which it operates. These are some of the commercial environments that an entrepreneurial architecture is designed to cope with:

➡ Markets where new technologies are important – Where new technological developments are highly valued by customers there is considerable 'first-mover advantage', reinforcing the importance of a rapid response to developments.
➡ Markets that value creativity – Many markets value creativity; for example, the video-gaming industry, which combines creativity with technological development. The creative industries generally should thrive within an entrepreneurial architecture.
➡ New or changing markets – This could be any market that is changing rapidly for any reason. New markets could be emerging and the whole structure of the market might be changing, with many mergers or take-overs. In these circumstances customers might be seen as promiscuous as their 'needs' change rapidly and, as a result, the industry spends increasing amounts on advertising in order to get their attention.
➡ Interconnected markets – The interconnectedness of markets and economies tends to amplify small initial changes – in customer needs or market trends – and this makes for instability and unpredictability, meaning that traditional forms of strategic planning no longer work. Speed of response is vital.
➡ Markets where information and knowledge are important – In markets providing up-to-date or real-time information and knowledge, rapid changes in both the information and market needs are important. This includes changes in technology that might impact on the ability to deliver this service.
➡ Price-sensitive markets – Markets might be highly price-sensitive, with low barriers to entry and high economies of scale. New competitors might be emerging all the time and these new competitors might be very price competitive and/or good at innovating.
➡ Markets coming to an end of their life-cycle – The ending of a product life-cycle may threaten the existence of a business or may just unbalance its product portfolio. Either way the company will need to innovate.

The appropriate entrepreneurial architecture can even vary with the nature of the entrepreneurial intensity required within the organizational unit. This implies the need to break down organizations into units that reflect their commercial purpose and external environment – possibly with structures within structures, subcultures within cultures and different approaches to leadership within an overall approach. Not all parts of a multi-product/market business may exhibit the same characteristics because of differences in their operational needs (for example, the stage in the life-cycle of products) and/or their market situations (for example, they do not operate in an entrepreneurial environment). The Virgin Group, for example, is a **conglomerate** that operates across different sectors and

conglomerate A diversified company with interests in a range of different industries

equires different architecture in each of its divisions or subsidiaries. However, the over-arching architecture of the holding company can still be entrepreneurial, allowing it to be esponsive to change. Entrepreneurial architecture is not a 'one-size-fits-all' blueprint. It eeds to be applied selectively, with thought and judgement.

CASE INSIGHT 2.2
Sulhail Bhawan Group

Oman

ENTREPRENEURIAL ARCHITECTURE

When they were still young Suhail Bhawan and his brother Saud Bhawan inherited a traditional wooden dhow (boat) from their father. They used it to trade goods such as fishing nets, building materials, dates and spices between India and Oman. The trade flourished and in 1965 both brothers moved to the capital, Muscat, where they set up a small shop in Muttrah souq, a traditional market frequented by traders and travellers. However, things changed when they obtained exclusive licenses to sell Seiko watches and Toyota vehicles in Oman. Toyota rapidly became the best-selling car in Oman, building on its reliability and backed by good service. As a result, the dealership expanded to other towns and cities in Oman.

However, in 2002 the brothers decided to go their separate ways. Suhail went on to expand and diversify the business into areas such as healthcare, construction, engineering, travel, oil and gas, manufacturing, agriculture fertilizers and information technology. By 2018, Forbes was reporting that Suhail Bhawan, who had become chairman of the Suhail Bhawan Group of companies (SBG), was worth $3.2 billion. The year before, he was awarded the Sheikh Issa bin Ali al Khalifa Award for voluntary work by the Arab League. The company is now headed by his daughter Amal Bahwan, his sixth child and second-eldest daughter. She is vice-chairman of the company and in 2018 was named by Forbes Middle East as one of the most influential Arab women.

SBG group now has a portfolio of over 40 companies in Oman and across the Gulf Region, North Africa and South Asia and has over 15,000 employees. Every company within the group continues to engage in related diversifications and develop core competencies in those sectors. For example, Bahwan Engineering has diversified into property development and construction. It has a division called Bilad Oman that specialises in providing a comprehensive steel structure build package – from design, detailing, procurement, manufacturing and surface treatment to the erection of the steel components for different structures. Similarly, its IT division has diversified into telecom and IT education, establishing the first educational institution in Oman to partner with a German university.

Suhail's leadership style has fed into the culture of the organization: 'We believe in working together, building positive relationships, celebrating diversity in business and culture and contributing positively to the communities we live in.' His daughter, Amal, shows her determination to maintain an entrepreneurial spirit in the company: 'As we look forward to a future brimming with new opportunities, we will continue to raise the bar and set new benchmarks for others to follow.' These messages aim to encourage a culture of opportunity-seeking, growth and innovation and to achieve it through teamwork, diversity and positive relationships with employees and business partners. The company has clear performance indicators and measurement criteria that encourage productivity and efficiency. However, there is a group in every division that monitors the market for emerging opportunities. Teamwork and collaboration is highly encouraged. Once an opportunity arises, the group is quick to exploit the opportunities, take risks and invest in the corporate spin-off.

The company's culture is driven by its values and philosophy. In Arabic, it is called 'Ahlan Wa-Sahlan' – where all customers are treated as guests and their expectations have to be surpassed. Further, the values of the company include statements like 'one-team–one-family' and 'our word is our bond' and the entrepreneurial nature of the company's culture is reflected through these core values:

➡ 'Inspired by the seafaring tradition of exploring new worlds . . . new horizons'
➡ 'Encouraged by endless opportunities . . . endless possibilities'
➡ 'Driven by the relentless pursuit of excellence, professionalism and dedicated service'
➡ 'Passionate about people and the quality of their lives'
➡ 'Innovative, contemporary, customer driven and caring'.

The organization structure, culture and leadership style support these values. SBG is a diversified company but with centralized systems. The management style of the company has evolved from being old school (hierarchical) to entrepreneurial. The business headquarters, which houses the corporate office and the human resource division, is located in Muscat. The human resource division manages the recruitment, training, performance and remuneration for all the companies. The group believes that having a centralized structure enables it to apply standardized processes and systems and ensure quality. For example, the quality of its customer service, around which its brand is built, cannot be compromised by any one company within the group. Every company must adhere to these standards and contribute its brand image of quality and service even if that company may be a small operator in its sector. The policy is designed to give the brand leverage to all its companies. However, companies within the group have the freedom to find new opportunities, diversify product and services and innovate based on their competencies and customer needs, as well as responding to competitor and market dynamics.

SBG's culture also drives the company's strategies. It aims to be a market leader in almost all the sectors it enters, using its size and resources to leverage its position. In the words of one employee: 'SBG has been a leader in many industries and because of its reputation and brand image enjoys considerable amount of bargaining power among suppliers, customers and competitors, even though it may be a small operator in that sector.' The company is aggressive in pursuing opportunities and entering new markets. It has produced innovations in many of its companies: engineering, logistics, information technology, oil and gas. For example, in logistics, which is one of the fastest-growing sectors in Oman, SBG has shown innovation in the entire value chain, providing its clients with end-to-end solutions in conducting global trade. Its strategy in dealing with its major competitor DHL has been to enter into a joint venture with it, called Bahwan DHL. As a result, SBG now has access to DHL's distribution network in 220 countries. The engineering group has also produced a number of engineering innovations, not only in Oman but also in United Arab Emirates. These include structural solutions for commercial projects as well in oil and gas fields. The energy and power division has also produced innovations in the treatment of sea water for various commercial purposes.

SBG leads the market in many sectors in Oman, operating in an environment which cannot boast of an innovative and entrepreneurial culture, particularly in a corporate world. Under family ownership and control, SBG has developed a diversified portfolio of businesses that have a homogeneous culture quite unlike most others in the country.

Visit the website: **www.suhailbahwangroup.com**

Questions:

1. Is Suhail Bahwan Group an entrepreneurial organization? If so, how does it achieve this? Is this part of an entrepreneurial architecture?
2. How might the environmental context in Oman over this period have influenced this?

Source: Wendel Samuel, 'From Humble Beginnings, Suhail Bahwan Became A Billionaire in Oman', *Forbes*, 11 April 2017. Retrieved 15 November 2018.
Case contributed by Dr Tahseen Arshi

BUILDING ENTREPRENEURIAL ARCHITECTURE

The personal character traits of the entrepreneur need to be reflected in the entrepreneurial architecture of an organization. As we have seen in Chapter 1, entrepreneurs are creative and innovative risk-takers. These are at the core of entrepreneurship. Their high need for achievement and internal locus of control gives them the drive and determination to push through projects when outcomes are uncertain. They value, and should therefore understand, the need for independence or autonomy of action. All of these character traits should be reflected in an entrepreneurial architecture (Table 2.1).

Chapter 1 also highlighted the key characteristic of the entrepreneur's approach to management and decision-making. All of these characteristics should also be reflected in an entrepreneurial architecture. These characteristics are listed in Table 2.2.

The challenge is to build all these characteristics into the architecture through its leadership and management, culture, structure and strategies. Entrepreneurial architecture

Table 2.1 Personal character traits of the entrepreneur that need to be reflected in an entrepreneurial architecture

An entrepreneurial architecture is one that replicates the character traits of the entrepreneur. It should:

➡ Encourage innovation and opportunity spotting.
➡ Embed within people a strong vision of what the organization can become.
➡ Motivate people to achieve, set goals and encourage achievement through public recognition and reward.
➡ Encourage people to belong to and 'own' the organization, ensuring that they share in its success, so that they are motivated to see it grow.
➡ Encourage a 'can-do' and 'work-is-fun' culture.
➡ Encourage delegation and decentralization, pushing decision-making down the organizational hierarchy.
➡ Empower staff to make the right decisions for the organization.
➡ Ensure there is a 'light touch' with management so that staff can exercise their sense of empowerment.
➡ Encourage organizational self-confidence and self-efficacy by celebrating achievement and success, but not at the expense of recognizing reality.
➡ Encourage open communication and the sharing of information and knowledge, so the organization can react quickly to environmental changes and capitalize on opportunities.
➡ Encourage continual learning (and unlearning) from this information and knowledge.
➡ Recognize change as the norm and something to be welcomed rather than avoided.
➡ Ensure success is celebrated.
➡ Recognize the importance of experimentation and balanced risk-taking.
➡ Not penalize failure unnecessarily, but always learn from it.

Table 2.2 Management characteristics of the entrepreneur that need to be reflected in an entrepreneurial architecture

An entrepreneurial architecture is one that replicates the characteristics of the entrepreneurs' approach to management. It should:

➡ Create a clear purpose for the organization, which is underpinned by a strong shared vision or strategic intent.
➡ Develop deep relationships with all stakeholders within and outside the organization – staff, customers, suppliers and partners.
➡ Rely on these strong relationships to give the organization identity and cement trust.
➡ Facilitate management through this relationship rather than relying on formal structures and hierarchies.
➡ Use these networks to gain information and knowledge so as to better manage the risks it faces.
➡ Encourage the sharing of this information and knowledge so as to allow strategizing.
➡ Encourage collaboration, for example through teamworking and partnership.
➡ Encourage continuous strategizing at all levels of the organization as well as the development of strategic options.
➡ Adopt an incremental, adaptive approach to decision-making, using small incremental steps, learning by doing, so as to better manage the risks it faces.

should provide the dynamic capabilities that allows the firm to 'achieve new resource combinations as markets emerge, collide, split, evolve, and die' (Eisenhardt and Martin, 2000) and, in so doing, create real shareholder value. Subsequent chapters will outline how this can be achieved.

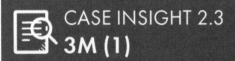 CASE INSIGHT 2.3
3M (1)

 USA

THE LONG GAME

3M has been known for decades as an entrepreneurial company that pursues growth through innovation. It currently generates a quarter of its annual revenues from products less than five years old. 3M started life as the Minnesota Mining and Manufacturing Company back in 1902. Its most successful product – flexible sandpaper – still forms an important part of its product line, but this now comprises over 60,000 products that range from adhesive tapes to office supplies, from medical supplies to traffic signs, from magnetic tapes and CDs to electrical equipment. Originally, innovation was encouraged informally by the founders, but over more than a century some of these rules have been formalized. But most important of all there has built up a culture which encourages innovation. For example, there is a 'hall of fame' of staff elected on the basis of their innovative achievements. And because this culture has built up a history of success, it perpetuates itself as well as helping the company to recruit people with innovative characteristics.

3M's best-known innovation is the Post-It Note® developed by the intrapreneur Art Frye in the 1980s.
Source: iStock/Christopher Dumond

3M started by selling a somewhat inferior quality of sandpaper. The only way it could promote this was by getting close to the customer – demonstrating it to the workmen that used it and persuading them to specify the product – an early form of relationship selling. This was the first strategic thrust of the fledgling business – get close to customers and understand their needs. And it still does this. For example, when it developed its overhead projector business it asked technical staff to contact users to find out how the product could be improved. To this day it encourages close links with users.

However, the company was desperate to move away from selling a commodity product and competing primarily on price, and its closeness to the customer led it to discover market opportunities that it had the expertise to capitalize on. The first such product was Three-M-Ite Abrasive – an abrasive cloth using aluminum oxide for durability in place of a natural abrasive. This was followed by waterproof sandpaper – an idea bought from an inventor who subsequently came to work for 3M. This was followed shortly afterwards by Wetordry – a product designed for use by the car industry in finishing bodywork. And with this the second strategic thrust of the company was developed – to seek out niche markets, no matter how small, which would allow it to charge a premium price for its products. The company began to realize that many small niche markets could prove to be more profitable than a few large ones.

In the 1990s this began to change somewhat, to the extent that some technologies became more sophisticated and the investment needed to develop new products increased. Therefore the return required became larger and markets needed to be correspondingly bigger. Luckily, the world was increasingly becoming a global marketplace. At the same time, competition was becoming tougher and the rapidity of technological change and shortening of product life-cycles made 3M recognize the need to dominate any market niche quickly – its second strategic thrust. Speed of response was vital. By the 1990s, many of the market niches 3M was pioneering were turning out to be not that small at all, particularly in the global marketplace. So, the approach remained the same, but the speed of response and size of market niche, world-wide, increased.

The company really started to diversify when it entered the adhesive tape market in the 1920s, but even this built on its expertise in coatings, backings and adhesives. What is more the way the first product evolved demonstrates perfectly how an entrepreneurial architecture works. By being close to its customers 3M saw a problem that it was able to solve for them through its technical expertise. In selling Wetordry to car-body finishers, an employee realized how difficult it was for the painters to produce the latest fad in car painting – two-tone paintwork. The result was the development of masking tape – imperfect at first, but developed over the years 'out-of-hours' by an employee to what we know it to be today and from that technology developed the Scotch range of branded tapes. So, the third strategic thrust was developed – diversify into the related areas identified as market opportunities by customers. Once 3M found a niche product to offer in a new market, it soon developed other related products and developed a dominant position in the new market.

In the 1990s 3M came to recognize that it did best when it introduced radically innovative products into a niche market in which it already had a toehold.

This experience also taught 3M the value of research, but in particular to value maverick inventors who were so attached to their ideas that they would push them through despite the bureaucracy of the company. As a result, it allowed researchers 15 per cent of their time to research pet ideas that might become new products for the company. If they could persuade a member of the board that the idea was worthwhile they would get the resources to develop it. This approach yielded a host of successful commercial innovations, but perhaps the best known is the Post-It Note® developed by the intrapreneur Art Frye in the 1980s (Case insight 13.1).

So the fourth strategic thrust of the company was developed – to pursue product development and innovation at every level in the organization through research. This was formalized when the Central Research Laboratory was set up in 1937, but maverick research continued to be encouraged. In 1940, a New Product Department was developed to explore the viability of new products or technologies unrelated to existing ones. In 1943, a Product Fabrications Laboratory was set up to develop manufacturing processes. In the 1980s four Sector Labs were created with a view to being more responsive to the market place and undertaking medium-term research (5–10 years): Industrial and Consumer, Life Sciences, Electronic and Information Technologies and Graphic Technologies. The Central Lab, later renamed the Corporate Lab, was maintained to undertake more long-term research (over 10 years). In addition most of the divisions had their own labs undertaking short-term, developmental research (1–5 years).

3M has always been admired for its ability to share knowledge across the organization and link technologies to produce numerous products that could be sold in different markets. It has a Technology Forum which seeks to encourage the 'free and active interchange of information and cross-fertilization of ideas'. One example of this interchange is Scotchlite Reflective Sheeting used for road signs, which was developed in the 1940s – in fact, as a result of failed research to develop reflective road markings. This combined research from three different laboratories to produce signs with a waterproof base onto which a covering of an opaque, light-reflecting pigment was added followed by microscopic beads. This was all sealed with a thin coat of plastic to ensure weather durability. Strategy five had emerged – get different parts of the organization to communicate and work together and, most important of all, to share knowledge. Sharing knowledge was formalized in the 1950s with the establishment of the Technical Forum, set up with the aim of sharing knowledge across the company. It held annual shows. Out of this came the Technical Council, made up of technical directors and technical personnel, which met several times a year to review research and address common problems. Alongside this the Manufacturing Council and then the Marketing Council were established. At the same time technical directors and researchers regularly moved around the different divisions. The fifth strategy was in place – share knowledge.

The culture in 3M evolved out of its place of origin and has been called 'Minnesota nice'. It has been described as non-political, low ego, egalitarian and non-hierarchical as well as hardworking and self-critical. It has also, at least in its earlier days, been described as paternalistic in its approach to employees. Above all, 3M is achievement-orientated and achievement, particularly in research, was rewarded, often through promotion. For example, successful new product teams were spun off to form new divisions. The leader of the team often became a general manager of the new division and this was seen as a great motivator. Lesser achievements were also acknowledged. Researchers who consistently achieved 'high standards of originality, dedication and integrity in the technical field' – as judged by their peers, not management – were invited to join the exclusive 'Calton Society'. The 'Golden Step' and 'Pathfinder' awards were also given to those helping develop successful new products. Achievement was lauded at all levels. Strategy six was emerging – encourage achievement through reward.

Today 3M faces many challenges to maintaining its reputation for innovation. As it becomes larger and more complex, involved in different markets with different products and technologies, at different stages of their life-cycle, it recognizes that different managerial approaches may be necessary. The 'maverick', high-risk approach to research and development may not be appropriate in certain sectors. The 25 per cent rule (the proportion of new product sales) may not be achievable by all divisions. 3M also faces stiffer competition, which means that cost economies have had to be made to maintain profitability. As a result, the 15 per cent rule is now described as more of an attitude than a reality. Nevertheless, 3M has for more than a century successfully practiced corporate entrepreneurship.

Visit the website on: www.3M.com

Questions:

1. List the four strategic thrusts of 3M. Are they appropriate for any company, even today?
2. Describe the organizational structures and devices 3M uses to encourage entrepreneurial activity. Why do they work?
3. How does 3M distinguish between incremental and fundamental innovations?
4. Describe, as best you can from the case, the culture of the organization. What does this depend upon?
5. Why has 3M been such a successful innovator for so long?
6. Can other companies just copy 3M's structures and culture and become successful innovators?

A series of case studies on 3M, tracking its history and development since its inception in 1902, have been written by Research Associate Mary Ackenhusen, Professor Neil Churchill and Associate Professor Daniel Muzyka from INSEAD. They can be obtained from the Case Clearing House, England and USA.

SUMMARY

➡ Corporate entrepreneurship is the term used to describe entrepreneurial behaviour in an established, larger organization, one that encourages entrepreneurial intensity. It includes terms such as entrepreneurial transformation, strategic renewal and strategic entrepreneurship. Organizations involved in these processes have been said to exhibit a sustained pattern of entrepreneurial behaviour over time which, in turn, has been called an entrepreneurial orientation. These patterns of behaviour are the result of an organizational architecture that can be described as entrepreneurial.

➡ Corporate venturing (both internal and external) is a major tool for encouraging corporate entrepreneurship and is part of an entrepreneurial architecture.

➡ The four pillars of organizational architecture are leadership and management, culture, structure and strategies. These can be crafted to make an entrepreneurial architecture, which becomes a network of relational contracts within or around an organization – its employees, suppliers, customers, partners and its network of other stakeholders.

➡ Entrepreneurial architecture creates within the organization the knowledge, learning and routines that allow it to respond flexibly to change and opportunity in the very way the entrepreneur does. It is not necessarily based on legal contracts and often only partly specified; therefore it is not easy to copy. It is based upon trust and mutual self-interest. Because it is complex, architecture can be a major source of sustainable competitive advantage.

➡ An entrepreneurial organization is also a learning organization. These thrive in environments of change, chaos, complexity, competition, uncertainty, even contradiction. Real knowledge means using the wheel of learning to understand the root cause of problems so as to put in place systematic solutions – knowing-how, knowing-why and doing something about it. This is real or double-loop learning. It involves challenging existing mental models or questioning the dominant logic of an organization. This learning is tacit and therefore also more difficult to copy by competitors.

➥ There is no prescriptive blueprint for entrepreneurial architecture. It depends on the context and environment that an organization faces. It can be sectorally and geographically dependent. It can also vary with the nature of the entrepreneurial intensity. For an organization to operate effectively, the style of leadership and management, its structures and culture need to be consistent and reinforce each other.

➥ An entrepreneurial architecture may not be appropriate for all organizations because they do not face an entrepreneurial environment.

 GROUP DISCUSSION TOPICS

1. What is entrepreneurial intensity and how can you increase it?
2. Why are some large firms not entrepreneurial?
3. What is corporate entrepreneurship?
4. What do you understand by the term 'entrepreneurial architecture' and how can it be shaped?
5. How does organizational architecture provide a theoretical framework for the 'entrepreneurial orientation' of a company? Why is a framework important?
6. Why do research studies into the 'entrepreneurial orientation' of companies highlight so many different factors as being important?
7. Why are relationships rather than legal contracts important within organizational architecture? Why does this provide a more sustainable form of competitive advantage?
8. How are leadership styles, organizational cultures and structures linked?
9. Why is corporate knowledge and learning important and how is it created?
10. How do you spread knowledge and learning in an organization?
11. Why is the concept of the learning organization important? Is it practical and achievable?
12. 'Learning organizations can be built only by individuals who put their life spirit into the task.' What does this mean and how can it be achieved?
13. Why does the 'dominant logic' within an organization constrain its thinking?
14. What are the pressures within an organization to conform to the 'dominant logic'?
15. Is building an entrepreneurial architecture easier for an entrepreneur than for a manager in a large organization? Explain.
16. Should all firms be entrepreneurial? Explain.
17. What are the advantages of bureaucratic procedures?
18. In what circumstances might a bureaucratic organization be more successful than an entrepreneurial organization?
19. What is an intrapreneur and how are they different than an entrepreneur? Is it easier to be an intrapreneur than an entrepreneur?
20. What is corporate venturing? Is external corporate venturing easier than internal corporate venturing?

 ACTIVITIES

1. List the criteria (and evidence) you would look for when interviewing for a manager position in an entrepreneurial firm. Conduct a mock interview with another member of the class for that job. What lessons have you learned?
2. Select an organization operating within a sector or environment where there is a *high* degree of market turbulence and write a report describing their organizational architecture. Link this to the success they have in their sector.

3. Select an organization operating within a sector or environment where there is a *low* degree of market turbulence and write a report describing their organizational architecture. Link this to the success they have in their sector.

4. List the sorts of activities where bureaucracy has some value and is important.

REFERENCES

Antoncic, B. (2006) 'Intrapreneurship: A Comparative Structural Equation Modelling Study', *Industrial Management and Data Systems*, 137(3).

Argyris, C. and Schön, D.A. (1978) Organizational Learning: A Theory of Action Perspective, Reading, MA: Addison Wesley.

Arshi, T. and Burns, P. (2018) 'Entrepreneurial Architecture: A Framework to Promote Innovation in Large Firms', *The Journal of Entrepreneurship*, 27(2).

Arshi, T. and Burns, P. (2019) 'Designing an Organization for Innovation in Emerging Economies: The Mediating Role of Readiness for Innovation', *Organizations and Markets in Emerging Economies*, 10(1) (19).

Birkinshaw, J.M. (2003) 'The Paradox of Corporate Entrepreneurship', *Strategy and Business*, 30, Spring.

Brizek, M.G. (2014) 'Explaining Corporate Entrepreneurship: A Contemporary Literature Investigation', *Journal of Management and Marketing Research*, 14.

Burgelman, R.A. (1983) 'A Process Model of Internal Corporate Venturing in the Diversified Major Firm', *Administrative Science Quarterly*, 28.

Burns, P. (2005) *Corporate Entrepreneurship: Building an Entrepreneurial Organization*, Basingstoke: Palgrave Macmillan.

Chesbrough, H.W. (2002) 'Making Sense of Corporate Venture Capital', *Harvard Business Review*, March.

Christensen, C.M. (1997) *The Innovator's Dilemma: When New Technologies Cause Great Firms to Fail*, Boston, MA: Harvard Business School Press.

Cogliser, C.C., Brigham, K.A. and Lumpkin, G.T. (2008) 'Entrepreneurial Orientation (EO) Research: A Comprehensive Review and Analyses of Theory, Measurement, and Data Analytic Practices', *Entrepreneurship Research Conference*, Wellesley, MA.

Covin, J.G. and Slevin, D.P. (1989) 'Strategic Management of Small Firms in Hostile and Benign Environments', *Strategic Management Journal*, 10(1).

Covin, G.C. and Wales, W.J. (2012) 'The Measurement of Entrepreneurial Orientation', *Entrepreneurship Theory and Practice*, 36(4).

Covin, J.G., Green, K. and Slevin, D.P. (2006a) 'Strategic Process Effects on the Entrepreneurial-Orientation Sales Growth Rate Relationship', *Entrepreneurship Theory and Practice*, 30(3).

Covin, J.G., Green, K.M. and Slevin, D.P. (2006b) 'Strategic Process Effects on the Entrepreneurial Orientation – Sales Growth Rate Relationships', *Entrepreneurship Theory and Practice*, 30(1).

Drucker, P.F. (1985) *Innovation and Entrepreneurship: Practice and Principles*, London: Heinemann.

Dubini, P. and Aldrich, H. (1991) 'Personal and Extended Networks are Central to the Entrepreneurial Process', *Journal of Business Venturing*, 8(3).

Eisenhardt, K.M. and Martin, J.A. (2000) 'Dynamic Capabilities: What Are They?', *Strategic Journal*, 21.

Forsman, H. (2011) Innovation Capacity and Innovation Development in Small Enterprises: A Comparison Between the Manufacturing and Service Sectors. *Research Policy*, 40, 739–750.

Foster, R.N. and Kaplan, S. (2001) *Creative Destruction: Why Companies That Are Built to Last Underperform the Market – And How to Successfully Transform Them*, New York, NY: Currency Doubleday.

Galbraith, J. (1982) 'Designing the Innovating Organization', *Organizational Dynamics*, Winter.

Ghoshal, S. and Bartlett, C.A. (1997) *The Individualised Corporation: A Fundamentally New Approach to Management*, New York, NY: Harper Business.

Hamel, G. (1999) 'Bringing Silicon Valley Inside', *Harvard Business Review*, September.

Kanter, R.M. (1989) *When Giants Learn to Dance: Mastering the Challenge of Strategy, Management and Careers in the 1990s*, New York, NY: Simon & Schuster.

Kay, J. (1995) *Foundations of Corporate Success*, Oxford: Oxford University Press.

Kim, D.H. (1993) 'The Link Between Individual and Organizational Learning', *Sloan Management Review*, Fall.

Kolb, D.A. (1984) *Experiential Learning: Experience as the Source of Learning and Development* (Vol. 1), Englewood Cliffs, NJ: Prentice-Hall.

Kuratko, D. and Audretsch, D. (2009) 'Strategic Entrepreneurship: Exploring Different Perspectives of an Emerging Concept', *Entrepreneurship Theory and Practice*, 33.

Kuratko, D.F. and Audretsch, D.B. (2013) 'Clarifying the Domains of Corporate Entrepreneurship', *International Entrepreneurship and Management Journal*, 9(3).

Lumpkin, G.T. and Dess, G. (1996) 'Clarifying the Entrepreneurial Orientation Construct and Linking It to Performance', *Academy of Management Review*, 21(1).

Markoczy, L. (1994) 'Modes of Organizational Learning: Institutional Change and Hungarian Joint Ventures', *International Studies of Management and Organizations*, 24, December.

Merx-Chermin, M. and Nijhof, W.J. (2005) 'Factors Influencing Knowledge Creation and Innovation in an Organization', *Journal of European Industrial Training*, 29(12).

Miller, A. (1996) *Strategic Management*, Maidenhead: Irwin/McGraw-Hill.

Miller, D. (2011) 'Miller (1983) Revisited: A Reflection on EO Research and Some Suggestions for the Future', *Entrepreneurship Theory and Practice*, 35(5).

Miller, D., and Friesen, P.H. (1977) 'Strategy Making in Context: Ten Empirical Archetypes', *Journal of Management Studies*, 14.

Morris, M., Kuratko, D. and Covin, J. (2008) *Corporate Entrepreneurship and Innovation*, Mason, OH: Thomson/South-Western.

Morse, C.W. (1986) 'The Delusion of Intrapreneurship', *Long Range Planning*, 19(2).

Nadler, D., Gerstein, M.C. and Shaw, R.B. (1992) *Organizational Architecture: Designs for Changing Organizations*, San Francisco, CA: Jossey-Bass.

Pedler, M., Burgoyne, J.G. and Boydell, T. (1991) *The Learning Company: A Strategy for Sustainable Development*, London: McGraw-Hill.

Peters, T. and Waterman, R. (1982) *In Search of Excellence: Lessons from America's Best-Run Companies*, New York, NY: Harper Row.

Rauch, A., Wiklund, J., Lumpkin, G.T. and Frese, M. (2009) 'Entrepreneurial Orientation and Business Performance: An Assessment of Past Research and Suggestions for the Future', *Entrepreneurship Theory & Practice*, 33(3).

Senge, P. (1992) 'Mental Models', *Planning Review*, March–April.

Sharma, P. and Chrisman, J. (1999) 'Toward a Reconciliation of the Definitional Issues in the Field of Corporate Entrepreneurship', *Entrepreneurship Theory and Practice*, 23(3).

Siguaw, J.A., Simpson, P.M. and Enz, C.A. (2006) 'Conceptualizing Innovation Orientation: A Framework for Study and Integration of Innovation Research', *Journal of Product Innovation Management*, 23.

Timmons, J.A. (1999) *New Venture Creation: Entrepreneurship for the 21st Century*, Singapore: Irwin/McGraw-Hill.

Tushman, M.L. and O'Reilly, C.A. (1996) 'Ambidextrous Organizations: Managing Evolutionary and Revolutionary Change', *California Management Review*, 38(4).

Wales, W.J., Gupta, V.K. and Mousa, F. (2013) 'Empirical Research on Entrepreneurial Orientation: An Assessment and Suggestions for Future Research', *International Small Business Journal*, 31(4).

Wilpert, B. (1995) 'Organizational Behaviour', *Annual Review of Psychology*, 46, January.

Zahra, S.A. (1996) 'Governance, Ownership, and Corporate Entrepreneurship: The Moderating Role of Industry Technological Opportunities', *Academy of Management Journal*, 39(6).

ONLINE RESOURCES AVAILABLE For further resources relating to this chapter see the companion website at **www.macmillanihe.com/Burns-CEI**

3 Innovation

CONTENTS

- The purpose of innovation
- Defining and measuring innovation
- Radical product/service innovation
- Business model innovation
- Challenging market paradigms
- Creativity and innovation
- Innovation intensity
- Innovation and risk
- Innovation, profitability and growth
- Innovation, company size and industry structure
- Summary
- Group discussion questions
- Activities
- References

CASE INSIGHTS

Learning outcomes

When you have read this chapter and undertaken the related activities you will be able to:

➡ Explain the meaning of innovation, its purpose and how it can be measured in a number of dimensions;
➡ Explain the links between creativity, invention, innovation and entrepreneurship;
➡ Explain how radical innovation might be stimulated and business models challenged so as to potentially cause a shift in market paradigms;
➡ Explain the relationship between innovation and risk, profitability and growth;
➡ Explain how innovation is reflected in different-sized companies and in different industry structures.

THE PURPOSE OF INNOVATION

Entrepreneurial architecture seeks to create within an organization an entrepreneurial ori entation that results in greater entrepreneurial intensity, measured in Figure 2.1 as fre quency and scale of entrepreneurial outputs. But what is the purpose of these outputs? What is the aim of innovation? Theories of 'industrial evolution', supported by empirica evidence, have linked entrepreneurship and economic growth directly (Audretsch, 1995 Ericson and Pakes, 1995; Hopenhayn, 1992; Jovanovic, 1982; Klepper, 1996; Lambson 1991). They focus on change as the central phenomenon and emphasize the role knowledge plays in charting a way through this. Innovation is seen as the key to market entry, growth and survival for an enterprise and the way entire industries change over time. Innovation therefore, is at the heart of entrepreneurship. Entrepreneurs use it to create change and opportunity. They use it to create profit and sustain competitive advantage. And, occasion- ally, they use it to create entirely new industries. Firms that grow do so because they inno- vate in some way. For all firms, of any size, innovation has become something of a Holy Grail to be sought after and encouraged, and the same applies to nations as they strive to see their economies grow. In the words of Michael Porter (1990): 'Invention and entrepre- neurship are at the heart of national advantage'.

However, innovation need not be just about economic or monetary benefit, as tradi- tional economists might define it. Innovation can contribute just as much to social and environmental well-being. Indeed the two can go hand in hand, with changes in business processes leading to increased profit. For example, by recovering and remanufacturing key component parts used in its products, the construction equipment manufacturer Caterpillar found that it increased its profits on those product lines by 50 per cent, whilst cutting its energy and water usage by 90 per cent. Economists such as Kate Raworth (2017) see this becoming the norm with industrial manufacturing beginning on a 'metamorphosis from degenerative to regenerative design', whereby products become part of a circular economy which makes greater use of naturally renewable materials and repairs, reuses, refurbishes and recycles existing products so as to recapture value at each stage of decomposition. Innovation can include the development of business models that include this concept of regenerative design. Raworth defines economic well-being far more broadly to encompass monetary, social and environmental well-being saying that 'the business of business is to contribute to a thriving world'. She also sees new organizational structures such as coopera- tives, not-for-profits and community interest companies as giving business a values-driven **mission** or 'living purpose' and distributing income more evenly. Innovation, therefore, can create many benefits for society as a whole, not just the organization that undertakes it.

mission The formal statement of business purpose – what the business aims to achieve and how it will achieve it

Furthermore, entrepreneurial innovation is not something to be undertaken just by the private sector. Ruttan (2006) argued that large-scale and long-term government invest- ment has been behind the development of almost every general purpose technology in the last century: for example, mass-production systems, nuclear power and aviation, space, information and internet technologies. Mazzucato (2018) argued that it is the State that funds, if not undertakes, much of the early-stage (i.e., the riskiest) innovation. For exam- ple, of all US government-funded R&D in 2008 (26%), more than half of that (57%) went to basic research. The private sector in 2008, meanwhile, funded 67% of US R&D but of that only 18 per cent went to basic research. She points out that the private sector has engaged more in the later stages of innovation but has often benefitted greatly from the research undertaken or funded by the public sector. She cites the big pharmaceuticals as articularly poor at basic research, preferring instead to 'buy-in' the research from small iotech firms or public labs and focus instead on the development and roll-out stages: 'it s especially the government labs and government-backed universities that invest in the esearch responsible for producing the most radical new drugs'. She points out that Apple's ighly successful iPhone and iPad capitalize on government investments in the technolo-ies that underpin them: the internet, GPS (global positioning system), touch-screen and ommunications technologies.

These views are echoed by many others. Janeway (2018) writes: 'From the first Industrial Revolution on the state has served as an enabler – sometimes an engine – of economic development, subsidizing if not directing the deployment of transformational technology and, more recently, taking responsibility for funding the advance of science and engineer-ing from which economically significant innovation has come to be derived.' He called it a Three-Player Game' in which 'state investment in fundamental research induces financial speculation to fund construction of transformational technological infrastructure, whose exploitation, in turn, raises living standards'. The private sector is seen as best at commer-cializing opportunities, but then they have a tendency to develop their monopoly power rather than focusing on further innovation, leaving the field open to new, smaller compa-nies. He cites the example of Xerox's patented and highly profitable position in the copier market causing it to refuse to commit funds to turn invention into commercially significant innovation, which in turn led many employees to leave to start their own businesses. Remember it was Xerox that invented, but failed to exploit, the graphical user interface that was managed by a mouse. Janeway sees the process as inherently unstable: 'a world in which bubbles and crashes in the financial system spill over and liquidate both the employed and their employers'. And yet these bubbles have been the vehicle for mobilizing capital on the scale needed to finance these new high-risk ventures.

DEFINING AND MEASURING INNOVATION

The literature on innovation is vast. This book focuses particularly on later-stage innova-tion, when it is more easily exploited commercially and it is therefore concerned not just with technology but also new ways of marketing. Innovation is probably most simply defined as 'new ways of doing something'. Kanter (1983) defined innovation as 'the genera-tion, acceptance and implementation of new ideas, processes, products and services . . . [which] involves creative use as well as original invention'. Schumpeter (1996) described five types of innovation, emphasizing 'newness':

1. The introduction of a *new* or improved good or service.
2. The introduction of a *new* process.
3. The opening up of a *new* market.
4. The identification of *new* sources of supply of raw materials.
5. The creation of *new* types of industrial organization. This would include organizational architecture, where the components are configured in new ways.

What constitutes 'newness' is debatable, often based more on perception than reality. More recently, Proctor (2014) defined innovation very narrowly as the 'practical application of new inventions into marketable products and service' – a definition that excludes the last three types of innovation on Schumpeter's list. The reality is that there are dozens of definitions of innovation. In the face of so many different definitions, Figure 3.1 depicts innovation very simply in three dimensions, with each dimension measured on a scale that ranges from incremental to radical:

radical innovation The creation of radically new products or services, including **market paradigm shift** (see definition)

Product/service innovation – A completely new product or service or improvements in its design and/or functional qualities. The internet was a radical innovation, whereas anti-lock brakes for cars were an incremental innovation. Some radical innovations, like the internet, can lead to the development of whole new industries. Any successful innovation needs to be safeguarded through intellectual property (IP) rights or they risk being copied. This is particularly important for radical innovations that may be the result of high up-front investment in R&D. For example, drug companies depend heavily on their IP rights to ensure sufficient income to justify the initial investment is generated from new break-through drugs.

Process innovation – Revisions to how a product or service is produced so that it is better or cheaper (e.g. by the substitution of a cheaper material in an existing product). The robot assembly line was a radical process innovation whereas merging two elements of assembly would be incremental. This is important because it can make a product or service difficult to copy.

marketing strategy How the value proposition is delivered to customer segments

Marketing innovation – Improvements in the marketing of an existing product or service, or even a better way of distributing or supporting an existing product or service. Selling direct to the public via telephone or the internet was a radical marketing innovation, whereas gorilla marketing or the use of social media was an incremental innovation. Innovation does not emerge just from R&D in products and processes. Entrepreneurial firms, in particular, are often innovative in their approach to marketing, finding more effective, often cheaper, routes to market. However, whilst innovations in marketing may be cheaper than other forms of innovation they are also more easily copied. Nevertheless, product/service innovations have a life-cycle, meaning that the most appropriate marketing strategy at each stage in the cycle is likely to be different and innovations in strategy need to take place especially later in this cycle (this is a topic we return to in Chapter 15).

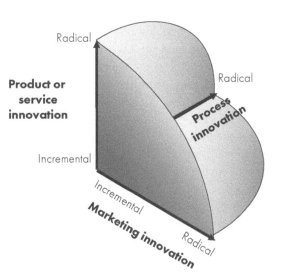

Figure 3.1 Product, process and marketing innovation

Linking these dimensions of innovation is business model innovation. This is about developing distinctively different business models – plans for how a business competes, uses its resources, structures its relationships, communicates with customers, creates value and generates profit. It may involve innovations in all three dimensions: products and processes as well as marketing. The development of iTunes has been called a breakthrough innovation that revolutionized the music business by linking technology in the iPod to a business model that monetarized recorded music at a time when CD sales were falling and it was being pirated and downloaded for free.

Innovation in the architecture of an organization, so as to make it more entrepreneurial, can make the organization more competitive and deliver higher levels of performance. Furthermore, whereas innovations in products, processes and marketing might be copied by competitors, architectural innovation is more difficult to copy, making it more sustainable. The rest of this chapter, however, is concerned with the more obvious forms of product, process and market innovation.

If defining innovation is difficult, so too is measuring it. There is no quantifiable scale for measuring innovation (Baregheh et al., 2009; Edison et al., 2013; Garcia and Calantone, 2002). What constitutes incremental or radical innovation in Figure 3.1 is a matter of judgement. To an economist, for a product to be completely or radically different from another the **cross elasticity of demand** must be zero (changes in demand for it do not affect demand for the other). Simply introducing a new product or service that is similar to others is not innovative, even if it is a replacement for an existing one. The cross elasticity of demand is not zero. New cars are rarely truly innovative, whatever the marketing hype might say. However, arguably the Mini was innovative because it changed the way cars were designed and changed the way people perceived vehicle size – a case of perception being just as important as reality.

cross elasticity of demand How demand reacts to changes in price

RADICAL PRODUCT/SERVICE INNOVATION

Radical innovation is usually associated with a 'mould-breaking' development of a 'new-to-the-world' product or process (the materials used, the process employed or how the firm is organized to deliver them). Radical innovation can be disruptive – changing markets, industries, even societies. New-to-the-world industries have been created for centuries; water power, textiles and iron in the eighteenth century, steam, steel and rail in the nineteenth century, and electricity, chemicals and the internal combustion engine in the early twentieth century. Now we have computers and mobile technologies which continue to disrupt entire industries, for example Google's driverless car (threatening the car industry) and Amazon's Fresh (threatening the fresh-food industry). The internet and cloud-based services have lowered the barriers to entry in many industries – facilitating market entry, offering automation and economies of scale and lowering capital costs. The next radical, disruptive innovations are likely to revolve around artificial intelligence and nanotechnology. The precise nature of the innovations in these areas is difficult to predict, but much of the basic research around them has already been undertaken and largely funded by governments. Now there are enormous commercial opportunities for the private sector to exploit. This will likely cause enormous economic booms that will eventually peter out as the technologies mature and market opportunities are fully exploited.

Invention is probably the clearest example of radical innovation. It is often linked with new technologies, often the product of research and sometimes a spin-off from other research or technological developments. For example, the 'invention' of the internet or 'World Wide Web' (www) by Tim Berners-Lee grew out of a small US Defense Department network project connecting researchers and was developed for computers installed at CERN (the European Organization for Nuclear Research). Examples abound of inventions that are not commercially successful and even more of inventors who did not benefit from their inventions. English scientist Charles Babbage outlined the principles of a mechanical analytical engine or universal calculator – a forerunner of the computer. It was programmed by punch cards, had a store of information (memory) and a calculating engine (processor). But he was forever tinkering with his design and could not find anyone to pay him to make the machine. Instead, he went on to try to devise a foolproof system for betting on horses. Thomas Edison, probably the most successful inventor of all time, was so incompetent at introducing his inventions to the marketplace that his backers had to remove him from every new business he founded. Even Tim Berners-Lee did not benefit directly from his invention. Others, like the founders of numerous internet firms, created businesses and made their fortunes from his invention.

So invention is only one extreme example of innovation and both are linked to successful commercialization. But market demand for a radically new product or service can be difficult to determine because potential customers have no experience of it and how it might be used. Traditional market research techniques appear ill-suited when it comes to predicting customer acceptance of more radical forms of innovation (Deszca et al., 1999). Because of this much of the basic research for this radical innovation is undertaken or funded by government. In addition, large companies with sunk costs in established technologies often appear unwilling to exploit radical innovations, even if the development has been undertaken by others and affects markets in which they are dominant (e.g. the established fossil fuel producers and the more sustainable forms of energy production and storage). Organizations that are able (and willing) to both explore and exploit innovations simultaneously have been called 'ambidextrous' – a term originally used by Duncan (1976) and popularized by March (1991). Much of the literature on **organizational ambidexterity** revolves around issues of structure, culture and leadership, and resonates with the approach taken by this book in developing an entrepreneurial architecture (e.g., Gibson and Birkinshaw, 2004; Tushman and O'Reilly, 1996).

organizational ambidexterity The ability to both explore and exploit innovations simultaneously

Organizational ambidexterity is not easy and often it is left to the entrepreneur to exploit the commercial application for an invention. Henry Ford did not invent the car but he did revolutionize the way cars were produced and sold, moving from craft-based to production-line manufacture, and from bespoke orders from wealthy customers to affordable cars sold through dealerships (Case insight 10.3). These approaches to innovation can be every bit as valuable as the more traditional invention. As we saw in Case insight 1.4, Steve Jobs never invented anything but he did apply technologies developed by others so as to revolutionize three industries – personal computers, music and film animations. He launched the Apple personal computer when market research told IBM that there was not a viable market for it. Jobs was able to foresee applications for personal computers that others could not. He never trusted market research or focus groups, preferring instead to rely on his own instincts. This entrepreneurial insight plays a vital role in the process of innovation. Entrepreneurs seem able to link technologies to market opportunities and in so doing make the technology more usable for, and therefore more attractive to, consumers. In their study of technology-based innovation, Phadke and Vyakarnam (2017) found this synthesis skill of critical importance in bringing an innovation to the market, but that it was in conflict with the scientific tradition which values analysis rather than synthesis.

CASE INSIGHT 3.1
Rolls-Royce and Finferries

UK  Finland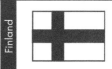

PARTNERSHIP WORKING

In 2018 Rolls-Royce Holdings and the Finnish state-owned ferry operator Finferries began collaborating on a research project called SVAN (Safer Vessel with Autonomous Navigation), implementing the findings from an earlier Advanced Autonomous Waterborne Applications (AAWA) research project, which had been funded by Business Finland (a government research-funding agency). SVAN saw the car ferry *Falco* (which already had Rolls-Royce engines) fitted with a range of Rolls-Royce Ship Intelligence technologies. Later that same year, after some 400 hours of sea trials, the ferry successfully completed a show-case voyage with some 80 VIPs in the Turku archipelago of Finland. The entire voyage was conducted under remote control and without human intervention.

The *Falco* was equipped with a range of advanced sensors which, combined with artificial intelligence, allowed it to build up a detailed picture of its surroundings, in real time and with a degree of accuracy beyond that of the human eye. This was relayed to Finferries' operations centre, some 50 kilometres away in the city of Turku, where a captain monitored the autonomous operations and could have taken control of the vessel if necessary. The autonomous navigation system includes an automatic collision avoidance and an automatic berthing system, which automatically alters course and speed when approaching the quay allowing the ship to dock safely, again without human intervention.

Visit the website: **www.rolls-royce.com**

Questions:

1. Who were the partners in this innovation and what were their roles?
2. What are the implications of having autonomous ferries in the near future? Is this a disruptive innovation?

BUSINESS MODEL INNOVATION

As already defined, business model innovation is about developing innovative plans for how a business competes, uses its resources, structures its relationships, communicates with customers, creates value and generates profit. It may involve changes to products and processes. As with all innovation, it can be anything from incremental to radical. Radical business model innovations create **market paradigm shift**. They change the way people think about products or services and create whole new markets where none existed before. Based on a sample of 108 companies, Kim and Mauborgne (2005) estimated that, whereas only 14 per cent of innovations created these new markets, these innovations delivered 38 per cent of new revenues and 61 per cent of increased profits.

A good example of market paradigm shift is the development of low-cost airlines like Southwest (USA), easyJet (UK) and Ryanair (Ireland). Before the launch of these airlines, flagship carriers like British Airways (UK) and Pan American (USA) offered a premium service targeted at businesspeople and the wealthy. Managers in these companies accepted this established way of doing things and, given their cost structures, did not believe air

market paradigm shift Changes in established market conventions associated with the creation of radically new markets

travel could be offered to everyone. They did not even consider changing their business model. The low-cost airlines created a whole new market for low-price air travel targeted at ordinary people by changing the airline business model to ensure the minimization of costs. Although the basic product remained unaltered (safe air travel from one point to another), the service offered to passengers was pared back to a minimum or charged as extra (e.g., no seat allocation, no food or drink, lower baggage allowances etc.), operations were re-engineered to minimize costs (e.g., fewer cabin crew, longer pilot air-time, fast airport turnaround etc.) and marketing altered so as to ensure that passenger numbers were maximised (e.g., aggressive promotion, differential pricing based on early booking virtual ticketing etc.). Everything about how the basic product was delivered to passengers was changed. As a result, a whole new market was created and many of the flagship carriers went out of business.

Often market paradigm shifts are made possible by developments in technologies, such as the internet, but they might arise through the emergence of new environmental conditions, untapped markets with different value expectations or even changes in legal requirements. Paradigm shift happens when the things customers value from a product or service are challenged. Sometimes doing things differently can add value for the customer without involving extra costs. Sometimes doing things differently can reduce costs whilst still allowing a high price to be charged. Sometimes additional revenues might be derived from sources other than the main activity of a business, allowing the price of a product or service to be reduced. This concept has been used to good effect by internet companies who offer 'free' services to customers but sell data on them to advertisers and others.

In most sectors, there are factors that managers believe are critical to the success of their business. These paradigms have probably endured for a long time and become part of the dominant logic of an industry. They filter the information managers receive, subconsciously interpreting environmental data in a certain way. Managers are constrained in their thinking by their prior knowledge (Venkatarman, 1997). They may consider only the information that they believe relevant to their prevailing dominant logic. As circumstances and the environment change, the managers running the industry may not adapt their way of thinking, leaving opportunities for others to capitalize on.

This blindness is the main reason existing businesses miss out on disruptive innovation. In his study of a number of industries, Christensen (1997) characterized this as happening in stable markets where companies were geared up to delivering more of what existing customers wanted. They did not want to disrupt an existing dominant market position. Reinforcing trends we noted in Chapter 1, he observed that with each generation almost all of the previously successful large firms failed to make the transition effectively and were often squeezed out of the market or into **bankruptcy**, despite the fact they were often exemplars of good practice – ploughing a high percentage of earnings into R&D; having strong working links with their supply chain; working with lead customers to better understand their needs and develop product innovations; delivering a continuous stream of product and process innovations that were in demand from their existing customers. The problem they had was their inability to identify and capitalize on the emergence of *new markets* with very different needs and expectations – one aspect of the problem of *market disruption*. Essentially, these firms were too close to their existing

bankruptcy When you are unable to pay your debts and a court order is obtained by creditors to have your affairs placed in the hands of an official receiver

ustomers, suppliers and technologies. The result was that they failed to see the long-term potential of newly emerging markets. What might have begun as a fringe business – often or something simpler and cheaper – moved into the mainstream and eventually changed the rules under which the mainstream businesses operated so, by the time the mainstream businesses realized this, they had lost their competitive advantage. Often, with the benefit of hindsight, the industry seemed to be driven by technological developments in their existing products rather than by developments in new technologies or changing market demand.

CASE INSIGHT 3.2
Bill Gates and Microsoft

USA

BARRIERS TO INNOVATION

Bill Gates and Microsoft is probably the most outstanding business success story of a generation. Now a billionaire, he stepped down as CEO of Microsoft in 2000 and retired as 'Chief Software Architect' in 2008. Five years before stepping down as CEO, he wrote an internal memo that has become increasingly pertinent:

> Developments on the internet over the next several years will set the course of our industry for a long time to come ... I have gone through several stages of increasing my views of its importance. Now I assign the internet the highest level of importance. In this memo I want to make it clear that our focus on the internet is crucial to every part of our business. The internet is the most important single development to come along since the IBM PC was introduced in 1981.

Unfortunately, he and the company did not seem to take any notice and, arguably, missed the internet revolution. By 2014, Microsoft had only just started to focus on its importance and was falling behind competitors. With sales of Windows and Microsoft Office falling sharply, it was forced to announce a 'far-reaching realignment of the company' to enable it to respond more quickly to change, 'focusing the whole company on a single strategy'. This involved disbanding product groups, making redundancies and reorganizing itself into functional lines such as engineering, marketing, advanced strategy and research. Since then it has been playing 'catch up' with the other US tech giants (see Case insight 15.4).

With its dominant market position and enormous resources, Microsoft could have dominated the search engine market rather than Google, but new developments that threatened to cannibalize their main source of revenue – the Window Operating System and the Microsoft Office suite – were not allowed to surface. The dominant logic within the company was to continue to exploit its extremely profitable existing product/market offering. Resources were therefore targeted at defending Microsoft's existing dominance of the software market rather than exploring more disruptive innovations.

Visit the website: www.microsoft.com

Questions:

1. How difficult is it to break away from the dominant logic within an organization?
2. How difficult is it to 'predict' the future in business?

CASE INSIGHT 3.3
Rolls-Royce and TotalCare®

UK

PRODUCT/SERVICE AND BUSINESS MODEL INNOVATION

The aero-engine manufacturer Rolls-Royce is known for the quality of its engines and the excellence of its after-sales service. It is also known for the innovations it has introduced in its engine designs, particularly with its newer 'lean-burn' and 'intelligent' engines, with sensors that predict when intervention is required – a service or the replacement of parts. This is beamed back so that parts can be delivered in advance to certain airports where the work can be undertaken. In the past this might have been undertaken by the airline or another service provider, priced on a time and material basis.

The introduction of the Rolls-Royce TotalCare programme was a radical innovation that changed the nature of what the company was selling – from a product to a service. Instead of buying a jet engine and a service package, Rolls-Royce enters into a contract with the airline based upon a fee for every hour the engine runs. Customers pay for engine power as they used it. Rolls-Royce then monitors the data from the sensors built into the engine to determine the need for service or parts replacement, which Rolls-Royce then arranges. They effectively guarantee engine availability. The airline is buying a service rather than a product, allowing it to move from investing significant fixed costs in engine maintenance to a variable cost – a business model that now dominates the industry and facilitated the growth of low-cost airlines. For Rolls-Royce, the TotalCare programme effectively 'locks-in' customers to the company and securing its parts business – a win-win situation for the company and its customers.

This new business model also had beneficial consequences for the environment. Rather than minimizing the initial engine cost, it created a strong incentive for the company to re-engineer its engines so as to minimize their total lifetime costs. That can mean factoring in higher quality so as to minimize service and repair time. Because the engines always belong to Rolls-Royce, it also means that they can design them so as to maximize the potential for reuse when the TotalCare contract comes to an end and, ultimately, recycling when the engines come to the end of their economic life. The TotalCare programme has proved so successful that most of Rolls-Royce's income now comes from this service, rather than the direct sale of engines.

Visit the website: **www.rolls-royce.com**

Questions:

1. How dependent on other forms of innovation was the development of the TotalCare programme?
2. What problems does a company face when it moves from selling a product to a service? Does this mean it has to change its business model?

CHALLENGING MARKET PARADIGMS

blue ocean strategy
The strategy of finding uncontested market space and creating new demand – essentially market paradigm shift

Chaston (2015) argued that you can challenge the market conventions on which established business models are based systematically and then develop new solutions and different models that are more attractive to customers. This is something that entrepreneurs do all the time as they seek to disrupt existing, already proven markets without incurring the often high cost and high risk of radical product innovation. Kim and Mauborgne (2005) called this 'blue ocean strategy' – finding market needs that are currently unrecognized and unmet. These approaches are outlined in Chapter 10. Both involve challenging the established status quo – the dominant logic of an industry – and asking whether customer needs can be better met in some other way.

> ❝ Reinventing the wheel is risky and usually money and time-consuming – both of which would-be entrepreneurs normally lack. However, improving something that is already on the market means there is a demand for the product and you can just do it better with some lateral, creative thinking. That's not to say entrepreneurs should be discouraged from trying something revolutionary. But if you look through history, almost every super successful entrepreneur took an existing idea or business and made it better. ❞
>
> Adam Schwab, founder Lux Group, Business Review Australia issuu.com, July 2014

Going to the heart of any challenge to the established conventions around business models is an approach to marketing called 'service-dominant logic'. In their award-winning paper, Vargo and Lusch (2004) argued that customers valued and purchased services rather than goods, and goods should therefore be viewed as a medium for delivering or 'transmitting' the firm's services. They defined service as 'the application of specialized competences (knowledge and skills) through deeds, processes, and performances for the benefit of another entity or the entity itself'. In this way companies manufacturing cars are not in the business of selling cars but in the business of providing 'mobility services' through the cars that they manufacture – a concept that could apply equally to aero-engines (see Case insight 3.3). Thus, all industries are service industries and it therefore becomes vital for firms to understand the service that consumers are seeking from them. This fundamentally different way of looking at business models questions the dominant logic surrounding any goods. It requires a shift in focus from the product to the **consumer** and a clear understanding of customer needs and how these translate into a service they value and are willing to pay for.

service-dominant logic The implications for the idea that, rather than the product, customers buy the services it delivers

consumer The person or organization consuming or using a product

Radical business model innovation is probably easier (and cheaper) than radical innovation based on new technological developments and can be just as profitable. It involves the ability to question dominant logic and think creatively outside the box, to generate and assimilate new ideas and knowledge, a vision of the future that links opportunities in diverse, fragmented and often geographically widespread markets to the key capabilities of the business. And these skills need to become part of the entrepreneurial architecture of the organization. One of the techniques for investigating the effectiveness of different business models is the Business Model Canvas (Osterwalder and Pigneur, 2010), which we look at in Chapter 12.

 CASE INSIGHT 3.4
Swatch

 Switzerland

MARKET PARADIGM SHIFT THROUGH DESIGN

Swatch created a whole new market for cheap watches by daring to be different. In the 1980s cheaper watches like those made by Citizen and Seiko competed by using quartz technology to improve accuracy and digital displays to make reading the time easier. The industry competed primarily on price and functional performance.

A selection of Swatch watches on display in an airport in Dubai, United Arab Emirates

Source: iStock/justhavealook

People usually owned just one watch. Swatch set out to change the watch market and make affordable fashion accessories that were also accurate timepieces. To do this they relied upon innovative design.

SMH, the Swiss parent, set up a design studio in Italy whose mission was to combine powerful technology with artwork, brilliant colours and flamboyant designs. For a start, Swatch had to be affordable so costs had to be kept low. Consequently, it was designed with fewer components than most watches. Screws were replaced by plastic moldings. It was made in large volumes in a highly automated factory, enabling labour costs to be driven down to less than 10 per cent of the selling price. Swatch changed the reason for buying a watch from the need to tell the time to the desire to be fashionable. They differentiated themselves not on the function of the timepiece but on its design and also its emotional appeal – a lifestyle image that made a statement about the wearer. In doing this they encouraged repeat purchases because each watch was a different fashion accessory making a different statement about the wearer. Because it was offered at an affordable price, people were encouraged to buy more than one watch. The company used innovative marketing techniques to bring the watch to the market under several different designs. Swatch has built up a core of loyal customers who repeat purchase their watches. New Swatch designs come out every year.

Visit the website: www.swatch.com

Questions:

1. How difficult is it to change the way you think about a product or market?
2. What role might design play in this?

CREATIVITY AND INNOVATION

Underpinning innovation is creativity but a prerequisite to all creative processes is knowledge and the openness to different ideas (Simmie, 2002). However, all too often people do not even seek out different ideas, remaining unaware of the information, knowledge and ideas being generated around them. Worse still, they surround themselves with people who think the same, generating their own dominant logic that is self-reinforcing – a well-known phenomenon on social media known as the 'echo chamber'. Of course, this tendency for like-minded people to cluster around each other is not new. It can have sound commercial reasons, such as the sharing of knowledge and other resources. It is one of the reasons we see clusters of small firms in certain geographic locations. And if these clusters represents outward-looking, creative people, such as Silicon Valley in the USA or Cambridge in the UK, then that creative culture will reinforce itself. Florida (2002; Florida and Tinagli, 2004) argued that some geographic locations (he highlighted cities like London and Barcelona) attract talented, creative people he called 'the new creative class' and these people, in turn, attracted creative, innovative firms. He claimed that rather than people following jobs (see Chapter 1: Geoffrey West, 2015), increasingly jobs will follow people with the appropriate talent, creating a virtuous circle of economic growth. He claimed that the ability to compete and prosper in the new global economy 'increasingly turns on the ability of nations to attract, retain and develop creative people', arguing that this new 'creative class' is drawn to a particular sort of place; 'open, diverse communities where differences are welcome and cultural creativity is easily accessed'. He argued that it is tolerance that attracts the creative class and that they have the talent to develop new technologies. New, technology-based organizations thrive in locations that combine three elements – technology, talent and tolerance.

The point is that ideas that are commonplace for one group can spark insight for another. It is all about being open to ideas from all and every source and not being inward-looking. It is not just about being aware of different approaches or perspectives on a problem, but also about getting the brain to accept that there are different ways of doing things – developing an open and enquiring mind. Large technology companies like Samsung and LG have active programmes to encourage staff to be exposed to ideas from a wide, and sometimes unusual, range of sources. Connectivity, therefore, extends beyond any industry or market context. This is one reason why partnering with other people can be so useful in stimulating innovation. One person exposes the other to different ways of doing things, different ideas, and from this there is the spark of creativity. However, many people almost have to give themselves permission to be creative – to think the unthinkable.

Knowledge and the exposure to different ideas encourage creativity, invention and radical and incremental innovation. 'Connectivity' is one of the key drivers of creativity – the connection we have with a wide range of different people and ideas (Johnson, 2010). This is about not just the scale and range of our network of contacts, but also our ability to spot connections between a problem in one context and a solution to it from another – a topic we shall explore in Chapter 9. Johnson observed that the driver of innovation over time has been the increasing connectivity between different minds. Luck may play a part in all this but, as he said, 'chance favours the connected mind'. He also makes the point that connectivity is not a one-off fix. Connectivity needs to be a continuous process – one that continually creates opportunities for ideas to collide and connect. There is an element of serendipity here – connecting as they do in the right place, and at the right time. This means that regular, frequent opportunities to connect need to be built into the structure and management of the organization and not just left to chance.

INNOVATION INTENSITY

We have seen how innovation is difficult to define and measure. It can come from changes in products, services, processes and marketing. It moves from radical innovation (including invention and market paradigm shift) through what might be called breakthrough innovations (where there are 'substantial' changes to products or services) to incremental changes. Few companies seem to achieve even 'breakthrough' innovations (Wagner et al. 2014), let alone radical ones. Indeed, there is evidence that the majority of commercially significant innovations are incremental rather than radical (Audretsch, 1995). The reality is that the most commercially successful innovations are really just improvements rather than ground-breaking inventions. Apple's sustained commercial success is based upon good design and improving product ease of use rather than invention. Apple 1 was a big improvement on other computers with its graphic user interface and 'mouse', the iPod was a big improvement on MP3 players, which had been available for years and the iPhone improved on mobile phones from Nokia and Blackberry. Google entered a crowded search engine market then dominated by AltaVista and simply created a better product by using an improved search algorithm. It became commercially successful after it introduced its AdWords bidding system – invented by Idealab. Facebook entered the market well after social networking sites such as Friendster and MySpace.

In 2018 the Boston Consulting Group produced their annual list of the 50 most innovative companies in the world (Table 3.1). The vast majority were based in the USA. The companies were judged on objective financial metrics as well as subjective criteria such as their speed, research and development processes; use of technological platforms; and exploration of adjacent markets based on a survey of 1,500 senior executives. As you can see, many of them have Case insights in this book (those that do are highlighted in bold).

Table 3.1 The world's most innovative companies

	Company	Country		Company	Country
1	**Apple**	USA	11	Airbnb	USA
2	**Alphabet (Google)**	USA	12	SpaceX	USA
3	**Microsoft**	USA	13	Netflix	USA
4	**Amazon**	USA	14	**Tencent**	China
5	Samsung	S. Korea	15	Hewlett-Packard	USA
6	**Tesla**	USA	16	Cisco Systems	USA
7	**IBM**	USA	17	**Toyota**	Japan
8	**Facebook**	USA	18	General Electric	USA
9	Uber	USA	19	Orange	France
10	**Alibaba**	China	20	Marriott	USA

21	Siemens	Germany	36	BMW	Germany
22	Unilever	Holland	37	Nissan	Japan
23	BASF	Germany	38	Pfizer	UK/USA
24	Expedia	USA	39	Time Warner	USA
25	Johnson & Johnson	USA	40	Renault	France
26	JP Morgan Chase	USA	41	3M	USA
27	Bayer	Germany	42	SAP	Germany
28	Dow Chemicals	USA	43	DuPont	USA
29	AT&T	USA	44	Intercontinental Hotels Group	UK
30	Allianz	Germany	45	Disney	USA
31	Intel	USA	46	Huawei	China
32	NTT DoCoMo	Japan	47	Procter & Gamble	USA
33	Daimler	Germany	48	Verizon	USA
34	AXA	France	49	Philips	Holland
35	Adidas	Germany	50	Nestlé	UK/Switzerland

Source: BCG (2018)

The notion that frequent incremental innovations in products, processes and marketing may be just as desirable as infrequent radical innovations brings us back to the question of what entrepreneurial architecture should encourage. And, of course, the answer is that it should encourage all forms of innovation, whether in products, processes or marketing and whether incremental or radical. Using the typology from Figure 2.1, which described entrepreneurship more generally, we might say entrepreneurship should specifically encourage **innovation intensity**, as shown in Figure 3.2a, by pushing this envelope of innovation as far as possible. These are the dimensions and definitions of innovation that Arshi and Burns (2018) used when they found entrepreneurial architecture associated with and antecedent to innovation intensity. They also found each form of innovation was independent of each other.

innovation intensity An increase in both the degree (or scale) and the frequency of innovation within an organization

You might also argue that an entrepreneurial architecture should encourage the speed with which an innovation is developed and brought to the market, so as to capitalize on first-mover advantage. The concept of innovation intensity therefore possibly requires a third dimension, as shown in Figure 3.2b.

A firm can undertake many different forms of innovation simultaneously and it is the innovation outputs, measured in the dimensions shown in Figures 3.2a and b, which reflect the outcomes of an entrepreneurial architecture. Incremental and radical innovations are not mutually exclusive and the entrepreneurial firm can gain competitive advantage from both. Indeed, it has been argued that a track record of successful incremental innovation is a prerequisite of radical innovation (Dunlop-Hinkler et al., 2010). Frequent, small incremental innovations may compensate for the occasional radical innovation or invention and are usually less risky. Furthermore, the sum of many small, incremental innovations can have an enormous impact on competitive advantage (Bessant, 1999). They might even add up to a revolution. As already mentioned, Henry Ford's revolution in the car industry involved extensive incremental changes – to products and processes, component and factory design and in the way labour was organized in his factories, not to mention his innovative way of selling cars through dealerships (Case insight 10.3).

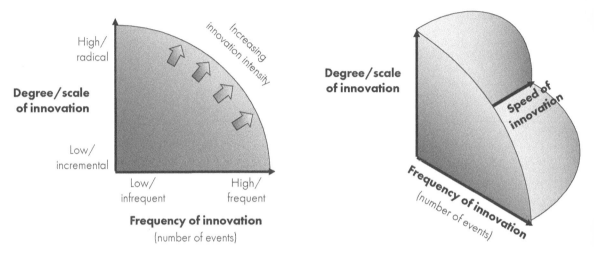

Figure 3.2a Innovation intensity (two dimensions)   **Figure 3.2b** Innovation intensity (three dimensions)

INNOVATION AND RISK

The survey by the Boston Consulting Group cited earlier found that many companies were risk-averse and that a risk-averse culture was a major barrier to innovation (BCG, 2018). However, whilst innovation is risky, in today's highly competitive environment not innovating is riskier. Incremental product or service innovation is generally less risky than radical innovation, not least because it builds on established knowledge and an established product or service. Established firms may have years of product or service experience, with established marketing channels and resource capabilities. Product or service innovation generally becomes more difficult the further an organization strays from its core competences. The risks in doing so also increase. Radical innovation might involve new technologies and unknown markets. As you might expect, the risks associated with product or service innovation are lowest for organizations that are good at innovation – practice breeds competence. However, they are also lowest for organizations whose core competences lie in building good customer relationships, often associated with effective branding – allowing for brand extension. The synergy of brand extension creates economies of scope, for example Virgin has successfully extended its brand over a diverse range of products and services from train to airplane transport and from broadband to financial services.

Once innovations start pushing an organization into new, unfamiliar markets, the risks increase. As you might expect, the risks associated with this sort of market extension are lowest for organizations that are good at sales and marketing. However, they can also be lowest for organizations whose core competences lie in the efficiency of their existing production methods where economies of scale may apply – for example, in the capital goods or extractive industries. So understanding the core competences of an organization is at the base of managing the risks of innovation. The further the organization strays from its core competences, the greater the risk. Figure 3.3 shows risk increasing as the degree of innovation and the unfamiliarity with the market increases. Selling incremental changes in products or services to existing customers should be low risk – the needs of customers should be well known and the organization should have the competences to innovate from its existing product or service base. However, selling radically new products or services into completely new markets involves many unknowns and is high risk.

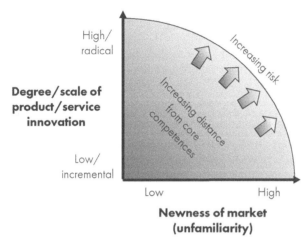

Figure 3.3 Innovation and risk

Most innovations take time to become accepted within a market, following an S-curve of innovation diffusion (see Chapter 14). The pace of diffusion is unpredictable, but is likely to be slower for more radical innovations. Both slow diffusion and rapid diffusion face risk – albeit different sorts. What is more, there are also issues about timing of the launch of an innovation – too early and you risk being ahead of the market; too late and you risk losing first-mover advantage and having many competitors (see Chapter 11).

The rapid pace of technological change today is constantly creating new markets – markets that are global and increasingly interlinked. These are not only attractive commercial opportunities, but also potential threats because a decision not to enter might threaten the organization's existence as these new markets consolidate as they mature. Consequently, high-growth firms are sometimes forced to expand geographically at the same time as their technology is changing – innovating as they enter new markets. For example, the five US internet giants started out offering different products or services: Amazon (internet retailer), Apple (computers), Facebook (social network), Google (internet search) and Microsoft (software). However, through a process of internal development, partnerships and acquisitions they are converging so as to offer a range of similar products and services via the internet. They are fighting to become monopoly providers of all their customers' digital requirements from the best online platform – a kind of digital utility. The more services they offer, the more customers, including advertisers, they seem to attract and the more data it can collect. If this can be done from their own branded hardware with their services wired in all the better. It all creates the opportunity to generate staggering profits (Case insight 15.4).

The keys to dealing with innovation risk are information, knowledge and learning about the products or services you are innovating and the markets you are entering. As we have seen in previous chapters, these are things that the entrepreneur understands very well and an entrepreneurial architecture must facilitate. Developing a set of organization-wide cognitive heuristics to aid risk assessment, information flows and decision-making is an important part of this. And, where knowledge or information is not available within the organization, it must be open to sourcing it from outside. Whilst an organization might understand the product or service it is innovating, it can find out more about the market it is entering by buying-in the knowledge – hiring consultants or recruiting new staff. It might consider partnering with or the acquisition of a firm already established in that market. Even new technologies can be bought-in. It might also consider the possibility of open-source innovation. The organization's network of relationships should also help with this process. Later chapters will demonstrate how innovation risk might be managed as part of an entrepreneurial architecture.

INNOVATION, PROFITABILITY AND GROWTH

Innovation is not usually an end in itself. There are usually other objectives. These may be related to economic, social or environmental outcomes. Numerous academic studies link innovation with competitive advantage. Whilst radical innovation is associated with *substantially superior* competitive advantage (Dunlop-Hinkler et al., 2010), frequent incremental innovation is associated with *sustained* competitive advantage (Avermaete et al., 2003; Dong, 2015; Norman and Verganti, 2014; Salavou, 2002). Of course, the two can be combined, particularly at different stages of a product/service life-cycle. But how do you measure competitive advantage? Is it through superior financial performance such as profitability or growth?

Just as there tends to be a link between risk and return (the higher the one, then the higher the other), you might reasonably expect for there to be a direct link between financial performance and innovation – greater innovation intensity leading to higher profits. You might also reasonably expect there to be a similar link with business growth – high-growth firms are more innovative than others. However, the linkages are not straightforward and finding evidence of a direct relationship between innovation and profitability or business growth is problematic because of both methodological and measurement issues:

➡ How do you measure innovation? Many studies simply use R&D spend as a proxy. However, there is no guarantee that this results in successful innovation and without that it is just an extra expenditure that will depress profits. For the R&D spend to be effective what is needed is an effective architecture that focuses the area of research and complementary assets that facilitates its commercialization (Freel and Robson, 2004).

➡ Although innovation is positively associated with growth in employment (Cosh and Hughes, 2007), any link with growth in profits is likely to be 'lagged', with innovation taking time, perhaps years, to feed back into growth in profits – the more radical the innovation, the longer the lag.

➡ The phenomenon of 'cycling' – the understandable tendency of firms to innovate in one period and then 'consolidate' in the next (Cefis, 2003) – can result in timing confusion. Improved performance might be the result of innovation but be observed and measured in the period of consolidation.

➡ Finally, there is the question of causation. Even if there were an observable link, it does not necessarily prove causation: 'while small innovators may in aggregate grow faster than non-innovators this is not to suggest that innovation is a necessary, nor less a sufficient condition for growth or superior performance' (Freel, 2000).

So, with these caveats, what does the empirical evidence tell us? McGrath (2001) observed that firms following 'conventional paths' have lower financial returns, while firms taking risks have variable outcomes ranging from medium to high returns and have potential for greater long-term profitability. Other studies have concluded that entrepreneurial risk taking positively influences both financial performance and business growth (Dess et al., 2011; Tang et al., 2014). What is more, radical innovation leads to market domination and firm growth (Atuahene-Gima, 2005; Tellis and Golder, 2002). However, while there is some empirical support for a link between innovation and business growth (Geroski and Machin, 1992; Yasuda, 2005), a number of studies have failed to find any direct *general* relationship (Coad and Rao, 2008; Lööf and Hesshmati, 2006; O'Regan et al., 2006). You might therefore conclude that the evidence linking innovation with financial performance, although intuitively likely, is inconclusive.

INNOVATION, COMPANY SIZE AND INDUSTRY STRUCTURE

Studies of innovation and company size can also appear contradictory. On the face of it, empirical evidence suggests that larger firms are more likely to be innovative than smaller ones. Indeed, EU data (European Union, 2007) showed that larger firms (250+ employees) were more likely to be innovative than smaller firms (10–49 employees). Data from the UK (Robson and Haigh, 2008) showed that larger firms (250+ employees) were more likely to conduct both internal and contracted-out R&D. They were also much more likely to introduce product, process or managerial innovations generally than smaller firms. By way of contrast, the same study showed that sales from new-to-market or new-to-the-business products – disruptive innovations – represent a higher percentage of turnover in smaller firms compared to larger firms. Another study found no difference between the innovative performance of small compared to large companies because, whilst R&D expenditure might be higher in large companies, small companies may have more innovative employees. Studies that use measures such as R&D expenditure or number of R&D employees must be treated with caution because of the inability of small firms often to separate these inputs out. Nevertheless it has been suggested that small firms conduct R&D more efficiently and introduce new products to the marketplace faster than big companies. For example, a US study found that small firms produce 2.4 times as many innovations per employee as large firms (Acs and Audretsch, 1990). Other studies have used measures such as number of patents – an accurate, but limited measure of innovative activity. These appear contradictory because they vary widely across different industry sectors.

Industry structure on the other hand does seem to influence the level of innovation (Santarelli and Piergiovanni, 1996). Studies have concluded that innovation is less likely in more mature industries that are highly concentrated and more likely in new industries that are less concentrated (Acs and Audretsch, 1988; Dolfsma and van der Panne, 2008; Symeonidis, 1996). Large firms are the dominant innovators in mature industries where you might speculate that the focus is on incremental product and cost-reducing process innovations. It is in new, less concentrated industries where small entrepreneurial firms are more important in terms of innovation and where an entrepreneurial architecture can be most advantageous.

Large firms seem to outperform small firms where resources are important – because of capital intensity or because of scale of spending on R&D, advertising, etc. – although there are typically fewer smaller firms in highly capital-intensive industries. Indeed, small firms generally have lower productivity than large firms. However, whereas larger firms have better access to both internal and external financing than smaller ones and are more productive, smaller firms have behavioural advantages – a closeness to the market, a greater willingness to take risks, an ability to act quickly. Nevertheless scale and resource availability matters, no less so than in industries or sectors that are facing disruption through innovation. For example, the retail sector is facing enormous disruption as online retailers compete against high street shops. The biggest disruptor is Amazon – and they spent some $27 billion on R&D in 2018. How many retailers spent anything approaching this? For context, the pharmaceutical multinational GlaxoSmithKline spent about $5.8 billion.

The evidence on the relationship between the size of established firms and innovation is inconclusive (Brynjolfsson and Kahin, 2000). This is despite the fact that large firms have many advantages: such as resources, funding, product and market knowledge and experienced management. So why are they not the main source of innovation? The main reason is probably that they become too focused on their existing products and established markets – making a change in direction more difficult.

What seems clear is that innovative behaviour is not entirely related to firm size. Smaller firms seem to have advantages in some industries, larger firms in others. What we learn from looking at industries rather than just size of companies is that:

➡ Smaller entrepreneurial firms play a significant role introducing radical, disruptive innovation. They spot the opportunity (perhaps coming out of basic research in the public sector), develop the innovation and move quickly into the market. If larger organizations wish to compete in these industries it requires them to show the same entrepreneurial flair as smaller companies by introducing an entrepreneurial architecture and create the same knowledge networks.

➡ Larger firms have a significant resource advantage over smaller firms and can be more productive generally. They have more resources of every kind to help with innovation and the costs of obtaining more resources are often lower than for smaller firms. However, smaller firms use the resources they have for innovation more efficiently than larger firms. Larger firms therefore have a potential competitive advantage over smaller firms in areas where the costs of innovation are high, particularly if they can develop an entrepreneurial architecture that enables them to use these resources as efficiently and effectively as smaller competitors.

➡ Smaller firms thrive in industries where economies of scale are less important to customers than other factors such as marketing, service quality or variety. Whilst these are often niche markets, they can be highly profitable. If larger organizations wish to compete in these markets they must at least match the factors valued by the target market. One way of doing this is to reorganize into smaller units, each with the entrepreneurial architecture that allows them to compete effectively. Alongside this it may be possible to develop different business models that would be more valued by these target markets, using resources that smaller competitors do not have.

➡ Smaller entrepreneurial firms are less important in stable, mature, high-concentration industries where the innovation focus has switched to efficiency and cost reduction. In these environments an entrepreneurial architecture may be counter-productive. However, by definition, these industries are probably nearing the end of their life-cycle and radical innovation or a move into other sectors is probably required to prolong the life expectancy of the larger organization.

It has been pointed out that the advantages of large firms are generally the disadvantages of small firms, and vice versa, and therefore collaboration or partnering between the two sizes of business can create powerful synergistic relationships (Vossen, 1998). This is a theme we shall return to many times.

CASE INSIGHT 3.5
Astex Therapeutics

UK

SMALL FIRMS AND INNOVATION

Astex Therapeutics was set up in 1999. It was founded by Dr. Harren Jhoti, who left GlaxoWellcome (now GlaxoSmithKline) and by two University of Cambridge professors – Chris Abell and Sir Tom Blundell. Located in Cambridge, UK, the company focused on the discovery and development of drugs, particularly in the area of oncology, using a technique called 'fragment-based drug discovery' – a technique pioneered by the founders and dubbed 'Pyramid'. It was partially seed-funded by the University of Cambridge and raised nearly £100 million of venture capital funds, working in partnership with larger pharma companies to develop a number of new drugs.

In 2011 it merged with a NASDAQ-quoted US company called Supergen, who then closed their US laboratory and concentrated its research in Cambridge, UK, where some 80 people were employed. Astex became a US-quoted company with James Manuso of Supergen as chairman and CEO until 2013, when it was bought by a Japanese pharmaceutical company called Otsuka for approximately $900 million. Its research and headquarters still operates from Cambridge with Harren Jhoti as president and CEO.

Visit the website: astx.com

Questions:

1. How important was the link with the University of Cambridge for Astex when it started?
2. In the age of the internet, how important is geographic proximity to sources of knowledge in encouraging innovation? Explain.

SUMMARY

➡ Innovation is difficult to define. It is about doing things differently. It can take different forms: product, process and/or market innovation. Although scale of innovation is important, competitive advantage can equally be gained by frequent, incremental innovations – a strategy that is less risky and from which the majority of commercially significant innovations have come.

➡ Innovation intensity is measured by the degree or scale of innovation and its frequency. This measure might be supplemented with the speed taken to innovate. The greater the innovation intensity, the higher the risks faced by an organization (but also the higher the potential profits).

➡ Invention is the extreme and riskiest form of innovation. Much early-stage innovation is funded by the public sector. But inventors and governments are not necessarily entrepreneurial and they may need the help of an entrepreneur or an entrepreneurial organization to link their invention to market demand and they, in turn, need the backing of financial institutions.

➡ Business model innovation is about developing innovative plans for how a business competes – plans that break from the dominant logic of a sector. This can lead to market paradigm shift, creating new markets where none existed before.

➡ Knowledge and the exposure to different ideas encourage creativity, invention and radical and incremental innovation. Connectivity is one of the key drivers of creativity – the connection we have with a wide range of different people and ideas – and this can be encouraged within an organization.

➡ Finding evidence of a relationship between innovation and business profitability and growth is problematic. The relationship between innovation and other factors is a complex one and therefore studies are inconclusive.

➡ The rate of innovation (however measured) seems to vary between firms of different size, across industries and sectors depending on industry age and stability, and even location. Small and large firms have advantages in producing different types of innovation. Large firms seem to outperform small firms where access to resources and markets is important. Small firms play a significant role in developing and introducing radical, disruptive innovations. They seem to innovate more efficiently than large firms, although they tend to do this in sectors where resources are less important (where they thrive).

GROUP DISCUSSION QUESTIONS

1. What does innovation mean? Give some examples.
2. How can innovation be measured? Explain how it might be undertaken.
3. What are the differences between creativity, invention and innovation? What are the links between these concepts and entrepreneurship?
4. Which countries are most associated with innovation? Why do you think this is?
5. Is there a best type of innovation?
6. How do you evaluate the commercial potential of a radical innovation?
7. How do you evaluate the commercial potential of a project that involves challenging proven business models that work well?
8. What are the risks associated with innovation?
9. What are the risks associated with market paradigm shift?

10. Is frequent incremental innovation better than infrequent radical innovation?
11. Why might large companies decide not to exploit innovations developed by others that affect their markets?
12. What are the challenges facing an organization seeking to become 'ambidextrous'?
13. If innovation is risky, then you need to take time to introduce it. Discuss.
14. What are the problems in linking innovation with profitability and growth?
15. What advantages and disadvantages do small firms have over large firms in innovation?
16. Why and how does scale influence innovation?
17. Why and how does sector influence innovation?
18. What does innovation mean for a social enterprise?

ACTIVITIES

1. Draw up a research proposal to measure innovations undertaken in an organization in the last year. Make sure you cover details of the measurement scale you propose to use (e.g., a copy of the questionnaire) and the methodology you would use to collect the data.
2. Find an organization that has introduced innovations over the last year and undertake this study, plotting your results on a diagram such as Figure 3.2(a) or (b).
3. Write a report explaining the commercial disruption caused by the internet and mobile technologies over the last decade.

REFERENCES

Acs, Z.J. and Audretsch, D.B. (1988) 'Innovation in Large and Small Firms: An Empirical Analysis', *American Economic Review*, 78(4).

Acs, Z.J. and Audretsch, D.B. (1990) *Innovation and Small Firms*, Cambridge, MA: MIT Press.

Arshi, T. and Burns, P. (2018) 'Entrepreneurial Architecture: A Framework to Promote Innovation in Large Firms', *The Journal of Entrepreneurship*, 27(2).

Atuahene-Gima, K. (2005) Resolving the Capability–Rigidity Paradox in New Product Innovation. *The Journal of Marketing*, 69, October.

Audretsch, D.B. (1995) 'Innovation, Growth and Survival', *International Journal of Industrial Organisation*, 13.

Avermaete, T., Viaene, E., Morgan, J., and Crawford, N. (2003) 'Determinants of Innovation in Small Food Firms', *European Journal of Innovation Management*, 6(1).

Baregheh, A., Rowley, J. and Sambrook, S. (2009) 'Towards a Multidisciplinary Definition of Innovation', *Management Decision*, 47(8).

BCG (2018) *The Most Innovative Companies 2018: Innovators Go All in on Digital*, Boston, MA: Boston Consulting Group. Available on: https://www.bcg.com/publications/2018/most-innovative-companies-2018-innovation.aspx.

Bessant, J. (1999) 'Developing Continuous Improvement Capability', *International Journal of Innovation Management*, 2.

Brynjolfsson, E. and Kahin, B. (2000) (eds) *Understanding the Digital Economy: Data, Tools and Research*, Cambridge, MA: MIT Press.

Cefis, E. (2003) 'Is there Persistence in Innovative Activities?', *International Journal of Industrial Organization*, 21(4).

Chaston, I. (2015) *Entrepreneurial Marketing: Competing by Challenging Convention* (2nd ed.), London: Red Globe Press.

Christensen, C. (1997) *The Innovator's Dilemma*, Cambridge, MA: Harvard Business School Press.

Coad, A. and Rao, R. (2008) 'Innovation and Firm Growth in High-Tech Sectors: A Quantile Regression Approach', *Research Policy*, 37(4).

Cosh, A.D. and Hughes, A. (eds) (2007) *British Enterprise: Thriving or Surviving?*, Cambridge: Centre for Business Research, University of Cambridge.

Dess, G.G., Pinkham, B.C. and Yang, H. (2011) 'Entrepreneurial Orientation: Assessing the Construct's Validity and Addressing Some of Its Implications for Research in the Areas of Family Business and Organizational Learning'. *Entrepreneurship Theory and Practice*, 35.

Deszca, G., Munro, H. and Noori, H. (1999) 'Developing Breakthrough Products: Challenges and Options for Market Assessment', *Journal of Operations Management*, 17(6).

Dolfsma, W. and van der Panne, G. (2008) 'Currents and Sub-currents in Innovation Flows: Explaining Innovativeness Using New-Product Announcements', *Research Policy*, 37(10).

Dong, A. (2015) 'Design × Innovation: Perspective or Evidence-Based Practices' *International Journal of Design Creativity and Innovation*, 3(3).

Duncan, R. (1976) 'The Ambidextrous Organization: Designing Dual Structures for Innovation', in R.H. Killman, L.R. Pondy, and D. Sleven (eds) *The Management of Organization*, New York, NY: North-Holland.

Dunlop-Hinkler, D., Mudambi, R. and Kotabe, M. (2010) 'A Story of Breakthrough and Incremental Innovation', *Strategic Entrepreneurship Journal*, 4(2).

Edison, H., Bin Ali, N. and Torkar, R. (2013) 'Towards Innovation Measurement in the Software Industry', *The Journal of Systems and Software*, 86(5).

Ericson, R. and Pakes, A. (1995) 'Markov-Perfect Industry Dynamics: A Framework for Empirical Work', *Review of Economic Studies*, 62.

European Union (2007) *Statistics in Focus: Community Innovation Statistics, Is Europe Growing More Innovative?, 61/2007*, Brussels: EU.

Florida, R. (2002) *The Rise of the Creative Class: And How It's Transforming Work, Leisure, Community and Everyday Life*, New York, NY: Basic Books.

Florida, R. and Tinagli, I. (2004) *Europe in the Creative Age*, London: Demos.

Freel, M.S. (2000) 'Do Small Innovating Firms Outperform Non-innovators?', *Small Business Economics*, 14(3).

Freel, M.S. and Robson, P.J.A. (2004) 'Small Firm Innovation, Growth and Performance: Evidence from Scotland and Northern Ireland', *International Small Business Journal*, 22(6).

Garcia, R. and Calantone, R. (2002) 'A Critical Look at Technological Innovation Typology and Innovativeness Terminology: A Literature Review', *Journal of Product Innovation Management*, 19(2).

Geroski P. and Machin, S. (1992) 'Do Innovating Firms Outperform Non-innovators?', *Business Strategy Review*, 3(2).

Gibson, C.B. and Birkinshaw, J. (2004) 'The Antecedents, Consequences and Mediating Role of Organizational Ambidexterity' *Academy of Management Journal*, 47.

Hopenhayn, H.A. (1992) 'Entry, Exit and Firm Dynamics in Long Run Equilibrium', *Econometrica*, 60.

Janeway, W.H. (2018) *Doing Capitalism in the Innovation Economy*, Cambridge: Cambridge University Press.

Johnson, S. (2010) *Where Good Ideas Come From: The Natural History of Innovation*, London: Allen Lane.

Jovanovic, B. (1982) 'Favorable Selection with Asymmetrical Information', *Quarterly Journal of Economics*, 97(3).

Kanter, R.M. (1983) *The Change Masters: Innovation and Productivity in American Corporations*, New York, NY: Simon & Schuster.

Kim, W.C. and Mauborgne, R. (2005) 'Blue Ocean Strategy: From Theory to Practice', *California Management Review*, 47(3), Spring.

Klepper, S. (1996) 'Entry, Exit, Growth and Innovation over the Product Life Cycle', *American Economic Review*, 86(3).

Lambson, V.E. (1991) 'Industry Evolution with Sunk Costs and Uncertain Market Conditions', *International Journal of Industrial Organisations*, 9.

Lööf, H. and Hesshmati, A. (2006) 'On the Relationship Between Innovation and Performance: A Sensitivity Analysis', *Economics of Innovation and New Technology*, 15, 4–5.

March, J.G. (1991) 'Exploration and Exploitation in Organizational Learning' *Organization Science*, 2.

Mazzucato, M. (2018) *The Entrepreneurial State: Debunking Public vs Private Sector Myths*, London: Penguin Books.

McGrath, R.G. (2001) Exploratory Learning, Innovative Capacity, and Managerial Oversight. *Academy of Management Journal*, 44(1).

Norman, D. and Verganti, R. (2014) 'Incremental and Radical Innovation: Design Research Versus Technology and Meaning Change', *Design Issues*, 30(1).

O'Regan, N., Ghobadian, A. and Gallear, D. (2006) 'In Search of the Drivers of High Growth in Manufacturing SMEs', *Technovation*, 26(1).

Osterwalder, A. and Pigneur, Y. (2010) *Business Model Generation: A Handbook for Visionaries, Game Changers and Challengers*, Hoboken, NJ: John Wiley & Sons.

Phadke, U. and Vyakarnam, S. (2017) *Camels, Tigers & Unicorns: Rethinking Science & Technology-Enabled Innovation*, London: World Scientific.

Porter, M.E. (1990) *The Competitive Advantage of Nations*, New York, NY: Free Press.

Raworth, K. (2017) *Doughnut Economics: Seven Ways to Think Like a 21st-Century Economist*, London: Random House Books.

Robson, S. and Haigh, G. (2008) 'First Findings from the UK Innovation Survey 2007', *Economic and Labour Market Review*, 2(4).

Ruttan, V. (2006) *Is War Necessary for Economic Growth? Military Procurement and Technological Development*, New York, NY: Oxford University Press.

Salavou, H. (2002) 'Product Innovativeness and Performance: A Focus on SMEs', *Management Decision*, 46(7).

Santarelli, E. and Piergiovanni, R. (1996) 'Analysing Literature-Based Innovation Output Indicators', *Research Policy*, 25(5).

Schumpeter, J.A. (1996) *The Theory of Economic Development*, Edition Copyright 1983, New Brunswick, NJ: Transaction Publishers.

Simmie, J. (2002) 'Knowledge Spillovers and Reasons for the Concentration of Innovative SMEs', *Urban Studies*, 39, 5–6.

Symeonidis, G. (1996) 'Innovation, Firm Size and Market Structure: Schumpeterian Hypotheses and Some New Themes', *OECD Economic Studies*, 27.

Tang, J., Tang, Z. and Katz, J.A. (2014) Proactiveness, Stakeholder-Firm Power Difference, and Product Safety and Quality of Chinese SMEs. *Entrepreneurship: Theory & Practice*, 38(5).

Tellis, G.J. and Golder, P. (2002) *Will and Vision: How Latecomers Grow to Dominate Markets*, New York, NY: McGraw-Hill.

Tushman, M.L., and O'Reilly, C.A. (1996) 'Ambidextrous Organizations: Managing Evolutionary and Revolutionary Change', *California Management Review*, 38.

Vargo, S.L. and Lusch, R.F. (2004) 'Evolving to a New Dominant Logic for Marketing', *Journal of Marketing*, 68(1).

Venkatarman, S. (1997) 'The Distinctive Domain of Entrepreneurship Research: An Editor's Perspective' in *Advances in Entrepreneurship, Firm Emergence and Growth*, Katz, J. and Brockhaus, R. eds., Greenwich, CT: JAI Press.

Vossen, R.W. (1998) 'Relative Strengths and Weaknesses of Small Firms in Innovation', *International Small Business Journal*, 16(3).

Wagner, K., Taylor, A., Zablit, H. and Foo, E. (2014) *The Most Innovative Companies 2014: Breaking Through Is Hard to Do*, Boston Consulting Group Report, October.

West, G. (2015) *Strategy + Business*, Issue 81, Winter.

Yasuda, T. (2005) 'Firm Growth, Size, Age and Behavior in Japanese Manufacturing', *Small Business Economics*, 24(1).

ONLINE RESOURCES AVAILABLE **For further resources relating to this chapter see the companion website at www.macmillanihe.com/Burns-CEI**

PART II

BUILDING ENTREPRENEURIAL ARCHITECTURE

This section looks at three of the pillars of an entrepreneurial architecture; culture, structure and leadership/management. Chapter 4 explores the dimensions of culture, what influences it and how an entrepreneurial organizational culture might be developed and even measured. Chapter 5 looks at the various structures that are used in organizations and develops an understanding of how they might be applied to a company undertaking different tasks and facing different environments. It explains the links between control, autonomy and motivation. It explores the trend towards down-scoping and outsourcing and new forms of organizing, including partnerships and joint ventures. Chapter 6 outlines the literature on leadership and, building on the environmental context facing an entrepreneurial organization, it defines the qualities needed for entrepreneurial leadership. Leaders also manage, and managers also lead in a variety of contexts. Chapters 7 and 8 address the issues in managing two major challenges for entrepreneurial organizations – managing change and risk. Chapter 6 looks at the challenge of managing a turn-around situation and developing environmentally sustainable entrepreneurship. Chapter 8 looks at the natural bias we have in decision-making before developing a simple risk management framework to overcome it.

It is easier to sustain architecture than to set out to create it.

John Kay, author

4 Culture in the entrepreneurial organization

Learning outcomes

When you have read this chapter and undertaken the related activities you will be able to:

➡ Critically analyze the meaning of culture, giving examples of the dimensions along which it can be measured;
➡ Critically analyze what is meant by the entrepreneurial culture of an organization, recognizing its most important elements, and how it can help create an entrepreneurial architecture;
➡ Construct the cultural web of an organization;
➡ Critically evaluate the culture of an organization and describe the managerial tools available to help construct or reconstruct it.

CULTURE

culture In an organization this is about the web of unspoken, prevalent norms, basic beliefs and assumptions about the 'right' way to behave. Sometimes simply described as 'how it is around here'

As we saw in Chapter 2, organizational **culture** is at the base of how many of the behavioural characteristics (or the 'organizational climate') of entrepreneurial orientation are defined: innovativeness, risk-taking, pro-activeness, competitive aggressiveness and autonomy. It is also one of the specific pillars of entrepreneurial architecture. Any group, family, organization, even a nation, has its own culture – each interacting and influencing the other. However, culture is an elusive concept. It is the personality of the group, the prevalent norms, basic beliefs and assumptions about behaviour that underpin it. There are many more detailed definitions. Hofstede (2001) defined it as the 'collective programming of the mind which distinguishes one group of people from another'. Culture is therefore based upon hidden and unspoken assumptions about the 'right' way to behave. It is a pattern of taken-for-granted assumptions and beliefs shared by individuals collectively about how they are. Schein (1990) said that it was 'invented, discovered, or developed by a given group'. Culture is important because it manifests itself in the way people are inclined to behave. Along with other factors like personality, rules and laws, it influences behaviour. It influences how individuals view life and underpins their mental models. It influences the dominant logic of a group.

Individuals are likely to belong to more than one group and therefore will be influenced by the sub-cultures created by these groups: family, nationality, religion, education, tribe, ethnic or social group, age etc. Each of these groups will have its own different and sometimes conflicting culture. One group culture might be strong – where people have a strong sense of the 'right' thing to do – another weak. Cultures evolve over time under this multitude of influences. They can therefore change and also be shaped and influenced over time. Individuals 'learn' the culture of the group (and sub-group) and it is passed down or taught to new members through the norms and conventions of the group.

As well as influencing behaviour, culture affects how different groups communicate and interact internally and externally. Unless recognized, this can cause misunderstandings between groups with different cultures. For example, Graham and Lam (2003) noted the following basic cultural differences between Chinese and US negotiators affected the way they approached those negotiations:

Chinese		**US**
Collectivist	⬌	Individualist
Hierarchical	⬌	Egalitarian
Relationship orientation	⬌	Information orientation
Holistic	⬌	Reductionist
Circular	⬌	Sequential
Seeks the way	⬌	Seeks the truth
The haggling culture	⬌	The argument culture

The collectivist approach of the Chinese stems from their agrarian background. The US individualistic approach stems from their pioneering and industrial backgrounds. The

Chinese preference for hierarchy has a long tradition, reinforced through the Communist Party, whereas the individualistic, egalitarian approach of the US has its roots in the Founding Fathers. However, the Chinese system involves reciprocal obligation and places responsibility on both followers and leaders.

Language is an essential element of culture since it transmits the view that the group has of itself and the world, but also because the words themselves help shape people's beliefs. Some cultures produce simple, clear and precise meanings and messages are taken at face value. In others, it is more nuanced and layered and messages are implied rather than stated explicitly. For example, Graham and Lam (2003) suggested that it was the use of pictograms in the Chinese language that caused Chinese negotiators to take a holistic and circular approach to negotiations – returning to issues – even when facing a number of tradable negotiating points. This compares to Americans' preference for dealing with one point at a time – a reductionist and sequential approach. Without the words to describe situations, values or beliefs, they cannot be communicated. In the same way some groups start to carve out their own vocabulary with a view to influencing culture. In some companies, like Gore-Tex in the USA, employees are referred to as 'associates'. In John Lewis in the UK they are referred to as 'partners' – and really do own the business. These words are value-laden and convey the organizations' view of their relationships with these people.

At the centre of any culture are the values that it holds. Some values are core, some are peripheral. Core values are stabilizing mechanisms that change only slowly over time, whilst peripheral values are less important and can change more quickly. Different nations have different cultures based upon underlying core values. Guirdham (1999) gave some examples: 'The status of women is a core value in Argentina, Chile, India and Israel, but less so in China, where the Confucian hierarchical concept of relations between individuals is more core . . . Similarly, to a third generation American, the value of the democratic right of free speech might be core, but to her Singaporean cousin it might be peripheral, something to be traded off against the value of having a low-crime, drug-free society to live in.'

Cultures might be visible on a fairly superficial level – the costumes or uniforms people wear distinguish them as belonging to a particular group that might be associated with the deeper things – the values and beliefs that the group holds and their view of themselves and the world. And often we make initial judgements about people based upon these superficial externalities. However, the simple fact that costumes or uniforms are worn does not necessarily guarantee a strong culture. The strength of a culture is rarely visible at the superficial level. Cultures become strong when they are reinforced in a consistent way by the different elements that influence them and, in particular, the rest of the organizational architecture.

THE DIMENSIONS OF CULTURE

Cultural models define characteristics of groups. These characteristics can create communication and interaction problems between different groups. Several cultural models have been developed in order to better understand these differences. These include the Hofstede Model (Hofstede 1981, updated 2001, Hofstede & Hofstede, 2005; Hofstede, 2007), studies by Schwartz and Bilsky (1987), Trompenaars (1993), and the GLOBE Model (House et al., 2004). Of these, it is the Hofstede Model that has been applied most often (Mooij & Hofstede, 2010). Hofstede undertook an extensive cross-cultural study, using questionnaire data from some 80,000 IBM employees in 66 countries across seven occupations. Drawing on his research, he established the four dimensions shown in Figure 4.1. This figure also shows the dominant culture he found in employees in particular countries at the extremes of these dimensions. This is instructive because you might expect the national culture of the USA to be highly entrepreneurial – one that fosters social attitudes that encourage entrepreneurship. Welsch (1998) described entrepreneurship as being 'ingrained' in North American culture. It is an achievement-orientated society that values individualism and material wealth. We might therefore use the national culture of the USA as a benchmark for one that encourages individual entrepreneurship.

Individualism versus collectivism – This is the degree to which people prefer to act as individuals rather than groups. Individualistic cultures are loosely knit social frameworks in which people primarily operate as individuals or in immediate families or groups. By contrast, collectivist cultures are composed of tight networks in which people operate as members of 'in-groups' and 'out-groups', expecting to look after, and be looked after by, other members of their 'in-group'. In the individualist culture, the task prevails over personal relationships and the atmosphere is competitive. In collectivist cultures it is co-operative within the 'in-group'; however, it may well be uncharacteristically competitive with 'out-groups' – a feature associated with the 'competitive aggressiveness dimension of an organization with an entrepreneurial orientation. Hofstede found that the 'Anglo' countries (the USA, UK, Australia, Canada and New Zealand) were the highest-scoring individualist cultures, together with the Netherlands, France and Germany, which just made it into the upper quartile of individualist cultures. At the other end of the spectrum, South American countries were the most collectivist cultures, together with Pakistan.

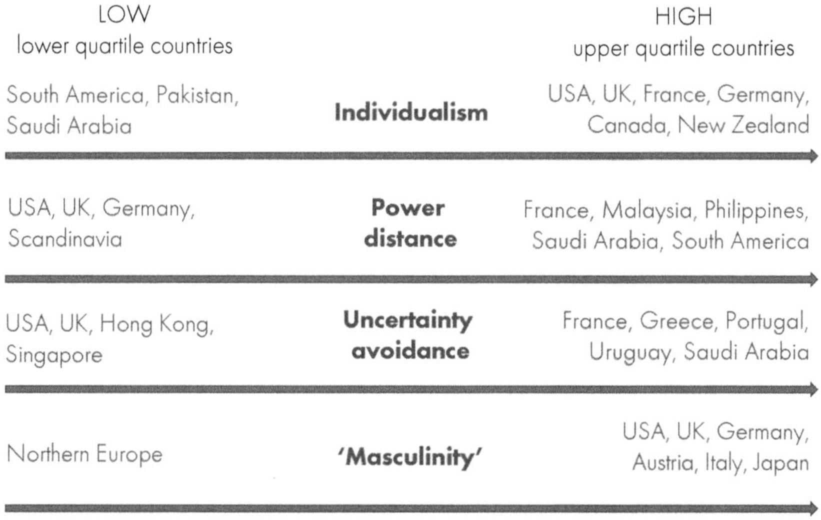

LOW lower quartile countries		HIGH upper quartile countries
South America, Pakistan, Saudi Arabia	**Individualism**	USA, UK, France, Germany, Canada, New Zealand
USA, UK, Germany, Scandinavia	**Power distance**	France, Malaysia, Philippines, Saudi Arabia, South America
USA, UK, Hong Kong, Singapore	**Uncertainty avoidance**	France, Greece, Portugal, Uruguay, Saudi Arabia
Northern Europe	**'Masculinity'**	USA, UK, Germany, Austria, Italy, Japan

Figure 4.1 Hofstede's dimensions of national culture

power distance The degree of inequality among people that the community is willing to accept

Power distance – This is the degree of inequality among people that the community is willing to accept. Low power-distance cultures endorse egalitarianism, with open and informal relations, functional and unrestricted information flows and organizations that tend to have flat structures. On the other hand, high power-distance cultures endorse hierarchies, with more formal relations, restricted information flows and organizations that tend to be igid and hierarchical. Individuals in high power-distance cultures have difficulty working n unsupervised groups whereas those in low power-distance cultures might be thought to exhibit a lack of 'respect' for authority. In Hofstede's classification the low power-distance countries were identified as Austria, Ireland, Israel, New Zealand and the four Scandinavian countries. The USA, UK and Germany also made it into the lower quartile. Among the high power-distance countries were Malaysia, the Philippines and four South American countries, with France also making it into the upper quartile in this respect.

Uncertainty avoidance – This is the degree to which people prefer to avoid ambiguity, resolve uncertainty and prefer structured rather than unstructured situations. Low uncertainty avoidance cultures tolerate greater ambiguity, prefer flexibility, stress personal choice and decision-making, reward initiative, experimentation, risk-taking and team-play and stress the development of analytical skills. High uncertainty avoidance cultures prefer rules and procedures, stress compliance, punish error and reward compliance, loyalty and attention to detail. The lowest uncertainty avoidance countries were Hong Kong, Ireland, Jamaica, Singapore and two Scandinavian countries, with the USA and UK also in the lowest quartile. The highest uncertainty avoidance countries were Greece, Portugal, Guatemala and Uruguay, with France also in the highest quartile group. Germany was about halfway.

'Masculinity' (versus 'femininity') – This defines quality of life issues. Hofstede defined 'masculine' virtues as those of achievement, assertiveness, competition and success. 'Masculine' cultures reward financial and material achievement with social prestige and status. 'Feminine' virtues include modesty, compromise and co-operation. 'Feminine' cultures value relationships. Issues such as quality of life, warmth in personal relationships, service and so on are important, and in some societies having a high standard of living is thought to be a matter of birth, luck or destiny, rather than personal achievement (an external locus of control – the opposite of internal locus of control). Hofstede found the most 'masculine' countries to be Japan, Austria, Venezuela, Italy and Switzerland, with the USA, UK and Germany all falling into the highest quartile. Four North European countries were the highest scoring feminine countries. France was about halfway.

At a later date, Hofstede and Bond (1991) added a fifth dimension – short/long-term orientation. A short-term orientation focuses on past and present and therefore values respect for the status quo. For example, they include an unqualified respect for tradition and for social and status obligations. A long-term orientation focuses on the future and therefore the values associated with this are more dynamic. For example, they include the adaptation of traditions to contemporary conditions and only qualified respect for social and status obligations. Entrepreneurial organizations both look forward to and embrace change. They therefore have a 'long-term' orientation on this dimension.

Notice one more thing from Figure 4.1. The UK sits alongside the USA – our benchmark for a national culture that encourages individual entrepreneurship. However, in the 1970s when these studies were conducted, the UK had a stagnant economy and could hardly have been held up to be the epitome of an enterprising nation. The explanation of the findings may lie in the timing of the study. Attitudes to enterprise were changing rapidly. In the UK and USA, political interest was focused on enterprise as a means of rescuing stagnant economies (O'Connor, 1973) and it was argued that structural change was needed to achieve an 'enterprise culture' (Morris, 1991; Carr, 2000). This happened in the UK with the arrival of the Thatcher government. The UK may not have been an enterprising nation at the time but cultural attitudes towards entrepreneurship were indeed changing rapidly, as subsequent economic performance indicated.

Hofstede's cultural framework is widely used and well respected and it remains important because of the scale of the sample. The GLOBE study (2004), by contrast, is more recent and covered more than one company. Designed to replicate Hofstede's work, it covered 17,000 middle managers from 951 organizations in three industries, across 62 societies. Although there is considerable academic debate about the subject, Hofstede (2010) believed the GLOBE researchers essentially adopted and verified his five dimensions of national culture, although they expanded them to nine: Power Distance; Uncertainty Avoidance; Future Orientation (all used by Hofstede); Institutional Collectivism; In-Group Collectivism (Hofstede used individualism-collectivism); Assertiveness; Gender Egalitarianism; Performance Orientation; and Humane Orientation (similar to Hofstede's 'masculine-feminine').

INTERNATIONAL INFLUENCES ON CULTURE

The USA shows us the anatomy of a national enterprise culture: one that encourages individual enterprise and entrepreneurship, one where there is the highest probability of an entrepreneur being made, rather than just born. This is the sort of culture that many other countries have been trying to promote and develop because it seems to encourage the characteristics that are needed to develop the largest number of entrepreneurs. As we have already noted, the UK also shares this profile. The USA emerges as a highly individualistic, 'masculine' culture, with low power distance and uncertainty avoidance. It is a culture that tolerates risk and ambiguity, has a preference for flexibility and an empowered culture that rewards personal initiative. It is a highly individualistic and egalitarian culture, one that is fiercely competitive and was then the home of the 'free-market economy'. Assertiveness and competition are central to the 'American dream'. If there is a key virtue in the USA it is achievement, and achievement receives its monetary reward. It is an informal culture with all people being created equal; however, they also have the freedom to accumulate sufficient wealth to become very unequal. The USA is the original 'frontier culture'. It actually seems to like change and uncertainty and certainly rewards initiative and risk-taking.

An entrepreneurial culture does not exist within an organization in isolation and an individual will be influenced by the cultures of the other groups to which they belong – their social, religious, national cultures, among others. Any organization must somehow reconcile the behavioural norms generated by these other cultures with that of its own. Sometimes the dominant national culture in which the company is based tends to discourage entrepreneurship. For example, Figure 4.1 shows Saudi Arabia (in the 1970s) to be at the opposite end of three of these dimensions to the USA (individualism, uncertainty avoidance and power distance) and France in two (uncertainty avoidance and power distance). An organization must also realize that it may need to develop a different culture to its own within certain groups such as venture teams (Chapter 13).

National culture remains a major influence on individual behaviour. An empirical investigation by Morris et al. (1994), which covered the USA, South Africa and Portugal, supported this. Powerful national cultures can overpower weaker organizational cultures. For this reason, Hofstede argued that is often difficult for organizational cultures to cross national boundaries. The fact he was able to identify national influences within IBM tends o support this. What is more, cultural comparisons and analyses are inextricably bound to a particular time and a particular place. Over time they change. The Hofstede study is some 40 years old and based on a technology company.

In this context it is worth remembering that most management theory and research was developed in the West in the second half of the twentieth century and that it is both culture- and gender-bound. It is written in English. It was developed for and about men. It reflects the 'scientific method' – emphasizing independence, lack of emotion, objectivity, rational- ty, logic. Hofstede (1991) himself stated that 'not only organizations are culturally bound; theories about organizations are equally culture bound. The Professors who wrote the the- ories are children of a culture: they grew up in families, went to schools, worked for employ- ers. Their experiences represent the material on which their thinking and writing have been based. Scholars are as human and culturally biased as other mortals.' There is no guarantee therefore that theories developed around the cultural context of one country at any par- ticular time can be applicable to another country or another time. So, for example, many of the early motivational theories were developed by American academics (e.g. Herzberg, Maslow, McClelland) and were based around self-interest and the satisfaction of personal needs such as money, status and 'self-actualization'. These theories are rooted very firmly in the Anglo-Saxon capitalist culture which values individualism and 'masculinity' (using Hofstede's dimensions) with low uncertainty avoidance.

Multinationals based in a number of different countries, each with different cultural profiles, may need to emphasize different things in different countries in order to combat the prevailing national culture. Often the prevailing national culture is such that the pos- sibility of achieving a homogenous organizational culture in a multinational is virtually impossible. Indeed, it might be argued that it is undesirable. Nevertheless, management is the art of the possible and Morden (1995) showed how national cultural issues might be addressed at a local level. Furthermore, Hofstede (1980) suggested that these characteris- tics themselves may confer competitive advantage by concentrating certain types of activities in particular countries. For example, highly 'feminine' countries (using Hofstede's terminology) such as the Netherlands or Denmark tend to be successful in consultancy, the service sector, helping relationships, horticulture and agriculture. He also observed that cultures can work in a complementary manner, citing the Anglo-Dutch multinationals Shell and Unilever where the values on power distance, uncertainty avoidance and individualism are similar, but where the people orientation of the Dutch complements the masculine, achievement orientation of the British.

Generally, people seem to prefer to be part of groups from their own culture (in-group) rather than from other cultures (out-groups) (e.g. Van Knippenberg et al., 2004; Van Knippenberg and Schippers, 2007). Therefore leading and managing multinational teams can pose some particularly complex problems which we shall return to in chapters 6–8. However, team diversity – including cultural diversity – offers many advantages, not least of which is an insight into national market needs that can be invaluable for innovation. Syed (2019) talked about 'cognitive diversity' being the real driver of innovation today – giving different perspectives on a problem and facilitating the recombination of ideas from differ- ent walks of life. This is particularly important for today's tech companies. For example, Waymo, the self-driving car technology company, needs to combine technologies from the internal combustion engine, computing, sensors, GPS map information and many more. Syed concluded that this comes from having an open, diverse and tolerant culture that facilitates the interaction of people with divergent views – a term we call 'connectivity' and return to in Chapter 9. He concluded:

> *[Organization and societal] cultures that encourage new ideas, foster dissent and have strong networks through rebel ideas can flow, innovate faster than those held back by cultures of intellectual conformity.*

The leader of a team may have an undue influence on team innovation. In one study, multicultural teams led by Chinese managers were found to be less innovative than teams led by people from other countries, suggesting that either the leader's national culture or the distance between the manager's and the team members' national cultures can have an impact on team innovation (Lisak et al., 2016).

MEASURING AN INDIVIDUAL'S CULTURE

One widely used tool for measuring an individual's culture was developed by Erin Meyer (2014). Based on research data from over thirty countries, it identified eight dimensions that she claims capture most of the differences among cultures that affect the way in which we communicate and understand each other:

➡ Communicating – This scale measures the degree to which a culture prefers low- or high-context communication. Low-context cultures (e.g., the USA, Germany, the Netherlands), favour simple, clear and precise communication, often with written confirmation. By contrast, high-context cultures (e.g., China, India and France) employ nuanced, layered communication with less put in writing and more left to interpretation.
➡ Evaluating – This scale measures the relative preference for direct versus indirect criticism. There is no direct link between this and the communication scale. Whilst France favours high-context communication, it also favours being much more direct with negative feedback, compared to the USA (low-context). Similarly, Spain and Mexico may both favour high-context, but Spain favours more direct criticism than Mexico.
➡ Persuading – This scale measures preference for principles-first (theory) vs applications-first arguments (practice). Germans and southern Europeans favour setting out generally accepted principles before presenting an opinion whilst the Americans and British typically start with opinions or practical observations, adding theory and principles later.
➡ Leading – This scale gauges the degree of respect and deference shown to authority figures (power distance). High power distance favours hierarchy (e.g., China, Russia, Nigeria and Japan). Low power distance favour egalitarianism (e.g., Scandinavia and Israel).
➡ Deciding – This scale measures how group decision-making is consensual compared to reliant on one person (the boss). There is no direct link between this and power distance (e.g., Japanese and Germans are hierarchical but are also consensual).
➡ Trusting – This scale balances task-based trust (from the head) with relationship-based trust (from the heart). In task-based cultures (e.g., the USA, the UK, Germany) trust is built through work. In relationship-based societies (e.g., Brazil, China, India) trust is built by personal networks.

hierarchy
Organizations' structures: tall structures have many managers with a narrower span of control (fewer people reporting to them); flat structures with fewer managers with a wider span of control (more people reporting to them)

➡ Disagreeing – This scale measures how confrontation is viewed – whether it improves or harms relationships. Some countries are comfortable airing differences (e.g., Germany, France, the Netherlands), others are not (e.g., Indonesia, Japan, Thailand).

➡ Scheduling – This scale measures whether time and time-keeping is as seen as flexible (e.g., in Switzerland, Germany, and the USA, time-keeping is expected, whereas in India, Brazil, and Italy it is viewed more flexibly).

These eight dimensions of culture affect the way individuals interact – with each other, within nations and within organizations. As we have observed, in multinational organizations they act as a filter that can distort communication and affect decision-making.

🔍 EXPLORE FURTHER

An assessment tool that allows you to see where you fall on Meyer's eight scales is free to use by individuals on hbr.org/web/assessment/2014/08/whats-your-cultural-profile. It also provides a comparison with the typical result from your own country allowing you to see the cultural profile of your own country.

ORGANIZATIONAL CULTURE

The culture within the organization helps shape its architecture (and vice versa). Bratton and Gold (2017) defined organizational culture simply as 'the set of values, understandings and ways of thinking that is shared by the majority of members of a work organization, and that is taught to new employees as correct'. In an earlier work, Schein (1983) extended this definition to include how these values and ways of thinking came about by defining it as 'the pattern of basic assumptions which a given group invented, discovered or developed in learning to cope with its problems of external adaptation and internal integration, which has worked well enough to be considered valid, and therefore to be taught to new members as the correct way to perceive, think and feel in relation to those problems'. Cornwall and Perlman (1990) added the observation that organizational culture reflected itself in the behaviour of the group and how it defined itself in relation to its external environment, an echo of the 'in-group' vs the 'out-group'. Organizational culture therefore reflects itself not only in behaviour but also in how the organization presents itself internally and externally through every form of communication, including its digital footprint.

Hofstede's mapping of national cultures gives us the USA as a benchmark for a culture that encourages *individual* entrepreneurship. However, whilst it may be obvious that a low power distance and uncertainty avoidance are desirable, there are two important differences when you transfer this to *organizational* culture:

1. Almost by definition, any organizational culture must involve a balance between individualism and collectivism. There must be a basis for working together, at the very least based on mutual self-interest. We discussed how an entrepreneurial architecture seeks to build a series of relational contracts that bond the organization together. This requires strong organizational identity. However, the spark of individualism needs to be kept alight. A cross-cultural, empirical investigation (Morris et al., 1994) suggested that

entrepreneurship appears to decline the more collectivism is emphasized, although dysfunctional high levels of individualism can have the same effect. In the place of individualism, the architecture should seek to promote a strong sense of 'in-group', with a clear identity and a feeling of competition against 'out-groups' (us against competitors).

2. At the same time, any organizational culture must involve a balance between Hofstede's 'masculine' and 'feminine' dimensions. Concern for others ('feminine') is a prerequisite to creating those relational contracts. The need for achievement ('masculine') must become achievement through co-operation in an entrepreneurial architecture. The aim is to build a culture of achievement by the 'in-group' against 'out-groups'.

As we have seen, organizational culture is just one of the many cultures that any individual may contribute to or be affected by. Even if a leader does not try to 'impose' an organizational culture, one will emerge. Therefore ignoring culture can be dangerous because the one that might emerge, if the process is not managed, may not help the organization meet its objectives. However, large organizations are complex. They contain many different environments (departments or operating units), each with differing cultures based on the different tasks, individuals, competitive environments, even time horizons. There is often competition between these cultures, resulting in different value choices. The role of management, therefore, is not just about selecting the culture to be emphasized; it is also about resolving these conflicts – emphasizing one or another and striking an appropriate balance between others. This is not an easy task and it is one that involves judgement, rather than being based on any sound scientific basis. Nevertheless, culture influences behaviour and is important as an alternative to rules and regulations. Indeed, the culture of an organization can be more important than any formal structure because it manifests itself in the way people are *inclined and likely to behave* rather than the way they are *supposed to behave*. Chapter 2 highlighted how 'innovativeness' is the most important dimension of an 'entrepreneurial orientation' and studies have confirmed that an organizational culture of creativity and innovation reflects itself in innovative behaviours by employees that lead to innovations being developed within the organization (Hogan and Coote, 2014; Sadegh and Ataei, 2012). It is important then to be able to describe organizational culture in a systematic way and understand how it might be influenced.

THE CULTURAL WEB

Johnson and Scholes (1999) introduced the concept of a cultural web that describes, but also shapes how a culture is formed within an organization. They talked about the 'cultural paradigm': how an organization thinks and acts. They represented this as a number of overlapping aspects of culture that help define it: organizational structures; control systems; routines; rituals; power; symbols; stories. Together, these both help to describe the organizational culture and can also help to shape it. They are interlinked, underlining the idea that culture is self-reinforcing. They make up the cultural web of an organization shown in Figure 4.2.

➡ Organizational structures – The structures of an organization should be consistent with its culture; if this is not the case then there is a disconnect between how people are inclined to behave and how they are supposed to behave. Structures might be

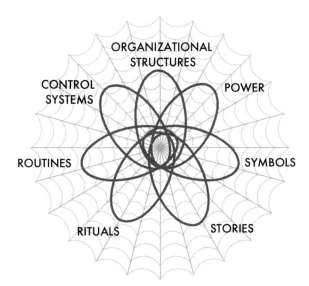

Figure 4.2 The cultural web

quick and easy to change, but that does not mean that there will be a change in culture, at least in the short term.

➡ Control systems – These are the systems that monitor, measure and incentivize the behaviour of individuals, including the metrics against which their performance is judged. They overlap with organizational structures and reinforce routines. We shall return to organization structures and control systems in the next chapter; however, there must be mechanisms that encourage employees to suggest innovative ideas and obtain the resources to investigate them.

➡ Routines – These are the ways in which people work and act towards each other. They enable the organization to run smoothly and perform routine tasks. They may be partly rule-based. For example, when they first join a firm many graduates have an induction programme which involves them undertaking routine 'shopfloor' tasks so as to get them to understand the different roles performed within it. However, not all rules may be written down and because of this they can be difficult to uncover and to change. On the other hand, because they involve this tacit knowledge they can be difficult to copy.

➡ Rituals – These are the regular events and traditions of the organization, such as annual appraisals, sales conferences etc. They are the things that indicate what the organization values. Employee innovation awards, 'seed-corn' funding and/or 'free time' for innovations indicate the importance an organization places on that activity.

➡ Power – This is also closely linked to the organizational structure, although people can also have power that is not shown in a hierarchical organization chart, for example because individuals have experience, information, knowledge or just charisma. Finding out where the real power lies in an organization can often lead to unexpected places. It can also lead to unintended consequences. It is therefore something intrapreneurs need to thoroughly understand.

➡ Symbols – These are often used to reinforce power, for example the 'guarded' office or designated parking spaces. However, they can also be used to help shape the organizational culture in an intended direction, for example, awards ceremonies, certificates, plaques etc. celebrating innovations. Many companies show-case their most recent innovations in highly visible ways. Ericsson, the Swedish telecoms company, gives a loaded credit card and one week to experiment to any employees who come up with an innovative idea. Famously, Google (now Alphabet) cultivates a vibrant, 'fun' working environment to encourage creativity and innovation

➡ Stories – Every organization will have stories that are told to new employees or visitors that reflect things that happen within it. Some will be constructive, others less so. Some might almost go down as part of the folklore of the organization because they are repeated so often. For example, the 'invention' of the ubiquitous Post-it notes reinforces 3M's reputation for encouraging intrapreneurship and innovation (Case insight 13.1). Buckler and Zien (1996) talk about 'innovative leaders' reshaping old stories to inspire the future.

Induction and training programmes have a large part to play in spreading and perpetuating the culture of an organization, although managing the change of culture can be very difficult (see Chapter 7). You can construct the cultural web of an organization by simply asking people what it is like to work within it – open questions around the key themes. You might similarly define what the desired web for an organization should look like, in each case noting down key words and phrases that describe it. Once this is done, you can start to determine the actions that need to be taken to make any changes. Based on the work of Harrison (1972), Handy (1985) popularized four organizational typologies that should be capable of being described using the typology of the cultural web in Figure 4.2:

Power culture – This is where power is concentrated in a single source, with communication and authority radiating out from the centre. Hall (2005) found that innovation did not occur in a power culture.

Role culture – This is where delegated power is exercised through clearly defined roles and strict procedures and individuals are judged by how well they adhere to these.

Task culture – This is where power is delegated to individuals and teams to perform given tasks and they are judged by how well they perform them.

Person culture – This is where the organization serves the individual and the individual thrives through their personal expertise.

Handy's work on organizational culture is closely linked to leadership styles, a topic we shall return to in Chapter 6.

 CASE INSIGHT 4.1
Dyson

CORPORATE CULTURE

James Dyson is the billionaire inventor of the bagless vacuum cleaner who challenged the market dominance of Hoover, and won. With some 12,000 employees worldwide, his company now designs and manufactures a range of household appliances such as vacuum cleaners, air purifiers, hand dryers, bladeless fans, heaters and hair dryers. He built the business in the UK only to announce in 2019 that he was moving manufacturing to Singapore. On a visit to the factory Hengky Wirawan explained: 'If you have a vacuum cleaner or hairdryer, the motor will have come from here. We make one every 2.6 seconds.' Pinky Leong added that the factory floor is 'live and con-nected to an App, so if James wants to look at it, he can'.

The quotes came from an article about the move, but it also contained some interesting insights by author Liam Kelly into Dyson's corporate culture, which he describes as 'quirky' and 'inward-looking' with teams being discour-aged from communicating. Kelly describes it as a 'cult of personality', explaining that Dyson is still involved with all products. One employee commented: 'It's really cool, because you get to have meetings with him, but also kind of annoying, because it's really hard to make decisions unless James Dyson makes them.' Some employees describe Dyson as 'a nice old grandad, friendly and approachable' and one who 'didn't dominate the conversation at all'. But at least one engineer appeared somewhat sceptical about his engineering ability: 'He's a great ideas man, I don't think he's a great engineer. Engineering is about getting the final solution with the smallest number of steps'. Kelly observed that Dyson famously took 15 years and 5127 attempts to make his first bagless vacuum cleaner.

Visit the website: **www.dyson.co.uk**

Question:

What insights into Dyson's corporate culture do you get from Kelly's article? What are the advantages and disadvantages of this sort of culture?

Source: Liam Kelly, *The Sunday Times*, 27 January 2019

CULTURE IN THE ENTREPRENEURIAL ORGANIZATION

Tables 2.1 and 2.2 described the elements of an entrepreneurial architecture, many of which need to come from the culture of the organization. The culture of the organization is par-ticularly important if it is to become a learning organization. For an 'entrepreneurial orien-tation' the cultural characteristics revolve around innovativeness, risk-taking and pro-activeness, competitive aggressiveness and internal autonomy. We have already observed that Hofstede's dimensions were not specifically designed to capture differences in organizational culture. However, in a later work Hofstede et al. (1990) looked at different dimensions of organizational culture in an attempt to discriminate between entrepreneur-ial and bureaucratic (or administrative) organizational cultures. Actually, these were not so much dimensions as descriptors of what an entrepreneurial culture might look like com-pared to an administrative one. They are shown in Table 4.1.

Table 4.1 Entrepreneurial vs bureaucratic cultures

Entrepreneurial	vs	Bureaucratic
Results	vs	Process orientation
Job	vs	Employee orientation
Parochial	vs	Professional interest
Open	vs	Closed system
Loose	vs	Tight control
Pragmatic	vs	Normative orientation

Source: Hofstede et al. (1990)

You might compare this to the list of cultures that enhance vs those that inhibit a learning organization in Table 4.2 (Schein, 1994). Starting from scratch you might be able to establish these features from the outset, but to change an established organizational culture is altogether more difficult since most established organizations tend to inhibit learning. Schein concluded that to nurture these qualities an organization needs to establish a 'psychologically safe haven' or 'parallel system' within it where learning – as we have defined it – can occur. And as we shall see in the next chapter, large organizations have responded to this organizational challenge with some success.

Table 4.2 Cultures that enhance vs cultures that inhibit learning

A culture that enhances learning	vs	A culture that inhibits learning
Balances interests of all stakeholders	vs	Believes tasks more important than people
Focuses on people rather than systems	vs	Focuses on systems rather than people
Empowers people and makes them believe they can change things	vs	Allows change only when absolutely necessary
Makes time for learning	vs	Is preoccupied with short-term coping and adapting
Takes an holistic approach to problems	vs	Compartmentalizes problem solving
Encourages open communication	vs	Restricts the flow of information
Believes in teamwork	vs	Believes in competition between individuals
Has approachable leaders	vs	Has controlling leader

Source: Derived from Schein (1994)

Many authors have tried to define an entrepreneurial culture. Rao and Weintraub (2013) defined it as one that 'cultivates engagement and enthusiasm, challenges people to take risks in a safe environment, fosters learning and encourages independent thinking'. Based on a synthesis of the work of Timmons (1999), Peters (1997) and Cornwall and Perlman (1990), Morris and Kuratko (2002) produced a list of features that they would expect to find in an entrepreneurial organization:

1. A people and empowerment focus.
2. Commitment and personal responsibility.
3. 'Doing the right thing'.
4. Value creation through innovation and change.
5. Hands-on management.
6. Freedom to grow and to fail.
7. Attention to basics.
8. Emphasis on the future and a sense of urgency.

Morris and Kuratko highlighted the importance of allowing failure, distinguishing between three types and how they should be handled:

➥ Moral failure – which occurs when there is a breach of ethics or moral standards. This should never be tolerated.
➥ Personal failure – which relates to inadequate skills, knowledge or understanding. This can be addressed through training, development and counseling.
➥ Uncontrollable failure – which happens because of events or conditions out of the control of the individual. This is bound to happen in an entrepreneurial organization and valuable learning can take place as a result of it.

> **❝** The guiding principles in a traditional corporate culture are: follow the instructions given; do not make any mistakes; do not fail; do not take initiatives but wait for instructions; stay within your turf; and protect your backside. The restrictive environment is of course not conducive to creativity, flexibility, independence, and risk taking. **❞**
>
> Robert Hisrich and Michael Peters, *Entrepreneurship: Starting, Developing and Managing a New Enterprise*, Homewood, IL: Irwin, 1992

As we saw in Chapter 2, one of the five dimensions of an 'entrepreneurial orientation' involves being 'risk-taking'. Making mistakes goes hand in hand with 'risk-taking' – making decisions in an uncertain, risky environment. To be 'risk-taking', an organization needs to tolerate mistakes. The skill is to manage those risks and to make more good decisions than bad ones (see Chapter 8). Whilst you might be able to manage risk, the danger of failure is always present. Rather than being viewed as the opposite ends of a spectrum, in the entrepreneurial firm success and failure can be viewed as the continuum shown in Figure 4.3 – a kind of score card. The difference between overall success and failure is for the organization to make certain the volume (or value) of successes outweighs the volume (or value) of failures. And that means that the lessons from every failure must be learned. It has been said

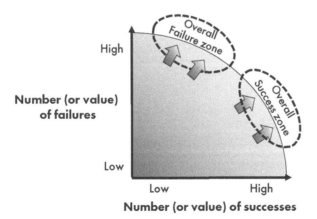

Figure 4.3 Success/failure score card

that the only way to avoid ever making a wrong decision is never to make a decision in the first place – not an option for the entrepreneurial organization.

The constant theme emerging from the literature is the need to empower and motivate employees to do 'the right thing' without having to be ordered to do so. This implies more of a consensus form of decision-making that takes time and can reduce the speed of action (see Chapter 6). However, in some circumstances this might just not be possible if an opportunity is to be seized quickly. This is when the organization should move back from collectivism to individualism, with the entrepreneur and leader asserting themselves. On the other hand, the different scenarios presented by an opportunity might have already been considered as the organization strategizes and evaluates the options open to it. However, ultimately there may be a problem here that only considerations of size and structure can address. If the decision-making group is too large, the organization may well be unable to react with sufficient speed to changing circumstances. We have already observed that size is a significant factor in constructing the management team to support the leader and project groups should also be small.

> **"** Empower your staff. 'People, people, people' is the mantra. If you do not have the right staff, fire them, quickly. Be nimble and act on your convictions. **"**
>
> Gururaj Deshpande, serial entrepreneur, *The Financial Times*, 21 February 2000

Figure 4.4 depicts what the cultural web of an entrepreneurial organization might look like: its structures, control systems, rituals, routines, symbols, stories and power. At the

Figure 4.4 The cultural web of an entrepreneurial organization

core of the web, highlighted in blue, is the organizational focus on creativity and innovation. Also highlighted in blue are the important cultural characteristics of: strong relationships at all levels inside and outside the organization; the sharing and using of information and knowledge; continual learning; measured risk-taking; the feeling of empowered decision-making that staff should have. This is a culture that welcomes change and thrives on the challenges it poses.

CASE INSIGHT 4.2
AirAsia

Malaysia

CORPORATE CULTURE

Former Time Warner executive Tony Fernandes set up Asia's first low-cost airline, AirAsia, in 2001 by buying the heavily indebted state-owned company from the Malaysian government for only 25c. He set about remodelling it as a short-haul, low-cost operator flying around Asia. It was the first low-cost airline in the Asian market, copying the idea from airlines in the West such as Southwest Airlines, easyJet and Ryanair. The company expanded rapidly from a fleet of only two planes in 2002 to a fleet of some 200 planes flying to over 165 destinations and 25 countries. Now with hubs in Kuala

Airasia Airbus planes parked at an airport in Kuala-Lumpur, Malaysia
Source: iStock/Brostock

Lumpur and Singapore, it has also established associate airlines in India, Japan, Thailand, the Philippines and Indonesia and AirAsia X affiliates in Thailand and Indonesia.

It created a completely new Asian market in low-cost air travel that is now enjoyed by millions of people. It claims to have the world's lowest unit cost of $0.023 per available seat kilometre and claims to have a break-even load factor of just over 52 per cent. It achieves this through a crew productivity level that is triple that of Malaysia Airlines and an average aircraft utilization rate of 13 hours a day, involving an aircraft turnaround time of just 25 minutes.

An article in *The Economist* ('Cheap, but Not Nasty', March 2009) said that on entering the airline industry Fernandes found it 'rigidly compartmentalized' and 'dysfunctional'. The article made a number of observations about his management style and its effect on the company's culture, saying that Fernandes wanted the culture to reflect his own 'unstuffy, open, and cheerful personality', observing that he is rarely seen without a baseball cap, open-necked shirt and jeans. Fernandes is proud of the lack of hierarchy within AirAsia, which the *Economist* says is very unusual, observing: 'Fernandes also practices what he preaches. Every month he spends a day as a baggage handler, every two months as a cabin crew, every three months as a check-in clerk.' It also means that there are no barriers to promotion. Some pilots started out as baggage handlers and others as stewards.

Fernandes believes this culture is central to the success of AirAsia and has established a 'culture department' to 'pass the message and hold parties': 'If you sit up in your ivory tower and just look at financial reports, you're going to make some big mistakes . . . Employees come number one, customers come number two. If you have a happy workforce they'll look after your customers anyway.' He believes that highly motivated people are the key to success in the airline business: 'You can have all the money you want in the world, and you can have all the brilliant ideas but if you don't have the people, forget it . . . I look for people who have drive, who have ambition, who are humble. I've hired many people at very strange places.' He also believes a company derives strength from a competent and motivated workforce and that good leadership is about training and recruiting others to replace you as leader: 'Good leadership is to know when to go and you only succeed as a good leader if you've transported someone else in and the company gets stronger. Then you've succeeded as leader.' (*BBC News Business*, 1 November 2010).

Visit the website: **www.airasia.com**

Question:

In commenting on AirAsia's success, what does Tony mean by 'culture, focus and discipline'? How has each of these contributed?

MEASURING ORGANIZATIONAL CULTURE

Hofstede gives us dimensions of national culture and an insight into the influence of sub-cultures. Similarly, the cultural web gives us an insight into how organizational culture can be described and influenced. Handy's typologies gives us a language with which to discuss the concept of organizational culture and how it impacts on, and is impacted by, leadership and structure. However, whilst these may be cultures that we can describe and recognize, it can be more difficult to measure them in any scientific way. One attempt to do this was Erin Meyer's eight dimensions of an individual's culture and its affect on communication and understanding. Another, this time looking at organizational culture, is called the Organizational Culture Assessment Instrument (OCAI). This is a simple, validated instrument developed by Robert Quinn and Kim Cameron that is free to download and use. Consequently, it is claimed to be used by over 10,000 companies worldwide since it can be used for most sizes of organizational units. The OCAI consists of six statements, each with four alternatives. Those who use it are asked to distribute 100 points between the alternatives, depending on the extent to which each alternative is similar to the organization now and how you might prefer it to be in five years' time. The six statements typify the dimensions of organizational culture:

➡ Dominant characteristics – The extent it is: a personal, sharing place; dynamic and entrepreneurial; aggressive and achievement-orientated; structured and controlling.
➡ Organizational leadership style – The extent it is: nurturing; entrepreneurial and innovative; aggressive and achievement orientated; organized and efficient.
➡ Management of employees – The extent it is: characterized by participation and team-working; innovation and individual risk-taking; competitiveness and achievement; conformity and predictability.
➡ Organization glue – The extent it is built on: loyalty and mutual trust; innovation and development; achievement and goal accomplishment; formal rules and policies.
➡ Strategic emphases – The extent it emphasizes: human development, including trust and openness; acquiring new resources and creating new challenges; competitive actions and achievement; stability and efficiency.

➡ Criteria for success – The extent it defines success on the basis of the development of: human resources and concern for people; having the most unique products; winning in the marketplace; efficiency.

The questions are designed to measure an organization's position on the Competing Values Framework (Quinn and Rohrbaugh, 1983) which measures the conflict between the internal and external focus of the organization and its preference for either stability and control or flexibility and discretion. The analysis in Figure 4.5 consists of four typologies:

➡ Adhocracy culture – This culture is mix of flexibility and discretion with an external focus – the one most associated with entrepreneurship. It is energetic and creative, innovative and risk-taking. It encourages freedom, individual ingenuity, experimentation and risk-taking. It has a long-term emphasis on growth. Leaders tend to be visionary entrepreneurs and innovators.

➡ Hierarchy culture – This culture is the more traditional one – an internal focus that emphasizes stability and control. It usually signifies a traditional organizational structure with hierarchical controls and structures that respect position and power, and emphasizes efficiency and cost reduction. It is characterized by formal procedures and policies that try to maintain uniformity and stability. Leaders tend to be coordinators, monitors and organizers.

➡ Market culture – This culture mixes stability and control with an external focus. It is results-orientated and emphasizes achievement. Consequently, this is a tough, highly competitive environment, one often associated with a sales- or marketing-orientated organization. Leaders tend to be hard drivers.

➡ Clan culture – This mix of internal focus and flexibility usually signifies a sociable organization held together by commitment, tradition and ethics with a sense of family (Hofstede's 'in-group') creating loyalty. Leaders tend to be facilitators, mentors and team builders.

The OCAI analysis includes a map like the one in Figure 4.5. This shows where you believe the organization to be now (solid blue line) and where you believe the organization might

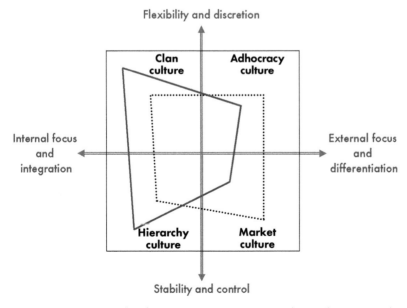

Figure 4.5 An Organizational Culture Assessment Instrument (OCAI) map. Used with permission from Kim Cameron and Robert Quinn

want to be on these typologies in five years time (dotted black line). The analysis also provides a brief explanation.

Quinn and Cameron state that most organizations employ multiple styles – which compete with each other – but that most have a leading or dominant style. They also say that flexible organizations are the most successful, depending on the environmental context. However, this sometimes leads to conflicts that need to be reconciled. In some sectors, however, one culture dominates; in the healthcare sector, for example, the dominant culture is said to be 'clan'.

🔍 EXPLORE FURTHER

The OCAI is free to use for individuals. It is available at: www.ocai-online.com.

CONSTRUCTING AND RECONSTRUCTING CULTURE

So, how do you go about creating an entrepreneurial culture in an organization – one that makes people feel empowered and emphasizes strong relationships, creativity and innovation, using and sharing information and knowledge, encouraging experimentation and measured risk-taking? If you look back to Figure 2.4, you will see that the answer is that it is predominantly created by the leader but reinforced by the structures the leader puts in place. Schein (1990) went so far as to say that the only important thing that leaders do may be constructing their organization's culture.

cognitive processes
The beliefs, assumptions and attitudes that staff hold in common and take for granted

Culture is shaped by **cognitive processes** – the underlying beliefs, assumptions and attitudes that staff hold in common and take for granted. These are embedded in and emanate from an organization's philosophies, values, morality and creed. Cognitive processes reflect themselves in how people behave – what actually happens in an organization and how it gets done. They influence whether outcomes are rational, transparent or the result of politicking. They influence whether the organization does actually follow rules, or is about bending them in the appropriate circumstances. Behaviour is also affected by vocabulary – job titles, slogans, metaphors, signals, even gossip. Language is laden with value judgements that we do not usually recognize – but they subconsciously influence the culture of the organization. Organizational culture and behaviours must be congruent and leadership and management are the prime influences on this.

The style of leadership sends signals about appropriate behaviour. How leaders behave, make decisions, treat people, react to situations, even allocate their time, sends powerful signals about priorities to which employees respond. Little things like 'guarded' or 'open' management offices, reserved or unreserved parking spaces, dress codes, normal methods of communication can all have an influence on the culture of the organization. An entrepreneurial organization should send out messages of egalitarianism with open relationships not based on status. Controls and rewards also send important signals about what the firm values. People take notice of what behaviours get rewarded (as well as what behaviours get punished) and behave accordingly. If salaries are based mainly on sales bonuses and there is a monthly league table of the best sales people, what does this tell you about the firm, its values and its goals? Criteria used for recruitment, selection, promotion and retirement are all important. Status, praise and public recognition are powerful motivators. We shall look at these issues in Chapters 6 and 7.

Organizational structure influences culture. Hierarchical organizations can discourage initiative. Functional specialization can create parochial attitudes and sends signals about which skills might be valued. Flat, decentralized structures with delegated decision-making send signals about encouraging local decision-making and empowerment. Organic structures with broader spans of control encourage creativity, innovation and entrepreneurship. We shall expand on this topic in Chapter 5.

> **❝** Creating a culture in which every person in your organization, at every level, thinks and acts like an owner means that you need to aim to connect individual performance with your company's most important objectives . . . A company composed of individual owners is less focused on hierarchy and who has a nice office, and more intent on achieving their goals. **❞**
>
> Michael Dell, founder Dell Corporation, *Direct from Dell: Strategies that Revolutionized an Industry*, New York: Harper Business, 1999

Constructing culture is like baking a cake. It takes the right ingredients and time for the mixture to bake. However the ingredients are far more volatile and unpredictable than a cake mix, particularly the relationships between individuals. Constructing the appropriate culture in a start-up is difficult enough, but that culture needs to shift and change as the organization grows. Most small firms start life with a 'task culture' – getting the job done. If the entrepreneur finds it difficult to delegate that may turn into a 'power culture' – where people vie to have power and influence over the entrepreneur. As this sort of firm grows, especially if the delegated authority is not genuine, there is a danger of developing a 'role culture' whereby job titles become too important – a culture that is quite different from the entrepreneurial culture outlined earlier.

But, whilst constructing and developing culture in a start-up is difficult enough, changing the culture in a large organization is altogether more difficult. It normally involves change at the top. Not just the MD or the CEO, but frequently the entire top team has to change. This is partly about bringing in new core values but also about sending the strongest possible signals to the workforce that things are changing. When companies merge or acquire other companies their inability to reconcile conflicting corporate cultures is a major reason why the merger might fail. Louis Gerstner is credited with turning around the ailing IBM in the 1990s. He claims management cannot change culture; it merely 'invites the workforce itself to change the culture'. His observations on the process are insightful (Case insight 4.3).

Reconstructing an existing culture is part of the skill involved in managing change, a topic to which we shall return in Chapter 7. But reconstructing culture can also be a painfully slow process. It involves many detailed changes that, considered in isolation, might not be considered significant, but, taken together, add up to the definition of 'how it is around here'. Consistent changes reinforce each other. Fundamentally, reconstruction involves a process of redefinition of values and priorities which then have to be communicated effectively. Many people will be unable to 'buy into' the changes in culture and will leave. Organizations with a strong culture, like Apple, tend to attract like-minded staff. In this way strong cultures become self-reinforcing. However, strong cultures are also the most difficult to change. The difficulty in changing culture is one reason why larger organizations create new, smaller organizational units to push through new initiatives, leaving the core business and the prevalent culture unchanged in the larger parent. Size and structure can be important influences on culture as well as a useful tool to facilitate change.

CASE INSIGHT 4.3
Louis Gerstner and IBM

CHANGING CORPORATE CULTURE

Louis Gerstner is credited with turning around the ailing giant IBM in the 1990s. He was brought in when the company lost $800 million plus write-offs in the first four months of 1993, eventually totalling $8.1 billion, and was facing a planned break-up. Today, IBM is one of the world's leading brands and features in the top ten most innovative companies in the world. His comments about changing culture are insightful:

'Changing the attitudes and culture of hundreds of thousands of people is very, very hard. Business schools don't teach how to do it. You can't lead the revolution from the splendid isolation of corporate headquarters. You can't simply give a couple of speeches or write a credo for the company and declare that the new culture has taken hold.

What you can do is create conditions . . . provide incentives . . . define the market place realities and goals. But then you have to trust. Management doesn't change culture. Management invites the workforce itself to change the culture.

My deepest culture-change was to induce IBMers to believe in themselves again – to believe they had the ability to determine their own fate, and that they already knew what they needed to know . . . at the same time I was working to get employees to listen to me, to understand where we needed to go, to follow me there – I needed to get them to stop being followers. It wasn't a logical, linear challenge. It was counter-intuitive, centered around emotion, rather than reason.

Change is hard work. It calls for commitment from employees way beyond the normal company–employee relationship . . . The best leaders create high performance cultures. They set demanding goals, measure results and hold people accountable. They are change agents, constantly driving their institutions to adapt and advance faster than their competitors.

Personal leadership is about visibility. Great CEOs roll up their sleeves and tackle problems personally. They don't hide behind staff. They never simply preside over the work of others. They are visible every day with customers, suppliers and business partners. Most of all, personal leadership is about passion. They want to win every day, every hour. They urge their colleagues to win. They loathe losing. It's not a cold intellectual exercise. It's personal.'

Questions:

1. Do you agree that changing culture is 'centered around emotion, rather than reason'?
2. What does this tell you about the leadership qualities needed to manage change?

Source: L.V. Gerstner Jr., *Who Says Elephants Can't Dance?* New York: HarperCollins, 2002

SUMMARY

➡ Most groups of people develop their own culture – a set of basic beliefs and assumptions regarding what it is about, how its members behave, and how it defines itself in relation to its external environment. It is the collective programming of the mind, a pattern of taken-for-granted assumptions that influence how people in an organization perceive, think and feel in relation to situations.

➡ Establishing an appropriate corporate culture is vital if you want to develop an entrepreneurial organization. However, the culture of an organization does not exist in isolation. An individual may participate in many different groups, each with its own dominant culture. Each group influences and is influenced by the other – and cultures can change over time. The dominant culture of the country in which the organization operates will be a major influence on individuals and may be a barrier to establishing an entrepreneurial culture.

➡ Culture within an organization is based on a firm set of enduring values. It can be constructed through organizational and cognitive processes and behaviours. It can be transmitted individually by the leader or through public relations (PR) activities, induction, training and good communications generally. Every organization evolves its own culture, be it strong or weak, and strong cultures attract like-minded people. They self-reinforce. However, they can be very difficult to reconstruct.

➡ Hofstede's dimensions can be used to describe the culture in an entrepreneurial organization:

- *Individualism vs collectivism* – An entrepreneurial culture involves a move from individualism to collectivism as an organization grows. This implies cooperation and the development of relationships and networks with a strong sense of 'in-group', a clear identity and a feeling of competition against 'out-groups';
- *Power distance* – An entrepreneurial culture has low power distance. This implies an egalitarian organization with flat structures and open, informal relationships and open, unrestricted information flows;
- *Uncertainty avoidance* – An entrepreneurial organization has low uncertainty avoidance. This implies a tolerance of risk and ambiguity, a preference for flexibility and an empowered culture that rewards personal initiative;
- *Masculinity vs femininity* – An entrepreneurial organization has balance between the masculine and feminine dimensions to build a culture of achievement against 'out-groups' through co-operation, networks and relationships with the 'in-group'.

➡ Figure 4.4 (see above) depicts what the cultural web of an entrepreneurial organization might look like; its structures, control systems, rituals, routines, symbols, stories and power. It uses the words that might describe the culture in an entrepreneurial organization.

➡ Reconstructing the culture of an organization is very difficult. It requires good change management skills. The difficulty is one reason why larger organizations often attempt to separate or spin off new initiatives so that they can create their own culture, leaving that of the core business unchanged. Size and structure matter.

GROUP DISCUSSION TOPICS

1. How do you describe culture? Can it be measured? What is the difference between description and measurement?
2. How does language affect culture? How does culture affect language? Are the two linked?

3. Is a strong culture good or bad? Give examples.
4. What are your core values? What are the core values of your national culture? What are the core values of entrepreneurship? What are the differences and can they be reconciled?
5. How do cognitive processes influence the culture of an organization? Give examples.
6. What organizational processes would reinforce the message that an organization is entrepreneurial?
7. What cognitive processes would reinforce the message that an organization is entrepreneurial?
8. What managerial behaviours would reinforce the message that an organization is entrepreneurial?
9. Do you notice any patterns in the national results of Hofstede's research?
10. What are the inherent biases in Hofstede's research?
11. The USA is normally seen as an entrepreneurial national culture. If this is the case, how would you describe an entrepreneurial culture? How would you describe the culture in your country?
12. What methodological problems might emerge when using a study that sets out to discriminate national cultures as a basis for discriminating organizational cultures?
13. What methodological problems might emerge when organizing a study which tries to discriminate an entrepreneurial culture from that of other organizations?
14. Why is the balance between individualism and collectivism significant? Why might it vary?
15. Is the culture of an entrepreneur the same as the culture of an entrepreneurial organization? Explain.
16. How would you describe an entrepreneurial organizational culture?
17. What actions of a leader might reinforce an entrepreneurial culture?
18. In what circumstances might an organization wish to see no mistakes or failures?
19. What particular problems face your country in developing an entrepreneurial organizational culture?
20. Why might it be better to separate or spin out new initiatives so that they can create their own culture, leaving that of the core business unchanged?

 ## ACTIVITIES

1. With the rest of your class, take the culture test developed by Erin Meyer (page 93). Discuss the results, trying to understand the reasons for similarities and differences.
2. Find an organization that is willing to learn about its culture (this could be your university department). Find a selected group of senior managers to complete the Organizational Culture Assessment Instrument (OCAI) (page 102–103). Write a report outlining your findings.
3. Select two organizations, one that you would describe as entrepreneurial, the other that you would describe as administrative or bureaucratic. Based upon the evidence available, describe their cultures in a report using a cultural web. Using the evidence you have collected, evaluate these cultures using the five dimensions of creativity and innovation, empowerment, strong relationships, continual learning and measured risk-taking.

REFERENCES

Bratton, J. and Gold, J. (2017) *Human Resource Management: Theory and Practice* (6th edn.), London: Red Globe Press.
Buckler, S.A. and Zien, K.A. (1996) 'The Spirituality of Innovation: Learning from Stories', *Journal of Product Innovation Management*, 13(5).
Carr, P. (2000) *The Age of Enterprise: The Emergence and Evolution of Entrepreneurial Management*, Dublin: Blackwell.

Cornwall, J. and Perlman, B. (1990) *Organizational Entrepreneurship*, Homewood, IL: Irwin.

Graham, J.L. and Lam, M. (2003) 'HBR Spotlight: The Chinese Negotiation', *Harvard Business Review*, October, Boston.

Guirdham, M. (1999) *Communicating Across Cultures*, Basingstoke: Macmillan (Now Palgrave Macmillan).

Hall, D. (2005) 'Insight from Facilitating Entrepreneurial Business Development Within Established Organisations', presented at *Institute for Small Business and Entrepreneurship Conference*, Blackpool, UK.

Handy, C. (1985) *Understanding Organizations*, London: Penguin.

Harrison R. (1972) 'Understanding Your Organization's Character', *Harvard Business Review*, May/June.

Hofstede, G. (1980) *Culture's Consequences: International Differences in Work-Related Values*, Beverly Hills, CA: Sage.

Hofstede, G. (1981) *Cultures and Organizations: Software of the Mind*, London: HarperCollins.

Hofstede, G. (1991) *Cultures and Organizations*, London: McGraw-Hill.

Hofstede, G. (2001) *Culture's Consequences: Comparing Values, Behaviors, Institutions and Organizations Across Nations*, Thousand Oaks: Sage.

Hofstede G. (2007) 'A European in Asia', *Asian Journal of Social Psychology*, 10.

Hofstede G. (2010) 'The GLOBE Debate: Back to Relevance', *Journal of International Business Studies*, 41.

Hofstede, G. and Bond, M.H. (1991) 'The Confucian Connection: From Cultural Roots to Economic Performance', *Organizational Dynamics*, Spring.

Hofstede G. and Hofstede G.J. (2005) *Cultures and Organizations: Software of the Mind* (2nd ed.). New York, NY: McGraw-Hill.

Hofstede, G., Neuijen B., Ohayv, D.D. and Sanders, G. (1990) 'Measuring Organizational Cultures: A Qualitative and Quantitative Study Across Twenty Cases', *Administrative Sciences Quarterly*, 35.

Hogan, S.J. and Coote, L.V. (2014) Organizational Culture, Innovation, and Performance: A Test of Schein's Model, *Journal of Business Research*, 67(8).

House, R.J., Hanges, P.J., Javidan, M., Dorfman, P.W. and Vipin, G. (2004) *Culture, Leadership and Organizations: The GLOBE Study of 62 Societies*, Thousand Oaks, CA: Sage.

Johnson, G. and Scholes, K. (1999) *Exploring Corporate Strategy* (5th edn.), Edinburgh: Pearson Education.

Lisak, A., Erez, M., Sui, Y. and Lee, C. (2016) 'The Positive Role of Global Leaders in Enhancing Multicultural Team Innovation', *Journal of International Business Studies*, 47.

Meyer, E. (2014) *The Culture Map: Breaking Through the Invisible Boundaries of Global Business*, New York, NY: Public Affairs.

Mooij M. and Hofstede G. (2010) 'The Hofstede Model Applications to Global Branding and Advertising Strategy and Research', *International Journal of Advertising*, 29(1).

Morris, P. (1991) 'Freeing the Spirit of Enterprise: The Genesis and Development of the Concept of Enterprise Culture', in R. Keat and N. Abercrombie (eds) *Enterprise Culture*, London: Routledge.

Morris, M.H. and Kuratko, D.F. (2002) *Corporate Entrepreneurship*, Orlando, FL: Harcourt College Publishers.

Morris, M.H., Davies, D.L. and Allen, J.W. (1994) 'Fostering Corporate Entrepreneurship: Cross Cultural Comparisons of the Importance of Individualism Versus Collectivism', *Journal of International Business Studies*, 25(1).

O'Connor, J. (1973) *The Fiscal Crisis of the State*, New York, NY: St. Martin's Press.

Peters, T. (1997) *The Circle of Innovation*, New York, NY: Alfred A. Knopf.

Quinn, R.E. and Rohrbaugh, J. (1983) 'A Spatial Model of Effectiveness Criteria: Towards a Competing Values Approach to Organizational Analysis', *Management Science*, 29.

Rao, J. and Weintraub, J. (2013) 'How Innovative Is Your Company's Culture?', *MIT Sloan Management Review*, 54(3).

Sadegh, M. and Ataei, S.V. (2012) 'Organizational Culture and Innovation Culture: Exploring the Relationships Between Constructs', *Leadership and Organization Development Journal*, 33(5).

Schein, E.H. (1983) 'The Role of the Founder in Creating Organizational Culture', *Organizational Dynamics*, Summer.

Schein, E.H. (1990) 'Organizational Culture', *American Psychologist*, February.

Schein, E.H. (1994) 'Organizational and Managerial Culture as a Facilitator or Inhibitor of Organizational Learning', *MIT Organizational Learning Network Working Paper 10.004*, May.

Schwartz S.H. and Bilsky W. (1987) 'Toward a Universal Psychological Structure of Human Values', *Journal of Personality and Social Psychology*, 53.

Syed, M. (2019) *Rebel Ideas: The Power of Diverse Thinking*, London: John Murray.

Timmons, J.A. (1999) *New Venture Creation: Entrepreneurship for the 21st Century*, Singapore: Irwin/McGraw-Hill.

Trompenaars K. (1993) *Riding the Waves of Culture: Understanding Cultural Diversity in Business*, London: Nicholas Brealey.

Van Knippenberg, D., and Schippers, M.C. (2007) 'Work Group Diversity', *Annual Review of Psychology*, 58.

Van Knippenberg, D., De Dreu, C.K., and Homan, A.C. (2004) 'Work Group Diversity and Group Performance: An Integrative Model and Research Agenda', *Journal of Applied Psychology*, 89(6).

Welsch, H. (1998) 'America: North', in A. Morrison (ed.), *Entrepreneurship: An International Perspective*, Oxford: Butterworth Heinemann.

ONLINE RESOURCES AVAILABLE For further resources relating to this chapter see the companion website at **www.macmillanihe.com/Burns-CEI**

5

Structure in the entrepreneurial organization

CONTENTS

- The need for hierarchy
- Organizational structures
- Limitations to hierarchy
- Organic structures
- Combining organic and hierarchical structures
- Structure, task and environment
- Control, autonomy and motivation
- New forms of organizing
- Network structures
- Down-scoping and outsourcing
- Partnerships and strategic alliances
- Joint ventures
- Summary
- Group discussion topics
- Activities
- References

CASE INSIGHTS

5.1   Enron
5.2   Tesla Motors
5.3   GVC and MGM Resorts
5.4   Alphabet (1)

Learning outcomes

When you have read this chapter and undertaken the related activities you will be able to:

➥ Explain and give examples of how size, structure and different organizational forms interact and how they are related to the tasks being undertaken and the environment in which an organization operates;

➥ Critically analyze new forms of corporate organizations such as networks and strategic alliances;

➥ Understand the balance managers need to have between controlling staff and giving them more autonomy and how that applies to different contexts;

➥ Creatively address how organizational structures can be used to help create an entrepreneurial architecture;

➥ Critically evaluate the structure of an organization.

THE NEED FOR HIERARCHY

Larger organizations have been trying to become more entrepreneurial and responsive to changing markets for some time by 'deconstructing' themselves – that is, breaking themselves down into smaller units. They seem to recognize that size can be the enemy of entrepreneurship and innovation. A number of trends have been apparent over the last few decades. The problem is that the bigger an organization becomes, the more it needs structure and, usually, that means hierarchy – and it is hierarchy, not necessarily size, that can inhibit speed of response and decision-making. Too much hierarchy or the wrong kind can become overly bureaucratic. Hierarchy is the fundamental feature of organizational structure, not only for humans, but for all complex systems (Simon, 1962). It marks the earliest influential theory of organizational design. Based on the work of Weber (1947), it stresses rationality and functional efficiency. The literature was broadened by Chandler (1962), as technical and organizational complexity increased, by the inclusion of divisions – a development that was seen as a rational solution to increasing scale and complexity. However, much of the later literature focused on the dysfunctional consequences of this structure where people got in the way of rational efficiency (Pugh and Hickson, 1976).

> ❝ In the management of creativity, size is your enemy. ❞
>
> Peter Chemin, CEO Fox TV, The Economist, 4 December 1999

Hierarchy creates structure and with it comes order. It gives managers confidence that they have the authority to manage (called the hierarchy of authority). Hierarchy facilitates the coordination of complex tasks whilst allowing specialization and cooperation, albeit with permission. Hierarchy, then, remains the basic structural form used by all companies today. Figure 5.1a shows a simple five-person hierarchy structure. Notice that there are only four interactions necessary to communicate to the four subordinates in the structure – and only four relationships to manage – an 'efficient' form of communication.

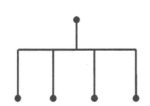

Figure 5.1a Simple hierarchy (5 people): 4 interactions

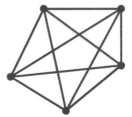

Figure 5.1b Self-organizing team (5 people): 10 interactions

Compare Figure 5.1a to Figure 1.4, which showed the typical spider's web organization of a small entrepreneurial firm. On the face of it, they are not that different – four interactions would still be necessary to communicate to four subordinates. Now compare it to Figure 5.1b, which shows the number of interactions possible with a group of five people in a self-organizing team – when there is no hierarchy. Five people need ten interactions to communicate a single message compared to only four in Figure 5.1a. In fact, the number of interactions needed in a self-organizing team can be represented by the mathematical formula:

$$n \times \left[\frac{n-1}{2} \right]$$ where n represents the number of people.

Simple hierarchy offers fewer interactions and relationships to manage. It is more efficient – faster and less prone to error. The problem comes when the manager at the top of the hierarchy or the entrepreneur at the centre of their spider's web can no longer control the number of staff they have. Managers and entrepreneurs can typically only manage about 15 to 20 people. Beyond that it becomes increasingly inefficient. At that point numerous interactions, albeit informal ones, begin to take place between staff and that is when there is the potential for delays, misunderstanding and conflict. Postulated by Northcote Parkinson, 'Parkinson's Coefficient of Inefficiency' proposes that the optimum *inefficient* number for a group is 21, at which point group interaction becomes impossible. From our formula, 21 people in a self-organizing group need a staggering 210 interactions to communicate a single message.

> 66 Once the business attains a certain size and critical mass, it inevitably becomes much more corporate, more regimented, and duller: staffed by bureaucrats and fewer pioneers. It is a less risky, but also less exciting venture. 99
>
> Luke Johnson, Chairman Risk Capital Partners, *The Sunday Times*, 2 September 2018

ORGANIZATIONAL STRUCTURES

As an organization grows, it needs structure to avoid this sort of chaos. Figure 5.2 shows a classic hierarchy involving departments (e.g., marketing, production, accounting, etc.), functions within the departments (e.g., sales, advertising, etc.) and individuals. Each level of hierarchy might represent a particular grouping or sub-grouping within the organization. This fosters stability and encourages efficient, rule-driven operation. It demonstrates a clear career path. However, while this may be efficient it says nothing about the quality of the interactions and the hierarchy structure can discourage collaboration and sharing of knowledge between the different departments, groups and/or individuals. As we noted in Chapter 3, innovation is underpinned by knowledge and an openness to different ideas (Simmie, 2002). When the organization grows beyond a certain size, there is a tendency for it to adopt a divisional structure – representing different product or market groupings – with each division then having its own departmental structure. This can be taken further by setting up each division as a subsidiary of the parent company, implying an even greater degree of freedom. There are no rules but four of the principal bases for grouping employees into departments and divisions are: common tasks, common products, geographic proximity and processes (sales, manufacturing, R&D, etc.).

There is no one 'best' structure. Some hierarchies might be 'tall' structures – with more managers each having a narrower span of control (fewer people reporting to them). Others might be 'flat' structures – with fewer managers each having a wider span of control (more

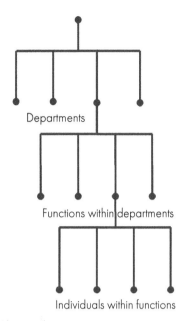

Figure 5.2 Organizational hierarchy

people reporting to them). Flat structures require fewer managers and there has been a tendency to 'delayer' – that is, to flatten structures and widen managers' span of control – thereby reducing managerial costs. This has been a recent trend, facilitated by improvements in information technology. The trend towards delayering and flattening organizational structures started in the USA in the 1980s and then spread to Europe. Associated with this trend is decentralization – the pushing down of decision-making to lower levels in the organization. Google, for example, has a relatively flat structure, with each manager having about twenty people reporting to them. Some Japanese manufacturing companies have only four layers of management; top, plant, departmental and section management. When vertical structures are de-emphasized it inevitably leads to greater cooperation and relationship-building as a basis for coordination, an approach supported by empirical evidence on the relationship between head offices and their subsidiaries (Roth and Nigh, 1992).

Since those early days the rapid pace of change has continued so that reorganizations are now just one of the natural things that managers do regularly, often in times of recession, simply to keep costs down. This is not just about deconstructing, it is about changing the attitudes of the remaining managers about the need for change and rooting out less efficient or effective managers. Flat structures are therefore something to be encouraged in an entrepreneurial organization.

> ❝ I believe in as flat a management structure as possible ... in leading without title ... I most certainly try to lead by example and I'm very much a big believer in making my mistakes public so that other people feel confident and comfortable to be able to air their own mistakes. ❞
>
> Shaa Wasmund, founder Mykindaplace and Brightstone Ventures, *Management Today* www.managementtoday.co.uk, 18 July 2008

A business that has multiple products, functions or geographic locations still needs to coordinate activities across all these dimensions. The organizational structure used to aid this is the matrix structure shown in Figure 5.3. This emerged from the **contingency school of management theory** (see Chapter 6). First posited by Galbraith (1973), it is based on the work of Lawrence and Lorsch (1967) and is essentially an overlay on what is still a bureaucratic structure with hierarchically distributed power and decision-making. In this structure people have multiple reporting lines – to their functional manager (e.g., accounting or sales) and their geographic or product manager. Determining which manager has the ultimate responsibility for an individual's performance can be problematic and it is often combined therefore with a hierarchical structure within functions (e.g., the accounting department might have a hierarchy). It is used to allow informal coordination within the formal structures, for example, within multinational companies that need to maintain functional consistency between geographic locations with formal reporting lines. Starbucks uses a matrix structure, combining functional and product-based divisions, with employees reporting to two managers. Matrix structures were widespread among large companies in the 1960s and 1970s, but became less popular in the 1980s and 1990s as their excessive complexity and slow responsiveness to change became apparent.

contingency theory A theory that emphasizes that the appropriate leadership style is contingent upon the group, task and circumstances

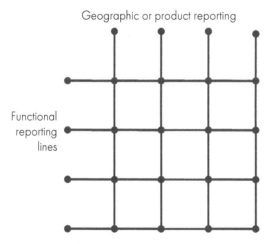

Figure 5.3 Matrix organizational structure

Nevertheless, the matrix structure laid the basis for much smaller project and venture teams – a topic to which we shall return. These comprise people with different skills from different functional departments, brought together to complete a defined project. As long as they are kept small, they are held to encourage communication, facilitate interaction and generally encourage creativity and innovation. Gore, the manufacturer of the famous high-tech Gore-Tex fabric, makes extensive use of project teams, with a minimum of top-down direction. Employees (called associates) either apply or are asked by other team members to join particular teams. Teams elect their leader, decide upon their own goals and manage themselves.

LIMITATIONS TO HIERARCHY

In its simplest form, the traditional hierarchical structure is mechanistic, bureaucratic and rigid. This has been called a 'machine bureaucracy' because it is most appropriate where the organization (or sub-organization) is tackling simple tasks with extensive standardization, in stable environments, and/or where security is important and where plans and programmes need to be followed carefully. Well-developed information systems reporting on production/processing activity need to exist for it to be effective. Staff must conform to set rules and power is concentrated in the top management. It is more concerned with production than marketing and is good at producing high volumes and achieving efficiency in production and distribution – that is, minimizing costs. As such, it is most appropriate for highly automated lines and, to a lesser extent, batch manufacturing and service businesses and/or when a product is in the mature phase of its life-cycle and is being 'milked' for profit as a 'cash cow' (see Chapter 15). For example, at the restaurant level, McDonalds is highly bureaucratized with high levels of job specialization and formal systems emphasizing rules and procedures. It is designed to stifle individual initiative and promote standardization and efficiency. However, the way in which its management operates at a higher level across restaurant sites is very different.

It was the contingency theorists of the late 1950s and 1960s that concluded there was no single best way of organizing a business. They concluded that the best model to adopt depended on the extent to which the structure furthers the objectives of the firm – its strategies and the tasks it undertakes to achieve them. It also depended on other factors such as:

➡ Its scale of operation (Pugh et al., 1969; Blau, 1970);
➡ The technology it uses (Woodward, 1965; Perrow, 1967);
➡ The environment the organization faces (Stinchcombe, 1959; Burns and Stalker, 1961; Emery and Trist, 1965; Haige and Aiken, 1967; Lawrence and Lorsch, 1967).

Chapter 1 painted the picture of the environment in which entrepreneurial organizations thrive: environments of change, chaos, complexity, competition, uncertainty and even contradiction, where innovation is essential. These are hardly the characteristics in which a machine bureaucracy, with its 'simple' (rather than 'complex') tasks and its 'stable' (rather than 'changing') environment, might thrive. A machine bureaucracy is the antithesis of an entrepreneurial structure. Layers of hierarchy impede information flows, lengthen decision-making and can kill flexibility and initiative.

> **❝** *Your organizational structure must be flexible enough to evolve along with your people, rather than work against them. This is one of the biggest and most challenging cultural issues we face as a fast growing company.* **❞**
>
> Michael Dell, founder Dell Corporation, *Direct from Dell: Strategies that Revolutionized an Industry*, New York: Harper Business, 1999

ORGANIC STRUCTURES

The structure of the organization can also affect the scale of innovation that needs to be encouraged (from incremental to radical). Whilst incremental innovation can be managed with more hierarchical structures, breakthrough and radical innovation may need more radical structures (Pfitzer et al., 2013). Angel (2006) highlighted the need for highly autonomous teams within these structures.

Covin and Slevin (1990) have argued that entrepreneurial behaviour within an organization was positively correlated with performance when structures were more 'organic' – a structure that is highly flexible and changing, with limited hierarchy; one that places greater emphasis on personal relationships and interactions than on structures; one in which power is decentralized and authority is linked to expertise, with few bureaucratic rules or standard procedures. In related work, Miller (1986) saw it as having limited hierarchy and a highly flexible structure, and being most appropriate when:

> *Groups of trained specialists from different work areas collaborate to design and produce complex and rapidly changing products. Emphasis is on extensive personal interaction and face-to-face communication, frequent meetings, use of committees and other liaison devices to ensure collaboration. Power is decentralized and authority is linked to expertise. Few bureaucratic rules or standard procedures exist. Sensitive information-gathering systems are in place for anticipating and monitoring the external environment.*

So, what does a simple organic structure look like? Unfortunately, that is difficult to answer because, by its very definition, it is constantly forming and reforming to meet the changes it faces as it undertakes those complex tasks. According to complexity theory, this forming and reforming whereby business units are continually being created, merged and redefined is typical of a complex system coping with unpredictability. In its simplest form, an organic structure might be thought of as a partnership of individual professionals. They are each highly autonomous and the organization exists simply to provide them with support rather than direction. It is the simplest of spider's webs, with no hierarchy and a flat organizational structure. Indeed, a large organic structure might comprise a series of spider's webs, each operating almost autonomously and collaborating in a loose and changing manner (Figure 5.4).

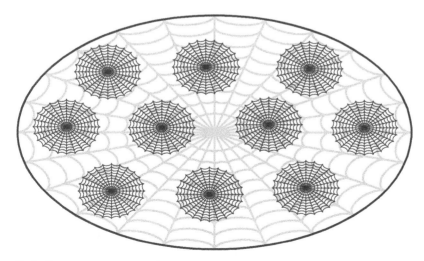

Figure 5.4 Organic structures within an organic structure

This may be seen more as a loose coalition of entrepreneurial teams or strategic partnership perhaps forming and reforming as opportunities appear. The danger is that each might operate with too much autonomy and too little direction, resulting in anarchy. In many organizations, particularly larger ones, more structure and hierarchy may be needed. In one example, Oticon, a manufacturer of hearing aids based in Denmark, famously reorganized into over 100 self-directed project teams, getting rid of most formal controls. Within six years, it was forced to dismantle what it called its 'spaghetti organization' and reintroduce more conventional hierarchical control.

COMBINING ORGANIC AND HIERARCHICAL STRUCTURES

Like the spider's web structure, the organic structure on its own probably only works with 15 to 20 people. It is therefore probably best used in combination with more traditional hierarchical structures, and with a designated leader. Figure 5.5 shows an organic project team formed from individuals from four departments within a hierarchical organization. This could be a venture team led by an intrapreneur. Teams can be either real or virtual, linked by technology and possibly in different countries. They can link individuals from departments or divisions in the same organization as well as individuals from partner organizations.

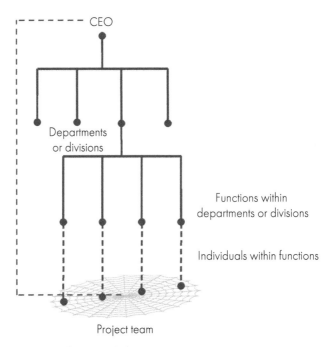

Figure 5.5 Organic multifunctional project teams

The divisional structure is the dominant organizational form for multi-product/multimarket business companies. Divisions can be organized in many ways, for example around products (3M), geographic regions (SAB-Miller) or vertically separate markets (market niches which have specialist needs) (oil companies such as ExxonMobil). Typically, divisions have a greater freedom of action than departments; in particular, each division might adopt a different organizational structure, along with the appropriate other elements of organizational archi-tecture, depending upon the basis for their existence. Figure 5.6 shows how an organic divi-sion – probably undertaking innovative **product development** – might be located within an otherwise hierarchical multidivisional organization.

product development
Developing a completely new or modifying product or service

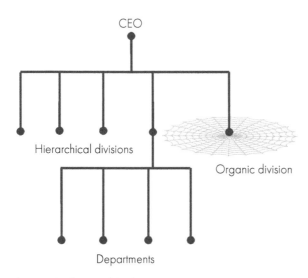

CEO

Hierarchical divisions

Organic division

Departments

Figure 5.6 Mixed organic/hierarchical structures

As an alternative, the holding company structure, with legally separate and more auton-omous subsidiaries, is common in these multi-product/multimarket businesses, especially conglomerates where each business is different, as, for example, with companies such as Tata, Samsung, Hyundai, Jardine Matheson, Mitsui and Mitsubishi. For example, the Virgin Group of companies, which is made up of over 20 separate umbrella companies, operates some 400 separate businesses across a wide range of industries, employing approximately 71,000 people in over 30 countries, with global brand revenue of about £20 billion (see Case insight 8.4). Virgin is a multinational conglomerate that describes itself as a 'branded **venture capital** company' – a big brand made up of lots of smaller, legally separate compa-nies each with different structures and with variations on the basic organizational culture. Virgin's subsidiaries have considerably more freedom of action than would typically be the case for separate divisions of the same company. One very real advantage of a holding com-pany structure is that it can help **compartmentalize risk**. If a legally separate part of a group of companies fails, it does not endanger the survival of the others.

Amazon is a giant multinational company employing some 60,000 people that is known for its commitment to innovation (it has an annual R&D budget of some $27 billion). Its organizational structure is hierarchical with a senior management team including two CEOs, three senior vice presidents and one worldwide controller, reporting directly to Amazon CEO Jeff Bezos. However, it manages to integrate many small teams that deal with various aspects of the business. New ventures can be set up by middle managers and run by small 'two-pizza' teams – that is, groups no larger than can be fed by two pizzas. The ven-ture capitalist Benedict Evans has said that Amazon was, in essence, many companies in one: 'It is hundreds of small, decentralized, atomized teams sitting on top of standardized

venture capital
Equity capital invested in the business by individuals or institutions other than the founders at an early stage in its development

compartmentalizing risk Setting up each operation as a separate legal entity

common internal systems . . . Amazon is a machine to make a machine – it is a machine to make more Amazon' (*The Sunday Times*, 9 September 2018).

The small managerial team in a holding company might be based on an organic organization structure whilst the subsidiaries might have other forms of organization structures (hierarchical, matrix or organic), each with its appropriate architecture (structures, cultures, leadership styles and strategies). This can mean organizational structures become multilayered and quite complex; in order to achieve this, companies may have to restructure and reorganize. Figure 5.7 shows an example of a holding company with subsidiaries, each of which has divisions, within which are departments. The holding company is an organic structure, and there are other organic structures at divisional and departmental levels.

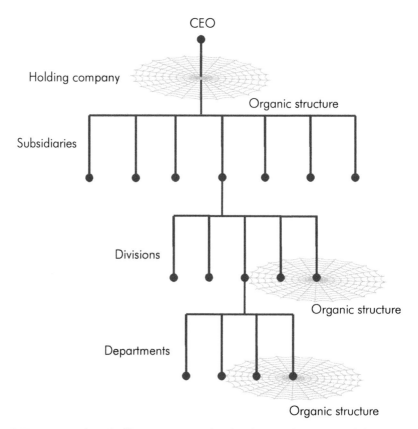

Figure 5.7 Organic head office structure with subsidiaries, divisions and departments

> To survive, big companies today are all deconstructing themselves and creating new structures, many as networks of autonomous units. Deconstruction is now a fashion, because it is the best way to search for survival.
>
> John Naisbitt, *Global Paradox: The Bigger the World Economy, the more Powerful its Smaller Players*, London: BCA, 1994

It is unlikely that one organizational structure – particularly an organic one – will suit all situations or will last for ever since organizations naturally change and adapt, so an entrepreneurial organization, like a chameleon, has to be prepared to change its organization structures to suit different situations and environments. Galbraith (1995) underlined the importance of being able to change organizational design rapidly and quickly in an entrepreneurial organization: 'Organizational designs that facilitate variety, change, and speed are sources of competitive advantage. These designs are difficult to execute and copy because they are intricate blends of many different policies.'

STRUCTURE, TASK AND ENVIRONMENT

The appropriate structure depends upon the nature of the tasks and the environmental uncertainty faced by individuals. Galbraith (1995) observed how task complexity increased with environmental uncertainty and the amount of information that needs to be processed by the decision-maker. Tasks involving cognitive skills can be complex. If the situation faced by individuals in completing these tasks is changing, the task becomes even more difficult. These two factors – task complexity and environmental uncertainty – have implications for both organizational structure and management style. The principles are straightforward. The simpler and more repetitive the task, the easier it is to impose control and the less need there is for initiative. Similarly, the more stable the environment, the less the need for initiative. But rigid control stifles initiative (and inhibits entrepreneurship), and therefore the more complex the task, the greater the need for flexibility and autonomy of action. Similarly, the more change or uncertainty in the environment, the greater the need for flexibility and autonomy. This is shown in Figure 5.8.

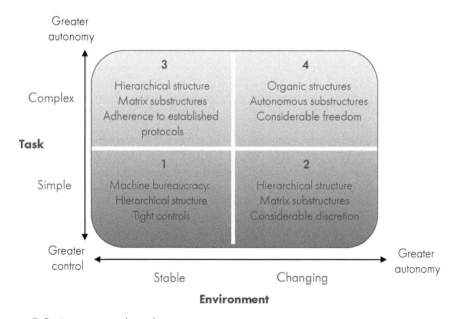

Figure 5.8 Structure, task and environment

Quadrant 1 – This is the machine bureaucracy with hierarchical structures and tight controls described earlier. It is most appropriate where the organization is tackling simple tasks with extensive standardization, in stable environments, and/or where security is important and where plans and programmes need to be followed carefully (e.g., in a McDonalds restaurant). Well-developed information systems reporting on the production/processing activity need to exist for it to be effective. Power is centralized. There is no slack. It is more concerned with production than marketing and is good at producing high volumes and achieving the efficiency in production and distribution needed for a low-cost/price business model. It is appropriate for continuous and most line production businesses.

line production Where there is a further increase in volume, with a regularity of order that justifies the investment in task analysis and dedicated resources

Quadrant 2 – As the environment becomes more changeable, standardization becomes less viable and responsibility for coping with unexpected changes needs to be pushed down the hierarchy. Staff usually have more autonomy, although within guidelines. The structure needs to be responsive to change – although hierarchical, it is relatively flat with few middle-management positions. A matrix substructure (teams) can be used to tackle unexpected projects. Culture is important because the workforce needs to be motivated to make frequent changes to their work practices. It is appropriate for most jobbing and batch production businesses (e.g., a team of skilled craftsman).

Quadrant 3 – Complex tasks performed in stable environments mean that it becomes worthwhile to develop standard skills to tackle the complexities. The matrix can be an effective substructure within a hierarchical organization. The matrix team can work on their complex tasks within set protocols, as they do, for example, in a surgical operation. In a changing environment, the matrix team must have a higher degree of autonomy because established protocols may be inappropriate to the changing circumstances, even for the simple tasks they face. It is appropriate for most jobbing and batch production businesses (e.g., the kitchen of a high-end restaurant).

Quadrant 4 – In a changing environment where there is high task complexity, organic structures are most appropriate. Team working is likely to be the norm to help deal with these complex situations, and matrix-type structures across different functional specialities may facilitate this. Staff autonomy needs to be high with authority for decision-making delegated down to enable staff to deal with changing circumstances. Clear job definitions should never lead to a narrowing of responsibilities so that people ignore the new tasks that emerge. In many ways, far more important than the formal organization structure for a firm of this sort is the culture that tells people what needs to be done and motivates them to do it. It is most appropriate for project-based production businesses, where tasks can be complex and specifications may change. It might also be appropriate in batch-production businesses where customer relations are vital. One of the characteristics of less hierarchical structures (such as team working) is that they rely on coordination by mutual adjustment rather than control through hierarchy. Individuals within them often have multiple roles and more freedom of action (e.g. a consultancy firm).

The principles from Figure 5.6 can be applied to different levels or organizational units within an organization. Generally, the less stable and predictable the environment an organization operates in and the more complex tasks that the staff face, the greater the autonomy staff should have, relying more on strong **entrepreneurial leadership** to give them direction and motivation. Which tasks are complex and which environments are uncertain? Both manual and cognitive tasks can have varying degrees of complexity. Innovation is a cognitive task that can be both complex and undertaken in an uncertain environment; however, that complexity can vary enormously. Innovation can be radical or incremental, continuous or discontinuous. Technological innovation is different than market innovation. Innovation in the pharmaceutical industry is of a different nature than that in the furniture industry. And not all parts of

entrepreneurial leadership Leadership that ensures an organization remains entrepreneurial

an organization may be involved in innovation to the same degree. So, while these principles may seem straightforward, their application in practice can be difficult. As with most areas of management, there are no set rules and their application involves judgement – not least in determining the 'balance' between control and autonomy. Nevertheless, hierarchy can hinder innovation and 'control by letting go' is generally seen as more effective than tight controls (Moss Kanter, 2008). Less hierarchy allows organizations to create value by making decisions faster than competitors (Blenko et al., 2010) and autonomy is a key element in this.

CONTROL, AUTONOMY AND MOTIVATION

Not only is the need for autonomy one of the personal character traits of entrepreneurs (Chapter 1), it is also explicitly one of the five dimensions of an 'entrepreneurial orientation' outlined in Chapter 2 (Lumpkin and Dess, 1996; Covin and Wales, 2012). Many authors have emphasized the need for autonomy in promoting creative and entrepreneurial behaviour (e.g. Amabile, 1997; Isaksen and Ekvall, 2010) and others have found links between job autonomy and innovative behaviour (e.g. Burcharth et al., 2017; De Spiegelaere et al., 2014).

It turns out that autonomy can be a great motivator for staff undertaking cognitive tasks where initiative and creativity are important. They enjoy the challenge of undertaking something that they find challenging but psychologically rewarding and use autonomy constructively. Pink (2011) quoted a number of studies across different countries which showed that, whilst monetary reward was a motivator for individuals undertaking mechanical tasks, it was not a motivator for individuals undertaking cognitive tasks involving complexity or creativity. This conclusion was reinforced by Phadke and Vyakarnam (2017) in their study of some 300 science- and technology-based firms, many of which were high growth. They concluded that the links between organizational performance and employee rewards were generally weak. Once monetary reward was sufficient to be 'taken off the table', other less tangible factors were far greater motivators and led to greater personal satisfaction and better performance. In particular, they highlighted self-direction and autonomy as important motivators if you want people to be innovative, engaged with their tasks and proactive rather than just compliant. For employees undertaking creative tasks there were three key motivators:

1. Autonomy – freedom of action and self-direction, not being told what to do or how to do it, which encourages people to enjoy what they are doing (e.g., Google's 20 per cent freedom policy).
2. Purpose – a reason for doing something based not upon monetary remuneration but upon a wider vision of what the organization can achieve (e.g., from CSR policies).
3. Mastery – the challenge of completing a complex or creative task. Pink cites Wikipedia and Linux as initiatives that have engaged highly skilled people in creative tasks without monetary remuneration.

> **❝** *Employees today should be encouraged to think for themselves. They should be cultivated to have an entrepreneurial, innovative spirit, and not just to implement orders.* **❞**
>
> Zhang Ruimin, CEO Haier Group, *Strategy + Business*, Issue 77, Winter 2014

The reason for this can be found in the literature on psychological ownership in organizations. Psychological ownership is when an individual 'feels' that they own the organization or part of it, even if they do not. And it is promoted by the three factors outlined above. Pierce et al. (2001) see autonomy or less control as important because it provides feelings of 'efficacy' and 'effectance'. They argue that it is also promoted by investing time, ideas and energy and acquiring an intimate knowledge of the task – which are all aspects of mastery. Furthermore, psychological ownership creates a sense of responsibility in the individual which is evidenced as stewardship and a sense of social responsibility – or purpose – for the organization.

So if autonomy is a motivator, the dilemma is the amount of autonomy to give. Too much, and anarchy or worse might result. Too little, and creativity, innovation and initiative will be stifled. Foster and Kaplan (2001) advocated a minimalist approach to control: 'Control what you must, not what you can: control when you must, not when you can. If a control procedure is not essential, eliminate it.' They promoted the need for 'divergent thinking' to encourage creativity which, according to them, said 'requires control through selection and motivation of employees rather than through control of people's actions; ample resources, including time, to achieve results; knowing what to measure and when to measure it; and genuine respect for others' capabilities and potential'.

The answer to the dilemma, provided by Birkinshaw (2003), was 'balance'. He outlined the model used by BP to help guide and control entrepreneurial action: direction, 'space' or 'slack', boundaries and support. All four need to be in balance. If they are not, either bureaucracy (constraint) or chaos might ensue. This is shown in Figure 5.9.

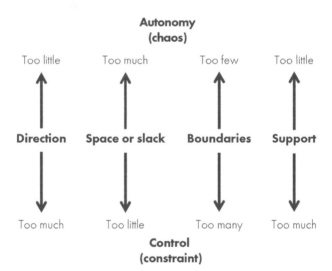

Figure 5.9 Control vs autonomy

Direction – This is the company's broad strategy and goals. Managers should have scope to develop the strategy for their own operating unit, in line with the company's general direction, values and mission. Pink agrees, saying creative people need a strong sense of 'purpose' in their work, which is not just about making profit. Birkinshaw gave two pieces of advice on getting this balance right:

➡ Set broad direction and re-evaluate periodically as markets and the environment change;
➡ Let the company's strategy inform that of the unit and the unit's inform that of the company.

Space or slack – This is to do with the degree of looseness in resource availability – monetary budgets, physical space and supervision of time. In a tightly run, highly efficient organization there is no time or other resources to think of or to experiment and innovate with. Creative organizations require a degree of space or slack to allow experimentation. Garud and Van de Ven (1992) confirm that entrepreneurial activity in a large organization is more likely to continue, despite negative outcomes, when there is slack in resource availability and a high degree of ambiguity about the outcomes. 3M allows researchers to spend 15 per cent of their time on their own projects. Google allows 20 per cent. However, if employees are given too much space, they run the risk of losing focus on the day-to-day detail of the job and it can be wasteful. Birkinshaw's advice was:

➥ Goal-setting should be carefully managed, clear and specific, but individuals should be given freedom in how the goals are to be achieved;
➥ Individuals should be allowed to learn from their own mistakes.

Boundaries – These are the legal, regulatory and moral limits within which the company operates. But rigid rules that are not shared beg to be circumvented. Boundaries should come from your values – which are shared by your staff. Not having boundaries courts extreme danger, particularly if breaking them might lead to the failure of the organization. Birkinshaw's advice was:

➥ Identify critical boundaries that, if crossed, threaten the survival of the organization and control them rigorously;
➥ Manage other boundaries in a non-invasive way through training, induction, codes of conduct and so on.

Support – This refers to the knowledge transfer systems and training and development programmes you provide to help managers do their job. Systems should encourage knowledge sharing and collaboration – a prerequisite for innovation. Training and career planning should be top-down. Both should be discretionary, however. The danger here is that knowledge will not be shared and there will be little collaboration, encouraging managers to go their own way. On the other hand, if there is too much support the manager will be 'spoon-fed' and initiative stifled. Birkinshaw's advice was:

➥ Put in place enough support systems to help managers and ensure they know where to go for help;
➥ Systems should encourage collaboration.

> ❝ Hyper-growth companies are quintessentially learn-by-doing organizations. Their survival depends on swift adaptation. Because resources and people are stretched, they most likely don't have excessive formal or overly structured systems in place. The key is to have enough structure in place that growth is not out of control – but not so much that the structure impedes your ability to adapt quickly . . . Balancing the need for supporting infrastructure without building infrastructure too far ahead of growth is one of the more difficult and on-going challenges any hyper-growth company will face. ❞
>
> Michael Dell, founder Dell Corporation, *Direct from Dell: Strategies that Revolutionized an Industry*, New York: Harper Business, 1999

The broad conclusions, therefore, are that the greater the complexity of tasks and the more staff have to use their cognitive abilities – creativity and initiative – to undertake these tasks within the context of a changing environment, then the greater the need for autonomy. Autonomy is not enough on its own, however. It needs to be combined with a sense of 'purpose' and the challenge of 'mastery' of that task. It can be influenced through giving individuals 'space' or 'slack' – looseness in resource availability, which allows employees to 'borrow' time, expertise, research, materials, equipment and other resources as they develop new concepts – but with direction, boundaries and support. However, too much autonomy can become licence and it needs to be combined with a strong accountability. It is for you to conclude whether, in the light of the Deepwater Horizon oil spillage in 2010, BP followed its own model. At the very least, financial control systems must be aligned with structures so that departments, teams and/or individuals can be held accountable for their actions.

At this point it is worth restating the importance of organizational culture being consistent with the organizational structures. They must reinforce each other and convey the same messages. This means that the more formal the structures the more formal the organizational culture should be. You cannot have an informal, flexible culture within a bureaucratic structure undertaking repetitive tasks with tight controls. The inconsistency is likely to lead to a dysfunctional organization that does not operate effectively because the message about how to behave is not conveyed consistently. An entrepreneurial culture will only thrive within appropriate structures, and with entrepreneurial leadership.

CASE INSIGHT 5.1
Enron

USA

AUTONOMY VS CONTROL

Enron Corporation was a US energy, commodities, and services company that was founded in 1985 before filing for bankruptcy in 2001 as a result of what subsequently became known as one of the biggest corporate scandals in US history involving fraud and corruption. Interestingly, *Fortune* magazine named Enron as 'America's Most Innovative Company' for six consecutive years. As a result, Birkinshaw (2003) raised the question about whether the failure of Enron might signal a rethink about the value of corporate entrepreneurship. The company had been held up as a model of entrepreneurship, attracting aggressive and creative managers and encouraging internal entrepreneurship to achieve its growth. Whilst hindsight is a wonderful thing that gives everybody 20:20 vision, he concludes that Enron does not merit such a rethink because the company was at the outer boundaries of all four dimensions of BP's model.

Too little direction: In the 1990s the company moved out of the natural gas sector into electricity trading, online trading, weather derivatives and broadband networks. It started out with the goal of being the 'best gas distribution company', this became 'the world's best energy company' and finally 'the world's best company'. Enron's lack of direction became a strength as managers were encouraged to pursue any opportunity that might help in its headlong rush for growth.

Too much space: Enron gave managers enormous freedom to pursue these opportunities. Top management practiced a philosophy of 'laissez-faire'. For example, one gas trader started an online trading business (EnronOnline) while still working at her original job. It had some 250 people working for it before the President of Enron became aware of its existence.

Too few boundaries: Enron had explicit rules about capital allocation and risk and had a Risk Assessment Control Unit. However, Enron managers regularly broke the rules, for example by setting up new subsidiary companies and financing activities off the balance sheet. Instead of being dismissed for these things, managers were often rewarded. The culture within the organization was one of rule breaking and there was no moral or ethical underpinning.

Too little support: Management at Enron were recruited from top US business schools. After a six-month induction working with different business units, they were largely left to their own devices. The reward system encouraged 'pushy', aggressive people and development start-ups or high growth opportunities. Support was not a function that was rewarded and 'steady performers' did not stay long in the company.

And the case of Enron and indeed BP itself underline the fact that being entrepreneurial is risky. And the line between too much and too little risk is never clear and forever moving and the concept of 'balance' is a subjective one. It also underlines that an entrepreneurial approach to management is not appropriate for every organization or department/division within it.

Question:

1. Do you agree with Birkinshaw's analysis of Enron?

NEW FORMS OF ORGANIZING

Over the last 50 years, firms have continued to organize based upon the enduring principles of Weber and Chandler. However, whilst the majority might use the traditional subsidiary, multidivisional and departmental hierarchical structures, this says little about the processes that go on under the surface – how managers actually behave – with real and virtual, informal team- and project-based structures being used alongside the formal structures. Over the last two or three decades, there has been a proliferation of writings on new organization forms that broaden our concepts of organizational structures. This reflects:

⇥ The increasing complexity of organizations as they struggle and experiment with different organizational forms in the ways outlined at the beginning of this chapter, so as to enable them to be more responsive to changing global markets. Traditional hierarchical reporting structures mask important informal lateral relationships that add increasing value to the firm.

⇥ The recognition that individuals increasingly perform multiple roles within organizations and can answer to different managers.

⇥ The changing nature of society in terms of social norms. There has been more of a focus on control by mutual agreement rather than command, and coordination rather than control.

➡ Improvements in mobile communication technologies. Computers, smartphones and the internet have made corporate boundaries permeable. They make communication easier and quicker and have changed the nature of work and its environment. People are better able to work at home and from a distance, driving changes in employment practices as well as how managers 'control' employees (or subcontractors and other partners).

➡ The shift towards a knowledge economy with competitive advantage becoming based more upon the organization's ability to assimilate and exploit information, knowledge and capabilities quickly. This has encouraged the development of real and virtual networks, partnerships and strategic alliances – informal lateral relationships that leverage the information, knowledge and capabilities of individual firms for mutual advantage. The internet has encouraged the development of **crowdsourcing** and **open innovation** to stimulate knowledge transfer and innovation, whereby an organization can benefit from the skills, knowledge and ideas of external individuals or organizations (see Chapter 9).

crowdsourcing A way of opening up collaboration to people connected on the internet to form a kind of online community

open innovation A process that links an organization with external individuals and organizations that wishes to generate new ideas, knowledge or to solve problems associated with an innovation

Although this burgeoning literature seems to have no overarching perspective or theory, it is fundamentally concerned with both structures and, more particularly, processes. As structures become more fluid and loose, the processes underlying them seem to take on greater importance. It has also broadened the perspective to recognize the importance of relationships in these informal structures – which is at the core of an entrepreneurial architecture. As Fenton and Pettigrew (2000) observed: 'It would seem that large organizations at the end of the twentieth century have the same structural characteristics as they did 50 years ago. The evidence appears to be that formal hierarchical organization is still present as an institutional backdrop but not so crucial in determining organizational activities or capabilities. Instead "new" subtle coordination mechanisms stress the informal and social processes of the organization. There is also a move away from defining organizations purely in distributional terms toward more relational notions. As firms add value via relationships and require ever greater internal and external interdependence to create, share and transfer knowledge, so the basis for organizational activity and configuration is centered on relationships and the wider social context within which firms are embedded.'

NETWORK STRUCTURES

What so much of this literature reveals is that the traditional organization chart is a poor representation of how many organizations really function. Informal structures are important, based on strong relationships – the word that appears again and again. Networks are important – in one context and then in another – flexing and changing over time. As soon as we identify one structure (and name it), another appears, perhaps reflecting the rapidly changing environment in which organizations today operate. And it has long been recognized that processes are just as important as structures, processes that are 'continually shaped and reshaped by the actions of actors who are in turn constrained by the structural positions they find themselves' (Nohria, 1992). What this literature does not give us is any clear agreement on how to think about these new structures. As with many things in management, firms are continually experimenting, both intentionally and unintentionally, both formally and informally, trying to face up to the organizational challenges they face. And organizational innovation often involves moving between extremes, yet maintaining business continuity as firms battle with the contradictions between hierarchies and networks, vertical and horizontal integration and sharing knowledge across units that both compete and collaborate and the dilemmas then posed in making decisions (Pettigrew, 1999). Management is an art, not a science. It involves judgement more than rule-following.

The literature also brings us to the realization that it is not always necessary to 'own' resources to be able to use them. Professional jobs, for example, can be contracted out and functions can be outsourced. Networks and other new forms of organizing allow different forms of expertise to be brought to bear in an organization. All these different ways of using resources without owning them allow firms to become smaller and more focused on their core activities and therefore simplifying their structures. The network structure comprises either an internal or external network of independent members (individuals or organizations), unified by a common purpose (often a job or project) and sharing in the benefits that stem from collaboration. Networks blur the boundaries of the firm, extending them to a community of interest, rather than restricting them to a legal or economic unit. They mean that resources and risks can be shared across economic units so that networks of small firms can compete more effectively against large firms. They can create distinctive capabilities, not available to each member individually. Network structures allow organizational units to be small, encourage knowledge sharing and an outward-facing culture and reduce risk. It is therefore not unexpected that they are embedded into the daily working life of the entrepreneurial organization.

For many firms, network structures can be more important than the formal internal organizational structures. And, unlike internal structures, which might reflect hierarchies and power structures, network structures are based on personal relationships which, in turn, are based on reciprocity and self-interest, underpinned by mutual trust, respect and reputation (Dubini and Aldrich, 1991; Larson, 1992). This can lead to tensions both inside and outside the organization if the two structures are based upon different values and cultures.

CASE INSIGHT 5.2
Tesla Motors

USA

ORGANIZING FOR INNOVATION

Tesla featured as one of the Boston Consulting Group's most innovative companies in its 2018 innovation survey (Chapter 3). The BCG believes that these organizations can innovate quicker and better than most others and it puts a lot of this ability down to the organizational structure at Tesla, which it describes as flat – aiding communication. Tesla makes extensive use of cross-functional team working, with incentives to encourage cross-functional interaction. Teams are organized to reduce coordination complexity and work on one integrated project plan at a time. Each project has a clear 'owner' and each project leader has the authority to establish cross-functional resource levels. Teams are accountable to a programme, not a function (such as marketing or engineering)

With no legacy structures to constrain it, Tesla organized itself for innovation . . . [It] looks nothing like other auto OEM [Original Equipment Manufacturer]. Its structure, rather than being functionally divided and hierarchical, is organized around small, agile-empowered teams that comprise a program executive who ensures cross-product integration; a product owner who is responsible for architectural definition, customer success criteria, and feature resource needs; feature developers; and end-to-end quality engineers. (BCG, 2018)

BCG also highlight Tesla's closeness to customers, observing that they are involved in testing and improving their cars influencing feature changes and priorities.

Visit the website: **www.tesla.com**

Questions:

1. Why do these structures make Tesla able to innovate quicker and better than other companies?
2. Are there any drawbacks of structures for Tesla now and in the future?

DOWN-SCOPING AND OUTSOURCING

down-scoping
When an organization restructures so as to focus on its core activities

The growth of network structures has developed alongside the trend towards **down-scoping** – when an organization restructures so as to focus on its core activities. This has, in turn, accelerated the trend towards outsourcing – subcontracting non-core activities. This enables a firm to reduce fixed costs and therefore risk. It allows them to flatten organizational structures and improve their response time to changes in the marketplace. It allows them to bring in expertise that they might not otherwise have – in information technology (IT), legal services, human resource management and payroll. At Google, 49 per cent of their workforce of 170,000 are now temporary workers, vendors or contractors (called internally TVCs). IT is the major area that firms outsource (estimated at some 73 per cent of the outsourcing market in the UK in 2017) and, whilst 69 per cent of UK IT outsourcing is seen by firms as a way of reducing costs, 64 per cent also see it as part of business transformation (PA Consulting, 2017). Little wonder outsourcing is popular with firms of any size. In fact, the smaller organization the more likely it is to buy-in IT support (including software) or form partnerships, compared with building in-house capability (Harvey Nash/KPMG, 2017).

Cost-cutting is a major reason for outsourcing. The gig workers, mentioned in Chapter 1, 'employed' in low-earning jobs but whose legal status as self-employed may be dubious, are an essential part of the low-cost business model of the firm 'employing' them – firms like Uber or Deliveroo. Gig workers are hired to undertake a single project (or 'gig'), with little resource other than, for example, their own means of transport. Many delivery firms, for example, outsource the final leg of the delivery and many taxi firms subcontract the actual transportation of the fee-paying customer. The success of this sort of outsourcing is built upon mobile technologies that mean people no longer have to be location-based to undertake tasks. Indeed, the mobility of the workforce is a definite advantage. These virtual networks come together to undertake specific jobs, forming and reforming in different groupings to exploit different opportunities. It is a structure that is best used to undertake specific tasks that do not need contact or the building of relationships with the workforce. It mirrors the self-employment status of many craftsmen and professionals. Because personal relationships are not established, it is likely to have a shorter life than a real network structure. With this exception, it shares many of the advantages of the network structure. Handy (1996) described it as a 'box of contracts' and, because of its lack of tangibility, it has profound consequences for how we think of organizational forms.

Outsourcing back-office activities has in the past been seen as a major way of cost-cutting, but this has sometimes led to reductions in customer service. For example, the rush to outsource call-centres to low-cost, off-shore locations has often proved unsuccessful and damaged brand reputations. As a result, many of these call-centres have been repatriated. Losing contact with customers carries with it the danger of losing information and data on their changing needs and buying habits. However, increasingly outsourcing back-office activities are seen as adding value rather than just cutting costs, particularly when specialist or high-skilled workers are required for the activities. Online labour sites like *Upwork*, *Peopleperhour* or *Freelancer* allow companies to source independent work from skilled people on a flexible, part-time basis. In a scarce labour market, with many firms reporting skills shortages, this can be extremely valuable.

The search for knowledge, skills and expertise is another driving reason for outsourcing – and one that is growing in importance, particularly as technology becomes more complex and the pace of development accelerates. Whilst information technology is currently the major area for outsourcing the area of artificial intelligence generally is growing rapidly and, in particular, robotic process analysis (RPA), which involves the programming of robots to mimic the way people use repetitive user-interface software applications like spreadsheets, data management or customer relations programmes. RPA promises to reduce costs, improve accuracy but also cause large-scale redundancies for those currently employed in these activities. A global survey by Harvey Nash/KPMG (2017) found that over one-third of all respondents were already investing in, or are planning to invest in, digital labour, including RPA and cognitive automation. This proportion increased to over 60 per cent in larger organizations. The most commonly outsourced technology functions are shown in Table 5.1.

Charles Handy (1994) predicted that many larger firms will become increasingly 'shamrock organizations' – the three leaves being core staff, temporary staff to ease them over

Table 5.1 Most commonly outsourced technology functions (%)

Software application development	64
Software application maintenance	51
Data centres	40
IT infrastructure	32
Service help desk	32
Networks	29
Systems integration	29
IT business systems	12
Human resources business systems	12
IT department	12
Knowledge process	6

Source: Harvey Nash/KPMG (2017)

peaks and troughs in work and small organizations supplying specialist services, deeply embedded in, and dependent upon, the larger firm. He predicted that many of us would mix five kinds of work: wage work, fee work, home work, gift work and study work. It is interesting to observe how many of his predictions have come true.

Amar Bhidé (2000) took the idea of down-scoping and outsourcing further. He suggested that, rather than trying to re-invent themselves, large firms should concentrate on incremental innovation and projects with high costs and low uncertainty – the areas outlined in Chapter 3 that they excel at – leaving smaller more entrepreneurial firms to concentrate on developing radical, disruptive innovations and projects with low costs and high uncertainty. It is at this point that the larger firm should 'adopt' the innovation, either by purchasing or licensing the intellectual property (patent, etc.) or by buying the small firm itself – the process of external corporate venturing that we shall explore in Chapter 14.

PARTNERSHIPS AND STRATEGIC ALLIANCES

partnership sourcing When firms engage in long-term outsourcing and build a long-term partnership with the outsource companies

When firms engage in long-term outsourcing, they are building a long-term partnership which, as we saw, is a network structure based on reciprocity and self-interest, underpinned by mutual trust. Poor performance by one partner can damage the other. The development of mobile technologies has allowed virtual networks to grow up in most industries – emphasizing this need to look beyond conventional organization charts to understand how organizations actually operate. This form of **partnership-sourcing** can bring advantages to both parties allowing each to build on their own skills and capabilities whilst leveraging those of the other. Perhaps the most famous of these was the network built up by Dell, with its integrated supply-chain management system linking customers' orders with suppliers to speed delivery, lower costs and therefore help keep prices low – a business model now copied not only in the computer industry. Indeed the manufacture of computers provides an excellent example of how partnerships underpin many of today's complex supply chains. Every element of the **value chain** might be located so as to provide the best combination of cost and expertise, as in the example shown in Table 5.2.

value chain The primary and support activities that add value to a product/ service

Table 5.2 Partnerships for a computer manufacturer

Component/process	Supplier location
Design	USA (in collaboration with third-party manufacturers)
Assembly	China
Microprocessor	Designed and manufactured in USA
Graphics card	Designed in Canada, manufactured in China
Screen	Manufactured in Korea
Hard disk drive	Designed in USA, manufactured in Malaysia
Lithium battery	Japan
Logistics	Subcontracted to third parties – some local, some global
Telephone sales/support	Subcontracted to third parties in key countries

Sarasvathy (2001), in her study of how entrepreneurs approached decision-making, found that they partnered with a wider range of stakeholders than professional executives. Partnerships can take many different forms. They can be set up for many different purposes. For example, partnering with another organization in setting up a new venture may simplify the operating tasks faced and mitigate the risks. Since assets are owned or contributed by all the partners, the financial resources needed and the associated risks are spread and flexibility is increased. True partners can become part of a team pursuing a particular opportunity, even though not part of the same legal entity. They can help in unexpected ways and often it is possible to leverage the capability and resources to both partners to their mutual advantage.

Strategic alliances are a form of partnership whereby separate organizations come together to pursue an agreed set of objectives. They can straddle countries, markets and hierarchies, providing a structure for cooperation. They might take the form of an informal collaborative arrangement, a **joint venture** through a newly formed organization or one party (or both) taking an equity stake in the other. They can be an effective way of sustaining competitive advantage and are particularly important in relation to innovation, where the partners have different competences that they can apply in pursuing a commercial opportunity. They have become a common business practice in many industries, primarily in response to globalization and technological change.

Alliances can create economic advantage by leveraging market presence (Lewis, 1990; Lorange and Roos, 1992; Ohmae, 1989). Alliances can also provide vertical integration and scale economies at a greatly reduced cost (Anderson and Weitz, 1992). There are usually explicit strategic and operational motives for an alliance. These might include gaining access to new markets, achieving economies of scale or leveraging complementary capabilities. In its simplest form, an alliance might be the arrangement a manufacturer has with a distributor for sole distribution rights in a particular country, or some form of **franchise** arrangement. Some firms have based their international expansion strategy almost entirely on foreign alliances. There are numerous examples of large firm alliances. For example, in the face of stiff competition from discount international retailers like Lidl and Aldi, the UK supermarket giant Tesco entered into a three-year strategic alliance in 2018 with the French supermarket giant Carrefour to give them greater international price leverage and buying power for everything from foodstuffs (particularly own-label) to till rolls.

Strategic partnerships and alliances are often formed by companies offering complementary products or services, where the attractiveness to customers is enhanced by the existence of the other product or service. These alliances can lead to cooperation in innovation and marketing. They can also be used to fight off competition. For example, Oneworld is a strategic alliance of a dozen airlines, including British Airways and American Airlines, whose primary purpose is to encourage passengers to use partner airlines. Alliances also facilitate organizational learning (Parkhe, 1993). As Karthik (2002) observed: 'alliances are pooling mechanisms combining diverse unique skills and capabilities, and thus are able to create potentially powerful learning opportunities for firms. In fact, learning opportunities create "learning organizations" that are able to increase their absorptive capacities and to assimilate new ideas easily to remain competitive.' In this way, strategic alliances increase the size and scope of the learning community and can improve the knowledge base of an organization. Alliances create value through

strategic alliance A form of partnership whereby separate organizations come together to pursue an agreed set of objectives

joint venture A more formal strategic partnership based upon a legal agreement, often involving a separate legal entity

franchise A business in which the owner of the name and method of doing business (the franchisor) allows a local operator (the franchisee) to set up a business under that name offering their products or services

synergy as partners achieve mutual gains that neither could gain individually (Teece, 1992). It is hardly surprising, therefore, that the most innovative companies have been found to incorporate external innovations through a variety of mechanisms, including acquisitions, partnerships, joint ventures and licensing (BCG, 2016).

Business priorities and motivations change over time and the specific reason for a partnership or alliance might cease to exist over time. Formal agreements might be time-limited and come to an end. In some cases, alliance partners can be torn between the advantages of cooperation and the temptation to behave opportunistically. There is always the risk that an alliance member who is also a competitor may, over time, be strengthened through the transfer or creation of knowledge and capabilities creating an incentive to dissolve the partnership or act unethically. Nevertheless, numerous academic studies have shown that there are real benefits from partnerships and strategic alliances for organizations of all sizes. A government survey in the UK concluded that: 'in both the UK and the US, we observe that the highest growth firms rely *heavily* on building relationships with other firms, either through supply chains or through formal strategic alliances' (DBER, 2008, emphasis added).

JOINT VENTURES

A more formal strategic partnership is called a joint venture. This usually has a degree of direct market involvement and therefore needs to be underpinned by some form of legal agreement that determines the split of resource inputs and rewards. Often the joint venture takes the form of a legal entity that is separate from either of the parties involved. Many joint ventures involve the coming together of companies with capabilities in completely different industries, often driven by accelerating developments in digital technologies – for example, the development of autonomous vehicles. A recent study found that the number of digital joint ventures increased by almost 60 per cent in the four years to 2018 (BCG, 2018).

Richard Branson has been particularly adept at using joint ventures as a basis for rolling out new business ideas. He partnered with Deutsche Telecom to create Virgin Mobile, and Singapore Airlines owned 49 per cent of Virgin Airlines. Swedish construction conglomerate Skansa AB formed a joint-venture partnership with furniture retailer IKEA called BoKlok to produce ready-built rooms in a highly automated factory, then to be assembled to form houses on-site. IKEA provided their expertise in internal room design and assembly, whilst Skansa provided their building expertise and access to construction sites. The partnership opened the door to large economies of scale, estimated to reduce the cost of erecting a fully furnished four-storey house by 35 per cent. By 2018, they were producing some 1,200 affordable houses per year. Some developing countries do not allow foreign companies to set up in their country, only allowing joint ventures with local organizations.

One common form of a joint venture, particularly in the retail sector, is the franchise. This is a licence to produce or sell a product or service. A franchise is a business in which the owner of the name and method of doing business (the franchisor) allows a local operator (the franchisee) to set up a business under that name offering their products or services. This allows the franchisee to capitalize on their local knowledge, but requires them also to

CASE INSIGHT 5.3
GVC and MGM Resorts

JOINT VENTURES

In 2018 the UK betting firm GVC (owner of Ladbrokes, Coral and Sportingbet brands) announced a 50/50 US joint venture with US hotel and casino operator MGM Resorts (best known for its Las Vegas brands such as MGM Grand and Bellingo). Only two months earlier, the US Supreme Court had overturned 1992 legislation that prohibited sports betting in the USA. The aim of the joint venture is to create a 'world-class sports betting and online gaming platform' in the USA with a separate headquarters and board of directors. Each company will invest an initial $100 million and plan to bring in leadership and expertise from both firms start the joint venture as soon as possible. MGM is arguably the biggest gambling brand in the USA, with physical gaming sites, and a customer base that includes 27 million 'M Life' members. The joint venture will be able to use MGM's brand to enter the online sports betting and gaming markets. GVC is known for its gaming technology and online capabilities, but it also will be providing a portfolio of complementary sports betting and gaming brands, including partypoker. Both companies are industry-leading gaming and consumer businesses in their own countries with a track record of joint ventures and partnerships.

Visit the websites: **gvc-plc.com** and **www.mgmresorts.com**

Questions:

1. What different attributes do the two partners bring to a joint venture?
2. Why are they moving so quickly after the ruling by the US Supreme Court?

take on many of the business risks. Their local market knowledge and dedication is vital if the market is to be penetrated effectively. For the franchisor, it is a way of rolling out a new product or an established business format rapidly without the need for large amounts of capital. It is popular with franchisees that may be less entrepreneurial but wish to run their own business. When entering the market in another country, a franchisor often appoints a head franchisee who will be responsible for finding other franchisees in their country. Table 5.3 summarizes the advantages and disadvantages of being a franchisor and franchisee.

As a variant on franchising, the UK opticians and hearing-aid specialists, Specsavers, operate a contract-based, joint-venture approach to retailing, tailored to professional practitioners, in this case opticians. It offers all the advantages of a franchise, but gives the local operator greater professional autonomy and responsibility. Specsavers is now the largest chain of opticians in the UK and is also expanding rapidly in other countries. Another example of the joint venture approach is the Danish price-point retailer Flying Tiger Copenhagen, who offer 50:50 partnerships with local national partners who are offered exclusive territories and are then responsible for store roll-out and day-to-day operations (Case insight 8.3).

Table 5.3 Advantages and disadvantages of being a franchisor or franchisee

	Franchisor	Franchisee
Advantages	➥ Way of expanding business quickly ➥ Financing costs shared with franchisees ➥ Franchisees usually highly motivated since their livelihood depends on success	➥ Business format proved; less risk of failure ➥ Easier to obtain finance than own start-up ➥ Established format; start-up should be quicker ➥ Training and support available from franchisor ➥ National branding should help sales ➥ Economies of scale may apply
Disadvantages	➥ There may be a franchise association with rules that need to be followed (in the UK, this is the British Franchise Association) ➥ Loss of some control to franchisees ➥ Franchisees can influence the business at the local level ➥ Failure of franchisee can reflect on franchise ➥ May be obligations to franchisee in the franchise agreement	➥ Not really your own idea and creation ➥ Lack of real independence ➥ Franchisor makes the rules ➥ Buying into franchise can be expensive ➥ Royalties can be high ➥ Goodwill built up dependent upon continuing franchise agreement; this may cause problems if franchisee wishes to sell ➥ Franchisor can damage brand

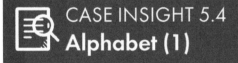 CASE INSIGHT 5.4
Alphabet (1)

 USA

ORGANIZATIONAL DESIGN AND RISK

Founded in 1996 by Larry Page and Sergey Brin when they were both PhD students at Stanford University, the original Google has moved beyond being a mere search engine. As well as information searches, it now also offers maps, images and many other services, including its own internet portal. Google also has Gmail, which is well established in the market, and has its Chrome internet browser. Google has become not only the name of a search engine and company, but also the name for what we do when we search the internet for information. Advertising generates 99 per cent of Google's revenues. Indeed, 70 per cent of all US online advertising now goes through Google or Facebook. Google effectively controls the means by which internet users find what they want online and in doing so it has been said to discriminate against rivals, harming competition. Its Android smartphone operating system now has more users than Apple's iPhones and accounts for most worldwide sales of smartphones, meaning that many other internet companies such as Facebook, Twitter and Snapchat are dependent on it. It now sells smartphones and tablet computers under its own brand, although manufacturing is subcontracted to partners.

It also has Google Music, which offers music downloads and owns YouTube, where you can watch and rent TV programmes and films, and has diversified into many technology areas, including the development of autonomous vehicle technology. It has its own online payment system called Google Wallet.

For a number of years, commentators observed that, if it were to continue to innovate quickly, the management structure at Google needed to change. In 2015, the company announced an overhaul of its structures, splitting it up into a number of subsidiaries and putting overall ownership in the hands of a new parent company called Alphabet with Larry Page as CEO and Sergey Brin as president. A newly reformed Google would remain the chief operating and income-generating subsidiary of Alphabet, with Sundar Pichai in charge (Page's number two in the old Google). The restructuring freed Page up from the day-to-day running of the business to allow him to focus more on 'the business of starting new things' and 'to continue to scale our aspirations' (*The Telegraph*, 12 August 2015). Alphabet runs over one million servers in data centres around the world and processes over one billion data requests every day. With a turnover in excess of $110 billion and a market capitalization in excess of $700 billion, it employs over 94,000 people worldwide and has its headquarters in Mountain View, California, in a campus called Googleplex, which it shares with Google. This Case insight explains how Alphabet is structured. In a later chapter, Case insight 7.2 looks at some of the consequences of the restructuring – changes in senior management and the culture of the organization.

In 2018 Alphabet had the following subsidiaries, shown in Figure 5.10: Google, Calico, Chronicle, Dandelion, DeepMind, GV, CapitalG, Google Fiber, Jigsaw, Sidewalk Labs, Verily, Waymo, Loon and X Development.

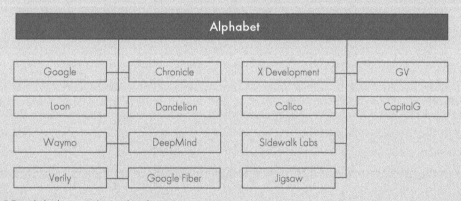

Figure 5.10 Alphabet and its subsidiaries

Google is the main subsidiary of Alphabet, generating the vast bulk of its revenue through advertising and related activities. Its search engine dominates the market in the USA and most Western countries. The reformed Google comprises a number of operating divisions representing the established Google product offerings – Search, Ads, Android, YouTube, Apps, Cloud Computing and Maps. It also includes a division called Advanced Technology and Projects (ATAP), which was set up to continually review developments in Google's highly competitive technology-based environment, its product/market offering and to speed up its strategic research projects.

Calico is a research and development biotech company founded in 2013 with the goal of combating ageing and associated diseases. As of 2018, it had still not developed any known drugs or biotechnology products.

Chronicle is a cybersecurity company that creates tools for businesses to prevent cybercrime on their platforms. Starting as a project in Google X, it became a subsidiary in 2018.

Dandelion is a company that offers geothermal heating installation in New York. Starting as a project in Google X, it became a subsidiary in 2017.

DeepMind is a UK artificial intelligence company founded in 2010 that was acquired by Google in 2014. It has created a neural network that learns how to play video games in a fashion similar to that of humans.

GV (formerly Google Ventures) is Alphabet's venture capital investment arm providing seed, venture, and growth-stage funding to technology companies. It operates independently from Google and makes financially driven investment decisions.

CapitalG (formerly Google Capital) is the late-stage growth venture capital fund financed by Alphabet. It focuses on larger, growth-stage technology companies, and invests for profit rather than strategically for Google. Since 2013, it has invested in 25 companies, in areas such as big data, financial technology, security, and e-learning.

Google Fiber provides a fibre-to-the-premises service for broadcast internet and Internet Protocol TV in the USA.

Jigsaw (formerly Google Ideas) is a technology incubator based in New York City. It is dedicated to 'understanding global challenges and applying technological solutions, from countering extremism, online censorship and cyber-attacks, to protecting access to information'.

Sidewalk Labs is a company that aims to improve urban infrastructure through technological solutions, and tackle issues such as cost of living, efficient transportation and energy usage.

Verily (formerly Google Life Sciences) is a research organization devoted to the study of life sciences. Until 2015 it was a division of Google X.

Waymo develops self-driving vehicle technology. Starting as a project in Google X, it became a subsidiary in 2016.

Loon uses high-altitude balloons in the stratosphere to create an aerial wireless network. Starting as a project in Google X, it became a subsidiary in 2018.

X Development (formerly Google X) is an ideas lab that identifies new physical products opportunities and develops and tests concepts (see Case insight 13.4).

Case insight 16.1 looks at how the original Google grew to be the dominant internet giant it is today and how it developed its organizational architecture.

To find out more about why Page and Brin reorganized visit the website: abc.xyz

Questions:

1. Why has Alphabet adopted this organization structure? What are the advantages and disadvantages?
2. Why is ATAP a subsidiary of Google when other research-based activities are subsidiaries of Alphabet?

SUMMARY

➡ Structures create order in an organization but there is no single 'best' organization structure. The most appropriate structure depends on the nature of the organization, the strategies it employs, the tasks it undertakes, the culture it wishes to encourage, the environment it operates in and its size.

➡ For larger firms, both hierarchical and matrix structures, or a combination of the two, can be appropriate in different circumstances, depending on the complexity of tasks and the degree of change. However, the traditional hierarchical structure can be mechanistic, bureaucratic and rigid. It is most appropriate for simple tasks in stable environments.

➡ Small organizational units are more responsive to change and large firms have responded to the entrepreneurial challenge by downsizing and deconstructing themselves. They are outsourcing non-core activities and down-scoping, including using smaller firms to 'outsource innovation'. Internally, they are making increased use of project teams, delayering and flattening their organizational structures and investing in information technology to improve communications.

➡ Entrepreneurial organizations typically face a high degree of competition and environmental turbulence. If the tasks they need to undertake are complex, they are best served by an organic organizational structure – one that can adapt and change to suit different circumstances.

➡ Different structures may be better suited to different segments of an organization facing different conditions. For example, there might be an organic head office structure but more traditional hierarchical structures within subsidiaries. Whilst the leadership of the subsidiaries might have autonomy in relation to head office, within these subsidiaries leadership, culture and structures should be appropriate, consistent and mutually reinforcing.

➡ Entrepreneurial firms typically have limited hierarchy and are highly flexible, decentralized with a minimum of levels within the structures. They are more horizontal than vertical. Authority is based on expertise not on role, and authority for decision-making tends to be delegated so that individuals feel empowered to make decisions. The organization is informal rather than formal, with loose control but an emphasis on getting things done. Spans of control are likely to be broader. Team working is likely to be the norm. There are structures within structures that encourage smaller units to develop, each with considerable autonomy, but there are also structures in place that encourage rapid, open, effective communication between and across these units and through any hierarchy.

➡ Entrepreneurial firms need looser control but tight accountability. Too much control stifles creativity, innovation and entrepreneurship. However, too little can lead to chaos. What is needed is 'balance' between:

- Space or slack – a looseness in resource availability, that encourages experimentation and innovation;
- Direction – a broad strategy and goals that gives innovation a focus;
- Support – knowledge transfer and training systems, which encourage innovation;
- Boundaries – not just rules but underlying morals and ethics, that underpin everything the firm does.

➡ Informal structures are becoming increasingly important, based on strong, mutually beneficial relationships. Networks, virtual or real, encourage resource sharing and the sharing and transferring of knowledge. Strategic alliances and partnerships are also important, particularly in the context of innovation and market penetration. Networks and partnerships therefore mitigate risk.

 GROUP DISCUSSION TOPICS

1. Why does size matter for an organization?
2. Should large firms concentrate on projects with high cost and low uncertainty and leave those with low cost and high uncertainty to small firms? Will this happen?
3. Will small firms become more important as time goes on?
4. Why do large firms deconstruct and downsize?
5. What factors determine the 'best' size of an organization and the 'best' way an organization is structured?
6. What is an organic structure? Can it be defined? Is it a useful construct?

7. Why does tight control stifle creativity, innovation and entrepreneurship?
8. Why, and in what circumstances, is autonomy important?
9. How do you achieve 'balance' between autonomy and control? Who makes the judgement? How easy is this to manage?
10. How can you have loose control but tight accountability? Give examples.
11. What are the advantages and disadvantages of the network structure – both real and virtual?
12. Why has globalization encouraged the growth of networks?
13. How has technology encouraged the growth of networks?
14. Why has the increasing importance of knowledge encouraged the growth of networks?
15. How can networking encourage innovation?
16. How can strategic partnerships encourage development of the innovation?
17. What are the prerequisites for an effective strategic partnership?
18. Why is organizational structure important?
19. Is there such a thing as an ideal organization structure for an entrepreneurial firm? If so, what is it?
20. What are the principles behind how you structure an organization with multi-product and markets?

 ACTIVITIES

1. Give some specific examples of an industry where a hierarchical, bureaucratic structure should be the 'best' way to organize. Select a company in this industry and investigate their organizational structure. Explain why their structure conforms or does not conform to your expectations, taking into account its relative commercial success.
2. List the type of organizations and market sectors that face high degrees of competition and turbulence. Select a particularly turbulent sector and research how the firms within it are structured and their relative success.
3. Describe the different ways large organizations break themselves down into smaller sub-organizations and explain their reasons for doing this.
4. Select a large company that has been broken up into at least two parts and explain the reasons for this.
5. Select a strategic alliance or joint venture and analyze and explain the reasons behind it.

REFERENCES

Amabile, T.M. (1997) 'Motivating Creativity in Organizations: On Doing What You Love and Loving What You Do', *California Management Review*, 40(1).

Anderson, E. and Weitz, B. (1992) 'The Use of Pledges to Build and Sustain Commitment in Distribution Channels', *Journal of Marketing Research*, 29, February.

Angel, R. (2006) 'Putting an Innovation Culture into Practice', *Ivey Business Journal Online*, January/February, at: http:/iveybusinessjournal.com/publication/putting-an-innovation-culture-into-practice/.

BCG (2016) *The Most Innovative Companies 2016: Getting Past "Not Invented Here"*, Boston, MA: Boston Consulting Group. Available on: https://www.bcg.com/publications/collections/most-innovative-companies-2016.aspx.

BCG (2018) *The Most Innovative Companies 2018: Innovators Go All in on Digital: How Digital Transforms Innovation Strategy*, Boston, MA: Boston Consulting Group. Available on: https://www.bcg.com/publications/2018/most-innovative-companies-2018-how-digital-transforms-strategy.aspx.

Bhidé, A. (2000) *The Origin and Evolution of New Businesses*, Oxford: Oxford University Press.

Birkinshaw, J. (2003) 'The Paradox of Corporate Entrepreneurship', *Strategy and Business*, 30.

Blau, P.M. (1970) 'A Formal Theory of Differentiation in Organizations', *American Sociological Review*, 35(2).

Blenko, M.W., Mankins, M.C. and Rogers, P. (2010) 'The Decision-Driven Organization', *Harvard Business Review*, 88(6).

Burcharth, A., Knudsen, P. and Søndergaard, H.A. (2017) 'The Role of Employee Autonomy for Open Innovation Performance', *Business Process Management Journal*, 23(6).

Burns, T. and Stalker, G.M. (1961) *The Management of Innovation*, London: Tavistock.

Chandler, A.D. (1962) *Strategy and Structure: Chapters in the History of the American Industrial Enterprise*, Cambridge, MA: MIT Press.

Covin, D. and Slevin, J. (1990) 'Judging Entrepreneurial Style and Organizational Structure: How to Get Your Act Together', *Sloan Management Review*, 31, Winter.

Covin, G.C. and Wales, W.J. (2012) 'The Measurement of Entrepreneurial Orientation', *Entrepreneurship Theory and Practice*, 36(4).

DBER (Department of Business, Enterprise and Regulatory Reform) (2008) 'High Growth Firms in the UK: Lessons from an Analysis of Comparative UK Performance', *BERR Economic Paper*, 3, November.

De Spiegelaere, S., Van Gyes, G., De Witte, H., Niesen, W. and Van Hootegem, G. (2014) 'On the Relation of Job Insecurity, Job Autonomy, Innovative Work Behaviour and the Mediating Effect of Work Engagement', *Creativity and Innovation Management*, 23.

Dubini, P. and Aldrich, H. (1991) 'Personal and Extended Networks Are Central to the Entrepreneurial Process', *Journal of Business Venturing*, 6.

Emery, F.E. and Trist, E.L. (1965) 'The Causal Texture of Organisational Environments', *Human Relations*, 18.

Fenton, E. and Pettigrew, A. (2000) 'Theoretical Perspectives', in A. Pettigrew and E. Fenton (eds), *The Innovating Organisation*, London: Sage.

Foster, R. and Kaplan, S. (2001) *Creative Destruction: Why Companies That Are Built to Last Underperform the Stock Market*, New York, NY: Doubleday/Currency.

Galbraith J.R. (1995) *Designing Organizations: An Executive Briefing on Strategy Structure and Process*, San Francisco, CA: Jossey-Bass.

Galbraith, J.R. (1973) *Designing Complex Organizations*, Reading, MA: Addison-Wesley.

Garud, R. and Van de Ven, A. (1992) 'An Empirical Evaluation of the Internal Corporate Venturing Process', *Strategic Management Journal*, 13(Special Issue).

Haige, J. and Aiken, M. (1967) 'Relationship of Centralization to Other Structural Properties', *Administrative Science Quarterly*, 12.

Handy, C. (1994) *The Empty Raincoat*, London: Hutchinson.

Handy, C. (1996) 'Rethinking Organisations' in T. Clark (ed.), *Advancement in Organisation Behaviour: Essays in Honour of Derek S. Pugh*, Aldershot: Ashgate.

Harvey Nash/KPMG (2017) *Harvey Nash/KPMG CIO Survey: Navigating Uncertainty*, London: Harvey Nash/KPMG, available at: https://home.kpmg.com/content/dam/kpmg/no/pdf/2017/cio-survey-2017.pdf

Isaksen, S.G. and Ekvall, G. (2010) 'Managing for Innovation: The Two Faces of Tension in Creative Climates', *Creativity and Innovation Management*, 19.

Karthik, N.S. (2002) 'Learning in Strategic Alliances: An Evolutionary Perspective', *Academy of Marketing Science Review*, 10.

Larson, A. (1992) 'Network Dyads in Entrepreneurial Settings: A Study of the Governance of Exchange Relationships', *Administrative Science Quarterly*, 37.

Lawrence, P.R. and Lorsch, J.W. (1967) *Organisation and Environment: Managing Differentiation and Integration*, Boston, MA: Division of Research, Graduate School of Business, Harvard University.

Lewis, J.D. (1990) *Partnerships for Profit: Structuring and Managing Strategic Alliances*, New York, NY: Free Press.

Lorange, P. and Roos, J. (1992) *Strategic Alliances: Formation, Implementation and Evolution*, Oxford: Blackwell.

Lumpkin, G.T. and Dess, G. (1996) 'Clarifying the Entrepreneurial Orientation Construct and Linking It to Performance', *Academy of Management Review*, 21(1).

Miller, D. (1986) 'Configurations of Strategy and Structure: Towards a Synthesis', *Strategic Management Journal*, 7.

Moss Kanter, R. (2008) 'Transforming Giants', *Harvard Business Review*, 86(1).

Nohria, N. (1992) 'Introduction: Is a Networking Perspective a Useful Way of Studying Organizations?', in N. Nohria and R.G. Eccles (eds) *Networks and Organizations: Structures, Form and Action*, Boston, MA: Harvard Business School.

Ohmae, K. (1989) 'The Global Logic of Strategic Alliances', *Harvard Business Review*, March/April.

PA Consulting (2017) *Results from the 2017 IT UK Outsourcing Study*, London: PA, available at: https://www.paconsulting.com/insights/2017/uk-it-outsourcing-study-2017/

Parkhe, A. (1993) 'Strategic Alliance Structuring: A Game Theoretic and Transaction Cost Examination of Interfirm Cooperation', *Academy of Management Journal*, 36, August.

Perrow, C. (1967) 'A Framework for the Comparative Analysis of Organizations', *American Sociological Review*, 32.

Pettigrew, A.M. (1999) 'Organising to Improve Company Performance', *Hot Topics*, Warwick Business School, 1(5).

Pfitzer, M., Bockstette, V. and Stamp, M. (2013) 'Innovating for Shared Value', *Harvard Business Review*, 91(9).

Phadke, U., Vyakarnam, S. (2017) *Camels, Tigers and Unicorns: Rethinking Science and Technology-Enabled Innovation*, London: World Scientific.

Pierce, J.L., Kovosta, T. and Dirks, K.T. (2001) 'Towards a Theory of Psychological Ownership in Organizations', *Academy of Management Review*, 26(2).

Pink, D. (2011) *Drive: The Surprising Truth About What Motivates Us*, New York, NY: Riverhead.

Pugh, D.S. and Hickson, D.J. (1976) *Organisational Structure in Its Context: The Aston Programme* 1, Farnborough: Saxon House.

Pugh, D.S., Hickson, D.J. and Hinings, C.R. (1969) 'The Context of Organisation Structures', *Administrative Science Quarterly*, 13.

Roth, K. and Nigh, D. (1992) 'The Effectiveness of HQ–Subsidiary Relationships: The Role of Coordination, Control and Conflict', *Journal of Business Research*, 25.

Sarasvathy, S.D. (2001) 'Causation and Effectuation: Toward a Theoretical Shift from Economic Inevitability to Entrepreneurial Contingency', *The Academy of Management Review*, 26(2).

Simmie, J. (2002) 'Knowledge Spillovers and Reasons for the Concentration of Innovative SMEs', *Urban Studies*, 39, 5–6.

Simon, H.A. (1962) 'The Architecture of Complexity', *Proceedings of the American Philosophical Society*, 106.

Stinchcombe, A.L. (1959) 'Social Structure and Organization', in J.G. March (ed.), *Handbook of Organizations*, Chicago, IL: Rand McNally.

Teece, D.J. (1992) 'Competition, Cooperation and Innovation: Organisational Arrangements for Regimes of Rapid Technological Progress', *Journal of Economic Behaviour and Organisation*, 18.

Weber, M. (1947) *The Theory of Social and Economic Organisation*, Glencoe, IL: The Free Press.

Woodward, J. (1965) *Industrial Organisation: Behaviour and Control*, Oxford: Oxford University Press.

 ONLINE RESOURCES AVAILABLE For further resources relating to this chapter see the companion website at www.macmillanihe.com/Burns-CEI

6 Leading the entrepreneurial organization

CONTENTS

- Leadership and management
- Defining the role of leader
- Personal attributes of leaders
- Building shared organizational values
- Building a shared vision and belief system
- Strategic intent
- Leadership style and contingency theory
- Leadership and national culture
- Leadership paradigms
- Entrepreneurial leadership
- Summary
- Group discussion topics
- Activities
- Leadership style questionnaire
- References

Learning outcomes

When you have read this chapter and undertaken the related activities you will be able to:

➡ Understand and explain the difference between management and leadership;
➡ Understand and explain what the job of leader involves;
➡ Understand and explain how leadership style can be tailored to different circumstances and evaluate your preferred leadership style;
➡ Understand and explain how conflict can be handled and evaluate how you handle it;
➡ Critically analyze the theories of leadership and how they contribute to an understanding of situational leadership in an entrepreneurial organization;
➡ Reflect on your own preferred leadership style.

LEADERSHIP AND MANAGEMENT

Organizational architecture may be based on structure and culture but the chief architect is the leader of the organization and the builders are their managers. Leading and managing an entrepreneurial organization is a distinctive challenge that requires some specific skills and capabilities. This chapter and the next are about these challenges and the skills needed to address them. Leadership and management are different and distinct terms, although the skills and competencies associated with each overlap and are complementary. According to Bennis (2009): 'Managers are people who do things right whilst leaders are those people who do the right thing'. However, the reality is that the two concepts overlap. Most leaders have to manage as well as lead and many managers have to lead as well as manage. A manager will find it difficult, if not impossible, to be entrepreneurial without an entrepreneurial leader. On the other hand, effective leadership is of little use without effective management to complement it and make things happen. Managers have to implement the policies and procedures to make an organization entrepreneurial. They may need an entrepreneurial architecture to thrive but they also contribute to developing and sustaining that architecture. The truth is that entrepreneurial leadership is a necessary but not a sufficient condition for entrepreneurial management to exist – and both are equally important, as much of the corporate entrepreneurship literature confirms. This chapter is about leadership and chapters 7 and 8 are about management.

Greiner's model in Chapter 1 highlighted how the skills of an entrepreneur need to change as the organization grows (Figure 1.2). The first crisis the firm is likely to face is caused by the changes needed for the entrepreneur to become an effective leader – a transition that is not always straightforward. Leadership is concerned with setting direction, communicating and motivating. It is about broad principles, emotion and less detail. If management is the head, leadership is the heart of an organization. It is therefore quite possible for an organization to be over-managed but under-led, or vice versa. An organization needs both good leadership and good management. The role of both leader and manager is normally based on some sort of authority. Authority can derive from role or status, tradition, legal position, expert skills or charismatic personality. Timmons (1999) believes that in successful entrepreneurial ventures leadership is based on knowledge and expertise rather than authority and many of the best-known, successful entrepreneurs, like Richard Branson or the late Steve Jobs, clearly also have charisma.

The characteristics needed for good leadership are not set in stone – they are situation-specific. Some leaders are good in one situation but not in others. Leaders can have roller-coaster careers as they exhibit successful leadership characteristics at certain discrete times, in certain circumstances, with particular people, but these characteristics do not work when things change. They fail to adapt. Winston Churchill, for example, was widely acknowledged as a great war-time leader but a poor peace-time leader. Therefore, entrepreneurs might be good leaders at the start-up stage but poor leaders as the business grows. At the same time, leaders of large organizations need to appreciate that their style of leadership must be adapted to suit the circumstances they face – and the style needed for a bureaucratic organization is not the same as that required for an entrepreneurial one.

The one certain characteristic that separates leaders from other people is the obvious one: that they have willing followers. Why is this? What is it about them that can persuade others to follow them? The characteristics and personality traits of good leaders tell us only a limited amount about good leadership. Leadership is not about who you are. It is more about what you do with who you are, and how you form relationships with your followers. Leadership effectiveness is influenced by the group, task and situation (or context) faced by the leader and their leadership style can be crafted to meet these different contexts. However, whilst it is too simplistic to state simply that leaders have certain enduring character traits, some individuals do seem to emerge as leaders across a variety of situations and tasks. This gives us some indications of the characteristics and particularly the behaviours needed to be a good leader. We are also beginning to better understand the importance of a leader's personal cognitive abilities, motives, social skills, expertise and problem-solving skills. What emerges is a complex interaction of many factors that underlines how good leadership is an art rather than a science – and is very dependent upon the situation or context. Whilst we can isolate the main factors that influence it and point to good practice in particular contexts, there is no magic formula.

DEFINING THE ROLE OF LEADER

Our traditional view of good leaders is that they are special people – often charismatic 'heroes' – who set the direction, make key decisions and motivate staff, frequently prevailing against the odds at times of crisis and, rather than going with public opinion, they lead it. They have vision – something most entrepreneurs have in abundance. They create the culture within the organization to reflect their priorities. As we observed in Chapter 4, Schein (1990) believes this to be the only important thing that leaders do. Leadership is more about guiding vision, culture and identity than it is about decision-making. Nevertheless they are also strategic thinkers and effective communicators. Most leaders also need to be good managers – or have good managers working with them. At the very least they need to be able to monitor and control performance. If there were ever a job description for a leader, therefore, it would probably include five elements:

➡ Having a vision for the organization – This gives people a clear focus on the direction of the organization, the values it stands for and the key issues and concerns it faces in achieving its goals. Visions are underpinned by the values of the organization and the values are reflected in the culture of the organization.

➡ Being able to develop strategy – It is one thing the leader knowing where they want to go; it is quite another to know how to get there. The heart of leadership is about being able to chart a course for future development that steers the organization towards the leader's vision. This is the essence of strategy – linking various actions and tactics in a consistent way that forms a coherent plan. There is a wonderful Chinese proverb:

> *Tactics without strategy is the noise before defeat.*

The proverb not only underlines the need for consistent, coherent strategy, but also that without it miscellaneous tactics – delegated actions – will just cause 'noise' or arguments among followers about what to do, why they should be doing it and whose responsibility it is.

➡ Being able to communicate effectively, particularly the vision – There is no point in having a vision and a strategy unless it can be communicated effectively in a way that inspires and motivates staff. Staff need to understand how the vision will be achieved, and believe that they can achieve it, particularly in an uncertain world. They need to understand where the organization is going and the strategies that are being adopted to take it there.

⮞ Creating the culture for the organization – The culture of an organization is the cement that binds it together. It influences how people think and how they act. Creating an appropriate culture is probably the single most important thing a leader has to do – but it is not an easy task (Chapter 4).

⮞ Managing and monitoring performance – Leaders still have to manage. This may be a routine task, but in an entrepreneurial organization there are special challenges such as dealing with rapid change, the balance between freedom and control and managing risk.

PERSONAL ATTRIBUTES OF LEADERS

strategic thinker
Someone who sees the broad, strategic, organizational perspective – the big picture. This involves taking a longer-term, holistic view of the organization

strategic learner
The learning from a 'strategy thinker' – looking at the big picture, trying to find patterns over time and looking for complex interactions so as to understand the underlying causes of problems

emotional intelligence An appreciation of yourself, your different circumstances and an ability to adapt your behaviour to meet them and relate to people

A key attributer of a leader is the ability to become a **strategic thinker**. Strategic thinkers are able to move away from day-to-day operational detail to see the broad, strategic, organizational perspective. This involves taking a longer-term, holistic view of the organization. Strategy sets a framework within which short-term actions can be judged. Leaders understand where they have come from – knowledge of the past – and also how it affects the current situation, where they are going to and how to get there. They are also engaged in perpetually 'scanning' the environment, both for opportunities and risks, strategizing and considering options. They therefore become **strategic learners**. This learning may involve looking at the big picture, trying to find patterns over time and looking for complex interactions so as to understand the underlying causes of problems. Based on this information, leaders can then envision a new and desirable future and reframe this new future in the context of the organization. This is their vision and strategic intent. During the process, they engage in synthesis as well as analysis.

Leadership is also about persuading people to become followers – and this is not just about a question of charisma. As we shall see later in this chapter, there are a number of styles that can be adopted to persuade people to do this; however, they all require empathy and **emotional intelligence** (Goleman, 1996). Emotional intelligence derives from four personal qualities:

⮞ Self-awareness – This is the ability of leaders to understand themselves, their strengths, weaknesses and emotions.

⮞ Self-management – This is the ability to adapt their behaviour to meet different circumstances, and requires control, integrity, initiative and conscientiousness.

⮞ Social awareness – This is the appreciation of different circumstances, both of people and the environment or context in which they find themselves, and requires empathy, sensing other people's emotions.

⮞ Social skills – This is the ability to relate to people and collaborate with them and, above all, build relationships with them.

A key skill in developing emotional intelligence is the ability and time to undertake honest reflection. This involves the leader cross-checking that their perception of themselves and of the situations they face corresponds with the perceptions of others. Perceptions can differ because people have different perspectives based upon their own values and interests. This may involve making a value judgement about which perception is most 'real'. And this involves a degree of mature judgement that is not easily taught, but develops over time and can be greatly enhanced by the leader having a supportive network of people around them, such as family or a close management team that they trust and are able to talk with.

> " You have to be self-critical and constantly aware of how you translate yourself to your staff. "
>
> Alex Head, founder Social Pantry, *The Times*, 25 February 2014

Trust and respect underpin the relationship that a leader needs to establish with those they wish to lead. Followers need to aspire to the leader's vision and buy into the strategies that will make it happen. But they also need to believe that the leader can be trusted to deliver it, and it is easier to trust someone who has high moral characteristics and ethical values that guides their decision-making and influences their behaviours; behaviours such as honesty, altruism, kindness, fairness, accountability and optimism (Luthans and Avolio, 2003; May et al., 2003). These are the leaders who really command our respect and loyalty; they generate more commitment from staff. Yet ethics are not just an 'add-on', since it is not easy to adopt personal attributes that do not represent the leader's real personality. Eventually, their guard will slip and their followers will see through the image they portray. And that will lead to distrust and resentment. Trust and respect come not just from words but also from actions. Leaders need to 'walk-the-talk' – they need to act as role models, aligning their goals and expectations with those of their followers (Shamir et al., 1993).

To sustain leadership, a leader needs to be 'authentic' – to believe in and act out these ethical underpinnings. Reflecting on interviews with 125 top leaders, George and Sims (2007) talked about '**authentic leadership**' coming from those individuals who follow their real values and beliefs – their internal compass. **Authentic leaders**:

authentic leaders Leaders who follow their real values and beliefs – their internal compass

➡ Have strong values and beliefs that they practise at work and at home – they 'pursued purpose with passion'. They had ethical foundations and boundaries and lead with their hearts as well as their heads.
➡ Build a support team of people with whom they have a close relationship (spouses, family members, mentors etc.) and have a network of professional contacts to provide counsel and guidance. These were people with whom they could reflect honestly on the issues they faced.
➡ Establish enduring relations with staff because they listened to them and demonstrated that they care.

George and Sims argued that, in this way, authentic leaders not only inspired those around them but also empowered people to lead. But they only do this by always being true to their own principles, values and beliefs. They were authentic – and that cannot be faked. Authentic leadership and transparent organizational communication have been found to generate a favourable reputation in the eyes of staff (Men, 2014). When the organization's senior leadership is viewed as trustworthy and credible, employees tend to have a higher opinion of the organization.

BUILDING SHARED ORGANIZATIONAL VALUES

The first task of a leader is to develop a vision for the organization that is built on shared **values** that are truthful and ethical. The values of the organization are an essential ingredient of its culture. A culture of creativity and innovation originates from the shared organizational

values Core beliefs

values and control and coordination structures within an organization (Büschgens et al. 2013) and, as Schein (1990) said, that culture is grounded in the leader's basic beliefs, values and assumptions. These are the foundations upon which an organization's culture is built. They are embedded and emanate from its philosophy, values, morality and creed. Values and beliefs create expectations regarding how the organization should operate and treat people – the 'relational contracts' referred to by John Kay in Chapter 2. They are likely to be strongest in firms that have a long history and where staff join at a young age and stay in the firm for most of their careers. Many of the most successful UK businesses founded in the Victorian age, such as Cadburys, Barclays Bank and John Lewis, were built around strong religious ethics whereby the success of the firm was shared with the workforce and many Victorian entrepreneurs went on to become great philanthropists (e.g George Peabody or Titus Salt). Values influence the cognitive processes that help shape and develop the culture of an organization. Shared values help cement relationships. They form a bond that binds the organization together – aligning and motivating people. Organizations with strong values tend to recruit staff who are able to identify with them. In this way those values are reinforced. Strong values can also help create the same bond with customers and suppliers. They can have great commercial value if used to underpin a strong brand identity.

 Our values are things that help us get in a state of mind and motivate us to get the results we want. You want something that attaches emotionally to each person in the team.

Barbara McNaughton, founder Elements, *The Times*, 25 February 2014

Values are articulated through actions, not just words. They are based in trust and need to be proved. It therefore follows that it is very difficult to pretend to have values that are not real. Like the leader, the organization will be caught out when it fails to carry them out in practice. Values are not negotiable and need to be reinforced through recognition and reward of staff. They need to be embedded in the systems, structures and norms of behaviour expected in the organization. These exist to enforce its values and ensure conformity with the culture. They should be reflected in the vision the organization has, the strategies it adopts and the decisions it makes. Every organization develops a distinctive culture that reflects certain underlying values, even if they are never made explicit. However, if these values are not made explicit – written down – there is always the risk that the culture that develops might be undesirable.

An entrepreneurial organization may struggle with norms of behaviour because one natural norm might well be to always ask the question 'Why?', and to question the norms themselves. If the norms are to be questioned, it is all the more important to have some deep values and beliefs that underpin them. Morris and Kuratko (2002) talk about entrepreneurial organizations having a culture of 'healthy discontent' – one where there is a constant questioning, critiquing and changing of the way things are done. However, they do point out that this requires a balancing act, since too much discontent can easily become negative and destructive and lead to political gamesmanship.

In a new entrepreneurial firm these beliefs can be moulded and developed by the enthusiasm and personality of the founding entrepreneur. They are strongly influenced by what the leader really pays attention to – not just by what they say. In larger firms, beliefs can be developed through more formal training and communication processes. However it is important that both internal and external communications are consistent and aligned; any disconnect can be disruptive. But the important point is that they take time to frame; they do not happen overnight.

The values of an organization should endure in the long term. They should be consistent and reflected in its **mission** (a statement of business purpose and scope – what it aims to achieve and how it will do it) and its vision (see next section). All three go hand in hand, with each reinforcing the others. Tactics are the actions that are undertaken day to day, such as promotions or sales campaigns. Strategies are groups of tactics that enable the goals to be achieved, which in turn take the organization towards its vision. As shown in Figure 6.1, while there may be rapid changes in strategies and tactics in an entrepreneurial organization, its vision and values are more enduring. Together, they form the 'road map' that tells everyone where the organization is going and how it might get there, even when one route is blocked in the short term. We return to strategic planning in Chapter 12.

> **mission** The formal statement of business purpose – what the business aims to achieve and how it will achieve it

Figure 6.1 Strategy development

![UK flag]

CASE INSIGHT 6.1
Lush

UK

CORPORATE VALUES

Lush is a privately-owned multinational retail chain founded in the UK in 1994 by Mark Constantine, who has become a multi-millionaire. It now has over 1000 stores in more than 50 countries. The company sells its own-brand, hand-made cosmetics – soaps, shampoos, shower gels, lotions, bubble bath and fragrances. Its value proposition and supporting marketing mix is heavily based upon the ethical and environmental values of the company.

Made in small batches based upon shop orders from fresh, organic fruit and vegetables, essential oils and safe synthetic ingredients in factories around the world, Lush cosmetics are 100 per cent vegetarian, 83 per cent vegan and 60 per cent preservative-free. In addition to making no use of animal fats in its products, Lush is also opposed to animal testing and tests its products solely with human volunteers. Moreover, Lush does not buy from companies that carry out, fund or commission any animal testing. The distinctive honeyed smell of a Lush shop first noticed by shoppers is caused by the environmentally sound lack of packaging on its products. It also offers a free face mask for customers who return five or more of their product containers. The aim is to have 100 per cent of their packaging recyclable, compostable or biodegradable.

Lush donates around 2 per cent of its profits to charity. In 2018, it contributed to 493 initiatives in the UK. It has a history of supporting many direct action groups such as Plane Stupid, a group against the expansion of UK airports, and Sea Shepherd, a group that takes action against Japanese whaling ships. It contributed £20,000 to seed-finance a group of environmental protestors that became Extinction Rebellion. The shops host regular campaigns around animal welfare, environmental conservation, human rights and climate change. Often, Lush launches products specifically to support these groups.

Lush's shareholders, who still include five of the original six founders, have some strong ethical beliefs that are reflected in their lifestyle and the values of the company. These values are stated on their website:

- We believe in buying ingredients only from companies that do not commission tests on animals and in testing our products on humans.
- We invent our own products and fragrances, we make them fresh by hand using little or no preservative or packaging, using only vegetarian ingredients and tell you when they were made.
- We believe in happy people making happy soap, putting our faces on our products and making our mums proud.
- We believe in long candlelit baths, sharing showers, massage, filling the world with perfume and in the right to make mistakes, lose everything and start again.
- We believe our products are good value, that we should make a profit and that the customer is always right.
- We also believe words like 'Fresh' and 'Organic' have an honest meaning beyond marketing.

Lush is listed regularly in *The Sunday Times* 100 Best Companies to Work For. The firm, based in Poole, Dorset and run from a small office above the first shop, remains family-run. Mark's wife designs cosmetics, one son is head perfumer and another is in charge of online marketing, his daughter works for the charity Reprieve, to which Lush donates. The Constantines have lived in the same house for 25 years. Mark, who does not hold a driving licence and has never owned a car, often cycles to work. His hobby is bird songs and he has published a book on the subject. Mark is proud of Lush:

Lush has been the most lucrative and successful thing I have ever done. There have been some innovative products that have helped propel the business, including bath bombs and the dream cream. The fact that the products don't have packaging helps boost profits. It is both an environmental and economic decision. The model is that if you don't package, you have enough money to put into your product and can give better value to the customer. (The Sunday Times, 20 April 2014)

Visit the website: uk.lush.com/tag/our-policies

Questions:

1. What are the advantages and disadvantages of having such a strong set of values?
2. What role do they play in the Lush brand and the marketing mix of the company?

BUILDING A SHARED VISION AND BELIEF SYSTEM

A vision is a shared mental image of a desired future state – an ideal of what the enterprise can become – a new and better world. It must be sufficiently realistic and credible that people believe it is achievable but at the same time be an attractive future that engages and energizes people (Nanus, 1992). It is usually *qualitative* rather than quantitative (that is, focusing on the firm's objectives). It can be intrinsic, directing the organization to do things better in some way, such as improving customer satisfaction or increasing product innovation. It can be extrinsic, for example, beating the competition. Vision is seen as inspiring and motivating, transcending logic and contractual relationships. It is more emotional than analytical in nature, something that touches the heart. As we shall see in Chapter 8, this 'right-brain' activity plays an important role in decision-making (alongside the more ratio-nal and analytic 'left-brain'). It gives existence within an organization to that most funda-mental of human cravings – a sense of meaning and purpose, which we have seen can be a strong motivator. As Bartlett and Ghoshal (1994) explain:

> Traditionally top-level managers have tried to engage employees intellectually through the persuasive logic of strategic analysis. But clinically framed and contractually based relationships do not inspire the extraordinary effort and sustained commitment required to deliver consistently superior performance . . . Senior managers must convert the con-tractual employees of an economic entity into committed members of a purposeful organization.

Visions should motivate people. Two strong motivations for people are fear and aspira-tion. Fear is probably the strongest motivation, galvanizing action and forcing people to change, but it tends to have a limited life. It worked well for Winston Churchill in the Second World War, but not thereafter. However, aspiration – that is, what we might become – has greater longevity and is an altogether more positive motivator. It is the one that underpins most entrepreneurial organizations. It emphasizes striving – a continuous journey of improvement.

Visions are living things that evolve over time. Developing the vision is a continuous process. It involves continually checking with staff to ensure that the vision has a resonance with them – modifying it little by little, if appropriate. Some entrepreneurial leaders can find this difficult and frustrating as they are more used to setting goals and seeking compli-ance. To succeed in a larger organization, however, leaders need to develop their listening as well as influencing skills.

Having your own individual vision is relatively easy and entrepreneurs often have a strong vision for their start-up. Building that shared vision with staff as the organization grows is an altogether more difficult achievement. It is not simply about going off and writing a vision statement that is circulated to staff:

> Building a shared vision is important early on because it fosters a long-term orientation and an imperative for learning . . . Crafting a larger story is one of the oldest domains of leadership . . . In a learning organization, leaders may start by pursuing their own vision, but as they learn to listen carefully to others' visions they begin to see that their own per-sonal vision is part of something larger. This does not diminish any leader's sense of responsibility for the vision – if anything it deepens it. (Senge, 1992)

Effective leadership involves mobilizing people around this shared vision, appealing to their hearts and their heads through a variety of images, signals and forecasts. The vision needs to be simple, easily understood, clearly desirable and motivating. One important way a leader can build a shared, empowering vision is by becoming a storyteller. Storytelling is a unique characteristic of mankind – Gardner (1995) maintained that this is *the* key leadership skill. Goffin and Mitchell (2017) said that managers 'can become "transformational leaders" if they develop and constantly tell enlightening stories about innovation at staff meetings, interviews and outside speeches'. This storytelling skill can be either verbal or written; however, in order to be credible, leaders must also 'walk-the-talk' – to model the behaviour they expect from others (Kouzes and Posner, 2007). Gardner said that the most successful stories are simple ones that have an emotional resonance with the audience, addressing questions of identity and providing answers to questions concerning personal, social and moral choices. Chapter 2 showed how a sense of reciprocal obligations – which instils ideas of fairness and generates loyalty – is important in order to build a strong organizational architecture. Collier (2018) observed that there were three types of stories that can fit together to forge a web of reciprocal obligations that combine to form a 'belief system': obligation, belonging and causality:

> *Our narratives of obligation instil fairness and loyalty to tell us why we ought to meet those that are reciprocal. Our narratives of shared belonging tell us who is taking part: reciprocal obligations apply only over a defined group of people who accept them. Our narratives of causality tell us why the action we are obliged to take is purposive. In combination, they are a belief system, changing our behaviour . . . The web of reciprocal obligations enabled by shared belonging delivers states that are more trusted, and so more effective. With the myriad tasks of meeting obligations distributed widely across society [or an organization], not only are the tasks better met, but people are more engaged and fulfilled.*

Collier cites ISIS as an exemplar of leadership. That organization used narratives of belonging, reciprocal obligation and causality within a network, and made particularly effective use of social media to achieve this. Used strategically in this way, stories linked with consistent actions (walk-the-talk) can build a complete belief system.

Identity is also important for an organization. This is a complex mix of many factors, including the values and vision of the organization, all linked through the stories that those in the network hear and tell. It is also about who the organization identifies with in terms of these values and its vision. Leaders pass this on to their followers. Those who have a sense of global identity – a sense of belongingness to the worldwide culture – tend to convey a sense of inclusion to multicultural teams (Lord and Hall, 2005). This influences both the team's culture and its way of working. They also tend to recognize innovation as being one of the most valued attributes of the global context (Erez and Drori, 2009) and therefore tend to encourage team-shared innovation goals, as perceived by culturally diverse teams (Lisak et al., 2016).

In order to motivate, storytelling should create tension within the organization by contrasting the shared vision with a constantly updated view of current reality. Too little tension produces inertia, but too much can create chaos. Senge (1992) called it a creative tension that energizes the organization:

> *The leader's story, sense of purpose, values and vision, establish the direction and target. His relentless commitment to the truth, and to inquiry into the forces underlying current reality continually highlight the gaps between reality and the vision. Leaders generate and manage this creative tension – not just themselves but in an entire organization. This is how they energize an organization. That is their basic job. That is why they exist . . . Crafting a larger story is one of the oldest domains of leadership . . . leaders may start by pursuing*

their own vision, but as they learn to listen carefully to others' visions they begin to see that their own vision is part of something larger. This does not diminish any leader's sense of responsibility for the vision – if anything it deepens it.

Senge explained how this tension can create within the organization a strong collective internal locus of control, one of the entrepreneurial character traits we considered in Chapter 1. This creates the belief in control over destiny:

Mastering creative tension throughout an organization leads to a profoundly different view of reality. People literally start to see more and more aspects of reality as something that they, collectively, can influence.

This is an important way in which individuals within the entrepreneurial organization deal psychologically with the uncertainty they face. You might also recognize it as one aspect of 'empowerment' – a motivation for people to do 'the right thing' (whatever that might be) to resolve a problem or secure an opportunity for the good of the organization, even if it is not in their job description. An entrepreneurial organization is an empowered learning organization. However, getting people to act as if they are empowered is not always as easy as it might seem. Managers in the USA may like to be given autonomy to run things as they see fit; in other cultures, however, they may prefer to defer to their superiors out of respect. Standing out may be perceived as face-threatening and managers may prefer to blend into and promote a group image. In these situations, 'empowerment' becomes a group rather than an individual process.

STRATEGIC INTENT

Sometimes leaders know what they want to achieve but not how they might achieve it. Ambitious goals might exceed the obvious resources available to achieve them. In other words, there is no obvious, logical way of achieving the vision and creative tension is stretched to breaking point. When this happens vision is replaced by strategic intent (Chapter 1) – a framework for achieving ambitious goals by energizing the organization into learning how to reach them. Ohmae (2005) used the Japanese word *kosoryoku*, explaining that it combined 'vision' with the notion of 'concept' and 'imagination': 'It is the product of imagination based on realistic understanding of what the shape of the oncoming world is and, pragmatically, the areas of business that you believe you can capture successfully because you have the means of realizing the vision.'

Strategic intent is not wishful thinking – which leads to terrible decision-making. It is more purposeful: identifying potential obstacles and how they might be overcome; setting staged goals that are achievable; and creating a route to a destination that followers see as both desirable and attainable. Strategic intent underpins creative tension and should act like the elastic band linking the two fingers in Figure 6.2. If you raise the upper finger it pulls on the lower finger and raises the hand gently, without forcing it. However, if the force exerted is too strong (control vs autonomy) or the distance between the two hands becomes too great (reality vs vision), then the elastic will snap.

Figure 6.2 Strategic intent

Entrepreneurial leaders using this approach have strategic intent that results in setting targets that stretch the organization to perform significantly better or differently from the present. The intent is the glue that binds the organization together and gets it to focus on achieving its goals. Staff need to be motivated to achieve these intents but also empowered to achieve them using knowledge from the marketplace. This approach is essential in an entrepreneurial organization that is looking to launch disruptive innovations or to challenge the dominant logic of existing market conventions or paradigms and create new markets or even industries.

Kotter (1996) recommended seven principles for successfully communicating a vision (or strategic intent):

1. Keep it simple – Focused and jargon-free.
2. Use metaphors, analogies and examples – Engage the imagination.
3. Use many different forums – The same message should come from as many different directions as possible.
4. Repeat the message – The same message should be repeated again, and again, and again.
5. Lead by example – 'Walk-the-talk'.
6. Address small inconsistencies – Small changes can have big effects if their symbolism is important to staff.
7. Listen and be listened to – Work hard to listen; it pays dividends.

However, leadership is not just about communication and must be more than just charismatic leadership if it is to perpetuate itself. Charismatic leaders deal in visions and crises but little in between. Entrepreneurial leadership is about the systematic and purposeful development of leadership skills and techniques at all levels within an organization. It is about developing enduring relationships based on trust and self-interest. It is about creating long-term sustainable competitive advantage by making the organization systematically entrepreneurial. All of which is dedicated, hard work and can take a long time.

> **❝** I am often asked what it is to be an entrepreneur . . . If you look around you, most of the largest companies have their foundations in one or two individuals who have the determination to turn a vision into reality. **❞**
>
> Richard Branson, founder Virgin Group, from J. Anderson, *Local Heroes*, Glasgow: Scottish Enterprise, 1995

LEADERSHIP STYLE AND CONTINGENCY THEORY

Three broad styles of leadership have been popularized, each involving different degrees of freedom or control for the employees (Figure 6.3):

➡ Authoritarian – This style focuses decision-making powers in the leader. It is most appropriate in times of crisis but usually fails to win 'hearts and minds'.
➡ Democratic – This style favours group decision-making and consensus-building. It is more appropriate in circumstances other than crisis.
➡ Laissez-faire – This style allows a high degree of freedom for followers. However, a leader adopting this style is often perceived as weak.

| Laissez-faire | Democratic | Authoritarian |

Increasing control – Decreasing freedom

Figure 6.3 Leadership styles and control

However, contingency theory emphasizes that there is no one 'best' style of leading. It depends on the interaction of all the factors in Figure 6.4 – leader, group, task and situation or context. The appropriate style to adopt depends upon the interaction between these factors and may vary from one department to another, one unit to another or one division to another. It can vary with the situation a leader faces within that department. They may personally prefer an informal, non-directional style, but faced with an inexperienced apprentice working a dangerous lathe they might be forgiven for reverting to a fairly formal, directive style with heavy supervision. In that situation, the change in style is appropriate. Try the same style with a group of experienced creative marketing consultants and there would be problems. Many different styles may be effective for different tasks, with different groups and in different contexts. Remember that there is no evidence of any single leadership style characterizing successful businesses. Furthermore, the ability of leaders to change and adapt their styles may vary enormously. By looking at the individual elements of these four factors, we can understand what style is best suited to different circumstances.

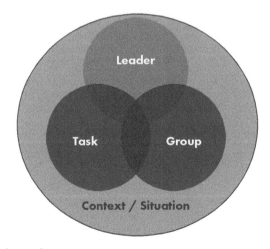

Figure 6.4 Leadership style

Don't underestimate the effect your management style has. It is not easy to motivate people because you can't do it with a large pay-packet in a small business, so you need to motivate with your vision and take people with you. Your labour turnover or attrition rate is the barometer of the culture of your business.

James Cain, MD Water Brands Group, *The Times*, 25 February 2014

Leader and task

Leaders have to work through others to complete tasks. The style they adopt will determine, in part, the degree of concern for the people they are leading compared to the task in hand. The leadership grid shown in Figure 6.5 shows style as dependent upon the leader's concern for task compared to the concern for people. At start-up, entrepreneurs are usually more concerned with completing the task (Timmons, 1999); as the firm grows, however, they must become more concerned with people if the tasks are to be accomplished. Task leadership may be appropriate in certain situations – for example, emergencies. However, concern for people must surface at some point if effective, trusting relationships are to develop. Low concern for both people and task is hardly leadership at all. High levels of concern for people – the country club style – is rare in business but can be appropriate in community groups, charities or social clubs where good relationships and high morale might be the dominant objectives. The questionnaire at the end of this chapter allows you to see where you might lie on this grid (also available on companion website: www.macmillanihe.com/Burns-CEI).

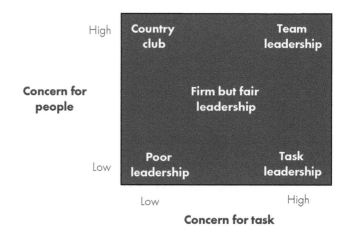

Figure 6.5 Leader and task
Source: adapted from R. Blake and J. Mouton, *The New Managerial Grid*, London: Gulf Publishing Company, 1978. Reprinted with permission

Leader and group

Successful leaders are likely to adopt different styles with different groups approaching the same task. Leadership style also depends on the relationship of the leader with the group they are leading. Figure 6.6 shows this in relation to the leader's degree of authority and the group's autonomy in decision-making. Because of its informality, the authority of leaders in entrepreneurial organizations will be derived from their abilities rather than their position in any hierarchy. If a leader has high authority but the group has low autonomy, the leader will tend to adopt an autocratic style, simply instructing people what to do. If they have low authority (e.g. because of past failure), they will tend to adopt a paternalistic style, cajoling the group into doing things, picking off individuals and offering grace and favour in exchange for performance. If the leader has low authority and the group has high autonomy, then they will tend to adopt a participative style, involving the whole group in decision-making and moving forward with consensus. If the leader has high authority, then they will seek opinions but make the decision themselves using a consultative style. Previous chapters have highlighted how autonomy is associated with the 'entrepreneurial orientation' of an organization, promoting a creative and entrepreneurial behaviour, so any organization hoping to be entrepreneurial should expect to operate along this axis. As you might expect, however, there is evidence that national culture influences the preferred as well as the acceptable leadership style and that the preferred leadership style changes anyway as the business grows, moving from being more autocratic to being more consultative (Burns and Whitehouse, 1996). We shall return to this issue later in the chapter.

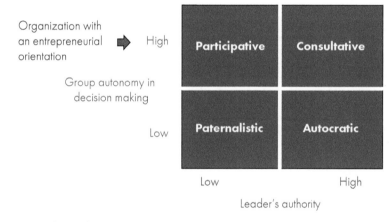

Figure 6.6 Leader and group

Leader and situation or context

The weight the leader should put on these different influences depends on the situation or context they face. However, taking an objective view of any context is always problematic because we view life through our own, biased lens and we might be tempted to 'construct' social contexts that legitimate our intended actions rather than viewing them objectively. Nevertheless, one situation that leaders are likely to face is that of conflict and entrepreneurs seem to be good at dealing with it. As Timmons observed:

> *There is among successful entrepreneurs a well-developed capacity to exert influence without formal power. These people are adept at conflict resolution. They know when to use logic and when to persuade, when to make a concession, and when to exact one. To run a successful venture, an entrepreneur learns to get along with different constituencies, often with conflicting aims – the customer, the supplier, the financial backer, the creditor, as well as the partners and others on the inside. Success comes when the entrepreneur is a mediator, a negotiator, rather than a dictator.*

> 66 *You can't avoid conflict. As well as rewarding people you need to be able to say 'that won't do'.* 99
>
> Alex Head, founder Social Pantry, *The Times*, 25 February 2014

The Thomas–Kilmann Conflict Modes instrument gives us an insight into how conflict might be handled. It shows how a person's behaviour can be classified under two dimensions:

- Assertiveness – The extent to which individuals attempt to satisfy their own needs.
- Cooperativeness – The extent to which they attempt to satisfy the needs of others.

These two dimensions led the authors to identify the five behavioural classifications:

1. Avoiding – This is both unassertive and uncooperative. It may involve side-stepping an issue or withdrawing from the conflict altogether. In this mode, any conflict may not be even addressed. This is not the way to handle conflict.
2. Competing – This is assertive but uncooperative. Individuals are concerned for themselves and pursue their own agenda forcefully, using power, rank or ability to argue in order to win the conflict. This can be seen as bullying with less forceful individuals or, when others use the same mode, it can lead to heated, possibly unresolved, arguments.
3. Accommodating – This is cooperative but unassertive – the opposite of competing. Individuals want to see the concerns of others satisfied. They might do so as an act of 'selfless generosity' or just because they are 'obeying orders', either way they run the risk of not making their own views heard.
4. Compromising - This is the 'in-between' route, involving some assertiveness (perhaps over the things that are important) and some compromise (over the things that are less important). This is the diplomatic and expedient solution to conflict which partially satisfies everyone. However, the outcome depends upon the styles adopted by those you are in conflict with and there is no guarantee that this solution is the 'optimum' one.
5. Collaborating – This is both assertive and cooperative, the complete opposite of avoiding. Issues get addressed but individuals are willing to work with others to resolve the conflict, perhaps finding alternatives that meet everybody's concerns. This is the most constructive approach to conflict for a group as a whole.

With the exception of 'avoiding', each style of handling conflict has its advantages and disadvantages and can be effective in certain situations. However, management teams or boards of directors, if they are to get the most from each member over a longer period of time, work best when all members adopt the collaborating and/or compromising modes. A team made up of just competitive individuals would find it difficult to get on and, indeed, to survive. A team made up of just accommodators would lack assertiveness and drive.

🔍 EXPLORE FURTHER

The Thomas–Kilmann Conflict Modes instrument is available on:
www.kilmanndiagnostics.com/assessments/

LEADERSHIP AND NATIONAL CULTURE

Many studies have shown significant national differences in leadership and management styles. Schneider and Barsoux (1997) observed that the culture in Nordic and Anglo-Saxon countries dictates that leaders and managers frequently adopt 'controlling' strategies – rational-analytical with a desire to control the external environment – strategies emanating no doubt from the 'scientific method' adopted by western management theorists. By way of contrast, Latin Europeans and Asians tend to adopt 'adapting' strategies – with a belief in a less certain and less controllable environment. Torrington (1994) highlighted some of the differences in manager–subordinate relationships in five countries – Britain, the USA, France, Germany and Japan – and in a number of Arab countries:

➡ British leaders are willing to 'listen' to subordinates (low uncertainty avoidance) and like 'old boy networks' (high masculinity).
➡ US leaders have a 'tough', results-orientated style in dealing with subordinates (high individualism and high masculinity).
➡ The French like formality (high power distance) and 'intellectualism' (high individualism).
➡ German leaders like routines and procedures and close control of apprentices (high uncertainty avoidance).
➡ The Japanese are high on both masculinity and collectivism, producing a 'nurturing father' style of management.
➡ Arab countries value loyalty and the avoidance of interpersonal conflict (high power distance).

The dimensions of an entrepreneurial culture have resonance in motivation theory, in particular in 'Theory Z' (Ouchi, 1981). 'Theory Z' is a development of 'Theories X and Y', popularized by the American academic Douglas McGregor back in the 1960s. McGregor contrasted his 'Theory X' – which assumes that employees have an inherent dislike of their work, taking an instrumental view of it, so that managers must exercise strong control over their activities because they cannot be trusted – with 'Theory Y' – which assumes that employees can like their work and can be motivated and then trusted to exercise discretion within a framework of rules. 'Theory Z' develops the participative nature of 'Theory Y' further by assuming that consensus and trust can be established within an organization, particularly through participative, team-based decision-making. These teams are responsible for achieving consensus and making decisions whilst the team's supervisor is still personally held responsible for the decision and its implementation. Relationships within the organization are based on trust and are long-term in nature. Career development depends on total commitment and a willingness to do whatever is needed to further the organization – flexibility. The organization builds upon the experience of individuals, internalizing it and using it in a way that parallels the learning organization. Management is based upon walkabout – 'walking-the-talk'. All of these characteristics have some resonance in the entrepreneurial organization.

The interesting thing about 'Theory Z' is the cultures in which it will or will not flourish. As Morden (1995) points out, 'Theory Z' would be difficult to establish 'in cultures characterized by large power distance, strong individualism, aggressive masculinity, strong uncertainty avoidance and a strong attachment to hierarchies'. Such cultures are clearly not entrepreneurial (refer back to Figure 4.1). Morden observes that these cultures include those of southern Europe and South America. He goes on to make the point that 'Theory Z' contains a tension between group power and individualism. This is exactly the problem facing the growing entrepreneurial organization as it develops from being very dependent on the entrepreneur. 'Theory Z' also ideally requires low individualism – or high collectivism – and low power distance. He observes that, whilst there are no such cultures recorded on Hofstede's culture maps, the nearest cultures shown are those of Austria, Israel and Finland.

So what sort of leadership style does a leader adopt in order to help promote an entrepreneurial culture? Do they simply adopt a style, such as 'Theory Z', that reflects the values contained in the organization's cultural web, even if the national culture in which the organization is placed finds this alien? Morden (1995) supports the view that it is unrealistic to take a 'one style suits all' approach to the principles and practice of management as they are applied from one country to another: 'What works well in one country may be entirely inappropriate in another.' He advocates adapting to suit local circumstances and that means remembering two things:

1. Management is the art of the achievable and it may be impossible to achieve the 'ideal' organizational culture within some strong national cultures. That means a suboptimal solution – 'not quite an entrepreneurial culture' – may be appropriate. However, there is no theoretical guarantee that this solution will be effective in delivering entrepreneurial activity.
2. It is one thing knowing where you want to get to, but quite another thing getting there. Leadership style can be adapted and changed gradually over time to suit circumstances so that it moves towards a more entrepreneurial style. There is a lot of evidence that it takes a considerable amount of time to change inherent cultures, whether we are talking about the impact of national cultures or changing the cultures of existing organizations.

Even in the context of a multinational organization, Morden does not advocate the development of 'geocentricity' – an international culture within the multinational. He sees this as only being an option when the multinational has clearly understood values and common technologies: 'the resources to create such a body of international managers, and the desire to maintain a high level of integration and control over diversity through its international management team'.

Meyer (2014) believes national cultural complexity is so great that Torrington's broad generalizations are far too simple and can lead to erroneous assumptions. He proposed an eight-scale cultural map onto which he placed management cultures in different countries. However, it was then up to the leader or manager to make the subtle, nuanced judgements about how those differences translated into actions by them, particularly if those actions involved multinational teams where they needed to apply multiple perspectives: 'If you are leading a global team . . . you learn to look through multiple lenses . . . where a culture falls on the scale doesn't in itself mean anything. What matters is the position of one country relative to another.' Understanding how different national cultures interpret the 'signals' that leadership and management words and actions send out is a vital first step in avoiding misunderstanding, but also capitalizing on the strengths of increased diversity. The problem of reconciling the different leadership styles and cultures needed in different contexts – not just related to geography – is one reason pushing companies to fundamentally rethink many of their organization structures.

LEADERSHIP PARADIGMS

Notwithstanding contingency theory's assertion that the appropriate leadership style depends on group, task and context, a number of leadership paradigms have emerged in the literature:

Transactional leadership – This style of leadership is about setting goals, putting in place systems and controls to achieve them and rewarding individuals when they meet the goals. It is about efficiency and incremental change, reinforcing rather than challenging organizational learning. It is associated with closed cultures, rigid systems, formal procedures and bureaucratic organization structures. Bass (1985, 1998) contrasts this with transformational leadership.

Transformational leadership – This is more emotional and is about inspiration, excitement and intellectual stimulation. It is a style best suited to highly turbulent and uncertain environments where crises, anxiety and high risk are prevalent (Vera and Crossan, 2004) – which tends to describe the entrepreneurial context. Unsurprisingly, this style of leadership is associated with open cultures, organic structures, adaptable systems, and flexible procedures. Transformational leaders are often seen as being charismatic, inspirational, intellectually stimulating and individually considerate (Avolio et al., 1999), and as having empathy and self-confidence (Egri and Herman, 2000). They inspire and motivate people with a vision, create excitement with their enthusiasm and get people to question the tried-and-tested ways of doing things and 'reframe' the future (Bass and Avolio, 1990).

Visionary leadership – Sashkin (1996) characterized this style as providing a clear vision which focuses people on goals that are part of that vision and on key issues and concerns. The visionary leader has good interpersonal and communication skills. They get everyone to understand the focus for the business and to work together towards common goals. They act consistently over time to develop trust and they care and respect others, making them self-confident, whilst having an inner self-confidence themselves. Finally, they provide creative opportunities that others can buy into and 'own' – empowering opportunities that involve people in making the right things their own priorities. Visionary leadership is often associated with the entrepreneurial school of strategy development, based around the single leader with full knowledge of all operations, which 'promotes a view of strategy as *perspective*, associated with image and sense of direction, namely *vision*' (Mintzberg et al., 1998).

visionary leadership
This is about providing a clear vision which focuses people on goals and key issues and concerns

🔍 EXPLORE FURTHER

Sashkin's *Leader Behaviour Questionnaire* is a 360-degree assessment instrument that measures visionary leadership behaviours, characteristics and contextual effects. It needs to be filled out by between three and six colleagues.

It is available on **www.hrdpress.com/Visionary-Leader-Self-5-Pack-VLSQ**

Dispersed leadership – This style draws on models of dispersed or distributed leadership which focus on leadership across all levels and in different forms (Bradford and Cohen, 1998; Chaleff, 1995; Mintzberg, 2009). It emphasizes the importance of 'emotional intelligence' in the leader and their ability to listen, empathize and communicate with those they lead (Goleman, 1996) – social skills essential to building effective relationships. As already mentioned, it emphasizes 'authenticity' (George, 2003; George and Sims, 2007) – leaders being true to their own beliefs (having an ethical underpinning) so that trust and respect can be built. The literature also emphasizes leaders as 'servants' of their workforce, acknowledging that self-interest is part of any relationship (Greenleaf, 1970) as well as 'educators' that develop organizational learning (Heifetz, 1994).

These paradigms are not, of course, mutually exclusive. They can overlap and need to be adapted to particular contexts. Nevertheless Kouzes and Posner (2007) summarized five core practices of good leaders:

1. They establish core values, principles and organizational goals by 'modelling the way'.
2. They motivate people and open minds to new possibilities by 'inspiring a shared vision' for the organization.
3. They change the status quo in innovative ways by 'challenging the process'.
4. They empower people to take responsibility and 'enable others to act'.
5. They give people faith that outcomes will be achieved by 'encouraging heart'.

ENTREPRENEURIAL LEADERSHIP

In leadership and management, context is everything, dictating the approach that needs to be taken. The context we are looking at is one that encourages and facilitates entrepreneurial innovation. So what does this say about how to lead an entrepreneurial organization and develop its entrepreneurial architecture? Firstly, entrepreneurial leaders probably need to be entrepreneurial themselves, sharing many of the character traits of an entrepreneur (see Chapter 1). However, their leadership needs to be both visionary and transformational but, importantly, they need to set out to build and embed leadership into the organization – and this is more than just dispersed leadership. Instead of concentrating just on acquiring the individual attributes of leadership, they take an architectural approach – building these leadership attributes into the organization itself and spreading them throughout it. An analogy by Collins and Porras (1994) illustrates the difference:

> Imagine you met a remarkable person who could look at the sun or stars at any time of day or night and state the exact time and date.... This person would be an amazing time teller, and we'd probably revere that person for the ability to tell the time. But wouldn't that person be even more amazing if, instead of telling the time, he or she built a clock that could tell time forever, even after he or she was dead and gone.

Being just a transformational, charismatic or visionary leader is 'time telling'. Being an entrepreneurial leader is about building an organization that can prosper far beyond the single leader, through multiple product life-cycles – it is 'clock building'. Authors have acknowledged that the role of leader is changing:

> The notion of the leader as a heroic decision maker is untenable. Leaders must be recast as social-systems architects who enable innovation ... Leaders will no longer be seen as grand visionaries, all-wise decision makers, and ironfisted disciplinarians. Instead they will need to become social architects, constitution writers, and entrepreneurs of meaning. In this new world, the leader's job is to create an environment where every employee has the chance to collaborate, innovate, and excel. (Hamel, 2009)

The entrepreneurial leader realizes that organizations are networks of individuals, all exercising some form of leadership and with no one person in total control, but with everyone open to influence through patterns of relationship (Raelin, 2003; Rost, 1991). The concept of entrepreneurial leader therefore draws on the previously outlined models of dispersed or distributed leadership, which emphasize the importance of 'emotional intelligence' and 'authenticity' in the leader as well as being 'servants' and 'educators' of their workforce. Entrepreneurial leaders learn to soften hierarchies, giving people more independence and autonomy but a clear sense of purpose and responsibility. They learn that they have just as much, if not more, responsibility as they have power and the real power they have is the ability to persuade, not command. These are all characteristics that we have already identified and themes we have explored.

They do this by building structures and a culture and developing strategies that combine with their leadership style to create an organizational architecture that is entrepreneurial – embodying all the entrepreneurial characteristics outlined in Chapter 1. This creates a willingness to work for the common good of the organization underpinned by Kay's 'relational contracts' – a series of reciprocal obligations which are built on trust and mutual self-interest, with the leader having an almost Confucian responsibility to care and protect those working for them (see Chapter 2). These increase compliance by creating a sense of obligation that is 'soft-wired' into the organization. But trust must be earned – and how this is done can be subtly different in different countries. In task-based cultures (e.g., USA) it is built cognitively (in the head) through actions. In relationship-based cultures (e.g., China) it is built by weaving a strong affective connection – spending time with each other on a personal level. In all cultures storytelling has an important part to play, weaving that web of reciprocal obligations through a narrative of belonging, obligation and causality. Rather than being 'commanders-in-chief', entrepreneurial leaders must be 'communicators-in-chief'. Building a top management team whose style complements each other and offers a consistent approach to entrepreneurial leadership can be a challenge.

> *Making an enduring company is far harder and far more important than making a great product*
>
> Steve Jobs, founder Apple Corporation, *The Real Leadership Lessons of Steve Jobs*, Walter Isaacson, HBR April 2011

The concept of the entrepreneurial leader is therefore subtly different to other leadership typologies. They are focused primarily on creating a willingness and ability to search for and exploit economic opportunity. They are both visionary and transformational but, importantly, they set out to distribute but also embed leadership into the organization. The challenge is to ensure that strategy development, like leadership, is also distributed rather than centralized and coordinated rather than controlled, that information and knowledge flows freely within the organization so as to encourage flexibility and adaptability. It is to ensure that intuition, judgement, wisdom, experience, insight are captured as part of the culture of the organization. These are qualities that Mintzberg et al. (1998) credited the entrepreneur as needing when they talked about the entrepreneurial school of strategy development. They are all part of a learning organization.

Kirby (2003) likened the entrepreneurial leader to the leader of a jazz band. He decides on the musicians to play in the band and the music to be played, but then allows the band to improvise and use their creativity to create the required sounds. In the process they have fun as the leader brings out the best in them. The leader's authority comes from his expertise and values rather than his position. Leaders of jazz bands lead by example – playing an instrument themselves. They empower their teams and nurture leaders at all levels – encouraging solo performances. There is an ancient Chinese proverb that still rings true:

> *The wicked leader is he who the people despise. The good leader is the one who the people revere. But the great leader is he who the people say 'we did it ourselves'.*

Drath et al. (2008) emphasized this new, more collaborative, approach to leadership, saying that effective leadership required three outcomes:

Direction – Agreement from the group being led about the overall goals, aims and mission.
Alignment – The organization and coordination of knowledge and work so that the group can work collectively as a single entity.
Commitment – The willingness of individuals in the group to align to this direction, because it is in their own interests.

Ensuring these outcomes requires a supportive culture, and creating this can be challenging – not least in well-established, mature firms (Ernst and Chrobat-Mason, 2011). However, this is all part of the entrepreneurial architecture that the leader needs to create. What is particularly interesting is that in a study of some 300 science and technology firms, Phadke and Vyakarnam (2017) found that this approach was prevalent in the media and entertainment, software and computer tools and education markets. They also found it prevalent in newer market spaces based on biotechnology, energy, lighting and financial services, suggesting that it was slowly gaining ground in high-growth market spaces such as telecommunications. They often found hybrid versions of this approach, blending it with the more traditional leader-follower-shared goals leadership paradigm.

Leadership has a crucial impact on innovation and entrepreneurial activity – for good or bad. The most important issue is for the leader to demonstrate a clear and visible commitment to innovation and an entrepreneurial architecture. What is more, Moss Kanter (2006) observed that companies that cultivate leadership skills are more likely to be successful innovators. She went on to advise that 'companies can avoid falling into the classic traps that stifle innovation by widening the search for new ideas, loosening overly tight controls and rigid structures, forging better connections between innovators and mainstream operations, and cultivating communication and collaboration skills.'

Chapter 1 described the type of environment in which an entrepreneurial architecture would thrive. Contingency theory says that it should be possible to have a leadership style that fits this general entrepreneurial context. What can be particularly difficult, however, is the leader constructs the architecture needed to encourage different types of innovation (incremental to radical), when the business has a portfolio of products or services (Tushman et al., 2011). Whilst incremental innovation typically requires the modification of existing ways of doing things, radical innovation requires the introduction of completely new ideas. It is important that the leader recognizes that breakthrough and radical innovations require new ways of thinking beyond the dominant logic of the industry in order to identify unmet needs or new opportunities (Prahalad, 2010). Simply adopting or enhancing best practice will not help. To do this they need to encourage a broad search for insights and ideas, providing focus for this search by identifying important unsolved problems with emotional or social needs, and facilitate experimenting with prototype solutions and new business models (Flur and Dyer, 2014).

However, there is always the further caveat that leadership style needs to be modified to fit specific groups, tasks and situations. Entrepreneurial leaders might also need to be able to adapt their style as the organization goes through different business cycles – from more visionary or transformational periods of rapid change, to more transactional periods of consolidation. In other words, the leader might need to change. Nobody said leadership is easy. These combinations of influences are shown in Figure 6.7.

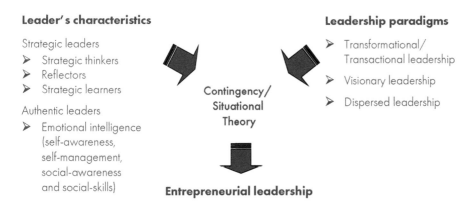

Figure 6.7 Entrepreneurial leadership

The defining characteristics of entrepreneurial leadership are the embracing of change and commitment to innovation. Innovation is at the centre of everything they do. In order to innovate continually, they need to evolve continually and change many aspects of the organization and, as we shall see in the next chapter, in managing change they will encounter many blocks and blockers. Middle managers may block innovation because they fear change. Sherman (2017) believes that many leaders tend to over-delegate the job of innovation, allowing middle managers to block progress. He points to the crucial difference at companies such as Apple (at least under Steve Jobs) and Amazon: the active, everyday involvement of their CEO in leading and pushing for breakthrough strategic innovation, not just renewing the company's existing products and services. These entrepreneurs demonstrate their commitment to innovation in everything they do and make its importance crystal-clear to all employees.

CASE INSIGHT 6.2
Steve Jobs and Apple (2)

USA

ENTREPRENEURIAL LEADERSHIP

Earlier, we looked at how Steve Jobs started Apple (Case insight 1.4). Jobs was the epitome of an entrepreneurial leader who became a Silicon Valley hero. By the time he died in 2011, Apple had become the second-most valuable company in the world measured by market capitalization, with a cash mountain of some $80 billion. This case examines his leadership qualities.

Steve Jobs delivers a keynote address at the 2005 Macworld Expo in 2005 in San Francisco
Source: Getty Images/Justin Sullivan

Many of Jobs' personal character traits did not endear him to others in business. He was a perfectionist who was highly secretive and had, at the very least, what might be described as a hard-driving management style. In 1993 *Fortune* magazine placed him on the list of America's Toughest Bosses for his time at NeXT, quoting co-founder Daniel Lewin as saying: 'The highs were unbelievable . . . but the lows were unimaginable' (18 October 1993). Fourteen years later, it described him as 'one of Silicon Valley's leading egomaniacs' (19 March 2007). He was notorious for micromanaging things, from the design of new products to the chips they used. In his obituary, the *Daily Telegraph* (6 October 2011) claimed

he was 'almost pathologically controlling' when it came to dealing with news reporters and the press, actively trying to stifle any reports that might seem critical of him or Apple. It went on to reveal some elements of his dark side:

> He oozed arrogance, was vicious about business rivals, and in contrast to, say, Bill Gates, refused to have any truck with notions of corporate responsibility. He habitually parked his car in the disabled slot at Apple headquarters and one of the first acts on returning to the company in 1997 was to terminate all of its corporate philanthropy programs . . . He ruled Apple with a combination of foul-mouthed tantrums and charm, withering scorn and flattery . . . and those in his regular orbit found he could flip with no warning from one category to the other . . . Yet members of Jobs' inner circle, many of whom came with him from NeXT, found working for him an exhilarating experience. To keep them on the board, Jobs eliminated most cash bonuses from executive compensation and started handing out stock options instead.

The *Sunday Times* (30 October 2011) was just as scathing about his personality, giving examples of his bad-tempered, often rude, tantrums with staff and suppliers. He had a propensity for tears and the article cited the example of him throwing a tantrum and crying when he was assigned No. 2 on the Apple payroll and Wozniak was assigned No. 1. Jobs insisted on being 'number zero'. It also cited examples of him often claiming the ideas of other Apple employees as his own and described him as 'selfish, rude, aggressive, lachrymose, unpredictable . . . a good candidate for the boss from hell'. It described Apple as 'a cultish, paranoid, joyless organization where public humiliations were a regular occurrence and cutthroat competition among the ranks was encouraged' (*Sunday Times*, 29 January 2012). And yet it also observed that Jobs could inspire incredible loyalty, albeit in the people he had helped to make rich.

Writing after Jobs' death, Adam Lashinsky (2012) gave us a rare insight into the effects this must have had in generating an organizational culture at Apple. As he said: 'you're expected to check your ego at the door' because there really is only room for one – that of Jobs, who, he says, exhibits 'narcissism, whimsy and disregard for the feelings of others'. Jobs emerges as a short-tempered, authoritarian dictator ruthlessly pushing, even bullying, staff to complete assigned tasks. On a (slightly) more positive note, Jobs is described as 'a visionary risk taker with a burning desire to change the world . . . charismatic leader willing to do whatever it takes to win and who couldn't give a fig about being liked'.

Central to Apple's culture was product excellence – a cult of product, in which employees did not want to let the company down by being the weakest link. And if they did, they could become collateral damage because of the aggressive, competitive environment. It was work-orientated and definitely not play-orientated – long hours, missed holidays and tight deadlines were expected and encouraged. However, Lashinsky admitted that 'by and large, Apple is a collaborative and cooperative environment, devoid of overt politicking . . . but it isn't usually nice, and it's almost never relaxed'. In his view, unquestioning collaboration and cooperation were necessary to ensure instructions were communicated and followed in this command-and-control structure. He believed that employee happiness was never a top priority for Steve Jobs. On the other hand, employees derived pride from Apple's products and in working for Jobs' vision. Jobs appeared omnipresent, or at least visible, around the campus, despite the fact that very few people had access to his office suite. A cultural web, based on the words used in Lashinsky's book to describe Apple's culture, is shown in Figure 6.8.

Secrecy, mistrust and paranoia seem to underpin the Apple culture. Apple under Steve Jobs emerged as a cultish, joyless organization, built on fear and mistrust, where competition and aggressive in-fighting between staff was encouraged and there was regular public humiliation. According to Lashinsky:

> Apple is secretive . . . Far from being empowered, its people operate within narrow bands of responsibility . . . employees are expected to follow orders, not offer opinions . . . Apple's CEO was a micromanager . . . and to an amazingly low level . . . Apple isn't even a nice place to work . . . . Jobs' brutality in dealing with subordinates legitimized a frighteningly harsh, bullying, and demanding culture . . . a culture of fear and intimidation found roots.

Apple's organizational structure encouraged secrecy – it did not have organization charts, although Lashinsky' attempted to draw one showing Jobs in the middle of a spider's web. He described Apple's organization as 'unconventional', with 15 senior vice presidents and vice presidents reporting directly to Jobs 'at the centre'. Staff were frequently organized around small project teams with teams isolated from each other and operating under strict secrecy rules. He described them as 'siloes within siloes'. Staff only knew about the elements of new product development that they needed to know about. The fact that there were no conventional organization charts limited the number of people employees knew outside their immediate environment – a cell-like structure.

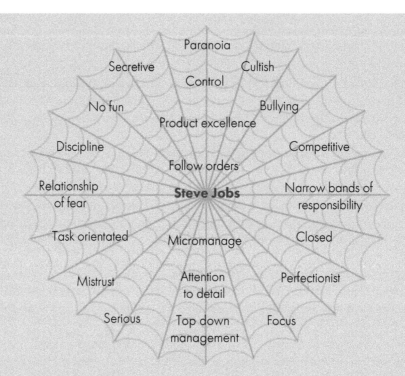

Figure 6.8 Apple's cultural web under Steve Jobs

In common with all entrepreneurs, Jobs' personality was integral to his leadership style. And he built an organization structure and culture to match his leadership style. However, it was almost the direct opposite of most successful high-tech businesses in Silicon Valley – Lashinsky frequently contrasted Apple with Google. And, at the time of Jobs' death, many commentators observed that this organization was so based upon one man that they questioned how long it would prosper without him.

Nevertheless, Jobs had many admirers and he certainly achieved enormous things in his life. Walter Isaacson (2012) believes that you should not 'fixate too much on the rough edges of his personality'. He said of Jobs that:

He acted as if the normal rules didn't apply to him, and the passion, intensity, and extreme emotionalism he brought to everyday life were things he also poured into the products he made. His petulance and impatience were part and parcel of his perfectionism.

Isaacson said there were 14 keys to his success:
1. Focus – Jobs was always able to focus and spend time on what he considered important, often to the frustration of others trying to get him to consider other things. As he explained to the 1997 meeting of the Apple Worldwide Developers Association: 'Focusing is about saying no . . . and the result of that focus is going to be some really great products where the total is much greater than the sum of the parts.'
2. Simplify – Jobs admired simplicity, and simplicity of use was a key design feature of all of Apple's products: 'It takes a lot of hard work to make something simple, to truly understand the underlying challenges and come up with elegant solutions.'

3. Take responsibility end to end – In his quest for simplicity, Jobs took end-to-end responsibility for the user experience, integrating hardware, software and peripherals – part of his controlling nature and drive for perfection.
4. When behind, leapfrog – Rather than copying competitors, Jobs would always try to create something better and different.
5. Push for perfection – Jobs was a perfectionist and would delay production until he thought the product was 100 per cent right.
6. Put products before profits – Because he was a perfectionist Jobs also wanted his products to be the best, whatever the price. He believed that if the product was great, profits would follow.
7. Don't be a slave to focus groups – Because Apple's products were so innovative, Jobs never trusted focus groups and market research, preferring his own instincts: 'Customers don't know what they want until we show them.'
8. Bend reality – Jobs' famous 'reality distortion field' persuaded people that his vision of the future would prevail. Some called it bullying and lying; others called it effective communication of strategic intent.
9. Impute – Jobs used the design of products and even its packaging to 'impute' signals to customers, signals that underpinned the brand identity.
10. Tolerate only 'A' players – Jobs' passion for perfection extended to employees and, perhaps, explains his rudeness to people who did not perform as he expected.
11. Engage face to face – Jobs was a believer in face-to-face meetings. His executive team met once a week, without an agenda, to 'kick around ideas'.
12. Know both the big picture and the detail – Jobs had both vision and a grasp of detail, or at least the detail he thought important.
13. Combine humanities and sciences – Jobs was able to connect ideas from different disciplines to create features in his products that customers valued (a creativity 'discovery skill' outlined in Chapter 9).
14. Stay hungry, stay foolish – Jobs never wanted to lose the drive he had in his youth and always wanted Apple to keep the culture of a start-up.

So was Steve Jobs a great entrepreneurial leader? He was certainly a great entrepreneur. And under his leadership Apple was certainly extremely successful. But has he created an organization that will endure entrepreneurially, one that can succeed and prosper without him? Only time will tell.

All information in this case study is collected and interpreted by its author and does not represent the opinion of Apple or its current management.

Questions:

1. Review your answers to the questions to Case insight 1.4. What elements of the entrepreneurial character did you spot in Jobs and how are these reflected in his leadership?
2. How did this this reflect itself in the culture and structure of Apple under his leadership? Are these organizational strengths or weaknesses?
3. Was Jobs a great entrepreneurial leader? Explain and justify.
4. Do you have to be a likeable character to be a great entrepreneurial leader? Explain and justify.

SUMMARY

➡ Management and leadership are different and distinct terms, although the skills and competencies associated with each are complementary. Management is concerned with handling complexity in organizational processes and the execution of work. It is about detail and logic, efficiency and effectiveness. Fayol defined the five functions of management as planning, organizing, commanding, coordinating and controlling. Leadership, on the other hand, is concerned with setting direction, communicating and motivating. It is about broad principles and emotion. It is particularly concerned with change.

➡ A vision is a desired future state. It must be attractive but credible – acknowledging the tension created by a realistic appraisal of the current situation. Developing vision is a continuous process, checking with staff that it resonates with them, modifying it to suit changing circumstances. It is best communicated as a 'story' that, in some way, appeals to emotions and motivates staff to achieve. It is formally communicated through a vision or mission statement.

➡ There were three types of stories that can fit together to forge the web of reciprocal obligations necessary to build a strong organizational architecture: obligation, belonging and causality.

➡ Leaders create, and should reinforce through their actions, the structure and culture of an organization.

➡ The ability to influence and build relationships requires certain characteristics in leaders – emotional intelligence; self-awareness, self-management social-awareness and social-skills. Leaders also need to be able to be strategic thinkers and learners and be able to reflect. They need to be authentic. However, they also need to be able to adapt to the situations or contexts that they face.

➡ Contingency theory tells us that the leadership style appropriate in one situation may be inappropriate in another. The appropriate leadership style depends on the leader, the group, the task and situation or context they face.

➡ The entrepreneurial context of leadership is one characterized by uncertainty, rapid change and risk-taking. There are leadership paradigms that inform us about leadership in this context – transactional leadership, transformational leadership, visionary leadership and dispersed leadership.

➡ The main aim of the entrepreneurial leader is to build an entrepreneurial architecture for the organization so that it can operate effectively on its own, without them. They are 'clock-builders' not 'time-tellers', building organizational sustainability.

GROUP DISCUSSION TOPICS

1. How does the role of leader differ from that of entrepreneur?
2. How does the role of leader differ from that of manager?
3. Leaders are born not made. Discuss.
4. Explain what the job of leader involves.
5. What personal qualities do leaders need? Explain.
6. What is the contingency theory and how does it affect leadership style?
7. What is vision? How can it be developed? How can it be communicated?
8. How is entrepreneurial leadership different from transformational and distributed leadership?
9. How does contingency theory relate to the theories of leadership discussed in this chapter? How does it relate to entrepreneurial leadership?
10. Is there such a thing as one 'best' leadership style for an entrepreneurial business?

11. What do you think are the prime tasks of a leader in an entrepreneurial organization? Why?
12. Why is 'walking-the-talk' important in an entrepreneurial organization?
13. Why is trust in the leadership of an organization important?
14. How do you build a relationship? Give examples.
15. How do you clarify ambiguity and uncertainty? Give examples.
16. Why is a 'light touch' important in an entrepreneurial organization? How is it achieved?
17. How do you build 'empowering opportunities'? Give examples.
18. Why is an ability to handle conflict important in the entrepreneurial firm?

ACTIVITIES

1. Answer the Leadership Styles Questionnaire at the end of this chapter or on the website and plot your score on the Leadership Grid. Do you agree that this is your preferred style? Explain and justify with examples of your behaviour.
2. Obtain the Thomas–Kilman Conflict Mode questionnaire (page 158) and evaluate how you handle conflict. Do you agree that this is your preferred approach? Explain and justify with examples of your behaviour.
3. Using detailed examples, show how the appropriate leadership style might differ for:

   a. three different tasks, given the same group and situation;
   b. three different groups, undertaking the same task in the same situation;
   c. three different situations, where the same group is undertaking the same task.

4. Research and write a profile of a successful entrepreneurial leader, emphasizing their leadership style.

LEADERSHIP STYLE QUESTIONNAIRE

Complete the Leadership Style questionnaire* on the companion website, reproduced below.

For each statement, tick the 'Yes' box if you tend to agree or the 'No' box if you disagree. Try to relate the answers to your actual recent behaviour as a manager and leader. If you are not a manager indicate how you believe you would respond to these situations. There are no right and wrong answers.

When you have completed the test score yourself against the answers on page 449. What does this tell you about your leadership style?

	Yes	No
1. I encourage overtime work	☐	☐
2. I allow staff complete freedom in their work	☐	☐
3. I encourage the use of standard procedures	☐	☐
4. I allow staff to use their own judgement in solving problems	☐	☐
5. I stress being better than other firms	☐	☐
6. I urge staff to greater effort	☐	☐
7. I try out my ideas with others in the firm	☐	☐
8. I let my staff work in the way they think best	☐	☐

9. I keep work moving at a rapid pace	☐	☐
10. I turn staff loose on a job and let them get on with it	☐	☐
11. I settle conflicts when they happen	☐	☐
12. I get swamped by detail	☐	☐
13. I always represent the 'firm view' at meetings with outsiders	☐	☐
14. I am reluctant to allow staff freedom of action	☐	☐
15. I decide what should be done and who should do it	☐	☐
16. I push for improved quality	☐	☐
17. I let some staff have authority I could keep	☐	☐
18. Things usually turn out as I predict	☐	☐
19. I allow staff a high degree of initiative	☐	☐
20. I assign staff to particular tasks	☐	☐
21. I am willing to make changes	☐	☐
22. I ask staff to work harder	☐	☐
23. I trust staff to exercise good judgement	☐	☐
24. I schedule the work to be done	☐	☐
25. I refuse to explain my actions	☐	☐
26. I persuade others that my ideas are to their advantage	☐	☐
27. I permit the staff to set their own pace for change	☐	☐
28. I urge staff to beat previous targets	☐	☐
29. I act without consulting staff	☐	☐
30. I ask staff to follow standard rules and procedures	☐	☐

*Adapted from Pfeiffer, J. and Jones, J. (eds) (1974) *A Handbook of Structured Experiences from Human Relations Training*, vol. 1 (rev.), University Associates, San Diego, California

REFERENCES

Avolio, B.J., Bass, B.M. and Jung, D.I. (1999) 'Re-examining the Components of Transformational and Transactional Leadership Using the Multifactor Leadership Questionnaire', *Journal of Occupational and Organisational Psychology*, 72.

Bartlett, C.A. and Ghoshal, S. (1994) 'Changing the Role of Top Management: Beyond Strategy to Purpose', *Harvard Business Review*, November/December.

Bass, B.M. (1985) *Leadership and Performance Beyond Expectations*, New York, NY: Free Press.

Bass, B.M. (1998) *Transformational Leadership: Industry, Military and Educational Impact*, Mahwah, NJ: Lawrence Erlbaum Associates.

Bass, B.M. and Avolio, B.J. (1990) 'The Implications of Transactional and Transformational Leadership for Individual, Team and Organizational Development', *Research in Organizational Change and Development*, 4.

Bennis, W. (2009) *On Becoming a Leader*, New York, NY: Basic Books.

Blake, R. and Mouton, J. (1978) *The New Managerial Grid*, London: Gulf.

Bradford, D.L. and Cohen, A.R. (1998) *Power Up: Transforming Organizations Through Shared Leadership*, New York, NY: John Wiley.

Burns, P. and Whitehouse, O. (1996) 'Managers in Europe', *European Venture Capital Journal*, 45, April/May.

Büschgens, T. Bausch, A. and Balkin, B. (2013) 'Organizational Culture and Innovation: A Meta-Analytic Review', *Journal of Product Innovation Management*, 30(4).

Chaleff, I. (1995) *The Courageous Follower: Standing Up, to and for Our Leaders*, San Francisco, CA: Bennet-Koehler.

Collier, P. (2018) *The Future of Capitalism: Facing the New Anxieties*, London: Allen Lane.

Collins, J.C. and Porras, J.I. (1994) *Built to Last: Successful Habits of Visionary Companies*, New York, NY: Harper Business.

Drath, W.H., McCauley, C.D., Palus, C.J., Van Velsor, E., O'Connor, P. and McGuire, J.B. (2008) 'Direction, Alignment, Commitment: Towards a More Integrated Ontology of Leadership', *The Leadership Quarterly*, 19.

Egri, C.P. and Herman, S. (2000) 'Leadership in the North American Environmental Sector: Values, Leadership Styles and Contexts of Environmental Leaders and their Organizations', *Academy of Management Journal*, 43.

Erez, M. and Drori, G.S. (2009) 'Global Culture and Organizational Processes', in R.S. Bhagat and R.M. Steers (eds) *Handbook of Culture, Organizations, and Work*, Cambridge: Cambridge University Press.

Ernst, C. and Chrobot-Mason, D. (2011) 'Flat World, Hard Boundaries: How to Lead Across Them', *MIT Sloan Management Review*, 52(3).

Flurr, N. and Dyer, J.H. (2014) 'Leading Your Team into the Unknown', *Harvard Business Review*, 93(12).

Gardner, H. (1995) *Leading Minds: An Anatomy of Leadership*, New York, NY: John Wiley & Sons.

George, B. (2003) *Authentic Leadership: Rediscovering the Secrets to Creating Lasting Value*, San Francisco, CA: Jossey-Bass.

George, B. and Sims, P.E. (2007) *True North: Discover Your Authentic Leadership*, San Francisco, CA: Jossey-Bass.

Goffin, K. and Mitchell, R. (2017) *Innovation Management: Effective Strategy and Implementation*, London: Palgrave-Macmillan.

Goleman, D. (1996) *Emotional Intelligence: Why It Can Matter More Than IQ*, London: Bloomsbury.

Greenleaf, R.F. (1970) *The Servant as Leader*, Mahwah, NJ: Paulist.

Hamel, G. (2009) 'Moon Shots for Management', *Harvard Business Review*, February.

Heifetz, R.A. (1994) *Leadership Without Easy Answers*, Cambridge MA: Harvard University Press.

Isaacson, W. (2012) 'The Real Leadership Lessons of Steve Jobs', *Harvard Business Review*, April.

Kirby, D. (2003) *Entrepreneurship*, London: McGraw-Hill.

Kotter, J.P. (1996) *Leading Change*, Boston, MA: Harvard Business School Press.

Kouzes, J.M. and Posner, B.Z. (2007) *The Leadership Challenge*, San Francisco, CA: Jossey-Bass.

Lashinsky, A. (2012) *Inside Apple: The Secrets Behind the Past and Future Success of Steve Jobs's Iconic Brand*, London: John Murray.

Lisak, A., Erez, M., Sui, Y. and Lee, C. (2016) 'The Positive Role of Global Leaders in Enhancing Multicultural Team Innovation', *Journal of International Business Studies*, 47.

Lord, R.G. and Hall, R.J. (2005) 'Identity, Deep Structure and the Development of Leadership Skill', *The Leadership Quarterly*, 16(4).

Luthans, F. and Avolio, B. (2003) 'Authentic Leadership: A Positive Development Approach', in K.S. Cameron, J.E. Dutton and R.E. Quinn (eds), *Positive Organizational Scholarship: Foundations of a New Discipline*, San Francisco, CA: Berrett-Koehler.

May, D.R., Chan, A., Hodges, T. and Avolio, B. (2003) 'Developing the Moral Component of Authentic Leadership', *Organizational Dynamics*, 32(3).

Men, L.R. (2014) 'Internal Reputation Management: The Impact of Authentic Leadership and Transparent Communication', *Corporate Reputation Review*, 17(4).

Meyer, E. (2014) 'Navigating the Cultural Minefield', *Harvard Business Review*, May.

Mintzberg, H. (2009) *Managing*, London: FT Prentice Hall.

Mintzberg, H., Ahlstrand, B. and Lampel, J. (1998) *Strategy Safari*, New York, NY: The Free Press.

Morden, T. (1995) 'International Culture and Management', *Management Decision*, 33(2).

Morris, M.H. and Kuratko, D.F. (2002) *Corporate Entrepreneurship*, Fort Worth, TX: Harcourt College Publishing.

Moss Kanter, R. (2006) 'Innovation: The Classic Traps', *Harvard Business Review*, 84(11).

Nanus, B. (1992) *Visionary Leadership: Creating a Compelling Sense of Direction for Your Organization*, San Francisco, CA: Jossey-Bass.

Ohmae, K. (2005) *The Next Global Stage: Challenges and Opportunities in Our Borderless World*, Upper Saddle River, NJ: Pearson Education.

Ouchi, W. (1981) *Theory Z*, Reading, MA: Addison-Wesley.

Phadke, U. and Vyakarnam, S. (2017) *Camels, Tigers and Unicorns: Rethinking Science and Technology-Enabled Innovation*, London: World Scientific.

Prahalad, C.K. (2010) 'Best Practices Get You Only So Far', *Harvard Business Review*, 88(4).

Raelin, J.A. (2003) *Leading Organizations: How to Bring Out Leadership in Everyone*, San Francisco, CA: Berrett-Koehler.

Rost, J.C. (1991) *Leadership for the Twentieth-First Century*, Westport, CT: Praeger.

Sashkin, M. (1996) *Becoming a Visionary Leader*, Amherst, MA: HRD Press.

Schein, E.H. (1990) 'Organizational Culture', *American Psychologist*, February.

Schneider, S.C. and Barsoux, J.-L. (1997) *Managing Across Cultures*, London: Prentice Hall.

Senge, P.M. (1992) *The Fifth Discipline*, London: Century Business.

Shamir, B., House, R.J., and Arthur, M.B. (1993) 'The Motivational Effects of Charismatic Leadership: A Self-Concept Based Theory', *Organizational Science*, 4(4).

Sherman, L. (2017) *If You're in a Dogfight, Become a Cat: Strategies for Long-Term Growth*, New York, NY: Columbia Business School Publishing.

Timmons, J.A. (1999) *New Venture Creation: Entrepreneurship for the 21st Century*, Singapore: Irwin/McGraw-Hill.

Torrington, D. (1994) *International Human Resource Management*, Hemel Hempstead: Prentice Hall.

Tushman, M.L., Smith, W.K. and Binns, A. (2011) 'The Ambidextrious CEO', *Harvard Business Review*, 89(6).

Vera, D. and Crossan, M. (2004) 'Strategic Leadership and Organizational Learning', *Academy of Management Review*, 29(2).

ONLINE RESOURCES AVAILABLE For further resources relating to this chapter see the companion website at **www.macmillanihe.com/Burns-CEI**

7 Managing the entrepreneurial organization

CONTENTS

- Management challenges
- Barriers to developing an entrepreneurial architecture
- Reactions to change
- Implementing change
- Cementing change
- Corporate turnaround and transformation
- Sustainable entrepreneurship
- Summary
- Group discussion topics
- Activities
- References

CASE INSIGHTS

Learning outcomes

When you have read this chapter and undertaken the related activities you will be able to:

➡ Understand the differences between leadership and management;
➡ Understand the barriers to developing an entrepreneurial architecture and how they might be overcome;
➡ Critically analyze how change can be facilitated, resistance reduced and blocks removed in an organization;
➡ Understand and explain the challenges faced and the critical actions needed in turning around a failing organization;
➡ Understand the importance of and ways to implement corporate social responsibility whilst maintaining or enhancing competitive advantage.

MANAGEMENT CHALLENGES

The previous chapter looked at the challenges of leadership in the entrepreneurial organization. This chapter looks at the challenges of management. Management is concerned with handling complexity in organizational processes and the execution of work. It is linked to the authority given to managers within a hierarchy. Back in the nineteenth century Max Fayol identified five functions of management: planning, organizing, commanding, coordinating and controlling. Today, these sound very much like the skills needed to lead a communist-style command economy. Fayol's work outlined how these functions required certain skills which could be taught and developed systematically in people. Management is therefore about detail and logic. It is about effective execution. As we said in the last chapter, it is the 'head' part of the organization. Without it, leadership is nothing more than blue-sky thinking.

There are many day-to-day challenges in managing an entrepreneurial organization. Often, these are the same as managing any organization; handling complexity in processes and the execution of tasks such as detailed planning, deciding on priorities, organizing, coordinating and controlling people to undertake tasks. Probably the most important skill is the ability to plan – and that is difficult enough in an uncertain, changing environment. Planning involves being able to decide which activities are most important and prioritizing them. These priorities vary from business to business and prioritization is a question of judgement. This involves deciding on, and ultimately compiling, a list of **critical success factors** (CSFs) – things that it is essential to get right if the task or project is to be successful. Failure to undertake actions to deal with CSFs risks failure. CSFs are distilled from **key operating activities** – key things that need to be done, although not all are critical. Which *activities* are *critical* is a question about identifying factors that might set the project back – there will be many of these. It is about deciding which things might fundamentally affect the success of the task or project and, ultimately, the business. The leader should have already decided on (and communicated) the overarching CSFs for the business; the other managers should then identify and support the CSFs for which they are responsible.

Indeed, everything managers say and do must be consistent with the overall objectives of the organization and the aim to develop and maintain an entrepreneurial architecture. An obstructive manager can block the transmission of the entrepreneurial ethos to staff working for them. It is important, therefore, that there is complete congruence between the leader's style and that of the manager. This means when managers lead others they should adopt the leadership styles outlined in the previous chapter – otherwise employees receive 'mixed messages' about what the organization is seeking to achieve, making it more difficult to create that entrepreneurial architecture. They will have to deal with the day-to-day tension between freedom and control that is inherent in giving staff the autonomy they need in this sort of organization (Chapter 5).

The context and operating environment facing an entrepreneurial organization is one of constant change, meaning that the skill of change management is an important one. Managers need to be adept at identifying barriers and blocks to change, dismantling them and then implementing the necessary organizational changes. This becomes a vital skill if managers are seeking to turn around an ailing company and change it quickly so as to become more entrepreneurial – a matter which this chapter will address.

critical success factors The activities upon which the success of the venture critically depend

key operating activities Important operating activities. These may become 'critical success factors'

The next chapter will address the management other issue that distinguishes an entrepreneurial organization – that because it is operating in this changing, uncertain environment and/or is introducing frequent or radical innovation, it probably faces higher risks. The skill of risk management is therefore a crucial one and understanding the CSFs, whether for the business as a whole or for a particular project, is an important aspect of this process. Remember that entrepreneurs appear to make extensive use of 'cognitive heuristics' based upon their past experiences (Chapter 1). This helps them make quick decisions and can lead to better decision-making with good information flows. However, they can also lead to over-optimism and underlines the need for realistic, but speedy risk assessment. What is needed in the organization are simple risk management processes based on open and accurate information flows that can replace these cognitive heuristics.

BARRIERS TO DEVELOPING AN ENTREPRENEURIAL ARCHITECTURE

Many traditional management techniques unintentionally discourage entrepreneurship. They dissuade individuals within the organization from using their initiative and behaving entrepreneurially. Examples of this include the way in which some organizations:

➥ Focus on efficiency or return on investment – An entrepreneurial organization is one that is going places, fast. It is probably first into a new market and needs to grow quickly, in order to penetrate the market, persuading customers to buy the product or service before competitors have time to react. It needs to focus on the CSFs that it faces to achieve this, rather than being managed like a mature company – a 'cash cow' – with the simple objective of generating maximum short-term profit through greater efficiency.

➥ Plan for the long term and then control against plan – In a turbulent, changing environment the future is uncertain, meaning that five-year plans are of little use. They inhibit freedom of action and become increasingly unrealistic. The entrepreneurial organization needs to have goals and a vision, but it also needs to learn from the changing reality as it moves towards its goals, changing the plans as appropriate. Interim milestones need to be set, but progress needs to be re-assessed after each one is reached and benchmarked against reality.

➥ Enforce standard procedures, rules and regulations – This tends to block innovation and lead to missed opportunities. The entrepreneurial organization needs to be flexible, creating simple rules for specific situations but then being prepared to ditch them when circumstances change. But too much freedom can lead to chaos. That means having a culture where rules can be challenged and are only accepted when proved to be for the good of the organization. It also means that there needs to be a balance between freedom and control.

➥ Avoid risk – Avoiding risk means missing opportunities. By way of contrast, an entrepreneurial organization will be willing to take measured risks. However, rather than launching headlong into the unknown, it progresses towards its goal in small steps, building an understanding of the risks it faces as it progresses. Risks need to be identified, even if they cannot be avoided. Once identified, they need to be monitored and early warning mechanisms put in place so that appropriate action can be taken in good time should the risk materialize.

> **"** To encourage people to innovate more, you have to make it safe for them to fail . . . Communicating is one of the most important tools in recovering from mistakes. When you tell someone . . . 'Look, we've got a problem. Here's how we're going to fix it,' you diffuse the fear of the unknown and focus on the solution. **"**
>
> Michael Dell, founder Dell Corporation, *Direct from Dell: Strategies that Revolutionized an Industry* New York: Harper Business, 1999

➥ Make decisions based on past experience – In a changing environment, the past is not always a good predictor of the future. Despite how entrepreneurs tend to act, relying on past experience is not a good way of moving an organization forward. These heuristics need to be tested. The entrepreneurial organization needs to take small steps, testing its assumptions as it goes, and learning from the changing reality.

➥ Manage functionally with rigid job descriptions – For many firms, this can be a barrier to creativity, which often relies on a holistic approach to problem-solving. Entrepreneurial organizations often create multidisciplinary teams to investigate and develop entrepreneurial opportunities – an approach called 'venture teams', which we shall explore in Chapter 13. Team working is an invaluable approach to breaking down barriers, encouraging information flows and innovation. However, some firms, like Apple, have managed to organize successfully on functional lines with a design/technological focus, although they avoid rigid job descriptions (Case insight 11.2).

➥ Promote individuals who conform – This is a certain way to lose innovators. An entrepreneurial organization must be able to accommodate, indeed encourage, those who do not conform. Ideas people and 'doers' need to be both encouraged and rewarded.

There is nothing wrong with these management techniques, in the right environmental context. However, they will not encourage the development of an entrepreneurial architecture. Operational structures are consistently identified as one of the most critical barriers to internal innovation (Srivastava and Agrawal, 2010). Based upon an extensive review of the literature on corporate innovation and entrepreneurship, surveys of medium-sized and large companies and in-depth assessments of three Fortune 500 companies, Morris (1998) concluded that there are six structural barriers to corporate entrepreneurship – all of which we would recognize as the opposite of the entrepreneurial architecture we are trying to build:

1. Systems – Inappropriate evaluation and reward systems, excessive and rigid control systems, inflexible budgeting systems, overly rigid and formal planning systems and arbitrary cost allocation systems. Formal systems evolve over a period of time and, in most organizations, are in place to generate order and conformity in a large complex organization. By way of contrast small, entrepreneurial companies rarely have strong systems. Their strategies evolve and planning becomes contingent, based upon different scenarios. The lesson is clear, if systems are too strong they can act as a disincentive for entrepreneurship.

2. Structures – Too many hierarchical levels, top-down management, an overly narrow span of control, responsibility without authority, restricted communications and a lack

of accountability. Hierarchy is anathema to an entrepreneurial organization; indeed, authority and responsibility should be pushed down to the point where they are most effective.

3. Strategic direction – No formal strategy for entrepreneurship, no vision from the top, no entrepreneurial role models at the top, no innovation goals, lack of senior management commitment. Visionary leaders with a commitment to make the entire organization entrepreneurial are essential. Equally tangible but achievable goals for product, process and marketing innovation are vital.

4. Policies and procedures – Long, complex approval procedures, excessive documentation requirements, unrealistic performance criteria and over-reliance on established rules of thumb. As with systems, small, entrepreneurial firms rarely have sophisticated policies and procedures – and this gives them greater flexibility. Yet these policies and procedures are needed as the firm grows. The problem is that, as policies and procedures grow in complexity, the lead time to make things happen increases and the temptation 'not to bother' grows. The entrepreneurial organization needs to build some slack and leeway into its procedures so that innovation is encouraged. More importantly, everybody needs to know, believe-in and take responsibility for doing what is good for the company.

5. People – Fear of failure, resistance to change, parochial bias, complacency, the protection of their own sphere of activity, short-term orientation, inappropriate skills and talents. People can be the greatest barrier of all. Changing people – their attitudes and the way they do things – is the biggest challenge facing management. It is never easy. There is a natural tendency to resist change and preserve the status quo, and nobody said generating an entrepreneurial culture was easy.

6. Culture – Ill-defined values, lack of consensus over priorities, lack of congruence, values that conflict with those of an entrepreneurial culture. As we have noted, culture is the cement that binds the entrepreneurial organization together. The stronger this is, the stronger the entrepreneurial architecture. Culture comes from the top, but it rests on a set of commonly held values and beliefs. If they are not commonly held, or not seen to be held by top management, there is little chance of success.

If confronted with these barriers you can choose to do one of three things. You can ignore them – but this only works with the less important barriers, otherwise nothing changes. You can work around them – intrapreneurs and venture teams are particularly good at this (Chapter 13), but this may result in the changes not being embedded in the organization and sustained over time. Finally, you can attempt to remove the barriers. An entrepreneurial organization is one that embraces change but often change is resisted by individuals within it. Unblocking barriers to change can be particularly difficult when it comes down to dealing with individuals – and that comes down to the interpersonal skills of its leader and managers.

REACTIONS TO CHANGE

Most animals do not like change because it often indicates risk and danger. This reaction is instinctive and deep-seated. We saw in Chapter 4 that some national cultures are risk-averse and that therefore change is likely to be resisted more in these countries. Many people find change unsettling or threatening and can become emotional over it. To some extent, this depends on their personalities. Individuals who are seen as reliable, steady or dependable often find change difficult, as do process-orientated people. And certain industries and disciplines can attract individuals with these characteristics. Indeed, would you want a nurse who was not reliable, steady and dependable? What is more, an individual's priorities and motivations are also different at different stages in their lives, for example with increasing family commitments, and this can be reflected in their approach to change. Resistance to change can also be deeply rooted in historical experiences, for example if people are rewarded for 'not rocking the boat' – that is, penalized for making bad decisions or rewarded for not making any decision at all. People may have good reason to fear change if they have always suffered as a result of it. In addition, fear of change can lead to stress – the single most frequent cause of absenteeism in most Western organizations.

An entrepreneurial organization will face change aplenty, often seeming like a succession of crises. As the organization passes through each change, individuals can encounter a roller coaster of human emotion as they find themselves facing a different role with new demands and responsibility rests with the managers of the organization. The skill of managing change is crucial and understanding the emotions an employee is likely to face can help both leaders and managers. The psychologist Kurt Lewin (1947) originally proposed a three-phase change model: unfreeze → change → refreeze. Subsequently, Kubler-Ross (1969) proposed a change model for patients approaching and/or surviving death, which was the basis for Kakabadse's (1983) three-phase managerial Change Curve (Figure 7.1).

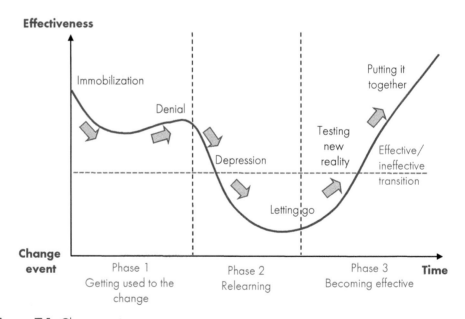

Figure 7.1 Change curve

1. Getting used to the new situation (unfreeze): After the shock of the change event, individuals might question or deny the need for change. The unfamiliarity with their new roles makes them feel anxious about their contribution and so their organizational effectiveness drops slightly. However, as they become used to the new circumstances and find support to help them, their effectiveness may improve and they may therefore start to believe that they do not have to change.

2. Relearning (change): Hard demands are now being made and individuals experience real stress as they realize that they do have to develop new skills to keep up with the job. They need to relearn their role. Although they may eventually learn how to do their new job, a period of anxiety and depression is likely to make them less effective because they can no longer rely on their old skills and they may believe that they can no longer cope. In fact this 'low' indicates that the person is realizing that they have to let go of the past and change. This is the most dangerous point in the change cycle as the individual feels highly stressed and may be tempted to give up. It is the point where they need the greatest support and encouragement if they are to progress through the cycle. It is also the point where they may be persuaded to leave the organization, if it is clear that they cannot change.

3. Becoming effective (refreeze): This is the stage when, having accepted the changes, individuals start learning and testing out new skills. They start to find out how effective they are in dealing with this new, changed reality. This can be as frustrating as it can be rewarding. In making the transition, individuals will inevitably make mistakes, causing them further stress. But, as newly learnt skills are brought into play effectively, their performance should improve and they should become happier. They should now have a new set of skills alongside their old ones.

Kubler-Ross's original model has been criticized for not being empirically based and being too generalized – each individual is different. However, it reminds us that most people need time to adjust to change and that the change process can be stressful. It also alerts managers to the support individuals need as they transition through the changes being asked of them.

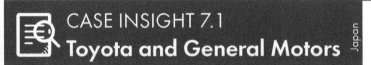

CASE INSIGHT 7.1
Toyota and General Motors

CULTURE AND BARRIERS TO CHANGE

The US car manufacturer General Motors (GM) was once the most successful in the world. By 2009, it was bankrupt. One of the reasons for this was increasing competition from the Japanese car manufacturers – in particular, Toyota – who was seen as producing more reliable cars. Initially, GM thought this was just down to Toyota's extensive use of robots so they introduced robots but sales continued to decline. Even when they entered a joint venture with Toyota producing identical cars but with different badges, customers continued to buy the Toyota version, even with a $3,000 price premium. Quality continued to be an issue. Why was quality control better at Toyota than GM? At the heart of the answer was the very contrasting culture to be found in the two organizations.

Toyota had good relationships with its workforce and a cooperative relationship with its suppliers, working together to improve quality rather than striving for a short-term cost advantage. Decades earlier, Toyota had pioneered the concept of 'quality circles' where small teams were given the responsibility for quality control. The team was to spot faults as soon as possible on their stretch of the assembly line and to rectify them if possible. If not, there was an 'Andon cord' that, if pulled, would stop the entire line. At a cost of some $10,000 per minute, this policy indicated the importance of rectifying faults but also that the management really trusted their workers to have a sense of purpose aligned with that of the company – the sense of reciprocal obligation referred to in the previous chapter.

By way of contrast, GM had a reputation for keeping costs to a minimum – squeezing suppliers and negotiating hard with the United Autoworkers Union over employee pay. Employee relations were poor and there had been a series of walkouts, culminating in a major strike in 2007. Ignoring the differences in organizational culture, when a new CEO was appointed at GM, he decided to address the continuing issue of quality control and imitate Toyota again by introducing Andon cords. At the time only a sample of completed cars were checked for quality and their faults rectified. The results were not what he expected, with the Andon cords being pulled repeatedly for spurious reasons. Unlike Toyota, employees clearly shared no sense of reciprocal obligation, preferring instead to disrupt production. Line managers were then held responsible by senior management for the resulting falls in productivity. To try to rectify this, the line managers then started tying the Andon cords to the ceiling – a very visible sign that they did not trust their workforce.

Questions:

1. What was the barrier to change in GM?
2. Why was there no sense of reciprocal obligation? Could this have been changed?

IMPLEMENTING CHANGE

An entrepreneurial architecture should embrace and encourage change. As we have seen, the key to a culture of continuous improvement and change is the acquisition of new knowledge – the development of what is called a learning organization. Learning organizations 'combine an ability to manage knowledge with an ability to change continuously so as to prove their effectiveness' (Jackson and Schuler, 2001). As Hamel (2000) observed, 'organizational learning and knowledge management are first cousins to continuous improvement'. In an entrepreneurial organization, change should be seen to be the norm and individuals should continuously question the status quo. In other words change should be easy to implement. As Machiavelli said, however: 'There is nothing more difficult to handle, more doubtful of success and more dangerous to carry through than initiating change.' And the bigger the change, the more difficult it is likely to be to implement. The literature on change management shows us ways to facilitate this.

Staff need to 'buy-into' change and be clear about what they have to do to achieve it. They need to be encouraged and rewarded if they act appropriately and trained to make the necessary changes. If they do not act appropriately, staff should be reprimanded and penalized. It is easier to change behaviour than beliefs. Change behaviour first, beliefs take longer. Any potential barriers to the changes need to be tackled in advance. There needs to be a compelling reason for change – often a crisis – and it needs to have the full and unequivocal commitment of all managers in the organization. And that compelling reason for change together with a vision for how the organization will look after the change is made must be communicated effectively by the leader – a narrative needs to be constructed around it. This is best done on a face-to-face basis rather than through emails or notices. Staff should be consulted, not so much on the need for change but on the process of change and in this respect project teams or task forces are invaluable. Change should not be piecemeal; as much as possible should be undertaken, as quickly as possible so that a clean break can be made with the past. The change should aim to achieve clear, tangible results quickly so that success can be readily demonstrated. Information about the changes and the change effort should be made freely available. Good communication is, arguably, the key to success but all these tactical measures can help managers to push through change,

Based on the work by Kotter (1996) and Kotter and Cohen (2002), Yukl (2002) suggests a framework for successfully implementing change that involves engaging in two overlapping sets of actions – 'political and organizational actions' and 'people-orientated actions' (Figure 7.2). However, there is an inherent tension in many of these actions between the possibility of having to impose change – often at speed and in a crisis – and the entrepreneurial architecture that is needed to replace it, which values autonomy of action.

CHANGE

Political and Organizational Actions

1. Remove blockers
2. Put in change agents
3. Build political support
4. Use task forces for implementation
5. Make symbolic changes
6. Demonstrate success quickly
7. Change structures as necessary
8. Monitor changes and ensure change is embedded

People-orientated Actions

1. Create sense of urgency
2. Communicate with briefings about effects of change
3. Communicate with briefings about progress of change – celebrate success
4. Help with training and counselling
5. Break up change into small parts
6. Empower staff to make changes
7. Demonstrate commitment

Figure 7.2 Framework for implementing change

The political and organizational actions shown in Figure 7.2 involve:

1. Deciding who might oppose change and doing something about them: Managers can try to convince sceptics and remove obvious barriers. They need to explain the need for change and staff need to buy-into the reasons. As we've already noted, some individuals inevitably resist change – even if it is ultimately in their own interest. They may even resist it to the point of trying to sabotage it. The organizational reasons for this could be because:

   ⇒ They think it will have a negative impact on them;
   ⇒ It affects their social relationships within the organization;
   ⇒ It means long-standing habits have to be changed;
   ⇒ The needs for and benefits of change have not been communicated properly;
   ⇒ Structures, systems, rewards are not aligned with the changes and inhibit them;
   ⇒ They feel coerced, rather than in control.

   If any, or all, of these reasons for resisting change can be removed, the likelihood of resistance will be reduced. However, understanding the reasons for resistance in one individual can be difficult and certainly requires a high degree of emotional intelligence.

The alternative is that the manager isolates the individuals, removes them from the change process – or just replaces them.

change agent
Somebody who believes in, and are committed to, certain changes

2. Put change agents into key positions in the organization: **Change agents** are managers who believe in and are committed to the changes. Often new people need to be brought into an existing organization in order to bring about major change, particularly when it involves shifts in culture. Change agents can employ any or all of the persuasive, political skills at their disposal. These sorts of changes need to start near the top and with the full approval of the board of directors; if not, they are likely to be frustrated by the prevailing inertia. The big advantage of 'parachuting in' change agents like these at a senior level is that they are likely to get results – one way or another – quickly. And time is important in business. Either they will change the status quo or those opposing them will leave. This sounds rather like using force instead of persuasion and that threat can be important – 'change behaviour or leave' is the ultimate threat to those blocking change. You only have to look to see how often a new managing director or CEO replaces the top management team to realize that this has almost become a standard procedure when major change is to be pushed through in a limited time span.

3. Build political support for the changes: This should be done with all the stakeholders, including board members, shareholders, employees, suppliers, and so on, whether inside or outside the organization, so as to ensure that there is a coalition of support for the changes. This needs all the emotional intelligence and persuasive skills of a leader.

4. Use task forces to push through implementation: The composition of the team depends on the nature of the task it faces and the resulting skills required. Team members need to be committed to the change and selection should have an eye to the personal characteristics for effective team working (see Belbin team roles in Chapter 13). Using multidisciplinary staff from different departments or units ensures a holistic approach to problems and helps subsequently to embed the changes within the organization.

5. Make dramatic, symbolic changes early on: Changing things like key personnel helps emphasize the importance placed on implementing the changes – and what might happen to blockers.

6. If possible, begin with small projects and demonstrating success quickly: This helps convince doubters. It also allows managers to learn from mistakes, without necessarily jeopardizing the larger project.

7. Remember to change relevant parts of the organizational structure as you go along: Changing the organizational architecture is not easy and can take time. Each step, however small, needs to be cemented into the organizational structure – a topic we shall explore in greater detail in the next section.

8. Monitor the process of change so as to learn from it and ensure that the changes are successfully embedded: Resistant people can reverse change all too easily if left to their own devices. On the other hand, some of the changes may actually prove to be inappropriate – so always learn from mistakes.

People-orientated actions focus on getting staff motivated to undertake the changes. This involves the need to:

1. Create a sense of urgency about the need for change: Organizations often embark on change as a result of a crisis that threatens its survival. Often the crisis is needed to jolt

managers out of their lethargy. It is a very real threat and the fear of the result of not changing outweighs the fear of change.

2. Prepare people for the effects of change by proper briefings: People need to understand the reasons for change. They also want to know how big changes will affect them personally – only this makes it real for them.

3. Keep people informed about the changes being made as they progress and the successes being achieved: Celebrate success so as to build confidence that the changes can be achieved and will work and help convince the sceptics.

4. Help people deal with change through proper training, counselling etc.: If you are asking people to undertake new or different jobs they will need to be trained. Putting this in place in advance gives them assurance that they will be able to cope. There is nothing more stressful than being asked to undertake tasks that you do not have the skills to undertake, particularly when coupled with the job uncertainties associated with change.

5. Break up the change process into small parts or stages: These provide opportunities to celebrate success as well as evaluate effectiveness. It also makes what might seem huge tasks overall, more achievable.

6. Empower staff to make the necessary changes themselves: In an entrepreneurial organization autonomy comes with responsibility and staff need to be made responsible and accountable for the changes that are being made. Task forces should have the necessary authority to undertake the tasks asked of them. There is nothing worse than being held accountable for something over which you have no authority.

7. Demonstrate continued commitment to the changes from the highest levels in the organization right until the project is complete: 'Walking-the-talk' is important, unblocking where necessary – all demonstrate that pushing through the changes is high on the agenda of senior management. Often a project is unsuccessful because management is diverted from it when the changes are only three-quarters complete and there is no final follow-through. The value of successful change should be reinforced through recruitment and promotion and change woven into the culture of the organization.

Implementing change takes time and it will take time to make all the changes needed to develop an entrepreneurial architecture. Clemmer (1995) sounded a note of caution about change management. He believed that whilst change can be created, it cannot be managed. 'Change can be ignored, resisted, responded to, capitalized upon, and created. But it cannot be managed and made to march to some orderly step-by-step process . . . Whether we become change victims, or victors, depends on our readiness for change.' This means that to some extent managers must realize they cannot always predict its course but rather need to 'go with the flow'. One thing for certain is that the course change takes is rarely smooth and continuous.

Managing change in a successful, growing organization is easier than in one that is contracting because change brings tangible results that reward everyone. And an entrepreneurial organization will be looking to grow. If it does not succeed at first it will readjust and try again. But whilst fear of failure and redundancy may be a strong short-term motivator, an organization can only experience downsizing for just so long. It will then start to lose some of its most valuable and entrepreneurial staff as they begin to doubt whether the changes being implemented will actually work. Indeed, trying to introduce an entrepreneurial architecture into an organization in permanent decline is probably not appropriate.

CASE INSIGHT 7.2
Alphabet (2)

USA

ORGANIZATIONAL DESIGN AND CULTURE CHANGE

Early in its life Google was known for its informal, innovative, 'just-try-it' culture. Phrases used to illustrate the culture included 'You can be serious without a suit', 'Work should be challenging and challenge should be fun' and 'You can make money without being evil'. It was a company with a conscience that treated its employees well. In 2015, the company restructured to become Alphabet. A reformed Google would remain the chief operating and income-generating subsidiary of the new holding company, Alphabet. Sundar Pichai, number two in the old Google, was appointed CEO of the 'new' subsidiary. The co-founders of the original Google 'stepped up' to be in charge of Alphabet; Larry Page became CEO and Sergey Brin became president.

From that point things seemed to change, albeit slowly. There were some subtle but significant signs. For example, over an extended period the famous 'Don't be evil' motto was changed to the less restrictive 'Do the right thing' for both Alphabet and later Google. But, even in 2016, both Alphabet and Google were at the forefront of the 'Black Lives Matter – we need racial justice now' campaign in the USA. In 2017 Google was still described by *Fortune* magazine as one of the best companies to work for in the country. But changes have started to become evident. The use of personal data from customers to allow targeted advertising, the abuse of its oligopoly powers to squeeze and ultimately eliminate competitors and its involvement with the US military showed there was a very serious competitive edge to Google.

In a 2018 article Google was described as moving from being 'one of the good guys' to becoming part of the 'evil empire' (*The Sunday Times*, 23 December 2018). The article highlights how things started to change when long-serving managers who had helped shape Google's original culture started to leave after the company's restructuring in 2015. New managers came in with a different ethos. Ruth Porat, an investment banker described as a 'Wall Street person', joined in 2015 to become CFO of both Alphabet and Google. She is credited with bringing greater financial discipline to Google and forcing it to become more commercially orientated. Her management style, and the financial discipline she introduced, seems to have been the catalyst for change. She is known as a cost-cutter; for example, she cut spending on Alphabet's 'moonshot' divisions, which account for less than 1 per cent of revenue. The article says that a board-level decision was made to make Google less political. The company started to exploit the data it held on customers and its dominance in online advertising (between them, Google and Facebook now account for 98 per cent of advertising spending in the USA). The company's long-serving head of public policy, Rachel Whetstone, left in 2015 to join Uber; the following year saw the departures of both the long-serving head of human resources, Laszlo Bock, and the chief executive of Alphabet and, before that, of Google, Eric Schmidt.

Employee discontent – unheard of before – is starting to show itself as the company charts an increasingly commercial course. In 2018, it emerged that Google had been appointed key contractor for the US government's Algorithmic Warfare Cross-Functional Team, which was to develop artificial intelligence systems to identify targets using drone imagery. However, employees protested that this goes against the ethos of the company and more than 3,000 employees signed a protest letter stating that 'Google should not be in the business of war'. As a result, Google withdrew from the contract. Diane Greene, head of Google's Cloud arm and long-time board member, who had been responsible for the contract, announced she would be leaving the company in 2019.

Also in 2018 it emerged that Google was planning to re-enter the Chinese market and was working to develop a search engine that did not recognize certain terms, blocked certain sites and required users to log in before searching – making it easier for the Chinese government to monitor activities as they can do with Chinese providers such as Tencent (Case insight 9.6). Hundreds of employees signed a protest letter, setting up a $200,000 strike fund, and several engineers left. Google announced subsequently that it had no plans to launch a search service in China. In the same year, some 20,000 Google employees walked out in protest after the revelation of a $90 million payoff to an executive who had been accused of sexual harassment. And other protests are also beginning to take shape. Almost half of Google's staff are TVCs (temporary staff, vendors and contractors) who have fewer employment rights and limited access to the other numerous benefits available to full-time employees. In 2018, they wrote to Pichai, claiming that they were 'disproportionately people from marginalized groups who are treated as less deserving of compensation, opportunities, workplace protections and respect'. They accused Google of 'institutional racism, sexism and discrimination'.

Visit the website: abc.xyz

Questions:

1. What has caused this change in organizational culture? Is it intentional or unintentional?
2. Is this change commercially necessary? If so, should it apply to all the Alphabet subsidiaries?
3. Do you agree that Google has gone from being 'one of the good guys' to becoming part of the 'evil empire'?
4. What do you think of the reaction of employees and how might customers react to these changes?

CEMENTING CHANGE

A final perspective on the scale of the task involved in leading and managing change was given to us by Mintzberg (1998). He agreed that to make change happen both strategy and organizational issues need to be addressed. He also observed that changes in strategy can range from the conceptual (abstract) to the concrete (tangible). The most conceptual element of strategy change is vision, followed by strategic positioning (repositioning, reconfiguring) then programmes (reprogramming, re-engineering), whilst the most concrete are products or services (redesigned, replaced). In the same way, organizational change can range from the conceptual to the concrete. The most conceptual element of organizational change is culture, followed by structures (re-organization), then systems (reworking, re-engineering), whilst the most concrete are people (retrained, replaced). Put another way, vision and culture are highly abstract, whereas products and people are highly concrete and can be changed or replaced relatively easily – without affecting any element above them. However if the conceptual elements (like vision or culture) are altered, to effect change, the other more concrete elements (like products/services or people) are also likely to have to change.

The complexity of the change process is increased by the recognition that these changes in strategy and organization can also be both formal and informal. For example, strategic positioning can be a formal process (deliberate strategy development) or an informal process (emergent strategy development). Similarly, people can change formally (training, coaching etc.) or informally (encouragement, mentoring etc.). Figure 7.3 shows the distinction between conceptual and concrete for changes in strategy (Vision → Positions → Programmes → Products/services) and changes in organization (Culture → Structure → Systems → People), whilst highlighting that each of these elements has both a formal and an informal dimension.

Mintzberg's point was that, in order to be effective and lasting, change in an organization must include all these elements of both strategy and organization: the conceptual and the concrete; the formal and the informal. This multidimensionality of change management makes it like a Rubik's cube – alter one element and you are likely to have to alter a number

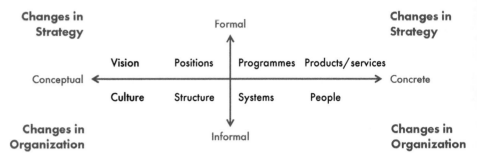

Figure 7.3 The multidimensionality of change management

of other elements because they are interconnected. For example, a change in strategic positioning may necessitate a change in organizational structures; if you change structures, you may change systems and people.

Sirkin et al. (2005) argued that, whilst the conceptual/abstract factors are important, it is the concrete/tangible (hard) factors that most determine the success or failure of a change programme. In a study based on 225 companies, they identified four key factors that they called the DICE variables: project *duration,* particularly the time between project reviews; performance *integrity,* or the capabilities of project teams to complete on time; the *commitment* of both senior executives and the staff whom the change will affect most; and the *effort* that employees must make to cope with the change. They developed a simple DICE framework that that involved asking key questions to managers and employees at various levels of the organization to help assess how a change project is progressing. They found that middle managers were generally willing to support change even if it put their jobs at risk, so long as they had sufficient input in shaping the initiatives; all too often, however, they lacked the tools and language to do so and the forums in which to comment.

Mintzberg's insight reminds us of the complexity of the task faced in changing the organizational architecture, comprising all the elements of leadership, structure, culture and strategies. It reminds us that changes must be both concrete/conceptual and formal/informal, each change being consistent with and reinforcing the other – change one and you may have to change another. And then over time these changes will be cemented into place and become the routine of how it is in the organization. However, the greater the organization is from being entrepreneurial the larger the task, the greater the number of changes and the longer the whole process is likely to take.

CASE INSIGHT 7.3
GlaxoSmithKline (GSK)

UK

MANAGING CHANGE

In the 1980s pharmaceutical companies regularly turned in operating margins of 40 per cent. These margins were the norm because the companies were able to extend patents almost at will and to charge very high prices for their drugs. A compound could be reformulated with only modest improvements in efficacy, but the regulators and courts seemed happy to grant and protect new patents. Things started to change in the 1990s, however, as companies producing generic imitations started to challenge patent extensions and regulators and courts sided with them. By the turn of 2000, more than 85 per cent of such patents were being overturned. The result was swift and predictable as generic imitations, often originating from low-cost developing countries, started appearing rapidly in the market. The result was that profits plummeted across the sector. At the same time, pharmaceutical firms were finding it increasingly difficult to discover pioneering new drugs at anything like the old rate of invention. With each new drug taking up to 15 years and costing up to $2 billion to develop, it was estimated that if you spent $1 billion a year on research, you needed one new drug approval a year (by the likes of the US Food and Drug Administration) in order to make a satisfactory economic return.

The UK pharmaceutical firm GlaxoSmithKline (GSK) was not immune to those winds of change with sales, profits and new drug approvals falling. As a consequence, in 2008 the company started to restructure and R&D was reorganized into smaller, more market-responsive units. Turnover initially increased before declining between 2010 and 2014, but it subsequently picked up in 2016 and 2017 to £30.2 billion (operating profit £4.1 billion; 13.6 per cent). At present, GSK has three areas of business: pharmaceuticals (57 per cent of turnover), vaccines (17 per cent of turnover) and consumer healthcare (26 per cent of turnover), but whilst consumer healthcare may be buoyant, analysts believe the drugs pipeline is dwindling.

In 2018 GSK announced that it had entered into an agreement with its US rival Pfizer to combine their consumer healthcare businesses into one joint venture, which is expected to lead to sales of almost £13 billion per annum – bringing together popular brands owned by the two firms such as Sensodyne toothpaste, Voltaren and Advil nonsteroidal anti-inflammatory drugs, Panadol painkillers and Centrum multivitamins and saving on distribution costs. GSK stated that the joint venture will become the global market leader in over-the-counter drugs at 7.3 per cent, more than 3 per cent ahead of its nearest competitor. GSK will hold the majority controlling interest of 68 per cent in the new business.

Within three years of closing the deal (expected to be agreed by shareholders in 2019), GSK intends to split into two separate businesses; one to be focused on consumer healthcare and the other for pharma and vaccines. GSK intends to place its debt into the new consumer arm, leaving the pharma/vaccine business with funds for R&D and to purchase emerging new drugs so as to bolster its drugs pipeline. GSK CEO, Emma Walmsley, commented:

> Through the combination of GSK and Pfizer's consumer healthcare businesses we will create substantial further value for shareholders . . . With our future intention to separate, the transaction also presents a clear pathway forward for GSK to create a new global pharmaceuticals/vaccines company, with an R&D approach focused on science related to the immune system, use of genetics and advanced technologies . . . Ultimately, our goal is to create two exceptional, UK-based global companies, with appropriate capital structures, that are each well positioned to deliver improving returns to shareholders and significant benefits to patients and consumers. (www.gsk.com/en-gb/media/press-releases/glaxosmithkline-plc-and-pfizer-inc-to-form-new-world-leading-consumer-healthcare-joint-venture)

Shareholders have been calling for the business to be split for some time. The deal was concluded after three months of secret talks about the possible acquisition of Pfizer by GSK, which failed because the price, at about $20 billion, was thought to be too high. Instead the joint venture was agreed on:

> Even though we knew the deal would be fantastic, the returns weren't what they needed to be. More importantly . . . it would cut across the capital allocation priority I had set since the day I came into the business, which was investing in pharma and the pipeline. I walked away, sadly, but expecting it to go to someone else, but thinking it was the right thing to do . . . [the joint venture] was obvious to me. It was a value creation, and we were able to negotiate it with a very tight, small team quickly and, most importantly, quickly. (The Sunday Times, 23 December 2018)

Earlier in 2018 GSK had bought out the Swiss pharmaceutical firm Novartis from its 36.5 per cent stake in a consumer healthcare joint venture at a cost of over $13 billion, announced a $300 million partnership with the US consumer genetics company 23andMe and bolstered its pharma business with a $5.1 billion acquisition of US oncology specialist Tesaro.

CEO Emma Walmsley only joined the company in 2017 and she had a background in consumer healthcare rather than pharma. She was brought in at a time when the company's share price was underperforming compared to that of its rivals – down 7.7 per cent between 2013 and 2018, compared to that of rivals such as AstraZeneca, which had risen by over 70 per cent over the same period. Despite her lack of pharma experience, she did more to transform the company in the 18 months leading up to joint venture in 2018 than her predecessor had done in the preceding decade. Walmsley's early comments about the pharma business were scathing, observing that GSK's scientists should produce more drugs with commercial prospects and 'stop drifting off in hobby-land'. She acted swiftly – axing some 80 drug programmes and replacing 40 per cent of her top managers. Hal Barron, the former chief medical officer at the Swiss drug manufacturer Roche, was brought in as chief scientific officer and president of R&D. Luke Miels moved from rival AstraZeneca to become head of pharma. These appointments were rumoured not to have gone down well with many research leaders. Although the changes were welcomed by investors, there is still a lot to be done to turn around the pharma side of the company.

Visit the website: **www.gsk.com**

Questions:

1. What are the differences between GSK's pharma and healthcare businesses? Do they require the same approach to management?
2. What are the reasons for this joint venture? Do they make sense?
3. Why did Walmsley say what she did about the pharma business and then make these top management changes? Would you describe her as entrepreneurial?
4. How vulnerable to being merged or taken over by another pharma group in the future do these changes leave GSK's remaining pharma/vaccine business? Explain.

CORPORATE TURNAROUND AND TRANSFORMATION

Chapter 1 highlighted how organizations often slip into bureaucracy as they grow. They stop being entrepreneurial and need a commercial shock to convince them of the need for change. Sometimes that can take the form of external events outside the control of the organization such as the lifting of import barriers, but the crisis is often caused by the company's consistently poor financial performance. It may be that the company finds itself running out of cash and approaching insolvency. Or perhaps the poor performance reflects itself in a plummeting share price and investors see the need to intervene. This crisis may then act as the spur to change that is required for the business to be turned around and transformed – to become entrepreneurial again.

The first thing that needs to be done is to stabilize the company and find sufficient cash to continue in business. This means retrenchment – selling off assets and reducing losses. Unprofitable product lines might be closed down and difficult markets abandoned. Departments, divisions or subsidiaries might be closed or sold off. No cost can be regarded as 'fixed' as the company chips away at its fixed cost base – downsizing and outsourcing. Boyne and Meier (2009) observe that retrenchment involves a focus on efficiency and a refocus on the core business to generate the cash flow needed for survival. What is required is a restructuring plan that addresses both survival and the root causes of failure in the first place so as to ensure that, if at all possible, the assets needed for the future are maintained. This involves undertaking a **strategic review** – a process we consider in Chapter 12.

Most companies facing this situation will need to seek additional finance, perhaps restructuring some of their existing debt by turning it into equity. This may take time, however, and that is often in short supply. There may not be the time to do all the things required amid the competing cash claims of creditors who may believe that if they are not paid quickly they may never see their money. That is why preferential creditors such as banks or, in the UK, tax authorities are often the first to push a company into compulsory insolvency. This involves a court appointing an official liquidator who will look very closely at the actions of the officers of the company; in some circumstances, such as in the mishandling of tax payments, the directors may become personally liable and may face legal consequences. The company will then be sold off, in whole or in part, as a going concern, or the assets of the company will be sold off, often at a discount, to pay the creditors as soon as possible. Most companies would seek to avoid compulsory liquidation and look to other alternatives such as:

> **strategic review** The process of reviewing the business model with a view to improvement

➡ A pre-packaged sale (pre-pack) – which allows the profitable part of the business to continue. The assets are bought out by a 'new' company, leaving the debts with the old company which is placed into liquidation. Eighteen per cent of US bankruptcies in 2016 were pre-packs.
➡ Company voluntary arrangements (CVA) – which, if all creditors agree, allows the company to continue but with creditors agreeing to take longer payment terms and/or reduced amounts.
➡ Administration – which places the company immediately under the protection of the court. It does not need the agreement of creditors and protects the company from any pending legal action. This is designed to provide protection for a limited period while the business is restructured and rescued.
➡ Creditors' voluntary liquidation (CVL) – which liquidates the company's assets, paying the proceeds to creditors.

In 2018 the UK department store House of Fraser entered a CVA. However, when the firm's creditors could not agree terms, it went into administration and its assets (stores, stocks / inventories and brand) were bought by the Sports Direct retail chain for £90 million in cash. This meant expensive store leases could be renegotiated or stores closed. What happened next was typical of company failure: all of the top management team was sacked and many stores closed. The existing management are always at risk when a company fails or is taken over. After all, they were responsible for its leadership and management. However, their departure also symbolizes a break with the past, a need for urgent change within the organization, and that no single employee is immune from this. There is no bigger symbolic action for the need to change. However, changes like this create enormous uncertainty for managers and employees as well as other stakeholders and rebuilding confidence and commitment in the company is a difficult and demanding leadership task. Implementing the changes needed in phase 3 of the Change Curve (Figure 7.1) is hard enough, but reigniting the flame of entrepreneurship can be even more difficult.

CASE INSIGHT 7.4
Nautitech

Australia

CORPORATE TURNAROUND

Founded in 2001, Nautitech is an Australian company that designs, develops, manufactures and installs special-ized mining equipment for extractive mining companies and multinational mining equipment manufacturers. Until the mining boom of 2010, its decision-making, management and administration systems remained largely informal and growth was slow with strategy guided by the founder's product/market knowledge – typical for an entrepre-neurial start-up. The mining boom brought accelerating demand with little pressure on prices. Within three years, turnover tripled and the number of employees increased by more than five times, to 33. However, the company failed to adapt. The lack of controls over product design and quality caused sales to collapse and the staff morale to decline. Having to deal constantly with crises caused by customer complaints, the founders failed to notice changes in the market which meant customers were seeking lifetime product support services, rather than simply the product itself. They failed to notice that their approach to leadership and management needed to change as the business grew. At the same time they failed to recognise the need for business model innovation.

In 2011, the company decided to bring in an independent consultant, to advise on systems for on-time delivery, cost reduction and continuous improvement. By then, however, coal sales were falling, mines were closing and the mining boom was coming to an end. Sales fell by 30 per cent each year for the next two years. And then one of the company's founders died. Rather than close the business, the remaining owner asked the consultant to take over as general manager and implement the turnaround strategy he had proposed. This involved:

➡ Re-engaging with customers to build a reputation for integrity, developing closer relationships with them and regaining their trust, rather than treating every order as a stand-alone transaction;
➡ Refocusing the value proposition on the needs of each individual customer, rather than just the product itself, so as to provide ongoing support for its installation, maintenance and improvement. This required building a direct relationship with end-users rather than relying on equipment producers to install and market the devices.

In the past, the causes of product failures, sources of costs or how designs reflected the priorities of customers was unknown. The company formed improvement teams across its functional areas, including product development, production and marketing to find the answers to these questions and implement quality improvement initiatives. As a result, product reliability improved and the company was able to cut costs. These were then passed on in lower prices and the company started to regain market share.

However, the stress caused by the crisis had led to morale dipping even further, despite staff being assured that there would be no redundancies. Because of the poor reputation of the company, the sales team were initially too reluctant to even go out and face customers. They had to be convinced that things were changing for the better. Revenue-sharing incentives and a bonus system were introduced. At the same time, the company's culture had to change. The new manager wanted to build one that was more values-based, a culture of innovation focused on customer solutions, rather than just products. To build a more open, inclusive and egalitarian culture, privileges based on seniority such as reserved car parking were removed, and career paths, based on merit, were clarified. Some staff felt that their status was being threatened, other that their benefits were being reduced, and they resisted these culture-change initiatives. Nevertheless, the new manager persevered despite the departure of some mem-bers of staff.

Over time, the changes began to take effect and profitability and growth began to pick up. Once this started the company began to recruit new staff, attracted by the success of the company – fresh talent that allowed it to cement its new culture and deepen its management and engineering capabilities. Staff were increasingly involved in decision-making and the recruitment of new staff was based on character and integrity rather than just skills. Success led to success. Growth in 2014–15 exceeded 30 per cent and the company continues to grow.

At the core of turnaround is a culture of disciplined innovation based on defined processes and focussed on customer priorities. Nautitech's portfolio of new products has grown and is now reviewed every two weeks, and the time to market has been more than halved. This culture change has led to growing self-confidence alongside greater openness and more collaborations. Nautitech now works with external engineering groups on aspects of new product development where they are faster or cheaper than an in-house team. It collaborates with a coal miner (Glencore), a mining equipment firm (Komatsu Mining) and two research organizations (CSIRO and the University of Technology Sydney). It keeps abreast of new technologies and uses them to deliver better solutions in the mining industry. It is also aware of the market limitations in Australia and is therefore looking to diversify its customer base to other countries through partnerships – for example, with Saminco in South Africa.

Visit the website on: **nautitech.com.au**

Questions:

1. List the things that needed to change in Nautitech in 2011:
   - in terms of urgency.
   - in terms of importance.
2. How do you reconcile urgency and importance?

Source: Australian Innovation System Report (2017), Australian Government, Department of Industry, Innovation and Science. Available at: publications.industry.gov.au/publications/australianinnovationsystemreport2017/index.html

CASE INSIGHT 7.5
The London School*

UK

MANAGING A TURNAROUND

London School is a multicultural, inner-city, state secondary school in the centre of London. Built in the 1980s to take more than a thousand pupils, a lack of maintenance and capital investment had led to many of the buildings showing signs of 'wear and tear'. One of the challenges for the school was that its catchment area was largely affluent and middle class and that its main competitors were local private schools. At the same time, pupil numbers had been dropping over a number of years, leading to budget cuts. This had, in turn, led to staff also leaving and most of the remaining staff had been in post for many years. Teaching standards and pupil performance were declining and, following an adverse report by the government inspectors (Ofsted), a new headteacher was appointed just as the school was placed under 'special measures', which meant that it required continuing monitoring of its teaching standards until they improved. If they did not, there was a risk that the school would be closed.

The headteacher immediately brought in a number of new senior managers. Together, they imposed a rigid set of demands on the teaching staff in order to get through the follow-up inspection – lesson plans, teaching styles, discipline etc. Classrooms even had to be laid out in a certain way. The initiatives introduced were quite simple, but designed to have a rapid effect on both the behaviour of students and the levels of learning in the classroom. Despite restricting their professional autonomy, staff were compliant, realizing the serious implications should there be no improvement. Within a couple of years, the school began to improve and it was taken out of 'special measures'. That led to increased levels of pupil enrolment and a change in the demographics of the school, in terms of the type of pupil.

Within this turnaround, the school needed to recruit new teachers and it chose to do so through a UK initiative called 'Teach First' which recruited high-achieving graduates and placed them in schools under the supervision of local universities. The school took in some ten new teachers. This is when a new set of problems started to emerge. As they settled into their career and qualified as teachers, these recruits became increasingly frustrated by the lack of autonomy teachers had within the school. Despite their enthusiasm to be creative and innovative in their teaching, the headteacher continued to demand that they stick rigidly to the school's teaching policies and practices. He was now used to operating as a leader in a school in crisis and found it hard to change his style in order to develop a different culture, one that would have allowed ideas to come from across the school rather than just from the senior staff and, if harnessed properly could have been instrumental in taking the school to the next level.

Questions:

1. Was the headteacher right to be authoritarian and impose such rigid teaching policies and procedures to turn the school around?
2. How easy is it to now change these policies and procedures? Should they be changed?
3. What are the dangers the school faces if they were to change?
4. What are the dangers if they were not to change?
5. What does this tell you about the context of leadership and management?

*The facts of the case are accurate but the name of the school has been changed.
Case contributed by Dr Jean Burns.

SUSTAINABLE ENTREPRENEURSHIP

Whilst survival may be a very immediate and compelling reason to justify change, the need to be more socially and environmentally responsible and sustainable (CSR) can be just as important for a company – and for society as a whole. Many business practices can have a negative social or environmental impact, yet because they have been in place for such a long time they can become part of the accepted way of doing things, the dominant logic of the organization. The threats and opportunities presented are enormous but may not seem as quite so immediate, which can make it more difficult to change an organization. Nevertheless, an entrepreneurial architecture needs to have sustainability embedded in it through its culture (values and beliefs) and its strategies.

> " *I think every business needs a leader that does not forget the massive impact business can have on the world. All business leaders should be thinking 'how can I be a force for good?' What I see is demand from our people to be a business that is good, makes a profit, but also does something for the planet and humanity. I think this is a trend we will see more of . . . CSR in my mind is defunct now. Compartmentalizing the social responsibility is not the way to go. I think the model for starting employee engagement activities has to be embedded in everything you do.* "
>
> Richard Branson, founder Virgin Group, *HRM Magazine*,
> 13 July 2010 on: www.hrmagazine.co.uk

Chapter 1 catalogued many of the threats posed by irresponsible ethical, social and environmental policies, from the corporate scandals to the environmental disasters. These damage brands and can threaten the very survival of some companies, let alone affecting the lives of investors, customers and society as a whole. However, as Kurucz et al. (2008) pointed out, high levels of CSR and awareness can actually enhance shareholder value by linking economic and social and environmental goals – creating commercial opportunities out of the needs of society. There are four reasons for this:

1. Many of the measures to become more sustainable and reduce pollution involve measuring and controlling inputs, and many environmental initiatives therefore also reduce costs (e.g., reducing waste and recycling, having better control of building temperatures or reducing use of agrochemicals). Yahoo saved 60 per cent of its electricity costs simply by opening windows where servers are located so as to let out the hot air. Similarly, Coca-Cola reduced gas usage by 10 per cent by simply installing a heat recovery system in its factory in Edmonton, UK. This is part of the company's 'Action on Climate' programme which aims to cut greenhouse gas emissions from its core business by 50 per cent by 2025. It is doing this by looking at its complete supply chain, its use of renewable energy and recycled materials and the use of more efficient coolers and vending machines. Waste-reducing cost savings can come from looking at raw materials usage, the manufacturing process, packaging requirements, transport needs, maintenance and the use of disposal methods. Many small steps can contribute to large savings for a company. For example, many companies are now following environmentally (more) friendly policies simply because it cuts their costs and keeps them competitive.

> " *More than ever, consumers expect brands to be environmentally aware. They want to invest financially and emotionally in a product and, at start-up, you can't ignore that.* "
>
> Chris Holmes, founder Woodbuds, *The Sunday Times*, 28 June 2015

2. The need to reduce waste alongside developing sustainable energy sources and means of using them can present opportunities for both radical and incremental innovation as consumers press for change. A whole new industry has been spawned in waste recycling. The Spanish company Plastic Energy, for example, has developed a patented thermal anaerobic technology (TAC) process that can be used to turn plastic waste into a renewable energy resource called TACOIL. It started production in Spain in 2014 and plans to expand, firstly in Europe, and then globally. China has recognized the opportunities created by the need to develop renewable energy sources and has pushed ahead in developing technologies for wind-farm turbines and solar power, at the same time as achieving the economies of scale to make the new technologies affordable, thus giving it a dominant market position. Battery technology is now improving to such an extent that electric-powered cars (and other products) will become a common sight on our streets over the next decade. Alongside this, developments in other technologies to reduce pollution should help us move (albeit slowly) towards a greener future – spurred on by the commercial opportunities. Innovation linked to sustainability often has major systems-level implications, demanding a holistic and integrated approach to innovation management. General Electric started an environmental sustainability programme in 2004. By 2008, this had yielded $100 million in savings and 80 new products and services that generated $17 million in revenues.

> **❝** *Doing good work for the planet creates new markets and makes [us] more money* **❞**
>
> Rose Marcario, CEO Patagonia, *FastCompany*, 21 February 2018 at:
> **www.fastcompany.com/company/patagonia**

3. Actions to improve working conditions, lessen environmental impact or increase employee involvement in decision-making can improve workforce productivity. For example, actions to improve work conditions in the supply chain have been seen to lead to decreases in defect rates in merchandise. Many social initiatives can increase employee motivation and cut absenteeism and staff turnover. An increasing number of graduates take CSR issues into consideration when making employment decisions.

4. Having a brand or a company associated with high levels of CSR can promote a more distinctive brand identity, attract new customers and increase loyalty by helping to differentiate it from competitors, as is the case for companies like Lush (Case insight 6.1) and Patagonia (Case insight 7.6). To be effective, these differentiating factors need to be real rather than just being reflected in marketing and PR. CSR needs to be built into the strategic decision-making of the organization.

> **❝** *We're really noticing people's perceptions changing. More than ever they want products that are sustainable but without sacrificing style or quality* **❞**
>
> Heather Wittle, founder Beyond Skin, *The Sunday Times*, 28 June 2015

We look at how entrepreneurial architecture creates sustainable shareholder value in Chapter 15, but is there any evidence that CSR specifically can help do this? Porter and Kramer (2002, 2006) believed that social and economic goals can be aligned. They believe that a firm's capabilities and relationships can be leveraged in support of social, environmental and philanthropic causes whilst at the same time creating shareholder value. But can this be proved? The quest to link corporate CSR directly to financial performance and/or share price performance spans some 40 years and the results have often been contradictory and confusing. Nevertheless, in a review and assessment of 127 empirical studies, Margolis and Walsh (2003) concluded that there was a positive relationship between CSR and financial performance, a result that is supported in a meta-survey by Orlitzy et al. (2003). Looking at investment portfolios, Ven de Velde et al. (2005) concluded that high-sustainability-rated portfolios (ones that integrated environmental, social and ethical issues) performed better than low-rated portfolios. Furthermore, an Economic Intelligence Unit Survey in 2008 showed that the vast majority of US business leaders and their boards of directors now accept a clear relationship between CSR and financial performance (Business Green, 2008).

In a review of the literature, Carroll and Shabana (2010) concluded that on the whole a positive relationship exists between CSR and financial performance, 'but inconsistencies linger'. This is because financial performance is affected by many other internal and external variables, not all controlled by the firm. In addition, 'the benefits of CSR are not homogeneous, and effective CSR initiatives are not generic'. They concluded that CSR activities need to be part of a coherent and consistent strategy that is directed at improving both stakeholder relationships and social welfare. They talked about 'a convergence between economic and social goals' – where social good is crafted into creating economic value. This requires an innovative approach to embedding CSR into the business model of any new products or services (Chapter 12). Sustainable entrepreneurship involves having CSR at the heart of the business and ensuring that creating social good and shareholder value go hand in hand.

🔍 EXPLORE FURTHER

Planet Mark is a mark that assures customers that the organization it is purchasing from is active in improving its environmental and social performance. Established in 2013 by the Eden Project and the sustainability consultancy Planet First, businesses achieving the mark are then helped to monitor their environmental impact and lessen it, as well as encouraging their employees, customers and stakeholders to take action.

Visit the website: theplanetmark.com

The Institute of Corporate Responsibility and Sustainability (ICRS) is a not-for-profit professional membership body established in 2014 by a number of leading companies to help promote CSR and sustainability through seminars and other events.

Visit the website: icrs.info

CASE INSIGHT 7.6
Patagonia

USA

RECONCILING CSR AND COMMERCIAL OBJECTIVES

The US outdoor apparel company Patagonia is an independent private benefit corporation* based in Ventura, California. Founded in 1973, it now employs some 1000 people and has revenues of over $209 million. It is well known for its high-profile CSR policies, mainly focused on environmental issues and climate change. For example, it set up the *One Per cent for the Planet* organization and each year it commits 1 per cent of its sales or 10 per cent of its profits (whichever is the higher) to environmental groups. But it came as quite a shock to find that in November 2018 its founder, Yvon Chouinard, had decided to give back a further $10 million in tax cuts to those same environmental groups. CEO Rose Marcario wrote in her LinkedIn announcement:

> *Based on last year's irresponsible tax cut [by US President Donald Trump], Patagonia will owe less in taxes this year. We are responding by putting $10 million back into the planet because our home needs it more than we do.*

Patagonia has also been politically active on behalf of the environment for some time, becoming the first US commercial brand to publicly endorse political candidates. It called President Trump a liar on the issue of public lands protection when, in 2017, he cut federal protection for 85 per cent of the Bears Ears National Monument (1.35 million acres of high desert designated a national monument by President Obama) and for almost 50 per cent of the Grand Staircase-Escalante National Monument (1.9 million acres, which includes The Grand Canyon). Together with others, it then filed suit to block the reductions, arguing that the president had no legal right to shrink a national monument. As part of its campaign, Patagonia changed its website to a black screen with the words: 'The President Stole Your Land'.

Marcario believes that a socially responsible and sustainable business can be both competitive and profitable. In 2016, at the instigation of its employees, it gave away all of the sales from its 'Black Friday' sales to environmental organizations. On that day, the company raised $10 million and signed up some 24,000 new customers. Marcario says she strives to embrace risk by acting 'quickly and decisively', but not by sacrificing the future, eschewing what she calls the business world's 'suicidal' addiction to quarterly earnings. According to her, 'Earnings per share is a like a chain around the neck of the country.' An article in *FastCompany* in 2018 said:

> *Patagonia's corporate campus in Ventura feels more like a beach town community college than home to one of the world's most influential apparel brands. Solar panels dot the parking lot, where surfboards and wet suits are splayed atop Priuses and beat-up trucks. The original tin shed where Chouinard first pounded out climbing pitons to sell still sits steps away on its original site, and accents the rustic vibe you'd expect from a company whose founder authored a book titled Let My People Go Surfing. [1]*

Patagonia uses its brand popularity to raise awareness around environmental issues such as climate change, investing in grassroots organizations and in companies developing technologies that will help make its supply chain and products more sustainable. It believes in fair trade and has invested in new recycling and sustainable materials initiatives while also challenging various government policies. It also invests in start-ups that complement Patagonia's mission.

Patagonia now has almost 500 fair-trade products, sewn in eight countries, including India, Thailand, Colombia, Vietnam, Nicaragua and Mexico. Factory workers receive collective bonus payments that can be distributed as cash or democratically used for a social investment like daycare. It has worked to reduce waste, eliminate packaging and increase its use of recycled materials. For example, it worked with the supplier Primaloft to develop a recycled insulation material for its jackets.

Worn Wear

By focusing on reducing waste and extending the life of its clothing, Patagonia has developed a new market for used goods. 'Worn Wear' started as a high street initiative with flagship stores accepting worn merchandise. This then developed into a 're-commerce' platform, which encourages customers to trade in old gear, offering them gift certificates for future purchases if they send in used clothing. It also attracts younger consumers for its more affordable, 'repurposed' clothing. As a result, the company has started its own clothing repair centre in Reno, Nevada. This initiative started in 2011 as a campaign by the company for people to repair and reuse clothing. In response to customer demand, they then created a market with eBay for customers to trade items they no longer needed (then called *Common Threads*). Within 18 months they had repaired over 30,000 items and, contrary to what you might expect, they also saw sales of new products increase by 30 per cent. Patagonia sold $1 million worth of used clothes via the new Worn Wear in the first six months of its site. The director of corporate development, Phil Graves, explained the company's strategy:

> [Worn Wear] makes our brand more accessible to college kids and others who are looking for lower price points . . . It was a cool idea to keep our gear in use longer but now it's this fledgling e-commerce business that we want to grow in a big way. The goal is to encourage every major brand to have their own re-commerce site behind their apparel. [1]

Tin Shed Ventures

Patagonia has its own venture capital arm called Tin Shed Ventures that invests in food, energy, water, waste, and apparel innovations. One of its investments, Yerdle, helped take Worn Wear online. Another portfolio company, Beyond Surface Technologies, developed environmentally-friendly textile treatments that use natural solutions to make fabrics water-repellent. The treatments are used in some of Patagonia's clothing.

Patagonia Provisions

By funding small, environmentally responsible initiatives, Patagonia has helped produce major strides in materials science as well as regenerative agriculture that produce lower carbon emissions, leading to it launching its own food line, Patagonia Provisions. The company considers it to be an 'innovation lab' for developing standards in regenerative organic agriculture – sustainable farming that uses fewer resources and is better for the soil.

Patagonia Action Works

Patagonia has created a digital hub called Patagonia Action Works, part social network, part recruiting tool, to connect stakeholders with the grassroots organizations the company supports. It is integrated into the company's e-commerce site and leverages up the brand image of the company, helping individuals connect and society more generally. As Marcario explains: 'This [is a] tool that helps people contribute skills, to volunteer, [attend] a city council meeting, run for office, start their own NGO.'

Visit the website: eu.patagonia.com

Questions:

1. How has Patagonia reconciled CSR with commercial viability?
2. How important is it to the brand image of the company? What are the strengths and weaknesses of this sort of brand?
3. If you wish to achieve a strong brand based upon CSR, how important is it that CSR is integrated into every aspect of a company's operations?

*A private benefit corporation is a private, for-profit corporation that includes positive impact on society, workers, the community and the environment in addition to profit as its legally defined goals.

[1] 'How Patagonia Grows Every Time It Amplifies Its Social Mission', *FastCompany*, 21 February 2018 on: www.fastcompany.com/company/patagonia)

SUMMARY

➡ People resist change even if it is for their own good; often a severe crisis is needed before changes are initiated in an organization. To facilitate change, 'political and organizational' and 'people-orientated' actions need to be undertaken simultaneously. Figure 7.3 demonstrates the complexity of what is required with all aspects of strategy and organization potentially having to change in both the concrete and conceptual dimensions and the formal and informal dimensions.

➡ In working through change, organizations experience three phases:

- Immobilization and denial;
- Depression and letting go;
- Testing the new reality and putting it together.

➡ Change starts at the top. It often needs a crisis before radical changes in top management are made are the resulting reappraisal of strategies, policies and procedures. New people are often brought in to effect changes quickly.

➡ Successful turnaround involves stabilizing the company and finding sufficient cash to continue in business. It needs a restructuring plan that addresses both survival and the root causes of past failure. This usually involves retrenchment – selling off assets, reducing losses with a focus on efficiency and a refocus on the core business so as to generate the cash flow needed. No cost can be regarded as 'fixed' as the company chips away at its fixed cost base – downsizing and outsourcing. However at the same time the company must look to the future - and that involves developing its entrepreneurial capabilities.

➡ As well as being worthwhile in its own right, CSR can add shareholder value by cutting costs, enhancing brand identity, creating commercial opportunity and improving staff motivation. Many companies need to change how they operate by developing CSR policies, recognising both the opportunities and threats that societal and environmental changes bring.

GROUP DISCUSSION TOPICS

1. Why might the seven conventional management techniques listed discourage corporate entrepreneurship? Can you think of other examples that fit with the classifications proposed by Michael Morris?
2. Looking back at Chapter 4, which countries are likely to be most resistant to risk-taking?
3. Looking back at Chapter 4, which countries are likely to be most resistant to change?
4. Meyer's research in (see Chapter 4) noted that Japanese culture is one of high power distance (which favours hierarchy) but is also consensual. It is also not comfortable airing differences. How do you reconcile this with Toyota's use of the 'Andon cord' in Case insight 7.1?
5. Does your national culture accept failure? Does it encourage success? What are the implications of your views for corporate entrepreneurship?
6. You can never change people. Discuss.
7. Change can be created, but never managed. Discuss.
8. Are the interrelationships in effecting change highlighted in Figure 7.3 so complicated that no major change initiative is ever likely to be 100 per cent successful?
9. Why is a critical event so often necessary for change to happen?
10. What are the critical factors in making a change initiative successful?
11. Is turning around a failing organization more difficult than starting up one?
12. Once an organization starts to be unresponsive to change there is no point in trying to change it. Discuss.
13. Why should you try to turn around a failing organization?
14. What moral and ethical boundaries would you place on business?
15. What constitutes sustainable entrepreneurship?
16. Does environmental sustainability put an organization at a competitive disadvantage?
17. The law defines the extent of a company's ethical and social responsibilities. Discuss.
18. What is CSR? How do you measure it and how do you judge whether it has been successfully implemented?
19. How might CSR add shareholder value?
20. Is it ethical to make profit from CSR?

ACTIVITIES

1. Using an example of a major change of which you have experience, chart how the changes were made, the problems encountered and the solutions put in place. Were the changes successful? Explain.
2. Find a company that has faced a crisis of some sort that required it to make major changes and. Write a report describing the changes, how they were managed, and analyzing their effectiveness.
3. Find a company that uses CSR as part of its marketing and write a report explaining how it does this and analyzing its effectiveness.

REFERENCES

Boyne, G.A. and Meier, K. (2009) 'Environmental Change, Human Resources and Organizational Turnaround', *Journal of Management Studies*, 46(5).

Business Green (2008) 'US Execs: CSR Initiatives Do Boost the Bottom Line', www.BusinessGreen.com.

Carroll, A.B. and Shabana, K.M. (2010) 'The Business Case for Corporate Social Responsibility: A Review of Concepts, Research and Practise', *International Journal of Management Reviews*, www.academia.edu.

Clemmer, J. (1995) Pathways to Performance: A Guide to Transforming Yourself, Your Team and Your Organization, Toronto: Macmillan Canada.

Hamel, G. (2000) 'Reinvent Your Company', *Fortune*, 12, June.

Jackson, S. and Schuler, R. (2001) 'Turning Knowledge into Business Advantage', in J. Pickford (ed.), *Mastering Management 2.0*, London: Prentice Hall.

Kakabadse, A. (1983) *The Politics of Management*, London: Gower.

Kotter, J.P. (1996) *Leading Change*, Boston, MA: Harvard Business School Press.

Kotter, J.P. and Cohen, D.S. (2002) *The Heart of Change*, Boston, MA: Harvard Business School Press.

Kubler-Ross, E. (1969) *On Death and Dying*, New York, NY: Macmillan.

Kurucz, E., Colbert, B. and Wheeler, D. (2008) 'The Business Case for Corporate Social Responsibility'. In A. Crane, A. McWilliams, D. Matten, J. Moon and D. Seigel (eds), *The Oxford Handbook of Corporate Social Responsibility*, Oxford: Oxford University Press.

Lewin, K. (1947) 'Frontiers in Group Dynamics: Concept, Method and Reality in Social Science; Social Equilibria and Social Change', *Human Relations*, June.

Margolis, J.D. and Walsh, J.P. (2003) 'Misery Loves Companies: Rethinking Social Initiatives by Business', *Administrative Science Quarterly*, 48.

Mintzberg, H. (1998) in H. Mintzberg, B. Ahlstrand and J. Lempel, *Strategy Safari*, New York, NY: The Free Press.

Morris, M.H. (1998) *Entrepreneurial Intensity*, Westport, CT: Quorum Books.

Orlitzy, M., Schmidt, F.L. and Rynes, S.L. (2003) 'Corporate Social Performance: A Meta-Analysis', *Organization Studies*, 24.

Porter, M.E. and Kramer, M.R. (2002) 'The Competitive Advantage of Corporate Philanthropy', *Harvard Business Review*, December.

Porter, M.E. and Kramer, M.R. (2006) 'Strategy and Society: The Link Between Competitive Advantage and Corporate Social Responsibility', *Harvard Business Review*, 12.

Sirkin, H.L., Keenan, P. and Jackson, A. (2005) 'The Hard Side of Change Management', *Harvard Business Review*, October.

Srivastava, N. and Agrawal, A. (2010) 'Factors Supporting Corporate Entrepreneurship: An Explorative Study', *Vision: The Journal of Business Perspective*, 14(3).

Ven de Velde, E., Vermeir, W. and Corten, F. (2005) 'Corporate Social Responsibility and Financial Performance', *Corporate Governance*, 5(3).

Yukl, G. (2002) *Leadership in Organizations*, Upper Saddle River, NJ: Prentice Hall Inc.

 ONLINE RESOURCES AVAILABLE **For further resources relating to this chapter see the companion website at www.macmillanihe.com/Burns-CEI**

8 Managing risk in the entrepreneurial organization

CONTENTS

CASE INSIGHTS

Learning outcomes

When you have read this chapter and undertaken the related activities you will be able to:

➡ Understand that people are naturally risk-averse for gains and risk-seeking for losses and explain the consequences of this bias;

➡ Understand the difference between 'known-unknowns' and 'unknown-unknowns' and the risk management techniques appropriate to the different situations;

➡ Use the risk management framework outlined in this chapter to identify risk, evaluate the probability of it materializing, quantify its impact and find ways to mitigating it;

➡ Understand and explain the nature of financing risk and how it might be mitigated or avoided.

BIAS AND RISK-TAKING

The previous chapter looked at the challenges of managing change in the entrepreneurial organization. This chapter looks at the challenges of managing risk. Because it operates in a changing, uncertain environment and/or is introducing frequent or radical innovation, the entrepreneurial organization probably faces greater risks than other organizations. The skill of risk management is therefore important. Remember from Chapter 1 how entrepreneurs appear to make extensive use of 'cognitive heuristics' based upon their past experiences (Delmar, 2000). This helps them make quick decisions and can lead to better decision-making with good information flows. However, entrepreneurs are inherently confident in their ability to influence outcomes and this can lead to over-optimism, perhaps reflecting itself in an inherent bias towards riskier projects (or at least a willingness to accept risks that others might not). This underlines the need for simple, speedy risk management processes in an organization, based on open and accurate information flows.

First it is worth exploring in greater detail how people in general arrive at risky decisions, and what role cognitive heuristics might play. The brain has two different systems or ways of working that are interlinked and complimentary but function in different ways. Different authors have used various names for these two systems, but largely agree on how they interact:

➡ System 1 (often referred to as 'right-brain*' and intuitively called 'the heart') – This is more intuitive and emotional. It is non-verbal, linking images together to get a holistic perspective (also called creative or lateral thinking). The right-brain (System 1) is most likely to engage first. It is automatic and involuntary. Dominant right-brain thinkers are more intuitive, value-based and non-linear in their approach. The right-brain is often the source of the 'hunch' or 'gut-feeling' that people refer to in coming to some decision or conclusion about a situation. It often relies on past experience for this and is probably the source of the cognitive heuristics used by entrepreneurs. It is therefore a source for quick decision-making, but can prove to be inaccurate once the left-brain is engaged and rational analysis is undertaken. Right-brain thinkers tend to prefer working in groups, experiencing things (for example, 'learning by doing') and generating lots of options in preference to focusing on making a speedy decision which might be based on incomplete data.

➡ System 2 (often referred to as 'left-brain*' and intuitively called 'the head') – This performs rational, logical functions. It tends to be verbal and analytic, operating in a linked, linear sequence (also called logical or vertical thinking). The left-brain (System 2) takes effort and concentration to engage. Although this is the analytical side, it can be distracted or disrupted when attention is drawn elsewhere. Because it takes effort, the mind does not always use this side, relying instead on the intuition of the right-side. Dominant left-brain thinkers tend to be rational, logical, analytical and sequential in their approach to problem-solving. This cognitive style is also reflected in their preferred working styles with left-brain thinkers tending to prefer working alone, learning about things rather than experiencing them and having the ability or preference to focus on making quick, logical decisions.

---

*NB: the division between right- and left-brain activities has no neurological foundation. In fact the brain comprises numerous different parts and is made up of innumerable neurons and axons.

You use both sides of your brain, shifting naturally from one to the other in different situations. Mostly they work together, although sometimes they can be in conflict. However, both sides are liable to bias and are not always rational. The right-brain reacts quickly and relies heavily on instinct. Instinct can be deep-seated. As we observed, for many animals change in the environment is treated with fear. It signifies risk and danger and puts the animal on its guard. The right-brain is therefore inherently risk-averse for most people. The left-brain takes more effort and therefore requires willpower to engage. To show this, Kahneman (2012) asked readers to make two concurrent or joint decisions by making two choices:

Decision 1:   A: A sure gain of $240, or
                        B: 25% chance to gain $1000 and 75% chance to gain nothing

AND

Decision 2:   C: A sure loss of $750, or
                        D: 75% chance to lose $1000 and 25% chance to lose nothing

He observed that most (but not all) people select options A and D – an instinctive right-brain reaction based on the certainty of A being a sure gain and D an uncertain (as opposed to certain) loss. Most people are risk-averse to gains – they prefer the certainty of a small gain [A] and risk-seeking for losses – they prefer to gamble and avoid the certainty of loss [D].

However, he also observed that most people do not calculate all the combinations of options open to them: [AC], [AD – as selected], [BC] and [BD]. This is a left-brain operation involving a calculation. If you make the calculation you find options [BC] and [BD] – not [AD] – offer the lowest loss:

Decision 1:   A: A sure gain of $240
$$= 100\% \times \$240 = +\$240$$
                     B: 25% chance to gain $1000 and 75% chance to gain nothing
$$= [25\% \times \$1000] + [75\% \times 0] = +\$250$$

Decision 2:   C: A sure loss of $750
$$= 100\% \times \$750 = -\$750$$
                     D: 75% chance to lose $1000 and 25% chance to lose nothing
$$= [75\% \times \$1000] \times [25\% \times 0] = -\$750$$

Option [AC]: +$240 − $750 = −$510
Option [AD]: +$240 − $750 = −$510
Option [BC]: +$250 − $750 = −$500
Option [BD]: +$250 − $750 = −$500

Kahneman (2012) then posed the following decision choice:

    [AD]: 25% chance to win $240 *and* 75% chance to lose $760
    OR
    [BC]: 25% chance to win $250 *and* 75% chance to lose $750

This time he observed that most people select [BC], which is, of course, the better (least worse) option:

    [AD]: (25% × $240) − (75% × $760) = −$510
    [BC]: (25% × $250) − (75% × $750) = −$500

The issue here, however, is that [BC] is just the combination of the rejected options in the previous decision problem. Not only do we have risk-averse biases, but our decision-making can be influenced by how the decision is presented or framed. Kahneman observes: 'Every simple choice formulated in terms of gains and losses can be decomposed in innumerable ways into a combination of choices, yielding preferences that are likely to be inconsistent . . . It is costly to be risk-averse for gains and risk-seeking for losses. These attitudes make you pay a premium to obtain a sure gain rather than a gamble, and also willing to pay a premium (in expected value) to avoid a sure loss.' As Kahneman showed, many other factors can affect our judgement and decisions such as our mood, norms, 'anchor' numbers which set expectations, associative thinking, triggers such as food and mood music, an exaggerated faith in small numbers or personal examples, even the font size on a report. All these factors can affect the cognitive heuristics individuals might use in making decisions involving risks.

It is also worth reflecting on the impact of having this sort of risk-averse decision-making across a large company. If all the projects it undertakes are risk-averse for gains and risk-seeking for losses, consider the effect on innovation – and the effect on earnings. As we shall consider in Chapter 14, a large company is likely to have a portfolio of projects, allowing it to spread some of the project risks (to fully spread risk the projects need to be independent). It therefore needs some higher-risk projects to balance off against lower-risk projects: it wins a few, it loses a few. A survey by the Boston Consulting Group found that many larger companies were risk-averse and this was a major barrier to innovation (BCG, 2018).

'KNOWN-UNKNOWNS' AND 'UNKNOWN-UNKNOWNS'

As we have seen, decision options need to be framed as broadly as possible, with all options and combinations of options considered. They also need to be evaluated systematically, using formal frameworks so as to force us to use the left- rather than just the right-brain – reconciling the apparent risk-taking of entrepreneurs with the risk-aversion of most people. However, they also need to be based upon as much information as possible – from both inside and outside the organization – perhaps phasing a project so as to allow more information about the risks associated with it to be collected and assessed as the project develops.

In 2002 Donald Rumsfeld, then US Secretary of State for Defence, famously said that there were 'known-unknowns' and 'unknown-unknowns'. This apposite observation underlines two approaches to risk management. The first is the more traditional, quantitative framework where the risks can be identified (the risks are known) and an attempt is made to quantify their probability of happening and the likely impact they will have. The risk management framework outlined in this chapter cover these 'known-unknowns'. This approach works best for projects involving incremental innovations where there is information that can be applied to the decision.

The second situation is where the risks cannot be identified (the risks are unknown) – for example, some natural disaster that has never struck before. When a project involves many unknown factors, such as whether or not a new technology might work and whether or not there might be a market demand for it, these are unknown risks where the impact cannot be quantified and their likelihood of occurrence is equally unquantifiable – 'unknown-unknowns'. This is often the entrepreneurial context, where there is very little information available. The approach involves setting stages for a project, limiting the financial exposure at each stage, and then deciding whether to continue, based on the information gained at each the end of that stage. At no point should the financial exposure threaten the financial viability of the firm. This is achieved by **compartmentalizing the risk** in some way. For example, there is an approach that involves setting an 'affordable loss' – an acceptable budget (or loss) for the project – and then letting the project run to gain more information. We shall consider this approach in Chapter 11. On a larger scale, an innovative project might be set up as a separate legal entity so that if it fails the holding company will not be jeopardized. This approach works for the most innovative projects and is probably the only realistic way to approach projects involving radical innovation.

compartmentalizing risk Setting up each operation as a separate legal entity

> " It's easy to take a risk when it's just a couple of founders working from a garage; risk taking is part of a start-up's DNA. When your business grows, you still need to take risks, except there's a lot more at stake. Sometimes 'betting the company' is essential, but other times the reward needs to be weighed up against the risks for shareholders, customers and clients. We take lots of risks but only when the odds are in our favour. "
>
> Adam Schwab, founder Lux Group, *The Sydney Morning Herald*, 28 April 2014

 CASE INSIGHT 8.1
BP and Deepwater Horizon
 UK

CONTROL VS RISK

Chapter 5 looked at the managerial 'balance' needed between autonomy and control. However, you might think that BP proved an unfortunate example for Birkinshaw (2003) to use when he looked at this, given the explosion in 2010 on the Deepwater Horizon offshore oil rig that cost 11 lives and caused a vast oil spillage across in the Gulf of Mexico. This disaster brought the notion of 'balance' into question when the risks faced were so great. Although financially very successful, at least in the period up to 2010, BP clearly got the balance wrong and took too many risks. In fact, it had already demonstrated this with the explosion in the Texas City oil refinery in 2005 that cost 15 lives with 170 injuries and the Prudhoe Bay pipeline burst in 2006 for which it was fined $20 million. So what went wrong and why?

In the 1980s, BP was seen as a cumbersome, bureaucratic organization spread across too many lines of business. In the late 1990s, BP slimmed down its range of activities and changed direction to focus its exploration activities on riskier, 'new frontiers' of oil and gas exploration that would also yield higher returns. It also flattened its organization and decentralized in the way Birkinshaw described, reducing the size of its headquarters and establishing a number of business units, so as to encourage entrepreneurship and risk-taking. BP encouraged the use of self-managed teams as a way of organizing the different layers of management and engineering, encouraging the horizontal rather than vertical flow of information. Heads of business units, which included managers of oil fields, were given more authority to run things the way they wanted to so long as they met performance targets. These were, in turn, linked to bonuses and rewards – loose control with tight accountability. As already observed, once targets were agreed they had 'free rein to deliver on their contract in whatever way they see fit, within a set of identified constraints'.

Birkinshaw's article was published in 2003, but BP's highly decentralized, entrepreneurial approach was reinforced when a new CEO, Tony Hayward, took over in 2007. He reorganized roles, reducing the number of senior executives from 650 to 500 (mainly in head office) and replacing almost a third. Despite the incidents in 2005 and 2007, he emphasized the need for operational efficiency and cost-cutting in what was, essentially, a commodity supplier that needed maximum efficiency. The continued slimming down of BP's layers of management and specialist expertise was accompanied by increasing subcontracting of operational activities. In this model the self-managed teams, including subcontractors, were responsible for all aspects of project management from costs to safety, with the inevitable tensions and conflict of interests that creates. However, this model continued to deliver good profits. Although BP regularly stated safety was its primary consideration, the team responsible for Deepwater Horizon (which included the subcontractor Halliburton, who installed the cement casings and caps that ruptured) clearly got the balance wrong. But why?

Visit the website: **www.bp.com**

Questions:

1. Was the risk behind this disaster a 'known-unknown' or a 'unknown-unknown'?
2. Given the reputational importance of safety at the corporate level, was there sufficient 'direction' from head office at project level? Was there too much 'direction' given regarding the importance of cost efficiency?
3. Was there any mechanism for resolving the conflict between safety and cost, within BP and with its subcontractors such as Halliburton?
4. Was there sufficient management and technical support at project level in what was generally regarded as a complex and challenging drilling environment? How does the involvement of subcontractors affect this?
5. How can a company make judgements about the degree of direction, support, space and boundaries? Does this change at different levels in the organization?
6. With such enormous risks to life and the environment, was it appropriate to adopt entrepreneurial management structures at the project level in BP? If so, what safeguards would you want to prevent this disaster happening again?

A RISK MANAGEMENT FRAMEWORK

Most organizational control systems are aimed at minimizing risk/uncertainty and promoting efficiency and effectiveness. However, efficiency and effectiveness can be the enemy of entrepreneurship and innovation. By definition, a highly efficient organization has no slack. Everything is tightly controlled, every penny accounted for, all jobs are defined and individuals made to conform. This environment might lead to high degrees of efficiency but it does not encourage entrepreneurship and innovation. On the other hand, entrepreneurship and innovation can be risky – and the more frequent and radical the innovations being introduced by an organization, the higher the risks it faces. The previous section highlighted the need to approach decision-making and risk assessment systematically. Any form of general risk management involves a four-stage process:

1. Identify the risks that might be faced (the known-unknowns).
2. Assess the likelihood, impact and controllability of those risks.

3. Decide on how the risks can be mitigated (reduced or avoided).
4. Deciding what early warning signs need to be monitored to identify when the risks start materializing.

The first step is to identify what the risks might be. Risks can either relate to a specific project – project risk – or to the business as a whole – corporate risk. Of course, you cannot hope to predict all eventualities, but the more you try to anticipate them, the more you are able to generate both plans to deal with these risks and strategic options about the changes in direction that might result. Risk can take a number of forms. The corporate risks an organization faces may come from:

➡ External incidents (e.g., flood, fire and pandemic illness, etc.): These can be difficult to predict and the probability of occurrence might be low. However, the possible impact might be so great – for example, loss of life – such that contingency plans are needed to deal with them. Some of these risks will constitute a generic risk to an industry. For example, the reaction of competitors.

➡ Internal incidents (e.g., loss of sources of supply, malfunction of a major machine and product contamination etc.): These can be many and varied, depending on the operations of the business. A good place to start looking for possibilities is in the key operating activities of the business.

If we are looking at a technology-based start-up project, for example, we might say that there are four key risks:

➡ Technology risk – Will it work?
➡ Market risk – Will anybody buy it (if it works)?
➡ Financing risk – Will anybody finance it until it generates a positive cash flow?
➡ Business risk – Is there a management team able to operationalize the business model and make this into a sustainable business?

Simply **brainstorming** the risks faced is one approach, but another that can be useful is **scenario planning** (Chapter 12). Based on the threats an organization faces, scenarios can be explored about the results of these threats materializing. However, no matter how thorough the analysis, it is impossible to identify every possible risk. As has been said, the only two certain things in life are death and taxes, and some multinationals are working to reduce the latter.

brainstorming
A group activity that generates as many ideas as possible without criticism

scenario planning
A technique that tries to assess how possible future situations might impact on a firm

ASSESSING RISKS

Identifying risks is only the start of the process of risk management, because not all risks are the same. Equally important is trying to estimate the probability and impact of the risk materializing. If the probability is very low, is there any point in preparing contingency plans? The answer may be 'yes' – if the impact on the business was large, but risk management is about prioritization. Ideally, the risks with the highest probability of occurrence and the greatest loss to the organization are handled first and those with the lowest probability of occurrence and the smallest loss are dealt with last. However, super-imposed on this is the issue of whether or not the risks are controllable – whether they can be mitigated or reduced in some way. Generally, the less the risk can be controlled or influenced, the greater the danger it poses.

> " Mapping the risks and opportunities for your business early on can make all the difference. "
>
> Richard Branson, founder Virgin Group, *The Guardian, Media Planet*, May 2015

Figure 8.1 shows how project or business risks can be classified in these three dimensions in order to form a risk matrix. This is a three-dimensional Rubik's cube measuring risk probability, impact and controllability. The first two dimensions are probability and impact. Any risks that have a major impact on the business are undesirable, but those which are very likely to happen pose the greatest risk (quadrant I). By way of contrast, risks with a low impact and a low likelihood of occurrence (quadrant A) pose the least threat. The third dimension is controllability. It may be possible to control or influence some risks; others might be completely out of the organization's control. Therefore, the quadrant posing the greatest danger to the organization are those in quadrant Q – highest impact, highest probability but least controllability. These risks cannot be mitigated but must be closely monitored. The risks that have the highest probability of occurrence and have a major impact on the organization but can be controlled (quadrant I) will be the focus of managerial action to mitigate and reduce them.

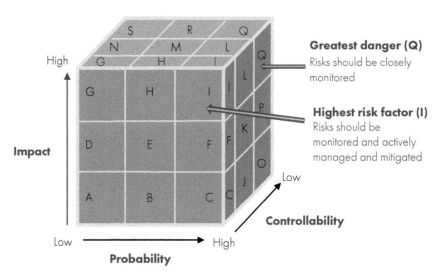

Figure 8.1 Risk classification

risk factor The probability of occurrence multiplied by the impact of the risk event

In reality, it is often very difficult to quantify the probability of a risk materializing beyond the simple low (A = 1), medium (B = 2) or high (C = 3) shown in Figure 8.1. The monetary impact of the risk materializing might be just as difficult to establish beyond a similar low (A = 1), medium (D = 2) or high (G = 3). The composite risk factor is defined as the probability of occurrence multiplied by the impact of the risk event. Using the simple classifications above, the highest composite risk factor is therefore 9 in quadrant I (3×3), the lowest is 1 in quadrant A (1×1). This 1 to 9 scale can then be reclassified as low (1–3), medium (4–6) and high (7–9). This low/medium/high classification is called a **risk index**. The higher the index number, the greater the impact and the probability of the risk happening.

You can add the dimension of controllability by reversing the simple 1–3 scale (1 = high, 3 = low controllability), e.g. A = 1, O = 3. A **danger factor** can be calculated by multiplying the risk factor (1–9) by the controllability factor (1–3). The lowest danger factor is 1 in quadrant A ($1 \times 1 \times 1$). The highest is 27 in quadrant Q ($3 \times 3 \times 3$); high impact, high probability and low controllability. This can be reduced to a **danger index** by reclassifying the danger as low (1–9), medium (10–18) and high 19–27).

risk index The composite risk factor reclassified in some simplified way

danger factor The risk factor multiplied by the controllability factor

danger index The composite danger factor reclassified in some simplified way

> *We take risks – but they're always calculated.*
>
> Emma Elston, founder UK Container Maintenance, *The Sunday Times*, 29 June 2014

MITIGATING RISKS

Once an organization has a risk and/or danger index (for projects or for the business as a whole), it can decide what to do about the risks it faces and start to develop key activities – things it needs to do in order to mitigate the risks. There are four options:

1. Attempt to eliminate the risk – It might withdraw completely from the area of activity that generates the risk – an unlikely course of action initially for an entrepreneurial organization. However, it needs to at least continue to monitor the risk because at some point in the future it might change this decision. By their nature, entrepreneurial organizations develop risky projects – all the more reason to accept this and attempt to reduce or share the risk.

2. Attempt to reduce the risk – It might attempt to reduce the risk of a project by selecting low-risk strategic alternatives within a business model, for example by using different **distribution channels**. It might also reduce risks by increasing internal controls, staff training or supervision, depending on the nature of the risk. Understanding the nature of the risk and putting in place the effective risk management processes outlined in this chapter will help.

channels of distribution The route your product or service takes to get to market – who you sell through

3. Transfer and/or sharing the risk – There are many useful techniques that can be used to transfer both internal and external risks such as insurance, foreign exchange or interest rate hedging. For example, companies constantly 'insure' against currency fluctuations – a risk they neither control nor influence – by buying forward in the currency market. Partnering in all its forms (e.g., subcontracting, outsourcing, franchising, etc.) is an extremely effective way of transferring risk. Partnerships and strategic alliances can be used to share the risks of a project as well as leveraging the strategic skills of the partnership. This helps a company to avoid over-commitment to any one project. The Virgin Group operates in this way with a holding company that owns, or partly owns, over 400 subsidiaries, each one set up in partnership with another company (see Case insight 8.4). Whilst Virgin contributes the capital of their brand and marketing

expertise, and possibly some financial capital, the partner contributes their operating knowledge and skills and the bulk of the financial capital.

4. Accept the risk – The organization might simply accept all the risks in quadrant A. If it accepts the risk completely, it needs to manage the risk and put in place early warning indicators of it materializing, although this might be uneconomic if the impact on the organization is small. Many industries have inherent risks that need to be accepted if the firm decides to operate in that sector. Even when a risk is accepted, entrepreneurs find ways of limiting the downside effects on the rest of the organization should the risk materialize. Entrepreneurs are expert at protecting themselves from the downside risk whilst capturing a lot of the upside profit. Partnering is a simple example of this. Another simple strategy is to compartmentalize the commercial risks by setting up each project as a separate legal entity. Should one fail, it will not endanger the whole organization. Serial entrepreneurs do this as a matter of course, partly because they intend to sell off each business at some point in the future. However, riskier off-shoots (divisions, etc.) – probably those developing more radical innovations – can also be set up as separate companies so as to safeguard the core business if the more innovative off-shoots fail. We look at this again in Chapter 13.

> 66 *If there are some obvious risks to your business model from the start, put in place some strategies to mitigate them.* 99
>
> Richard Branson, founder Virgin Group, *The Guardian, Media Planet*, May 2015

CASE INSIGHT 8.2
Eurostar

RISK MANAGEMENT

By necessity, the operations of a railway will be bureaucratic and you would be correct to think that they take risk management very seriously. Eurostar is high-speed rail service that runs between England and France under the English Channel. It has identified the risks it faces and has a business continuity plan for use in the event of disruption. Every one of Eurostar's departments has helped establish the risk register. Examples of risks on the register range from losing the main offices because of fire, bomb scares, train derailment, computer systems failure and even financial catastrophe. Using the techniques outlined in the text, Eurostar has developed a risk matrix showing the impact of a risk and its likelihood of occurrence. This allows the company to calculate a composite risk factor and consider what actions might mitigate those risks with a high impact. For example, Eurostar has a telephone contact centre at Ashford in the UK that handles sales, ticketing and customer service. In the event of a serious fire, the company would lose much of its booking capacity with a resulting impact on revenue and reputation.

Risk is mitigated through fire alarms, trip switches on electrical circuits, fire procedures and, ultimately, back-up locations that can be activated so that operations can be continued if the fire happens despite the other mitigations. The company has even carried out exercises using different locations in its own offices to simulate these actions.

Eurostar rescores the composite risk factor after considering the mitigations that have been implemented until an acceptable level has been reached. It revisits the risk matrix every six months just to check that the risks have remained unchanged and that the mitigating activities are working as planned.

Eurostar has a business continuity department, but implementing the continuity plan is firmly the responsibility of line management. Every line department has a business continuity champion. They are responsible for: assessing business impact, assessing the risk of the events, identifying who is responsible for ensuring that mitigating actions are carried out, considering what further mitigations might be possible, coordinating business continuity within the department, investigating failures and departmental risk training. Eurostar has a full training programme of exercises that simulates various 'disasters'. These might involve a range of approaches, from simple round-table discussions to practical simulations. For example, it has carried out major evacuation exercises in the Channel Tunnel with Eurotunnel and the emergency services and is constructing its own tunnel evacuation training simulator.

Visit the website: **www.eurostar.com**

Questions:

1. What are the business risks to Eurostar of not having a comprehensive risk management system?
2. Using the format shown below (see Figure 8.1), list the major risks that you think Eurostar faces and, on a scale of 1 (low) to 3 (high), estimate the impact that risk materializing might have on the business, the probability of it happening. Calculate the risk index. Evaluate the controllability of these risks reversing the scale of 1 (high controllability) to 3 (low) and calculate the danger index. What do the results tell you and what might you do with this information?

Risk	Impact	Probability	Risk index	Controllability	Danger index
	(1–3)	(1–3)	(1–9)	(1–3, reversed)	
1.					
2.					
3.					
4.					
5.					

MONITORING RISKS

All organizations have to accept some residual risk associated with their operations. However, each company will need to monitor those risks with the highest risk index numbers, particularly those that are least controllable. It needs to identify parameters or events that indicate an increased likelihood of the risk materializing – so-called **key risk indicators**. And this is where the information gathered by networking with customers, suppliers and other professionals is of vital importance. This can give it foreknowledge of risks materializing. These need to be monitored on a regular basis so the organization can then take remedial action.

To be effective, key risk indicators must be easy to monitor as part of the firm's regular activity, highlighting when corrective action is needed and providing guidance on what

key risk indicators
Parameters or events that indicate an increased likelihood of the risk materializing

action is needed. Cash flow is an obvious example of a potential key risk indicator. The risk is bankruptcy – any organization needs cash to pay its bills – and cash flow measures its ability to do this. If the reaction of competitors is a major risk to a business, it needs to develop a risk indicator that will measure this and put in place activities to ensure that it is monitored. For example, supermarkets regularly and routinely monitor the prices competitors charge for a typical basket of products. Without doing this they risk being uncompetitive and losing customers to rivals.

> ❝ As overwhelming as it might seem, if you have vision and you believe you have a unique product, then go for it. You need to take risks and accept that you will not succeed every time but that's part of the process. When it comes right, it's an amazing journey. ❞
>
> Wayne Edy, founder Inov-8, *The Sunday Times*, 15 March 2015

The most dangerous situation in business is where you have a high risk index in a situation over which you have little control – quadrant Q in Figure 8.1. In this situation it might consider any of options 1 to 3 on page 211, but even if it ends up accepting the risk it is vital that it monitors the risk and then takes corrective action if it materializes. Quadrant Q represents the situation it may face with competitors if a new product/service proves successful. An organization has no control over the competitive reaction of its rivals. If this is the case it needs to have some **strategic options** – plans for how to deal with this. Preparing scenarios of 'worst-possible' cases in advance of them happening allows it to prepare contingency plans, rather than trying to react after the event. It is about creating as many options for future courses of action as possible so as to better deal with an uncertain and rapidly changing commercial environment. The more strategic options it has, the less the likely impact of the risks it faces, should they materialize.

strategic options
Actions you might undertake if risks or opportunities materialize

Accepting the existence of risk may be part of an entrepreneurial architecture, but that does not mean that risk should be ignored. Risks needs to be understood, monitored and managed and decisions made based upon a realistic assessment of their likelihood, impact and controllability. These processes could be key or even critical activities for an organization practicing innovation. The primary way that entrepreneurs mitigate the risks they face is through their ability to react quickly to the knowledge and information they obtain through their extensive network of contacts both inside and outside the organization. Open information flows within the organization are therefore essential. They help inform decisions and mitigate risks. Project decisions might be made incrementally as a new product or service is developed, based upon up-to-date information or feedback – an approach outlined in Chapter 11.

Finally, it is worth pointing out that the risk management framework outlined in this chapter can be turned on its head and used to look at business opportunities and strategic options, seeking to identify those with the highest impact (profit), highest probability (of success) and highest controllability. In this business opportunity framework, quadrant I in Figure 8.1 becomes the most attractive, controllable opportunity. We shall return to the issue of finding business opportunities in Chapter 10.

CASE INSIGHT 8.3
Flying Tiger Copenhagen

Denmark

GROWTH AND RISK MANAGEMENT

The entrance to a Flying Tiger store in Lisbon, Portugal
Source: Getty Images/Jeff Greenberg

Flying Tiger Copenhagen – or just Tiger as the shops are called – is a Danish version of price-point retail concept. It sells a quirky, ever-changing range of cheap products such as toys and stationery, along-side hobby and craft goods like knitting needles and glitter glue. The products are own-branded, simple and colourful and most retail at less than £5 ($6). Global best-selling lines include low-value items like popping candy, pencil sets and soap bubbles, but the store also sells odd items at higher prices – for example, a record player at £100 ($120). Tiger taps into seasonal occasions like Christmas or Halloween. For example, it has sold an inflatable Santa suit. It also taps into lifestyle trends. For example, when the trend for crafting took off, it started offering knitting needles and brightly coloured wool.

The price-point business model is basically a low-cost/low-price one, enhanced by other elements such as a high footfall location. Tiger's website states that its business model is based on four elements: value proposition, assortment, store and customer experience:

➡ Value proposition: Tiger stresses their Scandinavian, functional but aesthetic design. Some 50 per cent of their new products are now designed, or have quirky design elements like packaging, added in-house. For example, Tiger received a Red Dot design award for its pink and green food containers. Their value proposition is as follows: 'To deliver everyday magic by providing a unique and playful experience in our stores, where customers discover a world of products that we carefully select and design. Flying Tiger Copenhagen stores are designed and curated to give our customers creative, fun and useful products. Our mission is to engage with people's lives, to help them live out their values and ideas and connect to the people that matter to them. While our products are offered at affordable round price points, it is a key objective that the quality should meet or exceed the customer's expectations as well as Zebra's corporate social responsibility requirements.'

➡ Assortment: Tiger's value-for-money products are changing continually. Each month, up to 300 new products can be introduced. They are primarily proprietary 'inspired by Danish heritage', often with a quirky twist.

➡ Store experience: The store itself is light, colourful and fun – laid out to be appealing to passers-by and to encourage impulse buys once inside as shoppers negotiate their way through the maze of stalls. It has been likened to an IKEA marketplace. The clean Scandinavian décor is a differentiating characteristic. The maze-like floor layout leads customers through pallet tables which display products with discreet price signs. The warm lighting creates stylish, but unpretentious product presentations. Stores are located in high footfall locations on high streets and in popular shopping malls. The store size is between 150 and 250 m².

➡ Customer experience: Tiger wants to provide a 'fun' customer experience derived partly from the shop and its products (which often just make you smile), but also from the attitude of the shop workers. In the UK, Tiger has been called the 'posh-Poundland'. However, whereas you might go to Poundland for necessities, you would go to Tiger for 'affordable indulgences':

> When we opened our first store in Basingstoke in 2005, some press called us a cool Scandi company. We hadn't seen ourselves like that. We were just a Danish store selling cheap items. It was a game changer because then Lennart hired the first in-house designer. The vision was to make design affordable (Tina Schwarz, Brand Director, The Observer, 18 December 2016).

Tiger has both a growth and an expansion model to facilitate its global rapid roll-out. Both rely heavily on effective partnerships. The company's growth model envisages growth coming from four elements:

➡ Increasing comparable store sales growth through the introduction of new products, conducting marketing campaigns to drive up the volume of purchases and the frequency of store visits.
➡ Increasing store penetration in existing markets by opening new stores through its expansion model.
➡ Geographical expansion into new markets by expanding into new territories through its expansion model.
➡ Increasing operating margins from scale advantage by investing in what it calls its 'corporate backbone' – its operating model – and leveraging its cost structure.

Tiger's expansion model relies on 50:50 partnerships with local partners who are offered exclusive territories that might be large cities, regions or even small countries. It stresses that this is not a franchise. For example, the UK is split into four territories: South-east, Midlands, Wales and Scotland (now run by Zebra A/S, the parent company of the Tiger brand). These joint ventures are owned 50 per cent by Zebra A/S (owner of the Tiger brand) and 50 per cent by the local partner. Within this arrangement Zebra owns the concept and brand and supplies the products, store interior and marketing material, while the local partner is responsible for store roll-outs and day-to-day operations including staffing, training and local marketing under specific guidelines set out by Zebra. Partners are expected to have comprehensive local retail experience, know-how and networks, an ability to run a minimum of 5–10 stores and access to at least €75,000. This model has enabled Zebra to grow rapidly. It has a contractually defined exit mechanism and it is part of Zebra's strategy to take full ownership of the local operating companies when this is assessed to be more beneficial than the partner model. Some operating companies, like the one in Scotland, are now wholly owned by Zebra.

Flying Tiger's ambitious growth targets are facilitated by its investment in what it calls its 'scalable corporate backbone', which aims to simplify operation and support future rapid growth. The operations model for their business units is anchored in a centralized, proactive management team that monitors and reviews the operational and financial performance of operating units. The team aims to take advantage of local or seasonal marketing opportunities and address problems which show up through underperformance. Tiger is presently investing substantial sums in a common IT system (using a Microsoft Dynamics AX ERP platform) so as to streamline their business processes and ensure a greater level of standardization. This not only increases efficiency but also makes it easier to scale-up operations quickly.

Because it operates a low-cost business model, it is important for Tiger that costs to be kept as low as possible. That mean it needs to have efficient supply chain operations and processes. Most Tiger products are produced by external suppliers. Tiger aims to minimize lead times from purchase to sale by making their sales forecasting process as efficient as possible. This minimizes working capital requirements as well as freeing up capital for further store expansion and future partner buyouts. Suppliers agree to Tiger's code of conduct and often, because Tiger have a hand in the design of many of the products, work under the direct supervision of the company. Most logistics is subcontracted to external operators, minimizing the investment in assets and making it easier to scale-up operations quickly. In 2015, warehousing was reorganized to reduce lead times to stores, minimize transportation costs and increase capacity. Whilst the company has its own warehouse in Greve (Denmark), the warehouses in Barcelona (Spain), Raunds (UK) and New Jersey (USA) are all operated by external partners. The company's transport is provided by freight forwarders.

Tiger has highlighted nine areas of risk that they monitor and for which they have put in place mitigation policies:

1. Financial risk – This is mainly foreign exchange and interest rate. This is mitigated by hedging foreign currency risk (agreeing to buy the foreign currency at a predetermined exchange rate) for 80 per cent of expected procurement for 12 months ahead, on a half-yearly basis. It also mitigates its exposure to interest rate fluctuations by maintaining a mix of borrowings between fixed and variable interest rates.
2. Liquidity risk – This is mitigated by monitoring its cash flow.
3. Competition risk – This is mitigated by investment in the business model. Initiatives include continued strengthening of creative capabilities within category management, product design and innovation, visual merchandising, marketing and branding as well as training of the store staff.
4. Expansion risk – This relates mainly to performance issues in local markets. This is monitored by business reviews and controls which aim to identify and then proactively address any potential disruptions in local markets.
5. Sourcing and supply chain risk – This is monitored on an ongoing basis. This is mitigated by the company's investment policy which aims to strengthen sourcing and supply chain systems, processes and capabilities so as to minimize disruption in supplies. Suppliers must adhere to the company's Code of Conduct and the company has a supplier audit programme.
6. Products, trademarks and legal risk – These are mitigated by having dedicated teams who focus on legal and compliance matters across the different legal jurisdictions in which the company operates.
7. Partner collaboration and buyout risk – This is mitigated by the partner business model, which entails a 'put' or a 'call' notice of one year. This allows the company to develop a detailed plan to transfer ownership and operations of the stores alongside the partner.
8. Infrastructure risk – This relates mainly to the implementation of the company's IT systems. This is mitigated by the strengthening of the company's project organization and project management capabilities, which is now monitored by the executive management.
9. People risk – This is about attracting, motivating and retaining qualified employees. This is mitigated through the work of Tiger's HR function, which supports the local operating companies and has rolled out various recruitment and training initiatives, including a recruitment kit designed to assist in local recruitment.

Visit the website: flyingtiger.com and corporate.flyingtiger.com

Questions:

1. Is Tiger's marketing mix consistent, with each element reinforcing the other? Does it reflect its value proposition?
2. List the strengths, weaknesses, opportunities and threats facing Tiger. Are the threats and weaknesses covered by the nine main risk areas they have highlighted?
3. List Tiger's critical success factors and the strategic options as it grows. Are these covered by the nine main risk areas they have highlighted?
4. Is the Tiger growth and expansion model consistent and coherent?
5. Why is this partnership model attractive to Tiger? What are the advantages and disadvantages of this model to partners?

FINANCING RISK

An organization faces both commercial risk – arising from the nature of the project and the commercial environment in which it operates – and financing risk – arising from how the activity is financed. Using external funds of any sort brings new risks and constraints. Entrepreneurs tend to keep the use of external funds – both loans and equity – to a minimum. This may be because of their inability to borrow or unwillingness to give up control. They may alter their business model so as to minimize the need for external funding. They keep capital investment and fixed costs as low as possible, sometimes renting or leasing assets, often subcontracting some activities. They might hire temporary, rather then part- or full-time, staff. Entrepreneurs prefer to commit costs to a project only after the opportunity has proved to be commercially viable – part of the approach called 'affordable loss' mentioned earlier. However, if the opportunity proves to be commercially viable they may then have to find external funds to finance the project.

Financing any project with external loans means that interest needs to be paid. This is a fixed cost, payable whether or not the project is generating income, although the actual rate of interest may vary as part of the loan agreement. The general rule of prudent financing is to match the term duration of the loan with the term duration of the use to which it is put. Hence long-term loans should be used to finance long-term projects or the purchase of fixed assets. However, lenders are usually unwilling to lend for the development of more innovative longer-term projects, where the return is uncertain and does not materialize until some way into the future. For these reasons, they see such projects as too risky. However, whilst financiers may be unwilling to lend against a specific project, they may be willing to lend to an established business which has a track record of successful trading on the basis that its portfolio of products or services generates sufficient income to cover the interest and loan repayments. The company may also have assets that can be used as collateral against the loan. An established company with a portfolio of products or services at different stages of their life-cycle may indeed be able to finance these projects from internal funds. This is the lowest risk financing strategy of all and we shall return to it in Chapter 15.

It is generally accepted that longer-term, riskier projects require equity finance. For an established company, this may come from venture capital firms, although they will be looking for a high annual rate of return (typically 30–60 per cent depending on the perceived risk) and will want to liquidate their investment within 5–10 years. If the company already has a stock market listing, it might also be possible to raise finance for a large-scale project by issuing additional shares. However, this varies greatly from sector to sector. The stock market is more understanding of lengthy periods of low or no profit for companies with proprietary technology. Similarly, it seems far more understanding of disruptor companies like Uber and Airbnb, perhaps sensing that these companies might develop new industries or come to dominate new, enormous markets and generate monopoly profits in years to come based upon their business models and network externalities. Nevertheless, the stock market can also be a cruel task master, with investors having a notoriously short-term orientation and requiring regular dividends or share buy-backs to boost share price. This focus on short-term performance influences the priorities in the allocation of resources within corporations and mitigates against more radical innovation. The incentive is to return capital to investors as quickly and efficiently as possible.

There have been two ways of avoiding this pressure. Firstly, there has been the practice of multiple share classes, some without voting rights. When the founders of Google and Facebook floated their companies on the stock market they held onto shares with extra voting rights so as to ensure that they kept control and were not subject to short-term shareholder pressures. This practice, although criticized by investment companies, continues today. When Snap, the Snapchat social media group founded in 2011, raised $3.4 billion in a float in 2017 the new share did not have voting rights, meaning that its founders maintained control.

The second way of avoiding this pressure has been to build up cash reserves. Once companies come to dominate their industries then the monopoly or oligopoly profits that are generated and the resulting mountainous cash reserves can insulate them from the short-termism of the stock markets. For example, as of mid-2017 Apple held some $77 billion in cash and short-term investments (plus $185 billion in marketable long-term investments). At the same time, Microsoft had $133 billion, Alphabet $86 billion, Facebook $36 billion and Amazon $26 billion. As Janeway (2018) observed: 'No doubt, a substantial portion of the financial reserves [of these companies] reflect the incentive to generate profits in low-tax regimes and hold cash receipts there, given the exemption from US taxation of profits held offshore nominally for reinvestment. But having accepted radical technological risk in the development of novel products and services, along with radical market risk to discover whether there are customers for their inventions, even the biggest winners in the innovation economy understandably choose to accept no financial risk whatsoever.'

Generally, there are two types of stock market investors. Firstly, there are those who focus on regular dividends and cash flow and less on growth potential and therefore prefer low risk. These prefer incremental innovation and process innovation, but may not object to partnering with other companies to spread the risks of other forms of innovation. Secondly, there are those who do not need the cash now and value growth potential instead. They can sell their shares when they wish to realize the capital gain. These are the ones who are prepared to back more radical product and market innovations. The CEO of a public company needs to understand its investor base.

As we noted in Chapter 3, the private sector is generally not good at financing early-stage, particularly radical, innovations and this applies to public as well as private companies. Mazzucato (2018) pointed out that over the last decade or so large pharmaceutical firms have been increasing the amount they spend on dividends and share buy-backs (that boost their share price) at the same time as decreasing the amount they spend on R&D,

claiming that 'most of the really "innovative" new drugs (i.e. new molecular entities with priority rating) come from publicly funded laboratories'. This short-term orientation, the loss of control and increased external accountability has led some entrepreneurs to withdraw their companies from stock exchanges. For example, Richard Branson withdrew Virgin from the stock market some years ago, buying back all of its shares.

The conclusion is that all forms of external finance bring with them a new set of risks that cannot be ignored. These may relate directly to projects being undertaken or to the portfolio of products or services that a business has. As we shall see in Chapter 15, having a balanced portfolio of product/service offerings can allow a firm to self-finance innovation. And having this diversified over products or services in different geographic markets, market sectors or industries can spread the risk of a market downturn in any one of them. However, as we shall also see, whilst a strategy of diversification may be attractive to a private company it can lead to other problems for a public company. Diversification and the formation of conglomerates (companies under one ownership but operating in entirely different industries) therefore remains a powerful driver of risk reduction strategy for private, unquoted companies. This is another reason Branson withdrew Virgin from the stock market. Virgin's scope of business now reaches into markets across the world and covers different industries from transport (airlines, trains and buses) to media (TV, radio, mobile phones and the internet), from health and lifestyle (health programmes to gyms) to financial services (credit cards, pension and insurance products and banking).

diversification
Moving away from core areas of activity into completely new and product/market areas.

 CASE INSIGHT 8.4
Virgin Group

 UK

ENTREPRENEURIAL ARCHITECTURE

Richard Branson is probably the best-known entrepreneur in Britain today and his name is closely associated with the many businesses that carry the Virgin brand name. He is outward-going and an excellent self-publicist. He has been called an 'adventurer', taking risks that few others would contemplate. This shows itself in his personal life, with his transatlantic power boating and round-the-world ballooning exploits, as well as in his business life, where he has challenged established firms like British Airways and Coca-Cola. He is a multimillionaire with what has been described as a charismatic leadership style. His company, the Virgin Group, is also probably the best-known brand in Britain, being closely associated with Branson and enjoying 96 per cent recognition. It is also a significant global player. The Virgin name has found its way onto aircraft, trains, cola, vodka, mobile phones, cinemas, a radio station, financial services, fitness studios and the internet. If there is any theme as to why Virgin set up in these sectors, it is simply commercial opportunity. Virgin Rail was a rail franchise bought from the government under its privatization policy. Virgin Atlantic was set up because of customer dissatisfaction with existing monopolistic suppliers such as British Airways. Virgin has also capitalized on the consumer telecoms and internet-based media boom with Virgin Mobile and Virgin Media (subsequently sold to Liberty Global). Branson has sold off many of his successful businesses and closed unsuccessful ones. He has also licenced the use of the Virgin brand.

Virgin Group is a privately owned, multinational conglomerate. It describes itself as a 'branded venture capital company' – a big brand made up of lots of smaller, legally separate companies each with different structures and with variations on the basic organizational culture. This structure mirrors a Japanese management structure called 'keiretsu', in which different businesses act as a family under one brand. In fact, it is made up of over 20 separate umbrella companies, operating some 400 separate businesses across a wide range of industries, and employing approximately 71,000 people in over 30 countries, with global brand revenue of about £20 billion: Branson described it in the following terms:

> *Virgin is not a big company – it's a big brand made up of lots of small companies. Our priorities are the opposite of our large competitors . . . For us our employees matter most. It just seems common sense that if you have a happy, well motivated workforce, you're much more likely to have happy customers. And in due course the resulting profits will make your shareholders happy. Convention dictates that big is beautiful, but every time one of our ventures gets too big we divide it up into smaller units . . . Each time we do this, the people involved haven't had much more work to do, but necessarily they have a greater incentive to perform and a greater zest for their work.(1)*

Companies in the Virgin Group are diverse and independent. In 1986 Virgin was floated on the stock market but later re-privatized because Branson did not like to be accountable for his actions to institutional shareholders. The structure of Virgin Group is complex and difficult to disentangle, involving offshore private companies and the existence of (unidentified) bearer shares (shares where the owner's name is not registered but ownership rests with whoever owns the physical share certificates). Equity interest in the umbrella organizations is owned by Virgin Group Investments. The Virgin trademark and logos are owned by Virgin Enterprises and these are licensed to companies both inside and outside the Virgin Group. Virgin Management is the management arm of the organization, appointing board members, senior executives and coordinates activities. Wikipedia highlighted the complexity of the Virgin organization and the difficulty in untangling it: 'Although Branson retains complete ownership and control of the Virgin brand, the commercial set-up of companies using it is varied and complex. Each of the companies operating under the Virgin brand is a separate entity, with Branson completely owning some and holding minority or majority stakes in others. Occasionally, he simply licenses the brand to a company that has purchased a division from him, such as Virgin Mobile USA, Virgin Mobile Australia, Virgin Radio and Virgin Music (now part of EMI).'

Virgin Group's headquarters are in London, but it also has offices in other countries each with sector teams, run by a managing partner, and employing a number of professional managers. Although the working environment is said to be informal, almost casual, there is a belief in hard work and individual responsibility. The Group is characterized as being information-driven. It sees itself as having minimal management layers, no bureaucracy, a tiny board and a small headquarters, an organization that is bottom-heavy rather than strangled by top-heavy management:

> *Our companies are part of a family rather than a hierarchy . . . They are empowered to run their own affairs, yet the companies help one another, and solutions to problems often come from within the Group somewhere. In a sense we are commonwealth, with shared ideas, values, interests and goals.(2)*

Branson is said to believe in delegation and be good at it, encouraging senior managers to be entrepreneurial. He sets direction and then steps back to allow them to get on with things, giving them the freedom and initiative to be creative. This willingness to delegate helps develop trust between him and his management team. Despite the informal, devolved structures, performance expectations are high. Managers at all levels in Virgin are given goals. Managers at headquarters are given overall goals to achieve, such as improving brand loyalty or expanding the business. Companies in the Group have different organizational structures, reflecting the different natures of their core businesses. However, managers in Group companies are given more specific goals associated with their own business. The further down the hierarchy you go the more specific and short-term the goals.

Virgin has an informal but complex culture based upon the Virgin brand – it is the brand that unifies the different companies in the Group. Branson believes that finding the right people to work with is the key to success and the Virgin brand is so strong that it helps attract like-minded staff. He believes that it is attitude, rather than qualifications, that matters in the selection of people. He refers to them as 'Virgin-type' people – staff who will enjoy their work and are customer-focused. And their enthusiasm for the brand rubs off on the customers. Branson said:

Our brand values are very important, and we tend to select people to work for us who share these values . . . For as much as you need a strong personality to build a business from scratch, you must also understand the art of delegation. I have to be willing to step back now. I have to be good at helping people run the individual businesses – it can't just be me that sets the culture when we recruit people . . . Our guiding principle is this: give individuals the tools they need, outline some parameters to work within, and then just let them get on and do their stuff . . . Our view at Virgin is that collective responsibility bonds the teams, and having pride in your work is a far better driver than a hierarchical culture where the boss calls the shots . . . I started Virgin with a philosophy that if staff are happy, customers will follow. It can't just be me that sets the culture when we recruit people. I have a really great set of CEOs across our businesses who live and breathe the Virgin brand and who are entrepreneurs themselves.(2)

The Virgin brand has been largely built through the personal PR efforts of its founder. Branson realized the importance of self-publicity very early on in his career when the BBC featured him in a documentary called 'The People of Tomorrow' because of his first venture, *Student* magazine. Since then he has become known for his often outrageous publicity stunts, such as dressing up as a bride for the launch of Virgin Bride. According to Branson: 'Brands must be built around reputation, quality and price . . . People should not be asking "is this one product too far?" but rather, "what are the qualities of my company's name? How can I develop them?" (1). As to what these qualities are for Virgin, Branson gave us a candid insight into at least one of them: 'Fun is at the core of the way I like to do business and has informed everything I've done from the outset. More than any other element fun is the secret of Virgin's success.' (2)

Virgin uses its brand as a capital asset in its joint ventures. Virgin contributes the brand and Branson's PR profile, whilst the partner provides the capital input – in some ways like a franchise operation – and often the operational expertise. It believes the brand stands for value for money, quality, innovation, fun and a sense of competitive challenge. It believes the company delivers a quality service by empowering employees and, whilst continuously monitoring customer feedback, striving to improve the customer's experience through innovation. According to Will Whitehorn, then director of corporate affairs at Virgin Management:

At Virgin, we know what the brand name means, and when we put our brand name on something, we're making a promise. It's a promise we've always kept and always will. It's harder work keeping promises than making them, but there is no secret formula. Virgin sticks to its principles and keeps its promises (The Guardian, 30 April 2002).

Branson's main skills are said to be networking, finding opportunities and securing the resources necessary for their exploitation. His network of personal influence and contacts is legendary. He hates formal meetings and prefers to make decisions on a face-to-face basis, albeit sometimes over the phone, but always developing and testing his personal relationships. Another of Branson's skills seems to be his ability to inspire staff and bring out the best in them. He can do this on a very personal basis and still regularly invites groups of employees to his house. Most people who meet him find him extremely likeable – charismatic – with boundless enthusiasm and an inquisitive mind. He can be a good listener, but says he never listens to critics. He encourages communication at all levels, using many different media. He seems to have an ability to 'connect' with people and loves challenges, whether related to the business or his own personal life.

If people are properly and regularly recognized for their initiative, then the business has to flourish. Why? Because it's their business, an extension of their personality. Everyone feels Virgin is theirs to keep and look after. And it runs deeper. I am a firm believer in listening to your staff at all times. The moment you stop doing this, you are in danger of losing your best people.(2)

Employees are encouraged to come up with new ideas and development capital is available. Once a new venture reaches a certain size, it is launched as an independent company within the Virgin Group and the intrapreneur takes an equity stake. Branson's personal approach is to listen to all ideas and offer feedback.

Many of our businesses run innovation schemes where employees can submit new business ideas to be considered by the strategic leaders. We also facilitate peer-to-peer nominations to recognize top performers around the four Virgin values of innovation, customer service, community and environment. One lucky person even gets to spend a week on [my] Necker Island.(2)

Branson's view on risk is interesting. He has been expert at minimizing his personal exposure. Indeed, in interviews one of the most prominent pieces of advice he gives entrepreneurs is to 'limit the downside':

Every time we launch a new business I know I'm taking a risk. For some it can seem like a leap into the unknown. However, I've always said business is like a game of chess – you have to learn quickly from mistakes. You have to adapt and be thinking two, three moves ahead . . . There are a number of different risks in business but the ones that stand out most are usually economic.(3)

His first record shop was 'given' to him rent-free. The Virgin Records business grew out of this, expanding into record production and music publishing. His Virgin Atlantic airline business, launched in 1984, was seen by Branson as high risk and was kept separate from other businesses:

The launch of Virgin Atlantic put financial pressure on the other businesses in the Virgin Group. I had to try to cover the downside by leasing the initial plane for a year, keeping the business separate from all our other companies. But even then we sailed close to the wind.(3)

He now uses partners to contribute both capital and expertise to his new business ventures. At the same time, he was not afraid to commit his own (or borrowed) money when needed, for example when Virgin Atlantic was re-privatized.

Branson is tolerant of risk taking within the Group and has seen some notable failures. It is estimated that he has started some 500 companies, but that he has also shut down some 200 of them that did not work. Probably the most widely publicised failure was Virgin Cola, launched in 1994 and closed down in 2012:

There are risks that don't pay off . . .Virgin Cola launched in 1994 and it's fair to say we made headlines . . . We wanted to smash our way past the competition. However it turned out we hadn't thought things through – declaring war on Coke [Coca-Cola] was madness . . . Virgin had become renowned as being a disruptor brand, entering new markets and shaking up the norm. But we'd forgotten one thing; we only do business where we can offer consumers something brilliantly different. Replicating what we'd done in the music industry and airlines was going to be difficult in the soft drinks sector. People were already getting a product they liked, at a price they were happy to pay – Virgin Cola just wasn't different enough. Although the business ultimately failed, it was a great learning experience.(3)

Virgin Vodka suffered the same fate as Virgin Cola and was part of the entire Virgin Drinks subsidiary that was eventually closed. Similarly, Virgin Vie was a cosmetics venture that was launched in 1997 and wound up in 2010.

Virgin Clothing was probably the shortest-lived venture. Offering men and women's clothing, it was launched in 1998 but wound up in 2000. Virginware, a venture selling female lingerie, was similarly disastrous, closing down in 2005. Indeed, some of Branson's companies have themselves 'subcontracted' the brand to insulate themselves from commercial risk. For example, when Virgin Atlantic launched Little Red in 2013 – a small UK-based domestic airline – it subcontracted all operations to the Irish company Aer Lingus on a 'wet lease' basis, meaning that they supplied the crew and aircraft, albeit in Virgin livery. Little Red closed down in 2014.

Whilst Branson may tolerate risk and accept failure because it goes along with being entrepreneurial, he continues to try to mitigate it throughout his business empire:

> One thing is certain in business; you and everyone around you will make mistakes. When you are pushing the boundaries this is inevitable – but it's important to recognize this. We need to look for new ways to shape up to the competition. So we trust people to learn from mistakes; blame and recriminations are pointless. A person who makes no mistakes, makes nothing. (www.hrmagazine.co.uk, 13 July 2010)

Visit the website: **www.virgin.com**

Questions:

1. Why has Virgin been successful?
2. What is the essence of the Virgin brand?
3. How would you describe the structure, culture and management of the Virgin Group? Does this reflect the brand?
4. Are these elements of an entrepreneurial architecture?
5. How do Branson and Virgin mitigate the risks they face?

Sources:
1. R. Branson, *Losing my Virginity*, London: Virgin, 1998.
2. J. Andersen, *Local Heroes*, Glasgow: Scottish Enterprise, 1995.
3. *Independent*, 24 April 2017.

SUMMARY

➡ Most people are biased in decision-making. They are risk-averse for gains and risk-seeking for losses. This means they are usually willing to pay a premium to obtain a sure gain rather than a gamble, and also willing to pay a premium (in expected value) to avoid a sure loss.

➡ Risk is an ever-present danger in an entrepreneurial firm. The 'known-unknowns' are where risks can be identified (they are known). The risk management framework outlined in this chapter cover these risks. It is appropriate for incremental innovation. The 'unknown-unknowns' are where the risks cannot be identified (they are unknown). These are dealt with using the approach called 'affordable loss', covered in Chapter 11. It is most appropriate for radical innovation.

➡ Risk management for 'known-unknowns' can be broken down into a five-stage process:

   • Identifying the risks (internal or external) associated with an action;
   • Evaluating the probability of the risk materializing;

- Evaluating the effects of that risk materializing;
- Mitigating the risk in whatever way possible;
- Monitoring the risk so as to ensure early warning, should the risk materialize.

➡ The riskiest situation is where there is a high likelihood of occurrence with a high impact in a situation but where you have little control. These can derive from internal factors or the external environment. Where risks can be identified it is important to monitor key risk indicators that give early warning signs of the risks materializing. Entrepreneurial firms need to identify the highest risks in the strategies they are following and then monitor the associated key risk indicators. Where a risk can be controlled it should be mitigated.

➡ Financing risk arises from how a project is financed. Using external funds of any sort brings new risks and constraints. Long-term finance (loans and equity) should generally be used to fund long-term projects, but interest and dividends may still need to be paid before a project starts generating cash flow. This is particularly a problem for radical innovations with extended pay-backs. Using internally generated cash flow from an existing portfolio of projects can avoid these short-term pressures.

GROUP DISCUSSION TOPICS

1. If managers focus too much on risk they will ignore opportunities. Discuss.
2. Are large companies doomed to always favour low-risk project opportunities?
3. Does high risk always go with high returns?
4. Is your own decision-making judgement always going to be biased?
5. What sort of risks fall into the category of 'unknown-unknowns'?
6. How can you deal with unknown risks?
7. What are the risks associated with global warming?
8. If you cannot measure risk, you cannot manage it. Discuss.
9. If you cannot manage risk, you might as well ignore it. Discuss.
10. Do entrepreneurs ignore risk?
11. The easiest way to avoid financing risks is to avoid using external finance. Discuss.
12. Are dual-right shares ethical?
13. Why does diversification and the formation of conglomerates remains a powerful driver of risk reduction strategy for private, unquoted companies?
14. If innovative companies face high risks, they are bound to face high capital costs. High capital costs just increase the risk these companies face. Discuss.
15. Risk is the biggest managerial issue for corporate entrepreneurship. Discuss.

ACTIVITIES

1. Set up Kahneman's decision experiment using a group of students who have not read this book. Do his results hold true? If there are students who do not make the expected decisions, explore with them their reasoning.
2. Describe the risks facing an organization of which you have experience (it might be your university). Classify them using the risk cube in Figure 8.1 and indicate what would be the key risk indicators that need monitoring.
3. List the risks you face in selecting a company to work for when you leave university. Classify them using the risk cube in Figure 8.1 and indicate what are the key risk indicators that you need to monitor.

REFERENCES

BCG (2018) *The Most Innovative Companies 2018: Innovators Go All in on Digital (Chapter 2)*, Boston, MA: Boston Consulting Group. Available on: www.bcg.com/publications/2018/most-innovative-companies-2018-how-digital-transforms-strategy.aspx.

Birkinshaw, J. (2003) 'The Paradox of Corporate Entrepreneurship', *Strategy and Business*, 30.

Delmar, F. (2000) 'The Psychology of the Entrepreneur' in S. Carter and D. Jones-Evans (eds) *Enterprise and Small Business: Principles, Practice and Policy* (1st edn.), London: Prentice Hall.

Janeway, W.H. (2018) *Doing Capitalism in the Innovation Economy*, Cambridge: Cambridge University Press.

Kahneman, D. (2012) *Thinking Fast and Slow*, London: Penguin Books.

Mazzucato, M. (2018) *The Entrepreneurial State: Debunking Public vs Private Sector Myths*, London: Penguin Books.

 ONLINE RESOURCES AVAILABLE

For further resources relating to this chapter see the companion website at **www.macmillanihe.com/Burns-CEI**

PART III

ENCOURAGING THE ENTREPRENEURIAL MINDSET

This section is about people and how they might be encouraged to develop an entrepreneurial mind-set – one that spots unmet needs in the market; opportunities to improve and innovate products or services; and is empowered to actually do something to make this happen. Chapters 9 and 10 show how creativity and innovation can be encouraged and business ideas generated in larger organizations by developing some simple skills and using some well-known techniques. Chapter 10 introduces the idea of 'creative synthesis' which builds on design thinking but integrates business model development with the technology perspective. Chapter 11 explains design thinking and sets out a low-risk way to develop concepts and market-test new products or services using lean start-up methodologies. Chapter 12 shows how the all-important business model can be developed, providing some simple frameworks that can be used alongside market testing (New Venture Creation Framework, Business Model Canvas and Lean Canvas), as well as explaining some of the most successful models already being used.

Lack of entrepreneurial spirit is a major reason for decreasing competitiveness – and even the eventual collapse – of big enterprises.

Zhang Ruimin, CEO Haier Group

9 Encouraging creativity and innovation

CONTENTS

- Creativity, innovation and commercial opportunity
- Understanding the creative brain
- Measuring creativity
- Blocks to creativity and innovation
- Connectivity
- Knowledge networks
- Crowdsourcing and open innovation
- Accelerators and incubators
- Creative environments
- Knowledge and learning
- Developing discovery skills
- Summary
- Group discussion topics
- Activities
- References

CASE INSIGHTS

Learning outcomes

When you have read this chapter and undertaken the related activities you will be able to:

➡ Understand and explain the factors that stimulate and critically analyze the factors that inhibit creativity and innovation both in individuals and across the organization;
➡ Critically assess the dimensions of your own creative potential;
➡ Understand and explain the importance of knowledge networks and the contribution that crowdsourcing can make to creativity and innovation;
➡ Critically analyze the factors that contribute to a creative environment;
➡ Develop creativity and discovery skills.

CREATIVITY, INNOVATION AND COMMERCIAL OPPORTUNITY

Innovation is the prime tool entrepreneurs use to create opportunity. It is underpinned by creativity, which is the ability to find or create something new – ideas, rules, patterns, methodologies etc. But if creativity underpins innovation, then entrepreneurship and the ability to perceive opportunities is the context in which it will flourish. For the entrepreneur, creativity is an essential tool that is used to seek out a business opportunity, identifying unmet needs in the marketplace and finding innovative ways of meeting these needs. In the words of Bolton and Thompson (2000): 'Creativity is the starting point whether it is associated with invention or opportunity spotting. This creativity is turned to practical reality (a product, for example) through innovation. Entrepreneurship then sets that innovation in the context of an enterprise (the actual business), which is something of recognised value.'

For an entrepreneurial corporation, innovation must be at the core of its strategy – encouraged and facilitated by its entrepreneurial architecture. This must permeate everything it does. This involves commitment from top management:

➡ That innovation is at the core of what the business does;
➡ That innovation is the responsibility of everyone, not just the R&D department;
➡ That innovation happens in everything, from developing new products/services to new processes and new approaches to marketing.

Innovation should not happen by chance or in a haphazard, piecemeal or tactical manner, with innovative projects being seen as burdensome additional work to 'business as usual'. Innovation must be encouraged, facilitated and just be a part of that 'business as usual'. This means encouraging creativity as well as innovation but linking it with commercial opportunity perception. This chapter will explain how creativity and innovation can be encouraged within individuals.

UNDERSTANDING THE CREATIVE BRAIN

The previous chapter gave us an insight into how the brain functions. These thinking styles also influence our creativity. 'Right-brain' thinkers (System 1 or the heart: also called creative or lateral thinkers) – who are more intuitive, emotional and creative – were characterized by Kirton (1976, 2003) as 'innovators' – divergent thinkers who discover problems by approaching tasks from unusual angles, and are less concerned with 'doing things better' and prefer 'doing things differently'. They are imaginative and often come up with more than one solution to a problem because they explore different approaches. They can take discontinuous leaps and often restructure the original problem.

By way of contrast, 'left-brain' thinkers (System 2 or the head: also called logical or vertical thinkers), who are more rational, logical and analytical, were characterized by Kirton as 'adaptors' – convergent thinkers who solve problems with a disciplined, rational approach, and are best at refining current practices and 'doing things better'. They always look for direct answers to problems and often converge on a solution, usually without questioning the premise upon it is based. They use existing structures and problem-solving approaches, concentrating on those approaches that they see as 'relevant'. Figure 9.1 shows some of the differences in the two approaches.

Logical		Creative
Seeks answers	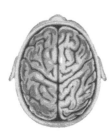	Seeks questions
Converges		Diverges
Asserts best or right view		Explores different views, seeks insights
Uses existing structure		Restructures
Says when an idea will not work		Seeks ways an idea might help
Uses logical steps		Welcomes discontinuous leaps
Concentrates on what is relevant		Welcomes chance intrusions
Closed		Open-ended

Figure 9.1 Right-brain, creative thinking (System 1) vs Left-brain logical thinking (System 2)

Kahneman (2012) pointed to the growing evidence that right-brain function is associated with moods, intuition, creativity and gullibility and left-brain function with vigilance, suspicion, analysis, increased effort and sadness. A happy mood (positive emotions) loosens the control of the left-brain over performance: 'when in a good mood, people become more intuitive and more creative but also less vigilant and more prone to logical errors'. Kahneman talked about a range of moods between 'cognitive ease', which encourages right-brain creativity (no threats, no need to redirect attention and mobilize effort), and 'cognitive strain', which encourages left-brain activity and discourages creativity (a problem exists which requires attention), noting that cognitive ease is both a cause and a consequence of a pleasant feeling. What is more interesting is that psychologists have found that cognitive ease influences, in particular, the important creative skill of association or connection that we shall highlight later in this chapter.

Oscillating between the two functions appears to improves *practical* creativity (Fox Cabane and Pollack, 2017) – which is why alternating between challenging cognitive tasks and activities with low cognitive loads (relaxing) enhances creativity. In fact, Fox Cabane and Pollack said that the best activity for encouraging creativity is walking, when both can be practiced. As we have observed, the two functions of the brain normally complement each other and people can (and do) switch between them for different tasks and in different contexts, although people may have a preference for one or other style of thinking.

Both are creative, albeit in different ways. The left-brain 'adaptor', however, is typically better at incremental innovation and the 'innovator' at radical or disruptive innovation. As with the character traits of entrepreneurs, these thinking styles can be influenced over time by environmental factors. Education, for example, encourages logic and conformity – left-brain functions – not only in terms of its values and encouraged behaviours but particularly in learning many of the basic life skills such as reading, writing and arithmetic. Kirby (2003) speculated that this may well explain why so many successful entrepreneurs appear not to have succeeded in the formal education system (e.g., Steve Jobs and Richard Branson). They are non-conformists and are prone to misbehaviour. He argued that entrepreneurs are right-brain dominant and went even further by speculating that there may be a link between this and dyslexia, observing that many entrepreneurs such as Branson are dyslexic and that language skills is a left-brain activity. This is an interesting but unproven hypothesis.

Mintzberg (1976) observed that effective leadership and management requires both right- and left-brain activity. Whilst leadership essentially appeals to peoples' emotions and requires emotional intelligence, a right-brain activity, much of management is concerned with logic, detailed analysis and planning, a left-brain activity. However, both also rely heavily on intuition and cognitive heuristics for decision-making. Mintzberg also observed that most managers divide their attention between a number of different tasks. They prefer to talk directly to staff rather than writing or emailing them, and this allows them to take a holistic view of the situation and 'read' non-verbal as well as verbal aspects of the interaction.

MEASURING CREATIVITY

The point is that most people are not creative; this is not by nature, but because of their upbringing. Society has certain values and norms of behaviour. It encourages us to conform, to follow these norms of behaviour. Not to do so brings the threat of sanction or penalty. It values logic, but particularly the dominant logic of the group and it has a tendency to reject non-conformist thinking – and thinkers. This is why creative types are often seen as rebels, disruptors or trouble-makers. They create change – and people and society generally do not like change. Majaro (1992) believed that, while stereotyping is to be avoided, creative types do exhibit some similar characteristics:

- Conceptual fluency – They are able to produce many ideas.
- Mental flexibility – They are adept at lateral thinking.
- Originality – They produce atypical responses to problems.
- Suspension of judgement – They do not analyze too quickly.
- Impulsive – They act impulsively to an idea, expressing their 'gut-feeling'.
- Anti-authority – They are always willing to challenge authority.
- Tolerance – They have a high tolerance threshold towards the ideas of others.

These characteristics mirror some of the character traits exhibited by entrepreneurs (see Chapter 1). This is unsurprising since entrepreneurs are creative, albeit in a way focused on commercial opportunity generation.

A range of online tests that measure creativity is provided below. They measure the respondent's preferred approach to creativity. That preference can change over time and with exposure to different environments. Creativity can be encouraged through an appropriate culture within an entrepreneurial architecture. It involves overcoming some personal blocks or barriers and can be developed through training and by practicing the discovery skills outlined in this chapter.

 EXPLORE FURTHER

Psychometric tests that measure general creativity

Kirton Adapter-Innovator (KAI) – This is a test that distinguishes between the two cognitive thinking styles described earlier: right-brain innovators (System 1) and left-brain adaptors (System 2). It uses a test, consisting of 32 questions, to assess the different dimensions of creativity, including originality, attention to detail and following rules. The scores range from 32 to 160 – one in the 60–90 range indicates an adaptive cognitive style and a score in the 110–140 range indicates an innovative style. Neither style is seen as 'better' than the other, each score is only different and complementary in the context of problem-solving and team working.

The test is available at: kaicentre.com.

AULIVE – This is a free-to-use online test, consisting of 40 questions, that measures the respondent's preferred general creativity across eight dimensions:

➡ Abstraction – the ability to apply abstract concepts/ideas.
➡ Connection – the ability to make connections between things that do not appear connected.
➡ Perspective – the ability to shift one's perspective on a situation in terms of space, time and other people.
➡ Curiosity – the desire to change or improve things that others see as normal.
➡ Boldness – the confidence to push boundaries beyond accepted conventions. It is also the ability to ignore what others might think of you.
➡ Paradox – the ability to simultaneously accept and work with statements that are contradictory.
➡ Complexity – the ability to carry large quantities of information and be able to manipulate and manage the relationships between such information.
➡ Persistence – the ability to force oneself to keep trying to more and stronger solutions even when good ones have already been generated.

The report generated by the test compares the respondent's creativity in these eight dimensions against the results from others with similar backgrounds and also provides the opportunity to reflect on the results.

The test is available at: www.testmycreativity.com.

Herrmann Brain Dominance Instrument (HBDI) – This is a test that measures and describes thinking preferences in four dimensions, based on a 120-question online test:

A: Analytical thinkers – These are the rational, logical, analytical and critical thinkers who prefer collecting and analyzing data, understanding how things work and judging ideas based on facts.
B: Sequential thinkers – These are the organized, structured, conservative thinkers who can handle complexity but prefer following detailed directions and step-by-step problem-solving and are good at organizing work and implementing ideas.
C: Interpersonal thinkers – These are the emotional, intuitive thinkers who prefer listening to and expressing ideas, group interaction and looking for personal meaning.
D: Imaginative thinkers – These are imaginative, intuitive, conceptual and holistic thinkers who can synthesize different ideas. They prefer looking at the big picture rather than dealing with detail, challenging assumptions and are good at creative problem-solving and long-term thinking.

Generally, dimensions A and B are more left-brain (System 2) thinkers – they are more 'rational'. C and D are more right-brain thinkers (System 1) – they are 'intuitive'. But A and D are more 'intellectual' and B and C are more 'instinctive'. In this model, a person may have more than one thinking preference at any one time. For example, a person may be dominant in both analytical and sequential styles of thinking (A and B) but weaker in terms of interpersonal or imaginative modes (C and D). Because of this, it has implications for whether and how creative ideas might get implemented. Figure 13.2 gives an example of an HDMI analysis.

The test is available at: www.hbdi.com/WholeBrainProductsAndServices/programs/thehbdi.php.

BLOCKS TO CREATIVITY AND INNOVATION

It has been said that Steve Wozniak presented his idea for a personal computer five times to his employers at Hewlett Packard before he left to start up Apple with Steve Jobs. People may be inherently creative, but this is not something that all organizations or society generally encourages. Furthermore, most of us stifle it because we find creativity involves questioning the status quo, questioning might lead to change, and change can be threatening. We all create rituals and routines that we feel comfortable with and these normally mitigate against questioning the status quo and it is these routines that help us through the day. Being creative often takes people outside their 'comfort zone', since it makes them feel uneasy. Here are some of these barriers to creativity:

➡ The belief that there is only one solution;
➡ The tendency to be practical and logical in looking for that solution;
➡ The tendency to think too narrowly and with too much focus – not thinking 'outside-the-box';
➡ The tendency not to question the premise on which a problem is based and therefore not to reframe it (not thinking 'outside-the-box' again);
➡ The tendency to accept the 'rules of the game' and the status quo unquestioningly;
➡ The reluctance to accept uncertainty and ambiguity;
➡ The unwillingness to appear foolish by suggesting unconventional approaches or ideas;
➡ The unwillingness to take risks in looking at different approaches or ideas;
➡ The lack of belief that a person can be creative.

Fox Cabane and Pollack (2017) believed that the three greatest barriers to creativity are the fear of failure, the experience of failure, and the pain of uncertainty. They argue that simply managing the anxiety and actual pain people feel in connection with the prospect and experience of both failure and uncertainty should result in a measurable increase in innovation. Individual managers can sometimes actively block creativity and innovation within their sphere of influence, despite the policies and procedures of the organization designed to encourage it. Kanter (2004) suggested ten ways that they could do this:

1. Regard new ideas with suspicion.
2. Enforce cumbersome approval mechanisms, rules and regulations.
3. Pit departments and individuals against each other.
4. Express criticism, without praise.
5. Treat problem identification as a sign of failure.
6. Control everything carefully.
7. Plan reorganization in secret.
8. Keep tight control over information.
9. Delegate unpleasant duties to inferiors.
10. Assume they (the higher-up) know everything important about the business.

It is never easy to change an inherent tendency in an individual. Sometimes the individual simply needs to be replaced. However, recognizing the blocks and blockers is the first stage in dismantling them (see Chapter 7). Only then can a more sympathetic culture be built.

CONNECTIVITY

One prerequisite to all creative processes is the generation of knowledge and the openness to different ideas (Simmie, 2002). This helps create the cognitive diversity that, as we observed in Chapter 4, is needed to provide the different perspectives on problems and situations that enable ideas from different walks of life to be recombined. As Syed (2019) pointed out, this diversity underpins much of modern, particularly technology-based, innovation. However, we are often constrained in our thinking not only by our dominant logic but also by our prior knowledge (Venkatarman, 1997), so we need to expand it. We need to actively seek out new knowledge, information and perspectives in as many ways as possible: through reading, travel, meeting and talking to others, even web browsing. We need to see how, and perhaps more importantly, why other people do things. However, all too often we are unaware of the knowledge and information generated around us. We then need time to mull over that knowledge and information. This subconscious 'incubation period' happens when a person is engaged in other activities and can focus their mind on the problem. The best activities are those that are instinctive and do not require left-brain dominance. Interestingly, sleep happens when the left-brain gets tired or bored and it is during this time that the right-brain has dominance. Incubation therefore often needs sleep. The old adage, 'Sleep on the problem', has its origins in an understanding of the workings of the brain. It is little wonder that so many people have creative ideas when they are asleep – the problem is trying to remember them. Creativity, therefore, can take time and needs 'sleeping on'.

 That's how we learned: by travelling, meeting people, setting up appointments, it's a continuous process.

Manish Agarwal, CEO Reliance Games, *The Guardian*, 22 April 2015

In a thought-provoking book, Johnson (2010) gave a good explanation that dispelled the romantic myth that good ideas are a result of serendipity – a 'eureka moment' for a lone genius:

> [Good ideas] come from crowds, from networks. . . . You know we have this clichéd idea of the lone genius having the eureka moment. . . . But in fact when you go back and you look at the history of innovation it turns out that so often there is this quiet collaborative process that goes on, either in people building on other people's ideas, but also in borrowing ideas, or tools or approaches to problems. . . .The ultimate idea comes from this remixing of various different components. There still are smart people and there still are people that have moments where they see the world differently in a flash. But for the most part it's a slower and more networked process than we give them credit for.

Johnson's central thesis was that new ideas rarely happen by chance. They take time to germinate and mature. The big idea often comes from the 'collision' of smaller ideas or hunches and the chance of these 'accidental collisions' is increased with the exposure to more people and different ideas. Thus, whilst creativity underpins the generation of ideas, a prerequisite of this is connectivity – a connection with, and an awareness of, what is going on in the world in general and an ability to transfer ideas from one context to another. It generates new ideas, knowledge and information. Connectivity is one of the elements of creativity measured in the AULIVE test.

The opportunity to practice connectivity can come from many sources. Reading newspapers, magazines, journals and books and surfing the web are examples of passive forms of connectivity. Essentially, however, it is a social process involving talking with people who hold different views of the world. Active connectivity involves meeting a diverse range of people – what we term networking. Networks are important structures that can provide information about markets, professional advice and opinion, often free of charge. This might involve attending meetings, clubs, seminars and conferences and it is likely to involve travel. Formal networks such as Chambers of Commerce and trade associations can also prove invaluable in this purpose. Universities can also provide opportunities for novel insights. Networks also offer opportunities to form partnerships, either formally or informally, with a range of different organizations so as to better exploit an opportunity (Chapter 5). The more exposed an organization is to these influences, the more likely it is to be creative and innovative and spot opportunities.

> **"** Contacts are important but you have to get out there and meet people. It can be difficult when you are absorbed in running a business. But there is always something to learn from meeting someone new and a lot to learn from meeting someone old. The right contacts can become an invaluable source of learning as well as an inspiration and support. **"**
>
> Jonathan Elvidge, founder Gadget Shop, *The Times*, 6 July 2002

Connectivity, therefore, extends beyond any industry or market context. It is not just about being aware of different approaches or perspectives on a problem, but also about getting the brain to accept that there are different ways of doing things – developing an open and inquiring mind. It is about being able to see the use of a novel idea in a different context, reusing or 'remixing' existing knowledge. For example, it is claimed that Steve Jobs' interest in calligraphy is the source for Apple's early development of a wide range of fonts on its computers.

Koestler (1964) talked about the creative act bringing new, previously unassociated frames of reference to bear on a topic with an existing frame of reference (patterns and rules that define boundaries of thought – dominant logic). Psychologists call it developing 'conceptual distance' from the dominant logic of a particular group and seeing things from a different perspective. It is not so much about seeing something new as about seeing something familiar in a new way – like the paintings of Picasso represented familiar objects in a very different way. Syed (2019) said this came about by meeting and mixing with people from different backgrounds, with different experiences who might think about problems (and solutions) in a different way. Flath et al. (2017) observed that most innovations do not emerge in isolation, but are at least in part recombinations of previously existing ideas – an assertion that can be traced back to Schumpeter (1942). This reuse or remixing of existing knowledge – sometimes called 'bricolage' in the context of entrepreneurship – is an indispensable part of the creation of novel ideas. In particular, intra-firm knowledge sharing, reuse and remixing are seen as key factors in the development of competitive advantage (Watson and Hewett, 2006; Carnabuci and Operti, 2013). Perhaps surprisingly, in a quantitative review of patents Strumsky and Lobo (2015) showed that most radical innovations come from the remixing and recombination of existing diverse knowledge – a conclusion supported by other research (Kaplan and Vakili, 2015; Nakamura et al., 2015).

> " I believe opportunity is part instinct and part immersion – in an industry, a subject, or an area of expertise . . . You don't have to be a genius, or a visionary, or even a college graduate to think unconventionally. You just need a framework . . . Seeing and seizing opportunities are skills that can be applied universally, if you have the curiosity and commitment. "
>
> Michael Dell, founder Dell Corporation *Direct from Dell: Strategies that Revolutionized an Industry*, New York: Harper Business, 1999

Burt (2004) showed that in many business contexts, good commercial ideas have social origins. He looked at a range of business sectors and measured the number of business ideas developed by staff. He found that the staff coming up with these ideas spanned 'structural holes' – they looked outwards for their ideas: 'This is not creativity born of genius; it is creativity born out of the import–export business.' Similarly, Lakhani (2006) found that it was 'outsiders – those with expertise at the periphery of a problem's field – who were most likely to find answers and do so quickly'. In other words, ideas that are commonplace for one group can spark insights for another. It is all about being open to ideas from all and every source rather than being inward-looking. For example, Cadbury, the chocolate-maker, was founded in 1824 on the basis of Quaker values, with the aim of persuading people to drink chocolate rather than alcohol.

Similarly, solutions to commercial problems or opportunities can come from unrelated disciplines. The ubiquitous Velcro fastening, for example, was conceived in 1941 by Swiss engineer Georges de Mestral. He got his inspiration from nature; after a walk, he observed that there were burrs of the burdock plant sticking to his clothes and his dog's fur. He looked at them under a microscope and observed they had hundreds of tiny 'hooks' that caught onto 'loops' on clothing or fur. Drawing on this observation, he conceived the possibility of two materials being bound together. This is why large technology companies such as Samsung and LG have active programmes to encourage staff to be exposed to ideas from a wide, and sometimes unusual, range of sources. This is one reason why partnering with other people can be so useful in stimulating innovation: One person exposes the other to different ways of doing things, different ideas, and from this emerges the spark of creativity.

CASE INSIGHT 9.1
Swarfega

UK

CONNECTIVITY

Not all ideas find a commercial application in the way that were originally envisaged, and observation and connectivity can change the direction of an invention. Swarfega is a coloured gel that is a dermatologically safe cleaner for the skin. It is now widely used to remove grease and oil from hands in factories and households. But the original product, developed in 1941 by Audley Williamson, was not intended for degreasing hands at all. It was intended as a mild detergent to wash silk stockings. Unfortunately, the invention of nylon, and its use for stockings and tights, rendered the product obsolete.

Watching workmen trying to clean their hands with a mixture of petrol, paraffin and sand, which left them cracked and sore, led Williamson to realize that there was a completely different commercial opportunity for his product. He *observed* a need to help clean grease from workmen's skin and *associated* the characteristics of Swarfega with the ability to solve that problem.

Visit the website: **www.swarfega.com**

Question:

1. How difficult is it to associate the characteristics of a product with the solution of a problem in a completely different context?

CASE INSIGHT 9.2
Great Ormond Street Hospital

UK

CONNECTIVITY

Ideas for innovations can come from unusual sources. The Great Ormond Street Hospital for children took its inspiration from watching the McLaren and Ferrari Formula 1 racing teams take only six seconds to turn a car around at a pit stop. Doctors at the hospital were concerned by the time they took to move patients from the operating theatre to the intensive care unit where they recovered. Delays in emergency handover could cost lives, so they contacted Ferrari to see how the process might be improved. Ferrari explained that their pit-stop procedure was kept simple, with minimal movements all planned in advance. In fact, it was so simple that it could be drawn on a single diagram. From that plan, every member of the Ferrari team knew exactly what they had to do and when to do it in a coordinated fashion. Ferrari videoed the hospital's handovers. When the doctors watched these back, they were shocked at the lack of structure. Ferrari concluded that, with an ever-changing team and unpredictable demand, the hospital's handover teams needed a simple formula they could understand and work to – just like a pit stop. And Ferrari helped the hospital to design it.

The hospital team *observed* the speed of the Formula 1 pit stop. They then *associated* this activity with the process that they undertook to move patients into intensive care. They *questioned* whether they could use similar processes. And finally they *experimented* to see if it would work.

Question:

1. What are the barriers to developing both personal and organizational connectivity? How might they be overcome?

KNOWLEDGE NETWORKS

Many authors have found that a strategic focus on creating intellectual, social and relational assets increases innovation (Bogers, 2011; Dobni et al., 2015; Lavie, 2006; Subramaniam and Youndt, 2005). The generation of information and knowledge is therefore a key component of any entrepreneurial strategy. A survey of 677 strategy leaders in the USA listed the ten most frequent sources of innovation ideas in order of priority as (CB Insights, 2018):

1. Customers.
2. Employees.
3. Competitive intelligence.
4. Supplier/vendors.
5. Academic partners.
6. Industry analysts.
7. Accelerators and incubators.
8. Corporate venture capital.
9. External ideation consultants.
10. Bankers & venture capitalists.

The range of sources may not be a surprise, although their order of priority may be. In the following chapter we consider how changes in customer needs are a vital source of ideas for innovation and this whole book is about encouraging innovation in employees. The other sources may be broadly characterized as 'knowledge networks'. These are a response to the need for connectivity in developing information and knowledge and promoting innovation in general and they can take many different forms. The way in which a commercial network operates depends on the type of network and the purpose it is set up to achieve. A study of 53 research networks by Doz et al. (2000) found two distinct dynamics of formation and growth: the first was through common interest and commercial interdependence, and the second was triggered by one dominant entity where other members are recruited to it.

Tidd and Bessant (2013) observed that operating a knowledge network can be difficult with the skill needed to manage one at the frontier of knowledge (where IP might be important and risks high) as being very different to one where there is an established innovation agenda. They identified four distinct types of network depending on how radical the innovation and the similarity of the companies. Figure 9.2 uses this typology to show the different types of real or virtual network that might be used.

Quadrant 1 has similar firms dealing with tactical innovation issues – 'good practice' forums. These are the easiest to develop and manage because of mutual self-interest.

Quadrant 2 has similar firms working together to create new products or processes by challenging existing boundaries, dealing with the issue of knowledge-sharing and risk-taking through the structures of strategic alliances/partnerships and formal joint ventures. We explored the value of these structures in Chapter 5. The dangers with these structures are that ideas might be copied or that that similar organizations may not question the dominant logic of the sector and therefore would be unlikely to come up with disruptive innovations.

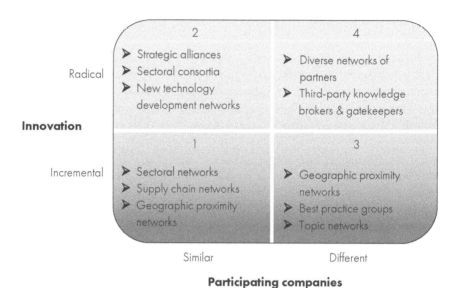

Figure 9.2 Innovation networks

Quadrant 3 has different firms bringing key pieces of information, perhaps from a wide range of disciplines, to the network. The risks of disclosure can be high so the ground rules for disclosure need to be set well in advance and any intellectual property rights issues resolved.

Quadrant 4 involves diverse organizations but uses third-party gatekeepers such as universities as neutral knowledge brokers because the stakes involved in unintended disclosure are even higher. The issue with radical and/or disruptive innovation is that networking too closely with existing customers and suppliers can lead staff to become blind to external developments. The organization's dominant logic is not questioned. The organization needs to build networks with new and different partners alongside the more traditional partners. Often knowledge brokers and gatekeepers such as universities are involved. These new networks may be different in nature and weaker. They are the most difficult to manage but the internet can help organizations with this.

CROWDSOURCING AND OPEN INNOVATION

Technology helps organizations extend their knowledge networks beyond their organizational boundaries. The internet has led to an enormous boost to connectivity. It makes communication and the transfer of knowledge and ideas on a global basis so much easier and quicker. Common design file standards can be sent to web-based on-demand commercial manufacturing services at the press of a button. This sort of network is now used extensively for supply chain management. In another example, General Electric has an extranet bidding and trading system to manage its 1,400 suppliers. In this context, risk revolves around chances of the loss of intellectual property. And with the emergence of open-license, online platforms that make it easy to access and share a wide range of user-generated ideas and knowledge, remixing has found its way from the world of music and art to the design of physical goods.

> **"** *I think as entrepreneurs we are driven by ideas . . . when I have my free time, I like to go onto the internet and really explore the different things that people are doing: what are the different ideas popping all over the world.* **"**
>
> Elim Chew, founder 77th Street, BBC News, 20 December 2010

Two developments that have been shown by Afuah and Tucci (2013) to encourage innovation are worth exploring in more detail – crowdsourcing and 'open innovation.' Crowdsourcing brings a new meaning to connectivity. It is a way of opening up collaboration to people connected on the internet to form a kind of online community. The community or crowd can be either self-selecting or formed from selected individuals such as customers. In this way, the organization can tap a wider range of talent than might be present in its own organization. The crowd might be rewarded or not. There are no rules about crowdsourcing; however, in essence it is about focused problem-solving, often with cross-crowd communication, rather than just a virtual suggestion box. The crowd might be used simply to generate ideas, perhaps through competitions, or might play a part in sorting through them. Either way, the community comes up with solutions or new perspectives to problems and this can be done a lot quicker and more cheaply in a virtual network than in a real network. Crowdsourcing has been used by many organizations such as Lego® (Case insight 16.2) to leverage up creative inputs, giving it a valuable perspective from outside the organization that is unfettered by any dominant logic. It can also have the added advantage of enhancing brand-building by building a feeling of being part of a community that is contributing to the brand's development.

Selected crowdsourcing is the essence of an approach called 'open innovation' (sometimes called 'distributed innovation'). The best-known example of this is Wikipedia, which was launched in 2001. Open innovation links external individuals and organizations with an organization that wishes to generate new ideas, knowledge or to solve problems associated with an innovation. Despite the patent or copyright issues, open innovation has been used by a number of companies to develop software in collaboration with outside organizations and sometimes with the help of customers: Procter & Gamble use the phrase 'Connect and Develop' (C&D) and see collaborative networks as crucial in helping them keep in touch with the research that they do not undertake themselves. Open innovation is at its most effective when innovation requires a diverse range of inputs and therefore is best organized by participants being able to select their own area of contribution. In addition, since physical control is impossible, participants are best left with high levels of autonomy – similar to our entrepreneurial organization.

Chesborough (2003) saw sourcing ideas from outside a company as vital to opening it up to new ideas and preventing it from becoming too inward-looking. He set out six principles behind the use of open innovation:

1. Smart people are everywhere – they don't just work for one organization.
2. To be successful an organization needs to get ideas from everywhere, inside and outside – this helps get behind its dominant logic and established ways of doing things.

3. It is important to get the business model right, not just to get to market first – the lean start-up methodology outlined in Chapter 11 is another way of doing this.
4. External ideas help create value but internal R&D helps the organization own some of that value – open innovation and R&D are not either/or options.
5. R&D should include knowledge brokerage as well as knowledge generation – knowledge has value that can be sold or leveraged up.
6. Never be afraid of buying intellectual property when it advances the business model – we look at the concept of external corporate venturing in Chapter 14.

The most developed example of open innovation is open source software (OSS) communities. OSS was the basis for the successful development of the Linux operating system (Case insight 9.4). In OSS, all contributed software is available to all users both within and outside the community. Some of the largest holders of intellectual property, such as Apple, IBM, Oracle and Sun, have encouraged staff to participate and have donated software and patents to OSS communities. OSS software has also been integrated into the product/service offerings.

Open or distributed innovation systems only operate within a receptive organizational architecture. As Lakhani and Panetta (2007) concluded: 'Traditional organizations should not, however, seize on distributed innovation systems as some silver bullet that will solve their internal innovation problems. Rather, these systems are an important addition to an organization's portfolio of innovation strategies. Those who would adopt or create a distributed innovation system, however, must be prepared to acknowledge the locus of innovation to be outside the boundaries of the focal organization. And this will require a fundamental reorientation of views about incentives, task structure, management, and intellectual property.'

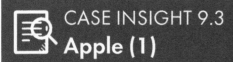 CASE INSIGHT 9.3
Apple (1)

 USA

OPEN INNOVATION

Apple's highly successful App Store is a good example of how open source innovation can be encouraged through partnerships. Apple allows people to develop applications for its iPhone and iPad by selling its own Software Developer Kit for a nominal fee. People can then develop their Apps and sell them for a price of their choosing at the App Store. In return, Apple takes a commission for each download. In its first year, Apple registered over 100,000 developers in the iPhone developer programme with the result that the App Store was able to offer over 65,000 applications and had over 1.5 billion downloads of those Apps – an average of over 23,000 for each App. Analysts estimate that App Store turnover in 2013 was some $2.4 billion; this had risen to $11.4 billion by 2017, an increase of 375 per cent. By comparison, iPhone sales increased by 53 per cent over the same period. Furthermore, the margin on the App Store sales is estimated to be 30 per cent.

Apple now relies heavily on the sale of virtual products. The App Store, iTunes, Apple Music, Apple Pay and iCloud storage generated some $31 billion in turnover in 2017, a figure that is projected to increase to some £50 billion by 2020. Analysts estimate that the overall margin on these sales is 85–90 per cent, making it a major profit generator.

Questions:

1. What are the pros and cons of this open innovation approach for the App Store?
2. What are the threats and opportunities Apple faces because of its success selling virtual products?

Sources: *The Sunday Times*, 29 April 2018 and *The Sunday Telegraph*, 6 January 2019.

 CASE INSIGHT 9.4
Linux

 USA

OPEN INNOVATION

Linus Torvald first suggested setting up a free operating system to compete with the DOS/Windows monopoly in 1991. It was out of the programming 'cooperative' set up to achieve this goal that Linux grew. It provided free source codes to all potential developers, thereby encouraging incremental development. The link with various user groups encouraged concurrent development and debugging. The growth of the internet and later web forms of collaborative working such as Web 2.0 facilitated the growth of Linux, which is now the best example of a successful Open Source Software (OSS) system. It has also spawned many commercial opportunities and is now to be found on servers, desktops and packaged software. Linux has been the platform of choice in the film industry for many years and it is now one of the leading operating systems, with over 90 per cent of the top 500 supercomputers running some variant of it.

Question:

1. Are there any commercial opportunities emerging from this approach to open source innovation? If so, what are they and how might they be organized?

Source: D. Lyons, 'Linux Rules Supercomputers', Forbes, 2005 at: forbes.com/2005/03/15/cz_dl_0315linux.html

ACCELERATORS AND INCUBATORS

One interesting approach to the challenge of acquiring new knowledge and skills as well as stimulating cognitive diversity are the 'accelerator programmes' sponsored by a number of large companies, such as Google for Entrepreneurs (based in Berlin, London, Madrid, Seoul, São Paulo and Warsaw), Disney Accelerator, Microsoft Ventures Accelerator (based in Tel Aviv), Barclay Accelerator, Nike + Accelerator (Techstars), Telefónica and others.

These are sponsored 'boot-camps' or training programmes for start-up teams, which offer training and support from mentors with different skills and investors with different backgrounds. They are designed to facilitate rapid conceptualization, prototyping and development of a business idea within a tight time frame – typically three months. Programmes also provide a wide range of networking connections. Selection is highly competitive (less than 5 per cent selected) and is usually based upon pitches or presentations of the business idea. Seed finance is usually offered by the sponsoring company in exchange for equity. At the end of the programme, teams are expected to demonstrate their product or service.

There are two types of accelerators:

➡ 'Start-up' or 'seed' accelerators, which are general programmes open to all start-ups;
➡ 'Corporate accelerators', which have objectives set by the sponsoring company. Some are open only to internal intrapreneurs or venture teams, whilst some might mix internal and external project teams to encourage cross-fertilization of knowledge and ideas. Some might be open to start-ups in specific areas of technology, allowing the sponsoring company to stay close to new developments and funneling start-ups towards corporate venture capital investment by the sponsoring company. Others might simply be generating good PR for the sponsoring company.

Many accelerator programmes are located in buildings where start-up teams share a range of advice and support such as training, mentoring and serviced office space – called 'business incubators'. These spaces are often designed specifically to facilitate interaction and knowledge exchange, although there are also some virtual, online incubators. There are many government- subsidized incubators open to any start-up, although some have a specific industry or technology focus and might be based in research and technology parks. Incubators do not require start-ups to offer equity involvement and have a continuous intake.

Phadke and Vyakarnam (2017) found that incubators were typically focused on providing support for technology start-ups facing early-stage problems such as the technology itself and framing the business proposition in the context of the competitive environment (customers and markets). By way of contrast, accelerators tended to take over from incubators once the technology was proven and specialized in specific product/market spaces or defined technology areas, typically providing expertise through mentors. They found that partnering with smaller firms was a powerful way for larger firms to 'acquire' innovative products and services through access to technologies they did not have, insights into market spaces and the ability to 'synthesize radically different products and services and to create new business models with the potential to transform the competitive marketplace'.

CREATIVE ENVIRONMENTS

Henrich (2015) observed that innovation 'does not take a genius or a village; it takes a big network of freely interacting minds'. Essentially, therefore, creativity is a social process. Accelerators and incubators recognize this. And the implications of this go beyond individual organizations. As we noted in Chapter 3, Florida (2002; Florida and Tinagli, 2004) observed how new, technology-based organizations thrive in locations such as Silicon Valley in the USA or Cambridge in the UK that combine three elements – technology, talent and tolerance – arguing that it was the diversity of people in these cities that helped spark and

South Africa

CASE INSIGHT 9.5
Stellenbosch LaunchLab

INCUBATORS AND ACCELERATORS

In recent years, an increasing number of incubators and accelerators have been established across the world in recent years. According to the World Bank, there are more than 90 in Africa. The Stellenbosch Launch Lab is supported by Stellenbosch University's Innovus programme, in collaboration with the University of the Western Cape and the University of Cape Town. It aims to facilitate university and industry spin-outs and start-ups by developing a community of entrepreneurs. It offers rental space ('hot-desks', offices and workspace), ICT infrastructure and training programmes, linking to students from the universities. Its 'Ideas' programme is a vehicle for taking concepts and early-stage start-ups from idea to reality with this support and with the connections available from a network of corporate partners. Corporate partners introduce innovation challenges from their industries to prospective entrepreneurs, and vice versa. Selected ideas move into the 'Build' and/or later-stage 'Countdown' programmes. The *LaunchLab* incubation programmes offer business skills training focused on the needs of the entrepreneur – developing their value proposition and business model alongside identifying target markets and customers. Its 'Makerspace' facility allows entrepreneurs to develop prototypes. It uses mentoring, business networking and funding events that introduce entrepreneurs to bankers, business angels, venture capitalists and other potential partners

LaunchLab has helped dozens of start-ups. For example, AzarGen is a biotech company that focuses on developing human therapeutic proteins using advanced genetic and synthetic biology techniques in plants. Sxuirrel is an online platform that helps you find and list different kinds of flexible space in your community – storage, parking, venues etc. Sudonum uses call tracking and data analytics to help businesses understand the effectiveness of their marketing and prove return on investment.

Visit the website at: **launchlab.co.za**

Questions:

1. How do incubators and accelerators facilitate corporate entrepreneurship?
2. What role do universities play in incubators and accelerators?
3. What benefits are gained by each of the stakeholders in incubators and accelerators?

maintain their creativity. The lesson for organizations wishing to build a creative environment is that they must work to develop this sort of physical and cultural environment. This involves bringing together people with different backgrounds and perspectives. It means allowing them to hold different opinions and disagree with each other – questioning the dominant logic of their community. These communities will then attract similarly minded questioning but tolerant people, developing a virtuous circle of creativity. This is not just the influence of the physical environment but also the influence of people – and this seems to be the case across a range of types of creativity. Building on Kirton's (1976, 2003) work, Jablokow and Booth (2006) used KAI (Kirton Adapter-Innovator) theory to increase the effectiveness of a high-performance product development organization. They assigned 'adaptors' in the group to the task of maintaining the current production system and 'innovators' to the task of research and design and total quality management. In both cases people exhibited greater creativity if placed within an environment that matched their cognitive style.

Johnson (2010) used the coral reef as the analogy for the perfect creative environment, be it workplace or city – one that encourages connectivity. The coral reef is a huge diverse eco-system where, despite competition for resources, existence is dependent on cooperation and everything is recycled on a matrix of calcium carbonate built up by the coral. A creative environment is one where ideas come into contact with each other and stimulation is continuous. To him, innovation is not something you do once a year. It is something you do continuously, but an activity that requires the right environment to facilitate it. Johnson goes on to make the point that invention is time- and environment-dependent. It depends on the right circumstances; so, for example, the internet depends on computers, microwave ovens on electricity and people on their environment.

Encouraging connectivity is vital and most organizations now realize that social spaces such as coffee bars, restaurants etc. can be more important than formal systems. Perhaps the best-known example of this is the headquarters of Google – Googleplex – where connectivity and experimentation are designed into the campus (Case insight 16.1). Because of the extensive social facilities, from free restaurants to launderettes, staff are encouraged to spend time on the campus as well as connecting and interacting with others. The 'playful' environment is designed to stimulate creativity. Similarly, much of Facebook's office space has moving walls and furniture so that it can be easily reconfigured to create open innovation labs and private spaces.

However, other organizations have taken a different approach, maintaining more traditional office designs for day-to-day work but establishing separate facilities where staff can go when they want to be more creative – where they are almost 'given permission' to think outside the box. For example, the UK Royal Mail Group developed a 'Creativity Laboratory' where creativity training was facilitated. This was made up of a number of open areas – facilitating groups forming, breaking out and coming together again – all with very informal seating arrangements. Standing and walking were encouraged. There was background music as well as toys and drinks and other distractions for the left-brain. All the walls were 'white walls' which could be written on with felt-tip pens when ideas were flowing freely. Pens were everywhere. There were computer systems that allowed ideas to be posted and voted on anonymously. And records were kept of the whole process – even the white walls were photographed – so that any agreed actions and outcomes could be followed up back in the workplace.

 CASE INSIGHT 9.6
Tencent

 China

WORK ENVIRONMENT

Tencent was founded in 1998 by Pony Ma Huateng and has become a multinational internet conglomerate – Asia's largest publicly traded company and the first to achieve a $500 billion valuation. It is the fourth-largest internet company in the world, after Google, Amazon and eBay and has also consistently been named by the Boston Consulting Group as one of the world's most innovative companies. Tencent started life as a copy of the ICQ

Tencent's headquarters in Shenzhen, China
Source: iStock/Yijing Liu

chatroom, targeting young people but has expanded into other areas. Its many services now include social network (WeChat), music (Tencent Music and QQ Music), web portal (QQ.com), search engine (Soso.com), mobile and multi-player online games (WeGame), internet services (Tencent Pictures, Tencent video and QQLive), payment systems (TenPay) and instant messaging (QQ).

Launched in 1999, Tencent QQ was Tencent's first instant messaging product and became a huge success. However, its biggest success is WeChat, launched in 2011. This is an 'all-in-one' social media platform, offering an ever-expanding range of smartphone services. It can be used to check the news, find a date, book a taxi, look up a restaurant review, make a reservation, and pay for dinner. With over a billion active users in 2018, the WeChat messaging app has seen explosive growth and is now so popular that it has more users than there are smartphones in China. It derives income from service fees and advertising and has recently opened up its advertising to western companies. Having such a diverse product and service offering through a single app, the most valuable thing WeChat owns is the rich lifestyle data it holds on its users (richer than even Facebook or Google), making it very attractive to advertisers – and the Chinese government, with whom Tencent has close links.

Tencent is also aiming to be a major digital content provider. It distributes music from the major global labels, and is now assisting Chinese musicians with copyright protection and promotion. Tencent owns the world's largest video-gaming company and has been successful in driving traffic to its games; it is now starting to create TV and film franchises based on its titles, as well as other intellectual property. For example, it turned the hit *Honor of Kings* mobile game into a celebrity game show called *Kings Attack* for its video-streaming service. In 2017 it launched its digital reading company, China Literature, which offers some 200 million customers sample chapters or complete books from its library of 10 million books – a library it intends to mine to develop films, TV series, etc. All of this content can be distributed through WeChat and it has huge potential.

In 2018, Tencent opened its new twin-tower, 50-storey skyscraper headquarters in Shenzhen, China, in a burgeoning tech district next to Shenzhen University. The eco-friendly building was constructed on reclaimed land and the company aims to create the same collegiate-style atmosphere for its 12,000 employees as its Silicon Valley competitors, albeit in a more compact footprint. These two towers are connected by links. The 'culture link' is at the base of the building. This houses the lobby and reception as well as a museum that aims to introduce visitors to Tencent's history and culture, an exhibition area and large auditorium as well as two levels of cafeterias. The 'health link' is on the 21st floor and houses health and gym facilities, including a running track, climbing wall, basketball court, dance studio, badminton courts, billiards tables and table tennis tables. There's also a juice bar.

The 'knowledge link' is on the 34th floor and houses conference rooms and a training centre called Tencent University as well as a dining hall. There is also a roof-top swimming pool. Buses from the complex connect to various parts of the city and drop employees off in the basement.

The building is very 'high-tech', with facial-recognition technology being used to identify employees and allow access to certain floors. Smart rooms adjust their temperature, based on the number of people present. Robot guides in the lobby show visitors to toilets and other facilities. A building-wide 'internet-of-things' system is also being developed to automate heating, air-conditioning, and security.

For a video tour of Tencent's headquarters, go to: www.cnbc.com/2018/06/07/inside-new-tencent-headquarters-in-shenzhen-china.html

Visit the website: www.tencent.com/en-us/index.html

Questions:

1. What does this building tell you about Tencent?
2. How might this environment affect the culture of Tencent?

KNOWLEDGE AND LEARNING

Knowledge creation is primarily an individual activity and the key role of the organization is to harness it for the production of goods or services. It is therefore logical that the organization's main focus is to stimulate individual creativity and learning and to translate that into products and services that the market values. However, just because an individual has knowledge it does not necessarily mean that it is embedded within an organization. It is often passed on in the form of information. Connectivity generates information, but to be really useful that information needs to be turned into knowledge by other individuals and this only happens through the wheel of learning (Chapter 2).

Figure 9.3 demonstrates this process. Information comes into the organization from a range of sources. It is conceptualized by other individuals through the wheel of learning in a way that is consistent with the organization's norms, cognitive frameworks, context and culture. This is learning, which in turn leads either to tacit knowledge (embedded in individuals' minds and activities) or explicit knowledge (stated in verbal communications or documents). Organizations need to integrate the knowledge generated so it can inform decisions, actions and behaviors and feed back into the processes creating the knowledge. Thus, the results of these decisions, actions and behaviours feed back in the form of information to the organization, which is then reprocessed in the wheel of learning.

Dissemination is the crucial element that distinguishes tacit learning from organizational learning. When information is disseminated, it develops a shared (organizational) interpretation – a consensus on its meaning and its implications for the organization. Firms that are able to do this and then apply it they are said to have a high 'absorptive capacity', defined by Cohen and Levinthal (1990) as the 'ability of a firm to recognize the value of a new, external information, assimilate it, and apply it to commercial ends'.

This brings us back to that aspect of the entrepreneurial architecture that mirrors a learning organization (discussed in Chapter 2) – the emphasis on organizational learning; the ability of the organization to understand the causes of a problem and question 'why';

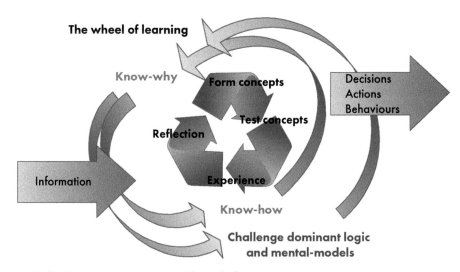

Figure 9.3 Creating organizational knowledge

its emphasis on tacit knowledge. Knowledge-creating companies constantly encourage the process whereby the tacit knowledge of individuals is made available to others to use to extend their own tacit knowledge base. This is facilitated by flat, non-hierarchical structures and might involve training as well as open information flows. A learning organization should therefore facilitate this whole process and the cross-fertilization of tacit and organizational knowledge. Rowley (2000) argued for greater integration of the learning processes with organizational systems (as emphasized in the learning organization literature but with the systems focus of the knowledge management literature). He argued that organizations need to build bridges between people (tacit knowledge) and the systems that transmit organizational knowledge. He coined the phrase 'knowledge entrepreneur' for an organization that can do this. This is vital in large organizations or multinationals, where systems are the only practical way to transmit most information and create knowledge. It is also vital in tackling the challenge of organizational sustainability.

DEVELOPING DISCOVERY SKILLS

Knowledge, awareness and connectivity are combined into what Dyer et al. (2009) called 'discovery skills'. These are skills that can be learned by individuals (tacit knowledge) but transmitted across an organization through training and practice. In a six-year study of more than 3,000 US CEOs, contrasting 25 well-known entrepreneurs (such as Steve Jobs of Apple, Jeff Bezos of Amazon, Pierre Omidyar of eBay, Peter Thiel of PayPal, Niklas Zennström of Skype and Michael Dell) with other CEOs who had no track record for innovation, Dyer et al. (2009) found five 'discovery skills' that made these entrepreneurs particularly adept at linking market opportunity and innovation. They echo Johnson's approach. The skills are:

discovery skills
Creativity skills practised by entrepreneurs: Networking, Observing, Questioning, Experimenting and Associating

1. Networking

These innovative entrepreneurs actively sought out new knowledge and information. They started with a problem they wanted to solve and spent time talking to a network of different people – different age, background, skills, countries, etc. – so as to get new insights and different approaches to finding a solution. They did not just network with like-minded people. They sought out different people from countries with diverse backgrounds not exposed to the dominant logic of their own. Networking is therefore about connectivity. It is a prerequisite for the other discovery skills.

> *Network. Meet people. Show a genuine interest in others. Don't talk too much. Listen more.* 🏻
>
> Raoul Shah, founder Exposure, *The Observer*, 29 September 2013

2. Observing

Innovative entrepreneurs observe common phenomena and people's behaviour – in particular, that of potential customers. They use all their senses; eyes, ears, nose and touch. They scrutinize these phenomena, noticing fine detail and gaining insight into new ways of doing things. Effective observing requires the ability to handle **complexity** and shift one's **perspective** – abilities also measured in the AULIVE test. Observing is coupled with the willingness to question why the things observed are that way. It is also a prerequisite to the skill of associating: you need to observe many different and diverse things so that you can make the associations – why the solutions to one problem may be associated with the solution to another problem. You need to observe detail to be able to associate it across boundaries.

creative complexity
The ability to carry large quantities of information and be able to manipulate and manage the relationships between such information

creative perspective
The ability to shift one's perspective on a situation in terms of space, time and other people

creative curiosity The desire to change or improve things that others see as normal

creative paradox
The ability to simultaneously accept and work with statements that are contradictory

creative boldness The confidence to push boundaries beyond accepted conventions. Also the ability to eliminate the fear of what others might think of you

3. Questioning

Innovative entrepreneurs have the **curiosity** to challenge conventional wisdom, asking 'Why?', 'Why not?' and 'What if?' Most people accept everyday conventions and ways of doing things. By contrast, innovative entrepreneurs ask themselves why they are like this. They also have a pressing problem to solve that gets them to try different approaches, asking again and again what might happen if they try this different approach. The iconic Apple iPod was developed at a time when MP3 players were well established. Staff developing Apple's iTunes software for use with MP3 players formed such a low opinion of the ease of use of MP3s that they decided that they could do better. Most of the innovative entrepreneurs in the study were able to remember the specific question they asked which had inspired them to set up their business. They were also able to imagine some different future state that includes their business idea as a success. They were also able to embrace real-world constraints so that these business ideas could became real business opportunities, so long as the constraints could be overcome. Questioning links the attributes of curiosity, **paradox** and **boldness** measured in the AULIVE test.

The 'Why?–Why?' diagram is a technique that encourages this sort of questioning systematically. For example, the technique could have been used to question why the domestic lock was designed in a particular way, taking nothing for granted. In this way, the technique should uncover the prime attributes that users seek. An alternative solution to the problem can then be constructed by asking the question 'Why not?' Figure 9.4 is an example of how the reasons for a fall in sales might be explored using the diagram. Although

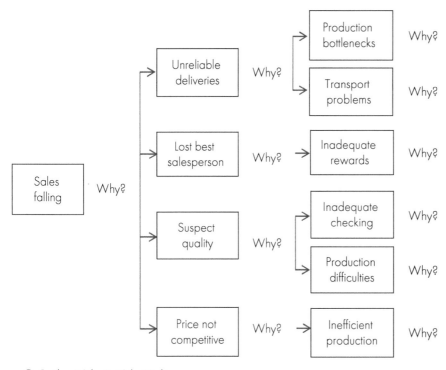

Figure 9.4 The 'Why?–Why?' diagram

not all trails have been followed to their conclusion, the root cause will lie at the end of one (or more) of the 'Why?' trails. Outcomes from asking 'Why?' might be eliminated if they do not reflect reality. Remaining options continue to be explored in this way until there are a number of final possibilities. At this point, we might start asking the questions 'Why not?' or 'What if?' So, for example, if one of the reasons for the fall in sales is unreliable deliveries due to transport problems you might ask the question 'Why not close the transport department?' and 'What if we subcontract deliveries?' Of course, other questions can also be asked.

4. Associating

Innovative entrepreneurs connect seemingly unrelated questions, problems or ideas from many different fields. They are able to recognize relationships among objects, processes, cause and effect, people and so on that others do not see, searching for different, unorthodox relationships that can be replicated in a different context. They link solutions to problems from one context to another – the problem they want to solve to launch their business idea. These relationships can lead to completely new business ideas, products or services that nobody else has thought about. This, the inconvenience of mixing different drinks to form a cocktail led to the (obvious?) idea of selling them ready-mixed; James Dyson was able to see that a cyclone system for separating paint particles could be used (less obviously?) to develop a better vacuum cleaner; and doctors at Great Ormond Street Hospital were able to see that the efficiency of Formula 1 pit stops could help them to improve patient care (Case insight 9.2). This often comes from mixing with people from diverse backgrounds and disciplines.

creative connection
The ability to make
connections between
things that do not
appear connected

The mind of the successful entrepreneur CEOs in the study was able to make **connections** between seemingly unrelated things, transferring questions, problems or ideas from one discipline to another. They capitalized on apparently divergent associations. In addition, this ability to associate seemed to be something that could be encouraged through stimulation: 'The more frequent people in our study attempted to understand, categorize, and store new knowledge, the more easily their brains could naturally and consistently make, store and recombine associations' (Dyer et al., 2009). Associating links the attributes of connection, **abstraction** and perspective in the AULIVE test.

creative abstraction
The ability to apply
abstract concepts/ideas

5. Experimenting

Innovative entrepreneurs actively try out new ideas, creating prototypes and launching pilots. Where these do not work, they learn from any mistakes and try to use the learning in different projects. The Apple iPod, for example, started life as prototypes made out of foam-core boards, using fishing weights to give it the right feel. Jeff Bezos, the founder and CEO of Amazon, is a firm believer in experimentation – but also seeing what can be measured and finding out what are the metrics that define success. All of the successful entrepreneur CEOs engaged in some form of active experimenting, ranging from 'intellectual exploration' to 'physical tinkering' – trying out new experiences, trying out new approaches (including business models), taking things apart, or building prototypes. They were motivated to do something about the problem that they are seeking to solve. One of their most powerful experiments was visiting, living and/or working in overseas countries. This was all part of being exposed to new ideas and mixing with people from diverse backgrounds. Experimenting is one aspect of curiosity.

> ❝ *Jeff [Bezos] has this great belief in experimentation . . . We did thousands of experiments and found out all kinds of things about human behaviour.* ❞
>
> Andreas Weigend, former Chief Scientist, Amazon,
> *The Sunday Times*, 9 September 2018

These discovery skills link closely with Johnson's idea of connectivity (Figure 9.5). They require an individual to be aware of, and engaged with, the world around them – exposed to as many diverse and different ideas, influences and people as possible. Even when exposed to diverse influences, most people walk through life as if on auto-pilot, blinkered to what is happening around them. They need to consciously (as opposed to subconsciously) *see* things. These skills require an open mind, one that is also questioning and willing to experiment. Staff can recognize market opportunities by observing how consumers go about their daily lives and questioning whether their needs can be met 'better' (or at all) in a different way. They need to think about things that are happening around them and how that might affect the future. Just *seeing* things is not enough. They need to question why things are like that – question the status quo and ask why things cannot be done differently. Importantly, they require the systematic coordination of both left- and right- brain systems.

Finally exercising these discovery skills requires staff to have the motivation and time to do something about their business idea or innovation. At their inception, not all new

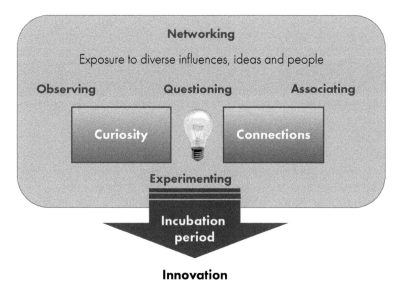

Figure 9.5 Connectivity and discovery skills

products or ideas work, and initially not all ideas are commercially viable. For example, Howard Head, the inventor of the steel ski, made some 40 different metal skis before he found one that worked consistently. Staff need to be motivated to formulate and reformulate their business idea or innovation so that a commercially viable business model can be developed. And all of this takes time – time to think and ponder, time to incubate ideas. Staff therefore need some autonomy over their everyday activities so that they have the slack in terms of time and other resources to take an idea further – which takes us back to the issues about autonomy and control outlined in Chapter 5, but also onto how this process might be facilitated in its later stages, which we cover in subsequent chapters. This process of reformulation of a business idea or innovation is one that repeats itself well into the concept phase of product/service development. It extends even into the phase of business model development. These discovery skills are active skills that need to be practiced. Over time, they become the accepted way of thinking and doing things – built into the architecture of the organization. They can be combined with a set of techniques that will actually help spot a commercial opportunity or develop an existing product or service.

CASE INSIGHT 9.7
Tata Group and Tata Consultancy Services (TCS)

India

STRUCTURES TO ENCOURAGE INNOVATION
Tata Group

The 120-year-old Tata Group is India's largest business, with a turnover of over $100 billion and employing some 700,000 staff. It is controlled by the Tata family through Tata Sons Ltd., the parent company to the group. The group is a conglomerate consisting of hundreds of subsidiaries, in many different industry sectors around the world, each with its own structure, culture and leadership and management style. These include Tata Steel, Tata Motors (the owner of Jaguar and Land Rover), Tata Global Beverages (the owner of Tetley Tea), Tata Communications, Tata Chemicals and Tata Consultancy Services (TCS).

Tata tries to create an environment that values and stimulates innovation throughout and across the entire group. It has the *Tata Group Innovation Forum*, which connects Tata Group companies all over the world, stimulating innovative thinking and fostering collaboration and research. The forum organizes events and workshops and facilitates interaction between Tata managers, innovation experts and academicians, inviting academics and experts to conduct workshops and seminars which introduce new innovation concepts and tools and stimulate innovative thinking among Tata managers. *InnoVerse* is a platform on which senior Tata executives can post problems and challenges facing the company in the hope of finding innovative solutions. *Interweave* is an innovation enabler, which triggers collaborative ideas across four business units. *InnoVista* is an annual Tata Group-level programme (replicated also at a TCS level) which aims to encourage middle-level managers to develop innovations by capturing details on a website, with awards being made for the best innovations.

Tata Consultancy Services (TCS)

TCS was set up in 1968, based in Mumbai, India. It is now a public company with 67 subsidiaries and has a turnover of over $19 billion, employing over 400,000 staff from offices in 46 countries. It is one of the largest Indian companies by market capitalization and is the world's second-largest information technology services provider. Its services include application development and maintenance, business process outsourcing, capacity planning, consulting, enterprise software, hardware sizing, payment processing, software management and technology education services.

TCS prides itself on building innovation into its culture and believes that, whether innovation is incremental or disruptive, there needs to be organizational structures and processes for moving the innovation forward and managers need to be able to direct employees down the appropriate route. It has a number of different structures to facilitate this. The major business units, such as insurance, banking and retail, have their own Innovation Units to develop and fund incremental innovations which improve current services closer to the customer. Platform-level innovations (those that can be extended beyond the present product/service offering), which help businesses adapt to changes in the next two to three years, are directed to 19 Innovation Labs focusing on specific technologies or business sectors. These are based in India, the USA and the UK. These labs also undertake longer-term research that produces disruptive innovations; for example, the provision of cheap agricultural data and information for India's farmers won an innovation award in 2008. They are focused on areas like genomics, metagenomics, integrated computational materials engineering (ICME), robotics and automation, and human-centric systems. Researchers can move between Innovation Labs and the Innovation Units at the business level.

TCS set up the first software research centre in India in 1981 (Tata Research Development and Design Center) undertaking research into software and process engineering and systems research. It runs a Research Scholar Program and in 2007 launched its Co-innovation Network (COIN) connecting to academic research, innovation labs, emerging tech companies, venture capital firms, strategic alliance companies and other Tata Group companies. It encourages collaboration with academia and other research bodies. Researchers have a distinct career path and role rotation from core research to research-related engineering, sales or co-innovation is encouraged. They are not given revenue targets, but are encouraged to explore new technologies, write papers, file patents. There are annual awards for innovation and support is given with patent filing. There is a centrally administered incubator fund that can be used to fund project development in the business units or the Innovation Labs.

TCS has a '4E model' for innovation management: explore, enable, exploit and evangelize. 'Exploration' is conducted in the labs. Once a concept has been tested and proved to be technically viable and to have market potential, it is 'enabled' by engineering application. This is the point at which a specialist team comes in to help with market inputs such as pricing models and distribution strategies. Those concepts that prove commercially viable are then scaled up by an 'exploit' team. Finally, the 'evangelize' team promote the development to stakeholders.

TCS tries to stimulate creative and innovative thinking in staff in a number of ways. TCS executives are expected to attend relevant high-level conferences so as to network and expose themselves to new ideas and developments. TCS has training programmes that focus on innovation, such as the four-day *Technovator* workshop. Staff have five hours of their 45-hour working week free for personal projects that can include either personal or idea development. Employees have annual reviews based upon nine areas, one of which is creativity and ideas generation. There is also a Young Innovator Award, which rewards staff with a salary rise and gives a boost to their career. TCS uses a social platform called *Knome* to encourage the entire organization to participate in focused 'conversations' on different topics. It has a crowdsourcing social network called *IdeaMax* that encourages staff to submit, comment and vote on new ideas. It has also run 'hackathons' (see Case insight 10.1) for clients involving TCS staff.

Visit the website: **www.tcs.com**

Questions:

1. Outline the structures TCS has for encouraging innovation and explain what each one aims to achieve.
2. Why is communication across Tata Group and within TCS important?
3. How might the organization and culture within the Innovation Labs in TCS differ from the business units? Why is this significant?

SUMMARY

➡ Dominant 'right-brain' thinkers are more creative, intuitive, imaginative and rule-breaking. Dominant 'left-brain' thinkers are more rational, logical and analytical. The ability to oscillate between the two modes improves practical creativity.

➡ Creativity can be inhibited by individuals or systems of control within organizations. Barriers to organizational creativity can be dismantled using the techniques for managing change outlined in Chapter 7.

➡ Connectivity – connecting with different ideas and ways of doing things – is a prerequisite to creativity. It generates new knowledge and information that can be transferred from one context to another and allows them to recombine previously existing ideas to solve new problems. It gets an individual to question their 'dominant logic'. But the creative process takes time to make the necessary linkages.

➡ Networking – both internal and external – is an important element in developing connectivity. Internal networking can be facilitated by an appropriate environment that allows staff to mingle and exchange ideas. Knowledge networks formalize this process for an organization. Crowdsourcing of ideas and open innovation can also bring fresh thinking and new ideas to an organization.

➡ Accelerators and incubators bring together individuals with new ideas that they want to commercialize through training and other forms of facilitation.

➡ Spotting and developing an original business idea requires creativity. You can improve this by developing discovery skills: networking, observing, questioning, experimenting and associating (connectivity). Discovery skills are active skills that can be practised. They require the systematic coordination of both left- and right-brain systems.

GROUP DISCUSSION TOPICS

1. Compare the barriers you face to being creative with the barriers faced by the rest of the group. Compile a list of the major barriers and how they might be overcome.
2. How is creativity and innovation shown in entrepreneurship?
3. Creativity favours the connected mind. Discuss.
4. What are the advantages and disadvantages of crowdsourcing?
5. What are the advantages and disadvantages of open innovation?
6. What constitutes a creative organizational environment? Why?
7. What constitutes a creative national environment? Why? What lessons are there for an organization?
8. Can you be creative on your own or in isolation?
9. Compare and contrast left- and right-brain thinking. How can you get them to work together?
10. Are you a predominantly left- or right-brain person? How does this show itself? Are you comfortable being creative?
11. Creativity is a more difficult skill than entrepreneurship to develop. Discuss.
12. Systematic is not a word you associate with creativity and innovation. Discuss.
13. Do you believe people can be trained to be more creative?
14. Is creativity the same as opportunity perception? What is the link?
15. How might creativity be both discouraged and encouraged?
16. Reflect on the need for freedom as well as slack time to encourage creativity. How is this affected by the issue of balance in autonomy and control, introduced in Chapter 5?
17. Is creativity good in all organizations? Give examples to support your case.
18. How are Dyer's five discovery skills – associating, questioning, observing, experimenting and networking – linked? Which ones are prerequisites for the others?
19. How can you improve your discovery skills?
20. Using your creativity test results as a base (Activity 1), discuss whether these dimensions adequately measure creativity compared to other measures covered in the text.

ACTIVITIES

1. Assess your creative potential by taking one of the online tests discussed in the text (e.g., AULIVE). Write a report outlining the implications of the results and provide evidence from your life to support (or otherwise) the results.
2. List the barriers that you feel inhibit you from being creative at home and at your college or university. How might they be removed or circumvented?
3. List the sources for awareness and new ideas you have at your disposal. What do you need to do to capitalize on them in a systematic way?
4. Select any day-to-day object (e.g., a paper clip). Undertake a group brainstorming session to see how many uses you can find for it. Repeat the activity with another object.

REFERENCES

Afuah, A. and Tucci, C.L. (2013) 'Capture and Crowdsourcing', *Academy of Management Review*, 38(3).

Bogers, M. (2011) 'The Open Innovation Paradox: Knowledge Sharing and Protection in R&D Collaborations', *European Journal of Innovation Management*, 14(1).

Bolton, B. and Thompson, J. (2000) *Entrepreneurs: Talent, Temperament, Technique,* Oxford: Butterworth-Heinemann.

Burt, S.B. (2004) 'Structural Holes and Good Ideas', *American Journal of Sociology*, 110(2), September.

Carnabuci, G. and Operti, E. (2013) 'Where Do Firms' Recombinant Capabilities Come From? Intraorganizational Networks, Knowledge, and Firms' Ability to in Novate Through Technological Recombination', *Strategic Management Journal*, 34(13).

CB Insights, (2018) *State of Innovation Report 2018: Survey of 677 Corporate Strategy Executives,* New York, NY: CB Insights.

Chesborough, H. (2003) *Open Innovation: The New Imperative for Creating and Profiting from Technology,* Boston, MA: Harvard Business School Press.

Cohen, W.M. and Levinthal, D.A. (1990) 'Absorptive Capacity: A New Perspective on Innovation and Learning', *Administrative Science Quarterly*, 35(1).

Dobni, C.B., Klassen, M. and Nelson, W.T. (2015) 'Innovation Strategy in the US Top Executives Offer Their Views', *The Journal of Business Strategy*, 36(1).

Doz, Y.L., Olk, P.M. and Ring, P.S. (2000) 'Formation Processes of R&D Consortia', *Strategic Management Journal*, 21(3).

Dyer, J.H., Gregersen, H.D. and Christensen, C.M. (2009) 'The Innovator's DNA', *Harvard Business Review*, December.

Flath, C.M., Sascha, F., Wirth, M. and Thiesse, F. (2017) 'Copy, Transform, Combine: Exploring the Remix as a Form of Innovation', *Journal of Information Technology*, 32.

Florida, R. (2002) *The Rise of the Creative Classes: And How It's Transforming Work, Leisure, Community and Everyday Life,* New York, NY: Basic Books.

Florida, R. and Tinagli, I. (2004) *Europe in the Creative Age,* London: Demos.

Fox Cabane, O. and Pollack, J. (2017) *The Net and the Butterfly: The Art and Practice of Breakthrough Thinking,* London: Portfolio/Penguin.

Henrich, J. (2015) *The Secret of Our Success: How Culture Is Driving Human Evolution, Domesticating Our Species, and Making Us Smarter,* Princeton, NJ: Princeton University Press.

Jablokow, K.W. and Booth, D.E. (2006) 'The Impact and Management of Cognitive Gap in High Performance Produce Development Organizations', *Journal of Engineering and Technology Management*, 23.

Johnson S. (2010) *Where Good Ideas Come From: The Natural History of Innovation,* London: Allen Lane.

Kahneman, D. (2012) *Thinking Fast and Slow,* London: Penguin Books.

Kanter, R.M. (2004) 'The Middle Manager as Innovator', *Harvard Business Review*, 82(7/8).

Kaplan, S. and Vakili, K. (2015) 'The Double-Edged Sword of Recombination in Breakthrough Innovation', *Strategic Management Journal*, 36(10).

Kirby, D. (2003) *Entrepreneurship,* London: McGraw-Hill.

Kirton, M. (1976) 'Adaptors and Innovators: A Description and Measure', *Journal of Applied Psychology*, October.

Kirton, M.J. (2003) *Adaption-Innovation: In the Context of Diversity and Change,* Hove: Routledge.

Koestler, A. (1964) *The Act of Creation,* London: Hutchinson.

Lakhani, K. (2006) 'Open Space Science: A New Model for Innovation', *Working Knowledge: Harvard Business School Newsletter*, November 20.

Lakhani, K.R. and Panetta, J.A. (2007) 'The Principles of Distributed Innovation', *Innovations*, Summer.

Lavie, D. (2006) 'The Competitive Advantage of Interconnected Firm: An Extension of the Resource Based View', *Academy of Management Review*, 3(3).

Majaro, S. (1992) 'Managing Ideas for Profit', *Journal of Marketing Management*, 8.

Mintzberg, H. (1976) 'Planning on the Left Side and Managing on the Right', *Harvard Business Review*, 54, July/August.

Nakamura, H., Suzuki, S., Sakata, I. and Kajikawa, Y. (2015) 'Knowledge Combination Modeling: The Measurement of Knowledge Similarity Between Different Technological Domains', *Technological Forecasting and Social Change*, 94.

Phadke, U. and Vyakarnam, S. (2017) *Camels, Tigers and Unicorns: Rethinking Science & Technology-Enabled Innovation,* London: World Scientific.

Rowley, J. (2000) 'From Learning Organization to Knowledge Entrepreneur', *Journal of Knowledge Management*, 4(1).

Schumpeter, J.A. (1942) *Capitalism, Socialism, and Democracy*, New York, NY: Harper and Brothers.

Simmie, J. (2002) 'Knowledge Spillovers and Reasons for the Concentration of Innovative SMEs', *Urban Studies*, 39(5–6).

Strumsky, D. and Lobo, J. (2015) 'Identifying the Sources of Technological Novelty in the Process of Invention', *Research Policy*, 44(8).

Subramaniam, M. and Youndt, M. (2005) 'The Influence of Intellectual Capital on the Type of Innovative Capabilities', *Academy of Management Journal*, 48(3).

Syed, M. (2019) *Rebel Ideas: The Power of Diverse Thinking*, London: John Murray.

Tidd, J. and Bessant, J. (2013) *Managing Innovation: Integrating Technology, Market and Organizational Change*, Chichester: John Wiley.

Venkataraman, S. (1997) 'The Distinctive Domain of Entrepreneurship Research: An Editor's Perspective' in J. Katz and R. Brockhaus (eds) *Advances in Entrepreneurship, Firm Emergence and Growth*, Greenwich, CT: JAI Press.

Watson, S. and Hewett, K. (2006) 'A Multi-theoretical Model of Knowledge Transfer in Organizations: Determinants of Knowledge Contribution and Knowledge Reuse', *Journal of Management Studies*, 43(2).

ONLINE RESOURCES AVAILABLE

For further resources relating to this chapter see the companion website at **www.macmillanihe.com/Burns-CEI**

10 Generating business ideas

CONTENTS

- Commercial opportunity
- New technology and market spaces
- Creative synthesis
- Creating blue-water opportunity
- Value-chain analysis
- Spotting opportunity
- Tools for exploring change
- Techniques for exploring product inadequacies
- Systematic inventive thinking
- Summary
- Group discussion questions
- Activities
- References

CASE INSIGHTS

Learning outcomes

When you have read this chapter and undertaken the related activities you will be able to:

➡ Understand and explain how 'creative synthesis' applied to technology is vital in bringing a new technology to the market;

➡ Understand and explain the importance of 'blue-water opportunities' and how to create them by challenging market conventions;

➡ Understand how exploring the value chain can highlight business opportunities;

➡ Use a range of techniques to scan the environment for changes that might highlight business opportunities;

➡ Use a range of techniques to explore product inadequacies that might highlight business opportunities.

COMMERCIAL OPPORTUNITY

Finding a new commercial business opportunity is about being able to find a solution to a problem – a solution that sufficient people are willing to pay for and one that competitors have not (yet) come up with. Successful entrepreneurs are able to match opportunities in the marketplace with innovative ways of meeting those opportunities. They link opportunity with creativity and innovation. But which comes first: seeing the commercial opportunity or the innovation?

That 'eureka moment', when a good business idea is born, rarely happens by chance. Successful entrepreneurial firms such as Google or Samsung also go about seeking out ways of developing innovations that match commercial opportunities in a systematic way. Their success is not just down to good luck. They systematically and actively stimulate individual creativity – connectivity and discovery skills – whilst integrating information and knowledge into organizational learning. They go about finding and developing business ideas in a similar systematic fashion.

> *Innovation has more to do with the pragmatic search for opportunity than the romantic ideas about serendipity or lonely pioneers pursuing their vision against all the odds.*
>
> Nicholas Valery, 'Innovation in Industry', *The Economist*, 5(28) 1999

Generating innovative ideas is a numbers game: the more ideas generated, the greater the likelihood some will see the light of day. It has been estimated that for every eleven ideas starting out on the process only one new product will be launched successfully. There is an element of randomness and serendipity about this, but with systems in place to encourage their generation and processing, there is a better chance of collecting them. Ideas may come from anywhere and at any time.

Many business ideas will never see the light of day because they prove to be impractical or commercially unviable. Commercial viability is important in the context of entrepreneurship. This means that the idea needs to be rooted in an entrepreneurial mindset – that ability to spot opportunity and link it to market need and value creation. Furthermore, developing and perfecting an idea can take some time. The product or service is unlikely to be exactly right straight away (it may not even work properly), so it will probably need to be modified. The business model that helps sell it may still need to be developed. And both may need to be tested in some way before the final launch. This means that options need to be generated and evaluated at each stage of development and even after launch. We shall return to this in the next chapter, but this chapter will focus on finding commercial opportunities.

NEW TECHNOLOGY AND MARKET SPACES

Not all innovation takes the same form. Companies following a marketing strategy of low price and low differentiation are likely to encourage innovations that reduce costs and encourage efficiency, but this may necessitate capital investment. These are likely to be incremental, process innovations. Companies following a strategy of high differentiation are likely to encourage innovation stimulated by information on user needs and technical inputs.

CASE INSIGHT 10.1
Hackathons

FINDING SOLUTIONS TO PROBLEMS

A hackathon is a time-limited (e.g., one-day), project-centred innovation event for computer programmers and others involved in software development. It has a very specific focus (e.g., to solve a specific problem) and often involves cross-functional teams (e.g. programmer, graphic designer, project manager, etc.). It can be either an 'open' event (often the source of more radical innovations) or a closed-company event focusing on specific product/markets. They might involve competing teams. The aim is to create a functioning piece of software or hardware at the end of the event. Usually, this involves demonstrations.

An early example of a hackathon was in 1999 when Sun Microsystems challenged attendees at the JavaOne conference to write a program in Java script for the new Palm V, using the infrared port to communicate with other Palm users. In a later example, the GroupMe company was born out of an open hackathon at the TechCrunch Disrupt conference in 2010. Yahoo! holds an annual open hackathon that focuses on apps for its websites. Google has run similar events. A closed-company hackathon was credited with coming up with the ubiquitous 'Like' button, originally developed for Facebook. Shutterstock hosts an annual 24-hour closed hackathon designed to allow employees to pursue any idea they have to improve the company. This approach has been so successful that the Australian software company Atlassian gives their employees a similar opportunity once every quarter, providing participants with refreshments and allowing them to work on whatever they want and with whoever they want so long as they share the outcome with the company.

Many companies have broadened the concept of a hackathon beyond software development to have a structured 'innovation day' for employees generally (within a department, division or even the entire small firm) that is designed around product/service innovation. Such events allow employees from different parts of the organization to meet and exchange ideas, problems that need to be solved, opportunities that could be pursued. They encourage the internal connections that are so important as part of a broader innovations strategy. Ideas coming out of these sorts of events are usually no more than that – ideas and concepts that need to be further developed.

Question:

1. Why do hackathons work so well? What lessons about innovation more generally do you take from this?

They are likely to implement major innovation frequently, although these will usually be well short of invention or paradigm shift. Encouraging large-scale innovation is not the same as encouraging incremental changes in products, processes and marketing. The risks faced in launching these different types of innovation are also very different. However, the reality in most multi-product businesses is that they will have to cope with both incremental and large-scale innovations – often on a continuous basis. And then there is the issue of invention and paradigm shift, which we call 'disruptive' or 'discontinuous' innovation, and which requires quite a different mindset; this is something to which we shall return later in this chapter.

Generally, the more radical the innovative ideas the more difficult they are to generate and then commercially validate. The idea may have originated from scientific research, but to be of interest to a business it must have a commercial application – hopefully one that has not been spotted by rivals and ideally one that can offer some sort of safeguard for the intellectual property.

Figure 10.1 shows three generic approaches to generating business ideas. The first approach is a technology-based approach relying on a good knowledge of new developments in technology and technology mapping (1). This may include analysing product/service inadequacies to understand and isolate commercial opportunities. It requires a deep understanding of the technology and can involve providing the product/service with greater or improved functionality and/or applying the technology to other applications. It can result in either incremental or radical innovation. However, unless it is linked to market needs it may prove to be commercially unsuccessful.

The second approach is the market-based approach relying on analysing market needs and trends (2). This involves spotting unmet needs and gaps in the market as well as analysing product/service inadequacies. Again the innovations in this instance may be either incremental or radical in their scope. The approach can be based on:

➡ Market research – This provides insights into existing customer behaviours and views. Generally, it provides a volume of broad data, rather than any depth. It is particularly useful in highlighting existing product inadequacies. It is less useful in providing insights about the future.

➡ Focus groups and key user analysis – These provide a deeper insight into how customers feel. They can be combined with market research. For example, market research might highlight a product inadequacy and focus groups or user analysis might provide greater details or insights into how the inadequacy might be addressed. They are also of limited use in providing insights about the future.

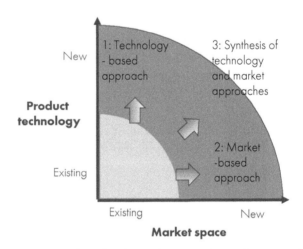

Figure 10.1 Technology- and market- based approaches to business idea generation

The third approach involves a synthesis of these two approaches – linking technological innovation with a market-based approach (3). This often involves linking new, often-emergent technologies with business model innovation to create new market spaces. This is disruptive innovation and is when new industries can be born. Whilst this may offer the greatest commercial opportunity, it is also the most difficult to achieve. Phadke and Vyakarnam (2017) observed the third approach required '**creative synthesis**' – blending an understanding of technology with an understanding of the market to create this new

creative synthesis
Synthesis of technological innovation with market-based innovation

market space. They talked about three levels of synthesis, consistent with increasing levels of market complexity and impact:

➡ Outcome-driven innovation – This is based on the premise that customer-valued performance can be identified and improved.
➡ Design thinking – A loose set of holistic concepts that approach design from the perspective of solving complex problems for people, rather than just creating distinctive objects or shapes. We cover this topic in the next chapter.
➡ Creative synthesis – This builds on design thinking but integrates business model development with the technology perspective. Again we will look at this in the next chapter. Creative synthesis applied to radical or disruptive innovation is the most likely approach to lead to the development of new-to-the-world industries (Figure 3.1).

Phadke and Vyakarnam saw **creative synthesis** applied to technology as vital in bringing a new technology to the market: 'Critical for science and technology-enabled innovation is the ability to synthesise new ideas, concepts, products and services: typically synthesis skills require the ability to understand and integrate a range of technologies and couple technology capability with potential users and customers.' Whilst acknowledging that this was a skill that could be taught, their research found that all too often it was missing.

creative synthesis Synthesis of technological innovation with market-based innovation

CASE INSIGHT 10.2
Sephora

France

INNOVATION IN RETAILING

While other cosmetic companies depend on department store sales, Sephora is revolutionizing retail by offering customers new in-store and on-line experiences such as trying on make-up virtually using augmented reality, matching their skin tone to a foundation using artificial intelligence (AI), and sampling a fragrance via a touchscreen and scented air. Founded in 1970, and acquired by the luxury goods conglomerate LVMH (Moët Hennessy – Louis Vuitton) in 1997, Sephora is a French retail cosmetics chain with some 2,300 stores operating in 33 countries and revenues of over $4 billion in 2013. It sells its own and other brands of cosmetics over-the-counter and online in a highly competitive and changing industry where brands like Glossier and Huda Beauty are rapidly building market share, almost entirely through the new channels of social media and user-generated content. To help it counter this competition and bridge the gap between its online and in-store experiences, Sephora set up an Innovation Lab in 2015 to help it develop, test and launch new offerings for shopping both in-store and online, using AI technologies such as natural language processing, machine learning and computer vision.

> We are very focused on our customers, and we know that her life is increasingly reliant on digital. So we know to be successful as a retailer, we've got to be where our clients are, and give her tools and experiences that meet her needs. It's about being open to new ideas, and working with partners to develop the right solutions – and being willing to do things that maybe our clients don't even know that they want yet. (Mary Beth Laughton, executive vice president of Omni retail, Sephora, IncubateIND, 18 February 2018)

One of the innovations coming out of the Lab was the Sephora Virtual Artist app, the product of a partnership with the facial analysis and visualization technology firm ModiFace. Launched in 2016, it allows customers to enjoy the

The cosmetics section of a Sephora store in Manhattan
Source: iStock/wdstock

personal attention they might have from an individual sales representative in-store and online using AI, but at a fraction of the cost. The Sephora Virtual Artist app is an augmented reality platform that allows users to upload a photo and then apply a virtual make-over, experimenting with different product and shade combinations for lips, eyes or cheeks. The app can be downloaded and used on a mobile device; in stores customers can also 'try on' any product virtually inside a kiosk by simply tapping on a screen. There is even a device that scans the surface of their skin and makes a precise match to foundation products. Alongside this, Sephora also developed a system called InstaScent, which allows a customer to test out 18 different kinds of scent groupings in-store.

With online shopping becoming more and more popular, particularly for the customers Sephora targets, the Sephora Visual Artist platform is an attempt to replicate an in-store experience for online shoppers. Hosting the app on Facebook Messenger, which has almost one billion daily users overwhelmingly on mobile devices hosting social media content, also helps it to target the same younger audience. Sephora advertises extensively on social media and is partnering with Dynamic Yield to provide personalized product ads for customers. These ads use algorithms that weigh factors like location, items previously viewed, and items purchased. With the employment of another product, called Storyboard, Sephora has also started blended its ads into the flow of articles, images, videos and blogs on Flipboard, a social media app that is focused less on connection to other users and more on the personal interests of the main user. This gives it a higher potential for targeting, since the user is providing a constant flow of data on the content that interests them.

Visit the website: **www.sephora.com**

Questions:

1. Who owns the technology being used by Sephora? How sustainable is this competitive advantage?
2. Is it important to have similar shopping experiences in-store and online?
3. Why is it important to have the same target market in mind when developing these new 'experiences' and then linking it a promotions strategy?
4. Are there any lessons here for other retailers?

CREATIVE SYNTHESIS

Radical innovation is riskier than spotting an existing market opportunity because there is no guarantee that the market need will materialize. It requires vision and self-belief aplenty, and is also likely to absorb both time and resources. It requires a high degree of creativity and innovation. However, the returns for success are also likely to be high. Disruptive innovation is a step change in products, processes or the framing of markets. Generated by major inventions, they can have large-scale disruptive effects on markets, industries and even economies. But many inventors fail to realize the commercial viability of their invention. When disruptive innovation creates radically new markets, fortunes can be made (and lost) quickly. There is no guarantee the product will work and there is no guarantee that it will have any customers. Even if it works, what will prevent competitors copying it? This form of innovation can be highly profitable, but also expensive and very risky. It requires a leap in creative imagination, from mere possibility to commercial reality. That can be difficult for many, if not most people. Many larger organizations prefer to rely on external corporate venturing to secure this sort of innovation – a way of buying-in these innovations once they are past the pure research and prototype stages. Big pharmaceutical companies do this all the time, buying-in the research from small biotech firms or public labs and focusing instead on the testing, development and market roll-out stages of drug development. We look at external corporate venturing in Chapter 14.

However, for every scientific innovation there could be dozens, if not hundreds, of commercial applications. Commercial value comes in matching the innovation with customer need. Case insight 1.4 highlighted how Steve Jobs was able to find commercial applications for the inventions and innovations of others. He never invented anything himself, being far more engaged in the commercial side of Apple's development. Apple's success is based upon good design and improving product ease of use rather than invention. What is more, many disruptive innovations did not come from scientific innovation – rather from radical market innovation often called 'market paradigm shift'. Case insight 10.3 shows how Henry Ford put together a series of incremental innovations to create the modern assembly line for production. Together these innovations were so disruptive that they created a new commercial market for affordable motor vehicles that did not exist before – a market paradigm shift.

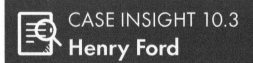

CASE INSIGHT 10.3
Henry Ford

MARKET PARADIGM SHIFT USING DISCOVERY SKILLS

Henry Ford did not invent the car, but he did revolutionize the way in which cars were produced and sold in the 1900s, moving from craft-based to production-line methods and from wealthy customers – a strategy all other firms were pursuing at the time – to supplying an affordable car for everyman – a vision he had to turn into a reality. He created a new commercial market for motor cars – a market paradigm shift that changed the rules of the game. And yet this involved only incremental changes – albeit on an extensive scale – to products and processes, component and factory design and also to the way labour in which was organized in his factories. This disruptive innovation created the mass market for cars that we know today. But from where did Ford get his vision of the future? How was he able to break away from the established thinking of how a car should be made and to whom it should be sold?

Henry Ford never believed in market research. He once said that if he had asked people what they wanted, they'd have said 'faster horses', rather than 'new-fangled' things called cars. And his vision led him away from car designs that reflected the old ways coachmen led horse-drawn carriages of the wealthy – chauffeurs separated from the wealthy that they drove – to the driver being part of the group in the car. Yet Ford had to find ways of making his vision a practical reality and developing a business model that would make it commercially viable. So where did he get his ideas from? Henry Ford was an 'active discoverer'. Firstly, he *questioned* why it was that only the wealthy could travel by car and came up with an alternative reality or vision. This all revolved around finding ways of producing cars cheaply – a low-cost business model with business strategies that reflected the need to mass produce and sell cars in high volumes. He *connected* this vision with a number of other situations he had *observed* through his *networks*.

Ford's key idea was to get workers to undertake repetitive tasks on a moving assembly line, rather than having craftsmen responsible for much of the assembly within a static garage. This idea came from observing how a slaughterhouse worked and connecting this to his vision. He implemented a system of profit sharing with front-line workers in order to motivate them to do this quickly (time was money) – a concept that had been used by a French printing company decades earlier. His strategy of making one standard product in one colour (the black Model T Ford) was designed to make the assembly line operate as fast as possible – and he knew through *experimentation* that black paint dried faster than any other colour. Finally, to get the volumes of cars coming off this production line sold quickly he started a novel network of car dealerships, partly paid on a commission basis – just as Isaac Singer had done to sell his sewing machines nearly half a century earlier.

Ford started with a problem – how to make an affordable motor vehicle. Building on this, he made new connections that led to novel solutions, and wrapped a successful strategy around the big idea – the moving assembly line. To use in his own words: 'I invented nothing new. I simply assembled the discoveries of others.'

Questions:

1. From the examples given, which discovery skills did Henry Ford exhibit and how were they used to make his vision a reality?
2. What do you have to do to develop these discovery skills?

CREATING BLUE-WATER OPPORTUNITY

Market paradigm shift happens when entrepreneurs challenge the conventional ways of marketing a product/service. In most sectors, there are factors that managers believe are critical to the success of their business. These paradigms become part of the dominant logic of an industry. But circumstances and the environment can change and the managers running the industry may not adapt their way of thinking, particularly if the company dominates an industry with its existing technologies. Case insight 3.2 highlighted how Microsoft almost missed the internet revolution because it was too focused on exploiting its main source of income derived from its dominance of the software industry with Microsoft Office.

Kim and Mauborgne (2005) coined the term 'blue ocean strategy' for one that seeks to meet market needs that are currently unrecognized and unmet. Companies creating blue-ocean strategies never benchmark against competitors, instead they make this irrelevant by 'creating a leap in value for both the buyers and the company itself'. They create uncontested market space, creating new demand and making competition irrelevant. Kim and

Mauborgne contrasted this to 'red-ocean strategy', which involves gaining competitive advantage in existing, often mature markets. They acknowledge that 'red oceans' cannot be ignored, but criticize conventional marketing strategy as being too focused on building advantage over competition in this way.

None of this was new. Based upon a study of firms that had challenged established big companies in a range of industries, Hamel and Prahalad (1994) claimed that these firms had succeeded in creating entirely new forms of competitive advantage by asking three key questions:

➡ What new types of customer benefits should you seek to provide in 5, 10 or 15 years?
➡ What new competencies will you need to build or acquire in order to offer these benefits?
➡ How will you need to reconfigure our customer interface over the next few years?

So how might a company go about creating completely new markets? Ian Chaston (2000, reprinted 2015) argued that they have to systematically challenge established market conventions – the dominant logic in an industry – and develop new solutions. Chaston's approach to this is simple: understand how conventional competitors operate and then challenge their approach by asking whether a different one would add customer value or create new customers. Sometimes doing things differently can add value for the customer without involving extra costs – indeed sometimes doing things differently can reduce costs – whilst still providing the opportunity to charge a high price. The company needs to ask the question '*why* are things done this way?' followed by the question '*why not* do them a different way?' This is one of the fundamental discovery skills outlined in the last chapter.

> 66 We learned the importance of ignoring conventional wisdom . . . It's fun to do things that people don't think are possible or likely. It's also exciting to achieve the unexpected. 99
>
> Michael Dell, founder Dell Corporation *Direct from Dell: Strategies that Revolutionized an Industry*, New York: Harper Business, 1999

An organization might dissect and challenge every element of its existing business model or those used by its competitors: 'Why is the product assembled, priced, promoted, distributed, etc. in this way?' Chaston suggested three broad categories of conventions that can be challenged:

1. Sectoral conventions: These are the strategic rules that guide the marketing operations of the majority of firms in a sector, such as efficiency of plants, economies of scale, methods of distribution and so on. Kim and Mauborgne talked about reorientating analysis from *competitors* to *alternatives*. So, for example, in the UK insurance used to be sold through high street insurance brokers until Direct Line challenged the conventional wisdom and began to sell direct over the telephone, then on the internet. Now this is the norm. We saw in Case insight 3.3 how Rolls-Royce redefined the nature of their business by offering the TotalCare® programme.

2. Performance conventions: These are set by other firms in the sector and include profit, cost of production, quality and so on. Kim and Mauborgne argued that both value enhancement and cost reduction can be achieved by redefining industry problems and looking outside industry boundaries, rather than simply trying to offer better solutions to existing problems as defined by the industry. In the 1960s, Japanese firms ignored Western performance conventions en-masse and managed to enter and succeed in these markets.

3. Customer conventions: These conventions make certain assumptions about what customers want from their purchases, for example price, size, design and so on. Kim and Mauborgne talked about reorientating analysis from *customers* to *non-customers*. The Body Shop redefined the cosmetic industry's 'feel-good factor' to include environmental issues. Companies like Southwest Airlines, Ryanair and easyJet pioneered low-price air travel and redefined the airline industry.

Creating opportunity through market paradigm shift is probably easier than radical product invention – and can be just as profitable. Both approaches need individuals to be able to think creatively – 'outside the box'. They need to be able to generate new ideas and knowledge, a vision of the future that links market opportunities to the key capabilities of the organization. They also need to be able to challenge conventions and be open to new ideas; to deal with rapidly changing and disparate information in a wide range of new technologies and in diverse, fragmented and often geographically widespread markets; to chart a way through often-uncertain political and unstable regulatory environments. And in these circumstances knowledge and information are powerful sources of opportunity and innovation. But remember, creating these sorts of opportunities can be risky. There is no guarantee that the market will agree with this vision of the future.

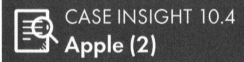 CASE INSIGHT 10.4
Apple (2)

 USA

DOMINANT LOGIC AND ITUNES

In 2019 Apple announced that it would be terminating iTunes and was going to split the software into three functional units dealing with music, podcasts and TV apps. It seemed logical as iTunes had become bloated by this time. Yet only 13 years ago iTunes had burst onto the market and revolutionized the music industry by making it easy to buy and download music. But how did this revolution happen?

Music has been on the internet since CDs made music digital in the early 1980s. Despite being huge (700MB), CDs could be copied and shared – despite the slow network connections. But it was not until the early 1990s when it was discovered how to shrink files that file sharing became practical. In 1994, the MP3 encoder was released, compressing three minutes of music into just 3MB. This opened the floodgates to music 'sharing'. Yet again it was not until Napster came along in 1999 – a free-to-use, internet-based software system that enabled computer user to 'share' music – that the music industry was turned on its head. Now files of music could be shared for free, albeit illegally. The dominant logic in the industry was based around a business model that involved selling CDs that were protected by copyright. Napster completely undermined that model. When they eventually managed to close down Napster in 2001, it left some 60 million users looking for, but unable to find, an internet-based substitute product. The industry continued to try to sell the CD.

It took Steve Jobs and Apple to recognise that there was a commercial opportunity for an internet-based music market. In 2001, Apple launched its own software which enabled music to be easily uploaded, organized and played, basing it on SoundJam MP, a software program that Jobs had acquired the previous year. The revolution was complete in 2003, when Apple finally launched the iTunes store, enabling tracks to be purchased and downloaded easily and legally. Apple had re-invented the business model for a music industry that had been fixated on selling physical products. In doing so, it leapfrogged competitors and quickly established itself as a dominant player in the music industry. Furthermore, because music was such an important part of the internet evolution, this also increased the functionality of its physical products such as computers, iPods and iPhones and was integral to their success.

Questions:

1. Why was the music industry fixated on selling CDs at the time?
2. How difficult is it to transfer knowledge and learning (along with market opportunities) from one industry to another?

VALUE-CHAIN ANALYSIS

One way to discover inadequacies in underlying processes or question market paradigms is by analysing the value chain of an industry. Behind this is the idea that real advantages in cost or product/service differentiation can be found in the chain of activities that a firm performs to deliver value to its customers. The value chain comprises five primary activities (Porter, 1985):

1. Inbound logistics (receiving, storing and disseminating inputs).
2. Operations (transforming inputs into a final product).
3. Outbound logistics (collecting, storing and distributing products to customers).
4. Marketing and sales.
5. After-sales service.

and four secondary or supporting activities:

1. Procurement (purchasing consumable and capital items).
2. Human resource management.
3. Technological development (R&D etc.).
4. Firm infrastructure (general management, accounting etc.).

Each generic category can be broken down into discrete activities unique to a particular firm or industry. By looking at the costs associated with each activity and trying to compare them to the value obtained by customers from that activity, mismatches can be identified. It might be possible to reduce costs through new technologies, different sourcing or work efficiencies. The internet has given business the opportunity to look at disintermediation – reducing the use of intermediaries – in order to reduce costs. Equally, however, if customers value certain stages of the chain more highly than indicated by the resources allocated to them, it may be profitable to offer an improved product/service by increasing the resources allocated to these stages. There may also be opportunities for complementary products or services to be developed either on your own or in partnership with other companies. In reality, it is difficult to do undertake this analysis with any precision, but often supply chains can remain unaltered simply because people fail to ask the question: 'Why are they like this?' Industries can be prone to this sort of 'dominant logic' when things have not changed for a long time despite customer discontent.

CASE INSIGHT 10.5
Bloom & Wild

UK

REIMAGINING THE VALUE CHAIN

Started in 2013, Ben Stanway and Aron Gelbard took the inspiration for their online florist business, Bloom & Wild, from the inefficiencies they found when they researched the supply chain for cut flowers. Flowers typically wilt within 14 to 16 days of being cut. And yet the supply chain from field to customer can involve up to four middlemen – exporter, auctioneer, wholesaler and retailer. Each middleman can take a couple of days to move the flowers on, which means that their life in the home is reduced to only a week or so. The founders realized that this supply chain for flowers not only added costs but also degraded the quality of the product. What they needed to find was a different and quicker route to market.

Bloom & Wild's business model involves customers ordering flowers online a few days in advance, so that growers can then cut them to order. They are then placed in small vials of water to keep them fresh and inside a net to keep the size down and then finally inside specially designed box that can fit through a standard letter box. Sending the flowers by post in this way means that customers do not have to be at home to receive them and they should last twice as long flowers bought in shops. There is one final advantage – the costs of the middlemen are cut out, making flowers from Bloom & Wild generally cheaper. So, at a stroke the new model solves issues of price, longevity and convenience. Videos on the company's website even give ideas about flower arrangement. In London the company can even deliver flowers within two hours.

Visit the website on: www.bloomandwild.com

Questions:

1. How important was industry knowledge to the development of this business model?
2. What are the critical success factors for Bloom & Wild?

SPOTTING OPPORTUNITY

It was Drucker (1985) who first said that innovation was 'capable of being presented as a discipline, capable of being learned and capable of being practiced', adding that 'entrepreneurs need to search purposefully for the sources of innovation, the changes and their symptoms that indicate opportunities for successful innovation'. The search for innovative opportunities can be practiced systematically through a creative analysis of change in the environment and the opportunities this generates. It is not the result of 'happenstance' or that rare 'eureka moment'. Firms can practice innovation systematically by using their discovery skills to search for change and then evaluate its potential for an economic or social return.

Drucker listed seven sources of opportunity for firms in search of creative innovation. Four can be found within the firm itself or from the industry of which it is part and they are therefore reasonably easy to spot. They are 'basic symptoms' – highly reliable indicators of changes that have already happened or can be made to happen with little effort. These are:

1. The unexpected – be it the unexpected success or failure or the unexpected event. Nobody can predict the future but an ability to react quickly to changes is a real commercial advantage, particularly in a rapidly changing environment. Information and knowledge are invaluable.
2. The incongruity – between what actually happens and what was supposed to happen. Plans go wrong and unexpected outcomes produce opportunities for firms that are able to spot them.
3. The inadequacy in underlying processes – that are taken for granted but can be improved or changed. This is essentially improving process engineering – especially important if the product is competing primarily on price.
4. The changes in industry or market structure – that take everyone by surprise. Again, unexpected change, perhaps arising from technology, legislation or other outside events create an opportunity to strategize about how the firm might cope and, as usual, first-mover advantage is usually worth striving for.

These changes produce sources of opportunity that need to be dissected and the underlying causes of change understood. A learning organization of the sort we have described would understand this. The causes of the changes give clues about how innovation can be used to increase value added to the customer and economic return to the firm. An entrepreneurial firm should be adept at this.

The other three factors come from scanning for change in the outside world:

5. Demographic changes – population changes caused by changes in birth rates, wars, medical improvements and so on.
6. Changes in perception, mood and meaning – that can be brought about by the ups and downs of the economy, culture, fashion etc. In-depth interviews or focus groups can also often give an insight into these changes.
7. New knowledge – both scientific and non-scientific.

Drucker (1985) listed the seven factors in increasing order of difficulty, uncertainty and unreliability, which means that he believes that new knowledge, including scientific invention, for all its visibility and glamour, is in fact the most difficult, least reliable and least predictable source of innovation. Paradoxically, this is the area to which government, academics and even entrepreneurial firms pay most attention. He argued that innovations arising from the systematic analysis of mundane and unglamorous unexpected successes or failures are far more likely to yield commercial innovations. They have the shortest lead times between start and yielding measurable results and carry fairly low risk and uncertainty.

Drucker's 'basic symptoms' revolve around the analysis of change. Change creates unexpected events and incongruities. It provides clues to the existence of commercial opportunities – unmet needs now or in the future – and can destabilize market structures.

And trying to analyse existing products and markets is probably easier than trying to invent new ones. It is certainly less risky. There may well already be existing commercial opportunities arising from:

➡ Unmet needs or the unsolved problems consumers face now (and in the future).
➡ Inadequate products/services where the product/service itself or the process undertaken to produce it can be improved.
➡ Products/services that can be reimagined and re-engineered to produce alternatives that also have value in the market.

CASE INSIGHT 10.6
Duplays

UAE

SPOTTING UNMET MARKET DEMAND

In many countries in the Middle East locals prize jobs in the public sector rather than in private business. It is unsurprising, therefore, that many start-ups originate from the large expatriate populations. And where better to find a business idea than from the unmet needs of the people in your community. Whilst working as expatriates in Dubai in the United Arab Emirates, Canadian-Indian-born Davinder Rao and Indian-born Ravi Bhusari wanted to make friends and play sports but found that most social activities revolved around going to bars or visiting shopping malls. They had already organized some 20 expat friends to play Frisbee on a regular basis and reasoned that if they wanted to do this, other expats might also be interested as well. Furthermore, there might be a business opportunity behind their idea. So, in 2007 they started Duplays. From this small beginning, the company has grown rapidly. It now organizes sports such as football (soccer), beach volleyball, basketball, touch rugby, netball, cricket, frisbee and golf, often with related social events. They offer nightly league matches and weekend tournaments organizing facilities, equipment, staffing and scheduling:

> Most of the institutionalised activity seemed to revolve around shopping malls or going for drinks or brunches. We figured plenty of people like to play sport and so the secret was to meet that need and build a website and a business that helped people discover what was out there.

The notorious 'red tape' in many countries of the Middle East can make it hard to start a new business. Duplays' founders discovered that the bureaucracy can be especially difficult for expats to negotiate without local connections. However, whilst many countries require expats starting a business to have a local partner, Dubai has a free-zone system that gets around this requirement, meaning that founders can own 100 per cent of the business. Nevertheless, Duplays' founders still found that raising finance was difficult:

> Attracting money can be harder as an expat. You can understand it from the investor's perspective. If an expat has a business and it goes belly-up, then they can walk away, go back home or to another country. They have less reputational risk, so for investors, that can be scary.

Since 2007 Duplays has grown to over 100,000 members playing over 29 recreational sports. It now has branches in cities in the UAE (Dubai, Abu Dhabi and Al Ain), Saudi Arabia (Riyadh and Jeddah), Qatar (Doha) and India (Delhi and Guraon) and claims to rank as one of the largest adult sport & social clubs in the world. In fact, much of its income now comes from organizing corporate events for international organizations such as Castrol, Gillette, Samsung, Volkswagen as well as local companies. Being based in an international business hub has proved crucial to Duplays' success in this market, while Dubai's tax-free status has not hurt either. The company has also expanded into what it calls 'corporate wellness', organizing events, leagues and complete wellness programmes for organizations to get employees healthy and active, using sport and activities to help with team-building. Duplays' clients now include Al Hilal Bank, Dubai Airport, Emirates Aluminium and First Gulf Bank.

We're proud that although we're expats, we're building a company that is good enough to export. That's a great feeling. (BBC News, 14 April 2013)

Visit the website on: **duplays.com**

Question:

1. What are the barriers to spotting this sort of opportunity?

TOOLS FOR EXPLORING CHANGE

There are a number of tools that can be used to explore change and uncover the resulting commercial opportunities.

PESTEL analysis

This is a widely used tool to aid thinking about changes in the wider environment. PESTEL is an acronym that stands for:

➡ Political changes like local or central government elections, political initiatives for example on price competitiveness, new or changed taxes, merger and take-over policy and so on.
➡ Economic changes such as recession, growth, changes in interest rates, inflation, employment, currency fluctuations and so on.
➡ Social changes such as an ageing population, increasing inequality, increasing work participation often from home, 24-hour shopping, increasing crime, increasing participation in higher education, changing employment patterns, increasing number of one-parent families and so on.
➡ Technological developments such as increasing internet bandwidth, the coming together of internet technologies, increasing use of computers and chip technology, increasing use of smartphones, increasing use of surveillance cameras and so on.
➡ Environmental developments such as climate change, waste and pollution reduction, species reduction and so on.
➡ Legal changes such as health and safety legislation, changes in employment laws, food hygiene regulations, patent laws and so on.

PESTEL analysis Tool to help thinking about future developments in the wider environment. An acronym for Political, Economic, Social, Technological, Environmental and Legal changes

The technique can be used to spot commercial opportunities that these developments generate. It is sometimes shortened to 'PEST' or 'SLEPT' by dropping the 'legal' and 'environmental' elements of the acronym.

Futures thinking

Once PESTEL has identified the broad environmental trends, futures thinking can be used to help paint a comprehensive picture of the future state of the competitive environment. It helps develop further insight into the changes that have been identified, ahead of defining the commercial opportunity. It tries to take an holistic perspective, developing a vision about the future state after the change has taken place. From this, the commercial opportunities can be identified, again using brainstorming. Current constraints to action are ignored and in this way the barriers to change are identified. Some barriers may indeed prove to be permanent or insurmountable, but many might not be. Objections are therefore outlawed and disbelief suspended at the initial ideas stage. Only later on might options be discarded, once the barriers are considered. The key to thinking about the future is not to assume it will necessarily be like the past. Change is now endemic and often discontinuous. So, for example, what will be the state of a particular form of retailing in five years' time, given the impact of the internet and smartphone? Will bricks-and-mortar retailing continue to exist? If so, how will it combine with these technological developments? What will it look like, where will it be located and what services will it need to offer? How will it attract customers? These and many more questions might help to 'flesh out' a picture of how it might look and what the company needs to do to survive and prosper in the future.

Scenario planning

This is another technique that tries to assess how possible future situations might impact on a firm. It allows you to take Porter's static **Five Forces** analysis and add to it the extra dimension of competitive reaction. If an innovation causes radical changes to markets it is particularly useful to 'game plan' how competitors might react. Trends and drivers of change identified from the PESTEL analysis can be built into the scenarios. These scenarios must be logically consistent possible futures, based around the strengths and weaknesses and other key factors influencing the firm and its competitors. Often three are constructed: an 'optimistic', a 'pessimistic' and a 'most likely' future. Optional courses of action or strategies can then be matched to these scenarios. In effect, the scenarios are being used to test the sensitivity of the business model and strategies that will be developed in Chapter 12. Scenarios allow assumptions about the status quo of the environment to be challenged. After the financial crisis of 2008, Lego started using scenario planning as part of its annual budgeting process, allowing it to build contingency plans for each 'crisis' scenario that it identified.

Brainstorming

Generating ideas is a numbers game. So it is worth distinguishing between those techniques designed to generate volume and those designed to improve the quality of the idea. **Brainstorming** is one of the most widely-used, basic techniques for facilitating the generation of volume of ideas around a topic. It is practised in a group, thereby encouraging connectivity. In the session participants do not question or criticize ideas. They suspend disbelief. The aim is to encourage the free flow of ideas – divergent thinking – and to come up with as many ideas as possible. Everyone has thousands of good ideas within them just waiting to come out. But people inherently fear making mistakes or looking foolish in front of others. Here making 'mistakes' and putting forward ideas which don't work is not only acceptable, it is encouraged. The group leader might start with a problem to be solved or an opportunity to be exploited. They will encourage and write down ideas as they come – there are no 'bad' ideas. All ideas are, at the very least, springboards for other ideas.

Brainstorming is often used as part of PESTEL analysis and futures thinking, firstly to generate the changes but then to help think through how these changes might create needs

Five Forces The five forces that affect the degree of competition in an industry: competitive rivalry; threat of substitution; threat of new entrants; power of buyers; and power of suppliers

brainstorming A group activity that generates as many ideas as possible without criticism

that are not currently being met and the related commercial opportunities. Take, for example, the development of the internet. The ability to download films and music has questioned the viability of shops selling DVDs and CDs, but created opportunities for new devices (netbooks, tablets, smartphones etc.) and services (particularly niche services) linked to the internet. The development of internet shopping generally might cause developers to rethink the purpose and structure of our town centres. It might cause individual shops to re-engineer the way they meet customer needs – most shops now have websites and many offer internet shopping alongside conventional shopping.

Mind maps

These are simple maps that link one idea to another. They can help develop and refine a business opportunity. They can be used by individuals or in a group. As with brainstorming, you have to suspend disbelief and simply generate related ideas that might not have been encapsulated in the original. It can help you 'think outside the box' and generate relationships that might not initially have been apparent. Creativity is about making connections between apparently unconnected things, and this technique can be particularly helpful.

mind maps a map of related ideas from one original idea

Figure 10.2 shows a simple four-stage, systematic process for spotting a commercial opportunity and generating a business idea based upon the techniques covered so far – PESTEL analysis, futures thinking, brainstorming and mind-mapping.

Figure 10.2 Spotting commercial opportunity arising out of change

TECHNIQUES FOR EXPLORING PRODUCT INADEQUACIES

Sometimes there may be problems for which no solutions – or rather no commercially viable solutions – have been found. More often perhaps existing products or services can be improved, providing better solutions to existing problems. There are a number of techniques that can be used to explore inadequacies in existing products or services.

Analogy

This is a product-centred technique that attempts to join together apparently unconnected or unrelated combinations of features of a product or service and benefits to the customer to come up with innovative solutions to problems. It is designed, therefore, to provide more focused ideas that create opportunity out of unsolved problems for customers. Analogies are proposed once the initial problem is stated. The analogies are then related to opportunities in the marketplace. They work in a similar way to brainstorming. Georges de Mestral's connection between the properties of burdock seed and the need to stick and unstick things is an example of **analogy** that led to the development of Velcro.

analogy Connections between apparently unrelated things

In building an analogy, basic questions might be asked such as:

➡ What does the situation or problem remind you of?
➡ What other areas of life or work face a similar situation/problem?
➡ Can the principles underlying the solution to the original situation/problem be adapted to the new situation/problem?

Often the analogy contains the words '... *is like* ...', encouraging you to ask why something 'is like' another. For example, why is advertising like cooking? Answer – because there is so much preamble to eating – anticipation from presentation and smell, even the ambience of the restaurant in which you eat, are just as important as the taste and nutritional value of the food itself. They 'advertise' the food to be eaten.

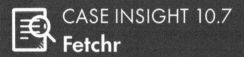

CASE INSIGHT 10.7
Fetchr

UAE

FINDING SOLUTIONS TO PROBLEMS

Joy Ajlouny was raised in the USA by Palestinian parents. She previously ran an e-commerce business called Bonfire that specialized in luxury footwear and she had become frustrated by the number of packages returned from customers in the Middle East marked 'address not found'. In many emerging markets, delivery of goods can be a problem because of the absence of a physical address. She discovered that delivery companies were literally sending the driver out with a piece of paper containing telephone numbers to call the customers one at a time to find out where to deliver the package. Joy first met Idriss Al Rifai at a tech conference in San Francisco in 2014. Idriss was born in Iraq and raised in France, and had experienced similar problems as head of operations of the Dubai-based e-commerce company Markavip. They started to discuss the problem and identified a technology-based solution.

Idriss and Joy came up with a novel mobile technology-based solution – a patented App that allows pick-up or delivery of merchandise to an exact GPS location based on the customer's smartphone signal. It means that there is no need for delivery directions. As a result, they launched their pick-up and delivery firm, Fetchr, in 2015 in Dubai, UAE before quickly rolling it out to Saudi Arabia and Bahrain. Their plan is to be an aggregator between couriers and customers, but to prove the concept saves time and money the company has been using its own fleet of vans in Dubai. Fetchr raised $11 million in venture funding in 2015, making it the first early-stage investment in an Arab start-up by a top US venture capital firm.

Visit the website on fetchr.us

Question:

1. What problems might you foresee with this business idea?

attribute analysis The features of a product/service are examined to see if they might be altered to provide the same or improved benefits to customers

Attribute analysis

Sometimes a product can be inadequate and simply not work properly, presenting a fairly obvious opportunity for a new, better product. However, sometimes the deficiencies can be more subtle. Attribute analysis is another more focused product-centred technique designed to evolve product improvements and line extensions – used as the product reaches the mature phase of its life-cycle. It can be useful, therefore, to spot opportunities arising from inadequate existing products or services. It uses the basic marketing technique of looking at the features of a product or service which, in turn, perform a series of functions but, most importantly, deliver benefits to the customers. An existing product or service is stripped down to its component parts and then you explore how these features might be altered, using brainstorming. The focus needs to be on whether those changes might bring valuable benefits to the customer. Nothing must be taken for granted. These changes can then be developed and refined using mind mapping.

For example, a domestic lock; this secures a door from being opened by an unwelcome intruder. The benefit is security and reduction/elimination of theft from the house. But keys can be lost or doors left unlocked, and some locks are difficult or inconvenient to open from the inside. A potential solution is to have doors that sense people approaching from the outside and lock themselves. There could be a reverse sensor on the inside – one that unlocks the door when someone approaches (which could be activated or deactivated centrally). The exterior sensor could recognize 'friendly' people approaching the door by means of sensors they carry in the form of 'credit cards', or the sensor could be overridden by a combination lock. The lock could be linked to a door that opens automatically.

Figure 10.3 shows a simple three-stage, systematic process for spotting a commercial opportunity and generating a business idea based upon analysing the attributes of an existing product or service and using brainstorming and mind-mapping techniques.

Figure 10.3 Spotting commercial opportunity arising out of an inadequate existing product or service

Gap analysis

This is a market-based approach that attempts to produce a 'map' of product/market attributes based on dimensions that are perceived as important to customers, analysing where competing products might lie and then spotting gaps where there is little or no competition. Depending on scale, this can be used to spot or create opportunity, particularly in the form of redefining market paradigms. Because of the complexity involved, the attributes are normally shown in only two dimensions. There are a number of approaches to this task:

➡ *Perceptual mapping* places the attributes of a product within specific categories. So, for example, the dessert market might be characterized as hot vs cold and sophisticated vs unsophisticated. Various desserts would then be mapped onto these two dimensions. This could be shown graphically (Figure 10.4). The issue is whether the 'gap' identified is one that customers would value being filled – and means understanding whether they value the dimensions being measured. That is a question for market research to attempt to answer.

gap analysis A 'map' of product/market attributes based on dimensions that are perceived as important to customers

perceptual mapping Maps the attributes of a product within specific categories

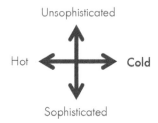

Figure 10.4 A perceptual map for desserts

non-metric mapping
Maps products in generic groups that customers find similar and then tries to explain why these groupings exist

➡ *Non-metric mapping* places products in generic groups that customers find similar and then tries to explain why these groupings exist. One classic example would be its application to the soft drinks market where products might be clustered and then described simply in terms of the widely-used generic groups, 'still' vs 'carbonated' and 'flavoured' vs 'non-flavoured'. The key here is also finding the appropriate dimensions that create opportunities for differentiating the product. The mapping of soft drinks on the two dimensions of a perceptual map is unlikely to reveal any gaps in the market.

repertory grid A more systematic extension of non-metric mapping that uses market research to group similar or dissimilar products and to explain the differences

➡ *Repertory grid* is a more systematic extension of this technique using market research. Customers are asked to group similar and dissimilar products within a market, normally in pairs. They are then asked to explain the similarities and dissimilarities. The sequence is repeated for all groups of similar and dissimilar products. The explanations are then used to derive 'constructs' which describe the way in which people relate and evaluate the products. These constructs form a grid that can be used to map the products, using the words used by the customers themselves.

Figure 10.5 shows a simple four-stage, systematic process for spotting or creating a commercial opportunity and generating a business idea based on mapping the attributes of an existing product or service, using brainstorming and identifying gaps in the market.

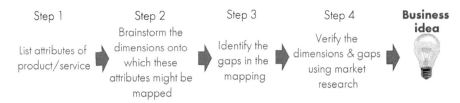

Figure 10.5 Spotting or creating commercial opportunity using gap analysis

delphi method
Questioning of experts about future developments until there is some convergence of opinion

Delphi method

This is useful where expert opinion is needed on aspects of future developments. It is often used to try to identify new technologies that might trigger discontinuities or disruption. First, relevant experts need to be identified. These might include experts in non-technological fields so that the economic, social and environmental impacts of the changes are not overlooked. The experts are then be asked to complete a carefully constructed questionnaire survey of their opinion on what the key future issues might be and their likelihood of occurrence. Having been analyzed, the questionnaire is then refined into a second more focused version and the experts resurveyed. The process is repeated until there is some convergence of opinion that yields a Delphi forecast of the probability and time scale of certain events. The process can be costly and time-consuming and depends upon the quality and appropriateness of experts and the questionnaires used.

CASE INSIGHT 10.8
Nikwax

UK

SPOTTING INADEQUATE PRODUCTS

Born in 1954, Nick Brown was a keen hiker who walked regularly in the Peak District and Scotland. But he was unhappy with the waterproofing products available in shops because they just did not keep his boots dry. He was also a bit of a scientist, having done A-level Chemistry at school. Consequently, as a teenager he used to mix together various ingredients from his shed and the local hardware store in a saucepan to form a boot wax. He would then use it to coat them with before going hiking. And it worked. He had dry feet and the boots did not soften up or lose their essential supportive feature.

However, it was a prolonged period of unemployment after leaving university with a third class degree in Anthropology at the age of 22 that forced him to turn his invention into a business. In order to earn some money, he boiled up the boot wax he had invented in his north London flat and sold it to a local shop at twice its cost of production. He manufactured the wax in a discarded tea urn, using a primus stove, a jug and materials bought from a local store. The wax was then poured into tins which he silk screened by hand.

> It was a low point for me. I stepped back and asked myself what I had done. I had done nothing well . . . I had already supplied a local store with a few pots of it. When they sold out quickly I realised this was something I could do. (Sunday Times, 25 May 2014)

He used a £200 overdraft to buy a van and travelled around, selling the wax directly to stores during the day, returning to make the wax at night. He focused on exports from an early stage, travelling to Europe on an InterRail card to sell directly to shops and going to trade shows to push his product. Turnover grew quickly and he started employing staff but the banks refused to provide finance, believing he was overtrading. He therefore financed the growth of the business internally through retained profits. Nikwax proved so effective that it set the standard for a range of aftercare products under the Nikwax brand. Nikwax was the first company in the world to produce a range of water-based products for restoring waterproofing in the home. The range grew to include products for many other uses where waterproofing was required, from ropes to tents.

Today Nikwax, founded in 1977, employs 114 staff and has a turnover of £10 million. Nick still owns 92 per cent with the rest owned by employees. 70 per cent of sales come from abroad and t has offices in the UK, USA, Australia and Poland.

Visit the website on: **www.nikwax.com**

Question:

1. How easy is it to explore the adequacy or inadequacy of an existing product?

SYSTEMATIC INVENTIVE THINKING

Boyd and Goldberg (2013) observed that there are many opportunities for innovation based upon existing products or services that do not adequately meet customer needs or where customer value can be enhanced through changes: 'The traditional view of creativity is that it is unstructured and doesn't follow rules or patterns. That you need to think "outside the box" to be truly original and innovative. That you should start with a problem and then "brainstorm" ideas without restraint until you find a solution. That you should "go wild" making analogies to things that have nothing to do with your products, services, or processes. That straying as far afield as possible will help you come up with a breakthrough idea. We believe just the opposite ... that more innovation – and better and quicker innovation – happens when you work inside your familiar world (yes, inside the box) using what we call templates.'

Their templates, which they called 'Systematic Inventive Thinking', involved five approaches to changing the attributes or features of a product or service:

1. Attribute dependency

   Bringing together or correlating two or more apparently unrelated attributes of the product can add value for customers. Examples include smartphones that provide information that depends on geographic location and in cars windscreen wiper speed or radio volume that varies with the speed of the car and headlights that dim automatically for oncoming cars.

2. Task unification

   Similarly, bringing together multiple tasks into one product or service can add value for customers. For example, sunscreen products added to facial moisturizers and make-up (and vice versa) to unify a task. Samsonite used this principle to redesign the shape of straps on backpacks so as to press softly at 'shiatsu points' on the back and provide a soothing massage sensation rather than causing back and neck strain from the weight of their contents. The heavier the contents, the deeper the sensation and the more stress-relieving for the wearer, thus using the heavy load carried as a comfort advantage.

3. Multiplication

   By way of contrast, duplicating some product feature or characteristic may enhance customer value. For example, 'picture-within-picture' TVs allow people to watch more than one programme at a time. Pearson Education has used this principle to create a new course designed specifically for students who failed algebra exams and needed a different approach to studying the subject.

4. Division

   Alternatively, dividing out the functions of a product might add value for some customers. For example, the dividing out of the control features on many electronic products and placing them into a remote control provided more convenience and allowed the products to become smaller, cheaper and easier to use.

5. Subtraction

   Finally, subtracting product features not valued by some **market segments**. This was the approach taken by low-cost airlines.

market segments
Groupings of
customers with similar

The term 'frugal innovation or engineering' has been used to describe the process of reducing product complexity by *subtracting* non-essential features from products (Radjou et al., 2012).

This is usually associated with cost and price reduction strategies that will make the product more attractive in low-income or developing economies. Of course, other changes to the product (e.g., improved durability) and business model (e.g., changes in distribution channels) will probably be needed alongside this. Subtracting features and selling at lower margins only tends to happen toward the end of a product life-cycle (Chapter 14), but the technique can help find new markets and, if volumes are sufficient, increase overall profits for an organization.

 SUMMARY

➡ Good business ideas come from creating opportunities or spotting them. You can create opportunities by creating change. You can spot opportunity by analysing change. In both of these cases, the idea must be linked to a market need, whether or not it is yet exhibited. Creative synthesis is needed to link any technological development to market need and a commercial opportunity.
➡ Creating change involves product or market innovation – changing the product/service or its market either incrementally or radically. Radical market innovation involves challenging industry paradigms by questioning sectoral, performance and customer conventions (e.g., the value chain). This is less risky than radical product innovation. Incremental product or market innovation is easier and less risky.
➡ Spotting change involves a systematic analysis of the environment to highlight changes (e.g., using PESTEL) and then developing an understanding of what commercial opportunities they might generate (e.g., using mind mapping, futures thinking and scenario planning).
➡ You can also spot opportunities by finding innovative solutions to existing problems (e.g., using analogy).
➡ Business opportunities also exist in questioning the value chain in an industry to see where additional value can be created (for customers and/or the firm) in some meaningful way.
➡ There are techniques that can help you can spot opportunities arising from inadequate products. These include the techniques of analogy, attribute analysis and gap analysis.
➡ 'Systematic Inventive Thinking' can be used in challenging the features of an existing product/service and see whether they can be reconfigured in a way that creates commercial opportunity.

 GROUP DISCUSSION QUESTIONS

1. How easy is it to come up with a business idea?
2. Why might a company decide not to develop a business opportunity, even if it is viable?
3. What factors decide whether a business idea is commercially viable?
4. Why it is so important that a product/service idea is different than competitors?
5. What attributes do you need to be able to apply creative synthesis to a technological development? How difficult is it to develop them?
6. How can you build CSR into a search for business opportunities?
7. The commercial viability of a completely new product/service is impossible to evaluate. Discuss.
8. How can you become more aware of the constant changes happening around you and the business opportunities they create?

9. How can a company use PESTEL to focus its search for business opportunities into areas where it has greatest competencies?
10. How can you find unsolved problems that may create a commercial opportunity in a systematic way?
11. How can you find out unmet needs that may create a commercial opportunity in a systematic way?
12. How can you uncover product/service deficiencies that may create a commercial opportunity in a systematic way?
13. How easy is it to disaggregate a supply chain?
14. How might a company ensure that staff have the opportunities to come up with new product/service ideas?
15. Coming up with new product/service ideas is the job of managers, not ordinary staff. Discuss.

ACTIVITIES

In groups:

1. Use the PESTEL acronym to explore major changes that your society will face in the next five years. From these, select one and, using brainstorming, explore the business opportunities that might arise out of it. Repeat the process for a number of these major changes.
2. Use analogy to come up with a business idea. Start with a problem to be solved and find the way similar problems might be solved in a different context. Alternatively find a natural solution to a problem and consider whether it can be applied to a different circumstance.
3. Use attribute analysis to come up with a business idea. Focus on an everyday product/service, select one feature or aspect of it and ask 'Why does it have to be that way – what benefit does it bring to the customer?' Try it a few times with different product/service features.
4. Use gap analysis to come up with a business idea. Select an everyday product/service, characterize it in two dimensions and use perceptual mapping to plot where competing products lie on these dimensions. Is there a gap in the market? Repeat the exercise for another product/service.
5. For the product/service ideas you came up with from previous activities, write down as clearly as possible:

   * A description of the product/service idea – its features;
   * A description of the types of customers that you think will purchase it;
   * The needs it will satisfy – the benefits it offers;
   * The names of competitors and why their product/service is not as good as this one;
   * The further development work still needed on you product/service;
   * Any other information that might be relevant to its commercial viability

REFERENCES

Boyd, D. and Goldenberg, J. (2013) *Inside the Box: A Proven System of Creativity for Breakthrough Results*, London: Profile Books.
Chaston, I. (2015) *Entrepreneurial Marketing: Competing by Challenging Convention* (2nd ed.), London: Red Globe Press.
Drucker, P. (1985) *Innovation and Entrepreneurship*, London: Heinemann.
Hamel, G. and Prahalad, C.K. (1994) *Competing for the Future: Breakthrough Strategies for Seizing Control of Your Industry and Creating the Markets of Tomorrow*, Boston, MA: Harvard Business School Press.
Kim, W.C. and Mauborgne, R. (2005) 'Blue Ocean Strategy: From Theory to Practice', *California Management Review*, 47(3), Spring.

Phadke, U. and Vyakarbnam, S. (2017) *Camels, Tigers and Unicorns: Rethinking Science and Technology-Enabled Innovation*, London: World Scientific Publishing.

Porter, M. (1985) *Competitive Advantage: Creating and Sustaining Superior Performance*, New York, NY: Free Press.

Radjou, N., Prabhu, J. and Ahuja, S. (2012) *Jugaad Innovation: Think Frugal, Be Flexible, Generate Breakthrough Growth*, San Francisco, CA: Jossey-Bass.

ONLINE RESOURCES AVAILABLE For further resources relating to this chapter see the companion website at **www.macmillanihe.com/Burns-CEI**

11 Encouraging concept development

CONTENTS

- Design thinking
- Lean start-up methodologies
- Affordable loss
- Risk and first-mover advantage
- Setting performance metrics
- Concept screening, development and testing
- Estimating market size
- Summary
- Group discussion topics
- Activities
- References

Learning outcomes

When you have read this chapter and undertaken the related activities you will be able to:

➡ Understand and explain the design thinking approach to new product/service development and its relationship to lean or agile start-up methodologies;

➡ Understand the risks facing the launch of a new product or service and how the concept of affordable loss can limit this;

➡ Understand how SMART performance metrics can be set and used to monitor the success of a new product or service launch;

➡ Critically analyze the criteria used to assess commercial viability of a new product or service at initial screening;

➡ Understand and explain the different measures of market size.

DESIGN THINKING

Coming up with a business idea or innovation is only the first step in the journey towards launching it onto a market. There will be many blocks and many blockers along the route – all of which have to be dealt with. Some of these will relate to how the new product/service fits into the company's existing portfolio. Some will relate to the costs of its development or whether there is a proven market for it. **Design thinking** (also called customer-centric design) is a different lens that is worth using to look at a new business idea. It is associated with agile or lean start-up methodologies, which are low-cost ways used by entrepreneurs to help identify market demand and refine a product/service so that it better meets the needs of the market. Applied to new projects being explored by entrepreneurial companies, they can help reduce the costs and risks associated with bringing new products/services to the market. They are particularly valuable when applied to radical innovations.

design thinking A loose set of holistic concepts that approach design from the perspective of solving complex problems for people, rather than just creating distinctive objects or shapes

Design generally is important as a way of identifying and differentiating a product and can be an important tool in both radical and incremental innovation. It is also an important weapon in the branding armoury. Good design can help not only to improve the functional performance of a product, but also to make it distinctive. It can be aesthetically pleasing and conveys emotions that functionality cannot. Studies have shown that for every £1 invested in design, businesses can expect turnover to increase by over £20 and profit by over £4 (Design Council, 2012). However, 'design thinking' is a term used to explain the creative process of finding solutions to problems from the perspective of the user of a product, rather than just creating distinctive objects or shapes. It is a holistic way of thinking rather than a clearly defined set of processes like the discovery skills outlined in Chapter 9.

The origins of design thinking can be traced back to Simon (1969). Although there are many versions of a design thinking process with numerous stages, Simon outlined a seven-stage process:

1. Define: Identify the real problem to solve – not necessarily the obvious one – and define the design brief in a way that is unconstrained by existing solutions.
2. Research: Observe how people deal with the problem and how similar problems in different contexts are handled.
3. Ideate: Think 'outside the box' – look at the problem from different perspectives and come up with as many different ideas and options as possible. This may involve a multi-disciplinary approach and periods of divergent and convergent thinking. Do not close down options too early. The stages so far are all concerned with finding a good idea – although not necessarily one that is commercially attractive.
4. Prototype: Experiment with prototype solutions to see which work.
5. Choose: This is a process of synthesis which helps select the one that works best or the *ones* that work best. Different solutions might be used to solve slightly different problems or meet the needs of different groups of people.
6. Implement: Try out the solution(s) and monitor effectiveness. Prototype solutions – both products and services – need to be tested, with iterations to develop and refine them.
7. Learn: Always learn from both success and failure.

Design thinking is evident in the design of some high-tech products where software and hardware are integrated and made intuitive, simple and even pleasurable to use. And to do this it needs to meet both peoples' practical (left-brain) and emotional (right-brain) needs – what is often called 'the user experience'. Companies that follow this approach develop value propositions that offer not only a promise of utility but also feelings or emotion. Kolko (2015) gives the example of automotive design which might offer both 'safe and comfortable transportation in a well-designed high-performance vehicle' and also a promise that 'you will feel pampered, luxurious and affluent'. Design thinking is not just confined to product design and value propositions, however; it is a holistic approach that seeks to integrate all the 'touch-points' a customer might have with the company rather than dealing with fragmented elements. Accordingly, Apple take as much care over the design of their packaging as they do with the product itself.

To achieve these ambitious objectives designers need to work in collaboration with users. This usually means that they need to build something before they can observe how users interact with it. It requires a customer focus and a willingness to learn from their needs and constantly refine a product/service offering to better meet them. The approach involves a number of principles, which are consistent with developing a coherent, integrated business model:

➡ Empathy with users – this goes to the core of finding a commercial business idea – understanding customer needs and finding solutions to the problems they face. These needs are both functional and emotional (heart and head). Companies like Samsung achieve this, in part, by sending designers out to see how customers use their products.
➡ Discipline of prototyping – this champions the use of prototypes to explore the effectiveness of potential solutions to problems. Kolko (2015) remarked that companies following this approach 'aren't shy about tinkering with ideas in a public forum and tend to iterate quickly on prototypes'.
➡ Tolerance of failure – innovation is risky and, as is the case with brainstorming, generating new ideas is a numbers game. The more ideas there are, the more likely it is that at least one of them will be a good one, yet that involves generating many ideas that are not. Failure is therefore to be expected in an organization that is innovating. Indeed, if a company generates no business ideas that fail, it is probably not generating sufficient business ideas. The trick with a failing project is to limit the company's exposure, terminate it quickly and learn from it – all principles of the lean start-up methodology we shall outline later in this chapter. To quote Thomas Edison, the inventor of the light bulb: 'I have not failed, not once. I've discovered ten thousand ways that don't work.'

 CASE INSIGHT 11.1
Zound Industries

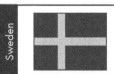 Sweden

DIFFERENTIATION BY DESIGN

Zound Industries was founded in 2008 by eight individuals coming from different backgrounds in design, product development, finance, marketing, sales and business. Despite its youth, it is already making a mark in the technology industry by bringing distinctive design to bear on headphones, merging the function of a sound source with fashion accessories targeted at different markets. It is one of the fastest-growing companies in Sweden, with offices in New York and Shenzhen, where most of the equipment it sells is manufactured. Co-founder and President Konrad Bergström explained:

> *The big dinosaurs of headphones or electronics still look at headphones as a technical product. If you search on the web, they are seen as a technical product. What we try to do is be the best in other aspects. Be best in design, be best in functionality but also be best when it comes to sound. What we are working really hard on is building these soft values, that if you use our products it says something more than just functionality. You are connecting in some way. (www.highsnobiety.com, 3 May 2013)*

Zound's mission is 'making electronics fashionable and fashion electronic'. Not that long ago it was the brand of trainers you wore that defined your lifestyle and 'tribe'. Today, it is your headphones, and Zound has helped to bring about this change. Zound produces four brands of headphones and mini-speakers, with each range being targeted at a different market, although you can only really appreciate these different products by viewing them on the website:

➡ Urbanears: Launched in 2009, this is the biggest brand. It is fashion-orientated, quirky and fun and is positioned at a mid-point price range. It was voted one of the 'CoolBrands' of 2014/15 in the *Sunday Times* annual survey. These headphones feature many useful functional design details as well as using a range of materials and textile wrap cords that give them a feeling closer to a garment than a technological product. There are also distinctively designed mini-speakers;

➡ Coloud: Targeted at the young and active, this range offers a colourful, cheaper alternative to Urbanears. It is essentially a headphone equivalent of a Swatch watch. Zound has partnered with Nokia to make these headphones from a smaller number of components and keep costs low. Triangularity is a distinctive theme that runs throughout the Coloud range, from the logo to the packaging to the angles in the head-phone design;

➡ Marshall: Launched in 2010, this is a brand licensed from the much-respected amplifier company. It is a quality range of headphones and speakers that sells to the high end of the market. It mirrors the distinctive look of Marshall amps and, by working with Marshall Amplification, also mirrors the distinctive sound quality;

➡ Molami: Launched in 2011, this is an ultra-high-end, female-focused fashion range, distinctively angular and incorporating materials like leather and silk. Zound boasts that the range can be worn as a stylish fashion accessory that complements any outfit, whether or not it is being used as a headphone. It was launched in cities around the world in the same way a fashion house might show off the latest season's designs and has featured regularly in fashion magazines.

To support and promote its products, Zound hosts high-profile Swegie events showcasing Swedish design, culture and creativity that coincide with fashion weeks in cities around the world, making certain they all have a 'celebrity' feel.

From its very beginnings, Zound has set its sights on becoming a global brand. Indeed, its vision is 'to be the world-leading lifestyle headphone manufacturer'. The company's strategy has been thought through systematically. Its distinctive design-led products are targeted at specific markets: 'From the time a product is developed to the day it is sitting on a store shelf, it has been strategically thought through how to create, market, and distribute it and which brand the product will be sold under. This way, multiple demographics are reached.' It has developed new products and new markets with relentless effectiveness.

Zound's success has also been based on its ability to partner with others. Starting at the very beginning, the founders had a range of skills and experience and they have described themselves as a 'collective'. At different stages of its growth, beginning in 2009, it has sought systematically to attract additional capital. It has partnered with different distributors in different countries and even produced joint-branded products with the retailer H&M. In 2014 Zound announced a partnership with the Swedish telecom operator TeliaSonera, which acquired a stake in the company. The aim of this project is to bundle fashion headphones, audio speakers and device accessories together with TeliaSonera's mobile telecommunications. At the time of writing, the company had sold more than 10 million pairs of headphones in over 20,000 stores globally, including Apple, Best Buy, HMV, Target, Urban Outfitters, Colette, FNAC, Media Markt, Telia, Deutsche Telecom, Orange and Tesco. The company's products have also been featured in thousands of articles in publications such as *Vogue* (US), *Elle* (US) and *Time*.

Visit the website on: **www.zoundindustries.com**

Questions:

1. Describe who you think are the target market customers for each of the four brands. How are they distinctive and different? How are their emotional (right-brain) and practical (left-brain) needs different? What are the implications for how each brand is marketed?
2. If this is a fashion brand, is it sustainable? If so, how?

Verganti (2009) observed that not all 'design-driven innovations' come from the market – making existing products better, easier to use or more distinctive. Design thinking can create whole new markets through market paradigm shift by giving products 'new meanings' – emotional, psychological and sociocultural rather than just utilitarian reasons for purchasing them. Customers come to view the product in a different light. He argued that for truly breakthrough products and services, you must look beyond customers to those he calls 'interpreters' – 'experts', like Steve Jobs, who have a deep understanding and an ability to shape the markets in which they work. Although in advance of their markets, they are absorbed in them, understanding trends, styles, materials and technology. However, they are able to rise above the dominant logic by recognising and questioning it. They are also able to influence the market through their insight, powers of persuasion and marketing skills. They have a vision and then take that vision to customers, persuading them that this new 'meaning' has value. However, this strength may also be a weakness because it can fail to take account of that prevailing market space and the business model required for a commercially viable business idea (Phadke and Vyakarnam, 2017).

🔍 EXPLORE FURTHER

The double-diamond design process

The UK Design Council uses a simple and relatively straightforward four-stage model to represent the design process. The 'double diamond' graphic in Figure 11.1 represents the alternatively divergent (right-brain) and convergent (left-brain) modes of thinking in the four phases of the process:

Phase 1 Discover – the stage when the initial idea or inspiration needs to be found, based on identifying user needs.

Phase 2 Define – when these needs are interpreted and aligned to business objectives resulting in the definition of the design project.

Phase 3   Develop – when design-led solutions are developed, iterated, built and tested. This will involve multidisciplinary prototype development and testing.

Phase 4   Deliver – when the resulting product is finalized, approved and launched, followed by evaluation and feedback.

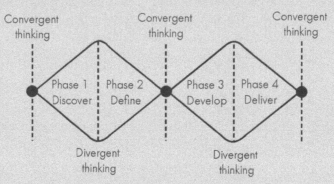

Figure 11.1 The double diamond design process

More information on the double diamond design process can be obtained from the Design Council: www.designcouncil.org.uk/news-opinion/what-framework-innovation-design-councils-evolved-double-diamond

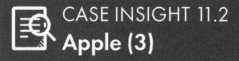 CASE INSIGHT 11.2
Apple (3)

 USA

DESIGN AND COMPETITIVE ADVANTAGE

The original Apple iMac (G3), with its teardrop or gum-drop shape, was designed by Jonathan Ive, a bathroom designer who rose to become chief design officer at Apple. It was launched by Steve Jobs in 1998 less than a year after his return to Apple. It was the first Macintosh computer to have a USB port but no floppy disk, allowing other hardware manufacturers to make peripherals that were compatible with the Mac. More importantly, however, its friendly, translucent candy-colours and futuristic form made it stand out from other desk-top computers of the time with their pervading beige colours. It quickly became a design icon, more of a 'futuristic home appliance' than an office machine. It was something to be admired – a bold statement and talking point that started to affect the things with which the home-owner surrounded it, things like lighting and furniture. It changed how people perceived computers and created demand because of its form rather than just its function. This was a classic instance of design driving innovation and creating a paradigm shift.

Apple has continually revolutionized the consumer electronics industry. It helped usher in the age of the personal computer in the 1980s with the sleek, affordable Macintosh; kick-started the age of digital music with the iPod and iTunes in 2001; and laid the groundwork for the now ubiquitous smartphone with

The original Apple iMac (G3)
Source: iStock/juniorbeep

2007's iPhone and iOS operating system. Apple has a track record of using outstanding design to create competitive advantage by combining high quality with easy-to-use product functionality and elegance. Whilst other makers of phones and tablets buy the same 'off-the-shelf' chips as their competitors, Apple designs its own chips, although they are manufactured largely in China. Consequently, an iPhone has a processor designed specifically optimized for Apple's operating system, apps, display, camera, and touch sensor. This attention to design detail even extends into the packaging of Apple products. The design features of Apple's products are promoted as part of their marketing strategy to create a functional but fashionable, distinctive and desirable brand that allows them to charge high prices for their products. For Apple, all of the elements of this marketing mix, including design, must be consistent, mutually reinforcing the brand identity and the value proposition of individual products. The functional qualities of the product/service can be enhanced through the aesthetics of design and reinforced by the emotional values associated with the brand. The more points of differentiation from competitors there are, the more sustainable the competitive advantage.

Nevertheless, there are limits as to how much customers are willing to pay for good design, even for an iconic brand such as Apple. 2019 saw a dramatic fall in Apple's stock market valuation as turnover shrank and sales of iPhones fell, particularly in the Chinese market, where competing Chinese brands offered similar or better functionality at more competitive prices. iPhones are available in China because, in contrast to competitors like Google, Apple agreed to store users' data on Chinese servers and offer only 'approved' Apps from its App Store. By 2015, Apple was selling more iPhones in China than in the USA. However, sales stagnated and, it is thought by analysts, started falling in 2017. Whilst iPhones account for around half of the smartphones in the USA and the UK, they now only account for 9 per cent of the Chinese market, placing it in fifth place behind the domestic manufacturers Huawei, Vivo, Oppo and Xiaomi. The global market for smartphones appears saturated and Apple's strategy of focusing on the Chinese market and constantly raising the price of its iPhones, trying to persuade customers to replace their existing models with the latest ones, seemed to be failing. Furthermore, in China many Apple services such as Apple Pay, and its iMessage App and the App Store more generally, are less widely used than in the West. In China, for example, the Android-based WeChat is the dominant messaging App. It is also used as a portal for finances, games and music because it can be used on a range of phones. This is a double problem for Apple, which also earns significant profits from sales on its App Store since it has been estimated by analysts that up to half of App Store's revenue between 2017/18 came from China, where gaming Apps are particularly popular.

The problem for Apple is that, despite massive investments in R&D, there appears to be few really innovative physical products to replace its now ageing portfolio. Although sales of the Apple Watch and AirPod headphones seem strong, sales of iPads and Mac computers are also down. Apple is said to be working on driverless cars, but is currently far behind Alphabet's Waymo. It has also invested in augmented reality, but this seems to have few immediate applications beyond gaming. The problem with the design of physical products more generally is that it can be copied and improved upon, even with protected IP. Increasingly, other factors need to be 'designed' into the product/market offering.

Visit the website: **www.apple.com**

LEAN START-UP METHODOLOGIES

Implicit in the design thinking methodology is the development and testing of a prototype. Throughout this process there is constant measurement of success (or failure) and feedback so as to learn from this and adapt the product or service. However, this process involves costs. These must be weighed against the risk of launching an untested product or service, one that is not attractive to customers and ultimately might fail. A good business idea has a window of commercial opportunity. Too early or too late and it is unlikely to be successful, and it will only have a finite life-cycle. Delay the launch and you risk losing that window of opportunity that gives 'first-mover advantage' in the market – a topic we shall return to in the next section.

Identifying the project risks associated with launching a new product or service, revolve around identifying the specific shortcomings in the product or service and its business model. These result in insufficient sales being generated. Market research and focus groups are likely to help with incremental changes to existing product/services. More radical innovations are more difficult since customers are often unable to understand how the new product or service might be used. If practical, what is needed is some form of limited market testing of the actual product or service and its business model. By collecting and analyzing this data the product/service and its business model can be evaluated and modifications made.

Ries (2011) developed what he called the lean start-up methodologies to address this problem. These were closely related to what has been called 'agile' methodologies, which were originally used by software designers, but have now found their way into other industries. Rather than developing a fully-finished product/service, it is an incremental approach to development that involves a continuous process of planning, experimentation, implementation, market testing, evaluation and integration of the results prior to proceeding to the next level of approval and development of a project – a continuous process until final launch.

Plan → Experiment → Implement → Market test → Evaluate → Integrate results

The lean start-up concept is simple. The product/service is not launched in a perfect, but rather in a pared-down, but workable, state. This **minimum viable product** (MVP) is one with just enough features to satisfy early customers. Customer feedback is then

minimum viable product (MVP) The minimum viable state of a product so that it can be launched and customer feedback then used to better tailor it to customer needs

used in an iterative fashion to further tailor the product or service to the specific needs of customers – a process Ries called **validated learning**. In this way, no valuable time or money are invested in designing features or services that customers do not value. The idea of small-scale market entry and testing to gain market information prior to full product launch, particularly for new entrepreneurial ideas, is well established (e.g., Chaston 2015). The process can be repeated as many times as is needed. This approach gives the company that important first-mover advantage and minimizes costs whilst also, importantly, reducing market risks when the product or service finally reaches a wider market.

validated learning Using customer to tailor your 'minimum viable product' (MVP)

AFFORDABLE LOSS

Associated with this approach is the concept of affordable loss, which entails entrepreneurs – or in our case the company – setting a loss or budget they can afford if the project proves unsuccessful and then launching the MVP to find out as much information as possible. This approach was based on a study of how 27 successful entrepreneurs approached business decisions compared to a group of professional executives (Sarasvathy, 2001).The study found that whilst executives wanted to research opportunities and assess potential returns before committing resources, the entrepreneurs were far more inclined to go to market as quickly and cheaply as possible and to assess market demand from that. Setting an affordable loss and then running the project allows a company to evaluate the opportunities produced by this investment, rather than trying to evaluate the attractiveness of the predictable (or unpredictable) upside of the project from its very inception – the 'unknown-unknowns' referred to in Chapter 8. The approach involves setting stages for a project, limiting the financial exposure at each stage, and then deciding whether or not to continue based on the information gained at each the end of that stage.

The company decides on the project budget for each stage, depending on the loss they are willing to suffer, rather than trying to predict from the outset the risks and returns associated with the entire project. The company therefore does not have to worry about the accuracy of predictions at this point. Affordable loss can be set with certainty, depending on the situation. It is a two-step process shown in Figure 11.2. Firstly, set the acceptable level of risk by setting the affordable loss, then push to maximize the information gained about the returns from the innovation. This process might be repeated as more information is obtained and the MVP modified accordingly. The final 'return' can then be evaluated more accurately. This approach can be combined with networking and/or partnering to leverage up the affordable loss or budget, not only through money, but through the other resources of the network or partners such as knowledge and skills, only finally using larger amounts of finance to develop a business model that best fits the project.

The lean start-up approach works well for some products such as software and web-based product development, particularly when new features can be trialled on the back of the core product. This is an approach often taken by Google. However, for high-investment (often disruptive) product innovations, the product itself may have to be substantially right the first time. Any imperfections in an MVP risk customer rejection and may damage the brand reputation. Imagine asking Apple if they would have been happy to launch a 'minimum viable' iPhone.

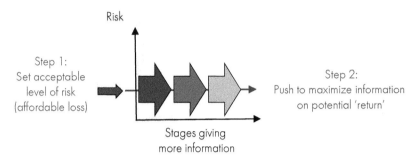

Figure 11.2 Setting risk and maximizing return

The lean start-up approach does represent an agile, low-cost/low-risk way to rapidly assess the potential risk and return of a business idea. It helps minimize this risk through the knowledge and information gained by a limited launch of the MVP. It mirrors the incremental approach entrepreneurs take to decision-making – gaining knowledge as they proceed – and the way they limit their financial exposure as much as possible. The key to the approach is close customer relationships and having mechanisms to receive their honest feedback. Ries (2011) gave the example of the start-up strategy of Nick Swinmurn, the founder of the US online shoe retailer, Zappos. Instead of building a website and a large database of footwear, he tested his business idea by taking pictures of shoes from local stores, posting them online and selling them through his website, buying the shoes from the stores at full price. Although he did not make a profit, this method quickly validated his business idea, at minimum cost and risk.

RISK AND FIRST-MOVER ADVANTAGE

Launch timing for any product or service is critical, but this is particularly the case for something innovative. Launch too late and first-mover advantage might be lost because there are already established competitors in the market. Launch too early, however, and the market might not be ready for a product that is 'just before its time', meaning that customers need to be educated about it before it goes into full-scale production – leaving the education costs with the early entrant and an opportunity to launch late with a competitor. There is also the risk of the product or service or marketing strategy being ill-prepared or untested and turning customers against it, leaving the market wide open for competitors. Either way, launching too early can often be even more disastrous than launching too late. In addition, every market is different. It is often the case that products launched first in the USA will not find a market in other countries until years later. Timing is crucial, which leads us to the link between risk and the time taken to get to market, shown in Figure 11.3.

One reason for getting the timing wrong arises from whether innovations come through technology-push or market-pull. Market-pull innovations are derived from customers' needs. They are more likely to succeed because the timing, by definition, is right. Innovation based upon technology-push may not yet meet a customer need simply because customers cannot visualize how the new product or service might be used. Market research can mislead when it comes to disruptive technology-push innovations. This was the case with IBM, when it found that market research into the idea of the personal computer suggested that customers were unwilling to pay for this product. History proved market research wrong

demand-pull The demand of customers for a product or service that 'pulls' it through your channels of distribution (see definition)

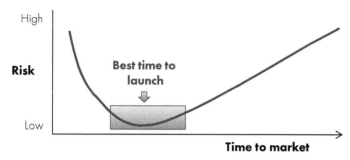

Figure 11.3 Risk and time to market

and entrepreneurs like Steve Jobs had the vision to see the potential of the personal computer, despite the opinions of customers at the time.

The idea of testing the market with an MVP does not solve these dilemmas entirely. An MVP may still not convince customers of the product or service's usefulness if it is simply too far 'before its time'. On the other hand, if the market exists it should throw up the modifications that need to be made to product prior to launch. The question then is: when is the MVP sufficiently ready to launch? If the MVP is so underdeveloped that it does not fulfill even the most basic functional requirements, then it might well be rejected by customers. This might result in a very different outcome to what might have occurred if they had been offered an MVP with greater functionality. Further, a MVP with poor functionality may spell disaster in the market for the fully-functioning final version if the reputation of the brand is tarnished. In addition, testing the MVP and modifying the prototype can take time, even if the company has sufficient resources. Modifying the MPV or waiting until there is a fully-functioning prototype risks losing that window of opportunity that gives first-mover advantage. These dilemmas revolve around the decision about what constitutes a 'minimum viable product' and the decision when to launch both the MVP and the final product remain judgement calls.

SETTING PERFORMANCE METRICS

Testing an MVP means decisions have to be made about how the tests are conducted and the information required from them. It could be that success or failure is based on simple binary outcomes such as whether or not a certain key activity or objective is achieved (e.g., development of website by a certain date). However, it might be more useful to measure performance through degrees of achievement (e.g., number of website views over a period). These quantifiable measures of performance are called **performance metrics**. They can involve the measurement of operating or financial metrics (e.g., profit, resources, quality, etc.) by a target date or within a given time frame. They can be inward (e.g., sales) or outward (e.g., market share) focused. Performance metrics for key activities are often called **key performance indicators** (KPIs) and can form the basis for bonuses for staff.

There are a whole range of financial metrics that can be used to control and measure the performance of a business as a whole. Performance can also be measured against non-financial metrics. A website business, for example, might monitor regular or active users/visitors; page views; or average page views per user/visitor. A call-centre might use metrics such as calls answered; calls abandoned; average handling time; average waiting time,

> **performance metrics** Measures of performance
>
> **key performance metrics indicators (KPIs)** The metrics that measure performance in the key operating activities. Often used as metrics to judge the performance of managers for calculating bonuses

among others. However, the appropriate performance metrics used to evaluate the success or failure of a lean start-up project needs careful thought. Maurya (2016) highlighted the problems of firstly selecting the right metrics to monitor and secondly finding the time and resources to gather and analyze them. Even then the link between cause and effect and any corrective actions needed may be unclear.

Often internet start-ups have focused simply on user numbers rather than income generation and many well-known internet companies have achieved a stock market listing without ever having made any profit. Like Ries (2011), Mauya was very much focused on internet start-ups and advocated the use of a metric that monitored 'traction' – 'the rate at which a business model captures monetizable value from its users' – in essence, linking the metrics to some target financial milestone(s). For example, an online magazine or newspaper could monitor webpage views as a key operational metric because they are directly linked to advertising revenue.

smart performance metrics are Specific for purpose; Measurable; Achievable; Relevant to the success of the organization; and Time-constrained

Performance metrics need to be 'SMART': Specific for purpose; Measurable; Achievable; Relevant to the success of the project and/or organization; Time constrained. Establishing a performance metric involves a three-step process:

1. Identify the process that needs to be monitored and controlled.
2. Establish the quantifiable outputs of that process.
3. Establish the targets against which to judge that performance.

There may be a number of lean/agile iterations or stages that are needed before a product or service is launched in the market. Each stage may need its own performance metrics to judge success or failure and take it to the next stage. Each set of metrics must provide information to improve the product/service offering.

Associated with the lean start-up approach is the concept of pivoting, defined by Ries (2011) as a 'structured course correction designed to test a new fundamental hypothesis about the product, strategy, and engine of growth'. This is where a company, based upon the validated learning it is obtaining from the limited launch, decides to make radical changes to its business model. We shall look at this in more detail in the next chapter.

CONCEPT SCREENING, DEVELOPMENT AND TESTING

Figure 11.4 sets out this whole process from idea generation to product or service launch. This concept development cycle involves six stages, building on design thinking and incorporating lean/agile methodologies. The product/service development phase (stages 1 to 5) incorporates a screening process using market/industry research to test for commercial viability. The screening process might also involve screening for compatibility with the existing skills and competencies of the company as well as its existing product/market offerings to ensure that the company has the capability to produce and market the product/service. Criteria used to evaluate this might include the operational relatedness and strategic importance of the project. A new product/service might be integrated into the existing company's portfolio. However, even if an idea is commercially viable, a decision might be made at a later date to licence it to another company better able to market it or even spin-out the development as a separate business. We look in more detail at the criteria for making these decisions in Chapter 13. The feedback loops between stages [1–2] and [3–4] allow the MVP to be improved. Stage 5 involves market testing of the MVP. We looked at the metrics that might be used to judge success or failure in the previous section. Stage 6 involves developing the business model (covered in the next chapter). This also requires testing before the final product launch. The feedback loops throughout the cycle allow learning to take place and the product/service to be improved. This continues after the launch and at any time pivoting – changing the business model – might take place (we also cover this in the next chapter).

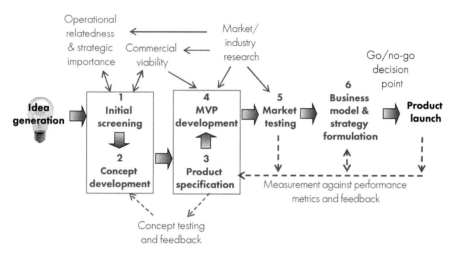

Figure 11.4 Concept development cycle

1. Initial screening

The first stage involves an initial screening of the idea. Assuming that the idea is technically feasible initial screening should be against two criteria:

i   Commercial viability – Probably the first screening to undertake is one of commercial viability. As previous chapters have highlighted, entrepreneurial organizations are looking for commercial opportunities. However, assessing commercial viability at this stage is a difficult task, especially for radical technology-based innovations. There are just too many unknown-unknowns. Anything other than rough assessments may not be possible for most innovations until the market-testing stage – and even then it may still be little more than a 'guesstimate'. To make this assessment, you need to estimate the market size for a product/service for which the business model has not yet been designed. Detailed financial assessments are therefore probably inappropriate at this stage for anything other than incremental, particularly cost-saving, process innovations. Table 11.1 sets out a checklist of criteria for evaluating the commercial attractiveness of a business idea or innovation. Companies might have their own criteria to add to the checklist.

> ❝ The ideal business has no overheads, commission only sales, large volume and low overheads. ❞
>
> David Speakman, founder Travel Counsellors, *The Sunday Times*, 6 December 1998

Table 11.1 Commercial viability checklist

➡ Identified market need or gap in market – the idea must meet a clearly identified market need to be commercially viable.

➡ No, few or weak existing competitors – the more innovative the product/service and markets into which it is sold, the fewer competitors, and the higher the price the company is normally able to charge. However, remember it is always possible that there are no competitors because there is no viable market for the product/service.

➡ New or growing market – it is always easier to launch a product/service into a new or growing rather than a declining market.

➡ Clearly identified customers – not identifying potential customers and their specific characteristics means that there is no way of knowing how best to sell to them, which means the product/service will probably not succeed. Building an effective business model starts by identifying the target market(s) for the product/service.

➡ High profit margins – the more innovative the product/service and the target market, the higher the profit margin is likely to be, but this does depend also on the business model.

➡ Not easily copied – if it can be, IP should be protected. However, often getting to the market quickly and developing a brand reputation is the best safeguard and if this is necessary it should be part of the business model.

➡ Identifiable risks that can be monitored and mitigated – identifying risks is the first step to understanding how they can be monitored and then mitigated.

scalability The potential to scale-up and grow

➡ Scalability – small projects can often get off the ground easily, but bigger projects can be problematic because they are just 'too big' and require too much resource. If this is a large-scale project see if it can be broken down into smaller projects that can be implemented when the original idea is proved. The idea is to avoid as much risk as possible for as long as possible – but to make sure the window of opportunity is not missed completely.

➡ Sustainability – the project must be built on solid foundations with lasting markets so that it has longevity. These might include CSR criteria.

➡ Financeable – the company should have the resources needed for the project's development.

➡ Viable business model – many of the issues come down to the viability and attractiveness of the business model, and this can be developed later unless there are any major obstacles.

ii Operational relatedness and strategic importance – At its heart this involves asking a simple question: 'Does the organization have the skills and capabilities to undertake this project?' In asking this question it is important to define the organization in terms of its unique capabilities rather than just the industry in which it operates; otherwise, it is restricting the opportunities it has to innovate by not considering new areas. For example, Google's AdSense was born out of Google's unique capability to understand what customers were looking for through their personal information, in particular their location, and their website browsing so as to enable advertisers to place targeted advertisements. If the answer to the question is 'yes', then the idea can be taken to the next stage.

Any new product or service should align with the organization's existing skills and capabilities. If it does not, but the project is of sufficient strategic importance, there may be ways that these skills and capabilities can be introduced through partnerships etc. (Chapter 5). Ideally it should also be sufficiently related to the current operations and product/market offerings to enhance the company's competitive position. But again there are options here. In fact, there are a host of options available for commercially attractive business ideas that do not 'fit' into the existing product portfolio of the organization. These are covered in Chapter 13.

Market and industry research will feed into both of these assessments. At this stage, this is likely to take the form of desk-based research involving market/industry reports etc. This screening process will continue throughout stages 2, 3 and 4. The task of trying to estimate market size is something that is likely to be repeated throughout the concept development cycle. We look at some of the terminology used in this process at the end of this chapter.

2. Concept development

If the initial screening proves the business idea is attractive the concept will have to be 'fleshed out' with more details about all aspects of the product or service – its physical looks, how it might be delivered and marketed. This may involve a simple text description, a computer simulation and/or storyboarding – something that can be shown to prospective users or bosses to see how they react. It should also involve minimal costs. Google provides a tool called *Sketchup* to help do this, but professional designers can help create storyboards and sample videos and the work can always be outsourced. They can also use computer-aided design (CAD) systems to draw up more detailed models of a concept.

 The beauty of being an entrepreneur is that, if the first idea doesn't work, you can come up with a second and a third until you come up with a workable concept.

Duncan Bannatyne, serial entrepreneur, *The Daily Telegraph*, March 2000

3. Product/service specification

Once the concept has been 'fleshed out', the product/service needs to be specified in detail. These specifications form the basis for the MVP and should give some indication of costs. The process of specifying the product/service may result in changes to the detail of the concept design to reflect ease or cost of manufacture, durability etc. For a service, the prototype is likely to be, in effect, this specification.

4. MVP prototype development

As we have seen, developing a product prototype is a process of experimentation, where numerous iterations of an idea are created and tested to see whether or not they provide the desired result. The MVP prototype needs to have just enough features to satisfy early customers. This might be a website or a physical product with minimal functionality. It might be possible through digitally enabled simulations or through 3D printed prototypes. At all times, practicality must be weighed against market needs and also what competitors are currently offering. Steve Jobs, for example, copied the idea of a computer mouse from Xerox. But whereas their mouse required expensive lasers to track its movements, Apple's MVP used the ball from a roll-on deodorant to track its movements on a flat surface and Apple went on to develop a simple low-cost alternative. The functionality of the MVP might be gradually improved if this process is repeated – producing what is often called a 'beta version'. Airbnb, Spotify and Zappos all tested beta products before launch. At some stage, thought needs to be given to whether or not the 'intellectual property' (IP) of the product or service can be safeguarded.

Feeding into this is research into the market or industry – the need to check the way other businesses may be approaching the market. Is the proposed approach viable? Who are the competitors? What is their supply chain? What are the plans to combat competition? How is this product/service different? Is this a real gap in the market? Is the required supply chain viable? If the product/service is a success, can it be scaled up? Can it be scaled up quicker than competitors? Is there anything to be learnt from the way competitors operate? The practicalities of producing the product or service must be weighed against the needs of customers and the commercial viability of the concept. Commercial viability is never certain, particularly at this stage, but studying the market and industry should give some clues.

This whole process is iterative and the product/service may need to be modified as more is discovered about customers and their needs.

CASE INSIGHT 11.3
FBR (Fastbrick Robotics)

Australia

PROTOTYPE DEVELOPMENT

People have been laying bricks to build houses for over 6,000 years, but that might be about to change. In 1994, Mark Pivac, a former aeronautic and mechanical engineer with experience in 3D computer-aided design (CAD) software, had an idea that brought together different technologies to produce a 'mobile dynamic stabilizing robot', which solved the problem of stabilizing a robot in a moving environment. This idea evolved over a long period, originally focused on an application that had no commercial potential. However, in 2005 there was a shortage of bricklayers in Australia and he started thinking about applying the concept to this problem. He obtained funding to develop his idea, and by 2008 he had built hundreds of prototypes, but, more importantly, he had also filed patents safeguarding his IP. The prototypes stood undeveloped for many years until he started working with his brother, Mike Pivac, to commercialize the idea. Mike had previously started and run a number of businesses, but at this time he was recovering from a serious back operation. His involvement proved pivotal in commercializing the company's technology, business plan and machine development strategy and he also forged relationships with investors, builders, suppliers and future customers.

It took almost eight years and some US$7 million, however, to finally develop a working commercial prototype. In 2016, the Hadrian 105 construction robot built the first cemented, multi-room block structure without human intervention from a 3D CAD model. This proved that the technology could work. By the following year, a commercial version, the mobile Hadrian X, was being produced for the market – a steel, aluminium and carbon fibre composite lorry-mounted machine capable of laying up to 1,000 bricks per hour in a fully automated process, making it possible to build the brick structure of a house in just two days. The robot element can also be mounted onto other bases, such as tracks, barges or cranes. It can work on its own for 24 hours a day, 365 days a year.

Bricks are fed onto a conveyor belt that travels along a long (28-metre) robotic arm, or telescopic boom, and are gripped by a claw-like 'hand' that lays them out in sequence on the pre-prepared groundwork, directed by a laser guiding system. A 3D CAD system works out the shape of the house, and the robot then calculates where each brick should go, leaving spaces for wiring and plumbing. It even scans and cuts the bricks if they need to be reshaped. Mortar or adhesive is then delivered under pressure to the hand of the arm and applied to the brick. Central to this process is FBR's Dynamic Stabilisation Technology (DST™), which measures movement caused by wind, vibration and inertia and counteracts it in real time, using algorithms to ensure precise placing of the bricks.

I invented DST™ to solve the problem of stabilising a robot at the end of a long moving boom, originally for an application that didn't have enough demand to justify its development cost. A decade later, a building boom converged with a shortage of bricklayers, driving the cost of laying a brick up to $1.25. I knew my idea's time had come. Once in a lifetime, if you're lucky, something you invent gets the opportunity to tackle a major global need. So we scaled up, built our own testing facilities and brought together brilliant minds from across the globe to bring this idea to life. (Mark Pivac, www.fbr.com.au/view/our-tech)

The home construction industry is notoriously resistant to innovation, but global demand for homes is growing and there are increasing shortages of bricklayers – which may make change inevitable. Potentially, this technology could make house building faster, safer and cheaper. As a result, in 2017 FBR signed a series of working agreements: with US giant Caterpillar, who invested US$2 million with an option to invest another US$10 million; with the Kingdom of Saudi Arabia, who were looking to purchase 100 robots; and with Mexico's GP Vivienda to develop social housing. The following year, it signed a partnership agreement with Wienerberger Group, a major European building materials producer, to develop, test and manufacture optimized clay blocks for the Hadrian X construction robot. These will subsequently be used in a pilot project in Europe and launched into Wienerberger's markets, together with the Hadrian X robot.

Visit the website: **www.fbr.com.au/view/our-story**

Questions:

1. What events were pivotal in taking this project forward? Were they predictable? What lessons are there in this for creativity and innovation?
2. Why was building a working commercial prototype so important?
3. Why is FBR seeking partnerships, rather than just rolling out the Hadrian X itself?

5. Market testing

Underpinning the process is the constant need to check the commercial viability of the business idea or innovation. Start with key stakeholders before testing with potential customers. These checks, together with market/industry research, will influence the form of the prototype product or service. The company will need to be assured that there is a viable market for it. Who are the customers and why will they buy the product/service? This begs the question about setting a price. The product/service may need to be modified to suit the price customers are willing to pay. Assessing commercial viability might be achieved through market research, focus groups or various forms of market testing. Gaining information in this way limits the risks faced and the information feeds back to influence the final form of the product/service. Market testing should provide a critical piece of the jigsaw puzzle about whether an innovation is viable – estimating the market size. We return to this in the next section. The founders of Innocent Smoothies in the UK market tested their drinks at a music festival. They set up two bins underneath a banner saying: 'Should we give up our jobs to start this business?' One said 'yes', the other 'no'. By the end of the festival, the 'yes' bin was overflowing. Their drinks business went on to become a great success.

> **❝** *The reality is that very few businesses invent a market for their products and services. Many, however go on to reinvent markets by filling gaps with standout offerings ... There's no other way to find out whether or not you will be successful other than just doing it. It just helps to test the water before you do.* **❞**
>
> Richard Branson, founder Virgin Group, 18 August 2015 on: **www.virgin.com/richard-branson/how-know-if-your-business-idea-good**

6. Business model development

This is the final pre-launch stage. With an MVP that potentially can be delivered at a commercially viable price, the next step is to map out the marketing strategy. This involves developing a full business model that can be market-tested, possibly through a limited launch of the MVP. The scenario planning technique outlined in Chapter 10 can also be used to construct possible future situations and help better understand how competitors might react to the successful launch of the product/service. They allow optional courses of action or strategies to be matched to these scenarios and can help identify critical success factors. Once again, the results may suggest changes in the business model or product/service – 'pivoting'. Despite extensive planning, the reality of the market can be very different and this process of obtaining and learning from the feedback of customers and evaluating the reaction of competitors should continue after the launch. We return to business model development and pivoting in the next chapter.

CASE INSIGHT 11.4
Dropbox

USA

LEAN START-UP

Dropbox is a file-hosting, cloud storage and transfer service founded by MIT students Drew Houston and Arash Ferdowsi in 2007 with initial funding from seed accelerator Y Combinator. It was launched in 2008. The beta phase of version 1.0 was offered to private clients in 2010 and Dropbox Business made the service available to larger teams in 2011. After further testing, a collaboration tool was introduced allowing users to collaborate in developing and processing text. Dropbox is now available to the general public using a freemium business model with free file storage and transfer up to a certain size with paid subscriptions available for extra storage capacity and additional features. Dropbox Business offers more functionality for teams, including collaboration tools, advanced security and unlimited file storage and recovery.

   Dropbox's development is a good example of lean start-up and the company is a keen advocate of the methodologies. Before bringing the product to market, Dropbox tested the concept in two stages. During these stages, there was no functioning prototype. Stage 1 tested the product with a limited number of users. Stage 2 involved the production of a video demonstrating the core features of the product – cloud-based storage and file transfer. This attracted some 75,000 views by early adopters and as a result the company received extensive feedback that helped it to simplify and develop the product's functionality. They used a product called Votebox – an online voting system based on open-source software – to establish a dialogue with users about product features. They continue to use this product to filter out the best features of various products.

Dropbox was also an early implementer of personalized applications. When they identified users who did not use a particular application, they would send them information about it and how it might be used. Users who had used up their allowable storage were emailed with offers of additional storage.

These techniques helped the company to gain valuable user feedback and to penetrate its market quickly. Regular communication helped build a loyal user base that was able to help with product development. In its early days Dropbox's attempts to increase users through traditional marketing methods proved unsuccessful. Instead, they offered free additional storage to existing users who successfully recommended Dropbox to new users. Within 15 months, the number of users grew from 100,000 to 4 million.

Based in San Francisco, Dropbox now has over 500 million users. Despite having never made a profit (although it reports positive cash flows), when it raised private capital through an Initial Public Offering (IPO) in early 2018 it was valued at $12 billion.

Visit the website: **www.dropbox.com**

Questions:

1. How have lean start-up methodologies helped Dropbox?
2. How much can these methodologies tell us about monetization and the financial return from the product?
3. Can the lessons from Dropbox be transferred to other start-ups not based on the internet?

ESTIMATING MARKET SIZE

Throughout the concept development cycle the development team will be seeking to establish the commercial viability of their new product/service. This will depend on the costs involved and the price they are able to charge, within the framework of the business model they decide upon (we cover this in the next chapter). However, it also depends upon the size of the market they think they can capture. Estimating the size of a new market created by disruptive innovation or market paradigm shift can be almost impossible. Even estimating the size of a segment of an existing market can be difficult. The market itself might be growing or declining and within it some segments might be growing whilst others are declining. Market research can provide only so much data. Inevitably, the final estimate will be based upon judgement and become a target for the company to aim for when the product/service is finally launched. For example, if you wish to introduce a new smartphone app, the fact that there are over 1 billion smartphones worldwide is not entirely relevant. That market is growing rapidly. However, your app might be in English, which limits the market size, and it might be developed for only one operating system. Then there is the question of the channels through which the app will be sold. All of these factors limit the market that you are attacking – even before the question of whether you are likely to achieve your target **market penetration**. Market size can be estimated in either value or volume (units), but the distinction needs to be made between the different types of market shown in Figure 11.5.

market penetration
Selling your original or existing product or service to the customers in the market segment you originally identified

303

➥ Potential market – The size of a general market that might be interested in buying a product/service (e.g., 1 billion smartphones);

➥ Total available market (TAM) – The size of the prospective market – those customers in the potential market who might be interested in buying this particular product/service. This reflects the total sales of competing products (e.g., English apps for a particular operating system);

➥ Served available market (SAM) – The size of the target market segment the innovation aims to capture within the TAM (e.g., particular app function);

➥ Penetrated market – The size of the SAM actually captured at any point of time.

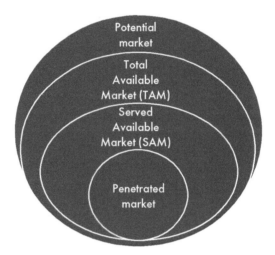

Figure 11.5 Market size definitions

Desk research should yield estimates of the size of the first two markets. SAM is the size of the market segment(s) the innovation is aiming to capture, given any restrictions such as demographics, geography, language, technology etc. This is the estimated market size that the business model should aim to capture and the target for the company to aim for when the product/service is finally launched. There is a dynamic to this as the size of the SAM is likely to increase over time as the product/service goes through its natural life-cycle (Chapter 14). Furthermore, if the product/service is successful it may attract customers from adjacent markets with similar product/services.

SUMMARY

➥ Design thinking is a holistic way of thinking rather than a clearly defined set of processes. It is an approach to new product/service development that seeks to marry the practical (left-brain) and emotional (right-brain) needs of customers.

➥ Lean or agile start-up involves developing a minimum viable product (MVP) with just enough features to satisfy early customers. Customer feedback is then used in an iterative fashion to tailor the product/service to the specific needs of customers – a process called validated learning. It is a continuous process until final launch:

Plan → Experiment → Implement → Market test → Evaluate → Integrate results

➡ Affordable loss involves setting a loss or budget that is affordable if the project proves unsuccessful and then launching the MVP to find out as much information as possible. This is a process that might progress over a number of stages.

➡ Timing of a product/service launch is crucial: too early and the market might not be ready for a product/service, too late and risk losing first-mover advantage.

➡ Performance metrics are quantifiable measures of performance that can be set to judge the success of a project by a target date or within a given time frame. They can be inward- or outward-focused. Performance metrics for key activities are often called key performance indicators (KPIs) and can form the basis for staff bonuses. Performance metrics need to be SMART: Specific for purpose; Measurable; Achievable; Relevant to the success of the project and/or organization; Time constrained.

➡ The concept development cycle involves the six stages shown in Figure 11.4:

1. Initial screening.
2. Concept development.
3. Product specification.
4. MVP development.
5. Market testing.
6. Business model and strategy formulation.

➡ The potential market is the size of a general market that might be interested in buying a product/service. The total available market (TAM) is the size of the prospective market – those customers in the potential market who might be interested in buying this particular product/service. The served available market (SAM) is the size of the target market segment the product/service aims to capture within the TAM. The penetrated market is the size of the SAM actually captured.

 GROUP DISCUSSION TOPICS

1. How important in the buying decision is design compared to other elements of the product such as its functional qualities and the marketing of it?
2. How important is emotion (right-brain) compared to logic (left-brain) in the buying decision?
3. How important is creativity (right-brain) compared to analysis (left-brain) in design thinking?
4. If all design-driven innovation comes from the market, then it is of no use for radical product innovation. Discuss.
5. What are the advantages of lean start-up compared to market research? Are they mutually exclusive? What are their different uses?
6. What does a minimum viable product mean?
7. Lean start-up only works for high technology businesses. Discuss.
8. If Steve Jobs had given customers pared-down, but workable versions of the first Apple computers, how do you think they would have reacted and what information might he have gained?
9. The amount of affordable loss varies from person to person and company to company and is therefore not an objective approach to risk management. Discuss.

10. Setting an affordable loss is like deciding on the stakes for a poker match – but it might mean that you cannot enter the high-stakes games and therefore miss out on the high returns. Discuss.
11. What are the advantages and disadvantages of setting an affordable loss compared to setting a properly costed out budget for market research?
12. Should you apply the affordable loss approach to the post-launch period?
13. How do you judge when it is best to launch a new product/service?
14. Is success always measurable?
15. Are performance metrics always objective or can they be influenced?
16. How can you judge the commercial viability of a project at the concept phase with any degree of accuracy?
17. How should a company deal with a good business idea that is neither operationally related to its activities nor strategically important to its future?
18. How can you market-test without having a price for a product/service?
19. You cannot estimate the size of the market for a radically innovative product/service. Discuss.
20. You cannot estimate the size of the market that a new product/service will capture without knowing the reaction of competitors. Discuss.

ACTIVITIES

1. For the product/service ideas you used for Activity 6 in Chapter 10, apply the criteria listed in Table 11.1 to try to assess their commercial viability. What does this tell you at this stage? How might you go about obtaining any information you need?
2. Select any recently introduced new product/service and apply the criteria listed in Table 11.1 to try to assess its commercial viability. What does this tell you? How did the company go about obtaining the information it needed to have sufficient confidence to launch the product/service?
3. Select a product or service market and, using desk research, estimate the TAM. Select the three major competing products or services within that market and estimate the SAM for each.

REFERENCES

Chaston, I. (2015) *Entrepreneurial Marketing: Competing by Challenging Convention* (2nd ed.), London: Red Globe Press.
Design Council (2012) *Design Delivers for Business: A Summary of Evidence from the Design Council's Design Leadership Programme*, London: Design Council.
Kolko, J. (2015) 'Design Thinking Comes of Age', *Harvard Business Review*, September.
Maurya, P. (2016) *Scaling Lean: Mastering the Metrics for Startup Growth*, London; Penguin.
Phadke, U. and Vyakarnam, S. (2017) *Camels, Tigers & Unicorns: Rethinking Science & Technology-Enabled Innovation*, London: World Scientific.
Ries, E. (2011) *The Lean Startup: How Today's Entrepreneurs Use Continuous Innovation to Create Radically Successful Businesses*, New York, NY: Crown Publishing.
Sarasvathy, S.D. (2001) 'Causation and Effectuation: Toward a Theoretical Shift from Economic Inevitability to Entrepreneurial Contingency', *The Academy of Management Review*, 26(2).
Simon, H. (1969) *The Sciences of the Artificial*, Cambridge: MIT Press.
Verganti, R. (2009) *Design-Driven Innovation: Changing the Rules of Competition by Radically Innovating What Things Mean*, Boston, MA: Harvard Business School Publishing.

ONLINE RESOURCES AVAILABLE For further resources relating to this chapter see the companion website at **www.macmillanihe.com/Burns-CEI**

12 Strategy and business model development

CONTENTS

- Levels of strategic planning
- Identifying core competencies
- Developing strategy
- Business model development
- The New Venture Creation Framework
- The Business Model Canvas
- The Lean Canvas
- Generic business models
- Business models for virtual products
- Project-level review – pivoting
- Corporate-level strategic review
- Summary
- Group discussion topics
- Activities
- References

CASE INSIGHTS

12.1 Quanta Computers
12.2 Fortnite: Battle Royal
12.3 Pinterest
12.4 wiGroup
12.5 audioBoom

Learning outcomes

When you have read this chapter and undertaken the related activities you will be able to:

➡ Understand and explain what makes an organization's core competencies and capabilities;
➡ Understand and explain how business strategy is developed and how business model frameworks can facilitate this;
➡ Critically analyze a business model using the New Venture Creation Framework;
➡ Understand and explain the importance of differentiation and customer focus or intimacy in developing a business model and their impact on the price a company is able to charge;
➡ Understand and explain the different sorts of business models that have been developed for internet businesses.

LEVELS OF STRATEGIC PLANNING

A business model is the plan for how a business competes, uses its resources, structures its relationships, communicates with customers, creates value and generates profits. For a company operating within a single product/market, it constitutes the main part of their strategic plan. For a company operating in a number of different product/markets, each product/market will have its own business model and plan. There may even be variations for different market segments. These must link and be consistent with the overall strategic plan of the organization. This overall strategic plan should 'inform' and give direction to the business model and plan for individual product/**market developments** (e.g. providing information about capabilities and competencies) but at the same time these business plans 'inform' and build into the overall strategic plan. The business plans for individual product/markets should aggregate into its overall business and competitive strategy. However, the business models and plans for individual projects can change the strategic direction of an organization, for example by taking the firm into new markets. The two plans are symbiotic.

market development
Finding new customers
or markets for
products or services

The strategy literature does make the distinction between two forms of strategy. The first is 'business' or 'competitive strategy', which is how the organization competes. The business plans for individual product/market developments feed into this. The second form is 'corporate strategy', which also includes the scope of the organization (i.e. the sectors within which it operates) and structure of the organization, including its overall architecture. New product/market developments can shift the scope of an organization, intentionally or unintentionally. In a multi-product/market organization, business or competitive strategy is usually determined at the divisional or subsidiary level whilst corporate strategy is decided on at the head office or holding company level.

> " The secret is to have vision and then build a plan and follow it. I think you have to do that, otherwise you just flounder about ... You change your game plan on the way, as long as you are going somewhere with a purpose. "
>
> Mike Peters, founder Universal Laboratories, *The Sunday Times*, 11 July 2004

This chapter is primarily about how the business model and plan can be developed for an individual project – usually a single product/market innovation. However, this should be informed by an understanding of the organization's overall strategic direction as well as how strategy might be developed more generally.

IDENTIFYING CORE COMPETENCIES

The secret to successful strategy development for any organization starts with identifying its unique set of core competencies and capabilities – the things it does best, its strengths. These might include skills, technical capabilities, pooled knowledge or market leverage such as branding or distribution. This is a portfolio of resources that can be combined in various ways to meet the opportunities or threats that the organization faces and give it competitive advantage. They could, for example, allow a firm to diversify into new markets by reapplying and reconfiguring what it does best. They therefore ought to underpin any new project being developed – the opportunities being pursued. Building upon these resources increases the chance of success.

The chief proponents of this approach were Prahalad and Hamel (1990). They saw core competency as the 'collective learning of the organization, especially how to coordinate diverse production skills and integrate multiple streams of technology ... [through] ... communication, involvement, and a deep commitment to work across organizational boundaries ... Competencies are the glue that binds existing businesses. They are also the engine for new business development.' They suggested that there were three tests which can be applied to identify core competencies:

1. They should provide potential access to a wide variety of markets rather than generating competitive advantage only in one.
2. They should make 'a significant contribution to the perceived customer benefits of the end-product' – they add value.
3. They should be difficult for competitors to copy. Products are easier to copy than processes and, as this book outlines, an entrepreneurial architecture should be particularly difficult to copy.

Identifying the core competencies of an organization underpins the process of strategic review and the SWOT (strengths, weaknesses, opportunities and threats) analysis used to aid it (this is outlined later in the chapter).

DEVELOPING STRATEGY

Once the core competencies of an organization are identified, it can start to plan how to respond to the opportunities and threats that it faces. A strategy is simply a plan as to how to achieve a longer-term goal. It comprises a series of interlinked actions or tactics. The specific goal in any time period should be quantifiable and measurable. It should help the organization towards achieving its long-term vision – what it might become. This is framed by the organization's mission – what it aims to achieve and how it will achieve it. The mission usually identifies the areas of activity of the business (its scope) and even the basis of its competitive advantage. What actions or tactics are needed to achieve the goal is a matter of judgement but they should be informed by the enduring values and beliefs of the organization (e.g. ethics, social responsibility, environmental sustainability etc.). These actions and tactics can themselves be made up from any number of other plans. This process was shown in Figure 6.1, which is reproduced in this chapter as Figure 12.1.

Enduring   Changing

VALUES → MISSION → VISION → GOALS → STRATEGY → TACTICS

Long-term   Short-term

Figure 12.1 Strategy development

In many ways how strategy is developed is the most distinctive feature of an entrepreneurial organization. In Chapter 6, we characterized the entrepreneurial leader as developing a strong *vision* that helps build a *strategic intent* within the organization; as someone who is continually *strategizing*, meaning that strategy will often be seen externally as *emergent*; and as someone who always has a number of *strategic options* that give the organization flexibility should circumstances change. They were also characterized as exercising dispersed or distributed leadership, which ensures that the process of strategy development is also dispersed rather than centralized and coordinated rather than controlled, and that information and knowledge flows freely within the organization so as to encourage flexibility and adaptability.

There are a number of views about how strategy is developed. Mintzberg et al. (1998) characterize what they call the 'Entrepreneurial School' of strategy as focused 'exclusively on the single leader' – the entrepreneur: 'Under entrepreneurship, key decisions concerning strategy and operations are centralized in the office of the chief executive. Such centralization can ensure that strategic response reflects full knowledge of the operations. It also encourages flexibility and adaptability: only one person need take the initiative.' For them, the entrepreneurial school 'stresses the most innate of mental states and process – intuition, judgment, wisdom, experience, insight. This promotes a view of strategy as *perspective*, associated with image and sense of direction, namely *vision*.' The challenge within an entrepreneurial architecture is to ensure that strategy development, like leadership, is distributed rather than centralized and coordinated rather than controlled. It is also to ensure that 'intuition, judgement, wisdom, experience, insight' – which are all part of a learning organization – are captured as part of the culture of the organization.

The 'Positioning School' treats strategy development as a rational, deductive, more deliberate process that can be depicted as a logical sequence of operations. By way of contrast, academics in what is called the 'Process School' (also associated with Mintzberg) would argue that the strategic process is so inextricably interlinked that what you need to do to understand strategy is to look at how it is *actually* developed, rather than how it *ought* to be developed. For them, the process is all and they pour cold water on the Positioning School, saying it neither represents the reality of what happens nor is it effective: 'No one has ever developed a strategy through analytical technique. Fed useful information into the strategy-making process: yes. Extrapolated current strategies or copied those of a competitor: yes. But developed a strategy: never' (Mintzberg et al., 1998).

A number of academics have observed that formalized strategic planning processes have not served companies well. In the words of Foster and Kaplan (2001): 'The conventional strategic planning process has failed most corporations ... New ways of conducting a dialogue and conversation among the leaders of the corporation and their inheritors are needed.' This hints at process being important. Indeed, Grant (2010) observed the spreading use of emergence in the strategic planning practices of large firms in recent years – reduced formality, emphasis on performance goals and a focus on direction rather than content – observing that it has its intellectual roots in complexity theory. Quinn et al. (1988) summed up the dilemma between the 'Positioning' and the 'Process' Schools rather well: 'One cannot decide reliably what should be done in a system as complicated as a contemporary organization without a genuine understanding of how the organization really works. In engineering, no student ever questions having to learn physics; in medicine, having to learn anatomy. Imagine an engineering student's hand shooting up in a physics class. "Listen, prof. It's fine to tell us how the atom does work. But what we want to know is how the atom should work".' Which did come first – the chicken or the egg?

So what do these established schools of thought have to contribute to how organizational and indeed project-level strategy might be developed in an entrepreneurial environment? The debate is essentially a false one. The development of strategy can be *both* deliberate and emergent, but at different times and in different circumstances. As we observed in Chapter 1, whilst executives tend to set goals and seek to achieve them sequentially and logically, entrepreneurs' goals are broad and evolved over time based on whatever personal strengths and resources they had, creatively reacting to contingencies as they occur – an approach which Sarasvathy (2001) calls '**effectual reasoning**' or '**effectuation**'. However, these strategies and goals must always be underpinned by a strong vision or direction – again one that is deliberate but also adaptable. Timely emergent strategy necessitates continuous strategizing, informed by good information flows which should lead to the development of strategic options for evaluation. This process is needed at both the organization and project level.

Continuous strategizing encourages the development of 'consensus strategy' – important for a project team developing a new product. It informs, involves and motivates a team. To quote Mintzberg et al. (1998): 'A successful strategy is one that committed people infuse with energy: they make it good by making it real – and perhaps making it themselves.' Continuous strategizing evolves from the process of learning (and making mistakes) but is focused by agreement to a common vision and mission. In that sense entrepreneurial strategy can also be both deliberate in overall vision and emergent in how the details of the vision unfold. Furthermore, strategy development and action can proceed side by side, recognizing that the future is not predictable and planning cannot, therefore, be a simple, linear process. It is non-linear and adaptive, even sometimes opportunistic. Actions (both successful and unsuccessful) feed into strategy development. Decision-making can be incremental and adaptive so as to maintain the maximum flexibility and adaptability needed to capitalize on change and make the most of any commercial opportunities that appear. Complexity theory shows how direction can be given to these individual decisions through the capacity to self-organize (through identity, information and relationships).

effectuation (effectual reasoning) An approach to decisionmaking that is not based solely on deductive reasoning

BUSINESS MODEL DEVELOPMENT

The business model is the route to taking a business idea to market and it will have a very large impact on whether or not the idea is successful. A good business idea can fail because of a bad model and a poor idea can survive because it has a good one. Some might say it is actually more important than the product or service idea itself. A business model is the strategic framework that gives the business idea direction and generates its competitive advantage. It is a commercial framework that creates a common language for the project team and a mechanism for communication as the commercial potential of the idea is developed. It helps with distributed strategizing. It allows the team to identify patterns and ask the important 'What-if?' questions and work through the likely consequences. These questions help identify strategic options, each option contingent upon different circumstances, using information to modify strategies to reflect the reality of these uncertain situations. The more options that can be identified, the more flexibility there is in formulating, or indeed pivoting and changing the strategy. Not all options should be constrained by current resources or the current competitive position. These constraints might change over time and sometimes the vision for the project might generate options that transcend these constraints anyway.

Developing a business model involves producing plans about how the product or service will be produced and marketed, the resources (both human and financial) needed to do this and the resulting costs and revenues. Developing the model involves iterations – going back over the building blocks to ensure consistency and coherence in the model. Alter how a product or service is produced or delivered and price may have to be altered, which in turn effects how it is marketed. This is a continuous process of refinement. What is important is that all of the elements of the business model are consistent and deliver the all-important **value proposition** to the target customers. The challenge is to develop a model that is attractive to customers as well as sponsors within the company. It is worth remembering that the two may not be mutually consistent. A business model that threatens to cannibalize the market for an existing product or service offered by the company may indeed have a viable market, but at the expense of the existing offering, and may therefore never see the light of day (at least in this company) either for commercial or political reasons.

value proposition
The marketing benefits offered to each target market segment

There are a number of generic business model frameworks that provide pictorial and/or verbal structures to aid understanding and development of a business model. The best are minimalist and simple – they force focused thinking and succinct communication. Nevertheless, the structure they use provides a coherent but flexible framework that helps the team develop their ideas. A framework needs to be flexible as it will probably change as feedback and market information becomes available. However, it also needs to ensure consistency, so that if one element of the model is altered another can be adjusted appropriately. As John Kay (1998) explained:

> *An organizational framework can never be right, or wrong, only helpful or unhelpful. A good organizational framework is minimalist – it is as simple as is consistent with illuminating the issues under discussion – and is memorable … [It] provides the link from judgment through experience to learning. A valid framework is one which focuses sharply on what the skilled manager, at least instinctively, already knows. He is constantly alive to strengths, weaknesses, opportunities, threats which confront him … A successful framework formalizes and extends their existing knowledge. For the less practiced, an effective framework is one which organizes and develops what would otherwise be disjointed experience.*

This chapter will outline three business model frameworks: the *New Venture Creation Framework*; the *Business Model Canvas*; and the *Lean Canvas*. All three models cover similar ground and are consistent, although they do use slightly different terminologies. However, the *New Venture Creation Framework* develops the elements of a business model in a sequential manner consistent with developing a new business or product/service, whereas the others work best with existing product/services. The advantage of developing any of these business models in this way is that they are (relatively) quick to develop and easy to change. The team can try out new business ideas. These frameworks allow them to:

➡ Modify target markets, value propositions and their marketing, operations and financial plans;
➡ Explore in a structured way innovative alternatives and options – always trying to understand the linkages and implications of different/product market offerings, whilst allowing them to test new models against established ones;

➥ Experiment with different versions to see which critical assumptions are most realistic (revenue model; pricing, sales, costs etc.);
➥ Identify patterns and ensure consistency in the elements of the business model.

Only when they are satisfied with the model created in this way would the team go on to 'fill-in' more of the details and perhaps write up a more formal **business plan**.

business plan A formal document setting out the business model for an organization

> « *Innovation matters, but it isn't everything. You need an economic model that makes sense – it's no good being original if there is no demand for your product or service at a price that generates a surplus.* »
>
> Luke Johnson, Chairman Risk Capital Partners, *The Sunday Times*, 21 May 2017

THE NEW VENTURE CREATION FRAMEWORK

The *New Venture Creation Framework* comprises the five sequential, linked stages shown in Figure 12.2 (Burns, 2014, 2018). This involves moving from the value proposition for the **target market segment(s)**, through the marketing and operations plans, to the resources available and/or needed to implement them and finally pulling the model together by developing the financial implications. Within each stage there are a number of critical building blocks. Each stage in the model is dependent on the other parts and the arrows imply a sequential process of development (the model was designed for a start-up and is linked to sequential chapters of a book). It can be used and modified as changes in the MVP prototype become necessary.

target market segment The key customers or groups of customers you are targeting with your marketing mix

1. Market segments and the value proposition – This stage involves identifying key customers or groups of customers (target market segments) and their specific needs so as to tailor the value proposition for each group. The value proposition is the bundle of products or services that satisfies customers' needs or solves their problems. This includes emotional as well as physical needs and therefore how customer relationships might be cemented through the values embedded in the product or service and its branding.
2. Marketing plan – The marketing plan describes how to target these customers and deliver the value proposition to them through a consistent **marketing mix** (product/ service, price, promotion, channels of distribution etc.), persuading them to purchase the product or service and then become loyal, repeat customers, and how the venture might be scaled-up beyond launch.
3. Operations plan – The operations plan highlights the practical things that need to be done to launch a new venture: the key activities, critical success factors and the strategic options, available if plans change. This involves identifying the risks facing the venture and how they will be monitored and mitigated, for example through partnerships.
4. Resources – This stage identifies the resources or capital available as well as needed for the venture: human, social and financial. The capital available and the capital needed influence and are influenced by the business model.
5. Financial plan – This stage involves pulling the plan together to show the financial consequences of the decisions made in developing the business model: sales, costs, profitability, breakeven and cash flow.

marketing mix The 'five Ps' that define your marketing strategy: Product/ service; Price; Promotion/ communication; People (service); and Place (distribution channels etc.)

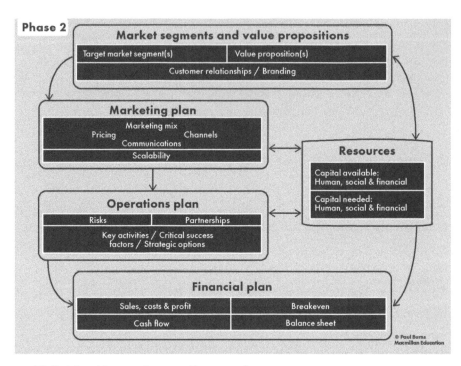

Figure 12.2 New Venture Creation Framework

Source: P. Burns, *New Venture Creation: A Framework for Entrepreneurial Start-ups* (2nd ed.), London; Red Globe Press, 2018

This framework is designed in a systematic, sequential process for a start-up launching a new product/service and can therefore easily be used to help develop the business model for any project. Figure 12.3 shows how this business model framework for a low-cost airline such as easyJet, Ryanair, Southwest Airlines or AirAsia might look.

THE BUSINESS MODEL CANVAS

Whilst the *New Venture Creation Framework* was designed to facilitate the development of a business model for a new product/service, the *Business Model Canvas*, developed by Osterwalder and Pigneur (2010) and shown in Figure 12.4, has more general application and is widely used for established product/services. For this reason, a variant called the *Lean Canvas* was developed (next section). Whilst *Business Model Canvas* covers the same ground as the *New Venture Creation Framework*, there is no sequential process and different elements of a business model are emphasized. It comprises nine interlinked building blocks, each influencing the other. At its core is the **Value proposition** [box 1]. On the right there are four blocks of the business model that are driven by value to customers: *Customer segments* [box 2], *Customer relations* [box 3], *Channels (of distribution)* [box 4] and the resulting *revenue streams* [box 5]. The remaining four blocks on the left are driven by business efficiencies: *Key activities* [box 6], *Key resources* [box 7], *Key partnerships* [box 8] and the resulting *Cost structures* [box 9]. This model was designed as a generic model for looking at an established product/service and is widely used by consultants and trainers.

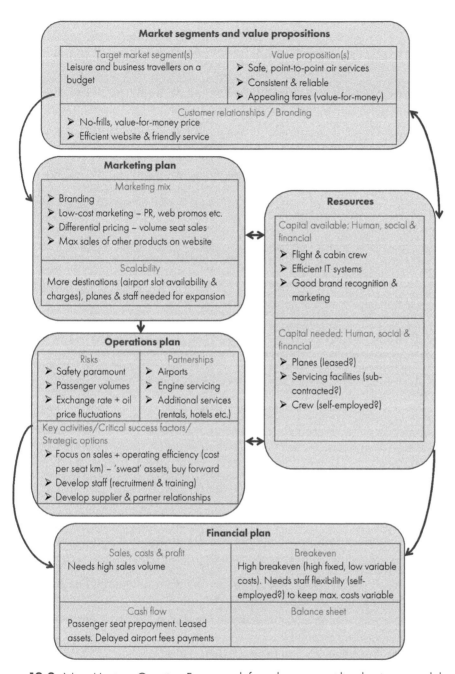

Figure 12.3 New Venture Creation Framework for a low-cost airline business model

Osterwalder and Pigneur's innovatively designed book certainly provides a stimulating pictorial structure for better understanding and developing business models as well as numerous examples of real business models for larger companies such as Apple, Google, Skype and Amazon and well-known products that can be sketched onto the Canvas so as to identify predictable patterns.

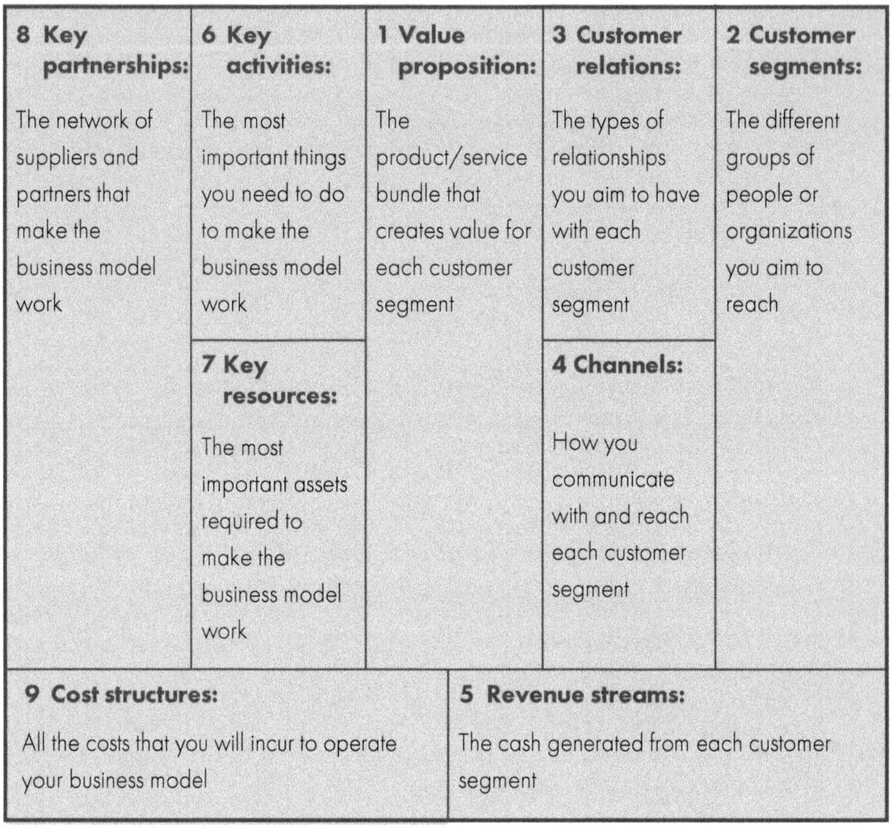

8 Key partnerships:	6 Key activities:	1 Value proposition:	3 Customer relations:	2 Customer segments:
The network of suppliers and partners that make the business model work	The most important things you need to do to make the business model work	The product/service bundle that creates value for each customer segment	The types of relationships you aim to have with each customer segment	The different groups of people or organizations you aim to reach
	7 Key resources: The most important assets required to make the business model work		**4 Channels:** How you communicate with and reach each customer segment	
9 Cost structures: All the costs that you will incur to operate your business model			**5 Revenue streams:** The cash generated from each customer segment	

Figure 12.4 The Business Model Canvas
Source: Strategyzer.com

Osterwalder and Pigneur encouraged the challenging of conventional business models using six techniques (all covered in this book) in conjunction with their Canvas:

➥ Generating new ideas – encouraging you not always to accept the 'dominant logic' of how to do things in a particular industry;
➥ Prototype development – encouraging you to explore alternative business models that might add value for customers;
➥ Storytelling – encouraging you to be able to articulate the concept behind the product/service and how it creates value for customers;
➥ Customer insights – encouraging you to develop a deep understanding of customer needs, even if they are not always derived directly from the customers themselves;
➥ Scenario development – building on customer insights and development in the competitive environment to make future possibilities more tangible;
➥ Visual thinking – encouraging you to draw or sketch out the business model on the Canvas and use sticky notes to explain it, thereby making abstract concepts more concrete.

🔍 EXPLORE FURTHER

New Venture Creation Framework

There is a Worksheet that replicates the five stages in the framework that can be downloaded from the companion website to the book, printed off and then written on. Also available is a Microsoft® PowerPoint slide showing the Worksheet that has simulated sticky notes that can be written on and 'posted' onto it.

These are available free on: www.macmillanihe.com/companion/Burns-New-Venture-Creation-2e/learning-resources/NVC-Framework

Business Model Canvas

The Canvas and other online tools to help apply it are available free on: strategyzer.com/canvas

THE LEAN CANVAS

The generic *Business Model Canvas* was developed for larger, established businesses. Rather than developing a new model, Maurya (2010, 2012) modified it to better suit web-based start-ups and similar small-scale projects. He acknowledged that 'it may have been easier to lay out a new canvas differently'. Shown in Figure 12.5, he called this the *Lean Canvas*. He modified four of the original nine blocks in the *Business Model Canvas*:

Box 3 *Customer relations* became '*Unfair advantage*'. This was just another name for 'competitive advantage', which is what any marketing plan should seek to gain. Despite its importance, he justified the exclusion of 'customer relations' on the grounds that it was included in 'channels' [original box 4].

Box 6 *Key activities* became '*Solutions*'. These were the solutions to the problems that Mauyer added to the canvas [new box 8]. He justified the exclusion of 'key activities' [original box 6] on the grounds that it was too 'outside-in' – 'helping outsiders looking in to understand what the start-up did'.

Box 7 *Key resources* became '*Key metrics*'. He defined this as 'the few actions that matter' – what we have called 'critical success factors'. He justified the exclusion of 'key resources' on the grounds that 'we need fewer resources than ever to get a product to market' – a claim that might be questioned.

Box 8 *Key partnerships* became '*Problems*'. These were the key problems that the value proposition seeks to solve for customers. Meyer admitted that 'key partnerships' was the hardest block to remove and, for me, partnerships remain an important way of identifying an approach to solving the problems of risk and resources faced by any start-up as well as signalling a way of working in the future.

Maurya highlighted the feedback loops needed to monitor customer feedback on an MVP – a learning cycle that turned ideas into products, measured customers' reactions for and against these products, and then decided whether or not to persevere or pivot the idea. The now-familiar process could be repeated as many times as necessary:

Idea → **Build** → *Product* → **Measure** → *Data* → **Learn**

8 Problems:	6 Solutions:	1 Value proposition:	3 Customer relations:	2 Unfair advantage:
The key problem(s) that the value proposition seeks to solve for customers	The solutions to the problems faced by customers	The product/service bundle that creates value for each customer segment	The types of relationships you aim to have with each customer segment	The advantage over competitors offered by this problem solution
	7 Key metrics: The few actions that matter – critical success factors		**4 Channels:** How you communicate with and reach each customer segment	

9 Cost structures:	5 Revenue streams:
All the costs that you will incur to operate your business model	The cash generated from each customer segment

Figure 12.5 The Lean Canvas

Schrage (2014) advocated using this 'agile' or 'lean' methodology more widely within larger organizations by organizing small teams to conduct multiple business experiments to test out new ideas, giving them a modest budget and a short time frame to achieve results. We shall return to this in the next chapter, when we look at how venture teams can develop innovations.

GENERIC BUSINESS MODELS

There are two strategic dimensions to any business models that combine to affect the price a company is able to charge (and therefore the profit it is likely to make) and have implications for how operations should be organized:

➡ Differentiation – where customers value the other elements of the marketing mix more than price and are therefore willing to pay a premium. Differentiation means setting out to be unique in the industry with regard to some dimensions that are widely valued by customers. These can be based upon the product or service and can be tangible (observable product/service characteristics such as function, quality, performance or technology etc.) and/or intangible (customer needs such as status, exclusivity etc.). Often, differentiation is more sustainable when based not just on tangible factors, which can be easily copied, but also on intangible factors, which cannot. These products or services offer high levels of product innovation, functionality and/or design and are usually associated with a strong brand identity (e.g., Apple

generic business models (or marketing strategies) The strategies of low cost, differentiation and/ or customer focus that form the basis of developing sustainable competitive advantage. Also called 'value disciplines'

differentiation Using the elements of the marketing mix to make your product/ service as different as possible from competitors. When valued by customers, this usually leads to being able to charge a higher price

smartphones and computers, Bang & Olufsen hi-fi, Mercedes Benz and Rolls-Royce cars, Dom Perignon champagne).

➡ Customer focus or intimacy – where knowledge of customer needs to be the greatest, allowing the product or service to be more closely tailored to their specific needs. The key to this is close customer relations and this approach goes hand in hand with effective market segmentation. It is often based on good customer service, but it can also be the result of effective marketing appealing particularly to the emotions of buyers.

customer focus (or intimacy) Having a clear understanding of all aspects of customer needs so that customers are satisfied with all aspects of the product/service offering. Usually involves having a close relationship with customers

The more a product or service is different to competitors and the closer and more focused the company is on the needs of customers, the higher the price it is likely to be able to command. These dimensions are important and can be applied to a wide range of businesses to produce fundamental ways of creating sustainable competitive advantage. Clear differentiation often goes with well-aimed market segmentation as it is easier to differentiate in a small, clearly identified market. The key to segmentation is the ability to identify the unique benefits that a product or service offers to potential customers. For example, there may be two electrical engineers producing similar products but, whereas one is a jobbing engineer producing a range of products for many customers with no particular competitive advantage, the other might differentiate itself on the basis of its market – that it sells to a few large companies with whom it has long-term relationships, being integrated into their supply chains.

A highly differentiated product or service offering, targeted at a focused market segment, is called a **niche business model**. Establishing a market niche is most effective when aimed at a narrowly defined market segment. The size of the segment might be limited but, because of the high price, profits are likely to be high. One problem with a niche market is its very narrowness. However, the environment can change: markets grow or shrink; technology changes and customers move around. As the picture changes, so do opportunities; what might offer a good niche in one decade may turn into a 'free for all' in another. However, one strategy is to develop a portfolio of products or services, each in its own distinct market niche, but thereby mitigating the risks associated with the individual size of each niche (see Chapter 15).

niche business model (or marketing strategy) A business model and strategy that involves high differentiation and customer focus

At the other extreme, an undifferentiated product selling to anybody – an unfocused market – is virtually a commodity. This sells mainly because of the price charged – the lower the better. This 'low-cost/low-price' strategy forms the third dimension to business models. Companies selling these products or services must have a way of maintaining lower costs than their competitors. Economies of scale are likely to be very important and this has implications for plant investment requirements and access to capital. It also has implications for capacity utilization and effective pricing policy to encourage the take up of otherwise unused capacity. Day-to-day control of all costs, but particularly overheads, will be important. This has implications for the design of processes and process R&D and innovation. It also has implications for the location of manufacturing (or outsourcing), where input costs for either labour or raw materials are significant. This has resulted in dramatic shifts in recent years. Similarly, transport costs for the finished product, if significant, may influence the choice of location. The emphasis on efficiency implies tight job descriptions and management control (quite the opposite of our entrepreneurial firm).

A number of academic authors have claimed that these are the only 'generic business models' that form enduring, core value propositions. Porter (1985) called them 'generic marketing strategies', whereas Treacy and Wiersema (1995) refer to 'value disciplines'. There is little difference between the two. These business models are summarized in Figure 12.6.

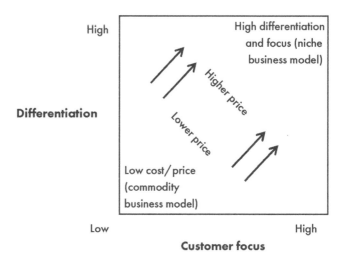

High

High differentiation
and focus (niche
business model)

Differentiation

Higher price

Lower price

Low cost/price
(commodity
business model)

Low   High

Customer focus

Figure 12.6 Generic business models

To decide on an appropriate strategy, Treacy and Wiersema stated that there were four questions that needed to be answered:

➡ For each dimension, what proportion of customers focus on it as their primary or dominant decision criterion? In other words, how important is each value discipline to each market segment?
➡ Which competitors provide the best value in each of these value dimensions? In other words, who is the major competitor in each discipline?
➡ How does the product/service compare to the competition on each dimension?
➡ If it falls short of the value leaders in each dimension of value, how can this be remedied? Of course, if it does fall short the real question is whether it can compete at all, or whether a sufficiently different value proposition must be constructed to create a new market – one that is not currently catered for.

> ❝ *If you set up a company selling widgets like the bloke down the road and the only difference is that's yours are cheaper, you'll make a living but that's all you'll achieve. If you can be truly differentiated and unique, then you've really got something.* ❞
>
> Martyn Dawes, founder Coffee Nation, *Startups*: www.startups.co.uk

There is no one 'best' business model – all of them have potential. There are many examples of successful firms following any of them. Different business models can exist successfully side by side in the same industry if it is sufficiently large and heterogeneous. For example, the business model for low-cost airlines like Southwest Airlines, easyJet and AirAsia is very different to that of flagship carriers like Delta, British Airways and Emirates. Yet both business models survive, each appealing to different target market segments. Similarly, Dell and Apple coexist in the personal computing market, but with completely different business models serving different market segments with different value offerings. It is often possible to unbundle the core business into market segments that reflect these generic business models. For example, most flagship carriers offer different 'classes' of service and accommodation and many use differential pricing – for example, depending on how early or late a booking is made.

There is certainly no 'golden formula' for success, but the choice of strategy has important implications for what the organization needs to be good at – its core competencies, capabilities, skills and knowledge base. The competitive advantage an organization is able to gain stems from these competencies. In a longitudinal study, Rasmussen et al. (2011) showed that the more unique these were, the more difficult they were to copy, hence the greater the firm's ability to differentiate itself and the more successful it was likely to be. The competencies can be combined with other valuable or unique assets, the organization might have such as equipment, trademarks, patents, brand etc. (called strategic assets) that allow the organization to differentiate itself and it is this that leads to more sustainable competitive advantage. The more unique and difficult the core competencies and strategic assets of the firm are to copy, the greater the potential to differentiate its product or service, and thereby the greater its ability to create sustainable competitive advantage. Both differentiation and customer focus provide significant opportunities to achieve economies of scope. This arises when the costs of intangible assets such as product development, market research or the cost of establishing a strong brand image (e.g., Apple, Mercedes Benz) can be spread across a range of products or services.

It is therefore the niche business model that has the greatest potential for success particularly for a start-up, so long as it is underpinned by the necessary core competencies and strategic assets. This high-differentiation strategy has a greater potential for success than the low-cost one – where economies of scale are unlikely to be as important. And this is more easily achieved when applied to a high-focus target market, where the economies of scale are unlikely to exist and market dominance is more easily achieved. However, the bigger the target market, the more vulnerable it is to further segmentation based upon even greater customer focus.

CASE INSIGHT 12.1
Quanta Computers

China

DIFFERENTIAL ADVANTAGE

Born in Shanghai and living much of his early life in Hong Kong, Barry Lam is the founder, chairman and chief executive of Quanta Computer Inc., the world's largest maker of notebook computers, with factories in both Taiwan and China. Quanta is now also the world's largest manufacturer of data storage servers. It has over 30,000 employees, of which some 3,500 are engineers. In 2006, Fortune Magazine recognized Quanta as one of the Fortune Global 500 companies. And yet few will recognize his name or that of his company because he keeps a low profile. This is because Quanta is a contract manufacturer – a company that designs and manufactures electronic equipment, but leaves the branding and marketing to others – Apple, Dell, HP, Compaq, Sony, Toshiba and many others. Indeed, Taiwanese companies now manufacture over half of the world's laptop computers, with Quanta being the largest, accounting for more than 30 per cent of the notebook market.

Quanta specializes in contract manufacturing. It is what he knows and what he does best. His entrepreneurial career started in the 1970s, when he started Kinpo, a company that went on to become the largest contract manufacturer of calculators. Quanta was set up in 1988 and by 2000 had overtaken Toshiba as the world's largest manufacturer of laptops.

Contract manufacturers tend to be providers of either electronic manufacturing services (EMS) or original design manufacturers (ODMs). EMSs build machines that others design. They look to achieve greater economies of scale with lower risk by amalgamating orders from several companies. However, they sell to fewer and fewer global brand names and have little bargaining power because they do not control design or marketing. Consequently, margins are becoming increasingly squeezed. Quanta, however, is an ODM; because it designs notebooks, it is able to charge a premium price, which reflects itself in the high profitability of the firm. Quanta's ability to design power and functionality into lightweight computers has been the key to its success. It allows customers to combine different features for each of its products. Once the design is agreed, production moves ahead quickly. These two elements, design capability and outstanding supply-chain management, are the basis of the long-term relationships. Quanta is not just a 'me-too' manufacturer; it invests in research and product innovation through the Quanta Research and Development Center at its headquarters in Taiwan. This is a vital element in the firm's success and it has links with many universities, including MIT.

Visit the website: www.quantatw.com/Quanta/english

Questions:

1. Which generic business model is most appropriate for Quanta?
2. What factors are likely to determine the company's success?

BUSINESS MODELS FOR VIRTUAL PRODUCTS

New business models are emerging all the time, particularly for businesses that produce virtual products such as computer programmes, apps, videos, etc. – often called 'knowledge products'. They face a particular set of challenges because, once developed, the product is available for downloading again and again at virtually zero cost to the producer – raising the issue of how to price this sort of 'product' since in theory, under competitive conditions, it should tend to be driven down to that marginal cost. Do you try to recoup the (often high) fixed cost of development by charging a high price for the product (at least initially) – thereby probably restricting the size of the market and inviting competition – or do you keep the price low and rely on wide distribution resulting in high levels of sales? Either approach risks generating operating losses. However, if the potential market is small the high price approach is probably more sensible, particularly when the IP is controlled. However, online content can often be easily accessed and copied by end-users, even if access is restricted. If the market is potentially large, investors seem more willing to face losses, at least in the short term, particularly if there is the prospect of dominating the market for this product/service.

It can take time to 'monetize' a new internet-based business idea – longer than it does to design the product or service itself. Nevertheless, it is often the case that users have to be found first in order to prove the concept and only afterwards can ways of monetizing it be found – underlining the attractiveness of the 'lean start-up'. Some companies generate revues directly from product/services sales (e.g., Amazon and Uber) whereas others generate revenue from attracting advertising and offering a free service (e.g., Google and Facebook). As the saying goes, however: 'if the service is free, you are the product.'

Here are just some of the better-known and more established business models that can generate income for internet companies. They are not mutually exclusive. Often more than one model is used alongside another, bringing together different market segments that derive value from the presence of the other. This is called a **multi-sided market** or **platform**.

multi-sided markets
Using different business models to sell to more than one customer

➡ Direct sales model – where products or services are sold directly online and delivered by post (e.g., Amazon);
➡ Bricks-and-clicks model – where traditional retail is combined with the direct internet sales model, either with postal delivery or customer collection (e.g., most large retailers such as John Lewis);
➡ Affiliate model – where a company helps sell a product or service, without necessarily taking ownership, in return for commission (e.g., Amazon);

> 66 *Publishers shouldn't be so dependent on anyone else's platform. It's a bad business decision. You don't own your audience, you're renting your audience – and that can turn off any time. When the algorithm shifts, everybody feels it.* 99
>
> John Avlon, Editor-in-Chief of The Daily Beast, *The Sunday Times*, 7 May 2017

➡ Auction model – where online shoppers bid for products (e.g., eBay).
➡ Flash sales model – where daily deals are offered to registered customers (e.g., Groupon);
➡ Advertising model – where the company is paid for ads being placed on their website (e.g., Facebook, Google and YouTube). There is a tension between advertising and website content as advertising can restrict available screen content. To persuade advertisers to place ads, the company needs to have high levels of focused website traffic. Advertising therefore works particularly well for popular niche sites but examples such as YouTube illustrate how hard it can be to monetize free content even when there is significant website traffic. The market is also becoming increasingly competitive with more and more websites and most of the ad revenue going through just two internet giants. In 2016, it was estimated that 99 per cent of the US and 89 per cent of the UK growth in digital advertising expenditure went through Google and Facebook. This growth has been mainly in the mobile market; it is now estimated that 90 per cent of Facebook's turnover now comes from mobile ads. This brings its own problems as content has to be tailored for mobile devices where the opportunity for advertising is even more space-limited;
➡ Pay-per-click model – where a company is paid for clicks onto an advertiser's link (e.g., Google). This is just a variant on the affiliate and advertising models;
➡ Subscription model – where customers subscribe for the online product or service (e.g., newspapers such as *The Times*). This requires specialist content that is of real value to the online customer and is often coupled with some sort of 'free-trial' usage to demonstrate its value. Because of the surge in 'fake news' in 2017, many newspapers saw a resurgence in their subscriptions levels;
➡ Freemium model – where the company gives away something for free such as a 'basic' service but extras or premium services are charged for (e.g., Spotify). This is most

common in service-based businesses, where the marginal cost of an additional customer is very small;

➡ Bait and hook model – where special deals are offered that lock customers into buying a particular product or service because the costs of switching are high (e.g., smartphones);

➡ Open business models – where value is created through collaboration between partners (e.g., price comparison websites);

➡ Pay-as-you-go model – where customers pay for what they use or consume (e.g., some smartphone contracts).

➡ The long tail – whereby a company offers a large number of small-volume, niche products at a relatively high price – what we have called a niche marketing strategy.

Alongside these models, some of the 'free-to-use' services have sold the data they have on users, creating a new source of value for the companies but also questions over ownership and usage as well as an ethical dilemma for regulators.

CASE INSIGHT 12.2
Fortnite: Battle Royal

China USA

MONETIZING A FREE-TO-PLAY COMPUTER GAME

The free-to-play computer game Fortnite became a cultural and financial phenomenon in 2018 with some 125 million people reported to have played it that year, generating an estimated revenue of $2.4 billion in the calendar year. The game was developed by Tim Sweeney and his company Epic. Whilst in development, in 2012 the Chinese technology conglomerate Tencent purchased a 48 per cent stake in the company for $330 million. Fortnite went live in 2017.

The business model for free-to-play computer games is simple. You offer the game for free and attract a wide player base, but sell in-game powers, abilities, clothes, etc. for a few dollars. The more players, the more the number of add-on sales – and they can add up to millions of dollars. In the game Fortnite drops 100 players onto an island and lets them build forts, scavenge for supplies and weapons and fight to the death. Gamers can play either individually or in teams. By mixing elements like the strategy of building forts for defence as well as just shooting opponents, it seems to attract a diverse range of players: young and old, professional and amateurs. The building element encourages problem-solving and the game encourages learning through experimentation. Players say that it is great fun. Income is derived from buying trivial things like 'skins' (costumes for the characters) or 'emotes' (expressions of emotion like a victory dance), rather than gaming advantage. Dances featured in the gameplay, such as the 'floss', have become real-world crazes. These are expensive, some three or four times the normal price in games. And the company creates demand – some skins are only made available for a limited time. Fortnite accounts with the rarest skins have been resold on eBay for up to $3,000. Epic feeds this enthusiasm. In 2018, it announced that it would give out $100 million in tournament prizes in 2019 – the most ever offered by a computer gaming company.

Serious players train regularly and many of the better-known Fortnite players offer their services as coaches using Skype. Ali Hassan, aka SypherPK, a 22-year-old from Austin, Texas earns some $150,000 a month from playing, coaching and live-streaming his Fortnite games on Twitch, an Amazon-owned broadcast channel that streams live video games (*The Sunday Times Magazine*, 21 October 2018). The channel is free, but some fans pay $5 – $25 a month to form allegiances with their favourite players. Of this fee, Twitch keeps between 30 and 50 per cent. Hassan now has some 17,000 Twitch subscribers, plus 1.5 million followers, not to mention a further 1 million on YouTube.

Visit the website: www.epicgames.com/fortnite/en-US/battle-pass/season-6

Questions:

1. How many income streams are there connected with Fortnite?
2. What are the keys to generating this income for Epic?

Generally, the more novel the business model the more likely it is to have some form of competitive advantage – at least in the short term. The question is how easy it is to copy and therefore how sustainable the competitive advantage might be. Unlike product inventions or innovations, it is unlikely that a novel business model can have its intellectual property safeguarded in law. And the more successful the business model, the more likely it is to be copied. There are three major weapons to help secure sustainability – all of which have implications for the design of the business model:

1. **The speed to market.** There is a lot to be said for first-mover advantage. This is one reason why so many of the digital giants (such as Amazon, Google, Facebook, etc.) buy up smaller players;
2. **The speed needed to dominate that market** and gain oligopoly power to influence price. The digital giants have learned that market dominance gives market power, so it is generally better to dominate a small market than to be a small player in a big market;
3. **The strength of the brand within that market.** The digital giants have also learned that this is the marketing tool that helps them carve out that dominance.

CASE INSIGHT 12.3
Pinterest

DEVELOPING A BUSINESS MODEL FOR A RADICAL INNOVATION

Founded in 2010 by Ben Silbermann, Paul Sciarra and Evan Sharp, Pinterest has attracted investments that value the company at $12.3 billion, despite the fact it has only just begun to generate revenue. Pinterest is a visual discovery app that helps people discover and save creative ideas. Users save (or 'pin') ideas they find on Pinterest or the web to themed digital boards – for example, fashion, photography, cooking, home or garden improvements etc. The site is highly visual, contrasting with many other text-heavy social networks. These 'Pinners' are given recommendations for 'Pins' and boards that interest them based on what others with similar interests have saved. There are more than 175 million monthly active users on Pinterest.

The inspiration for the idea came when Silbermann and Sciarra were working on a failed idea for a shopping app called Tote. They noticed that instead of buying through the app, users emailed pictures of products to each other. People liked pictures and they wanted to get ideas and inspiration from them. The challenge was to turn this into something that made money.

There has been so much remarkable work on search – on making it so that you can find what you're looking for and you can retrieve it really quickly. But there has been little work done on helping people discover things when they may not know exactly what they are looking for . . . From very early on with our investors, we were clear that the goal of the service was to help people discover things that were meaningful to them. That motivation falls closely in line with the goals of lots of businesses and advertisers. *(The Sunday Times, 6 July 2014)*

Because Pinners have an obvious hobby interest, advertising can be highly relevant and targeted, thereby commanding a premium price. Because Pinners browse Pinterest for attractive images and ideas, it has a very different feel to conventional search engines, such as Google, which are designed to deliver specific information. Sites like Google build profiles of their users by mining the data they generate. But that means that their targeted advertising can often feel intrusive and therefore counterproductive for advertisers. People come to Pinterest specifically to plan the things that they would like to do in the future – whether it is something they would like to buy, a recipe they would like to make, or a place they would like to go to. They just click on the pins they wish to investigate further. Therefore, it is a huge opportunity for marketers to be a part of the process

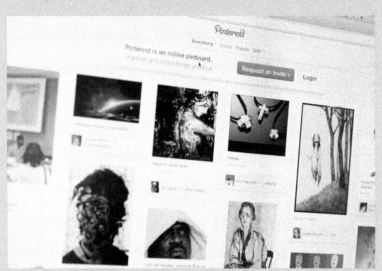

An example of a board on Pinterest
Source: iStock/sematadesign

in helping Pinners take action on the Pins that they find online. And, whilst Pinterest also has pins promoted by companies, a Promoted Pin looks just like any other Pin in the system with the exception of a note that says 'promoted', making a Promoted Pin less obtrusive than other ads. Companies have been Pinning for years, setting up their own pinboards on Pinterest to showcase their own products. In 2014, the company launched a self-serve platform that enables companies to create their own Promoted Pins that can be posted to other boards.

With more than 175 million regular users, Pinterest has caught the attention not only of investors but also of the big advertisers. However, now that they have devised a revenue-generating business model, the question is: how will the search engines that they hope to take revenue from react? In the past, they have often bought up the best new ideas.

Visit the website: **www.pinterest.com**

Questions:

1. Which business models would you apply to Pinterest?
2. The inspiration for Pinterest came from a failed idea for an app called Tote. What are the potential effects on an entrepreneur of a failure like this?

PROJECT-LEVEL REVIEW – PIVOTING

Associated with the lean start-up approach is the concept of **pivoting**, defined by Ries (2011) as a 'structured course correction designed to test a new fundamental hypothesis about the product, strategy, and engine of growth.' This is where a company, based upon the validated learning it is obtaining from the limited-launch MVP, decides to make radical changes to its business model. At any point in the process outlined in Figure 12.2, the business model may need to be changed as it crashes up against the realities of the market and the commercial environment. This is why setting appropriate metrics to evaluate the project is so important. Even after launch of a product/service the business model may need to change. The first year of a project start-up has been called the real validation phase – when it is proved that the business model works. Twitter, Instagram and WhatsApp all radically changed their start-up business model when they found it was not working in practice.

pivoting Changing your business model and/or strategy

> *No plan survives first contact with customers.*
>
> Steve Blank, serial entrepreneur, 8 April 2010: **steveblank.com/category/customer-development-manifesto**

There could be dozens of ways of changing a business model, so this process may involve multiple iterations before the financial outcome is satisfactory. However, never forget that the ultimate test of viability rests with the customers: Does the business model deliver what customers want, at a price they are willing to pay – the value proposition? The reality is that whilst planning may have been meticulous and market-testing rigorous, the only certain way of finding out whether this is a viable product/service is to launch it and then monitor its progress.

Pivoting probably involves undertaking a strategic review of the whole project so as to learn any lessons from the feedback coming from customers. This process is shown in Figure 12.7. The review is informed by the overall strategy of the organization and how this project fits within it. The metrics against which the performance of the project is judged should reflect this as well as the vision the project team had for it. The review starts by looking at the project outcomes compared to these metrics, the assumptions on which they were based and any reasons why they might not have been valid. The assumption that is most likely to be wrong concerns competition since this is a factor that is hard to anticipate in a changing market. If the product is successful, new competitors may have already emerged and their performance needs to be assessed, perhaps using market research.

> *Any plan will collide with reality and something else will emerge. People have to adjust their models to the market, the competition and events.*
>
> Luke Johnson, Chairman Risk Capital Partners, *The Sunday Times*, 20 April 2014

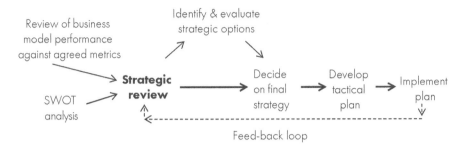

Figure 12.7 Project-level strategic review

The review will try to identify any deficiencies in the product/service and/or its business model (compared to competitors). One technique often used is the classic SWOT analysis (strengths, weaknesses, opportunities and threats) of the current market position. A SWOT analysis can be carried out at a number of levels in the organization. In this case, it is being used at the product/market level. Some of the tools that can be used in a SWOT analysis are listed in Table 12.1. The strengths and weaknesses of the project (or business) can be ascertained using tools like both desk- and field-based market research into customers and competitors, benchmarking against performance metrics, industry norms (including financial criteria) and CSFs, value-chain analysis, product/service life-cycle analysis (used later in the project's life and covered in Chapter 14) and product/market portfolio analysis (used predominantly to address weaknesses and covered in Chapter 15). The threats and opportunities facing the project (or business) can also be ascertained through market research (typically shorter-term) but also longer-term through the PESTEL analysis and the other futures-thinking techniques outlined in Chapter 10. Porter's Five Force analysis (Chapter 14) is a tool used for market analysis and judging competition within an industry. It can be used to ascertain the strength or weakness of a project (or business) within an industry, although it is predominantly used to understand the shorter-term threats it faces. If competing products or services have emerged since the launch, assessing performance against them on the dimensions of the generic business model in Figure 12.6 (price/cost; quality/differentiation; customer focus/intimacy) will be particularly significant. The business model provides a framework for the tactical planning and implementation that subsequently takes place.

The whole process of strategic analysis is an art rather than a science and there is no prescriptive approach. It should give strategic direction to the project (or the business) and help provide a clear understanding of which elements of strategy have worked, which have not and how they might be improved. It may even identify new, emerging opportunities. However, in developing the initial business model for the project, critical success factors should have been highlighted and, out of this, strategic options developed. These may cover the reasons for needing to review the business model and provide 'ready-made' contingency plans. As we have seen, strategic options are important and valuable in an unpredictable commercial environment.

Table 12.1 Tools for a SWOT analysis

➡ Market research
➡ Benchmarking against performance metrics, industry norms and CSFs (Chapter 11)
➡ PESTEL analysis and other futures-thinking techniques (Chapter 10)
➡ Value-chain analysis (Chapter 10)
➡ Product/service life-cycle analysis (Chapter 14)
➡ Product/market portfolio analysis (Chapter 15)
➡ Porter's Five Forces analysis (Chapter 14)
➡ Business models

CASE INSIGHT 12.4
wiGroup

South Africa

PIVOTING

Bevan DuCasse was keen to find a technology-based business opportunity and he realized that Africa was becoming the largest and fastest-growing mobile money market in the world. He therefore thought that anything that built on this opportunity would be a winner and he launched wiWallet in 2007. This was a mobile transaction payment App that linked to credit cards, which DuCasse claims was the first of its kind. However, on its own it proved to be unsuccessful partly because of competition from existing banks and retailers and partly because it was targeting the wrong customers – the App users. At the time, there were very few Apps and there were no App stores.

In 2008, Bevan was joined in the business by Basie Kok and they decided to 'pivot' the business model to one offering an integrated range of enhanced benefits to a range of different customers. The company changed its name to wiGroup and developed two core offerings:

➡ wiCode – an integrated platform that allows merchants to accept payments via their point-of-sale (POS) devices from mobile phones linked to a wide range of credit or payment providers (including mobile-based payment options such as Vodacom's M-Pesa or MTN's Mobile Money)
➡ wiBlox – a card-free service that allows companies to offer customers a range of mobile-based benefits, including loyalty, rewards, vouchers, coupons and gift programmes. At the same time, companies receive data on customer transactions. While many large retailers have card-based loyalty and rewards programmes, wiGroup's technology allows for all of this to be integrated into one App offering payments, loyalty points redemption, coupons and vouchers.

These offerings were then targeted at four different types of customers:

➡ App users – who now usually download the App free and can then use it for payments and to obtain and monitor their rewards or points status;
➡ Retailers and merchants – facilitating payment, enabling them to track purchases and offer promotions;
➡ Product manufacturers, particularly those of fast-moving-consumer-goods (FMCG) – also allowing them to offer promotions and track purchases;
➡ Banks and other credit providers – enhancing their customer service.

This change in direction meant the company had to work collaboratively with POS providers to integrate their systems. It also developed a small reader that merchants could plug into their POS terminal to accept payments and transactions from Apps. The change also meant that the company had to sell the benefits of the platform to a range of different customers. Key to their success was gaining wide market coverage in South Africa as quickly as possible. wiGroup's mobile transacting network has grown to over 55,000 POS outlets in South Africa. It is used by five large retail chains (including Shoprite, Checkers, KFC and Pick n Pay), more than 10 hospitality groups, 50-plus FMCG brands and 8 mobile money issuers. wiGroup now describes itself as an 'ecosystem play, enabling everything from SnapScan to Zapper to integrate with banks and retailers' and, with significant financial backing from Investec Asset Management, it is now looking to expand globally.

See how wiCode and wiBox work: www.youtube.com/watch?v=RDHc53k5ooc
See an interview with Bevan DuCasse: www.youtube.com/watch?v=OpJXumYS9HA&t=59s
Visit the website: www.wigroupinternational.com

Question:

1. Why was the old business model for wiGroup unsuccessful and why has the revised business model worked?

CORPORATE-LEVEL STRATEGIC REVIEW

As we have seen, the success or failure of individual projects (and their business models) can affect the overall strategy of an organization, for example by taking the firm into new markets. This means that the review of individual projects needs to feed into the regular strategic review of the organization. This is one of the mechanisms for making distributed strategizing a reality. The process is similar to the one outlined earlier, but at the corporate level. This is the distinction between 'business' and 'corporate' strategy, which is shown in Figure 12.8. The process is given direction by the vision for the organization overall and underpinned by its core values and beliefs. At the corporate level, the SWOT analysis can use the same tools as shown in Table 12.1. It seeks to identify an overlap between the business environment and the firm's resources – a match between the organization's core competencies, capabilities and resources and market opportunities. Again, this gives the whole organization a strategic direction that can then be translated into detailed tactical and operating plans.

Figure 12.8 Corporate-level strategic review

Kotter (2012) suggests that, in today's rapidly changing and complex world, large companies need to undertake this sort of review at least annually in a way that echoes the approach that entrepreneurs take to strategy development. He advocates what he calls a 'second operating system, devoted to the design and implementation of strategy that uses an agile, network-like structure [that] continually assesses the business, the industry, and the organization [that] constantly seeks opportunities, identifies initiatives . . . and completes those initiatives swiftly and efficiently . . . an ongoing process of searching, doing, learning and modifying'. He adds that this system needs to be operated by many change agents (devolved strategizing) who feel empowered to make decisions – a system that relies on an emotional commitment to the organization rather than rules. These are all characteristics of an entrepreneurial architecture.

 Review your strategy constantly to ensure you are meeting market demands.
Elizabeth Gooch, founder EG Solutions, *Launch Lab*, 13 January 2009:
www.launchlab.co.uk

The business model frameworks in this chapter provide structure and focus for any strategic review but are particularly valuable when strategizing is conducted within a group such as a venture team focused on a single product/service. They provide a set of commonly-known and understood techniques and processes. They generate a common language and mechanism for communication. They help to come to the right decisions, consistently. Strategic frameworks replicate good practice. They provide the link from judgement through experience to learning. They ought to be logical and apply common sense. They are not in the nature of a scientific discovery. They are, to quote a colleague, 'a glimpse of the blindingly obvious' – something you knew all along but were never quite able to express in that simple way. In that sense, they help organize and develop what might otherwise be a disjointed and unsystematic process.

 CASE INSIGHT 12.5
audioBoom

PIVOTING

Audioboom is the audio equivalent of Netflix. The business was launched in 2009 in the UK and already has almost four million listeners. It is also quoted on the London Stock Exchange after its reverse takeover of One Delta, an AIM (Alternative Investment Market)-listed shell company in 2014. Later the same year, the company raised £8 million in a share placing with a number of blue-chip institutional investors, valuing it at over £73 million.

The reason Audioboom has attracted so much attention is because so many analysts believe it has tremendous potential for future growth outside the UK, particularly in markets like the USA, Australia and India. The company's strategy and business model have changed a number of times since its launch:

Stage 1: Amateur users were allowed to record, post and share audio clips – spoken word, not music – for free. Because there was no music, Audioboom did not have to pay performance royalties. This phase attracted many celebrity users and generated a loyal listening. The problem was that audioBoom had not yet worked out how to generate income.

Stage 2: This was to persuade professional organizations to make audio content, such as news, reviews and interviews, available on the site. By 2014, it had developed some 2,000 commercial partners such as the BBC, Sky Sports, talkSport, the Premier League and also many newspapers and magazines. At the same time, it started to develop a new business model that would allow it to generate income; to enable this to happen, however, it also had to develop a new software platform and it was this that was to account for much of the financial investment.

Stage 3: The next stage, in late 2014, was to relaunch, allowing for content embeds on the user's own website, Twitter, Facebook or Tumblr feed. This allowed users to create their own personalized feed by download-ing content that interested them. Content could range across sport, news, financial markets and entertain-ment. Users could select the content they wished to receive and this could be downloaded automatically at times they select – a system called 'content curation'. In this way, a sports fan could download up-to-date selected content and listen to it as the news breaks or store it to listen to on the way to work. At the same time, the original idea of allowing users to post their own audio clips via mobile devices was made easier. Just as YouTube does not pay for content, Audioboom does not pay for most audio clips and it generates income by selling and inserting advertising before, during and after a clip.

Audioboom, which has over 60 million listens per month, is now the leading podcasting and on-demand audio plat-form for hosting, distributing and monetizing content – hosting thousands of podcasts from around the world from orga-nizations such as the Associated Press, BBC and Red FM. Content can now be shared via iTunes, iHeartRadio, Google Play, Spotify, Stitcher, Facebook and Twitter as well as users' own websites and mobile apps. The company is still based in London, where most of its users are to be found, but it also now has offices in Melbourne, Mumbai and New York.

Visit the website: audioboom.com

Question:

1. What lessons do you learn from Audioboom about changing your business model?

SUMMARY

➡ An organization's core competencies and capabilities are the things it does best, a portfolio of resources that can be combined in various ways to meet the opportunities or threats that the organization faces and give it competitive advantage. They should underpin a new project.

➡ A strategy is simply a plan as to how to achieve a longer-term goal. It comprises a series of interlinked actions or tactics. It should help the organization towards achieving its long-term vision – what it might become. This is framed by the organization's mission – what it aims to achieve and how it will achieve it. Strategy development can be both deliberate and emergent but at different times and in different circum-stances. Timely emergent strategy necessitates continuous strategizing, must always be underpinned by a strong vision or direction and informed by good information flows which should lead to the development of strategic options for evaluation.

➡ A business model is the plan for how a business competes, uses its resources, structures its relationships, communicates with customers, creates value and generates profits. The chapter outlined three generic business model frameworks that provide pictorial and/or verbal structures to aid understanding and development of a business model: the *New Venture Creation Framework*; the *Business Model Canvas*; and the *Lean Canvas*. They are minimalist and simple and force focused thinking and succinct communication.

➡ There are two strategic dimensions to any business models that combine to affect the price a company is able to charge: differentiation and customer focus or intimacy. The higher the differentiation and focus, the higher the price, but low price can also be an attractive business model so long as it is based on low costs. There are many variants that can be used for novel, often technology-based, products. Different business models can exist happily side by side in the same industry, appealing to different target markets.

➡ There are three major weapons to help secure sustainability, all of which have implications for the design of the business model: speed to market, speed to dominate market and the strength of a brand.

➡ Pivoting is where a company, based upon the validated learning it is obtaining from the launch of its MVP, decides to make radical changes to its business model. This involves undertaking a strategic review of the project aimed at identifying deficiencies in the product/service and/or its business model. A strategic review can also be carried out at the business level.

 GROUP DISCUSSION TOPICS

1. At what level(s) should strategy be developed and how should it be coordinated?
2. What is the difference between business strategy and competitive strategy? How do they relate to each other? How are they coordinated?
3. Give examples of the things that might be the core competencies and capabilities of an organization? How do you make the judgement?
4. How should strategy be determined?
5. What might cause the core values and beliefs of an organization to change? How easy is it to actually change them?
6. Do you agree that the debate between the 'Positioning' and 'Process' schools of strategy development is false? Explain.
7. What are the advantages and disadvantages of using a framework like the *New Venture Creation Framework* or the *Business Model Canvas* to help develop a business model?
8. Which of the frameworks outlined in the book do you prefer? Explain.
9. If your business model is constantly changing to suit changing circumstances, when (if ever) should it be formalized into a business plan?
10. What is the difference between the marketing mix, the value proposition and the business model?
11. What are the advantages and disadvantages of a business model relying on customer focus?
12. What are the advantages and disadvantages of a business model relying on low cost/low price?
13. What are the advantages and disadvantages of a business model relying on differentiation?
14. What are the advantages and disadvantages of the niche business model?
15. Customers always want the cheapest product. Discuss.
16. Different customers are happy to pay different prices for the same product. Discuss.
17. How can you make a SWOT analysis as objective as possible?
18. In different contexts, strengths can be weaknesses and opportunities can be threats. Discuss.

19. How do you generate strategic options? Which techniques might help?
20. If a project meets all the performance metrics set for it do you need to undertake a strategic review?

ACTIVITIES

1. Critically analyze the business model in Figure 12.3, fleshing out the details of what the bullet points under the five headings involve. What are the model's strengths and weaknesses? Is anything missing? Looking at the 'key operating activities' section of the Operations Plan, what are the critical success factors and are there more strategic options?
2. Select ten internet-based product/services and explain their business model(s).
3. Prepare a SWOT analysis on your course, college, university or university department.
4. Prepare a SWOT analysis on a selected product/service or company.
5. Undertake a full strategic review on a selected company. What are the company's core capabilities and competencies?

REFERENCES

Burns, P. (2018, 2014) *New Venture Creation: A Framework for Entrepreneurial Start-Ups* (2nd edn., 1st edn.), London: Palgrave.
Foster, R.N. and Kaplan, S. (2001) *Creative Destruction: Why Companies That Are Built to Last Underperform the Market – And How to Successfully Transform Them*, New York, NY: Currency Doubleday.
Grant, R.M. (2010) *Contemporary Strategy Analysis* (7th edn.), Chichester: Wiley.
Kay, J. (1998) *Foundations of Corporate Success*, Oxford: Oxford University Press.
Kotter, J.P. (2012) 'Accelerate!', *Harvard Business Review*, November.
Maurya, A. (2010) 'Why Lean Canvas vs Business Model', https://blog.leanstack.com/why-lean-canvas-vs-business-model-canvas-af62c0f250f0.
Maurya, A. (2012) *Running Lean: Iterate from Plan A to a Plan That Works*, The lean series (2nd edn.), Sebastopol, CA: O'Reilly.
Mintzberg, H., Ahlstrand, B. and Lampel, J. (1998) *Strategy Safari*, New York, NY: The Free Press.
Osterwalder, A. and Pigneur, Y. (2010) *Business Model Generation: A Handbook for Visionaries, Game Changers and Challengers*, Hoboken, NJ: John Wiley & Sons.
Porter, M. (1985) *Competitive Advantage: Creating and Sustaining Superior Performance*, New York, NY: Free Press.
Prahalad, C.K. and Hamel G. (1990) 'The Core Competence of the Corporation', *Harvard Business Review*, 68(3).
Quinn, J.B. Mintzberg, H. and James, R.M. (1988) *The Strategy Process*, Hemel Hempstead: Prentice Hall International.
Rasmussen, E., Mosey, S. and Wright, M. (2011) 'The Evolution of Entrepreneurial Competencies: A Longitudinal Study of University Spin-Off Venture Emergence', *Journal of Management Studies*, 48(6), September.
Ries, E. (2011) *The Lean Startup: How Today's Entrepreneurs Use Continuous Innovation to Create Radically Successful Businesses*, New York, NY: Crown Publishing.
Sarasvathy, S.D. (2001) 'Causation and Effectuation: Toward a Theoretical Shift from Economic Inevitability to Entrepreneurial Contingency', *The Academy of Management Review*, 26(2).
Schrage, M. (2014) *The Innovator's Hypothesis: How Cheap Experiments Are Worth More Than Good Ideas*, Cambridge, MA: The MIT Press.
Treacy, M. and Wiersema, F. (1995) *The Discipline of Market Leaders*, Reading, MA: Addison-Wesley.

 ONLINE RESOURCES AVAILABLE For further resources relating to this chapter see the companion website at **www.macmillanihe.com/Burns-CEI**

PART IV

CORPORATE VENTURING

This section is about how large organizations organize themselves so as to encourage innovation and new venture development internally and how they can go about it through a process of systematic external corporate acquisition. Chapter 13 is about internal venturing; how intrapreneurs and intrapreneurial teams can be facilitated, developed and encouraged; the role of innovation functions, departments, units or divisions; and how the outcomes of these ventures might then be organized. Chapter 14 is about how the existing portfolio of products and services might be developed and the effects of diversification. It looks at the reasons for corporate acquisitions, how they might be facilitated and the risks posed by this strategy. Chapter 15 explores the consequences of diversification, particularly in relation to the emergence of new product/markets, and how shareholder value might be created in conglomerates. Finally it explores how corporations following this strategy might be best organized.

Intrepreneurship is focused on not just inventing but also seeking ways to make ideas commercially viable.

Kevin DeSouza, author

13 Venture teams and intrapreneurs

CONTENTS

- Corporate venturing
- Intrapreneurs
- Facilitating intrapreneurship
- Handling internal politics
- Selecting a venture team
- Team development
- Innovation departments or functions
- Innovation units or divisions
- Corporate accelerators and incubators
- Strategic 'fit'
- Deciding what to do with new ventures
- New venture success and failure
- Summary
- Group discussion topics
- Activities
- References

CASE INSIGHTS

13.1 3M (2): The Post-It Note®
13.2 W.L. Gore
13.3 Lockheed Martin
13.4 Alphabet (3): X Development

Learning outcomes

When you have read this chapter and undertaken the related activities you will be able to:

➡ Understand and explain the role of the intrapreneur and venture teams in larger firms and how they might be encouraged and facilitated;

➡ Understand and explain the character traits of intrapreneurs and how they might be developed;

➡ Critically assess whether you have an entrepreneurial tendency;

➡ Understand and explain the basis on which to select a venture team;

➡ Critically assess your own preferred team role;

➡ Understand and explain how teams develop;

➡ Critically analyze the role of innovation departments, innovation units and corporate accelerators and incubators;

➡ Understand and explain the structures used for dealing with new venture developments.

CORPORATE VENTURING

Corporate venturing can be viewed simply as a series of tools or techniques that can help bring about entrepreneurial outcomes. They help generate and maintain strategic renewal. Some of these tools and techniques relate to how the organization structures and manages itself internally (called internal corporate venturing) whilst others relate to how it structures itself externally (called external corporate venturing). An entrepreneurial architecture encourages and facilitates the development and use of these tools and techniques.

Internal corporate venturing is concerned with how the organization encourages and manages innovative, entrepreneurial projects – how it encourages new businesses to develop internally whilst aligning them to the company's existing activities (Burgelman, 1983; Drucker, 1985; Galbraith, 1982). Internal corporate venturing might be undertaken by an individual – who is known as an intrapreneur. More often it is now undertaken by a team, often called a venture team. One reason for this, particularly in tech firms, is the importance of cognitive diversity to facilitate the recombination of skills and ideas from different areas. This may be an ad hoc team formed for a specific project from staff with different skills from different departments. Some companies have permanent departments dedicated to innovation. Some projects might be so close to the companies' core competencies and relate directly to its core operations or be of such strategic importance that they are eventually assimilated into mainstream operations. Some projects may be sufficiently different that they need to be set up with some degree of separation from the mainstream activity – the degree of separation is important. Other projects might be so distant from the core activities of the organization that they are spun-off or sold.

External corporate venturing is concerned with how the organization structures itself externally to encourage innovation and develop new business areas. This may be through partnerships, strategic alliances and joint ventures, which we considered in Chapter 5. It may also be through investments and acquisitions in strategically important smaller firms and the corporate venturing units needed to undertake this role (Chesbrough, 2002). This topic will be covered in Chapter 15.

INTRAPRENEURS

The term intrapreneur is generally used to describe the individual charged with pushing through innovations within a larger organization, in an entrepreneurial fashion – a salaried 'entrepreneur' in a big company that they do not own. The key is that they work in an entrepreneurial way, with an entrepreneurial mindset. At the same time, they must be sufficiently adept (and patient) at manoeuvring their way through the bureaucracy of a large organization. Pinchot (1985) defined them as 'dreamers who do; those who take hands-on responsibility for creating innovation of any kind within an organization; they may be the creators or inventors but are always the dreamers who figure out how to turn an idea into a profitable reality'. Actually, they are rarely the inventor of the product; they usually work with teams to cut through the bureaucracy of the organization in order to bring it to the marketplace as quickly as possible. Like entrepreneurs, they turn the dream into reality. The practice of intrapreneurship can be undertaken at many different levels – corporate, divisional, functional or project level. Whilst not dependent upon the size of the organization (Antoncic and Hisrich, 2003), intrapreneurship appears to become more difficult to sustain as the firm grows (Ross, 1987).

Innovative behaviour can occur in a random, unsystematic way. Gillis Lundgren was a driver trying to deliver a table in 1953 when he discovered that it wouldn't fit into the back of his small car. His solution was to remove the legs. He worked for a small mail-order furniture company in Sweden called IKEA, and this idea was taken up by the company, leading it to develop the flat-pack, self-assembly furniture for which it is known today. At the time, Lundgren was only IKEA's fourth employee, and he certainly did not regard himself as an intrapreneur. He just had a problem to solve and he told his boss what he had done. He later became IKEA's head of design and played a major role in the company's success. The difference between this random behaviour and intrapreneurial behaviour is that giving it the label 'intrapreneurial' recognizes and legitimizes it so that it can be systematically encouraged and facilitated.

> **❝** While it is true that every company needs an entrepreneur to get it under way, healthy growth requires a smattering of intrapreneurs who drive new projects and explore new and unexpected directions for business development. Virgin could never have grown into the group of more than 200 companies it is now, were it not for a steady stream of intrapreneurs who looked for and developed opportunities, often leading efforts that went against the grain. **❞**
>
> Richard Branson, founder Virgin Group,
> **www.entrepreneur.com/article/218011**, January 2011

Successful intrapreneurs share many of the character traits of entrepreneurs outlined in Chapter 1 – a need for achievement, a need for autonomy, drive and determination, a high internal locus of control, creativity and innovativeness and an ability to live with risk and uncertainty. Although they have a desire for autonomy and a willingness to live with risk and uncertainty (Hornsby et al., 1993), this does not translate into a desire to be completely independent and set up their own business – they are probably too risk-averse. Autonomy, and in particular the 'psychological ownership' of their intrapreneurial project, can be seen as a strong personal motivator encouraging that feeling of efficacy outlined in Chapter 5. Their project also gives them a sense of purpose and mastery – which are both important motivators. It demonstrates their willingness to take limited risks and to cope with uncertainty within the framework of a regular job. However, they probably have sufficient belief in their abilities that were they to lose their job they believe they would quickly find another. However, they remain less willing to take personal risks than entrepreneurs.

Nevertheless, intrapreneurs are comfortable with change and are able to cope with uncertainty (Kanter, 2004). They are able to perceive an opportunity and have a vision for what it might become (Kanter, 2004; Pinchot, 1987). They are motivated to pro-actively take the initiative and run with it and are action-orientated: 'Vision and imagination make up half of "the dreamers that do". Action is the other half' (Pinchot, 1987). They are also results-orientated (Pinchot, 1985; Ross and Unwalla, 1986). Pinchot (1985) characterized them as follows: like entrepreneurs they are self-confident and optimistic, but probably cynical about the bureaucratic systems within which they operate, although they believe they can circumvent or manipulate the 'system' to achieve their goals; like entrepreneurs they are strongly intuitive (right-brain thinkers), but because of their corporate background less willing to rely solely on intuition and more willing to undertake research into a new business idea (left-brain thinking).

> **❝** *We inadvertently developed this role [intrapreneur] at Virgin by virtue of the fact that when we've chosen to jump into a business about which we have little or no real knowledge, we've had to enable a few carefully selected people who do know which end is up. ... Perhaps the greatest thing about this form of enabled intrapreneurship is that often everyone becomes so immersed in what they're doing that they feel like they own their companies. They don't feel like employees working for someone else, they feel much more like, well I think the only word to describe it is 'belongers'.* **❞**
>
> Richard Branson, founder Virgin Group,
> **www.entrepreneur.com/article/218011**, January 2011

According to Ross and Unwalla (1986), the best intrapreneurs are ambitious, rational, competitive and questioning. They dislike bureaucracy and are challenged by innovation, but they have an understanding of their organization and a belief in their colleagues. Unlike many entrepreneurs, they need to be adept at politics and good at resolving conflict as they navigate their way through the blocks and blockers in other operational units in their organization (Govindaranjan and Trimble, 2010). Pinchot (1985) observed that intrapreneurs are adept communicators with strong interpersonal skills that make them good at persuading others to do what they want. They are also sensitive to the need to disguise risks within the organization in order to minimize the political cost of failure. At the heart of the intrapreneurs' skill is this process of influencing without authority, based upon some form of reciprocity (Cohen and Bradford, 1991). Intrapreneurs need to identify potential allies and understand the language they use and their values and motivations. By doing this, they are able to develop a personal relationship and are better able to influence allies through exchanges of value – a process of give and take. According to Kanter (2004), intrapreneurs prefer to use a participative management style and have an understanding that they needed to work with others to achieve their goals.

Pinchot (1985) and Morris and Kuratko (2002) suggested that intrapreneurs should approach their role in a certain way. They should:

➥ Have a vision for what they want to achieve and be willing to do anything to achieve it, regardless of their personal job description and including disobeying orders that might block the project – even if it involves the risk of getting fired.
➥ Find a high-level sponsor. Be loyal and truthful to them and build a solid relationship. Nevertheless, manage expectations and never over-promise. It is better to promise less and deliver more.
➥ Be true to their goals, but realistic in how they can be achieved. Set the parameters of what they do and how they do it – in other words, to change the rules of the game – so that they start to control as much of the project and how it is evaluated as they can.

➥ Show a few early wins with tangible deliverables in order to create confidence. Small wins can evolve into significant accomplishments and develop a momentum for the project that becomes difficult to stop.

➥ Select and build a highly motivated but flexible project team and a network of internal and external supporters who are willing to help.

➥ Work 'underground' for as long as possible; once they 'go public' blocks and blockers will emerge.

➥ Remember, when action is needed quickly it is often better to ask for forgiveness than permission.

Whilst there are psychometric tests that measure entrepreneurial tendency (see boxed section), Pinchot (1985) said that if a manager could answer 'yes' to six or more of the following questions they were probably already behaving like an intrapreneur:

1. Does striving to make things work better occupy as much of your time as working on existing systems and duties?
2. Do you get excited about work?
3. Do you think about new business ideas in your spare time?
4. Can you see what needs to be done to actually make new ideas happen?
5. Do you get into trouble sometimes for doing things that exceed your authority?
6. Can you keep your ideas secret until they are tested and more developed?
7. Have you overcome the despondency you feel when a project you are working on looks as if it might fail and pushed on to complete it?
8. Do you have a network of work colleagues you can count on for support?
9. Do you get annoyed and frustrated when others cannot execute your ideas successfully?
10. Can you overcome the desire to do all the work on a project yourself and share responsibility with others?
11. Would you be willing to give up some salary to try out a business idea, provided the final rewards were adequate?

🔍 EXPLORE FURTHER

The General Enterprise Tendency (GET) test is a 54-question, validated, online psychometric test of entrepreneurial character (Caird, 1991a, b; Stormer et al., 1999). It measures character traits in five dimensions:

➥ Need for independence (high in entrepreneurs);
➥ Need for achievement (high in entrepreneurs);
➥ Internal locus of control (high in entrepreneurs);
➥ Creativity (high in entrepreneurs);
➥ Accepting of risk and uncertainty(high in entrepreneurs).

The Results are analyzed automatically and a personal report on your entrepreneurial traits is then produced, which includes whether you have the character traits of intrapreneur rather than an entrepreneur.

The test is free and can be taken online at: www.get2test.net

FACILITATING INTRAPRENEURSHIP

Intrapreneurs and venture teams should thrive within an organization with an entrepreneurial architecture – an architecture created and nurtured by the leader of the organization. However, for an intrapreneurial project to succeed it needs a number of other facilitating elements:

➡ An intrapreneurial team – The team needs to have the necessary skills, knowledge and competencies to undertake the project. It also needs to have appropriate team skills – a topic we shall expand on this later in this chapter. Underpinning this, the team needs to have an intrapreneurial culture, defined by Hisrich (1990) as one that develops visions, goals, and action plans; takes action and rewards action; encourages suggesting, trying and experimenting; encourages creating and developing regardless of the area; and encourages the taking of responsibility and ownership. This strong sense of purpose or 'shared cognition' improves collective understanding within a group, and helps individuals with different functional backgrounds to reach consensus. This can improve both decision-making quality and the overall performance of the team (Smith et al., 2005; West III, 2007). It should also create a strong sense of identity and cohesion (Hofstede's 'in-group').

shared cognition
The sharing of goals, effective communication and transfer of knowledge between partners in a business

➡ High-level sponsor – Since it may be inappropriate for the architecture around the core activity of an organization to be entrepreneurial (see Chapter 2), the intrapreneur and their team may need to be shielded in some way and made to feel that they are different and protected. Every project needs a high-level sponsor with sufficient authority both to protect them when times are difficult or vested interests are upset and to help them unblock the blockages to change as they occur. The sponsor should help secure resources, provide advice and contacts and help give them the organizational freedom they need. They will need to nurture and encourage the intrapreneur and their team, particularly early on in the life of the project or when things go wrong. They will need to handle the internal politics, endorsing the project and creating visibility for it at the appropriate time. Underpinning this must be a trusting relationship between the sponsor and the intrapreneurial team and a clear vision for the future of the project either inside or outside the organization.

➡ Resources – Resources of all kinds are needed for any project – particularly in terms of time and freedom or slack from day-to-day responsibilities. Other resources may include money, materials and access to information, knowledge and skills that other managers may be guarding jealously. The high-level sponsor may need to facilitate cross-departmental transfers of staff to provide the team with the necessary skills to undertake the project as well as press departments to provide information to the project team.

➡ Tolerance of uncertainty and risk-taking – The team need to believe that they can take risks in pushing through the project without any fear of penalties. These risks may relate not only to the success or failure of the project but also to potential damage to interpersonal relationships if the team is perceived as circumventing the authority of certain managers. The internal politics of an organization may need to be managed by the high-level sponsor.

➡ Reward – We have seen how monetary reward is not necessarily a motivation for those undertaking cognitive tasks, although regular pay and security of employment offer important security to intrapreneurs. Gardner (2017) argued that companies should measure the inputs of individuals, not just their outputs, so as to reinforce the behaviour they want to encourage. They should prioritize intrinsic motivators, such as recognition, promotion, expanded job responsibility and personal development, over extrinsic motivators such as money. Rather than offering bonuses to individuals, companies should have a single profit pool and use frameworks and guidance, rather than formulas, to determine pay. She cautioned against rewards that discouraged collaboration. However, simple competitions can send clear signals to the organization about what behaviour is valued. For example, the Chinese firm Tencent offers cash prizes for ideas that translate into innovations, (Case insight 2.1) and Chinese consumer electronics and appliance manufacturer Haier has competitions where teams of employees pitch their ideas for projects against other teams to obtain prestigious recognition as well as resources (Case insight 9.6). Haier now considers itself to have some 3,000 micro-businesses.

Intrapreneurs and venture teams need to be aligned around one important goal – a specific, measurable achievement within a specific time frame. However, they need to have strategic intent to allow them to 'regroup' if they are pushed off-course. Such teams need not only to feel that they have autonomy, but also to actually have that autonomy. However, since they will inevitably end up 'breaking the rules', they also need to be shielded from the politics of the organization. At the same time, they need to be held accountable for their results, which implies that a certain amount of control is necessary. This means three things:

1. A budget needs to be set for the project and then monitored;
2. Metrics need to be established to judge the progress of the project within specific time frames. Wherever possible, these metrics should be quantifiable and measurable rather than qualitative and vague, and should use objective, respected data (see Chapter 11). Google, for example, has 'Objectives and Key Results' (OKRs) that are set by a project team and can be seen by all Google employees. It is expected that teams should achieve about 80 per cent of their OKRs since 100 per cent is rarely achievable and would therefore be a demotivating objective;
3. The risks associated with the project need to be identified, monitoring set in place and contingencies planned (Chapter 8). These include both internal and external risks. Should any of the risks materialize, it may impact on the progress of the project and may result in the performance metrics not being achieved. Indeed, achieving some of these metrics may be contingent upon the delivery of certain resources from other parts of the organization. Highlighting this sort of goal interdependence within an organization emphasizes an important aspect of successful intrapreneurship.

Once these are established, progress can then be monitored within this framework with regular review meetings using the agreed data. The blocks and blockages arising might be dealt with on an ad hoc basis or within these meetings. This is best conducted in a transparent way using some form of score card, although commercial confidentiality must always be respected. These regular review meetings provide the opportunity to establish a sense of urgency and celebrate successes as milestones are passed. They also provide the opportunity to shut down a project and compartmentalize any risks should the need arise.

CASE INSIGHT 13.1
3M (2): The Post-It Note®

USA

INTRAPRENEURS AND 'BOOTLEGGING'

3M has been known for decades as an entrepreneurial company that pursues growth through innovation (see Case insight 2.3). In the late 1920s, it developed a policy of allowing researchers to spend up to 15 per cent of their time working on their own projects. To this day, it tries to make innovation part of the corporate culture by encouraging staff to spend some of their time working on pet ideas that may one day become new products for the company. Staff are encouraged to 'bootleg' (borrow) resources early in its development; once an idea is accepted they can be allocated a budget to buy equipment and hire extra help. To get an idea accepted, they must first get the personal backing of a member of the main board. An interdisciplinary team is then set up to take the idea further. Membership of these teams is encouraged and often voluntary. Failure is not punished, but success is well rewarded.

Perhaps the best-known contemporary example of the success of this policy is the development of the Post-it Note® by Art Frye in the 1980s. The story of this invention has become one of the best-known examples of how intrapreneurs work. Frye was looking for a way to mark places in a hymn book – a paper marker that would stick, but not permanently. At the same time, the company had developed a new glue for the aerospace industry which, unfortunately as it seemed at the time, would not dry – a glue that would not stick firmly, but left no residue. Art spotted a use for the product; what was different, however, was the way he went about persuading his bosses to back the project. He produced the product, complete with its distinctive yellow colour, and distributed it to secretaries who started using it throughout 3M. Art then cut their supplies, insisting that there would be no more unless the company officially backed the product. The rest is history.

Questions:

1. Why is 'bootlegging' important for intrapreneurship?
2. What other lessons might you learn from how Art Frye went about getting the company to back his product?

CASE INSIGHT 13.2
W.L. Gore

USA

INTRAPRENEURS AND 'DABBLE-TIME'

W.L Gore is a company best known for its Gore-Tex fabric. It is also associated with the idea of giving staff slack time to explore new product ideas and personal projects; in 3M it was 15 per cent (now described as more of an attitude of mind than a reality); in Google it is 20 per cent (once a project is approved); in W.L. Gore the 10 per cent is called 'dabble-time'. Using 'dabble-time' a Gore employee called Dave Myers identified that one of their products – 'ePTFE' – a coating for push-pull cables, could be used to make guitar strings more comfortable to use. The coated strings proved to be only marginally more comfortable, but the unexpected bonus was that they kept their tone longer than uncoated guitar strings. Launched under the brand name ELIXIR Strings, they are now the best-selling acoustic guitar strings.

Visit the website: **www.gore.com**

Question:

1. Why is 'dabble-time' important for intrapreneurship?

 **CASE INSIGHT 13.3**
Lockheed Martin

INTRAPRENEURS AND 'SKUNK-WORKING'

'Skunk-works' is a term associated with Lockheed Martin. It is another name for the Advanced Development Programs Lockheed allowed Kelly Johnson and Ben Rich to establish as an autonomous organization – a company within a company – with a small, focused team. This team created some of the most innovative aircraft models, including the U-2, Lockheed SR-71 Blackbird, Lockheed F-117 Nighthawk, Lockheed Martin F-22 Raptor and the Lockheed Martiin F-35 Lightening II – all of which had been used by air forces in several countries. Lockheed learned that successful intrapreneurship happens when team members are given autonomy and are allowed to define a clear path themselves for their idea and they are given the authority to modify and innovate as needed without going through bureaucratic approval processes. 'Skunk-working' is now a term widely used in business to describe a group working in a similar way.

Visit the website: **www.lockheedmartin.com**

Question:

1. Why is 'skunk-working' important for intrapreneurship?

HANDLING INTERNAL POLITICS

Intrapreneurs face many blocks and blockers – some internal, others external. They need to navigate the internal politics of the organization from the very start and that can sometimes be the most difficult part of getting a new product or service to market. Based on interviews with 100 intrapreneurs, Price et al. (2009) concluded that success depends critically upon viewing the political challenge as part of the project from the very start and engaging with it: '[Intrapreneurs] apply a wide variety of political influence actions to help move the organization. They actively engage people across their organization. They position the product and the project in the context of the organization in a way that others could see the value and benefits. Then, they use both soft and hard influence actions to help others move with them. Politics, almost, becomes a natural part of what they do in order to ensure that their innovations reach the market and address the customer needs they so thoroughly understand.'

There are often numerous individuals or groups of stakeholders to an intrapreneurial project that may influence its outcome. Each needs to be handled in a different manner, some being potential allies and others enemies of the project. However, Auster and Hillenbrand (2016) highlighted six broad categories that make handling them easier:

early adopters The second group of customers to buy a new product – people with status in their market segment and opinion leaders

1. Early adopters – stakeholders that are likely to welcome the innovation (see Chapter 14). These are the ones who should be contacted early so as to identify how the project might be shaped in order to overcome any early objections and benefit them most.
2. Advocates – stakeholders with political power who are likely to promote the project. These might easily be external stakeholders such as customers, partners or industry regulators. They are likely to have been advocates of other innovations. They are the key to unlocking the path of the project through their political influence and should also be contacted early.
3. Positive fence sitters – stakeholders who are open to the innovation but are too busy to get involved. These could be staff in the departments that will eventually support or benefit from the project but who do not see it yet as a priority. They may be customers or external partners who will benefit from the project. Contacting this group is not an immediate priority.
4. Cautious fence sitters – stakeholders who are uncertain about the innovation and are therefore open to influence from others. These could be customers or partners for whom any benefit from the project is uncertain or not immediate and are therefore unlikely to back it immediately. However, they could easily turn against the project if sceptics emerge.
5. Positive sceptics – stakeholders that have justifiable concerns about the impact the innovation may have on the organization or market. These may be from the legal and finance departments or regulators. These are people that need to be engaged with early on so as to accommodate or overcome their concerns and win their support.
6. Negative sceptics – stakeholders who may be hurt in some way by the innovation – for example, through the loss of political power and influence in the organization. They may simply be natural blockers to change. They may be competitors with the most to lose from the project's success. These stakeholders are unlikely to change their views. If possible, avoid their attention, influence or involvement and plan for their active disruption.

The ability to influence individuals in these groups depends upon the character and track record of the intrapreneur and their team. Price et al. (2009) concluded that 'their political actions usually emanate from a foundation of trust and respect, which must be built over time and across people in multiple functions at multiple levels of the organization' – a leadership characteristic highlighted in Chapter 6. However, not every individual or group will have the same degree of political influence over the project. The power they have to potentially help or hinder the project needs to be assessed. It may be possible to place the project under the direct hierarchical control of its high-power advocates – or move it away from the control of high-power sceptics. Similarly, more time generally may need to be spent with all high-power influencers. Auster and Hillenbrand (2016) recommend identifying early adopters, advocates and positive sceptics early so that the intrapreneur can consult them to build their support or extract their concerns – particularly those with the greatest power to influence the project. They also recommended identifying negative sceptics early so that the intrapreneur can avoid them and not attract their attention too early. Chapter 7 outlined some ways of dealing with blockers of change that may also be useful.

SELECTING A VENTURE TEAM

Team working is commonplace now across most businesses and is particularly valuable in pushing through innovations. A single intrapreneur on their own rarely has all the skills required to see a project through to completion. They often need a team to work with them – a venture team. The most innovative companies use cross-functional teams and agile ways of developing innovations (BCG, 2017). Venture teams are ad hoc, forming and reforming to tackle different projects. At Google, all staff are involved in product development work in some form. They work in small teams of three or four people. Larger teams get broken down into smaller sub-teams, each working on specific aspects of the bigger project. Each team has a leader that rotates depending on the changing project requirements and most staff work in more than one team.

The ability to work effectively as a team is important. Venture teams need all the freedom and support that would be given to an intrapreneur. As we have noted, research suggests that the most important factors in team effectiveness are how the team functions and their commitment to achieving overall goals (shared cognition). How the team functions is often down to the personal chemistry between members of the team. In order to be successful, the team needs to have:

➡ The skills, knowledge and competencies to undertake the project, probably from a wide range of different disciplines such as computer programming, engineering, marketing or finance. Phadke and Vyakarnam (2017) note that experience of 'different market spaces' is particularly important for teams to develop 'creative synthesis' (Chapter 10). The problem with cross-functional teams is that they need to be managed (for example, to resolve conflict) and this can be difficult if the team leader does not have direct authority over the team members. Conflict of interest can be difficult to resolve if the team leader (or who ever they report to) does not have sufficient authority and power within the organization. The issue of authority can lead to duality of loyalty within the team and can affect motivation;

➡ A balance between creativity and project execution is necessary and has direct implications on the project's outcome. For example, using the *Herrmann Brain Dominance Instrument* (HBDI) outlined in Chapter 9, a person or team may be dominant 'imaginative thinkers' (type D) and weak 'sequential thinkers' (type B) – meaning that they are highly creative but are less able to organize their work and implement their ideas. An example of this is necessary is given in the next section.

➡ Complementary personal characteristics so that their 'team roles' complement each other's (see below). The team needs to build trust and this can be helped if the team has prior experience working together.

> ❝ It takes real team spirit to take on challenges and win, and it also builds true camaraderie. It is this togetherness, above and beyond any other factor, that set great businesses apart from the also-rans. ❞
>
> Richard Branson, founder Virgin Group, *The Sunday Times*, 7 December 2014

Based upon research into how effective teams work, Belbin (1981) identified three 'personal orientations': thinking, people and action. Each of these translates into three 'team roles' – functions naturally undertaken by the individual – giving a total of nine team roles. Each team role has positive qualities but also some allowable weaknesses.

Thinking orientation

➡ Plant – This is the team's vital spark and chief source of new ideas – creative, imaginative and often unorthodox. However, they can be distant and uncommunicative and sometimes their ideas can seem a little impractical.

➡ Monitor-Evaluator – This is the team's rock – introvert, sober, strategic and discerning. They explore all options and are capable of deep analysis of huge amounts of data. They are rarely wrong. However, they can lack drive and are unlikely to inspire or excite others.

➡ Specialist – This is the team's chief source of technical knowledge or skill – single-minded, self-starting and dedicated. However, they tend to contribute on a narrow front.

People orientation

➡ Coordinator – This is the team's natural chair – mature, confident and trusting. They clarify goals and promote decision-making. They are calm and have strong interpersonal skills. However, they can be perceived as a little manipulative. Indeed, this person is naturally suited helping with the challenge of handling the internal politics of the project.

➡ Team-Worker – This is the team's counsellor or conciliator – someone who is mild-mannered and social, perceptive and aware of problems or undercurrents, accommodating and has good listening skills. They promote harmony and are particularly valuable at times of crisis. However, they can be indecisive.

➡ Resource Investigator – This is 'the fixer' – an extrovert, who is amiable, using six phones on the go, with a wealth of contacts. The fixer picks other peoples' brains and explore opportunities. However, they can be a bit undisciplined and can lose interest quickly once their initial enthusiasm has passed.

Action orientation

➡ Shaper – This is usually the self-elected task leader with lots of nervous energy – extrovert, dynamic, outgoing, highly strung, argumentative, and seeking ways around obstacles. They do have a tendency to bully and are not always liked. However, they generate action and thrive under pressure.

➡ Implementer – This is the team's workhorse – disciplined, reliable and conservative. They turn ideas into practical actions and get on with the job logically and loyally. However, they can be inflexible and slow to change.

➡ Completer-Finisher – This is the team's 'worry-guts', who makes sure things get finished – sticklers for detail, deadlines and schedules. They have relentless follow-through, picking up any errors or omissions as they go. However, they sometimes just cannot let go and are reluctant to delegate.

Most individuals are naturally suited to two or three roles, but to be effective all nine roles must be present within a team. Chell (2001) suggested that the 'prototypical entrepreneur' might be a mix of three Belbin roles: plant (creative, ideas person), shaper (dynamism, full of drive and energy) and resource investigator (enthusiastically explores opportunities). However, by implication an effective team needs three to five people, whether or not led by a 'prototypical entrepreneur'.

The challenge is to select the team and then to build cohesion and motivation. A cohesive team works together effectively because of its collective commitment to an agreed goal. There may be different views about how that goal is achieved and this involves analysing the options and building a consensus while balancing multiple viewpoints and demands. However, too great a reliance on achieving consensus can lead to slow decision-making, so a balance is needed that may strain the interpersonal skills of the team leader and their high-level sponsor.

 ## EXPLORE FURTHER

Belbin Team Roles – This test is not free. The questionnaire can be obtained from: www.belbin.com.

Meyers-Briggs Type Indicator (MBTI) – This is a commonly used psychometric test that looks at general personality. It is based upon Jung's typologies, which postulate four cognitive functions: thinking, feeling, sensing and intuition. Each of these has two polar orientations: extraversion or introversion. The test combines these to produce five personality types: mind, energy, tactics and identity:

➡ Mind (introvert vs extrovert) – shows how you interact with your surroundings (e.g., introverts tend to prefer solitary activities whereas extroverts tend to prefer group activities).
➡ Energy (observant vs intuitive) – determines how you see the world and process information (e.g., observant people tend to be highly practical, focused on the present whereas intuitive people tend to be more open-minded and creative).
➡ Nature (thinking vs feeling) – determines how you make decisions (e.g., thinking people tend to be more rational whereas feeling people tend to be more sensitive and emotional).
➡ Tactics (judging vs prospecting) – reflects how you approach work and decision-making (e.g., judging people tend to be decisive and prefer structure whereas prospecting people can be more flexible, spontaneous better at spotting opportunities).
➡ Identity (assertive vs turbulent) – reflects how confident you are in your abilities and decisions (e.g., assertive people tend to be more self-assured, easy-going and more resistant to stress whereas turbulent people are more self-conscious, success-driven and stress-prone).

The MBTI test can be taken free on-line at: www.16personalities.com

TEAM DEVELOPMENT

All personal relationships are based upon trust – it is the cornerstone of a good team. It binds them together. This involves being open and spontaneous, honest and direct, being supportive of individuals and having their interests at heart. But trust needs to be earned, it does not come as a right and therefore needs to be built up between individual members of the team over time. It needs to be demonstrated with real outcomes, but can be lost very quickly by careless words or actions and then takes even longer to rebuild. Effective teams do not just happen; they have to be developed, and that can take time. Teams go through a development process, shown in Figure 13.1:

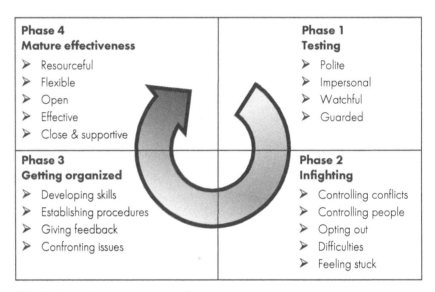

Figure 13.1 Team development wheel

Phase 1   The group tests relationships. Individuals are polite, impersonal, watchful and guarded.

Phase 2   In-fighting starts in the group and controlling the conflict is important. However, whilst some individuals might be confrontational others might opt out and avoid the conflict altogether. Neither approach is good. Collaboration is best. This is a dangerous phase from which some groups never emerge. The Thomas–Kilmann Conflict Modes instrument gives us an insight into how conflict might be handled (Chapter 6).

Phase 3   The group starts to get organized; developing skills, establishing procedures, giving feedback, confronting issues.

Phase 4   The group becomes mature and effective, working flexibly and closely, making the most of resources and being close-knit and supportive.

The whole process of team formation and development has been likened to courtship and marriage, involving decisions based partly on emotion rather than logic. For that reason, it is important that the team shares the same values and is committed to the same goals. They may disagree on tactics but they all agree on the destination and how they are going to get there. It is also important that team roles are clearly defined, although given the uncertainty involved with rapid growth, it is also important that flexibility is maintained. An effective team will generate team norms of behaviour that can be a powerful force for conformity but developing an effective team needs skilful handling.

> **❝** The best teams stand out because they are teams, because the individual members have been so truly integrated that the team functions with a single spirit. There is a constant flow of mutual support among the players, enabling them to feed off strengths and compensate for weaknesses. They depend on one another, trust one another. A manager should engender that sense of unity. He should create a bond among his players and between him and them that raises performance to heights that were unimaginable when they started out as disparate individuals. **❞**
>
> Alex Ferguson, former Manager Manchester United FC,
> *Managing My Life*, London: Hodder & Stoughton, 1999

INNOVATION DEPARTMENTS OR FUNCTIONS

An innovation department is a permanent organizational structure set up for the purpose of originating and/or developing innovations. These innovative ideas might originate from within the department or from other sources, including intrapreneurs. The department then needs the resources to develop the idea. Innovation may also simply be a function within a department – for example, an innovation function might be located within the marketing department of a company. The distinction between function and department is important in signalling to others in the organization the authority and autonomy its management has and the importance of innovation within the organization. Being part of an existing organization, these functions or departments can be subsidized from other activities.

Being part of an existing organization, these structures allow existing skills and competencies to be leveraged at the same time as maintaining the potential to learn and/or hire in new ones. They allow revenues from existing, successful products and services to finance innovations which might take some time to become profitable. However, by separating out the development of innovation the hope is that the division or department will be able to establish its own organizational architecture which encourages and facilitates innovation as a continuous process. Mainstream activities can then continue as 'business as usual' in the rest of the organization.

There are a number of issues with innovation departments or functions:

➡ They may find it difficult to think 'outside the box' in searching for innovative ideas because they share the same 'dominant logic' with the rest of the organization but are likely to have narrower horizons. Indeed, rather than allowing skills and competences across the organization to be leveraged, they may cause them to be compartmentalized. If the innovation function is part of the production department, the innovations are likely to relate to production. If it is part of the marketing department they are likely to relate to marketing.

➡ They may not have the skills and capabilities to take a promising idea forward, despite it being in some way strategically important to the future of the organization. New ideas may need resources and investment beyond the normal budget of a department or function within a department. In these circumstances, the intervention of top management may be required to provide the resources and degree of organizational separation and/or support needed by the department.

➥ They may be unduly susceptible to political in-fighting because of the seniority (or otherwise) of its managers and, even if it has an entrepreneurial architecture itself, it may face a hostile architecture elsewhere in the organization.

Innovation departments are therefore most successful when taking forward incremental innovations relating to existing activities. Typically, they have limited skills, knowledge and competencies compared to an ad hoc team drawn from across an organization. To address this, one variant is to second individuals from that wider organization on an ad hoc basis.

Another problem facing permanent departments, particularly smaller ones with limited scope, is that they attract similar people rather than the diversity of people that typically encourage creativity and innovation. For example, the innovations department of a UK high street retailer was frustrated that many of the good ideas they were coming up with were not being implemented. As part of a training programme on creativity, staff were asked to take the *Herrmann Brain Dominance Instrument* (HBDI) (explained in Chapter 9). The results are shown in Figure 13.2. Individual results are represented by the large dots and the overall result profile by the solid black line. As can be seen, the department is strongly skewed towards Type D Imaginative thinkers – which you would expect to be good for an innovations department. However, the profile is also skewed away from Type B Sequential thinkers, who, as you might remember from Chapter 9, are the ones who are good at organizing work and implementing ideas. This analysis made the retail chain think whether the problem lay within the department rather than outside and what would be needed to develop or recruit more 'implementers'.

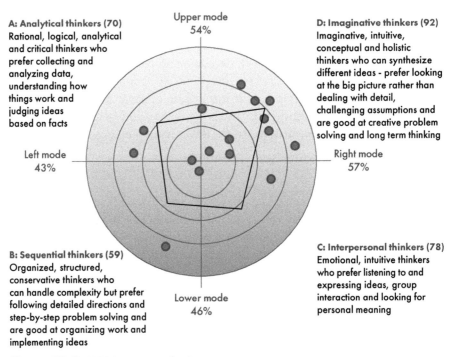

Figure 13.2 HBDI mapping for Innovation team

INNOVATION UNITS OR DIVISIONS

Because of these issues, innovation departments or functions are most likely to come up with incremental innovations to products, processes or marketing that, because of their operational relatedness, will probably be quickly adopted by the organization. What is really needed for large organizations that are seeking to encourage both incremental and radical innovation, particularly through the intrapreneurial teams is an organizational capability that is more flexible, has more resources and greater perceived and real authority within the organization. This may come by simply giving that department more resources, greater autonomy and more senior management – perhaps linking it to innovation across different divisions that straddle different product/market sectors.

Many of the most innovative companies have therefore set up separate innovation units or divisions, often in a separate location, reporting directly to the CEO. Studies indicate that radical innovations are best placed in separate locations, led by a high-level manager with greater autonomy and free from the bureaucracy of the main organization (e.g., Gwynne, 1997). The distinction between department/function and division/unit is important – it indicates greater importance and autonomy – and depends to a large degree on volume and scale of activity, but might also reflect scope of activity and strategic importance of innovation within the organization. For example, Alphabet has its own secretive early-stage ideation and development division called X Development whereas its major subsidiary, Google, has its own product development group and in-house incubator called Advanced Technology and Projects (ATAP) (Case insight 13.4).

The annual BCG survey of the most innovative companies found that 70 per cent of the 'strong' *digital* innovators had either a centralized organization that controlled and drove innovation or one that drove R&D and passes the results to business units (BCG, 2018). They recommended an approach to developing and implementing digital innovations:

> In our experience, a centralized digital innovation unit has a mix of several critical responsibilities. It creates a digital innovation roadmap that guides the digitization of the company's innovation function and monitors progress. It manages cross-functional digital projects. A chief data officer is responsible for using external and internal data for improved decision making, including developing tools, methodologies, and platforms; identifying and prioritizing data sources; building a data engine to gain insights; and developing and managing data policy. A customer experience team seeks to create superior and seamless customer experiences across digital and non-digital channels. This includes mapping customer journeys, designing customer interfaces, and putting in place an e-commerce strategy, if needed. This team also helps business units implement digital tools and best practices. A team responsible for driving digital innovation brings in the technology. It manages relations with the startup community, including seed investments; fosters internal innovation; oversees digital incubators, accelerators, and labs; and supports deployment of innovation initiatives. Finally, a partnerships team develops an ecosystem of business development ventures that can generate new sources of revenue.

CORPORATE ACCELERATORS AND INCUBATORS

Whilst often intrapreneurial teams are left to work on their own within existing structures, albeit with a high-level sponsor, another approach is to move them into a corporate accelerator. These are development programs, often linked to resources and facilities such as incubators, designed to facilitate rapid conceptualization, prototyping and development of a business idea within a tight time frame. They might be open to company-only teams or mixed with outside projects teams – the aim being to encourage the cross-fertilization of ideas and knowledge. Projects selection is usually based upon recommendation but the team will also usually be required to make a pitch to senior managers. If successful they might be extracted in whole or in part from their day-to-day jobs and allocated a budget and a timeframe for completion of the project. The intrapreneur and their venture team might be moved to the incubator to develop the project until the organization decides what to do with it – a topic we return to later. Once completed, the project team might decide to join any spin-off from the project or move back into mainstream operations, where it is hoped that they will have developed that entrepreneurial mindset that can then be applied to another innovation project.

Corporate accelerators and incubators usually span all the divisions of an organization. They therefore have a scale and scope that innovation departments do not have. They should have access to all the resources needed to develop the project prior to launch and expertise in facilitating a successful outcome. Maletz and Nohria (2001) found that placing innovative projects in these sort of organizational 'whitespace' outside the formal organization – with its usual rules and procedures about planning, organizing and controlling – accelerated natural experimentation and generally nurtured project development. The broader the boundaries of this 'whitespace' the more radical the innovations are likely to be.

Corporate accelerators and incubators are cost centers rather than short-term revenue generators but are strategically important for future developments in the organization. Their success depends very much upon the resources they command, the autonomy they are granted and therefore the seniority of their management. Ultimately they will be judged by the success or otherwise of the projects they help to develop. The manager of the accelerator or incubator needs to have the seniority that facilitates a close relationship not only with the leader of the organization but also with each of the high-level sponsors of the projects that they house. Indeed the manager of the accelerator or incubator may be the sole or joint high-level sponsor of the project, involved in project selection and monitoring.

Innovation departments or divisions and corporate incubators are not the same as traditional research and development (R&D) departments. R&D departments are staffed by technical staff and dedicated to taking existing products further in their technical sophistication. In the R&D department the focus is entirely on technological advancement. The work is research-based and technology-driven. Many R&D departments are better at inventing than innovating. Innovation departments and corporate accelerators and incubators should be technology-enabled but market-focused and market-driven – where are the opportunities and how can we capitalize on them? Part of their work may be technology based but the emphasis is on how this will be delivered to a market and how it will best meet a real market need. This has been one of the real successes of both Apple and Alphabet, where the two functions are separated into different divisions.

Because of their fundamental difference from the routine operations of a business, most in-house R&D departments are kept separate. Their productivity depends heavily upon the organizational conditions that encourage creativity and the systems that allow their innovations to find their way into the market place. They often face pressure to pursue short-term commercial opportunities. Where R&D returns can be identified, they are often long-term. This makes it difficult to decide on the scale of investment in R&D and to evaluate the return received. For example, it has been estimated that it can take 15 years to research and develop a new medicine and cost up to $1.7 billion to get it into production. This has led many larger organizations, particularly in the pharmaceutical industry, to look to other smaller organizations to undertake the research and then buying-in that research through patents or company acquisition, reducing the risks they face and leaving the development and the marketing of the product to them, where they consider their real skill and capability to lie. We look at this strategy in the next chapter. However, it must be emphasized that internal and external corporate venturing are not mutually exclusive options and they can be carried out very successfully side by side.

CASE INSIGHT 13.4
Alphabet (3): X Development

USA

NEW PRODUCT/SERVICE IDEATION AND DEVELOPMENT DIVISIONS

Case insight 5.4 (Alphabet 1) explained how Alphabet had become the holding company for Google and other subsidiaries: Calico, Chronicle, Dandelion, DeepMind, GV, CapitalG, Google Fiber, Jigsaw, Sidewalk Labs, Verily, Waymo and X Development. Located on the edge of the Google campus in Mountain View California, X Development (formerly Google X) is where new ideas are identified and new products developed. It is focused on making actual objects that interact with the real world and have commercial value and it prides itself on being able to build the bridge between idea and proven concept. X is a secretive organization. However, among the projects that have graduated out of X to become subsidiaries of Alphabet are Google Glass, driverless cars (project Waymo), high-altitude Wi-Fi balloons (project Loon) and glucose-monitoring contact lenses (project Verily, which includes other life science projects).

X was originally set up in 2010 to build a driverless car, but its aim is now broader – to find and develop other major revenue streams to the highly successful Google search engine, which finances its current activities. Alphabet has unimaginable resources of money and talent, and it is bringing them to focus on the opportunities brought about by the coalescing of networks, computing power and AI – areas where it has skills, competences and market presence. Because of this, unlike many companies that fund only research with a short-term payback, most of X's projects are medium- to long-term in nature. Most projects originate inside Google, but it does buy-in some ideas – for example, a current project called Makani that produces wind energy using kites was purchased in 2013.

X has more than 250 employees from diverse backgrounds – former park rangers, sculptors, philosophers, and machinists. One X scientist has won two Academy Awards for special effects; another spent five years of his evenings and weekends building a helicopter in his garage. This diversity of backgrounds helps them bring different perspectives to problems and ideas since none are particularly experts in any field. Astro Teller, for example, is CEO or 'Captain of Moonshots', and reports directly to Serge Brin (co-founder of the original Google and president of Alphabet). Teller himself has written a novel, worked in finance, and has a PhD in AI. All of the projects are called moonshots – defined as the intersection of a big problem, a radical solution and breakthrough technology. Unsurprisingly, most moonshots never see the light of day. Teller explained:

> If one of Google X's projects were a home run, became everything we wanted, I would be really happy. I would be overjoyed if it happened with two (Fast Company, May 2014).

X projects cover an extremely wide spectrum, across a wide variety of technological domains. Unconstrained by Google's core activity, there are three broad criteria to become an X project. Firstly, they must address a problem that affects millions of people (and therefore has the potential to generate millions of dollars). Secondly, they must utilize a radical solution that has not been considered so far. Finally, they must use technologies that are now (or very nearly) obtainable. Despite the risks in this approach, X is not interested in incremental projects. Rich DeVaul, the head of its Rapid Evaluation team, explained that this is as much because of practical as ideological reasons:

> It's so hard to do almost anything in this world. Getting out of bed in the morning can be hard for me. But attacking a problem that is twice as big or 10 times as big is not twice or 10 times as hard. If there's a completely crazy, lame idea, then it's probably come from me (Fast Company, May 2014).

The generation of wild, off-the-wall ideas – the so-called moonshots – is encouraged, and staff are celebrated and rewarded for both project success and failure. Projects graduating from X are celebrated, with teams being awarded diplomas and wearing mortarboards at the ceremony. Uncovering good ideas is a numbers game – the more ideas you have, the more likely you are to find a good one – and X is as much about failure (or failing-fast) as success. At X, failure is the norm. Teller has said that he sometimes hugs people who admit mistakes or defeat in group meetings. In the words of DeVaul:

> Why put off failing until tomorrow or next week if you can fail now? (Fast Company, May 2014).

X monitors ideas from anywhere, both inside and outside Alphabet, and particularly in academia. Ideas are brainstormed and often scenarios are built around how products might be used in the future. Each moonshot comprises a small core team supplemented by in-house staff with expertise in particular, relevant fields such as design or mechanical engineering. To help build and develop prototypes, X has its own Design Kitchen next to the main building – a large-scale fabrication shop filled with 3-D printers, sophisticated lathes, table saws and other sophisticated machinery. Obi Felton is the so-called 'Head of Getting Moonshots ready for Contact with the Real World' – meaning she is in charge of bringing an idea to market. She explained that not all the projects have to evolve into large revenue earners:

> The portfolio has to make money [but] not necessarily each product. Some of these will be better businesses than others, if you want to measure in terms of dollars. Others might make a huge impact on the world, but it's not a massive market (Fast Company, May 2014).

The Rapid Evaluation team test out the most promising moonshots by doing everything they can to get the idea to fail – theoretically, practically and commercially. This method emphasizes rejecting ideas more than affirming them and it occurs in three separate stages. Firstly, the team get a few weeks and a few thousand dollars to try to understand a moonshot's biggest risks. Overcoming those risks becomes the team's milestones and will unlock more budget or permission to grow the team. This kills many ideas quickly. In the second stage, the team are given a few months and more money to build prototypes, focusing on the hardest and riskiest parts of the technology to better understand the problem they're trying to solve. At the same time, they must also build a techno-economic analysis that proves this idea could survive in the real world as a large business with a real market potential. Even fewer ideas survive this stage. Finally, under the direction of Obi Fenton, the project goes to the Foundry to iron out any technology issues and decide whether or not the project can eventually be turned into a product and business in a reasonable time span. This can last about a year and even then the project might be returned to the Rapid Evaluation team for reimagining. X also uses kill signals. These are metrics agreed with the team at the start of the project, such as viability within a certain time frame. If triggered, these metrics will mean the immediate death of the project. Only about half of these projects graduate from the Foundry stage. For example, the Loon Wi-Fi delivery system project went through the following process:

1. **Problem identification:** Whilst the Rapid Evaluation Team was discussing issues and ideas related to communication generally and internet connection in particular, the project started life as an idea involving connections between mobile devices. In 2011, however, DeVaul decided to shift focus towards increasing internet access for rural or poor areas – areas currently lacking any connection.
2. **Idea development:** The team discovered that Lockheed was working on a high-altitude communication airship that could stay in one place, but keeping such a craft stationary was proving extremely difficult. DeVaul had the insight of, rather than keeping a single airship in place, replacing it quickly and cheaply with more airships – or rather balloons.
3. **Solution testing:** DeVaul bought a batch of high-flying weather balloons and assembled a radio transmitter in a cardboard box that he attached to one of them. He launched it over a reservoir, following in his car to see if it worked. One early milestone was to manufacture balloons that could last for three months. Having achieved that, the next milestones became to lower the total cost of the balloons.
4. **Prototype building:** Loon was commissioned as an official project in 2011 and a team was recruited to build a small fleet of prototypes. X's Design Kitchen began to work on a Loon antenna, building a small house in their workshop to see how the antenna might attach to customers' residences. They developed wireless routers that could be placed in these balloons that could fly high in the stratosphere.
5. **Product introduction:** Entrepreneur Mike Cassidy was brought in to manage the project's rollout as an actual business, first in 2013 as a pilot in New Zealand. In 2018, Loon graduated to become a subsidiary of Alphabet. In this system, balloons are manoeuvred by adjusting their altitude in the stratosphere so that they float up to a wind layer that is blowing in the appropriate direction and speed. Users connect to the balloon network using their home antenna. The signal then travels from balloon to balloon, finally connecting to a ground station connected to an internet service provider. The aim is to enable everyone to access the internet, even in remote areas.

You will recall from Case insight 5.4 that Alphabet has a number of other research or innovation-focused subsidiaries. Google also has its own research division, called Advanced Technology and Projects (ATAP), which was set up to continually review developments in Google's highly competitive technology-based environment, its product/market offering and to speed up its strategic research projects. One example of its work is on issues related to developing new unique user interfaces (UIs) for small smartwatches and other wearables where, in a project called Jacquard, they have shown how to weave a multitouch input panel like a mouse pad into regular cloth using processes available in the existing textile industry.

Case insights 15.3 and 16.1 will look at the strategies that helped Google grow to become the dominant internet giant it is today.

Visit the website: **x.company**

Questions:

1. How does Alphabet mitigate the risks associated with innovation?
2. What lessons are to be learned from X's approach to turning ideas into proven concepts? What is required to launch the proven concept onto a market?
3. How does the work of X differ from that of other research subsidiaries and, in particular, from ATAP? Why is the company organized in this way? Are there any disadvantages to this form of organization?
4. Can any company imitate Alphabet's approach to organizing innovation, or is this model heavily based upon technological innovation?

STRATEGIC 'FIT'

We should never underestimate the ability of large corporations with dominant market positions to ignore internal developments. They might have the funds to invest in R&D on the one hand, but on the other their existing product/markets might dominate their attention. And heaven forbid if an innovation should potentially threaten that market position. Xerox's Palo Alto Research Center (PARC) is a good example of how innovation might be successfully encouraged but not commercially exploited. PARC was a separate R&D entity, fully funded and resourced by Xerox but kept organizationally separate. In the 1970s, PARC became a leader in invention and innovation, developing many of the fundamental computing technologies that were later commercialized by other Silicon Valley companies such as Apple, Adobe, and 3M. However, with the one (major) exception of the laser printer (Xerox was in the copier business), Xerox failed to exploit most of the innovations because it could not see their relevance to its existing business. The company watched on passively as entrepreneurs left to set up their own businesses because it refused to commit the funds needed to turn inventions into commercially significant innovations. The paradox here was that a company with enormous resources generated by its patented, dominant position in the copier market was unable to successfully commercially exploit the innovations generated by the research funded by these resources.

The reason for this seems to be because innovations were kept in-house. There were no mechanisms and organizational structures for dealing with innovations in a systematic way. It was only in 1989 when Xerox set up a separate corporate division, Xerox Technology Ventures (XTV), located almost as far away in the USA as you can get from both Xerox head office and PARC that things began to change. XTV was established to exploit technologies that did not into Xerox's product portfolio. It worked much like an internal venture capital firm, using some $30 million of funding given to it by Xerox. If a product was turned down by head office, it could be offered to XTV. Once a working model was perfected, the founders were moved out of the plush PARC laboratories and into low-cost commercial premises and professional management put in to bring the product to market. 80 per cent of the gains from the spin-out would go to Xerox, while the XTV principals would share the remaining 20 percent among themselves.

Xerox is not alone in facing this problem. Whilst there are areas of innovation where large firms have the resources to develop innovative technologies to the point of commercial exploitation, they have often failed to take it that one, entrepreneurial step further, seemingly unable to handle the risk and uncertainty associated with it. As Janeway (2018) observed: 'All too often the broad-based firm with multitudes of established market positions and ample financial resources has failed to lead, even when its own laboratories have been primary sources of the very innovation in question.'

DECIDING WHAT TO DO WITH NEW VENTURES

Once the flow of innovative ideas has started, the question will arise as to what to do with them, in particular, whether they are kept in-house or spun-out in some way. The two factors that influence how an incremental or a radical product/service innovation is handled by an organization are operational relatedness and strategic importance. Operational relatedness refers to how close the innovation is to the existing product/service portfolio and its market footprint, reflecting the core skills, competences and capabilities of the organization. This is not necessarily related simply to a company's own industry. For example, Google's AdSense was not an internet search product, but rather leveraged Google's unique ability to gather data on what users were browsing so as to help better target advertising. Most incremental innovations will have high operational relatedness. Strategic importance refers to how important the innovation is to the future development of the organization. There could be many reasons for this, but one factor is the current strategic orientation of the organization and the business model it adopts in meeting the needs of customers. This might also provide some insights into its capabilities and competences that underpin its business models (e.g. product quality, process efficiency or cost and customer focus – see Chapter 12). Both these factors involve making judgements – there are no hard-and-fast rules to apply. Figure 13.3 shows how these innovations are likely to be treated.

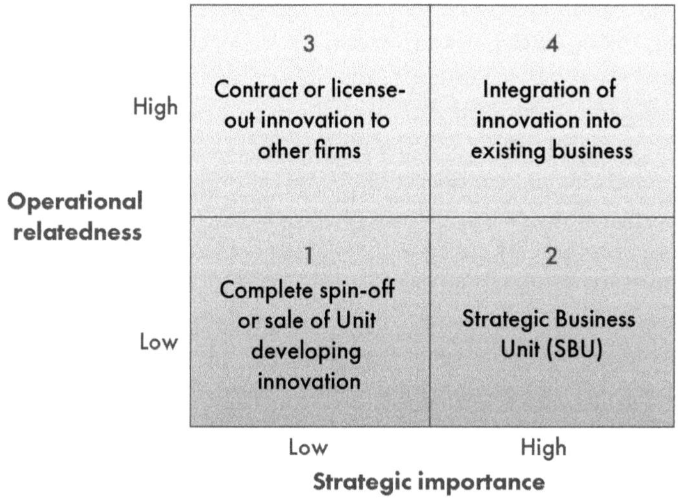

Figure 13.3 Organizing innovations

Box 1   Spin-off – The less the innovation is related to existing operations, the more likely it is to be separated out in some way. If it has no strategic importance then it is likely to be spun-off or sold, with the organization retaining little or no ownership or control. For example, in 2003 McDonald's launched Redbox, a business that operates DVD-rental kiosks primarily located outside grocery stores. Despite its success, between 2005 and 2008 it was sold off to a company called Coinstar because it was neither operationally related nor strategically important to McDonald's. The most important values in a spin-off are the skills, competencies and knowledge of the staff rather than the physical assets (Garvin, 1983). Spin-offs can create significant shareholder value, particularly for diversified firms (conglomerates). In 2016, there were 35 spin-offs in the USA worth some $100 billion in initial market value and these spin-offs seem to perform particularly well once freed of the constraints of their parent. Cornell (2017) observes that between 2002 and 2016, spin-offs as a group outperformed the broader US stock market – the Bloomberg US Spun-Off Index returned 714 per cent, while the S&P 500 Index returned 155 per cent.

Box 2   Strategic Business Unit (SBU) (also called an Independent or Special Business Unit or New Venture Unit) – If it is uncertain whether the innovation may have some strategic importance to the organization, perhaps because it is based on new technology or emerging markets, then it could be placed within a separate Unit with a high degree of independence and autonomy until its fate is decided. Indeed, it may already have some degree of independence as a separate legal entity because of this importance or because legal separation allows any risks associated with it to be contained within the Unit. Sometimes, these projects are grouped together in a separate division or legally separate company such as X Developments (Case insight 13.4). The innovation might have originated from a Corporate Incubator or directly from an intrapreneurial team. It might be the result of a partnership or joint venture with another firm and therefore already enjoys a legal separation and independence from the organization. It might already have new staff with different skills. Because the innovation may lead to new strategic directions for the organization (i.e., diversification – a topic to we shall return in the next chapter), it needs to retain full or partial ownership and control of the development until decisions can be made about the future of the SBU. It also needs to attract a high level of top-management involvement.

Box 3   Contract- or licence-out – If the innovation is of little strategic importance but highly related to current operations, it might eventually be offered to other firms under contract or licence. This is appropriate where the IP is embodied in a physical product or process that is owned by the company and that IP has commercial value, but is not critical to the competitive advantage enjoyed by the mainstream operations. These innovations are also likely to be incremental and have originated from either ad hoc intrapreneurship teams or internal innovation departments.

Box 4   Integration – The more the innovation is related to existing operations, the more likely it is to be integrated into the existing business, particularly if it is also strategically important. These innovations are likely to be incremental and have originated from either ad hoc intrapreneurship teams or internal innovation departments. They will be absorbed into the mainstream activities of the organization and are likely to have an immediate impact.

Foster and Kaplan (2001) argued for a radical approach to innovation. They suggested that companies should create and spin off new businesses continuously and should also sell off or close down those parts of the organization where growth was slowing. Only in this way will the organization survive. They called these 'transformational strategies' of 'creative destruction'. However, the closure of product lines that are nearing the end of their life is a strategy that should be approached with caution. It risks selling off assets that may be key to future developments and not having access to the cash generated by products later in their life-cycle – a topic to which we shall return in the next chapter.

NEW VENTURE SUCCESS AND FAILURE

As we have seen, the appropriate outcome and organizational structure for a successful innovative project depends on its strategic importance and operational relatedness. Tidd and Bassent (2009) claim that, on average, around half of all new ventures coming out of larger organizations survive to become operating divisions and they will typically achieve profitability within two to three years. They also suggest that internal corporate venturing is a less risky strategy for diversification than acquisition. They say that four factors characterize firms that are consistently successful at internal corporate venturing:

➡ New venturing is seen as a learning process, learning from both success and failure;
➡ Distinction is made between bad decisions and bad luck in failed ventures;
➡ Metrics and milestones are agreed in advance and monitored regularly, learning from experience and redirecting or resetting strategies as necessary;
➡ The venture itself is seen as a learning process or experiment and there is a willingness to terminate the venture if necessary, rather than making further investments.

However, success is not guaranteed for these ventures. They claim that the main reason for failure is not simply their poor commercial prospects, but rather 'strategic reversal':

➡ When the timescales for the new venture conflict with those of the existing business, for example it does not generate profit or cash flow quickly enough;
➡ When internal politicking undermines the venture and it faces difficulties of some sort created by these tensions rather than external commercial influences.

Even if a venture has a high-level sponsor, it needs to minimize the possibility of strategic reversal. If the parent company fails to define and articulate the role of the venture and the metrics and milestones that will be used to evaluate its success, there is the probability of conflict arising – and that might lead to the failure of the venture (or at least its sale).

Corporate venturing is about regenerating an organization by giving it new skills and competencies and new strategic directions. Internally, it can manifest itself in various degrees through the structures outlined in this chapter. Unsurprisingly, the success of internal corporate venturing does seem to vary from company to company, depending on the environmental conditions encountered. However, many companies also practice external corporate venturing through partnership, strategic alliances and joint ventures (Chapter 5) and through strategic acquisitions, which we consider in the next chapter. The appropriateness of these strategies depends upon how far the parent company is straying from its core skills and competencies, and, in particular, how far it is straying from its existing products and markets.

 **SUMMARY**

➡ Internal corporate venturing is concerned with how an organization encourages and manages innovative, entrepreneurial projects and how it encourages new businesses to develop internally whilst aligning them to the company's existing activities. External corporate venturing is concerned with how the organization structures itself externally to encourage innovation and develop new business areas. In both cases, the ultimate aim is to extend the organization's product/market scope and its core competencies.
➡ Intrapreneurs and venture teams push through innovative projects within larger organizations, in an entrepreneurial fashion.

➥ Intrapreneurs have many of the characteristics of entrepreneurs. They are results-orientated, ambitious, rational, competitive and questioning. They must be adept at handling conflict and the politics of the larger organization in which they operate. They are motivated primarily by intrinsic factors, in particularly autonomy, purpose and mastery. Autonomy is particularly important because it is the mechanism that allows them to feel they 'own' the project. Intrapreneurs need to be adept at handling internal politics.

➥ A venture team should be small but have appropriate skills; senior management support; resources (including time); tolerance of uncertainty and risk-taking; and appropriate rewards if successful. The team needs to have an agreed budget, metrics that measure success and appropriate risk management systems.

➥ Picking a venture team is not just about selecting people with appropriate functional skills. It is also about assembling a mix of different personalities and a balance between left- and right- brain thinkers. Belbin identified nine characteristics, divided into three orientations, that need to be present to form an effective team: a thinking orientation (plant, monitor-evaluator, specialist); a people orientation (coordinator, team worker, resource investigator); and an action orientation (shaper, implementer, completer-finisher).

➥ Innovation departments or functions are permanent organizational structure set up for the purpose of originating and/or developing innovations. Typically, they are most successful in taking forward incremental innovations relating to existing activities.

➥ Innovation units or divisions have greater autonomy, wider scope, more resources, and more senior management. They often link innovation across different divisions that straddle different product/market sectors.

➥ Corporate accelerators and incubators are development programmes, often linked to resources and facilities. They are designed to facilitate the rapid conceptualization, prototyping and development of a business idea within a tight time frame.

➥ The more strategically important an innovation project and the more operationally related to existing activities, the more likely it is to be kept in-house. The less strategically important and less operationally related, the more likely it is to be spun-out. Strategic Business Units are a way of deferring a decision until the strategic importance of a development becomes clearer.

➥ Firms that are consistently successful at internal corporate venturing view it, and any project conducted within its framework, as a learning process. They make the distinction between bad decisions and bad luck in failed ventures, using agreed metrics to help monitor and review the progress of projects. The main reason for the failure of a project is strategic reversal – when timescales conflict with those of the existing business or when it is undermined by internal politicking.

 GROUP DISCUSSION TOPICS

1. Is an intrapreneur the same as an entrepreneur? If not, how do they differ?
2. Is it easier to be an intrapreneur or an entrepreneur?
3. Under what conditions might intrapreneurship thrive?
4. How are intrapreneurs and venture teams motivated?
5. How much autonomy or 'space' is needed by an intrapreneur or a venture team?
6. What does an organization need to do to encourage intrapreneurship?
7. The number of people leaving to set up their own business is a sign of a real entrepreneurial organization. Discuss.
8. Does there always have to be at least one intrapreneur in a venture team?
9. What constitutes a 'good' team?

10. A good team never argues. Discuss.
11. How does a venture team differ from any other team? What are the similarities?
12. What are the advantages/disadvantages and strengths/weaknesses of an innovation department or function?
13. What are the advantages/disadvantages and strengths/weaknesses of an innovation unit or division?
14. What are the advantages/disadvantages and strengths/weaknesses of a corporate accelerator and/or incubator?
15. How can a corporate accelerator and/or incubator encourage change within an organization?
16. How does an innovation unit or division differ from a R&D department?
17. Why are operational relatedness and strategic importance important determinants of what to do with new ventures?
18. Why should new product/service ideas not simply be integrated into an existing business?
19. Why should a large company want to spin out a new venture with good opportunities?
20. Chapter 1 talked about companies having a defined life, which eventually ends. Is this true? If so, what constitutes the end of a company's life?

ACTIVITIES

1. Take the GET2 test. Discuss the results with other students in your group to see whether they recognize these characteristics in you. Write a report either supporting or questioning the results, based upon evidence of your behaviours in life.
2. Take the MBTI test. Discuss the results with other students in your group to see whether they recognize these characteristics in you. Write a report either supporting or questioning the results, based upon evidence of your behaviours in life.
3. Using the Belbin Team Roles questionnaire, evaluate your preferred team role(s). Discuss the results with other students in your group to see whether or not they agree with your results. Write a report either supporting or questioning the results, based upon evidence of your behaviours in life.
4. Using the results of these tests, discuss how venture teams might be best formed from the students in your group, justifying why particular students should go into particular venture teams.
5. Select a large company spin-out. Research and write up its history and describe its success or failure. What lessons are to be learnt from this?

REFERENCES

Antoncic, B. and Hisrich, R.D. (2003) 'Clarifying the Intrapreneurship Concept', *Journal of Small Business and Enterprise Development*, 10(1).
Auster, E.R, and Hillenbrand, L. (2016) *Stragility: Excelling at Strategic Changes*, Toronto: University of Toronto Press.
BCG (2017) *Taking Agile Way Beyond Software*, Boston, MA: Boston Consulting Group. Available on: https://www.bcg.com/publications/2017/technology-digital-organization-taking-agile-way-beyond-software.aspx.
Belbin, R.M. (1981) *Management Teams – Why They Succeed and Fail*, London: Heinemann Professional Publishing.
Burgelman, R.A. (1983) 'A Process Model of Internal Corporate Venturing in the Diversified Major Firm', *Administrative Science Quarterly*, 28.
Caird, S. (1991a) 'Self Assessments on Enterprise Training Courses', *British Journal of Education and Work*, 4(3).
Caird, S. (1991b) 'Testing Enterprising Tendency in Occupational Groups', *British Journal of Management*, 2(4).
Chell, E. (2001) *Entrepreneurship: Globalization, Innovation and Development*, London: Thomson Learning.
Chesbrough, H.W. (2002) 'Making Sense of Corporate Venture Capital', *Harvard Business Review*, March.

Cohen, A.R. and Bradford, D. (1991) *Influence Without Authority*, New York, NY: Wiley.

Cornell, J. (2017) 'The Top 15 Spin-Offs of 2016', *Forbes*, January 5. Available on: https://www.forbes.com/sites/joecornell/.

Drucker, P.F. (1985) *Innovation and Entrepreneurship: Practice and Principles*, London: Heinemann.

Foster, R. and Kaplan, S. (2001) *Creative Destruction: Why Companies That Are Built to Last Underperform the Stock Market*, New York, NY: Doubleday/Currency.

Galbraith, J. (1982) 'Designing the Innovating Organization', *Organizational Dynamics*, Winter.

Gardner, H.K. (2017) *Smart Collaboration: How Professionals and Their Firms Succeed by Breaking Down Silos*, Boston, MA: Harvard Business Review Press.

Garvin, D.A. (1983) 'Spin-Offs and New Firm Formation Process', *California Management Review*, 25(2).

Govindaranjan, V. and Trimble, C. (2010) 'Stop the Innovation Wars', *Harvard Business Review*, 88(7/8).

Gwynne, P. (1997) 'Skunk Works, 1990s-Style', *Research-Technology Management*, 40(4).

Hisrich, R.D. (1990) 'Entrepreneurship/Intrapreneurship', *American Psychologist*, 45(2).

Hornsby, J.S., Naffziger, D.W., Kuratko, D.F. and Montagno, R.V. (1993) 'An Interactive Model of the Corporate Entrepreneurship Process', *Entrepreneurship, Theory and Practice*, 17(2).

Janeway, W.H. (2018) *Doing Capitalism in the Innovation Economy*, Cambridge: Cambridge University Press.

Kanter, R.M. (2004) 'The Middle Manager as Innovator', *Harvard Business Review*, 82(7/8).

Maletz, M.C. and Nohria, N. (2001) 'Managing in the Whitespace', *Harvard Business Review*, 79(2).

Morris, M.H. and Kuratko, D.F. (2002) *Corporate Entrepreneurship*, Fort Worth, TX: Harcourt College Publishers.

Phadke, U. and Vyakarbnam, S. (2017) *Camels, Tigers and Unicorns: Rethinking Science and Technology-Enabled Innovation*, London: World Scientific Publishing.

Pinchot, G.H. (1985) *Intrapreneurship*, New York, NY: Harper & Row.

Pinchot, G.H. (1987) 'Innovation Through Intrapreneuring', *Research Management*, 13(2).

Price, R.L., Griffin, A., Eccles, D. Vojak, B.A., Hoffmann, N. and Burgon, H. (2009) 'Innovation Politics: How Serial Innovators Gain Organisational Acceptance for Breakthrough New Products', *International Journal of Technology Marketing*, 4(2–3).

Ross J. (1987) 'Intrapreneurship and Corporate Culture', *Industrial Management*, 29(1).

Ross, J.E. and Unwalla, D. (1986) 'Who Is an Intrapreneur?', *Personnel*, 63(12).

Smith, K.G., Collins, C.J. and Clark, K.D. (2005) 'Existing Knowledge, Knowledge Creation Capability, and the Rate of New Product Introduction in High-Technology Firms', *Academy of Management Journal*, 48(2).

Stormer, R., Kline, T. and Goldberg, S. (1999) 'Measuring Entrepreneurship with the General Enterprise Tendency (GET) Test: Criterion-Related Validity and Reliability', *Human Systems Management*, 18(1).

Tidd, J. and Bessant, J. (2009) *Managing Innovation: Integrating Technological, Market and Organizational Change*, Chichester: John Wiley.

West III, G.P. (2007) 'Collective Cognition: When Entrepreneurial Teams, Not Individuals, Make Decisions', *Entrepreneurship Theory and Practice*, 31(1).

 ONLINE RESOURCES AVAILABLE For further resources relating to this chapter see the companion website at **www.macmillanihe.com/Burns-CEI**

14 Product/market development

CONTENTS

- Product/market expansion
- Diffusion of innovation
- Developing existing products and markets
- Finding new markets
- Diversification
- External corporate venturing
- Acquisitions and industry life-cycles
- Reasons for corporate acquisitions
- Risk and corporate venturing
- Attractions and dangers of corporate acquisitions
- Venture funds
- Summary
- Group discussion topics
- Activities
- References

CASE INSIGHTS

Learning outcomes

When you have read this chapter and undertaken the related activities you will be able to:

➡ Understand and explain how internal and external corporate venturing impacts on product/market development and how risk might be mitigated through continuous, incremental diversification;

➡ Critically analyze the role of corporate acquisitions in the context of innovation and product/market development;

➡ Understand and explain why some corporate acquisitions succeed and others fail;

➡ Understand and explain how diversification is central to the process of corporate evolution can how it can add shareholder value;

➡ Use Porter's Five Forces analysis to assess the competitiveness of an industry.

PRODUCT/MARKET EXPANSION

Innovation involves moving into new products and/or new markets and the risks involved increase the further the firm moves from its core competencies. This point was made in Chapter 3 and Figure 3.3 is reproduced as Figure 14.1a. The greater the degree of innovation and the greater the unfamiliarity of the market, the higher the risk. Below it in Figure 14.1b is a simplified way of presenting the options of product and/or market development: Product development, market development and diversification. Companies will follow combinations of these routes as they grow, through both internal and external developments.

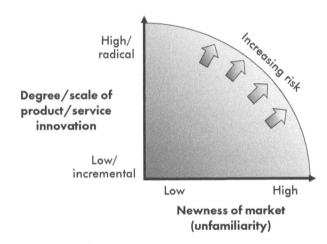

Figure 14.1a Innovation and risk

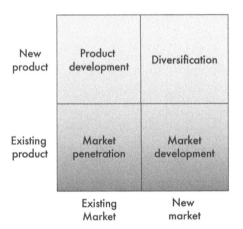

Figure 14.1b Product/market development

Once an innovation has been developed, it needs to be marketed and sold – the market penetration in Figure 14.1b. Over time, however, the product will age, competition will increase and new markets or products will have to be found.

➥ Market development is most successful for companies whose core competencies lie in the efficiency of their existing production methods, for example in the capital goods industries, and are seeking economies of scale, or for firms adept at sales, marketing and developing close customer relationships. One way of lowering the risks associated with finding new markets is through strategic alliances/partnerships and joint ventures.

➡ Product and process development is most successful for those companies whose competencies lie in building good customer relationships, often associated with effective branding. However, of equal importance could be the ability to innovate. Again, one way of lowering the risks associated with product innovation is through the formation of strategic alliances/partnerships and joint ventures.

➡ Diversification – introducing new products into new markets – is a high-risk strategy for most companies. This is why, in the previous chapter, it was said that this sort of development should either be spun off and sold or set up as SBUs until a final decision about strategic importance is made. This can be likened to radical or disruptive innovation that might create a new-to-the world industry. Whilst some firms might see these innovations coming from within, frequently they pursue this growth option through a strategy of acquisition. We shall consider diversification in more detail later in this chapter.

To some extent, deciding which option(s) to pursue depends on the strengths and weaknesses of the organization, linked to its core competences and capabilities – replicating the process of opportunity spotting outlined in Chapter 10. This will give a strategic direction to the search for growth. However, the options shown in Figure 14.1b are not mutually exclusive. Some companies might follow all four strategies in pursuit of growth. However, the best companies pursue a strategy of continuous innovation – the incremental, step-by-step development of both the product and the market. Dynamic, continuous innovation builds upon existing products and services so that customers understand the nature of the offering; this contrasts with discrete innovation, which may address a need but one that has to be explained and accepted by the customer.

DIFFUSION OF INNOVATION

Market penetration can take time. Some customers may even be adopting an innovation for the first time at the end of its commercial life. The diffusion of an innovation takes time as different types of customers adopt it at different stages of its life-cycle. Rogers (2003) argued that the adoption of innovations by consumers follows channels of communication within society and is not steady. It can be represented by a simple S-curve (Figure 14.2). He argued that successive groups with distinguishing characteristics adopt innovations sequentially as they communicate its proven benefits (solid blue line). Adoption begins slowly, accelerates to a peak rate of growth and then slows. Eventually, the market share of the innovation will reach saturation level as it nears the end of its life. He classified customers into five groups:

Innovators (estimated at 2.5 per cent) – These are risk-takers, typically with high social and financial status, who are interested and understand the innovation and are willing to experiment.
Early adopters (estimated at 13.5 per cent) – These are opinion leaders, typically again with high social and financial status, who are sufficiently well connected and educated to learn about and understand the benefits of the innovation. It is important for any innovation to impact favourably on this group.

Early majority (estimated at 34 per cent) – These form the majority of customers with average social and financial status. They have contact with early adopters and are likely to be influenced by them.

Late majority (estimated at 34 per cent) – These adopt the innovation after the average person, approaching any innovation with scepticism. Typically, they have below-average social and financial status.

Laggards (estimated at 16 per cent) – These are the last to adopt an innovation. They are traditionalists who dislike change. Typically, they are older, with limited contacts outside their close network and also have below average social and financial status.

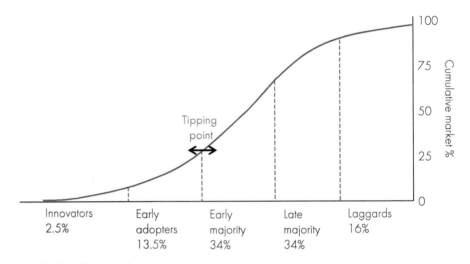

Figure 14.2 Diffusion of innovations

Figure 14.2 shows that for products or services that are successful, there is a tipping point where demand for a product or service suddenly takes off, with explosive growth as the early adopters give way to the early majority. This is greatest when there are strong network effects – where the value of the product or service is increased as more people in the network use them. This is the point where investment in capacity and distribution is particularly required. Demand for an innovation eventually plateaus and slows down, usually as the late majority adopt it or new innovations come to replace it. We shall examine how a company might manage a product or service at this stage of its life in the next chapter.

DEVELOPING EXISTING PRODUCTS AND MARKETS

Innovation is not just about finding entirely new product/market offerings. Existing products and markets can be adjusted innovatively so that their life is extended or their market expanded. These innovations can start at the growth phase of the life-cycle by expanding the product offering and meeting the needs of selected market segments so as to counter the threat of competition. Expanding the offering means developing product variations. So, for example, a car manufacturer might start offering sports or estate variants of a model. A soft drink manufacturer might start to offer sugar-free variants or new flavours. The original product might also be modified in terms of quality, function or design so as to address any weaknesses or omissions in it. Even service levels might be improved.

At the same time, the company might want to try to find new distribution channels so that more customers gain exposure to the product. Sometimes they move from a selective distribution network to a more intensive network. Associated with this is a more aggressive promotion and pricing strategy that encourages further market penetration ahead of the rapidly emerging competition. Building the brand is important and this will be a vital part of the advertising message.

Further growth may even be possible in the mature phase of the life-cycle. In many cases, a mature market presents opportunities to start segmenting the market and tailoring the product range that was expanded in the previous phase through **product modification**, so as to better meet the different needs of the different market segments that purchase them. This might lead to further expansion of the range and further product modification in terms of quality, function or style. Although essentially a defensive strategy to counter competition, **product expansion** can also be used as a strategy to seek out new markets for similar products. As we shall see in Case insight 15.4, Amazon, Apple, Facebook, Google and Microsoft are all doing this as part of a battle to become internet utilities.

Another technique is called **product extension** whereby a successful brands extended to similar but different products that might be purchased by the same customers. In this way a number of chocolate bar manufacturers have successfully extended their brand into ice cream. The key to success here is having a strong brand, one that actually means something to customers, and with values that can be extended onto the other products. Thus, Timberland, a company well known for producing durable outdoor footwear, extended its product range to include durable outdoor clothing. Many so-called new products are in fact line extensions. This strategy is generally a less expensive and lower-risk alternative for firms seeking to increase sales.

Chapter 10 highlighted how frugal innovation can be used to simplify products, cheapening their cost of manufacture and therefore allowing the price to be brought down. Allied to changes in the business model, this can be an attractive strategy to help penetrate new markets in developing countries.

product modification
Small and evolutionary modifications of existing products in terms of quality, function or style

product expansion
Developing product or service variations that meet the needs of different market segments

product extension
Extending a successful brand to similar but different products or services that might be purchased by the same customers

FINDING NEW MARKETS

Increasing numbers of businesses now sell their products internationally from day one. Selling to a very small target or niche market in one country can raise issues of viability. Selling to the same niche market globally can dramatically change the equation and offer the opportunity of high profits, because of economies of scale (also important if the product is perceived as a commodity and cost leadership is dependent upon achieving them). The internet has made it easier to sell internationally, particularly for virtual products that can be transmitted on the internet (e.g., music or apps). Physical products can use global internet retail platforms like Amazon or eBay to sell their product, take payment by credit card and use distribution networks like FedEx.

Finding new markets can be an important way of extending the life of a product or service. This is often important for companies whose key competencies lie with the product, for example with capital goods like cars, and therefore the continued exploitation of the product by market development is the preferred route for expansion. Most capital goods companies follow this strategy – opening up new overseas markets as existing markets become saturated – because of the high cost of developing new products. By way of contrast, many service businesses, such as accounting, insurance, advertising and banking, have been pulled into overseas markets because their clients operate there.

In seeking new overseas markets, the lowest-risk option is to seek out and target customers or market segments that are similar to those the firm already sells to, thereby reducing the unfamiliarity and the risk. However, the structure of the industry in that market is also important – the customers, suppliers, competitors and the potential substitutes and barriers to entry. These determine the degree of competition and therefore the profitability likely to be achieved. Porter (1985) developed a useful structural analysis which looked at five forces that affect the degree of competition for an industry, forces that determine the underlying economic and technical characteristics of the industry. They can change over time, but the analysis does emphasize the need to select industries carefully in the first place.

1. Industry rivalry – The competitive rivalry of an industry is central to the analysis. Rivalry will depend on the number and size of firms within it and their concentration (**fragmented** vs **consolidated**), its newness and growth (the point in the life-cycle) and therefore its attractiveness in terms of profit and value added together with intermittent overcapacity. Crucially important is the extent of product differentiation, brand identity and **switch costs**. The greater the competitive rivalry, the less the ability of a firm to charge a high price. Hypercompetitive industries not only exhibit destabilizing price-cutting but also expensive marketing and frequent product/market innovation. They can emerge from oligopolistic industries. A lack of competitive rivalry tends to be evidence of the existence of monopolies and oligopolies. Some industries tend towards monopoly because of the importance of economies of scale, others because of 'network effects' – where value is derived from the number of people using a product/service (e.g., Microsoft Office, Facebook).

2. Threat of substitutes – How likely are customers to stop buying your product/service? This revolves around the relative price performance of substitutes, the switch costs and the propensity of the customer to switch, for example because of changes in tastes or fashion. Innovation might bring with it the threat of substitutes. The greater the threat of substitutes, the less the ability of the firm to charge a high price. So, for example, a small firm selling a poorly differentiated product in a price-sensitive, fashion market would find it difficult to charge a high price.

3. Threat of new entrants – Barriers to entry exclude new entrants from an industry. These can arise because of legal protection (patents and so on), economies of scale, proprietary product differences, brand identity, access to distribution, government policy, capital or R&D costs, switch costs and so forth. Switch costs are the costs of switching to another product. A firm whose product is protected by patent or copyright may feel that it is relatively safe from competition. The greater the possible threat of a new entry

fragmented market A market where there are a large number of competitors of about the same size, usually in a mature or declining industry

consolidated market A market where there are a few, large competitors, usually in a mature or declining industry

switch costs The costs of switching the company you buy a product or service from

to a market, the lower the bargaining power and control over price of the firm within it. Entrepreneurs might choose to enter a market with low barriers to entry.

4. Bargaining power of buyers – This is determined by the relative size of buyers or customers and their concentration. The fewer there are, the higher their buying power. It is influenced by the volumes they purchase, the information they have about competitors or substitutes, switch costs and their ability to backward integrate or develop their own source of supply. The extent to which the product they are buying is differentiated in some way also affects relative buying power. The greater the power of the buyers, the weaker the bargaining position of the firm selling to them. So, for example, if buyers are large firms, in concentrated industries, buying large volumes with good price information about a relatively undifferentiated product with low switch costs, they will be in a strong position to keep prices low. Thus, if you are selling to the big supermarket chains they will squeeze your margins.

5. Bargaining power of suppliers – This is also determined by the relative size of firms and the other factors mentioned above – the fewer there are, the higher their power. So, for example, if suppliers are large firms in concentrated industries, with well-differentiated products that are relatively important to the small firms buying them, then those small firms are in a weak position to keep prices, and therefore their costs, low.

One of the issues with this analysis is defining the correct industry to look at. Industries can be segmented in many ways, not just geographically, each with differing competitive forces. Technological innovation can cause industries to converge and the boundaries to competition may shift (e.g., the camera company Kodak went bankrupt because of the competition from mobile phones). Johnson et al. (2017) have argued for the inclusion of a 'sixth force', that of complementary (rather than competitor) organizations, whose product or service enhances the attractiveness to customers of another product or service (e.g., the McAfee computer security system complements the Microsoft Office suite of software). In these situations, it pays for companies to work together. Identifying companies with complementary products or services may also therefore help to identify strategic alliances or partnerships for the future.

In considering new markets to enter, we might add to Porter's analysis the need for an economic appraisal of the environment of the country being considered – domestic demand, local laws and regulations, government policies, exchange rates, related and supporting industries etc. Of course, success in the new market depends upon competitive advantage and, as we have noted, this is achieved when there is a match between a firm's internal strengths in resources and capabilities and the key success factors of the industry – but we would add that this is in the context of the particular national environment.

There are many ways to enter a foreign market. If the firm's competitive advantage is based on resources located in its home country, then the form this takes should be to pursue an exporting strategy. Exporting is also often a low-cost, low-risk way of finding out about the market. It can take the form of spot sales – now much easier to achieve for some firms with the advent of the internet. But to achieve market presence in local distribution channels a local distributor in the selected country may well be needed. This distributor might influence changes in the product or other elements of the marketing mix to suit local needs. The company might be expected to finance advertising and promotion itself and with no certainty of a profitable return. Finding a distributor can be difficult enough but if, for whatever reason, the distributor does not push the firm's products then there is little the firm can do other than change distributors, unless they are willing to take on the job of marketing in the country themselves – and that can be both expensive and risky.

Another option is to form a strategic alliance, partnership or joint venture with another firm, whereby the partner brings different resources to the joint venture and shares the profits as well as the risks. This can be a particularly effective strategy to overcome the potential deficiencies in resources and capabilities that are faced as a start-up. Partners can provide vital insights into effective market entry and competitive strategies. In some developing economies, the only way to enter the market may be through a joint venture with a local firm. Used properly, strategic alliances, partnerships and joint ventures can leverage up competencies and capabilities with limited risk (Chapter 5).

The riskiest and most expensive option of all when entering a foreign market is direct investment. This involves the setting up of a wholly-owned subsidiary which may involve simply marketing and distribution but may also involve full integration. Clearly, this is an expensive option, normally only taken by larger companies. These different degrees of involvement in foreign markets and the increasing risk associated with them are shown in Figure 14.3. There is no prescriptive best approach to internationalization and often the degree of involvement in the foreign market increases with the success of the product or service.

Increasing resource commitment
Increasing risk

Figure 14.3 Degree of involvement in foreign markets

CASE INSIGHT 14.1
Mobike

China

BUSINESS MODELS AND COMPETITIVE ADVANTAGE

Invented in 1817, bicycles used to be the most common means of transport in China. These days, however, they have been overtaken by cars, leaving China's roads, particularly in its cities, heavily congested. This heralded the return of the bicycle. Many Chinese cities started municipal bike-rental schemes years ago, allowing users to pick up and drop off their bikes at designated stations, similar to hundreds of programmes around the world. However, Mobike offered a different approach. Launched in Shanghai in 2016, it was the idea of David Wang who left his job as general manager of Uber in China to start the venture. Mobike uses a bike-sharing App for mobile phones

Rows of shared bikes parked in Downtown Nanchang, China

Source: iStock/Sean Xu

that allows you to pick up and leave a Mobike wherever you need to go. It was the world's first cashless and station-free bike-sharing platform. Mobikes have a patented design that uses an internet-controlled wheel-locking system that links to the smartphone App. Each bike carries a unique matrix bar code which requires being scanned in order for it to be unlocked. Every bike also has GPS tracking. The pedal bikes are powered by a small generator installed on the rear wheel hub to power the lock. Mobikes share a time-lapse graphic that tracks user rides using its GPS system.

The Mobike App requires customers to register using their mobile number and some form of identification. They must open an account and make a pre-paid, refundable deposit against deliberate damage. The software automatically disqualifies users under the age of 14 and tracks not only where customers go but also how they behave, giving them a Mobike score, which penalizes behaviour such as forgetting to lock the bike after use and affects future charges and the use of the system. Once the fee has been paid, the App allows customers to locate the nearest bike not in use. Customers then unlock the bike by scanning the matrix bar code. They can then use the bike and leave it where they choose. The distance travelled, time spent, energy used and cost of using the bike is then displayed on the bike, which will be deducted from customer's account.

Mobikes are distinctive, with a bright orange livery and a fashionable, modern design. They are built for durability and low maintenance. The classic bike has a shiny aluminium V-shaped chassis, with puncture-proof tyres and a shaft transmission system. The wheels have five sets of double metal, bright orange spokes. The 'lite' version has wire spokes and a conventional chain drive. An electric version was launched in 2018.

Mobikes are intended for short urban trips, solving the 'first-mile/last-mile' problem of moving to or from public transport points. A one-hour journey can cost as little as 1 yuan (about 15 cents). With over 700 million mobile phone users in China, Mobike was an instant success. Its only rival was Ofo, which was launched in 2015 but targeted a different demographic by offering a cheaper, and far more conventional and basic, bright yellow bike. Building on its success in China, Mobike very quickly made the most of its first-mover advantage in order to expand internationally. Initially funded by venture capitalists, it raised $600 million in Series E funding led by Tencent, bringing the firm's fund-raising in 2017 alone to nearly $1 billion. In 2018, it was acquired by the Chinese web company Meituan-Dianping. By 2018, Mobike could be found throughout Asia, Europe and the Americas – in over 200 cities and 19 countries around the world.

However, this rapid global rollout has not been unproblematic. The bikes do not require docking stations and many cities have complained about the bikes being left in places that cause obstruction or clutter. In Beijing, they can be seen piled on top of each other in public places. The bikes are not treated well and there have been many reports of vandalism in some countries where the Mobike score system is less effective than in China (where the social pressures to conform may be greater). As a result, the company has reduced coverage and it has even withdrawn its bikes from some cities in the UK.

Visit the website: mobike.com/global/

Questions:

1. The investment needed for such a rapid global rollout must have been very high. Was the company right to do this, rather than doing more market research in different countries first?
2. What, if anything, is the uniqueness of the Mobike? What is the basis for its competitive advantage?
3. What threats does the company face? Is its competitive advantage sustainable? What does the company have to do to maintain any advantage?

DIVERSIFICATION

Diversification involves moving from core areas of activity into completely new and unrelated product and market areas (Figure 14.1). The opportunity for diversification may come from a corporate acquisition, but it might also come from internal venturing that resulted in a SBU being set up (Chapter 13). Many academics have pointed out that diversification is a high-risk strategy and one that often fails to increase shareholder value, at least in publicly quoted companies. Grant (2010) went further, suggesting that diversification has probably caused more value destruction than any other type of strategic decision. He described it as being 'like sex: its attractions are obvious, often irresistible. Yet the experience is often disappointing. For top management it is a mine field.' The business risks generated by diversification depend upon two things: Firstly, the willingness and ability of the new organization to actually implement the merger between the two companies and gain the so-called synergy associated with it. Also at issue is the ability of management to actually manage the new, larger organization effectively, whatever its structure. The second factor is the nature of the diversification, which determines the associated risks. The literature distinguishes between unrelated and related diversification.

Unrelated diversification – Unrelated diversification happens when the firm develops beyond its present 'industry' or 'sector' into new products/services and markets that, on the face of it, bear little relationship to the one it is in. Whether arising from internal development or acquisition, there is little or no operational relatedness with the innovation (Figure 13.3). The risks are said to be high because the firm understands neither the product/service nor the market the innovation is to be sold into and therefore might overvalue it and not understand how to deploy it. The further the company strays from its core competencies, the higher the risks because of problems with implementation, particularly when this is coupled with an implementation strategy involving acquisition (Bowman and Faulkner, 1997). Companies that pursue a strategy of diversification over time end up with a number of units or subsidiaries operating in different product/market sectors. Called conglomerates, if these companies are traded on stock markets they have tended to be traded at a discount, for reasons explained later. In other words, not only is there is no added shareholder value from the companies operating jointly, but there actually appears to be a reduction.

Related diversification – Related diversification is when development (or acquisition) is beyond the present product and market, but within the confines of the industry or sector in which the firm operates. In these circumstances, there is likely to be some operational relatedness that offers the opportunity for economies of scale, scope (synergy) or the expansion or extension of the firm's existing product range – in other words, there is some added benefit from the move. There are three variants of related diversification:

1. *Backward vertical integration* – This is where the firm becomes its own supplier of some basic raw materials or services or provides transport or financing. For example, the UK supermarket Waitrose originally subcontracted its home delivery service to Ocado; once it proved popular, however, it took full control of the operation.
2. *Forward vertical integration* – This is where the firm becomes its own distributor or retailer or perhaps services its own products in some way. For example, Timberland, which was famous for its sturdy, waterproof boots, opened a number of speciality stores and factory outlets selling its boots alongside Timberland-branded outdoor clothes and other products whilst continuing to sell predominantly through distributors, franchisees and commissioned agents.
3. *Horizontal integration* – This is where there is development into activities which are either directly complementary or competitive with the firm's current activities. For example, the Ford motor company diversified into financial services to facilitate car purchase and now earns more from this source than from the manufacture of the vehicles themselves.

The literature suggests, therefore, that related diversification is more likely to be commercially successful than unrelated diversification. Only then might it be worth buying another company in unrelated product/market areas. The problem with this view is that it militates radical innovation that may result in developing new product/market areas (diversification) – whether it originates internally or externally, through a corporate acquisitions strategy.

*Diversification makes very little sense for anyone that knows what they're doing...
Diversification is protection against ignorance.*

Warren Buffett, investor, Berkshire Hathaway annual shareholders meeting, 1996

EXTERNAL CORPORATE VENTURING

Rather than just expanding products and markets through internal development and innovations, companies have the option of trying to acquire other companies that might already occupy those market spaces. Combining businesses in similar industries offers opportunities for creating economies of scale and scope and increase pricing power through market leadership. The Belgian company AB InBev is the world's largest brewer of beer, with some 30 per cent of global market share. They achieved this through a series of acquisitions that both increased their market share and generated cost savings of between 14 and 21 per cent of acquisition sales value.

But corporate acquisitions are made for reasons other than just buying market share. They are also used to buy-in innovation. Bhidé (2000) took the concept of down-scoping and outsourcing (see Chapter 5) to its ultimate conclusion by suggesting that, rather than trying to re-invent themselves, large firms should effectively outsource innovation. Smaller, more entrepreneurial firms should be left to concentrate on developing radical, disruptive innovations and projects with low costs and high uncertainty, at least in the earliest stages of development. As we saw in Chapter 3, these are areas where small firms play a significant part, particularly where technology is continuing to evolve (Deakins and Freel, 2006). Bhidé said that once innovations are proved to work and their associated risks and rewards become more quantifiable large firm should buy-in (or buy-out) the innovation. Large firms should concentrate on developing internally what they were good at – incremental innovations and projects with high costs and low uncertainty.

Buying-in intellectual property (IP) can take many forms – for example, the purchase of licences, patents, copyright or simply acquiring distribution rights rather than outright acquisition of a company. It all depends on what stage the innovative development has reached and how the larger company can best add value. Larger firms may be better at the development phase (rather than research) or be better able to bring the product to the market quickly because of their market dominance and extensive distribution networks. This is where their real competitive advantage lies. The purchase of a smaller firm may also give its acquirer access to a new or rapidly developing market that it has been slow to recognize. It may help a larger firm in consolidating an existing dominant market position, particularly if the focus of that market is shifting in some way, for example as a result of technological developments. External corporate venturing is about this strategy of acquisition and how it is operationalized.

Although large firms seem to innovate more than small firms in industries where resources are important (because of capital intensity or because of the scale of spending on R&D, advertising etc.), external corporate venturing can still prove cost-effective. In the pharmaceutical industry, there are many smaller entrepreneurial organizations, often linked to universities, conducting early-stage research (particularly in biotechnology) and selling on to large pharmaceutical firms when they reach the expensive, clinical trial stage of development –where large-scale trials are necessary. Sometimes these firms are bought out, but more often the technology they have developed is licensed to the larger firm. Large pharmaceutical firms enjoy significant market advantage because they have global sales and distribution networks. About one-third of the revenue of these large pharmaceutical firms now comes from licensed-in technology. As an alternative, particularly at the development stage of a new product, many organizations are forming strategic alliances, pooling skills and resources and minimizing risk.

Unsurprisingly, the acquisition of small firms by larger ones is particularly popular in technology industries. However, this is a strategy that is apparent in sectors ranging from telecommunications to consumer goods to engineering and is particularly common in the pharmaceutical industry. It is also a strategy that is particularly popular in the USA. It has seen booms in the late 1960s, late 1980s and late 1990s and now seems to be re-emerging.

In 2010, external corporate venturing represented $1.9 billion (or around 9 per cent) of total venture capital investment in the USA (National Venture Capital Association).

ACQUISITIONS AND INDUSTRY LIFE-CYCLES

Deans et al. (2003) observed that there is increasing acquisition and merger activity as industries mature and that this leads to increased industry concentration. This is consistent with the limited corporate life expectancy noted in Chapter 1. They claimed that an industry typically has the four distinct phases shown in Figure 14.4 and that the main factor determining corporate survival and success is the speed with which the company actively moves towards the final phase – the endgame curve – through a series of mergers and acquisitions.

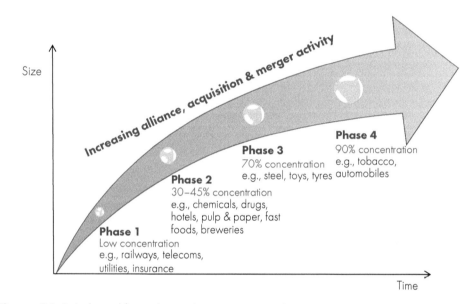

Figure 14.4 Industry life-cycles and acquisitions and mergers

Phase 1   In this phase, there is heavy competition from start-ups, spin-offs, firms in deregulated industries and smaller companies. As a result, there is low market concentration – less than 20 per cent, measured by the combined market share of the three biggest companies. This phase typically lasts at least five years.

Phase 2   The authors called this the 'scale phase' because size begins to matter. Corporate acquisitions increase and leading companies start to merge. Concentration increases to 30–45 per cent.

Phase 3   In this phase, companies extend their core business, eliminating secondary operations or exchanging them with other firms for assets closer to their core business. Concentration increases to almost 70 per cent.

Phase 4   This final phase sees concentration reaching 90 per cent and large companies forming alliances in order to boost growth.

CASE INSIGHT 14.2
Lenovo

China

ACQUISITIONS AND INDUSTRY CONCENTRATION

Founded in 1984, Lenovo is one of China's biggest computer firms. Unlike many Chinese firms, it is run like a private company with little state interference from two head offices, one in Beijing, China, and the in Morrisville, USA, with its research centre in Japan. In 2005, it acquired IBM's PC arm and quickly grew to become one of the world's biggest PC makers, capitalizing on its low-cost manufacturing base. In 2014, it purchased Motorola smartphones from Google for $2.3 billion. Although Google had failed to make profits from Motorola in the three years it owned the company, Lenovo felt that the potential for economies of scale and scope would enable it to consolidate its market position and threaten Samsung and Apple in the growing smartphone market. In the same year, it purchased IBM's low-cost server unit for $2.9 billion, believing that these units would be needed to store ever-increasing amounts of data.

By 2018 it was clear that both of these acquisitions were unsuccessful. At this time it was selling 17 per cent fewer smartphones than in 2014, despite market growth of 15 per cent, and the smartphone business had made a loss every quarter since the takeover, a total of almost $2 billion, forcing it to shed staff. The company blamed rising costs and mature markets saying that 'component costs continue to present challenges', but that it was trying to strengthen its position in Latin America and 'drive breakthrough in mature markets' (*The Observer*, 13 May 2018). But analysts also pointed out that there had been a long internal struggle to decide which brand should drive business – Lenovo or Motorola – and selecting one brand in territories where they overlapped (China, South-East Asia and India) lost key business for the other.

By 2018, the server business had also lost over $700 million, largely as a result in the growth of cloud services from Google, Amazon and Microsoft, allowing clients to store data without the need for their own hardware. Being a Chinese company, security was also an issue for Western companies. Analysts point to some $2.7 billion of goodwill related to these acquisitions, which is still carried on the balance sheet and speculate whether it may have to be written off. For Lenovo, expensive acquisitions have proved very costly in a cut-throat global tech market.

Visit the website: **www.lenovo.com**

Questions:

1. Was the company right to make these acquisitions when it did?
2. Were these outcomes foreseeable? What would you have done differently?

REASONS FOR CORPORATE ACQUISITIONS

The strategic acquisition of small firms by larger ones is probably the most visible form of external corporate venturing. It can also be a powerful accelerator of growth. However, there are many motives for corporate acquisitions other than the introduction of new technologies and innovation. Stock markets expect growth and an aggressive acquisition strategy can be a way of disguising a lack of growth in the core business. Sometimes the motive is sheer opportunism – seeing a business that can be purchased for less than its value and then resold at a profit. Furthermore, all too often acquisitions have too much corporate ego tied up in the deal, particularly when one competitor buys out another, and that can lead to a loss of business logic. Nevertheless, there are four strategic reasons why companies acquire another 'going-concern' business (Figure 14.5).

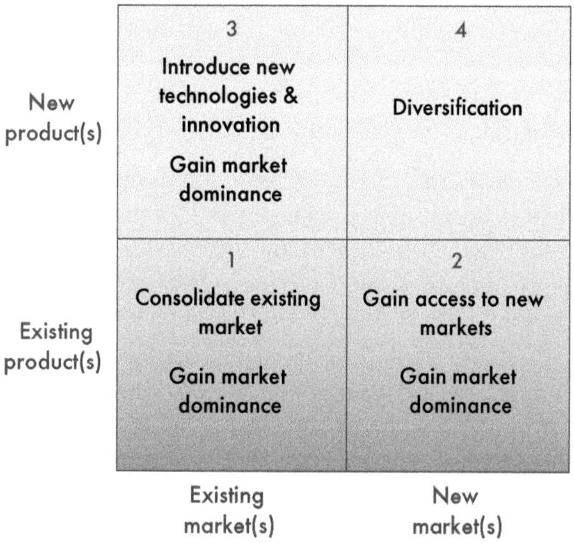

	Existing market(s)	New market(s)
New product(s)	**3** Introduce new technologies & innovation Gain market dominance	**4** Diversification
Existing product(s)	**1** Consolidate existing market Gain market dominance	**2** Gain access to new markets Gain market dominance

Figure 14.5 Reasons for corporate acquisitions

Box 1   Existing product(s) and market(s) – Market dominance provides organizations with the opportunity to charge oligopoly prices and the acquisition of competitors may have a role to play in this, albeit at the price of acquiring the competitor. The company purchases a customer base and eliminates a competitor at the same time. We see this sort of acquisition activity in newly emerging markets where no clear dominant brands have yet been established. We see it also in mature markets as products approach the end of their life-cycles and there is a decline in the number of customers. Some firms will decide to exit the market through a corporate sale; others may simply cease trading. Dominant companies may seek to consolidate their competitive position, albeit in this declining market, with the aim of closing the competitor's factories, transferring production to their own factories and achieving better economies of scale and therefore higher profits.

Box 2   Introducing existing product(s) into new market(s) – The purchase of another firm may be a way of buying market share – buying into a new market, possibly in another country. Once more, the aim is to achieve global market dominance quickly by buying competitors in foreign markets. The purchase might also help gain economies of scale where this is important – for example, with technology and internet-based businesses that face high fixed costs in development and low variable costs in selling their product or service. There might also be economies of scope or synergy.

   Economies of scope or synergy can come about because:

➡ Tangible assets and their related fixed costs, such as sales and distribution networks or R&D facilities, are spread across more products or services. This is the claim made for large pharmaceutical companies buying innovative small companies in order to sell their products through their extensive distribution networks;

- Intangible assets like brands can be profitably extended across more products or services (called brand extension). This is the claim made by Virgin in the UK and Reliance in India for their acquisition strategies;
- Organizational capabilities, such as general, sales or technological management, can be extended across more products or services;
- Network effects are important in the market because customer value is added by increasing the volume of customers or users (e.g. Facebook and Linkedin).

Because it generates extra profit, synergy is often referred to as '1 + 1 = 3'. It is a strategy that is particularly attractive in newly developing markets, for example in developing countries, where local brands may have pioneered the development of a market but are not as well known as the big global brands which then enter it as it starts to grow.

For this strategy to work best the key competency of the business should lie with their product or service, for example with technology-based products in which there is IP that can be exploited by finding new markets to sell the product into within a limited window of opportunity. Most technology-based companies follow this strategy – opening up new overseas markets as existing markets become saturated – because of the high cost of developing new products. By way of contrast, many service businesses such as consultancies have been pulled into new overseas markets because their clients operate there. Economies of scope can be exploited by simply selling or licensing the product or service. For example, banks have long supplied back-office capabilities for branded store and credit cards such as those of John Lewis, Tesco or Sainsbury. This is one reason why some companies might decide to sell or license their product to another in a foreign market whilst others decide to establish themselves in the country. The appropriate course of action depends upon a cost–benefit analysis of particular circumstances. However, the importance of economies of scope in shared resources and capabilities is likely to be a reason why related diversification is likely to be more profitable than unrelated diversification.

Box 3   Introducing new product(s) into existing market(s) – Any acquisition of another business with new products or technologies will involve finding markets for the innovations. One important motive in the purchase will be that the product is attractive to existing customers. It could be that these products replace existing ones, but it could also be the case that they offer the opportunity for product expansion (product variations that meet the needs of different market segments) and/or product extension (where a successful brand is extended to similar but different products). If the new products are complementary, it may be possible to integrate them into an existing range, thereby offering a more comprehensive range at the same time as gaining access to new customers. Synergy can also apply to the introduction of new products into an existing market. This strategy builds on the core competency of customer relations and may offer a cost-effective way of increasing the sales to every customer through the consolidated distribution channels.

The key to success here is having close customer relations and a loyal customer base, often associated with a strong brand with clear brand values that can be extended to the other products. Apple started with computers but moved into tablets, smartphones and smartwatches, extending its brand values of attractive design and ease of use. Mercedes-Benz is a brand that has a strong association with quality, and the company has capitalized on this by producing an ever wider range of vehicles, always, like Apple, being able to charge a premium price for its product. This has allowed it to move into new and different segments of the vehicle market. Virgin and Saga are two examples of UK brands that have been applied to a wide range of diverse products and services, mainly successfully, linking customers and their lifestyle aspirations rather than product characteristics. Both rarely undertake 'production' themselves, relying instead on partners with existing expertise.

> ❝ Capital needs to be deployed into areas where you are able to reap the highest returns. If a business segment isn't successful you need to be able to quickly divert valuable capital. ❞
>
> Michael Schwab, founder Aussie Commerce Group, *Business Review Australia*, issuu.com, July 2014

Box 4   Diversification: Introducing new product(s) into new market(s) – As we have seen, there are many reasons for both internal and external corporate venturing – not least changing or enhancing the core capabilities of the firm, even changing its business scope fundamentally. However, the acquisition of another business with new products or technologies may result in the acquiring firm having to find new markets for these new products which require a set of skills and knowledge it does not currently possess. In this case, it is essential that these are assimilated as quickly as possible and in a way that minimizes disruptions to the current activities. This strategy of diversification therefore carries with it a number of risks that we shall explore shortly.

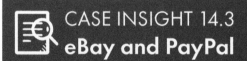 **CASE INSIGHT 14.3**
eBay and PayPal

ACQUISITIONS AND SPIN-OFFS

PayPal is a US online payments system for online vendors, auction sites and other commercial users. It was founded in 1998 as Confinity, a company that developed security software for handheld devices, and merged in 2000 with Xcom, an online banking company, taking its current name in 2001. PayPal allows customers to register details of their credit card or bank account. Then, when customers buy something on the internet, they simply enter their email account and the purchase price. The amount is then taken from their credit card or bank account. The advantage is that these details are not disclosed to the vendor.

PayPal had its IPO in 2002; one year later, it was purchased by eBay for $1.5 billion – giving a valuation of over $23 a share, or 77 per cent above the IPO price. The high premium reflected the potential commercial synergy between two companies – customers buying or selling on eBay could secure their payments using PayPal. It was attractive to customers because they could fund PayPal accounts using credit or debit cards without divulging the numbers and it was attractive to sellers since most were unable to accept credit cards because they did not have merchant accounts. It became a wholly owned subsidiary of the auction and retail site and rapidly became the dominant form of payment on eBay (it was offered as the default payment choice).

PayPal's business model expanded its customer base and volumes in three phases:

1. Expanding its services among eBay users in the USA through an aggressive marketing campaign.
2. Expanding PayPal to eBay's international sites. This involved using currencies other than the US dollar and therefore meeting local regulations and laws.
3. Extending PayPal's business beyond eBay. In 2003, PayPal launched a business unit called Merchant Services that offered services to e-commerce merchants other than eBay. From 2011, it became possible to make payments via PayPal in stores.

Like many internet firms, PayPal has pursued a strategy of enhancing its product and extending its market through the following acquisitions:

2005: Verisign to expand its market and provide added security support.
2008: Fraud Sciences, a start-up with expertise in online risk tools, in order to enhance its fraud management systems; Bill Me Later, a US online payments company, which was rebranded as PayPal Credit
2011: Where.com, a US location-based media company connecting merchants with customers; FigCard, a mobile payments start-up; Zong, a mobile payments company where the charge is to the mobile.
2012: card.io, a start-up that developed a scanning App for mobiles;
2013: IronPearl, a start-up offering engagement software; Braintree, a US mobile payment gateway; Venmo, a US mobile payments company; StackMob, a mobile platform development App.
2015: Paydiant, a cloud-based service for merchants; CyActive, an internet security start-up; Xoom Corporation, an international money transfer company; Modest Inc., a mobile shopping platform for retailers.
2017: TIO Networks, a payments processor; Swift Financial, an international payments transfer service.
2018: iZettle, a Swedish payment processor; Hyperwallet, a payments service for commission distribution; Simiity, a fraud prevention service.

PayPal has also partnered with many other organizations. For example, in 2007 it partnered with MasterCard to launch PayPal Secure Card service, a software facility that allows customers to make payments on websites that do not accept PayPal directly. In 2012, it partnered with Discover Card to allow PayPal payments to be made at any of the stores in Discover Card's network. In 2017, it partnered with Baidu to allow the Chinese firm's 100 million mobile wallet users to make payments to PayPal's 17 million merchants through the Baidu service.

In 2014, eBay announced plans to spin off PayPal into an independent company. It was said that this was due to shareholders wishing to realize PayPal's value, which, it was thought, was not reflected in eBay's stock market valuation (at the time PayPal was thought to be worth some $50 billion and eBay as a whole only $69 billion). The split was completed in 2015. After 2020, it is intended that PayPal should remain a payment option on eBay, but that it would no longer be featured ahead of other card options; at this point it would cease to process payments for eBay. Payments would then be handled by a Dutch back-end payments firm called Adyen, who can handle over 200 different payment methods. It was estimated that this might add some $2 billion to eBay revenues, lowering costs to sellers and creating more payment options for buyers.

PayPal reported earnings of $1.795 billion in 2017, on revenues of US$13.094 billion – an increase of 21 per cent over the previous year. As of 2018, PayPal operated in 202 markets and 25 currencies and had some 244 million active, registered accounts worldwide. Its market value is now some $100 billion.

Visit the website: www.paypal.com/

Questions:

1. Why did eBay purchase PayPal?
2. What do you think of PayPal's business model?
3. What is the strategic logic behind PayPal's acquisitions?
4. Why did eBay decide to spin out PayPal and then stop using it as a featured payment system?
5. Is there any benefit to PayPal from this proposed separation in 2020?

RISK AND CORPORATE VENTURING

Any acquisition strategy needs to be thought through, starting with the reasons behind it. Nothing that we have said so far changes the fact that, generally, risk increases as you increase the distance from the firm's core competencies by increasing the degree or scale of product or service innovation and the newness of the market. The risks associated with the four strategies shown in Figure 14.5 are therefore not the same.

Box 1   This is the lowest-risk acquisition strategy. The company should understand its core product and market and therefore be better able to judge the risks involved and the value of the company it is acquiring.

Box 2/3 There are risks involved in these acquisition strategies since they involve moving into either new product(s) or new market(s). However, entering into partnerships, strategic alliances, joint ventures (Chapter 5) or the acquisition of another company, where the other organization has capabilities and experience, can reduce these risks.

Box 4   Diversification is the highest-risk acquisition strategy of all, particularly if it involves radical innovation in either products or markets. The company may have little product or market knowledge and be straying furthest from its core competencies. However, the risks might be mitigated and financial exposure reduced by entering into partnerships, strategic alliances or joint ventures with another company. It might be further reduced by acquiring a company and their personnel with the knowledge and capabilities required for this new product and market.

In reality, these strategies are not mutually exclusive and can be used alongside each other, as circumstances dictate. This keeps open as many strategic options as possible. If the company moves into new product and new market areas (Boxes 2 and 3) through an active acquisition strategy (a lower-risk strategy), and then absorbs and assimilates the knowledge and capabilities of the individual acquisitions, it is in effect diversifying albeit incrementally, but without facing the higher risks associated with going into both new product and new market areas simultaneously (Box 4). Figure 14.6 shows how different approaches to corporate venturing might be best used in connection to the risks associated with these strategies.

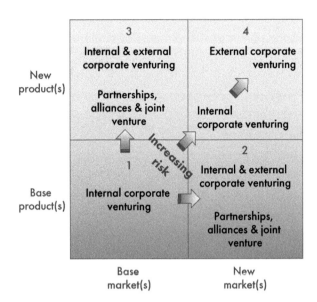

Figure 14.6 Corporate venturing and risk

The consultancy McKinsey favours organic growth rather than growth through corporate acquisitions. Using estimated results for prototypical organic growth in the consumer packaged goods industry, it concluded that strategies directed at organic growth – maintaining or growing market share in a growing market (Box 1 in Figure 14.6), new product/market developments (Boxes 2 and 3) and expanding into adjacent markets (Box 2) – would create far greater shareholder value than those directed at acquisition:

> *In our experience, executives would be better off recognising the limitations of size and revisiting the fundamentals of how growth creates shareholder value. By understanding that not all types of growth are equal when it comes to creating value for shareholders, even the largest companies can avoid bulking up on the business equivalent of empty calories and instead nourish themselves on the types of growth most likely to create shareholder value. (Lawler et al., 2004)*

As we saw from Figure 13.3 in the previous chapter, operational relatedness and strategic importance are important factors in determining what to do with an internally generated innovation. The degree of operational relatedness will often also influence how far a company is able to move into new products and markets on its own through internal corporate venturing. This is where external corporate venturing can have an important strategic role. Partnerships, strategic alliances and joint ventures are particularly valuable when the partners have complementary capabilities and are wishing to develop strategically important innovations. In the absence of a willing or suitable non-competing partner, the acquisition of another company may be the only way a company has of gaining these capabilities and developing the innovation, at least in the short term. These factors also influence whether a corporate acquisition should be integrated into the existing business or kept separate. Acquisitions are likely to have strategic importance (why else would they be made?). The greater the operational relatedness, the more likely it is that the acquisition will be

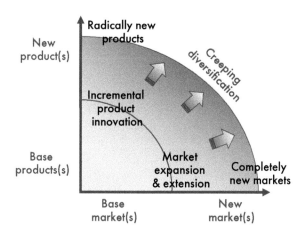

Figure 14.7 Diversification creep

integrated into the existing business. The lower the operational relatedness, the more likely it is to be kept separate as a Strategic Business Unit or subsidiary.

This form of continuous, incremental diversification through both internal and external corporate venturing can result in significant change. Diversification creep (Figure 14.7) can be a very effective way of reducing the risk of developing new product/markets. It is also a strategy that entrepreneurial firms, with their distinctive architecture, should have a competitive advantage in pursuing. It can deliver economies of both scale and scope and can also lead to significant growth in both sales and profit. It is a strategy that the US tech giants (Alphabet, Amazon, Apple, Facebook and Microsoft) have used very effectively. The next chapter will show how these combinations of new products and new markets can be bundled together into synergistic portfolios that create shareholder value now and for the future.

ATTRACTIONS AND DANGERS OF CORPORATE ACQUISITIONS

For an entrepreneur facing the possible purchase of their firm by a larger company there are a number of tempting advantages. It can yield an immediate capital gain and the possibility of a role within a larger organization, whilst removing the need for further investment that may have meant using personal funds or offering personal guarantees for a bank loan. For the smaller company, it offers access to resources to enable further development of the innovation (money, skills and knowledge). More importantly, it might offer access to markets that the smaller company might not otherwise enjoy, allowing it to roll out the innovation more rapidly.

The purchase of a small business can be very attractive to larger companies. It can be completed quickly. It is often easier to find funds for this than for R&D and innovation – particularly if the entrepreneur accepts shares for the purchase. We have seen how obtaining external funding for innovations can be difficult, where the outcome is uncertain and the pay-back is over the long term. The purchase can help the larger company enter new markets or consolidate existing market dominance. This can be particularly attractive when the focus of a market is shifting and the scope of a firm's activity has to shift with it. Bringing in new operating units or even autonomous subsidiaries with their own cultures, incentives and business models can be part of a broader strategy of business transformation.

> **"** *Mergers are like marriages. They are the bringing together of two individuals. If you wouldn't marry someone for the 'operational efficiencies' they offer in the running of a household, then why would you combine two companies with unique cultures and identities for that reason?* **"**
>
> Simon Sinek, author, Huffpost, 21 March 2010

However, there are also dangers attached to corporate venturing. The acquisition of any firm by another involves risks, not least because of information asymmetry – one party having more knowledge than another. The fact that the buyer knows less about the company and its innovative technology than the seller can lead to overvaluation. For example, the purchase of the British company Autonomy by the US multinational HP for $10.3 billion in 2011 resulted in an acrimonious legal battle lasting many years and an $8.8 billion write-down of the purchase because of 'accounting irregularities'. This underlines not only the importance of undertaking due diligence before any purchase but also understanding the market and industry as well as any technology being purchased. There is the danger that the venturing company might be just copying what competitors are doing, rather than following a well-thought-out strategy. Even after the purchase, the technology or the market prospects of the purchased firm may prove to be badly understood and outcomes, timescales and future development costs might escalate. Indeed, the acquired unit may prove such a bad 'fit' with the organization that it is eventually closed or key staff leave. Furthermore, all these problems may distract management from day-to-day business and damage short-term performance. Searching out potential companies to purchase requires specialist skills and larger firms often need to set up specialist in-house venture units. Table 14.1 shows the main advantages and dangers of undertaking corporate acquisitions.

Table 14.1 Attractions and dangers of corporate acquisitions

Advantages	Dangers
➥ It facilitates innovation and knowledge transfer from external sources, where there are gaps in the venturing company's internal performance.	➥ The venturing company may not fully understand the innovation or technology purchased and overestimate its attractiveness and potential value.
➥ It can be quick to execute.	➥ The venturing company might be just copying what competitors are doing, rather than following a well-thought-through strategy.
➥ External sources of finance may be easier to access for an acquisition rather than for internal innovation (particularly when there is a long and/or uncertain payback).	➥ If this is to be part of a strategy, it requires the venture company to invest in mechanisms that set up venture management and networks that search out, evaluate and generate deal flows.
➥ It can help the venturing company enter new markets or consolidate existing market dominance.	➥ The purchase needs to be paid for. This might be in cash (eating into other investment opportunities) or shares (diluting ownership).

➡ It facilitates the creation of semi-autonomous operating units with their own cultures, incentives and business models and can therefore be part of a strategy of business transformation.

➡ It is often highly motivating to the staff involved.

➡ The venturing company may not be in complete control of the development of the innovation and outcomes, timescales and future development costs might change.

➡ The acquired operating unit may not be assimilated successfully resulting in staff leaving and loss of their intrinsic knowledge and skills.

➡ The acquisition might distract management from day-to-day business and damage profitability in the short term.

The major reason why acquisitions fail is because of a failure of implementation. Claimed synergies may not be achieved; perhaps rationalization is insufficiently ruthless. Resources might not be shared and capabilities not transferred more efficiently than before the acquisition or merger. In other words, additional value is not created. It might also be the case that the costs of additional management outweigh the benefits of these linkages. Implementation fails because management fails to push through the required changes. This might be because clear management lines and responsibilities have not been laid down. Of course, short-term profit or growth targets may have been unrealistic in the first place.

Internal politicking is not uncommon in merged organizations, with managers from the two companies vying for dominance. Underpinning this there may be a clash of organizational cultures. The clash causes conflict and impedes communication and might result in the merged organizations being unable to work together effectively. This clash of cultures is not uncommon when larger firms acquire smaller ones and the entrepreneurial owner stays on. The entrepreneur may be unwilling to take orders and report to other managers; or they may feel undervalued and that their status is diminished. There was certainly a clash of cultures, for example, when the internet giant Facebook acquired Instagram and WhatsApp. This led to the departure of both of the companies' founders (Case insight 14.4). In fact, the departure of managers in an acquired company within a short space of time is a common outcome. They may, of course, be pushed rather than leaving of their own volition, but nevertheless this means that the timescale for proactive management of the assimilation and/or integration can be very short. Management of a merger or acquisition is difficult and requires all of the skills of change management outlined in Chapter 7.

CASE INSIGHT 14.4
Facebook: Instagram and WhatsApp

USA

ACQUISITIONS AND FOUNDERS

Launched in 2004 by Mark Zuckerberg, Facebook is probably the most successful of the so-called Web 2.0 start-ups. It has over two billion active users and revenues of over $40 billion. Over the years, Facebook has made relatively fewer corporate venturing acquisitions than other internet firms. In 2012, it purchased Instagram, the photo and video sharing social networking site, for $1 billion in cash and stock, retaining its founders, Kevin Systrom and Mike Krieger. In 2014, it purchased WhatsApp for over $19 billion in cash and stock, also keeping on its founders Jan Koum and Brian Acton. The founders from both companies were attracted by the prospect of their companies being able to grow more quickly with the backing of resources from the social media giant. However, despite their companies' continuing success and lucrative salaries, in 2018 the founders of both of these companies decided to leave because of disagreements with Mark Zuckerberg, the chairman and CEO of Facebook.

After their decision, Instagram's founders remarked that: 'We're planning on taking some time off to explore our creativity again. . . Building new things requires that we step back, understand what inspires us and match that with what the world needs; that's what we plan to do' (*The Observer*, 30 September 2018). However, speculation soon spread a different story. By 2018, it was estimated that Instagram generated $6 billion in revenue for Facebook – its second-largest income stream after News Feed. Originally, Zuckerberg had promised that Instagram would be allowed to grow independently. However, events were leading the founders to believe that this might be changing as Zuckerberg tightened his control over the company. Zuckerberg started 'meddling' in design decisions, despite this being seen as one of Systrom's strengths. Earlier in the year, for example, Facebook had removed a short cut link to Instagram from its bookmarks menu inside the Facebook App, eliminating the traffic flow from Facebook to Instagram. At the same time, Zuckerberg stopped the founders reporting directly to him, having them report instead to Chris Cox, the chief product officer. After their departure, Adam Mosseri, the former head of Facebook's News Feed, was appointed head of product. At the same time, Facebook absorbed Instagram's marketing department. It also removed the Instagram branding from photos shared on Facebook.

When Koum and Acton, WhatsApp's owners, left Facebook, not only did they leave behind lucrative salaries, but they also forfeited unvested stock options reportedly worth millions of dollars. The trigger this time was one of principle. With its end-to-end encryption, WhatsApp is synonymous with message safety, security and privacy. Even after joining Facebook, Koum had undertaken to keep users' data private: 'Respect for your privacy is coded into out DNA and we built WhatsApp around the goal of knowing as little about you as possible. You don't have to give us your email address. We don't know your home address. We don't know where you work. We don't know your likes, what you search for on the internet or collect your GPS location. None of that data has ever been collected and stored by WhatsApp and we have no plans to change that' (*The Observer*, 30 September 2018). However, once again things seemed about to change as Zuckerberg wanted the App to start making money by merging Facebook and WhatsApp data, thereby ditching all of Koum's assurances. Acton's response was to plough $50 million in another end-to-end encrypted messaging service called Signal. The funds were used to establish a not-for-profit foundation, making Signal free from advertising and monetization pressures.

The motivation behind Facebook's actions seems to be financial – allowing it to generate even more advertising revenue by assimilating even more data about its users. But is this what its customers want? And will entrepreneurs in the future be willing to sell their companies to Facebook, knowing how it is likely to operate?

Visit the website: investor.fb.com/home/default.aspx

Questions:

1. What do you think were the motivations behind these decisions to resign?
2. What does this say about Facebook?
3. What does this say about the ability of founders to stay on when their company has been bought out by Facebook? Is this generally the case? If not, why?

VENTURE FUNDS

If the acquisition of small innovative companies is to be a core part of a larger firm's strategy, it needs to have mechanisms that search out and evaluate potential venture investment and/or acquisitions. Venture funds are used by many large organizations to invest in areas of innovation that are of strategic interest. If the investment does not become strategically important to the investing company, it may be sold off – much like a spin-off. However, if that innovation proves successful and becomes strategically important then the investing company may move to acquire the IP or assimilate the company. Networks such as accelerators, incubators, strategic alliances and partnerships can be used to identify potential external investments and acquisitions. Venture funds can also be used to finance investment in internal innovations that might become Strategic Business Units. The Intel Corporation has Intel Capital, where investment professionals work alongside Intel business units to identify potential venture investments. We saw in Case insight 5.4 how Alphabet, in addition to its commitment to internal corporate venturing, has two subsidiaries: GV (formerly Google Ventures) providing seed, venture, and growth-stage funding to technology companies; and CapitalG (formerly Google Capital) providing late-stage growth venture capital funding. Both are independent venture funds and make financially driven investment decisions.

The key to success in external corporate venturing is 'strategic fit' – when there is synergy between the venture company and its smaller 'partner'. As shown in Figure 13.3, this is greatest where there is high operational relatedness and/or strategic importance. However, it is not simply about targeting the right sort of investment. For a venture fund to be successful, a number of other things need to be in place:

➡ As with most initiatives, the venture fund needs the commitment of senior management;
➡ The investments need to be consistent with corporate strategy, in such a way that an investment 'roadmap' can be produced, listing the areas to be investigated and invested in, the rationale for this and the mechanisms for searching out investments. However, the search mechanism needs to be sufficiently flexible to react to unexpected opportunities. It is important that the strategy is integrated into the overall corporate strategy for growth and innovation. A company can only beat venture capitalists at their own game if it adds value to the process in some way and the venture portfolio is aligned to its overall corporate strategy. It is this ability to share and leverage industry knowledge between portfolio companies and the business units of the investing company that creates true added value;
➡ If the investment results in an acquisition, there needs to be effective HR policies in place within the venturing company in order to encourage the retention of talented staff in the acquired company and encourage continuity. There is little point in acquiring a company only to find that key staff leave shortly after acquisition. Effective knowledge transfer is at the heart of successful corporate venturing for commercial purposes and many mechanisms can be used to facilitate this. For example, within Motorola, Motorola Ventures has a knowledge transfer team that is tasked with developing relationships between the acquired company and the Motorola parent. In this way, engineers can monitor whether or not the technology acquired meets expectations and identify opportunities between it and existing business units. The same team works with Motorola's own start-ups and spin-offs.

➡ The investing firm needs to have access to sufficient capital to use corporate venturing in this strategic way. This capital might, at least in part, be from external sources but this can create a conflict of interest should the firm decide to acquire the company concerned.

Some large companies also run venture funds with wider social investment criteria, such as creating jobs in areas where the company has made redundancies. Many of these funds have not-for-profit objectives and are part of a larger social or environmental agenda for the company. Clearly, in these cases the criteria for searching out and investing in projects are completely different and there is no prospect of the investment being integrated into the commercial activities of the larger company

SUMMARY

➡ Innovation often involves product and/or market development and creates increasing risk, as the organization moves away from its core competencies. Market penetration takes time as customers take time to adopt innovations.

➡ Finding new markets for an existing product/service is an important growth strategy which can extend the life of a product/service. It often involves entering overseas markets which can be risky and often is best done on a staged basis involving increasing degrees of commitment: export; sales agent; license or franchise; and joint venture. New markets can be assessed using Porter's Five Forces: industry rivalry; threat of substitutes; threat of new entrants; bargaining power of buyers; and bargaining power of suppliers.

➡ The riskiest strategy is when the organization moves into completely new and unrelated product and market areas at the same time – called diversification. This is most risky when the firm develops beyond its present 'industry' or 'sector' into new products/services and markets that, on the face of it, bear little relationship to the one it is in – called unrelated diversification. Related diversification is less risky and is when there is likely to be some 'operational relatedness' that offers the opportunity for economies of scale, scope (synergy) or the expansion or extension of the firm's existing product range.

➡ Synergy is often described as '1 + 1 = 3'. It comes about through economies of scope – spreading an asset (tangible or intangible) or capability over multiple activities.

➡ External corporate venturing is concerned with how the organization structures itself externally to encourage innovation and develop new business areas. One prominent aspect of this is corporate acquisitions which are used to buy-in IP related to product/service development, gain access to new markets and/or consolidate market share with the aim of dominating the market. Sometimes corporate acquisitions involve diversification – combining all of these motivations.

➡ Corporate acquisition can be a quick way to shore up gaps in the venturing company's internal performance. However, it carries dangers, not least that the venturing company may not fully understand the innovation or technology purchased and overestimate its attractiveness and potential value. There is also the danger that the acquired business may not be successfully assimilated and any planned gains not realised.

➡ For a corporate acquisitions strategy to work it needs: the commitment of senior management; consistency and integration with corporate strategy; to add value through effective knowledge transfer, leveraging knowledge from the larger company and the firm it acquires; effective HR policies to encourage the retention of talented staff; and finally to provide access to sufficient capital.

➡ Diversification is central to the process of corporate evolution and part of the process of corporate entrepreneurship. It can create new industries. Organizations can develop new product/services and new markets through internal or external corporate venturing. Partnerships, alliances and joint ventures can mitigate the risks of both types of developments, but particularly diversification.

➡ Continuous, incremental diversification through both internal and external corporate venturing can result in significant change and diversification creep can be a very effective way of reducing the risk of developing new product and markets and sometimes creating completely new ones.

GROUP DISCUSSION TOPICS

1. Penetrating the market is just about selling more. Discuss.
2. How useful are the labels of 'innovators', 'early adopters', 'late adopters' and 'laggards' to customers at different stages of the life-cycle? How long are each of the stages?
3. The life-cycle of products and services is speeding up and it is becoming increasingly more difficult to label different stages. Discuss.
4. What is the logic of gradually increasing commitment to a foreign market? Under what circumstances might you wish to establish a wholly owned subsidiary straight away?
5. What are the advantages in acquiring an existing company if you want to enter a foreign market?
6. In what circumstances might company acquisition(s) help you achieve market dominance? How important is speed of acquisition?
7. Why are big pharma companies so keen to purchase innovative start-ups?
8. What needs to be done ahead of purchasing another company (called due diligence)?
9. Under what circumstances might diversification be an attractive option? Explain.
10. Diversification is inevitable for a company that is innovating. Discuss.
11. Are there any differences between a Strategic Business Unit (SBU) and a corporate acquisition?
12. Can a company become a dominant market force by the mature stage of its life-cycle, other than through mergers and acquisitions? Explain.
13. What needs to be in place for a corporate acquisition strategy to work?
14. Why is effective knowledge transfer important in corporate acquisitions? How can it be achieved?
15. Why might related diversification work best for entrepreneurial companies?
16. What is synergy and how might it be achieved?
17. Why do so many mergers and/or acquisitions fail? Give examples.
18. Why do so many founders of successful businesses sell up once the business model proves successful?
19. Why do founders stay on after acquisition by a larger company? Why do so many leave quickly afterwards?
20. Why might a strategy of internal growth be less risky than one of acquisition? In what circumstances might it be more attractive?

ACTIVITIES

1. For the department in your university or college, use the product/market matrix (Figure 14.1b) to list the growth options that it faces for the courses on offer.
2. The top ten Pharma companies by turnover are Pfizer (USA), Roche (Switzerland), Merck (USA), Johnson & Johnson (USA), Sanofi (France), Novartis (Switzerland), Abbvie (USA), AstraZeneca (UK), Gilead (USA) and Amgen (USA). Select two companies and write a report outlining their acquisitions over the last five years, the reasons for them and their success. Compare and contrast the two companies.

3. Select a company that has grown rapidly over the last five years. Analyze the strategies it has followed to secure this growth, comparing its use of internal with external corporate venturing.
4. Find an example of a successful corporate acquisition and analyze why it has worked. Repeat this for a corporate acquisition that has proved unsuccessful.
5. Select an industry and assess its competitiveness using Porter's Five Forces.

REFERENCES

Bhidé, A. (2000) *The Origin and Evolution of New Business*, Oxford: Oxford University Press.

Bowman, C. and Faulkner, D.O. (1997) *Competitive and Corporate Strategy*, London: Irwin.

Deakins, D. and Freel, M. (2006) *Entrepreneurship and Small Firms* (4th edn.), London: McGraw Hill.

Deans, G., Zeisel, S. and Kroeger, F. (2003) *Winning the Merger End Game*, New York, NY: McGraw-Hill.

Grant, R.M. (2010) *Contemporary Strategic Analysis* (7th edn.), Chichester: John Wiley.

Johnson, G., Whittington, R., Regnér, P., Scholes, K. and Angwin, D. (2017) *Exploring Strategy: Text and Cases*, Harlow: Pearson Education.

Lawler, N.F., McNish, R.S. and Monier, J.-H.J. (2004) 'Why the Biggest and Best Struggle to Grow', *McKinsey Insights*. Available at: https://www.mckinsey.com/business-functions/strategy-and-corporate-finance/our-insights/why-the-biggest-and-best-struggle-to-grow.

Porter, M.E. (1985) *Competitive Advantage, Creating and Sustaining Superior Performance*, New York, NY: Free Press.

Rogers, E.M. (2003) *Diffusion of Innovations* (5th edn.), New York, NY: Simon and Schuster.

ONLINE RESOURCES AVAILABLE — For further resources relating to this chapter see the companion website at **www.macmillanihe.com/Burns-CEI**

15 Shareholder value in the multi-product/market firm

CONTENTS

- The multi-product/market firm
- The product/market portfolio
- Cash flow and the product/market portfolio
- A portfolio approach to risk
- Multi-product/markets and conglomerates
- Shareholder value and diversification
- Shareholder value in conglomerates
- Organization structure and product/market portfolios
- Summary
- Group discussion questions
- Activities
- References

CASE INSIGHTS

Learning outcomes

When you have read this chapter and undertaken the related activities you will be able to:

➡ Understand and explain the effects of product life-cycles on marketing strategy and how the life-cycle can be lengthened through product modification, expansion and extension;

➡ Use the growth-share matrix to communicate marketing strategies for a portfolio of products;

➡ Critically analyze how companies and conglomerates use the cash flows from their product/ market portfolios;

➡ Show advance knowledge of how the product portfolio can be managed;

➡ Understand and explain how diversification can create shareholder value;

➡ Understand and explain how multi-product/market conglomerates can create shareholder value.

THE MULTI-PRODUCT/MARKET FIRM

Most large firms have a portfolio of different product/market offerings. The portfolio grows over time through corporate venturing in its different forms. Even as successive waves of innovation might bring in new products or new markets, however, the old product/market offerings still need to be managed – and innovation, albeit probably only incremental – continues to have a part to play. Having a product/market portfolio creates managerial complexity with each product/market offering potentially at a different stage in its life-cycle and with its own business model and marketing strategy. That complexity increases again if the business is a multinational and operates over a number of countries.

If the product/market range becomes so diverse that the company effectively operates in different industries, it is said to be a conglomerate. This can happen because the company, either intentionally or unintentionally, follows the strategy of diversification that we looked at it the last chapter. This can be the result of radical, disruptive innovations that create opportunities to develop whole new industries. Whilst a multi-product/market firm might be organized along divisional lines, if it becomes a conglomerate it is far more likely to operate as a parent company (a holding-company with a head office) and subsidiaries.

Creating a portfolio of different product/market offerings may add managerial complexity but it can offer some advantages. We saw in Case insight 5.4 how Google, the core business of Alphabet, was a cash generator that financed its other innovation activities. Within Google, there are a number of product/market offerings such as Search, Ads, Android, YouTube, Apps, Cloud Computing and Maps, each with its own business model and marketing strategy, which is coordinated across all the Alphabet subsidiaries by head office.

This chapter will provide some tools that can help to manage the complexity of a portfolio of products and markets. It looks at some of the issues surrounding public companies and their stock market valuation. In particular, it looks at how an entrepreneurial firm that expands into emerging products and markets can create and sustain shareholder value – even if it becomes a conglomerate – by minimizing risk and maximizing opportunity. It also explores how new product/market developments might be organized within the organization so as to maximize shareholder value.

THE PRODUCT/MARKET PORTFOLIO

The growth-share matrix is a simple tool for showing the important issues facing products at different stages of their life and the implications for strategy (Figure 15.1). The vertical axis measures the market attractiveness – the growth and profit potential (rather than historic growth rate) of the market. The horizontal axis measures the strength of the product/service in this market – its sales, relative market share etc. A product/service is launched into an attractive market (otherwise why do it?), but its market position is likely to be weak to start with. This is called a Problem Child. If the market continues to be attractive, sales will grow and its market position will strengthen. This is called a Star. Eventually, however, the market will mature, becoming less attractive, and the product/service will become a Cash Cow – a market leader with a lot of stability, but little potential for additional growth because it is approaching the end of its life. Eventually, it will become a Dog and its life will be terminated. Sometimes the market a product is launched into proves to be unattractive – then its life is very short as it becomes a Dog. A Cash Dog might prolong its life because it covers its costs, at least for a time. The arrows show the trajectory of travel in the matrix and the size of the circle represents the value or volume of sales.

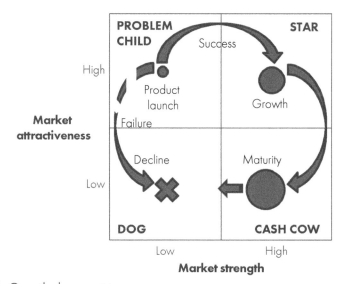

Figure 15.1 Growth-share matrix
Source: Adapted from *The BCG Portfolio Matrix* from the *Product Portfolio Matrix*,
The Boston Consulting Group, 1970

There are a number of measurement issues with this simple framework. How do you define the market so that market share or market growth can be measured? You might use just one factor on each axis or a number of them weighted in some way. Nevertheless, the problem of measurement remains. The matrix is therefore probably best used as a loose conceptual framework that helps to clarify complexity. Anything that simplifies complexity and therefore helps our understanding must be of value.

Product modification, extension and expansion opportunities can be represented in the growth-share matrix. An example of this is shown in Figure 15.2. Again, this is a useful visual aid to understanding strategy options.

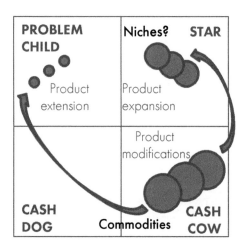

Figure 15.2 Product modification, extension and expansion
Source: Adapted from *The BCG Portfolio Matrix* from the *Product Portfolio Matrix*,
The Boston Consulting Group, 1970

PROBLEM CHILD	**STAR**
Develop opportunities	Invest for growth
➢ Be critical of prospects ➢ Invest in selected products ➢ Basic product ➢ Encourage customer trial & evaluate response ➢ Price low (encourage trial) or price high (novelty) ➢ Develop brand ➢ Selective distribution	➢ Sell aggressively & penetrate market ➢ Differentiate product ➢ Promote brand loyalty ➢ Modify product & expand range ➢ Price competitively to combat competition ➢ Wide distribution
CASH DOG	**CASH COW**
Generate cash	Manage for earnings
➢ Monitor carefully - judge when to discontinue ➢ Maintain customer loyalty ➢ Reduce costs (e.g., minimize promotions) ➢ Improve productivity ➢ Price low (stock disposal) or price high (little competition) ➢ Look for 'easy' new markets (e.g. overseas)	➢ Maintain market position with successful product(s) ➢ Differentiate & maintain brand loyalty ➢ Heavy promotion ➢ Price defensively ➢ Selective marketing with special offers & promotions ➢ Intensive push on distribution (including trade discounts)

Figure 15.3 Strategy implications of the growth-share matrix

Similarly, generalized marketing strategies for different product/service offerings in a portfolio can be shown in the growth-share matrix (Figure 15.3). If you can place each product/market offering within the matrix, these bullet points should summarize elements of the marketing strategy, all things being equal. However, it should be remembered that, while this framework reflects general strategies that are appropriate at different stages of the product life-cycles, it does not reflect the generic business models that underpin them, which were outlined in Chapter 12: price, differentiation and degree of customer focus. These need to be incorporated into any overall marketing strategy.

CASH FLOWS AND THE PRODUCT/MARKET PORTFOLIO

As a product moves through this matrix there are implications for cash flow and the different business skills required. In the Problem Child phase, it is the entrepreneurial and marketing skills that are of most value. This phase consumes cash for development and promotional costs at a rate of knots, while at the same time generating little cash by way of revenues. In the Star phase, these skills are also important and marketing costs will continue to be high but at least the product should be generating revenues that will at least meet these costs. Once the product is in its mature phase, it needs to be managed as a Cash Cow – costs tightly controlled and the product milked for all the cash flow it can generate.

That means high levels of efficiency are needed, probably achieved through a high degree of control and direction – things that are not characteristic of an entrepreneurial architecture. There are two kinds of Dogs. One is a Cash Dog, which covers its costs and might be worth keeping, for example if it brings in customers for other products or services or if it shares overheads. The other is the Genuine Dog, which is losing money – both in cash flow and profit terms – and should be scrapped. These cash flow implications are shown in Figure 15.4. Remember that most firms will need additional cash to finance the innovations that have not yet reached the market.

PROBLEM CHILD		STAR	
Revenue	+	Revenue	+ + +
Expenditure	- - -	Expenditure	- - -
Cash flow	- - (negative)	Cash flow	neutral
CASH DOG		CASH COW	
Revenue	+	Revenue	+ + + +
Expenditure	-	Expenditure	- -
Cash flow	neutral	Cash flow	+ + (positive)

Figure 15.4 Cash flow implications of the growth-share matrix

> *Fast growth normally means being unprofitable because you have to invest heavily in staff and marketing. Then there is aiming to be profitable and living within your means, which means you are not going to grow. That's the classic tightrope for technology businesses.*
>
> William Reeve, co-founder Lovefilm, *The Sunday Times*, 2 April 2017

In a multi-product/market firm the organizational architecture appropriate for each phase is different and therefore the challenge for management can be complex. However, having a portfolio means that, ideally, the cash flows might balance out so that the surplus cash from Cash Cows can be used to invest in the Problem Children. This ideal firm is self-financing. The problem that arises with an unbalanced portfolio is that there is either a surplus of cash (no new products) or a deficit (too many new products). If there are too many Problem Children and Stars in the portfolio (too many good, new ideas), then further cash injections will be required, underlining the paradox that you can be profitable and still run out of cash. The growth-share matrix is a convenient way of showing this. Each circle in Figure 15.5 represents different product/market offerings and the size of these could be represented by the sales or profit they generate. Figure 15.5a shows a balanced portfolio with three new products, four growth Stars and three Cash Cows. Figure 15.5b shows an unbalanced portfolio with four new products (Problem Children) and two growth Stars. This latter portfolio is unlikely to generate sufficient cash to finance the marketing of the new

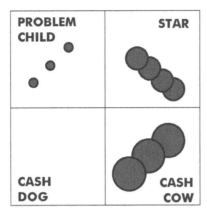

Figure 15.5a A balanced portfolio

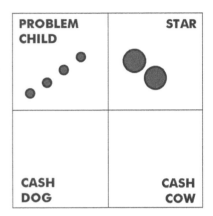

Figure 15.5b An unbalanced portfolio: Insufficient cash/Too many new products

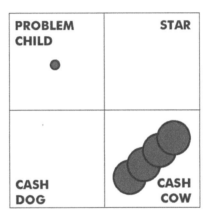

Figure 15.5c An unbalanced portfolio: Too much cash/Too few new products

products, meaning external finance may have to be sought. Figure 15.5c shows an unbalanced portfolio with only one new product (Problem Child) but four Cash Cows. This portfolio generates a lot of cash but the launch of only one new product is unlikely to use it all up. It might be paying high dividends but the future does not look good for this company unless it has a number of innovations coming through, which do not yet feature on the matrix.

Again, the added complexity in these situations is the generic marketing strategies that need to be factored into the strategy. For example, if the Star and Cash Cow product/market offerings in15.5a are all commodities, selling mainly on price, with low margins under intense pressure, it has implications not only for strategy but also for the cash flow available to invest in the Problem Children and any other innovations not yet shown in the matrix.

It is important to establish any linkages that might offer economies of scale or scope between different product/markets in a portfolio. Synergistic linkages might create completely new markets and prolong the life of individual products.

Although we have been talking about applying this type of analysis to each product/market, it can also usefully be applied to individual units, divisions or even subsidiaries of a company.

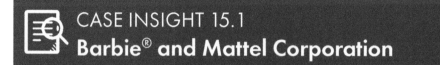

CASE INSIGHT 15.1
Barbie® and Mattel Corporation

USA

EXTENDING THE PRODUCT LIFE-CYCLE

Barbie was born in 1959, but she has never aged because it is a doll. To date, more than a billion Barbies have been sold by the US company that owns it, Mattel Corporation, making it their largest and most profitable line. Mattel is the world's second-largest toymaker after Lego. Ruth Handler, who founded the company along with her husband, Elliot, modelled the doll on an 11.5-inch plastic German toy called Lilli sold to adult men. She named the adapted doll after her daughter, Barbara. But how has this plastic doll endured for so long in an industry notorious for its susceptibility to fickleness and fashion? Surely it must have come to the end of its life-cycle? The answer lies in innovative marketing and product extension.

When originally introduced into the market, Barbie was competing with dolls that were based on babies and designed to be cradled and cared for. Barbie was unique in having an adult appearance, with an exaggerated female figure normally with blonde hair and pouting lips. Barbie was seen as adult and independent – a child of 'liberated' times, one that could become anything or anyone the child wanted. Mattel describe Barbie as a 'life-style, not just a toy . . . a fashion statement, a way of life'. Barbie was not only innovative, it was also intended to be more than just a doll.

Barbie is not just a doll – it comes with a range of clothes and accessories. Every year, Mattel devises hundreds of new Barbie dolls and outfits as it continues to re-invent the brand. She was a 'mod' in the 1960s and a hippie in the 1970s. Her hairstyle has also changed often over the years: from ponytail to bubble-cut, and from page boy to swirl to side-part flip. The doll has also taken on various roles in life – from holidaying in Malibu to being an astronaut. Barbie has had a career as a soldier, an air force pilot, a surgeon, a vet, a doctor, a dentist, an engineer, a fire-fighter, a diplomat, a fashion model, an Olympic athlete, a skier, a scuba diver, a sportswoman, a TV news reporter, an aerobics instructor, a rock star, a rap musician and even a presidential candidate. Each role has had numerous associated accessories – from cars to horse and carriage, from jewellery box to lunch box. Barbie even has a partner called Ken, as well as (multicultural) friends, siblings and cousins. Dressing and undressing, grooming and making-up (and going out with Ken and her family and friends) is what Barbie is made for.

Mattel has worked hard to generate brand extension. There are a large range of Barbie branded goods, including books, apparel, cosmetics, and video games. Mattel also licences production of hundreds of different Barbie products, including make-up, pajamas, bed clothes, furniture and wallpapers. There have been TV specials, TV series (the latest, *Dreamhouse Adventures*, was launched in 2018) and almost 40 Barbie computer animated videos, selling in the millions, usually accompanied by special dolls, other accessories and product tie-ins. Tim Kilpin, the senior vice-president for girls marketing at Mattel, explained the strategy: 'What you see now are several different Barbie worlds anchored by content and storytelling. A girl can understand what role Barbie is playing, what the other characters are doing, and how they interrelate. That's a much richer level of story that leads to a richer level of play' ('Barbie's Midlife Crisis', *Brand Strategy*, 14 May 2004). The first video, based on Barbie in the Nutcracker in 2001, grossed $150 million in sales, including associated products. A new 'live-action' Barbie film is currently in production.

Mattel has tried to segment the market – trying to find new markets into which to sell the doll and its accessories product extensions attempt this. But selling beyond the basic market, for example to older girls, is problematic. The main problem is that 'age compression' – that girls are getting older sooner – means that it is increasingly hard to hang on to the basic market, let alone trying to extend it.

Over the years, Barbie has become a cultural icon. The doll is seen by many as the ideal vision of an American woman. Mattel has cultivated and defended these images. In 1976, the USA included Barbie in the bicentennial time capsule. There are sociology courses in the USA based upon her, speculating on the layered meanings of the Barbie image. There are Barbie exhibitions, conventions, fan clubs, magazines, and websites. A 'Barbie Café' has even been opened in Taiwan. It is also estimated that there are over 100,000 collectors of Barbie dolls – recently, one collector paid $17,000 for a vintage Barbie model.

The problem remains that Barbie is getting old and must be nearing the end of her product life-cycle. In a changing world, young girls will continue to want the Barbie fantasy world. Sales peaked at $1.8 billion in 1997. Since then they have fallen continuously in every subsequent year. So the question is how long can innovations sustain Barbie?

Visit the website: **www.mattel.com**

Questions:

1. Why has Barbie been so successful?
2. Barbie is hardly a high-tech product, but has Mattel been innovative in how it has developed the product and extended its lif-cycle?
3. What are the lessons for product innovation?

A PORTFOLIO APPROACH TO RISK

Chapter 8 showed how we are biased towards risk-aversion for gains and risk-seeking for losses. This tendency can result in the spread of projects and product/market offerings in a portfolio being biased against riskier projects and adversely affect earnings. An understanding of portfolio risk is therefore an essential part of understanding how risk might be managed. By holding a balanced portfolio of stocks and shares you can eliminate all but the overall market risk (the risk that affects all shares). Similarly, by holding a portfolio of projects (or product/market offerings) *that are independent of each other*, you can spread their risk and achieve higher earnings. The portfolio therefore needs some higher-risk projects to balance off against lower-risk projects: it wins a few, it loses a few. Although the risk associated with a new-to-the-world project may be high, as part of a balanced portfolio of innovations and activities that business risk is mitigated by the other, less risky, projects. The role of failure is recognized and accepted as part of the cost of achieving winning innovations and a balanced portfolio. Some innovations will be major and others moderate winners, but some will be failures.

For example, consider the hypothetical company whose portfolio of projects is represented in Figure 15.6. This is a snapshot at a point of time, or for one operating period, that changes over time. Each letter represents an innovation project. The company's highest-risk project is project A, a new-to-the-world innovation that will require careful management and risk assessment. This diversification takes it into completely new products and markets. There are only two projects, B and C, that are, on the face of it, in the area of

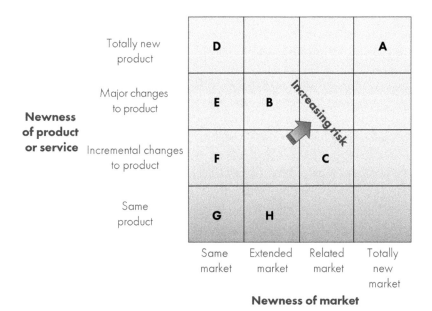

Figure 15.6 A specimen risk portfolio

'diversification creep' where entrepreneurial firms might operate to greatest competitive advantage and we might seek to question why that is the case. More worrying is the fact that there are so few new market developments. Why is this? And does project G really involve no innovation of any sort? There might be a good reason, for example that this is a new product and in this period what is required is further market penetration. But the analysis acts as a prompt for the question. For each project a better understanding of the strategic fit with the company's core competencies is central to understanding the risks the firm faces overall. However, for this company the risk portfolio does not appear to be balanced. It would appear to be risk-averse and focused on its current market. What will happen if that market disappears?

SUPPLY CHAIN INNOVATION AND MARKET ENTRY

Based in India, TutorVista was launched in 2006 by Krishnan Ganesh. He came up with the idea when he was travelling around the USA and was shocked to hear a media debate about 'the crisis in the US school education system'. He investigated (asking the question 'Why?') and realized that personal tutors in the USA were charging $40–60 an hour and were regarded by most people as unaffordable. That got him to ask the question: 'Why not link teachers from India, where wage rates are lower, to the market demand in the USA?'

TutorVista is an intermediary. It uses the internet to connect students in high wage-cost countries such as the USA and Britain with private tutors from low wage-cost countries such as India. It is completely dependent on the internet and the widespread availability of home computers. The part-time tutors are mainly employed full-time as teachers in Indian schools and work from home for TutorVista in their free time as gig workers. This remote business model allows the company to keep capital and running costs to a minimum and minimize risks. Teachers are vetted and quality is monitored. The company markets the service directly using Google search advertisements. When somebody searches for tutor support in any subject, an advertisement for TutorVista pops up. When they click on the website they can talk to staff about the service. By 2017, TutorVista had some 2,000 teachers and had served over 5 million online tutorial sessions.

In 2011, the British-owned multinational education company Pearson plc increased a smaller stake in the company to a 76 per cent majority stake, paying $127 million. In 2013, it acquired the remaining shares. Pearson plc is the largest education company in the world and is the owner of the publishers Pearson Education, as well as other imprints. It has invested heavily in digital learning but has experienced financial difficulties resulting in redundancies and the sale of some of its subsidiaries. In 2017, it sold TutorVista to Byju's, an Indian online education company. Byju's is best known for its learning app that creates 'personalised learning programmes' for students, allowing them to learn at their own pace and style. At the time of writing it has over 8 million users in India

Visit the website on: byjus.com

Questions:

1. Why do you think Pearson bought TutorVista?
2. Why might a global company like Pearson not have come up with the idea behind TutorVista themselves?
3. Why do you think Byju's bought TutorVista?

MULTI-PRODUCT/MARKETS AND CONGLOMERATES

There is no clear distinction between a company operating in diverse product/markets and a conglomerate, which is said to operate in different industries. The distinction revolves around the degree of connection between the different markets and when they are sufficiently distinct to become separate industries. However, the new era of technology is blurring these boundaries. Hardware and software are increasingly linked, with the US tech giants (Alphabet, Amazon, Apple, Facebook and Microsoft) able to offer virtual and physical, goods and services, marketed (in real time) using algorithms based on information they have gained from intelligent systems embedded in the software we are using (cookies).

In the past, conglomerates grew up through a conscious strategy of diversification. Today, they can come out of a strategy of promoting innovation as radical innovations spawn new-to-the-world industries. Diversification through the acquisition of other companies was a major feature of post-war Western corporate activity until the 1980s. Conglomerates became popular because it was thought that they would reduce risk and therefore increase shareholder value. The idea was that different product/markets have different cycles of growth and decline; by combining them, you can reduce or smooth the effect of these differences, particularly upon the overall cash flow of the organization (Figure 15.6); this form of risk reduction appealed to managers, whose jobs depended on the company continuing to operate. These acquisitions were often financed by high levels of borrowings. But the great conglomerate-merger wave did not generally lead to improvements in performance for the firms that were involved. The trend was reversed by the large-scale selling of unrelated businesses in the 1980s, encouraged by high interest rates. Porter (1987), in his study of 33 major corporations between 1950 and 1986, concluded that more often than not acquisitions were subsequently sold off rather than retained, and the net result was a dissipation of shareholder value rather than an increase.

A focus on the core business at the corporate level was emphasized in the 1980s by academics (e.g. Abell, 1980). They stressed that the unique elements of a company's differentiation strategy are likely to be based on distinctive capabilities and that these, applied to a relevant market, become its competitive advantage. This area will become the company's core business, the one in which it has a distinct advantage by adding the greatest value for its customers and shareholders. Many studies showed that more focused firms performed better than diversified ones (e.g., Wernerfelt and Montgomery, 1986). This focus on the core business was popularized by Peters and Waterman (1982) as 'sticking to the knitting'. Although some studies were subsequently disputed (e.g., Luffman and Reed, 1984; Michel and Shaked, 1984; Park, 2002), Peters and Waterman (1982) concluded:

> Organizations that do branch out but stick to their knitting outperform the others. The most successful are those that diversified around a single skill. . . . The second group in descending order, comprise those companies that branch out into related fields. . . . The least successful are those companies that diversify into a wide variety of fields. Acquisitions especially among this group tend to wither on the vine.

Developments in financial theory, in particular the **Capital Asset Pricing Model** (CAPM), also showed that conglomerates did not create shareholder value by reducing risk in stock markets, even if their product/market offerings were independent of each other (e.g., Levy and Sarnat, 1970; Weston et al., 1972; Mason and Goudzwaard, 1976). In particular, diversification did not reduce **systematic risk** – the part of risk associated with how the share price performs compared to the overall market (measured by the company's beta coefficient). Shareholders can simply buy shares in undiversified companies representing the diversified interests of the conglomerate. This spreads their risk, and probably with lower transaction costs. Therefore, at the corporate level diversification does not create shareholder value and, if badly managed because of the increased organizational complexity, can destroy it. This is why conglomerates often trade at a discount on the value of their component parts.

Despite academics, the formation of conglomerates remains a powerful driver of strategy for private, unquoted companies, particularly when family wealth is tied up in them. For example, the Virgin Group is a private company. Its scope of business reaches across the world and ranges from transport (airlines, trains and buses) to media (TV, radio, mobile phones and internet), from health and lifestyle (health programs to gyms) to financial services (credit cards, pension and insurance products and banking). Sometimes these businesses are established in partnership with other companies better able to manage operations and sometimes they are bought as going concerns. Richard Branson (Virgin's owner) withdrew the company from the stock market some years ago, buying back its shares. Publicly quoted conglomerates continue to exist and prosper, particularly in developing economies; for example, Tata Group and Reliance Industries – two of the largest publicly traded companies in India (by market capitalization). One reason for this may be the higher share transaction costs in these markets. Another might be the high concentration of ownership in family hands. Ultimately, however, the reason probably boils down to inefficiencies in the markets. So, traditional forms of diversification and the formation of conglomerates still have a role to play, particularly in private companies.

capital aasset pricing model (CAPM) A theoretical model used to determine the required rate of return for an asset

systematic risk That part of risk associated with how the share price of a company performs compared to the overall market (measured by the company's beta coefficient)

> ❝ The approach to running a group of private companies is fundamentally different to that of running public companies. Short-term taxable profits with good dividends are a prerequisite of public life. Avoiding short-term taxable profits and seeking long-term capital growth is the best approach to growing private companies. ❞
>
> Richard Branson, founder Virgin Group, letter to *The Economist*, 7 March 1998

SHAREHOLDER VALUE AND DIVERSIFICATION

The problem is that, although it is traditionally viewed as risky, diversification is central to the process of corporate evolution – whether through incremental or radical shifts in product/markets. As products come to the end of their natural life-cycles, the longevity of any particular organization will depend on its ability to innovate and in so doing eventually redefine the business it is in, applying existing capabilities to developing new products and markets, perhaps even new industries, and buying-in those capabilities when necessary. And opportunities for diversification are the natural outcomes of internal and/or external corporate venturing within a firm with an entrepreneurial architecture. The challenge is to make clear how diversification can create shareholder value.

The arguments against diversification revolve around risk and not straying from a firm's core skills, knowledge and capabilities, applied to a relevant market. However, products, markets and society are changing rapidly and in this context shareholder value can indeed be created in a systematic process that includes diversification. Listed below are the ways in which an entrepreneurial multi-product/market business (a conglomerate) can create real value for its shareholders:

➥ The distinctive capabilities of a firm with an entrepreneurial architecture relate to its ability to innovate, again and again. These capabilities can be extended across more products or services. In effect, the firm's core business is innovation through both internal and external corporate venturing, including acquisitions. Operationally related innovations can be integrated into existing operations or licensed out to other firms depending on their strategic importance (see Figure 13.3), thereby creating shareholder value. Those innovations that are not can be spun off and sold, also creating shareholder value.

➥ Markets are changing rapidly and new product/market opportunities are emerging, particularly with regard to new technologies. Radical innovation creates the product/markets of the future, not the past, meaning that the core skills, knowledge and capabilities needed to exploit them have still to be determined. An innovating firm with an entrepreneurial architecture should be able to combine its portfolio of core competencies in various ways to meet opportunities. Furthermore, it will have first-mover advantage and be well placed to dominate the new product/market (industry) it creates, exploit its monopoly or oligopoly position and create shareholder super-value.

➥ An aggressive acquisition strategy can be combined with internally generated innovations to produce diversification creep, minimizing the risks associated with new product/market development. The speed at which an acquisition can be executed allows rapid entry to these new product/market opportunities.

➡ By combining incremental and radical innovation, internal and external corporate venturing, and adopting a portfolio approach to product and business organization the risks associated with diversification can be minimized.

What might be described as related or unrelated products and markets is not always clear-cut, shading into grey, particularly in the areas of rapidly developing new technologies, where new markets are being created where none existed before. Five of the most successful entrepreneurial companies of the last couple of decades – the US tech giants Alphabet, Apple, Amazon, Facebook and Microsoft – have adopted strategies of diversification that are probably beginning to redefine their business scope (Case insight 15.4). This is happening through a combination of organic growth, internal corporate venturing and acquisition. Their moves into new areas have been incremental, bundling additional services to sell to existing customers, finding out about market acceptance of their new products experimentally – a form of market-testing. Often they have used acquisition to buy new customers as well as innovations. To see the proof that these processes create shareholder value in this new digital era you need look no further than the stock market success of these companies. They are all becoming multi-product/multimarket businesses. In the past, we might have described them as multinational conglomerates. In this new era where markets are redefining themselves, this is no longer a criticism.

SHAREHOLDER VALUE IN CONGLOMERATES

Investors are increasingly understanding of lengthy periods of low or no profit for companies with proprietary technology or companies (such as Uber and Airbnb) which might be creating new, enormous industries that they are able to dominate and then benefit from monopoly or oligopoly profits. In developing into conglomerates, the tech giants have often deployed both strategies. They have also found both economies of scale and scope to add further value for shareholders. The scale and scope of their activities are allowing them to dominate markets, wield excessive market power and stifle competition, often buying-out local competitors. For example, in 2017 Google was fined €2.4 billion by the EU Antitrust Commission for abusing its market position through promoting its own shopping service in search results. The following year, it was fined a further €4.34 billion for using its Android operating system to restrict competition by requiring smartphone and tablet manufacturers that use Android to exclusively pre-install several of Google's own applications (e.g., its search engine). Investors now expect some of the EU regulations to become law in the USA, ending these restrictive practices. When a market becomes too large, the strategy of market domination can threaten public good. However, these enormous profits can also insulate the tech giants from the short-term vagaries of the stock markets and allow them to push through with innovations that might have a longer-term payback. This conflicting role that the restrictive practices and price-setting power of monopolists and oligopolists can have, on the one hand creating market inefficiency but on the other encouraging innovation (for themselves and for others), is a paradox that is inherent in Schumpeter's 'perennial gale of creative destruction'.

> *Across every industry there is a creeping but relentless consolidation. Technology, globalization, finance and economies of scale drive even more mergers and rising market share for multinationals. Most big sectors – from oil to automotives to banking to airlines to supermarkets –are now highly concentrated. Many are, in effect, oligopolies.*
>
> Luke Johnson, Chairman Risk Capital Partners, *The Sunday Times*, 2 September 2018

Synergy also offers these multi-product/market businesses the opportunities to create shareholder value. Synergy can be obtained by creating linkages between activities, processes, knowledge and/or information which have been previously unconnected, or where the connection has been of a different type. To justify the claim of synergy in an acquisition, the acquiring company must really be able to create value by operating across multiple businesses and multiple markets and leveraging these synergies. The mere potential or existence of the linkages is insufficient; they must be operationalized. The venturing company must be able to coordinate management, reconciling conflicting cultures. It must be able to share resources and transfer capabilities more effectively than otherwise. The justification for the continuing existence of conglomerates relies on them adding real shareholder value in this way. And the opportunities for this are also increasing, with the tech companies mining data on our internet linked behaviors that can be used or even sold. The combination of these data with artificial intelligence is creating new opportunities and potential markets. The more data the better the algorithms and the better the services offered by the tech giants. Conventional sources of economies of scale and scope are being supplemented by this driver of competitive advantage.

However, creating shareholder value begs the question of 'How much value?' What is acceptable to a shareholder who values low-risk might not be acceptable to those willing to take high-risk. Are these speculators the investors the company should seek to attract? The issue here is to make clear what risks the company is facing and the things it is doing to mitigate them. But even then the frontier of where innovation meets financial markets is not calm, instead regularly generating financial 'bubbles'. Indeed, Janeway (2018) believes speculation and financial 'bubbles' are a necessary part of gaining the finance innovation needs:

The most powerful enabler of risk-taking at the frontier of innovation is the possibility of winning financially even if the funded project fails.

The unknown-unknowns are increasing and investors realize that they can never know enough and they only have a short window of opportunity to invest before others beat them to profits. Stock markets are a rough place.

What is more, creating shareholder value can create tensions with other stakeholders. Monopolies and oligopolies create value for shareholders, but usually at the expense of customers, competitors and society at large. Polluters create shareholder value by imposing costs on others and causing environmental degradation. Shareholder value might be increased, in the short term at least, by taking commercial risks or by unethical behaviour. (Is data mining unethical?) You might argue that none of these situations is sustainable and that corporations should be aiming to create sustainable shareholder value whilst adhering to CSR principles. Again, the issue here is to make it clear to stakeholders what those principles are.

CASE INSIGHT 15.3
Alphabet (4)

ACQUISITIONS, MONETIZATION AND KNOWLEDGE TRANSFER

Alphabet (previously Google) has become a technology conglomerate as it tries to work out which of the business opportunities it is pursuing, from driverless cars to healthcare, will produce a sustainable source of revenue in the future (see Alphabet (1): Case insight 5.4). None of this, however, guarantees that its search for a long-term future beyond internet advertising will yield results, or that the 3 per cent of revenues it spends on what it calls its 'other bets' will not be money wasted. Alphabet is trying to prolong its life by giving birth to other successful ventures, financed by the dominant market position of its major revenue-generating subsidiary, Google (whose history we chart in Case insight 16.1). However it is it is still trying to find business models that monetize the innovations it has developed. Despite its financial strength, the lack of a precedent for the type of technology conglomerate it is trying to create, the strength of its competitors and the vagueness of Alphabet's long-term aims add to the risk of failure (see Alphabet (2): Case insight 7.2). Alphabet's individual ventures do not have their own boards, and there are no equity arrangements to tie employees' rewards to the success of their units – and to Alphabet. Instead, Alphabet offers cash bonuses based upon the success in achieving significant milestones. Perhaps as a result, many engineers in the driverless car division are said to have left, often going to competitors offering more money.

Many of Alphabet's product/services originated through its long history of aggressive acquisition of smaller start-up companies – a history that antitrust regulators are beginning to see as stifling potential rivals. In the 18 years between 2001 and 2018, it acquired some 220 companies – an average of one every month. The company has proved to be excellent at creating linkages that transfer knowledge and capabilities within its structure – linkages that create synergy between existing market offerings and innovations that may prove to be the market offerings of the future. For example, the video-sharing website YouTube (now part of Google) was founded in 2005 and was purchased by Google some two years later for $1.65 billion, despite never having made any profits. Google monetized YouTube by introducing advertising. YouTube now earns advertising revenue from another Alphabet subsidiary, AdSense, which targets ads according to site content and audience. The majority of YouTube's videos are free to view, but there are exceptions, including subscription-based premium channels, film rentals and YouTube Premium, a subscription service offering ad-free access to the website and exclusive content.

These knowledge-transfer linkages extend to individuals and organizations such as universities that are not part of Alphabet and can take many years to yield results. Take, for example, the self-driving technology developed by Google and now established as a stand-alone subsidiary called Waymo. Its origins can be traced back to a Google-sponsored project coming out of the Stanford (University) Artificial Intelligence Laboratory. The director, Sebastian Thrun, is credited as the co-inventor of Google Street View, a technology now featured in Google Maps and Google Earth. He became the project leader for the self-driving technology project in Google's X Lab in 2009.

However, not all of the business and personal linkages prove successful. For example, Nest is a US manufacturer of smart home products including thermostats, smoke detectors, and security systems that Google purchased for $3.2 billion in 2014. The purchase was lauded as taking Google into new product/markets far removed from its core business, as well as being a significant business in its own right. Its founder, Tony Fadell, was thought to be held in high regard within Google and had been thought to be destined to become head of hardware for the entire group, particularly since he had been put in charge of Glass, Google's ailing 'smart-glass' venture. With the restructuring of Google, however, came a change in top management and a refocusing on the importance of revenue generation. Nest was given a narrower set of business goals and Fadell left in 2016. It is thought that the company even considered selling off Nest.

Alphabet is also seeing some internal politicking about where innovation is undertaken. Google itself has created its own hardware division and Sundar Pichai, Google's CEO, has assumed some of Fadell's responsibilities. Glass is now located within Google's hardware division. It is also developing virtual reality headsets as well as a device called Head – a voice-activated device that can act as a gatekeeper to the internet for traditional search functions but also as a hub for controlling the home – a market that Nest originally was set up to attack.

Visit the website: abc.xyz/investor

Questions:

1. Why is monetization and knowledge transfer important?
2. What role does corporate acquisition play in innovation within Google and Alphabet? How do you keep the entrepreneurs associated with an acquired company?
3. What are the strengths and weaknesses of Alphabet's approach to innovation? Do you foresee any problems ahead?

Most of the tech giants, arguably, have become conglomerates. The Chinese tech giant Tencent (Case insight 9.6) controls hundreds of subsidiaries and associates across a diverse range of businesses, from social media to film production, internet services to film production. It is also one of the most active investment corporations in the world, focusing on Asian tech start-ups. And technology can pull more traditional industries into domains with which they are unfamiliar. For example, internet-connected cars are pulling the automotive industry into the software business at the same time as autonomous vehicles are bringing the tech companies into the automotive and transport business – often resulting in partnership between companies in the two sectors. In financial services, most companies are also now investing heavily in digital innovations. For example, global insurer AXA has invested €100 million into a Venture Lab, called Kamet, with the goal of developing disruptive new insurance tech businesses; and the Santander Group has set up a $100 million fund called InnoVentures to make strategic investments in fintech products and services.

However, there are many examples of low-tech conglomerates that are able to obtain synergy across different products/markets. For example, the French company LVMH (Moët Hennessy Louis Vuitton) is the world's largest supplier of branded luxury goods. Its portfolio includes Moët et Chandon champagne (as well as other brands), Hennessy cognac, Louis Vuitton accessories and leather goods, Dior, Givenchy and Guerlain fashion clothes and perfumes, TAG Heuer and Chaumet watches, and Sephora (Case insight 10.2), to name but a few. Its distinctive capability is its ability to manage these luxury brands through market analysis, advertising, promotion, retail management and quality assurance. Economies of scope have emerged from these organizational capabilities. LVMH comprises some 60 subsidiary companies, often independently managed. Interestingly, whilst it is a public company, some 41 per cent of LVMH is owned by Christian Dior SE, a company owned by Bernard Arnault, who is Chairman and CEO of both companies.

Another example is the UK Virgin Group – a private company comprising a conglomerate of apparently disparate businesses. However, in reality it is a good example of a brand that has been applied to a wide range of diverse products, largely successfully, linking customers and their lifestyle aspirations. Economies of scope came from brand extension. The core competency of Virgin lies in the brand and associated marketing which often uses the founder, Richard Branson, to gain PR instead of expensive advertising – an approach that has been used by a number of start-ups. All Virgin companies sell to final customers. Virgin rarely undertakes 'production' in a new venture, relying instead on partners with developed expertise. Instead, it brings the strong Virgin brand and its associations to the partnership. No wonder it now describes itself as a 'branded venture capital company'.

CASE INSIGHT 15.4
New-to-the-world industries
USA

CONVERGING MARKETS: REDEFINING BUSINESS SCOPE

The boundary between markets/industries can become very blurred in the fast-moving technology-driven world of the internet, making the identification of competitors sometimes difficult. This is particularly the case when the real fight is for an emerging market that, as yet, is not formally defined. This is the case with the battle currently under way between the five US tech giants of the digital age: Amazon, Apple, Facebook, Google and Microsoft. In the past, these companies have provided hardware, software and various products and services, each content to 'stick to the knitting' and focus on its core market. However, new hardware such as smartphones and tablet computers linked by Wi-Fi and 4G/5G networks, and new software in the form of Apps, are breaking down these barriers and forcing the convergence of old markets. At the same time, the value of the personal data these companies have on their customers is coming to be realized.

The battle now is to become the sole provider of all our digital and physical requirements, offering a vast range of services tailored to our 'needs', all day, every day, anywhere, from the best online platform – a kind of 'digital utility' offering of 'universal internet services' that is also a portal to the physical world. That portal might also direct customers to the provider's own digital and physical products in preference to those of their competitors. The more products and services these companies offer, the more customers they are likely to attract, and the more advertising and 'click-through' revenue they are likely to earn. Add to that the recommendations and 'likes' that social media users might pass onto family and friends and sales might be further leveraged.

Yet the reward is not just the profit from the goods and services sold but also the digital footprint of users and customers (identified by their IP address) – their internet surfing and buying habits, likes and dislikes, times of day on the internet and even their location. All of this is collected automatically in real time. It is very valuable to both advertisers and salespeople, allowing algorithms to be used to offer targeted advertising at particular times of day in particular geographic areas, to particular users, based upon their digital histories. It can even anticipate their whims, allowing companies to send them unsolicited products on a 'trial-or-return' basis with a high probability of a sale being made. The more data that are collected and combined, the more powerful it becomes. For example, combining it with financial data (e.g., from credit cards) could provide opportunities for selling investments or personal credit scoring; similarly, combining it with health data could be valuable to insurance companies. The possibilities increase daily as our ability to use the data increases. To quote a recent newspaper article: 'Once we searched Google, but now Google searches us. Once we thought of digital services as free, but now surveillance capitalists think of us as free' (The Observer: The New Review, 20 January 2019).

Each of the US tech giants is coming to this new market from different existing markets with new products and services and very different strengths and core competences. All but Apple have been voracious acquirers of smaller tech companies, allowing them to develop new technologies and/or enter new markets. They are examples of networks that tend towards natural global monopoly in their particular niches. Most dominate and have monopoly power in their main markets and exploit this advantage. Alphabet and Facebook dominate the internet advertising market, securing well over 90 per cent of the revenue, and have been accused of stifling competition. The European Commission fined Google €2.4 billion in 2017 for abusing its market dominance as a search engine by giving illegal advantage to its own comparison shopping service, Google Shopping, whilst demoting the results of rival sites.

➡ Alphabet (formerly Google) started life as a search engine but Google has become the name for what we do when we search the internet for information. It is estimated to have 90 per cent of the search engine market. The company now offers many other services, such as maps and images. There is Gmail, Gmail+ which is designed to make this more social, in direct competition with Facebook, and the Google Chrome internet browser, not to mention its cloud-based services. Its Android smartphone operating system dominates the market with an estimated 87 per cent market share. The company now sells smartphones and tablet computers under the Google brand, although their manufacturing is subcontracted. It has Google Play offering music, games and other downloads. It owns YouTube, where you can watch and rent TV programmes and films, and has plans to launch Google TV. It also has its own online payment system called Google Wallet.

➡ Amazon started life selling books online and now sells almost everything and is even looking to break into the food market. It is exploring how to deliver physical products using land and air-based robots. With the introduction of the Kindle, which allowed the purchase and reading of books and films online, it entered the hardware market (it also subcontracts production). Models come pre-loaded with the customer's Amazon account details, making purchases easier, and with social networking that encourages interaction with others who purchase the same books and films. Amazon also has an App shop, an online payment system, TV and video streaming and a cloud computing facility. Through Amazon Prime it hopes to reach out to more of the market for digital products.

➡ Apple started life designing and manufacturing computers and has now become an iconic designer brand, offering premium-priced electronic gadgets ranging from computers to the iPod, iPad, iPhone and Apple Watch. It has its own closed operating systems: macOS for desktops, with 13 per cent market share and iOS for smartphones, with a 12 per cent share. Apple redefined how music was sold through iTunes. It has an App Store selling music, games and other Apps for its devices. There is also the web-enabled Apple TV and its own cloud computing facility. Apple is also established in China (although sales have stalled) and is sitting on a large mountain of cash, more than any of the other four companies. However, unlike the other companies, Apple has a track record of working on its own to grow. It is the only one of the tech giants with its own 'closed' operating system, iOS. It also has its own retail outlets.

➡ Facebook, the ubiquitous social network site, is the newcomer to this group. It has its own email system and photo- and video-sharing platform. It also offers a search service, based on the data provided by Facebook subscribers rather than computer algorithms. Although scandals in recent years have caused users to close accounts, it remains the dominant network and has expanded its reach with the acquisitions of Instagram and WhatsApp. It is constantly improving itself and now offers many of the features of Google+.

➡ Microsoft predates the other four companies and its MS-DOS operating system dominates the desktop market, with an 83 per cent share. It is also the supplier of the ubiquitous Windows Operating System and the Microsoft Office suite of software. It has the web browser Microsoft Edge, the search engine Bing, with 3 per cent market share, the MSN internet portal and the email system Outlook Express. Many computers come with its software and browser pre-loaded. It offers server applications and cloud computing services. It has the Xbox video gaming and entertainment system. It also markets computer hardware and game controllers. Arguably, it missed the internet revolution, and since then it has been playing catch-up by acquiring companies such as the search engine Bing and the video communications company Skype. It has also imitated Apple by opening its own retail outlets.

A similar pattern is emerging in China with three tech giants: Alibaba Group (Case insight 1.1), Tencent (Case insight 9.6) and Baidu. Baidu is similar to Google and offers a search engine (2 per cent market share), audio files, images and video, an encyclopaedia similar to Wikipedia and, importantly for China, a search service for government information and laws as well as access to shopping and e-commerce. Between them, these companies offer hardware and systems that control most of the internet search, social media and e-commerce transactions in China and as a result they hold even more data on users than their western competitors. The critical difference is that these companies operate in what is in effect a closed market and they have close links with the Chinese government. For example, whilst Google refused to renew contracts with the US Pentagon following extensive employee protests at the use of AI for military purposes, Baidu welcomes its military partnerships. They are also amassing large amounts of sophisticated data on Chinese citizens and, in contrast to their western counterparts, are willing to share it with the government. They are even using a tradeable social-credit system to incentivize citizens to 'do good'.

So, Amazon started life as an internet retailer and remains probably the largest retailer of physical products. Apple started as a tech hardware supplier and remains the premium brand for tech products. Facebook started as a social network and remains the dominant network. Google started as an internet search engine and is now established in most tech markets. Microsoft started as a software developer and remains the dominant operating system and provider of software. But questions still remain: Where will this convergence of competition lead? What will be needed to gain competitive advantage? Will there be only one winner? Will the winner(s) have a monopoly? If so, will they be more powerful than governments?

Questions:

1. Why are these product/markets converging?
2. How might you describe this new industry? What is its potential?
3. Do these new, emerging industries need government regulation? Explain.
4. The US and Chinese tech giants are in the same industry. However, they are not yet direct competitors. How do their markets differ? How might this change in the future? What might be the consequences?

ORGANIZATION STRUCTURE AND PRODUCT/MARKET PORTFOLIOS

This book has argued that the organizational architecture of an operating unit will be a key determinant of its success. In particular, an entrepreneurial architecture will be a key source of competitive advantage in a highly competitive and changing market. Although innovation will be part of the fabric of the organization, different forms of innovation may well require different organizational structures to encourage their development. For example, as we have seen, the organization structure required to facilitate continuous process development of a product in the mature stage of its life-cycle is quite different from that required to encourage radical innovation or a new-to-the-world invention. Strategies need to be developed for sourcing these new ideas. Do they come from internal or external sources, or both? Financing also needs to be addressed since the needs of different types of innovation, in terms of volume and nature (internal vs external finance and equity vs loan finance), may be quite different.

Diverse product/market portfolios can insulate a company from the risks associated with individual markets. As we have seen, a balanced portfolio can also provide the cash flow to finance innovation, and that can insulate it from the demands of the stock market. Having a portfolio of different product/market offerings begs the question as to how they might be organized. Should divisions with products at different stages of their life-cycle be segregated into different, separate organizations? Perhaps they should be grouped together to make the most of entrepreneurial expertise? And what happens as they progress through their life-cycle? Are they transferred to different organizations, delineated not by their product specification but by the stage they are at in their life-cycle and the managerial style therefore required, and at what point is the transfer made?

Management is an art not a science, so there are no prescriptive solutions to these problems – and there is often more than one solution to a problem. But there are some clues. As we have seen, size matters and new initiatives or ventures are better off – for all sorts of reasons – starting small. Small organizations can more easily encourage entrepreneurship. Whether they combine at some later stage depends on the synergy that might be obtained from combining them and their operational relatedness. 3M has different divisions into which new ventures are expected to be merged. Divisions might comprise different operating units or companies, each with product/market profiles that are different in significant ways, but they can be combined in some overriding way. New products might spawn new companies or be swallowed up into existing operating units or companies. Xerox has so many completely different new ventures that it is far more relaxed about spinning out completely different companies. The point is that, currently, synergy is unlikely to be achieved by combining them. Indeed, in these circumstances completely spinning off, and even selling off, subsidiaries that are not core to the business may be an appropriate option. There is no prescriptive blueprint. Furthermore, when these changes take place is an even more complex judgement that depends on individuals as well as products, markets and competitors combined with an array of external factors, many of which will be outside the control of the company.

The real issue, then, is the form of the umbrella organization – head office, parent company, whatever it is called. Unless it is essentially entrepreneurial, this diversity will just not happen. The organizational solution outlined in Chapter 5 is the use of a hybrid organic structure that combines different organizational forms within an overall organic structure (Figure 5.7). The umbrella organization must be able to handle this heterogeneous approach to management with different styles of leadership, structures and cultures in different subsidiaries or divisions. Essentially, it must be willing to delegate day-to-day management, within defined parameters, to these subsidiaries or divisions and it must be able to deal with the apparent inconsistencies this can generate. However, there are different approaches to this, each of which produces a different dominant culture. Case insight 8.1 (BP) showed one approach – that of trying to maintain balance within each operating unit belonging to one organization. By way of contrast, as we saw in Case insight 8.4, the Virgin empire thrives on entirely separate organizations sharing the same culture and brand, but little else.

An entrepreneurial public company operating in a range of different product/markets faces the danger of being seen as a conglomerate of unconnected operations. If it is, then its share price is likely to be discounted. The company must, therefore, be able to unify diverse management and share resources and capabilities more effectively than otherwise. It needs to be adept at communicating its core competencies and strategies to shareholders what are and to explain how its entrepreneurial architecture contributes to its ability to innovate and create competitive advantage. It needs to be able to explain the synergies it is currently achieving from its diversified position and those that might evolve as the product/markets it is pioneering develop. It needs to be politically astute, particularly if it is aiming to dominate newly emerging market spaces. That involves being adept at dealing with governments and the general public: paying appropriate taxes, and acting in an ethical and socially responsible manner. Commercial success brings with it new responsibilities.

CASE INSIGHT 15.5
Planet Innovation

CORPORATE ENTREPRENEURSHIP

Planet Innovation (PI) is seen as one of the most innovative companies in Australia. It was founded in 2009 by Stuart Elliott, Sam Lanyon, Troy O'Callaghan and Eduardo Vom, initially as an innovation and commercialization consultancy but it pivoted to manufacturing in 2014. The founders had previously started up the cancer diagnostics manufacturer Vision Biosystems, whose parent, Vision Systems, sold it to the US conglomerate Danaher Corporation for $815 million in 2006. PI remains a private company and now has over 250 employees, with an office in the USA and its own portfolio of businesses.

PI focuses on providing technology-based solutions to niche, but critical problems within large, fast-growing global markets, such as energy consumption and healthcare. It uses its skills and capabilities to incubate, grow and, at the right time, spin-off new ventures as independent entities, including securing direct capital funding to provide financial independence. Its approach involves the creative synthesis of markets and technology by gathering market insight before building the technology solutions. PI's broad-based team offers expertise in research, design, engineering, manufacturing, funding and marketing new products globally. It uses a methodology it calls the PI Playbook™ to develop and launch new ventures. This involves five stages: Incubation (identifying the niche opportunity); Developing the MVP; Market-testing and data gathering; Data analysis for machine learning; and Launch. It also partners with other organizations to help them create innovations to grow their business.

PI has four business divisions:

PI Design services – which provides services for the development of regulated biomedical products and technology-based connected devices; exploiting the technology convergence between sectors such as diagnostics, life sciences, medical devices, digital health, industrial and consumer products. Its clients include larger biotech companies.

PI Manufacturing services – which manufactures its regulated products.

PI Labs – which incubates early-stage ventures. It specializes in providing market insight and rapid time-to-market and lean methodologies so as to quickly generate early customers.

PI Businesses – PI's strategy is to incubate, grow and, at the right time, spin off high-value technology businesses as independent entities. As each venture reaches an appropriate level of maturity it is spun off from PI as a stand-alone entity, including securing direct capital funding to provide financial independence. PI already has a portfolio of four high-growth ventures that were spun out from PI Labs:

➡ Zen Ecosystems: An intelligent cloud-based energy management solution, connected to a smart thermostat, targeting commercial buildings, particularly in the USA. It is a low-cost alternative to Alphabet's Nest and contributed Aus$3.7 million to PI's Aus$47.8 million revenue in 2016–17.

➡ Lumos Diagnostics: A platform technology that combines low-cost point-of-care diagnostic testing for a wide range of applications (e.g., infectious diseases, cardiac, cancer, drug abuse and fertility) with solutions.

➡ Vitalic Medical: A connected health monitoring platform that helps to improve patient management.

➡ Atmo Biosciences: A ingestible gas–sensing capsule that provides a low-cost way of diagnosing and treating common gastrointestinal disorders via a hand-held receiver and mobile app. The capsule is licenced from RMIT University.

PI has delivered 10 years of consistent profitability and growth and in each of the past two years has delivered more than Aus$7m in free cash flows; however, its profit of Aus$4.1 million in 2016–17 was dwarfed by its R&D investment of Aus$5 million. It approaches innovation with six principles that it believes aligns its goals and behaviours with those of its clients:

1. Consider the whole journey, start with the end in mind – an idea for how the product will be commercialized.
2. Assume nothing, let the market drive your innovation – this allows you to identify the MVP needed to enter a market.
3. Resist the temptation to design while you innovate – early-stage research and proof of concept doesn't have to look like a designed product.
4. Align your goals, focus on products, not projects – treat partners as partners sharing goals, risks and incentives.
5. Reduce risk by turning big projects into small projects – each with its own set of clear objectives, activities and deliverables. The initial stage is all about proving the technical and commercial feasibility.
6. Reuse rather than reinvent – integrating existing components or systems can reduce development costs and deliver more reliable products to market faster.

PI describes its employees as 'friendly, talented and experienced':

> We have some of the brightest people on the planet, who also happen to bike, bake, ski and play together. And if you like a bit of friendly competition you will find a basketball game or robot challenge with your name on it.

PI describes its leadership style as 'open, accessible and authentic – we know that our success comes from your success'. Nevertheless, it wants employees to 'push' themselves and 'explore new roles and new opportunities'. It describes its focus on medical and energy innovation as 'areas where we can make a positive impact on society'. It believes that, since its business is entrepreneurial innovation, it should recruit entrepreneurial people with a 'start-up spirit':

> We believe that to attract and retain the best people in the world, we need to provide an environment that is fun, challenging and allows people's talents to shine. We encourage all our staff to look deeply into growing markets and challenge the status quo. We support them as they find unmet market needs and suggest new product and commercial ideas. This is the true spirit of entrepreneurship and the heart and soul of Planet Innovation. (https://planetinnovation.com/about/)

Visit the website: **planetinnovation.com**

Questions:

1. What elements of an entrepreneurial architecture can you spot in PI?
2. From the information given, how would you describe the culture in PI?
3. What similarities and/or differences do you see between the PI Playbook™ and the lean methodologies outlined in this book?
4. What do you think of PI's six principles? Are they consistent with the methodologies outlined in this book?
5. What are the synergies in PI's portfolio of activities?
6. What pressures would the company face if it were to become a public company?

SUMMARY

➡ Most firms have a range of products and services at different stages of their life-cycle, each tailored to the particular needs of their market place. These can be represented in the growth-share matrix – a loose conceptual framework that helps clarify the complexity of the portfolio. The two axes of the matrix represent market attractiveness and market strength. Products at different points in the matrix have different strategic imperatives and different marketing strategies.

➡ The product life-cycle and its journey through the matrix can be extended through product modification, expansion and extension.

➡ The growth-share matrix has cash-flow implications; Problem Children use cash, Stars are cash-neutral, generating but also using large amounts, and Cash Cows generate cash. Only when the portfolio is balanced will cash flow be stable. If the portfolio comprises independent product/market offerings the risks facing the company are reduced.

➡ Companies operating in multi-product/markets are called conglomerates and traditionally trade on stock markets at a discount, even if their product/market offerings are independent of each other, because they are seen as difficult to manage with synergistic gain often not realized.

➡ Internal and/or external corporate venturing often leads to diversification and this leads to the development of a conglomerate. However, in entrepreneurial firms this can create shareholder value. Unwanted innovations or SBUs might be sold off and/or new product/markets might offer high margins through first-mover advantage or the possibility of creating new-to-the-world industries. By combining incremental and radical innovation, internal and external corporate venturing, encouraging diversification creep and adopting a portfolio approach to product and business organization the risks associated with diversification can be minimized.

➡ Entrepreneurial multi-product/market conglomerates such as the tech giants can also create synergy by developing linkages between activities, processes, knowledge and information which have been previously unconnected or where linkages were not considered possible.

➡ In order to achieve this, multi-product/market conglomerates must be able to operate effectively across all their operating units – unifying diverse management and sharing knowledge, capabilities and other resources more effectively than might otherwise be the case. They must develop an entrepreneurial architecture.

GROUP DISCUSSION QUESTIONS

1. In practical terms it is impossible to find out where a product is at in its life-cycle. Discuss.
2. How would you go about creating a scale for each axis of the growth-share matrix that reflects a range of relevant factors? Give a practical example.
3. In what circumstances might you not want to 'shoot a Dog'?
4. Give some examples of product expansions and extensions.
5. Can a Problem Child be profitable? Explain.
6. Will a Star always be profitable? Explain.
7. In what circumstances might you retain a Cash Cow that is unprofitable? What would you do with it?
8. Is there a relationship between the growth-share matrix and organizational architecture? Explain.
9. What part does luck play in both internal and external corporate venturing?
10. Why is diversification creep low risk and how does it create shareholder value?
11. Diversified companies underperform focused companies. Discuss.
12. What is a conglomerate? How do you define an industry?

13. There are many examples of private family firms that are conglomerates. Why are these any different than companies quoted on the stock exchange?
14. What is needed for a conglomerate to be successful and create shareholder value?
15. What is synergy? Give examples of how it might be created.
16. How do you go about creating the linkages needed to facilitate knowledge transfer?
17. How do you go about creating a hybrid organic structure for an organization? How can it be sustained?
18. Even a hybrid organic organizational structure needs a leader. How do they go about leading subsidiaries or divisions that may not be entrepreneurial and have more traditional bureaucratic structures?
19. What information synergies can the tech giants create? What is the commercial opportunity they create?
20. What are the characteristics of the new industry or industries being formed by the tech giants? What are the implications?

ACTIVITIES

1. For your university, college or department, analyze the course portfolio using the growth-share matrix. What are your conclusions?
2. For a selected company, analyze the product portfolio using the growth-share matrix. What are your conclusions?
3. Select a well-known product/service that is now in the mature phase of its life-cycle and it is now a Cash Cow and analyze how the cash it generates is being used in other parts of the product/market portfolio. If it is being used to buy back shares, why do you think this is?
4. Select a conglomerate quoted on the stock exchange and analyze the profitability/cash-flow of its subsidiaries. Overall, is it generating surplus cash and where is this going? If it is being used to buy-back shares, why do you think this is?
5. Select a conglomerate quoted on the stock exchange and evaluate the reasons it claims to create added value for its shareholders. Is the company successful?

REFERENCES

Abell, D.F. (1980) *Defining the Business*, Hemel Hempstead: Prentice Hall.
Bowman, C. and Faulkner, D. (1997) *Competitive and Corporate Strategy*, London: Irwin.
Janeway, W.H. (2018) *Doing Capitalism in the Innovation Economy*, Cambridge: Cambridge University Press.
Levy, H. and Sarnat, M. (1970) 'Diversification, Portfolio Analysis and the Uneasy Case for Conglomerate Mergers', *Journal of Finance*, 25.
Luffman, G.A. Reed, R. (1984) *The Strategy and Performance of British Industry*, Basingstoke: Macmillan.
Mason, R.H. and Goudzwaard, M.B. (1976) 'Performance of Conglomerate Firms: A Portfolio Approach', *Journal of Finance*, 31.
Michel, A. and Shaked, I. (1984) 'Does Business Diversification Affect Performance?', *Financial Management*, 13(4).
Park, C. (2002) 'The Effects of Prior Performance on the Choice Between Related and Unrelated Acquisitions', *Journal of Management Studies*, 39.
Peters, T.J. and Waterman, R.H. (1982) *In Search of Excellence*, London: Harper & Row.
Porter, M.E. (1987) 'From Competitive Advantage to Competitive Strategy', *Harvard Business Review*, 65(3).
Wernerfelt, B. and Montgomery, C.A. (1986) 'What Is an Attractive Industry?', *Management Science*, 32.
Weston, J.F., Smith, K.V. and Shrieves, R.E. (1972) 'Conglomerate Performance Using the Capital Asset Pricing Model', *Review of Economics and Statistics*, 54.

ONLINE RESOURCES AVAILABLE For further resources relating to this chapter see the companion website at **www.macmillanihe.com/Burns-CEI**

Summary: The Corporate Entrepreneurship Audit

16

CONTENTS

- Entrepreneurial architecture
- Cultural characteristics of an entrepreneurial organization
- Structural characteristics of an entrepreneurial organization
- Leadership characteristics for an entrepreneurial organization
- Strategies for an entrepreneurial organization
- Environment for an entrepreneurial organization
- Corporate Entrepreneurship Audit
- Group discussion topics
- Activity
- References

CASE INSIGHTS

Learning outcomes

When you have read this chapter and undertaken the related activities you will be able to:

➡ Synthesize the elements of an entrepreneurial architecture and understand the environment where it is appropriate;

➡ Undertake an audit of the architecture of an organization;

➡ Critically analyze the architecture of an organization and determine whether it is 'entrepreneurial';

➡ Critically analyze the environment within which an organization operates and determine whether an entrepreneurial architecture is appropriate.

ENTREPRENEURIAL ARCHITECTURE

Entrepreneurial architecture comprises four elements or pillars: leadership and management, culture, structures and strategies (Figure 2.3). Combined so as to match the challenges of the competitive environment, they form a powerful force to develop sustainable competitive advantage and in particular the ability to innovate continuously. Kay (1995) identified three capabilities that he said formed the basis for sustainable competitive advantage. All three may be viewed as part of the entrepreneurial architecture defined in this book. The three capabilities are:

➡ Reputation – This is often encapsulated in brand identity but equally can be communicated through the relationships embedded in the architecture.
➡ The way the organization innovates – This is one of the defining characteristics of the organization's entrepreneurial architecture enabling innovation to take place again and again and again.
➡ The organization's strategic assets – These are the ones to which competitors do not have access. However, the most valuable is likely to be its entrepreneurial architecture because it is a multilevel activity and therefore difficult to copy.

So just what does an entrepreneurial organization look like? Whilst there is no one-size-fits-all blueprint, there are some elements that mean you really will know one when you see one. To start with, it will be creative and innovative, priding itself on its ability to thrive in a competitive, changing environment. Indeed, it will see itself as helping to shape that environment. And it will be successful. But there will be other internal characteristics reflecting an organizational architecture that encourages entrepreneurial, innovative activity at all levels. Remember, however, that not all parts of a multi-product, multimarket business organization may exhibit these characteristics because their operational needs (for example, the stage in the life-cycle of products) and/or their contextual situations are different (for example, they do not operate in an entrepreneurial environment). We have characterized the entrepreneurial environment as highly competitive, one of rapid change and uncertainty where speed of response and innovation are vital and knowledge and learning are of paramount importance. Where a multi-product, multimarket business has different organizational needs in its various operating divisions or subsidiaries, what is important is that the overarching structure linking the operating divisions or subsidiaries has an entrepreneurial architecture.

CULTURAL CHARACTERISTICS OF AN ENTREPRENEURIAL ORGANIZATION

Establishing an appropriate corporate culture is vital if you want to develop an entrepreneurial organization. Based on values, norms and beliefs, it influences individual and social behavioural norms. The culture should see change as the norm, certainly not something to be feared. Above all, it should value strong relationships, creativity and innovation, empowerment, measured risk-taking through experimentation and continual learning. It should value relationships sufficiently to generate a strong sense of group identity. It should have confidence in its future. It should be egalitarian but slightly anti-authoritarian – always daring to be different.

It will tolerate mistakes and should encourage learning from them. Individuals should feel empowered and motivated to make decisions for the good of the organization. Indeed, decision-making will be delegated down, as far as possible, and information will be shared rather than hoarded. There will be a 'can-do' attitude around that values achievement.

A strong organizational culture is particularly necessary because of the informal organization structure and loose management control. The culture needs to build a strong identity (Hofstede's in-group). This can be built around the vision for the organization as well as its recognizable values, norms and beliefs. It needs to be consistent with the leadership and management style adopted within the organization.

In Hofstede's dimensions, the organizational culture should exhibit:

➥ Balance between individualism and collectivism, implying that whilst individual initiative is valued so too are cooperative relationships and networks with a strong sense of 'in-group', and a clear identity and a feeling of competition against 'out-groups';
➥ Low power distance, implying an egalitarian organization with flat structures and open and informal relationships and open, unrestricted information flows;
➥ Low uncertainty avoidance, implying a tolerance of risk and ambiguity, a preference for flexibility and an empowered culture that rewards personal and team initiative;
➥ Balance between masculine and feminine dimensions, implying encouragement to build a culture of achievement against out-groups through co-operation, networks and relationships within the in-group.

Tables 1.1 and 2.2 listed the entrepreneurial characteristics that need to be replicated in an entrepreneurial architecture. These are reflected in the checklist in Table 16.1. They are characteristics that should encourage personal empowerment and general innovation. Some of these characteristics will be replicated in the other three pillars of architecture as it is important that the pillars are consistent and reinforce each other.

Table 16.1 Culture characteristics of an entrepreneurial organization

1. The organization encourages entrepreneurial risk-taking.
2. The organization is an empowering one.
3. The organization sees change as normal.
4. The organization encourages staff to build relationships at all levels.
5. The organization encourages creativity and innovation.
6. The organization encourages continuous innovation.
7. The organization is egalitarian.
8. The organization is tolerant of mistakes.
9. The organization encourages and facilitates delegated decision-making.
10. The organization encourages team working.
11. The organization encourages internal information and knowledge sharing.
12. The organization encourages building networks of relationships with external people and organizations.

13. The organization encourages continual learning from both inside and outside.

14. The organization encourages experimentation.

15. The organization celebrates success.

16. The organization is informal.

17. The organization is achievement-orientated.

18. There is time for learning and innovation.

19. The organization encourages strategizing.

20. People are valued in the organization.

21. Staff feel responsible for the future of the organization.

22. Staff feel they 'belong' to the organization.

23. The voice of the customer is important.

24. The voice of the supplier is important.

25. The organization encourages open communication, top-down, bottom-up and across the organization.

Figure 16.1 reproduces the typical cultural web for an entrepreneurial organization (Figure 4.4), with the core elements highlighted in blue at the centre of the web.

Figure 16.1 The cultural web of an entrepreneurial organization

STRUCTURAL CHARACTERISTICS OF AN ENTREPRENEURIAL ORGANIZATION

Structure is needed to create order within an organization but the most appropriate one depends on many other factors, such as the nature of its tasks or operations and the culture it wishes to encourage. There is no single 'best' structure. Entrepreneurial organizations typically face a high degree of environmental uncertainty and turbulence. If the tasks or operations they need to undertake are complex, they are best served by an organic organizational structure that may well change and evolve in different situations. An organic structure is like a spider's web made up of smaller spider's webs – teams working with other teams – with membership based upon expertise, not role, and each with considerable autonomy. It works well with an empowered, entrepreneurial culture.

The common themes are that an entrepreneurial structure must be flexible to fit changing circumstances, with structures within structures that encourage smaller, often informal, organic structures to develop, each with considerable autonomy (see for example Figures 5.5, 5.6 and 5.7). As the levels of formal hierarchy are reduced, the managerial span of control will widen, with an emphasis on getting things done. The processes underlying how the different levels of hierarchy interact and communicate is just as important as the structure itself. They should encourage rapid, open, effective communication across and throughout the organization, so that decision-making can be delegated as much as possible, giving staff greater autonomy and looser control, albeit with greater accountability. Structures, behaviours, even controls are likely to be more informal than formal, based on strong relationships. It certainly will not be bureaucratic in any way. There should be an emphasis on flexible team working and open communication, with team-based, project-based and process-based structures.

Entrepreneurial organizations are likely to exhibit other organizational characteristics or forms:

➡ Structures to encourage and facilitate intrapreneurship, including project and venture teams;
➡ Facilities that can be used to encourage creative thinking and project experimentation and development;
➡ Structures to encourage and facilitate internal and external corporate venturing;
➡ Participation in numerous formal and informal, real and virtual networks, including crowdsourcing and open innovation;
➡ Strategic alliances/partnerships and joint ventures with other organizations, including licensing of technologies etc.;
➡ Relatively autonomous Strategic Business Units and a track record of spin-offs.

Organic structures are not appropriate for all organizations and it is probable that a multi-product multimarket business will need to have different operating divisions or subsidiaries with more traditional structures, reflecting their different capabilities and operating environments. What might emerge is a hybrid-organic structure with operating divisions or subsidiaries being relatively autonomous but linked to head office through an organic structure with entrepreneurial architecture.

Tables 2.1 and 2.2 listed the entrepreneurial characteristics that need to be replicated in the structures of an entrepreneurial architecture. These were combined with characteristics taken from other chapters and are reflected in the checklist in Table 16.2. Some characteristics will be replicated in the other three pillars of architecture as it is important that the pillars are consistent and reinforce each other.

Table 16.2 Structural characteristics of an entrepreneurial organization

1. The senior management team (head office) are organized organically.
2. The organization is broken down into small sub-structures.
3. The organization is *not* hierarchical.
4. The organization is *not* bureaucratic.
5. The organization structure is flexible.
6. Spans of management control are broad.
7. There is loose organizational control but tight accountability.
8. Team working is encouraged and facilitated.
9. The organization participates in strategic alliances, partnerships and/or joint ventures.
10. The organization has developed and participates in a number of professional networks.
11. There is a new venture unit, department and/or division.
12. Intrapreneurs and/or cross-functional venture teams are used to take new business ideas forward.
13. Structures encourage intrapreneurship.
14. Structures encourage delegated decision-making.
15. Operating divisions or subsidiaries are relatively autonomous.
16. There are facilities that encourage creative thinking.
17. There are facilities that encourage and facilitate internal and external corporate venturing.
18. Crowdsourcing and open innovation are encouraged and facilitated.
19. There have been spin-offs from new venture activities.
20. There are structures that provide resources for new venture activities.
21. There are structures to facilitate continuous innovation.
22. There are structures to encourage and facilitate training and development.
23. There is an R&D department and/or budget.
24. Entrepreneurship is recognised and rewarded.
25. There are structures to monitor and manage risk.

LEADERSHIP CHARACTERISTICS FOR AN ENTREPRENEURIAL ORGANIZATION

We know that effective leadership and management styles depend upon a range of contextual factors, including group, task and situation. Whilst there is therefore no blueprint for success, we have characterized good leadership in an entrepreneurial environment as visionary, transformational but distributed (team-based). The high-level leadership team ideally comprises just half a dozen executives who trust each other, share information and cover for each other. That model is replicated across the entire organization. To be effective, leaders need to have good emotional intelligence – both self- and social awareness as well as good social skills. The 10 characteristics of a good leader in an entrepreneurial organization are set out below:

1. Visionary – They should be driven by a strong vision, underpinned by equally strong values. However, this vision should be grounded in sufficient reality to make the vision appear achievable, albeit causing some tension.

2. Good communicator/motivator – They should be able to communicate this vision effectively, through many mechanisms, but particularly informal influence. They should lead by example – 'walking-the-talk'. They should, somehow, embody the vision and values that they have for the organization. Staff motivation should be underpinned by loyalty to both the leader and the organization.

3. Strategic thinker and learner – They should be a strategic thinker, able to rise above day-to-day crises and see the bigger picture, perpetually scanning the environment for both opportunities and risks. They should be a strategic learner, trying to find patterns in the environment over time and looking for complex interactions so as to understand the underlying causes that give clues about the opportunities and risks. They should be continually strategizing and developing strategic options for the organization.

4. Emotionally intelligent with strong interpersonal skills – They should be able to listen, to influence others rather than to direct, and therefore be able to manage 'with a light touch'. They should be adept at reconciling conflict and dealing with ambiguity and uncertainty. To be emotionally intelligent, they should be self-aware and reflective. They also need to exercise a degree of self-management. And again, they should walk-the-talk, modelling the behaviour they expect from others.

5. Relationship builder – They should be adept at using their emotional intelligence and interpersonal skills to building strong personal relationships with all the stakeholders in the organization. This will have been built up by acting consistently over time based upon a dominant set of values, so as to generate trust. The leader should be firm but fair with staff and care and respect them.

6. Team player – They should value team working and be a team player, willing to share information and delegate to the team. They should have built a cohesive, open and trusting top management team, although that might comprise just three or four individuals who share knowledge. Furthermore, although having specialized roles, they are able to cover for one another. This team structure should be replicated throughout the organization.

7. Builder of confidence – They should be able to encourage organizational self-confidence and self-efficacy in the face of uncertainty and risk-taking. They should be able to inspire others to share their visions and dreams through their emotional intelligence and ability to build relationships.

8. Builder of an open organization that shares information – They should encourage the sharing of knowledge, information and ideas. They should encourage staff to develop the discovery skills of associating, questioning, observing, experimenting and networking. Staff will require a degree of space or slack to be able to do this. The leader

should encourage staff to question their own mental models through continual learning and also the dominant logic of the organization. Staff should be involved in networks both inside and outside the organization and there should be organizational initiatives that bring outsiders with different ideas and perspectives into the organization. Experimentation should be encouraged and failure learned from rather than penalized.

9. Clarifier of ambiguity and uncertainty – They should be able to give a clear focus on the key issues and concerns facing the organization in the face of rapid change. This comes from their ability to be a strategic thinker and an effective communicator.

10. Builder of empowering opportunities – They should be able to make staff want to do 'the right thing' for the organization without necessarily being asked. Staff should feel empowered to do this, having the knowledge, skills, and motivation, without fearing that they will be countermanded or penalized for using their initiative or making an unintended mistake.

Table 16.3 lists the characteristics that need to be shown by the leader of an entrepreneurial organization. These were taken primarily from Chapters 6 and 7. They are characteristics that reinforce other pillars of the organizational architecture. These characteristics do, however, need to be adapted to suit the circumstances facing particular organizations, consistent with contingency theory.

Table 16.3 Leadership characteristics of an entrepreneurial organization

1. There is a clear vision for the organization.
2. Senior managers model the vision and values of the organization – they walk-the-talk.
3. The vision for the organization is clearly communicated.
4. There are clear values underpinning everything the organization does.
5. There is a clear strategy for achieving the vision.
6. The vision is realistic and achievable but stretching.
7. There is an understanding of the opportunities and threats that the organization faces.
8. The organization has strategic options for the future.
9. Senior managers work as a team.
10. Senior managers are accessible and approachable.
11. Senior managers listen.
12. Senior managers influence rather than direct; they manage with a 'light touch'.
13. Senior managers are good at reconciling conflict.
14. Senior managers are good at clarifying uncertainties going forward, focusing effort on important things.
15. Senior managers are reflective and self-aware.

16. Senior managers have good relationships with staff.
17. Senior managers show care and respect for staff.
18. Senior managers are trustworthy.
19. Senior managers are consistent in their behaviour with staff.
20. Senior managers think and act strategically.
21. Team working is encouraged in the organization.
22. Cross-functional team working is commonplace in the organization.
23. Information and knowledge is shared in the organization.
24. Senior managers empower people to deal with problems and opportunities.
25. Decision-making is delegated.

STRATEGIES FOR AN ENTREPRENEURIAL ORGANIZATION

The strategies that an organization pursues are particular to its situation and difficult to generalize. However, an entrepreneurial organization faces a complex and inherently unpredictable environment and is likely to develop strategy in a certain way and to be pursuing a number of typical strategies. These are the common themes:

1. Strategy development might be either emergent or deliberate, but characterized by continuous strategizing at all levels in the organization, underpinned by a strong vision and sense of direction. This vision should be ambitious but rooted in reality, creating a tension sufficient to motivate the organization to change. The organization will be good at scanning the environment for opportunities and threats. Strategic options will be available and there may be a strong strategic intent if the vision is particularly challenging. Strategy will come from both the top and the bottom of the organization with a strong involvement of all levels of management.
2. Decision-making will tend to be decentralized, incremental and adaptive, so as to maintain maximum flexibility. But it should be underpinned by the strong vision and an understanding of the strategies being adopted to achieve the vision. There may be some simple rules that provide guidance, but staff will know enough about the organization and be motivated to do the best they can. Mistakes will be tolerated and learned from. In this way, the organization will be able to respond speedily to opportunities or threats.
3. The organization will understand its strengths and its core competencies at both corporate and business levels. At the corporate level, a major strategic imperative will be the continuing development of its entrepreneurial architecture, and all that entails. If it is pursuing a policy of acquisition this should be part of a coherent strategy (for example, as part of buying into new markets, product developments or developing industries). If it is a multi-product multi-market business, it will create value by operating effectively and creating synergistic linkages across all the operating units – unifying diverse management and sharing resources, capabilities and knowledge more effectively than might otherwise be the case.

4. At the business level, this will display itself as having an inherent understanding of the basis of its competitive advantage and an understanding of how customer and shareholder value can be enhanced. There will be an understanding of marketing issues such as differentiation, branding, pricing, customer focus and product life-cycles. Customer needs and competitors will be monitored continuously. If there is a portfolio of products/ services, these will be managed strategically as a coherent portfolio.

5. The organization should have strategies to encourage internal growth through innovation, new product or service developments and entry into new markets. These developments should be continuous and incremental with some discontinuous or radical innovations. Both types of innovation are required, often simultaneously. This requires facilitating structures. There should also be an emphasis on continual improvement. The organization should be willing to experiment and take measured risks, but should identify and monitor them, learning from any mistakes. Revenue and profit growth is likely to come mainly from these internal developments and then used for the more radical innovations.

6. There should be a strategy to encourage creativity with a commercial focus. Strategies to encourage creativity are likely to encourage development of the discovery skills of associating, questioning, observing, experimenting and networking, in particular they bring diverse outside influences into the organization. They should encourage the questioning of existing marketing paradigms, questioning sectoral, performance and customer conventions.

7. There should be a strategy to encourage innovation. Strategies to encourage innovation are likely to include internal and external corporate venturing, networking, strategic alliances/partnerships and joint ventures. There should be a strategy for mitigating the risks associated with innovation, particularly disruptive innovation, such as experimentation, limited launches, joint ventures and compartmentalization. The organization should take a portfolio approach to its innovative activities.

Just because an organization has an appropriate entrepreneurial architecture does not guarantee that it will be successful. Survival might be a badge of success in some circumstances. Bad luck, in particular completely unpredictable events, always plays a part. There is no certainty in life, no matter how thorough an organization might be in trying to predict and prepare for the future. All we can ever do in business is play the odds. In order to better understand the architecture, it is quite probable that we will need to delve deeper into the organization.

A good starting point is always to better understand the degree of innovative intensity within the organization, measured in terms of scale and frequency of innovation. Figure 16.2 shows a map of all the incidents of innovation over the last year for a hypothetical company. This tells you about the nature and extent of innovative activity taking place in the organization. It shows that our hypothetical company had four small-scale innovations in addition to one major and one radical innovation. You can then investigate these innovations in further detail and arrive at an assessment. For example, numerous incremental innovations may not have been a sufficient response in an industry facing disruptive innovation. However, if they relate to products at the end of their life-cycle it may be the appropriate product strategy. The innovation strategy needs to be

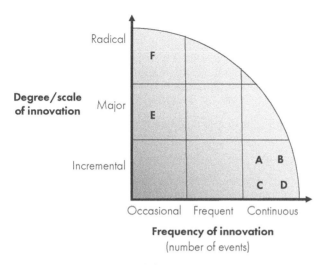

Figure 16.2 A specimen innovation portfolio

placed in the context of the company's product portfolio and the market challenges it faces.

The next step is to better understand the organization's growth strategy and, in particular, the nature of its shifts in developing new products and new markets (Figure 16.3a) and the strategies it has pursued to develop these (Figure 16.3b). As well as looking at the past (the last year), we need to look to the future and the planned outcomes of the existing strategies represented in these Figures. This should be built upon an understanding of the

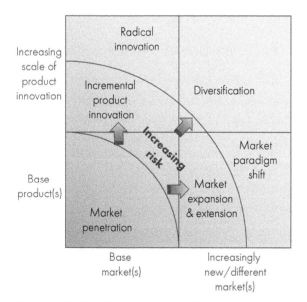

Figure 16.3a Product/market development typologies

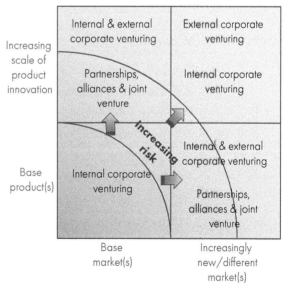

Figure 16.3b Corporate venturing and risk

organization's existing product/service portfolio and how it might be developed. You can then critically evaluate these strategies, the risks associated with them and the safeguards to provide early warning signs and deal with them. Are the strategies coherent and consistent with the firm's vision/mission and its core strengths or competencies? Is there a coherent strategic rationale for any acquisitions? Does the organization have the resources to undertake these strategies?

It is one thing to describe this 'mythical beast' of an entrepreneurial organization, but quite another to create one. And the most difficult task of all is to turn around an existing organization so as to become one – a really challenging exercise in change management. This sort of turnaround is often only possible when the organization itself faces an imminent crisis, such as one of survival. If entrepreneurs are the super-heroes of the business world, what does that make those who practice corporate entrepreneurship?

Whilst the strategies being pursued by an organization will be specific to the circumstances it faces, Table 16.4 lists some of the general characteristics of the strategies and approaches to strategy development that are likely to be seen in an entrepreneurial organization.

Table 16.4 Characteristics of strategies likely to be seen in an entrepreneurial organization

---

1. There is a clear vision for the organization that is realistic and achievable but stretching.
2. There are clear values underpinning everything the organization does.
3. There is a clear strategy for achieving the vision.
4. The vision is realistic and achievable but stretching.
5. There are clear strategic objectives.
6. Staff are encouraged to strategize.
7. Staff are encouraged to spot commercial opportunities for the organization.
8. Strategy development is both top-down and bottom-up, involving everyone.
9. There is an understanding of the opportunities and threats that the organization faces.
10. There are strategic options for the future.
11. Decision-making is decentralized, incremental and adaptive.
12. There is an understanding of the organization's core competencies.
13. Encouraging entrepreneurship is central to the organization's strategy.
14. There is an understanding of the basis for competitive advantage in the organization's different markets.
15. There are strategies to encourage and facilitate innovation.
16. There are strategies to encourage and facilitate commercially orientated creativity.
17. There are strategies and structures to get customer feedback.

18. Strategies are aimed at achieving year-on-year growth.

19. Resources and capabilities are shared across the organization.

20. Benchmarking against competitors is regular and continuous.

21. The risks associated with strategic options are identified.

22. The organization identifies and implements risk-mitigation strategies.

23. The product/market portfolio is managed strategically.

24. Environmental developments in the future are reviewed regularly.

25. Strategy can be implemented quickly.

ENVIRONMENT FOR AN ENTREPRENEURIAL ORGANIZATION

Management is an art not a science and the appropriate form required for an effective architecture depends on the environment. It can be sectorally and/or geographically dependent. It can vary with the nature of the entrepreneurial intensity undertaken. The point is that there can be no prescriptive blueprint. This means structuring the organization so that each operating unit can be organized in such a way as to best deal with the environment it faces possibly with structures within structures, sub-cultures within cultures and different approaches to leadership and management within an overall approach.

Entrepreneurial firms thrive in environments of change, chaos, complexity, competition, uncertainty and even contradiction. Their interconnectedness tends to amplify small initial changes. This rapid, continuous interconnected change makes for instability and unpredictability and it means that traditional forms of strategic planning no longer work. These sorts of markets are likely to be characterized by rapid technological change in markets where this is important and valued by customers – for example, because of their need for knowledge and information. Such markets offer considerable first-mover advantage and reinforce the importance of a rapid response to developments. Markets might be highly price-sensitive, with low barriers to entry and high economies of scale. New competitors might be emerging all the time and these new competitors might be very price-competitive and/or good at innovating. New markets could be emerging and the whole structure of the market might be changing, with many mergers or takeovers. In these circumstances, customers might be seen as promiscuous as their 'needs' change rapidly and, as a result, the industry spends increasing amounts on advertising in order to get their attention. As product life-cycles shorten, all this can lead to an unbalanced product/service portfolio. Adding to all these problems might be rapid economic and social change, pressures for greater corporate social responsibility and problems in attracting suitable staff. This is the sort of environment that an entrepreneurial architecture is designed to deal with. These characteristics are shown in Table 16.5.

Table 16.5 Characteristics of an environment where an entrepreneurial architecture would be beneficial

1. The commercial environment is highly competitive.
2. The commercial environment is unstable and unpredictable.
3. The commercial environment changes rapidly and continuously.
4. Technological change is rapid and strongly influences the market.
5. The structure of the market is changing.
6. There are no barriers to entry in the market.
7. New competitors are emerging all the time.
8. The future is highly uncertain.
9. Predicted economic and societal changes will greatly impact the industry.
10. There are continual innovations in the industry.
11. Innovation is valued by customers.
12. There is considerable 'first-mover advantage' with innovation.
13. The market is highly price-sensitive.
14. There are large, achievable economies of scale.
15. Customers are *not* loyal.
16. Customer needs are changing all the time.
17. Competitors innovate continuously.
18. Competitors are very price-competitive.
19. There is heavy expenditure on marketing within the industry.
20. There are many mergers and takeovers in the industry.
21. New markets are emerging continually.
22. The product/service portfolio is unbalanced.
23. Suppliers exert a great deal of power.
24. Good managers and staff are difficult to attract.
25. Developments in the industry depend very much on knowledge and information.

CORPORATE ENTREPRENEURSHIP AUDIT

The Corporate Entrepreneurship Audit (CEA) offers a structured, research-based approach to assessing the entrepreneurial orientation of organizational architecture. This diagnostic tool can be applied to any level of organization – the organization as a whole, a division, a department and so on. It provides a means of analyzing potential areas for improvement based upon issues flagged in this book, rather than a crude pass/fail test. This involves making informed judgements about certain criteria and, as such, is subjective rather than objective. It does not answer the question as to why things are the way they are.

➥ **Part 1** catalogues the observed characteristics of an entrepreneurial organization using the four dimensions of organizational architecture – leadership and management, culture, structure and strategies – in 100 statements concerning the organization. These statements are derived from the checklists in Tables 16.1, 16.2, 16.3 and 16.4. Respondents are asked to circle the appropriate score for each statement from 0 (= not true at all) to 6 (= very true). Scores are totalled and mapped onto a CEA Results Grid, which shows results in percentages. This allows the company profile to be compared against competitors in the industry (if available).

➥ **Part 2** lists 25 statements concerning the commercial environment the organization faces, to help assess whether it 'fits' with an entrepreneurial architecture. These statements are based on Table 16.5. Respondents are asked to circle the appropriate score for each statement from 0 (= not true at all) to 6 (= very true). Scores are then totalled and mapped onto the results grid. The higher the score, the more competitive the commercial environment. This can then be compared to the company CEA profile and a judgement made about whether this 'fits' with the environmental profile.

A paper-based version of the CEA and the Results Grid is available on the companion website. There is also an interactive version that will analyze the responses and provide a company and an environmental profile similar to the one below (web address). The profile in Figure 16.4 shows an organization with a high entrepreneurial orientation but an uneven profile: Leadership and management 70 per cent; Culture 90 per cent; Structure 50 per cent; Strategy 60 per cent. It should be possible to determine the reasons for the low 'structure' score by reviewing the score to individual statements, thus highlighting areas of 'weakness'. Similar analysis can be applied to the other areas of organizational architecture. The profile also shows a commercial environment score of 80 per cent, indicating it is highly competitive. It would be expected that an organization in a highly competitive environment would have a high CEA score and a uniform profile over the four architectural areas.

The CEA is a snapshot at a point in time based upon your judgements, and possibly those of others within the organization. It weights each characteristic and/or criteria equally. Research indicates that some characteristics and/or criteria influence innovation more than others and the importance of these characteristics and/or criteria is therefore likely to vary from firm to firm and depend on the environment within which the firm operates. It is therefore not a simple pass/fail test of entrepreneurial orientation. It requires interpretation and interrogation. Combining the detailed results with an understanding of the strategic direction the organization is taking and in the context of its portfolio of operations gives the respondent the opportunity to really understand, not only the entrepreneurial orientation of the organization, but also how this might be improved. This involves making informed judgements about certain characteristics and/or criteria and, as such, the CEA is a subjective rather than an objective tool. It does not answer the question as to why things are the way they are. It should be used as a basis for a detailed discussion about the architecture of the organization – understanding what the underlying causes of the CEA results are and why they are important. In looking at this detail, never forget to also look at the commercial results generated by the organization – whether or not it is performing well in its industry.

Organizational architecture and environment profile

Figure 16.4 An example of a CEA profile

CASE INSIGHT 16.1
Alphabet (5): Google

USA

ENTREPRENEURIAL ARCHITECTURE

In 2015 the ubiquitous internet giant Google changed its name, under a corporate restructuring, to become Alphabet. Google remained the name of Alphabet's chief operating subsidiary and revenue earner. There have been four previous Alphabet Case insights that have looked at aspects of the new company:

➡ 5.4 looked at the reasons for Google's restructuring.
➡ 7.2 looked at the managerial and cultural consequences of this restructuring.
➡ 13.4 looked at how X Development operates.
➡ 15.3 looked at how Alphabet monetizes and transfers knowledge from acquisitions.

This case considers how Google achieved its dominant market position prior to the restructuring in 2015.

Growth strategies

Google is known for the power of its search engine algorithm and the elegance of its business model that matches text ads to searches. Its spectacular growth has come through organic growth combined with new product development, acquisitions and partnerships to take it beyond its core search engine business. Google exhibited many of the internal architectural features of an entrepreneurial organization as well as following many widely used entrepreneurial growth strategies. Its strategy has always been to develop or enter and then dominate new and related markets as quickly as possible. It has expanded into new geographic markets and, at the same time, developing (or buying into) new products/services that can be delivered on the internet into these markets. It has absorbed knowledge and learning from these acquisitions very efficiently and effectively.

Google has become the dominant internet browser used in the West. It has made effective use of the vast information it has on users, allowing it to provide 'real-time' advertising, tailored to the search history of users and the advertiser's message, and directing users to Google-related websites for purchases. It has sought to become the dominant player in all the related markets it has entered as quickly as possible and, in doing so, aspired to become what might be described as an 'internet utility', supplying everything customers might want to purchase on the internet as a 'one-stop shop'). This has brought it into direct competition with other tech giants such as Amazon (which started in online retail), Apple (which started in computer hardware), Facebook (the ubiquitous social network) and Microsoft (which started as the supplier of software and operating systems). All of these companies have moved from their origins to converge and compete in this emerging 'internet utilities' market (Case insight 15.4).

Culture

Google is known for its innovative culture. It has an informal corporate culture and regularly features in Fortune magazine's list of the best companies to work for. It still likes to think of itself as still 'small', despite the fact it is anything but. Phrases used to illustrate the culture included 'you can be serious without a suit', 'work should be challenging and challenge should be fun' and 'you can make money without being evil'. It thinks of itself as humorous and has a tradition of creating April Fools' Day jokes. This started in 2000 when it launched MentalPlex, called 'Google's ability to read your mind and visualize the search result you want' (change 'ability' to 'predict' and this is not far short of what Google's algorithms can now do. It tried to add humour to its services). In 2008, it announced 'Gmail Custom' time where users could change the time that the email was sent and in 2011 'Gmail Motion', a way of controlling Gmail with body movement. It has even included 'Klingon' as a language selection for its search engine.

Google tries to encourage creativity and innovation in a number of ways. For many years, it was known as one of the best companies to work for in the USA. Many companies that work on building successful teams or encouraging creativity are known to facilitate playful environments. The lobby in Googleplex has a piano, lava lamps, old server clusters and a projection of search queries on the wall. The corridors have exercise balls and bicycles. Other playful elements include a slide and a fireman's pole. Recreational facilities – from video games and ping-pong tables to workout rooms – are scattered throughout the campus. It also has functional elements that aid idea generation and dissemination. For example, it has enclosed, noise-free projectors that can be left on at all times and employees can automatically email meeting notes to attendees. As one newspaper commented:

> To visit Google's headquarters in Mountain View, California, is to travel to another planet. The natives wander about in T-shirts and shorts, zipping past volleyball courts and organic-vegetable gardens while holding their open laptops at shoulder height, like waiters' trays. Those laptops are gifts from the company, as is free food, Wi-Fi-enabled commuter buses, healthcare, dry cleaning, gyms, massages and car washes, all designed to keep its employees happy and on campus. (Ken Auletta, The Guardian, 4 March 2010)

Pictures and videos of the campus can be seen on their website. For an alternative view, go to: www.youtube.com/watch?v=43wZNGzXjFg.

Google staff are allowed 20 per cent of their time to work on new projects. Services such as Gmail, Google News, Orkut, and AdSense all emerged from this initiative. Staff are encouraged to explore new technological developments and unmet market needs and 'experiment':

Google's "just-try-it" philosophy is applied to even the company's most daunting projects, like digitizing the world's libraries. Like every new initiative, Google Book Search began with a makeshift experiment aimed at answering a critical question; in this case: how long does it take to digitize a book? To find out, Larry Page [co-founder of Google] and Marissa Mayer [a former senior Google executive] rigged up a piece of ply-wood with a couple of clamps and proceeded to photograph each page of a 300 page book, using a metronome to keep pace. With Mayer flipping pages, and one half of Google's founding team taking digital snap shots, it took 40 minutes to turn the ink into pixels. An optical character recognition program soon turned the digital photos into text, and within five days the pair had ginned up a piece of software that could search the book. That kind of step-wise, learn-as-you-go approach has repeatedly helped Google to test critical assumptions and avoid making bet-the-farm mistakes (Gary Hamell, The Future of Management, Boston MA: Harvard Business School Press, 2007).

Google has promoted a benevolent image, as embodied in its 'Do no evil' motto. It supports philanthropy. The not-for-profit Google.org creates awareness about climate change, global public health and poverty. The company is also a noted supporter of network neutrality. In 2011, it donated €1 million to the International Mathematical Olympiad and has supported gay rights. However, this aspect of the organization has been seriously dented by a range of recent revelations, for example about its use of the personal data it holds on individuals, its tax minimization practices, its attitudes towards sexual harassment and other employment practices. Many of these predate the 2015 restructuring. There can also be little doubt that it has exploited its dominant market position.

Structures and team working

Google has a flat, decentralized organization structure with lean hierarchies. There is low job specialization, emphasizing principles rather than rules and horizontal communication. It is highly democratic and tightly interconnected – like the internet itself. It has been said that this comes the founders' own dislike of authority. Each manager has about twenty people reporting to them. Almost half of Google's employees are involved in product development working in small multidisciplinary teams of three LINK four people. All of the staff involved in product development work in small teams of between three or four people. Larger teams get broken down into smaller sub-teams, each working on specific elements of the bigger project. Each team has a leader that rotates depending on the changing project requirements. Most staff work in more than one team and are allowed 20 per cent of their time to work on new projects.

Innovation strategies

Marissa Mayer was one of Google's earliest employees. She helped launch over 100 products and features, including Gmail and Google Instant, before being promoted to head up the newly formed Geographic and Local Services, as Vice President Search Products. She developed Google's 9 Principles of Innovation (20 February 2008, www.fastcompany.com):

1. Innovation, not instant perfection: Google has a low-cost, try-it-out, experimental approach to new product development. Because of the mould-breaking nature of many of Google's innovations, it wants its products to be launched early and then developed and perfected as it learns what the market wants: 'The beauty of experimenting in this way is that you never get too far from what the market wants.

The market pulls you back.' The problem has been that many of these products have been far from perfect when launched.

2. Ideas come from everywhere: The company has several technology-enabled solutions to foster creativity amongst employees. Google Ideas acts as a repository for innovative ideas. It enables employees to share new ideas on products, services and to comment on the ideas of others. The tool also has a feature to rate the ideas submitted on a scale of 0–5, 0 denoting 'Dangerous or harmful if implemented' and 5, 'Great idea! Make it so': 'We have this great internal list where people post new ideas and everyone can go on and see them. It's like a voting pool where you can say how good or bad you think an idea is. Those comments lead to new ideas.'

3. A license to pursue your dreams: Google has built in slack to encourage creativity through its 70/20/10 Rule – staff spend 70 per cent of their time working on their core projects, 20 per cent on ideas that are closely related to their projects, and 10 per cent on any other ideas they would like to pursue. Half of Google's new product launches have originated from this scheme, including two of Google's best-known products, Gmail and Google News. Google News was created by Krishna Bharat. After the 9/11 terrorist attacks, he found himself tracking information from several news sites. This caused him to come up with the idea of creating a tool that could trawl through different news sites to cluster the type of information he wanted to read. Google magnified this idea to form a complete news service on their site. Google also encourage rapid, low-cost experimentation early in the life of projects so as to continually check feasibility.

4. Morph projects, don't kill them: Google believes that every idea that makes it to its labs must have the kernel of a good idea somewhere, even if the market does not respond to it, and the trick is to see how it can be used. And few innovators are able to succeed every time. Consider, for example, the case of Lars Rasmussen and Jens Rasmussen, who created Google Maps. The Rasmussen brothers also created Google Wave – billed as a tool that would transform online communication and collaboration – which failed spectacularly to live up to its promise to be a social collaborative platform that would replace email and was closed down in 2009. However, Google was positive about learning from such failures, stressing that, whilst there may not have been the user adoption they would have liked, the knowledge from the technological developments would not be lost. Indeed, it viewed Wave almost as an experiment. Indeed, the first of Google's Principles of Innovation is to launch early then develop the product into what the market really wants – only sometimes the market really does not want the product.

5. Share as much information as you can: Google has its own intranet called MOMMA which allows staff to share information. Every week staff jot down the five or six things they have been working on. These are indexed and made into a giant web page allowing anyone to search to find what staff are working on that week. Google also encourages employees to pay attention to what is happening in the outside world – new ideas from many different sources. For example, it hosts regular 'Tech Talks' with speakers including distinguished researchers from around the world and experts in other fields, such as artists, writers, and chefs. Google shows that it values these talks by including the number an employee has hosted in staff performance reviews.

6. Users, users, users: Innovations need users, since it is users that generate a marketplace. With a marketplace, a business model will emerge. This is Google's market focus.

7. Data are apolitical: Google believes design is a science, not an art, relying on data: 'Run a 1 per cent test (on 1 per cent of the audience) and whichever design does best against the user happiness metrics over a 2-week period is the one we launch.'

8. Creativity loves constraints: Google engineers love to be told something cannot be done and then proving you wrong. Google also recognizes the tension between staff freedom and control and the need to have a senior supporter for any project going forward for development. It believes staff need a sponsoring manager to be a 'guardrail' – setting reasonable boundaries within which they can be creative and experiment with

ideas. The sponsor and employee must develop an experimentation plan that covers details such as expectations, timelines and resource commitments. Key milestones for the development of the idea are agreed and regular check-in points scheduled where the employee can update the sponsor on the experiment's progress. Sponsors build 'dashboards' to capture the key metrics of their programmes. They take any opportunity to share these metrics with their peers and superiors so as to remind them about the value of their programme.

9. You're brilliant? We're hiring: Google employs only people who it thinks are exceptionally talented. It believes you need to attract the right sort of people to build a successful innovating organization – people with ambition and a high regard for themselves. Then you need to build the team.

Partnering

In contrast to Apple, which jealously guards its iPhone operating system (iOS), Google's Android system is open access and it is interesting to compare the success of these two very different strategies. Anyone can write Apps for Android, compared to Apple's strict control of its Apps store and a resulting problem is that quality can be variable. Manufacturers can use the operating system free of charge, thereby encouraging the development of a wide range of phones, compared to Apple's limited range. As a result, the Android system now accounts for some 87 per cent of smartphone sales worldwide (mainly by Samsung) compared with Apple's 13 per cent. However, in 2015 it was estimated that whilst about 70 per cent more Apps are downloaded from Google Play than Apple's App Store, the revenue generated by the Apps Store was about 70 per cent higher. However, App sales through Google Play do not tell the full story as Google expects income to come from advertising, capitalizing on a user's location. Unlike Apple's monopoly on Apps, Android's open access means any company can set up an App store. Ironically, when Amazon opened what it called the 'Appstore' in 2011 (named despite the best efforts of Apple) it was a closed system, monitored and controlled by Amazon, just like Apple's own App Store.

Google has also partnered with numerous organizations, involved in a range of activities, from research to advertising. Examples include Sun Microsystems to share and distribute each other's technologies, AOL to enhance each other's video search services, Fox Interactive Media (part of News Corporation) to provide search and advertising, and GeoEye to provide satellite images for Google Earth.

Corporate venturing

Google has pursued an aggressive policy of acquisition, focusing mainly on small venture capital-backed start-up companies. By 2017, it had acquired over 200 companies, which have resulted in some key developments: Google Earth, for example, came out of the acquisition of Keyhole in 2004 and Google Voice out of the acquisition of Grand Central in 2007. It also purchased YouTube in 2006, DoubleClick in 2007 (which developed technology that allows Google to determine user interests and target advertising), video software maker On2 Technologies and social network Aardvark in 2009 and, in 2010, hardware start-up Agnilux and web-based teleconferencing company Global IP Solutions. Case insight 15.3 looked at how these companies were 'absorbed' within Google and 'monetized'.

Google had its own venture capital arm, Google Ventures (now called GV), which provided seed, venture, and growth stage funding to technology companies that were thought might be strategically important to the company. Between 2008 and 2010 it invested in some 30 firms in areas as diverse as educational software and biotechnology. Its annual budget of $100 million was invested in amounts of between $50,000 and $50 million and companies are often sold off (for example, the gaming company, Ngmoco) or floated on the stock market (for example the holiday rentals and bed-and-breakfast portal Home Away). Google also had Google Capital (now called Capital G) which was a late-stage growth venture capital fund focused on larger, growth technology companies.

These structures were separate from the finance for Google's in-house projects, which in turn had projects as diverse as driverless cars and new sources of alternative energy.

Future growth

In 2015 Google still generated most of its revenue through advertising with over 40 per cent from clicks (cost per click). This included sales of Apps, purchases made through Apps, digital content on Google and YouTube, Android and licensing and service fees. Whilst its core search business was an enormous revenue generator, it was felt that there were limits to this and the need to find other sources of income for the future was seen as paramount.

Whilst future income might come from internal development like driverless cars that could move the company into new products/markets and change its scope of activities, it was thought that existing products/markets offered additional opportunities. For example:

➡ The Android operating system – this had become as ubiquitous as the Google search engine and other mobile technology companies were now dependent on it. The question was 'how'?
➡ YouTube – increasingly television was becoming an on-demand service and moving onto mobile platforms.
➡ The web browser Chrome – this already had 15 per cent of the market with more than 120 million users and was being developed into a whole PC operating system that would compete with Microsoft Windows. Google already had contracts with Acer and Samsung.
➡ Cloud services – selling computer applications like email and word processing directly to business users.
➡ China – this was the largest and fastest-growing market for mobile technologies in the world and Google was not represented there. Apple had agreed to various government restrictions (such as housing its servers in China) and had gained market share against local rivals. It was tempting to do the same.

However, probably the biggest opportunity Google faced was how to exploit the treasure chest of personal information it held on users and the algorithms it used to target messages to them. Many analysts argued that the company's real future revolved around information-intensive services, rather than around matching platforms for advertising and here they might adopt a two-pronged strategy:

1. Learning as much as possible about each and every user of its services by offering heavily subsidized services. These data allow Google to predict our information needs in a way that does not always require us to type in a search query – for example, from information in our emails or about our location – and then sending it to us through a smart device of any kind.
2. Leverage all these data to build advanced services, many based on artificial intelligence, which can be sold to other companies and governments. For example, it might be used to send users unsolicited, free product trials based upon the things they browse, buy and can afford, or it could offer 'smart healthcare' powered by this intelligence and paid for either by individuals or governments. It was suggested that Google extend its customer base from companies to governments, and not just for healthcare. It already had close links with the US government through its work on government-related contracts and subsequent press reports raised the question whether this work was for the intelligence services, to which it also appeared to have close links (*The Guardian*, 20 December 2018).

The sheer scale of Google's data treasure trove and its dominance in that market gives it an advantage over competitors, but the virtual world is changing rapidly and Google's lack of success in getting into the social networking market is an area of weakness often commented on in the press. Millions of Facebook users navigate from page to page according to friends' recommendations, in contrast to the complicated algorithms underpinning the Google search engine. And the data generated by Facebook is every bit as valuable, and you might say dangerous, as that generated by Google. As one newspaper commented; 'Google looks positively ancient to the whiz-kids at Facebook and Twitter. . . . Google is the establishment now, plugged into government and Wall Street' (*The Sunday Times*, 3 April 2011). But then Facebook also now seems to be losing market share to other social network platforms. Furthermore, in the longer term the rapid rise of the Chinese internet giants (Tencent, Alibaba and Baidu) and their links to government may prove to be far more threatening than anything else.

Visit the website: abc.xyz/investor

Questions:

1. List the main elements of Google's growth strategies up to 2015.
2. Has the strategy of expanding into new markets at the same time as developing new products or services been wise? If so, why?
3. How has Google mitigated the risks of this strategy?
4. How has Google encouraged creativity and innovation?
5. Analyze the Strengths, Weaknesses, Opportunities and Threats facing Google in 2015.
6. Analyze the pros and cons of the growth opportunities facing Google in 2015. Which of these has Alphabet pursued and why?

All information in this case study is collected and interpreted by its author and does not represent the opinion of Alphabet or Google.

 CASE INSIGHT 16.2
LEGO®

ENTREPRENEURIAL TRANSFORMATION

LEGO, the well-known children's building system, has been around for a long time and in an age when new toys come and go with astonishing rapidity and technology-based toys like computer games are reaching astonishing heights of sophistication, it might be difficult to understand the enduring market appeal of these basic building bricks. Now called LEGO Systems in Play, over 60 billion LEGO bricks and other elements are made every year: indeed, if all the LEGO bricks ever produced were divided among the world's population each person would have at least 100 bricks. The name LEGO is an abbreviation of two Danish words 'leg godt', meaning 'play well'. The company was founded by Ole Kirk Kristiansen in 1932 and it remains a privately owned fourth-generation family business. It is now one of the world's largest and most profitable manufacturers of toys, with its head office in Billund, Denmark and branches throughout the world. The traditional interlocking LEGO brick has twice been named toy of the century – first by *Fortune* magazine and then by the British Association of Toy Retailers.

The LEGO range

The brick was launched In its present form in 1958. However, the LEGO Group's product range is now far wider than just the world-famous LEGO Classic brick. It also includes LEGO DUPLO and LEGO Juniors, which are targeted at younger children, extending the target market age from 1½ to 11 years. Since the late 1970s, LEGO products have been sold not just as building bricks but as medium of creative expression for children to start stories around various themes. The company has developed numerous play themes for all of its products, including fire stations, police, airports, knights, castles and racing cars. LEGO City consists of sets of bricks, together with mini-figures, that can be used to build these themed scenes. Characters and scenes from movies or cartoons like LEGO Harry Potter, Spiderman, Bob the Builder, Star Wars and Batman – produced under licence – are also available. There are also newer products like BIONICLE, which allows children to construct action figures like knights and to develop a detailed online world into which they can be placed to play within a story. The LEGO Group has also moved into different market segments. In 2012, LEGO Friends was introduced, aimed at young girls, allowing them to construct scenes from everyday life or from the world of fairy tales. LEGO Group now produces video games (e.g., LEGO Star Wars) and even produces its own movies. These developments have evolved through four eras:

1. The first was developing construction and building as the central elements in play, augmented in 1962 by the introduction of the LEGO wheel.
2. The second era evolved as LEGO products gained motion through wheels, small motors and gears through the introduction of LEGO Technic in 1972.
3. The third era, which evolved alongside the second in the 1970s, was role play, which saw the launch of LEGO mini-figures. This heralded the development of a new business model called 'System within the System' based upon play themes, the first ones being LEGOLAND® Town, LEGOLAND® Castle and LEGOLAND® Space.
4. The fourth era introduced intelligence and behaviour like the LEGO MINDSTORMS (robot building sets).

The 2003 crisis

However, LEGO Group's current success has been hard-won. In 2003, the company reported a record loss of $240 million, spawning rumours that it might be taken over. It had lost confidence in the brick as the core of its product offering and many of its efforts to innovate with the aim of becoming a lifestyle brand for families with children – both within and outside its traditional business – had proved to be unprofitable or outright failures. Furthermore, costs were not being controlled effectively, with sales of individual components not being matched to production in the supply chain. LEGO's CEO and owner, Kjeld Kirk Kristiansen (grandson of the founder), decided to stand down, appointing Jorgen Vig Knudstorp in his place in 2004. Knudstorp (known as JVK), a one-time management consultant, had joined the company as director of strategic development in 2001. Upon his appointment, he was given a clear mandate for radical change by the Kristiansen family who injected additional funding of $178 million, giving the company space for a turnaround. And although Kjeld Kirk Kristiansen stood down as CEO, he worked closely with JVK and other members of the board and the leadership team to pinpoint the company's problems.

The turnaround involved a number of parallel initiatives to halt the decline in sales, cut costs and focus on improving cash flow. Cutting costs and improving cash flow was vital. Without this, the company might not have survived. At this time, competition from similar, lower-priced products was eating into sales. Based in the high-cost country of Denmark, LEGO Group's supply chains were long and expensive. They were also geared to supplying small retailers rather than the big-box stores, resulting in high levels of stockholding. To address this, the company had to eliminate inefficiencies and re-gear to compete in the new retail world. The team decided to approach this issue holistically, analyzing the entire process from product development to sourcing, manufacturing and finally distribution. Whilst the team believed the company was good at innovating, it also believed that there were just too many innovation projects and that they were not being well-managed. It discovered that each successive generation of innovation in established product lines seemed to deliver slimmer margins as product complexity increased. Designers were simply not factoring in the price of materials or costs of manufacture when they developed new products.

The first thing they did was to reduce the number of unique pieces manufactured from more than 13,000 to 6,000 and to establish new manufacturing bases in the lower-cost countries of Hungary and Mexico (by 2014, this had been extended to the Czech Republic, with a new factory planned for China to cover the growing Asian market). Individual products were cut as a review revealed that just 30 per cent of products were responsible for 80 per cent of sales. A pirate kit included eight pirates with 10 different legs, developed without a thought of the cost of manufacture or stockholding. Indeed, two-thirds of the company's stock turned out to be items that were no longer manufactured. With more than 11,000 suppliers, growing all the time as designers sought new materials to develop new products, there was plenty of scope to rationalize sourcing and leverage the buying power of the company. The Danish factory was one of the largest injection-moulding operations in the world and yet it operated a fragmented, batch production system, responding to frequent changes in production demands. This was inefficient and capacity utilization was only 70 per cent. Although the 200 largest toy chains generated over two-thirds of sales, LEGO Group devoted as much effort to supplying the thousands of smaller shops that generated the balance, often supplying them with small orders at short notice.

A team approach to driving transformation

JVK adopted a twin-track approach to driving the transformation, each involving different multidisciplinary teams. A leadership team developed the strategies and a management team, consisting of managers from sales, IT, logistics and manufacturing drove the changes at an operational level. The management team held daily meetings in a war room to prioritize and coordinate the changes, assigning responsibility for specific initiatives to individual managers. They tracked progress, anticipating resistance and dealing with obstacles as they arose. The room itself had whiteboards and often these were covered in action lists and schedules. JVK himself would visit the war room regularly, checking on the status of various initiatives and always pushing to get the changes through as quickly as possible. The teams worked in a very open way, debating how to change in the first place but, once agreed, only deviating from it should the approach prove ineffective.

The leadership team also operated in an open way, taking time for consensus building, between themselves and the management team. The workforce was also involved and the need for the changes – including redundancies – was made clear. The policy was one of transparency, including debate around the realities of the situation. The workforce was involved in how redundancies would be implemented. The belief was that, although this process took time, the changes would be more effectively implemented and the benefits more lasting if they were understood and, as far as possible, staff bought into them.

Early wins

The team piloting changes to sourcing was headed by LEGO Group's former chief financial officer, Jesper Ovesen, with the intention of signalling the importance of this initiative. The first task it tackled was the cost of the different coloured resins that went into the production of the bricks – the largest material cost the company faced. The team also included the head of product innovation and the manager of the company's supply chain. It cut the number of coloured bricks by almost half, cut back on slow-moving lines and slashed the number of different suppliers by 80 per cent. By leveraging its buying power, LEGO Group was able to cut resin costs by a massive 50 per cent. The rapid success of this initiative and its effect on the finances of the company led to an early sense of optimism – a quick win for the change initiative that increased confidence that they would succeed.

Integrating cost into design

One management team took on the task of encouraging designers to consider costs in their new product decisions. They developed a cost matrix that allowed them to see the costs associated with making changes to established bricks. In this way, designers were encouraged to think about designing to price points, using existing bricks as far as possible and generally reducing product complexity. Cutting the number of resins and bricks made it easier to simplify the production cycles. Specific moulds were assigned to specific machines and set production cycles established based upon monthly sales schedules. The leadership team assigned decision rights and protocols for changing production schedules so that accountability for changes was clear. The manufacturing of some of LEGO Group's simpler products was outsourced. At the same time, manufacturing was also moved to lower-cost countries. However, by selecting countries close to its main markets at the time it cut its delivery lead times, resulting in a further net saving. Logistics were also rationalized, with providers reduced from 26 to 4, reducing costs by a further 10 per cent.

Partnering with retailers

Finally, the marketing team started working more closely with the large retailers. LEGO Group had previously failed to marry up sales forecasts of individual components with production in the supply chain, resulting in high levels of stockholding. By working more closely with these large retailers and offering customized, big-box products, it was better able to match supply with demand. It was also better able to provide marketing support. There was the added advantage of this partnering providing a greater insight into buyer behaviour and market trends – helping with product development.

The various efficiency gains were forecast to yield savings of over $200 million. As a result, the LEGO Group returned to profitability in 2005 – a rapid turnaround by any standards. Restoring profitability and getting the core business right – product development, sourcing, manufacturing and distribution – allowed JVK and his team to focus once more on creativity and innovation, the elements that would give the company sustainable competitive advantage.

Embedding innovation in the organization

Perhaps the most interesting of the changes JVK introduced was the more focused approach to innovation – despite the fact that it was thought to be an inherent strength. Over the decades, the LEGO Group has proved to be good at innovation, which was deep-rooted in the corporate culture. By 2003, however, customers and retailers felt it had wandered too far away from its original concept of a 'creative building experience' and had to get back to basics whilst continuing to innovate. As a result, it developed its Innovation Matrix to help identify, staff, and coordinate the different types of innovation needed to develop new products over the crisis period. This acted as a guide for restructuring the company and clarifying the specific innovation responsibilities of each department. The company assigned responsibility for innovation to four groups or departments;

➡ The functional groups – such as sales or manufacturing;
➡ The Concept Lab – which developed fundamentally new products and play experiences;
➡ Product and Marketing Development (PMD) – which developed the next generation of existing products and innovated on existing play themes, packaging and marketing campaigns;
➡ Community, Education and Direction (CED) – which supported customer communities and tapped them for product ideas, managed the retail chain, the online store and educational-market offerings and created on-line play experiences.

It also introduced a cross-functional Executive Innovation Governance Group to coordinate the process of innovation – to decide on the portfolio of innovation projects to be undertaken, delegate authority for each new development across the four groups, and allocate resources and monitor developments.

These four groups or departments influenced eight areas of innovation. The functional groups were given responsibility for innovation in areas where the degree of innovation could vary widely:

1. Core processes – sales, operations and financial planning, performance management.
2. Enabling processes – forecasting, marketing planning.

The Concept Lab (with its high degree of innovation) and PMD (with its medium degree of innovation) were given responsibility for innovation in:

3. Messaging – advertising campaigns, websites.
4. Offerings – products and packaging.
5. Platforms – toys' technology elements.

CED was given responsibility for wide-ranging innovation in:

6. Customer interaction – communities, customer services, including the Creativity Labs.
7. Sales channels – retailers, direct to customers.
8. Business models – revenue, pricing.

Current organization

The company is now organized into four strategic business areas, each represented on the Management Board: Operations (manufacturing, procurement, supply chain planning and distribution, engineering and quality, etc.); Marketing Management and Development (organized by geographic areas plus shopper marketing and channel development); Product and Marketing Development (organized by product group plus innovation and consumer marketing); and finally Business Enabling (IT, finance, legal etc.).

Concept and product development now take place primarily within the Product and Marketing Development, which is based at the company's headquarters in Billund. Its creative core is made up of over 200 set-designers recruited from around the world, most coming from an art school background. Applicants attend a workshop at Billund where they go through a process that allows them to demonstrate their creative skills using LEGO bricks. The company plays great store on learning from the creativity of its customers – children – and how LEGO bricks can be used to play games. It has what it calls 'listening posts' in a number of cities around the world. These take children from different countries and encourage them to try out different combinations with the same LEGO pieces and create worlds of their own, which the company can incorporate into its 'play themes' – often then developed further on the company's website. The Labs try to spot trends in children's play, understanding the motivations behind them and translating them into what it means for the company and new product development – effectively trying to systematically understand children's' creativity by observing them at play – also drawing on inputs from customer communities.

Open innovation and crowdsourcing

The story of LEGO MINDSTORMS shows the evolution of LEGO Group's policies to encourage innovation. Strategic partnerships have played an important part in LEGO Group innovations over the years; more recently, however, the company has also relied on customer involvement to leverage innovation (area 6 in the innovation matrix) and has turned to policies of 'open innovation' and 'crowdsourcing'. The story of MINDSTORMS starts in 1984, before digital development really took off, when LEGO entered into a partnership with Media Laboratory at the Massachusetts Institute of Technology. By blending physical and virtual worlds into an integrated play universe, the company came up with new products. LEGO Technic Computer Control was the first tangible product of the partnership, launched in 1986. These programmable bricks paved the way for the introduction in 1998 of LEGO MINDSTORMS, integrating robot technology, electric motors and sensors with LEGO bricks and LEGO Technic pieces such as gears, axles and beams. It enabled children to create and program intelligent LEGO models and rapidly became one of the company's bestselling lines.

The programmable brick at the heart of LEGO MINDSTORMS has undergone several updates. LEGO MINDSTORMS NXT, launched in 2006, includes sensors that detect touch, light, sound and ultrasonic waves. It allows children to build and program their own robot so that it can see, hear, speak, feel and move – in as little as half an hour. The original brick was programmed using proprietary, copyrighted software that ran only on PCs, but in the early 1990s Chris Rogers, a professor at Tufts University in the USA who was using MINDSTORMS for teaching purposes, adapted it to run on Macs using a program produced by a company called National Instruments, later licensing this development back to the LEGO Group. The complexity of these original programs was a key limitation which, curiously, probably explained why over 70 per cent of users were, in fact, adults. Simplification was a key objective for NXT.

The capabilities of the MINDSTORMS have also been used to help develop prosthetic limbs for children. Designed in collaboration with LEGO's Future Lab, the modular prosthetics incorporate myoelectric sensors that register the activity of the muscle in the limb and send a signal to control movement in the attachment. A processing unit in the body of the prosthetic contains an engine compatible with LEGO MINDSTORMS, which allows the wearer to build an extensive range of customized, programmable limbs.

Early in its development, the LEGO Group had decided to use an open innovation approach involving customers. It discovered early in the life of MINDSTORMS that adults like Chris were illegally hacking into their original software and changing it; rather than trying to control or restrict this, however, the LEGO Group decided to facilitate it by making source codes available and allowing hacking as part of the software license. They decided that it would be impossible to predict how customers might use MINDSTORMS and decided instead to encourage experimentation and innovation. The LEGO Group also facilitated the development of online communities and organized robot competitions. For example, in partnership with a US non-profit organization called FIRST (For Inspiration and Recognition of Science and Technology), the LEGO Group established FIRST LEGO League, a worldwide tournament in which children compete by designing their own robots and participate in a series of scientific and mathematical or technical projects. These vibrant user communities comprised not just customers but also suppliers and partners who earn a living from the product, as well as professors, teachers, consultants and others who used MINDSTORMS as part of their day-to-day job. They acted as promoters and champions of MINDSTORMS. The LEGO Group identified this group as vital to the development of NXT and had a development team member whose sole responsibility was to manage this community and ensure they were listened and responded to. But the LEGO Group went further. It identified 'lead customers' and then involved them – without payment – in the development of NXT. Lead customers were among the most advanced users of MINDSTORMS – each inventing new ways to extend the functionality of the original product – and reflected the large customer base of adults. Chris Rogers was designated a lead customer and he reintroduced the LEGO Group to National Instruments, the company that eventually developed the software platform for NXT. Lead customers also helped develop complementary products like sensors, software, books and educational programs. NXT has become the bestselling LEGO product ever.

LEGO Communities

As a result of the success of this open innovation approach, the LEGO Group now has some forty LEGO Ambassadors in over twenty countries representing user communities. They provide dialogue and initiate activities between the LEGO Group and some 220 communities of adult LEGO users called AFOLs (Adult Fans of LEGO). There is also LEGO Club, with some 5 million members across 18 global markets. These communities have their own websites, blogs and discussion forums and organize face-to-face meetings on a regular basis. The LEGO Group also organizes events and exhibitions for them and encourages them to get directly involved in product development. It also has a crowdsourcing website on which these communities are encouraged to suggest ideas for new LEGO products. In 2014, four LEGO Ideas products were launched based on user-developed projects uploaded to the LEGO Ideas website.

LEGO Group has also set up 'Lego Serious Play', a business training/consultancy that aims to foster creative thinking. Participants build metaphors of their organizational identities and experiences and work through imaginary scenarios using LEGO bricks.

LEGO philosophy and values

One of the reasons for LEGO Group's continuing popularity is that it has changed with the market. The company continues to invest large sums around the world to understand changes in children's tastes and to explore new product developments based around its mission 'to inspire children to explore and challenge their own creative potential'. Central to the LEGO philosophy is its ideas about what play is about and its importance. It sees LEGO play as both a way of learning structure and something that can stimulate creative thinking. This effectively spells out how children use LEGO building experiences to build a model and play out an adventure with it.

LEGO Group's brand values can be summed up in six words, with explanations taken from the company's website:

Imagination – Curiosity asks 'Why?' and imagines explanations or possibilities (if. . . then). Playfulness asks 'What if?' and imagines how the ordinary becomes extraordinary, fantasy or fiction. Dreaming it is a first step towards doing it. Free play is how children develop their imagination – the foundation for creativity.

Creativity – Creativity is the ability to come up with ideas and things that are new, surprising and valuable. Systematic creativity is a particular form of creativity that combines logic and reasoning with playfulness and imagination.

Fun – Fun is the happiness we experience when we are fully engaged in something that requires mastery (hard fun), when our abilities are in balance with the challenge at hand and we are making progress towards a goal. Fun is both in the process, and in the completion. Fun is being active together, the thrill of an adventure, the joyful enthusiasm of children and the delight in surprising both yourself and others in what you can do or create.

Learning – Learning is about opportunities to experiment, improvise and discover – expanding our thinking and doing (hands-on, minds-on), helping us see and appreciate multiple perspectives.

Caring – Caring is about the desire to make a positive difference in the lives of children, for our partners, colleagues and the world we find ourselves in, and considering their perspective in everything we do. Going the extra mile for other people, not because we have to but because it feels right and because we care. Caring is about humility – not thinking less of ourselves, but thinking of ourselves less.

Quality – From a reputation for manufacturing excellence to becoming trusted by all – we believe in quality that speaks for itself and earns us the recommendation of all. For us quality means the challenge of continuous improvement to be the best toy, the best for children and their development and the best to our community and partners.

The LEGO Group is adamant that the business is about a greater purpose than just making money, and that these values stem from its ownership structure as a privately-owned family business. These values are in its DNA. Employees become part of the LEGO family and the company is seen in Denmark as almost a religious group – secretive with employees always 'on message' and wary of the outside world (an in-group). JVK has said that he tries to guide things in the company through role modelling and relationships rather than regulation and that he believes this allows the company to be more 'purposeful'.

Toy sales are heavily influenced by movies and TV series and LEGO has been able to tie in many of its sets to successful ones like Harry Potter or Star Wars. However, none of these included LEGO figures, so it was always the company that had to make the association – and pay licence fees. In 2013, the company broke new ground with *The LEGO Movie*. It was an instant success in cinemas and subsequently on DVDs. With this, the LEGO Group took control of its future, becoming less dependent on other non-LEGO movies that might be popular with children. All at once the LEGO figures took on a life of their own.

Change of leadership

Under the leadership of Knudstorp, LEGO was turned, regaining its focus on its core values of product quality, the LEGO legacy and a value for money proposition for both retailers and customers. Clear leadership with an effective management structure focused on profitability based on a premium pricing strategy and a high return on sales.

Revenue growth slowed in 2016, down from 25 per cent in 2015 to 6 per cent, the lowest annual increase in 9 years, hit by weaker demand in its established markets. As a result, the company looked to expand overseas, particularly into China, where it opened a new factory in late 2016. On 1 January 2017, Bali Padda took over as chief executive of LEGO. Aged 60, he had been at Lego for 14 years and had previously served as the company's chief operations officer. Jorgen Vig Knudstorp became chair of the newly created LEGO brand group, whose deputy chair became Thomas Kirk Kristiansen, the great-grandson of the founder. However, Padda did not last long in his new role. In August of the same year, it was announced that he was to be replaced in October by Niels Christiansen, a 51-year-old former chief executive of Danfoss, a Danish manufacturing and technology company, although Padda would stay on in an advisory role.

In September, before Christiansen could arrive, LEGO announced that its revenues had actually fallen 6 per cent in the first half of 2017 – the first time since 2004. Net profits were also down 3 per cent, despite reported double-digit growth in China. As a result, Lego announced plans to cut 1,400 jobs. The company said that the revenue losses were due to a more competitive environment, where the company had to compete not only against its major competitors Mattel and Hasbro, but also against technology companies such as Sony or Microsoft as more children turned to mobile devices for entertainment. Vig Knudstor explained:

We have added complexity into the organization which now in turn makes it harder for us to grow further. As a result, we have pressed the reset-button for the entire group. . . We will build a smaller and less complex organization than we have today, which will simplify our business model in order to reach more children. It will also impact our costs. . . Finally, in some markets the reset entails addressing a clean-up of inventory across the entire value chain. (The Guardian, 5 September 2017)

The Guardian commented that the company was 'paying the price for allowing ranges to proliferate [through over-licencing]. . . and giving cheaper competitors the chance to woo customers.'

Lego Financial information

Billion DKK	2018	2017	2016	2015	2014	2013	2012	2011	2010	2009
Sales	36.4	35.0	37.9	35.8	28.6	25.3	23.1	18.7	16.0	11.7
Gross profit	26.0	24.8	27.4	26.0	20.6	17.9	16.3	13.2	11.6	8.2
GP (%)	71.4	70.7%	72.2	72.6	71.8	70.7	70.6	70.5	72.4	70.3
Overheads	15.2	14.4	15.0	13.7	10.8	9.5	8.7	7.5	6.5	5.2
O'head (%)	41.8	41.1	39.4%	38.4%	37.8	37.7	37.6	40.3	40.5	44.6
Operating profit	10.8	10.4	12.4	12.2	9.7	8.3	7.6	5.7	5.1	3.0
Profit before tax	10.5	10.2	12.4	12.1	9.5	8.2	7.5	5.5	4.9	2.9
Profit %	28.8%	29.1%	32.7%	33.7%	33.2%	32.4%	32.5%	29.4%	30.6%	24.8%
Total assets	31.5	29.9	29.9	27.9	21.4	18.0	16.4	12.9	11.0	7.8
Return on total assets	33.3%	29.1%	37.9%	43.4%	34.0%	44.4%	45.6%	42.6%	44.5%	37.2%

Visit website www.lego.com to see some of the features described in this case. This is more than just a showcase for the company's products; it also allows children to play games, enjoy stories and undertake activities, stimulating ideas and creativity. This is important because stories spur children to play games – and the website encourages those games to include LEGO.

Questions:

1. Does LEGO have an entrepreneurial architecture? Explain.
2. How did LEGO transform itself?
3. How important was the commitment of top management? How did this show itself?
4. How has LEGO embedded creativity and innovation into its DNA?
5. What form does partnering with stakeholders take at LEGO?
6. What lessons do you learn from the development of MINDSTORMS?
7. LEGO is still owned by the Christiansen family. What do you learn from LEGO about the advantages and disadvantages of being a private company?
8. What do you learn from the events in 2017? Research what has happened to LEGO subsequently.

All information in this case study is collected and interpreted by its author and does not represent the opinion of the LEGO Group.

GROUP DISCUSSION TOPICS

1. How does the idea of an 'entrepreneurial orientation' fit with an entrepreneurial architecture?
2. In what circumstances is an entrepreneurial architecture not appropriate?
3. The concept of organizational architecture is an artificial construct. Discuss.
4. The CEA replaces judgement with a simplistic checklist. Discuss.

5. How do you judge where to score an organization on individual questions in the CEA?
6. Should the questions within the CEA be weighted? If so, how do you determine the weightings?
7. Can you really simply add the scores from each question in the CEA to get a meaningful overall score?
8. How can you use the CEA with a multi-product/market organization?
9. How can you use the CEA in a holding company with subsidiaries?
10. How do you decide on the appropriate environment for the CEA? Is it market-, sector-, industry- or geographically-related?
11. How might the CEA be used to undertake research into firm behaviour?
12. What are the shortcomings of the CEA? How might they be remedied?

ACTIVITY

Select an organization and, using the CEA, undertake an audit of its architecture and the environment in which it operates. Assess its strategic direction in more detail using the framework outlined in this chapter. Write a report on your findings that critically analyses the company's architecture.

REFERENCE

Kay, J. (1995) *Foundations of Corporate Success*, Oxford: Oxford University Press.

ONLINE RESOURCES AVAILABLE For further resources relating to this chapter see the companion website at **www.macmillanihe.com/Burns-CEI**

SCORING THE LEADERSHIP STYLE QUESTIONNAIRE

To obtain your leadership orientation rating, score one point for the appropriate response under each heading. If your response is inappropriate you do not score.

Concern for PEOPLE score (maximum score 15)
'Yes' for questions: 2, 4, 8, 10, 17, 19, 21, 23, 27.
'No' for questions: 6, 13, 14, 25, 29, 30.

Concern for TASK score (maximum score 15)
'Yes' for questions: 1, 3, 5, 7, 9, 11, 15, 16, 18, 20, 22, 24, 26, 28.
'No' for question: 12.

Total your scores and plot your position on the Leadership Grid below. As a guide, a score of 5 or less is low and 12 or more is high.

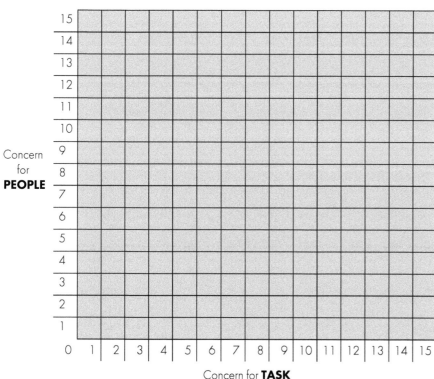

Glossary of Key Terms

Affordable loss The maximum loss you are willing to accept should the venture fail.

Analogy Connections between apparently unrelated things.

Attribute analysis The features of a product/service are examined to see if they might be altered to provide the same or improved benefits to customers.

Authentic leaders Leaders who follow their real values and beliefs – their internal compass.

Bankruptcy When you are unable to pay your debts and a court order is obtained by creditors to have your affairs placed in the hands of an official receiver.

Blue ocean strategy The strategy of finding uncontested market space and creating new demand – essentially market paradigm shift.

Brainstorming A group activity that generates as many ideas as possible without criticism.

Business model A plan for how a business competes, uses its resources, structures its relationships, communicates with customers, creates value and generates profits.

Business plan A formal document setting out the business model for an organization.

Capital Asset Pricing Model (CAPM) A theoretical model used to determine the required rate of return for an asset.

Cognitive heuristics Simplifying strategies or approaches to decision-making, often based upon past experiences. Not guaranteed to be optimal.

Cognitive processes The beliefs, assumptions and attitudes that staff hold in common and take for granted.

Compartmentalizing risk Setting up each operation as a separate legal entity.

Competitive advantage The advantage a firm has over its competitors, allowing it to generate higher sales or profit margins and/or retain more customers than its competitors.

Conglomerate A diversified company with interests in a range of different industries.

Consolidated market A market where there are a few, large competitors, usually in a mature or declining industry.

Consumer The person or organization consuming or using a product.

Contingency theory A theory that emphasizes that the appropriate leadership style is contingent upon the group, task and circumstances.

Core competencies and competences The skills, multiple resources and technologies that enable a company to provide benefits to customers and distinguish them in the marketplace.

Corporate social responsibility (CSR) The combination of business ethics, social responsibility and environmental sustainability.

Creative synthesis Synthesis of technological innovation with market-based innovation.

Critical success factors The activities upon which the success of the venture critically depend.

Cross elasticity of demand How demand reacts to changes in price.

Crowdsourcing A way of opening up collaboration to people connected on the internet to form a kind of online community.

Culture In an organization this is about the web of unspoken, prevalent norms, basic beliefs and assumptions about the 'right' way to behave. Sometimes simply described as 'how it is around here'.

Customer focus (or intimacy) Having a clear understanding of all aspects of customer needs so that customers are satisfied with all aspects of the product/service offering. Usually involves having a close relationship with customers.

Customers Those people who buy your product/service

Danger factor The risk factor multiplied by the controllability factor

Danger index The composite danger factor reclassified in some simplified way.

Delphi method Questioning of experts about future developments until there is some convergence of opinion.

Design thinking (Customer-centric design) A loose set of holistic concepts that approach design from the perspective of solving complex problems for people, rather than just creating distinctive objects or shapes.

Differentiation Using the elements of the marketing mix to make your product/service as different as possible from competitors. When valued by customers, this usually leads to being able to charge a higher price.

Discovery skills Creativity skills practised by entrepreneurs: Networking, Observing, Questioning, Experimenting and Associating.

Dispersed leadership Focus on leadership across all levels and in different forms.

Disruptive innovation Introducing radically new products or services into existing markets. See also **radical innovation.**

Diversification Moving away from core areas of activity into completely new and product/market areas. It can be either 'related' or 'unrelated' to their core activities. Moving into complementary or competitive areas is called horizontal integration. Moving into the supply chain it is called backwards vertical integration. Moving into the distribution chain it is called 'forwards vertical integration'.

Dominant logic Paradigms or conventions that establish a status quo that is rarely questioned.

Double-loop learning A learning cycle that moves from 'knowing-how' to 'knowing-why'. Often called the 'wheel of learning'.

Down-scoping When an organization restructures so as to focus on its core activities.

Early adopters The second group of customers to buy a new product – people with status in their market segment and opinion leaders.

Echo chambers A metaphor describing a situation where beliefs are amplified or reinforced by communication and repetition inside a closed system such as news or social media.

Economies of scale The cost advantages obtained due to the scale of operation, where cost per unit of output decreases with increasing scale.

Economies of scope (synergy) The term used when less of a resource is used because it is spread across multiple activities. Often referred to as '1 + 1 = 3'.

Effectuation (effectual reasoning) An approach to decision-making that is not based solely on deductive reasoning.

Emergent strategy Strategy development that is characterized by reactive solutions to existing problems.

Emotional intelligence An appreciation of yourself, your different circumstances and an ability to adapt your behaviour to meet them and relate to people.

Entrepreneur A person who creates and/or exploits change for profit, by innovating, accepting risk and moving resources to areas of higher return.

Entrepreneurial architecture Organizational architecture that encourages entrepreneurship and innovation on a sustainable basis.

Entrepreneurial intensity An increase in both the degree (or scale) and the frequency of entrepreneurial activity within an organization.

Entrepreneurial leadership Leadership that ensures an organization remains entrepreneurial.

Entrepreneurial orientation (EO) Organizations involved in processes to encourage entrepreneurship and have exhibited a sustained pattern of entrepreneurial behaviour over time.

Entrepreneurial transformation See **strategic renewal.**

External corporate venturing Strategic partnerships, alliances etc. and the investment and acquisition by large companies in strategically important smaller firms.

First-mover advantage The competitive advantage gained by being the first into a market.

Five Forces The five forces that affect the degree of competition in an industry: competitive rivalry; threat of substitution; threat of new entrants; power of buyers; and power of suppliers.

Fragmented market A market where there are a large number of competitors of about the same size, usually in a mature or declining industry.

Franchise A business in which the owner of the name and method of doing business (the franchisor) allows a local operator (the franchisee) to set up a business under that name offering their products or services.

Frugal innovation (or engineering) The process of reducing product complexity by subtracting non-essential features from products.

Futures thinking A holistic perspective that develops a vision about the future state after a change has taken place.

Gap analysis A 'map' of product/market attributes based on dimensions that are perceived as important to customers.

Gazelles Young, high-growth firms.

Generic business models (or marketing strategies) The strategies of low cost, differentiation and/or customer focus that form the basis of developing sustainable competitive advantage. Also called 'value disciplines'.

Gig workers (and economy) Workers seeking temporary, short-term work 'gigs' or projects.

Hierarchy Organizations' structures: tall structures have many managers with a narrower span of control (fewer people reporting to them); flat structures with fewer managers with a wider span of control (more people reporting to them).

Information asymmetry When parties have different levels of information.

Initial public offering (IPO) The stock market launch of a company, where shares are sold to institutional and usually also retail investors

Innovation intensity An increase in both the degree (or scale) and the frequency of innovation within an organization.

Innovation team See **venture team.**

Internal corporate venturing Organizational structures needed to encourage new businesses to develop internally whilst aligning them with the company's existing activities.

Intrapreneur Someone developing new products or businesses and operating within a company that is not owned by them.

Joint venture A more formal strategic partnership based upon a legal agreement, often involving a separate legal entity.

Key operating activities Important operating activities. These may become '**critical success factors'.**

Key performance indicators (KPIs) The **metrics** (see definition) that measure performance in the **key operating activities** (see definition). Often used as metrics to judge the performance of managers against.

Key risk indicators Parameters or events that indicate an increased likelihood of the risk materializing.

Kosoryoku A Japanese word Ohmae used to describe what is needed to develop entrepreneurial strategy in an uncertain environment – something that combined 'vision' with the notion of 'concept' and 'imagination'.

Leadership This is concerned with setting direction, communicating and motivating staff.

Lean start-up The launch of a **minimum viable product** (see definition), then using customer feedback in an iterative fashion to tailor it further to the specific needs of customers.

Life-cycle Stages of life – can refer to a product, market or industry.

Management This is concerned with handling complexity in organizational processes and the execution of work.

Market development Finding new customers or markets for products or services.

Market paradigm shift Changes in established market conventions associated with the creation of radically new markets.

Market penetration Selling your original or existing product or service to the customers in the market segment you originally identified.

Market segments Groupings of customers with similar characteristics.

Marketing mix The five Ps that define your marketing strategy: Product/service; Price; Promotion/communication; People (service); and Place (distribution channels, etc.).

Marketing strategy How the value proposition is delivered to customer segments.

Mental models See **dominant logic.**

Metrics Measures of performance.

Mind maps A map of related ideas from one original idea.

Minimum viable product (MVP) The minimum viable state of a product so that it can be launched and customer feedback then used to better tailor it to customer needs.

Mission The formal statement of business purpose – what the business aims to achieve and how it will achieve it.

Monopoly The exclusive possession or control of the supply of or trade in a commodity or service by a company or group of companies.

Multi-sided markets Using different business models to sell to more than one customer.

Niche business model (or marketing strategy) A business model and strategy that involves high differentiation and customer focus.

Non-metric mapping Maps products in generic groups that customers find similar and then tries to explain why these groupings exist.

Oligopoly A market or industry dominated by a small number of large sellers.

Open innovation A process that links an organization with external individuals and organizations that wishes to generate new ideas, knowledge or to solve problems associated with an innovation.

Organizational ambidexterity The ability to both explore and exploit innovations simultaneously.

Organizational architecture The infrastructure needed to build processes that deliver an organization's vision. It comprises: (leadership and management, culture; structure including systems; and strategies.

Partnership sourcing When firms engage in long-term outsourcing and build a long-term partnership with the outsource companies.

Penetrated market The size of the SAM you capture.

Performance metrics See **metrics.**

PESTEL analysis Tool to help thinking about future developments in the wider environment. An acronym for Political, Economic, Social, Technological, Environmental and Legal changes.

Perceptual mapping Maps the attributes of a product within specific categories.

Pivoting Changing your business model and/or strategy.

Potential market The size of a general market that might be interested in buying a product.

Power distance The degree of inequality among people that the community is willing to accept.

Product development Developing a completely new or modifying product or service.

Product expansion Developing product or service variations that meet the needs of different market segments.

Product extension Extending a successful brand to similar but different products or services that might be purchased by the same customers.

Product modification Small and evolutionary modifications of existing products in terms of quality, function or style.

Radical innovation The creation of radically new products or services, including **market paradigm shift** (see definition).

Related diversification Diversification into related areas where you have some product or market knowledge and/or expertise.

Relational contracts The strong, long-term relationships between stakeholders. Based on trust, despite being unwritten they form tacit contracts concerning how to behave.

Repertory grid A more systematic extension of non-metric mapping that uses market research to group similar or dissimilar products and to explain the differences.

Risk factor The probability of occurrence multiplied by the impact of the risk event.

Risk index The composite risk factor reclassified in some simplified way.

Scalability The potential to scale-up and grow.

Scenario planning A technique that tries to assess how possible future situations might impact on a firm.

Served available market (SAM) The size of the target market segment you wish to serve within the TAM.

Service dominant logic The implications for the idea that, rather than the product, customers buy the services it delivers.

Shared cognition The sharing of goals, effective communication and transfer of knowledge between partners in a business.

SMART performance metrics SMART performance metrics are: Specific for purpose; Measurable; Achievable; Relevant to the success of the organization; and Time-constrained.

Social networks and media Communication hosted on the internet or on smartphones, such as texting, tweeting or blogging, includes social networking sites such as Facebook, Twitter and YouTube.

Strategic alliance A form of partnership whereby separate organizations come together to pursue an agreed set of objectives.

Strategic entrepreneurship See **strategic renewal.**

Strategic intent A strong underlying vision of what a company might become.

Strategic learner The learning from a 'strategy thinker' – looking at the big picture, trying to find patterns over time and looking for complex interactions so as to understand the underlying causes of problems. See also **double-loop learning.**

Strategic options Actions you might undertake if risks or opportunities materialize.

Strategic renewal Changing the strategic direction of the organization so as to better cope with change and innovation. Often linked to a company attempting a turnaround. Also called 'strategic entrepreneurship' and/or 'entrepreneurial transformation.'

Strategic review The process of reviewing the business model with a view to improvement.

Strategic thinker Someone who sees the broad, strategic, organizational perspective – the big picture. This involves taking a longer-term, holistic view of the organization.

Strategizing Continuous assessment of the options about how to make the most of opportunities or avoid risks as they arise.

Switch costs The costs of switching the company you buy a product or service from.

SWOT analysis An analysis of your Strengths and Weaknesses and the Opportunities and Threats that you face.

Synergy (economies of scope) See **economies of scope.**

Systematic risk That part of risk associated with how the share price of a company performs compared to the overall market (measured by the company's beta coefficient).

Target market segment The key customers or groups of customers you are targeting with your marketing mix.

Total available market (TAM) The size of your prospective market. Those in the potential market who might be interested in buying your particular product.

Transactional leadership This is about efficiency and incremental change, reinforcing rather than challenging the status quo; setting goals, putting in place systems, controls and rewards to achieve them.

Transformational leadership This is about inspiration, excitement and intellectual stimulation.

Unicorn A high-growth private company valued at over $1 billion.

Validated learning Using customer to tailor your **minimum viable product (MVP)**.

Value chain The primary and support activities that add value to a product/service.

Value disciplines The strategies of low cost, differentiation and/or customer focus that form the basis of developing sustainable competitive advantage. Also called 'generic business models' and 'generic marketing strategies'.

Value proposition The marketing benefits offered to each target market segment.
Values Core beliefs.
Venture team A group developing new products or businesses and operating within a company that is not owned by them.
Venture capital Equity capital invested in the business by individuals or institutions other than the founders at an early stage in its development.
Vision What the business might become.
Visionary leadership This is about providing a clear vision which focuses people on goals and key issues and concerns.

Subject Index

E

economies of scope, *see* synergy

effectuation   311

emotional intelligence   146, 161, 163, 183, 184, 231, 423

entrepreneurial
  architecture   35–36, 38–50, 418
  character traits   14–17
  intensity   32–33, 37
  leadership   162–165
  orientation (EO)   34–38
  structural characteristics   421–422
  transformation (*see* strategic renewal)

F

financial metrics   295–296

financing risk   218–220

first mover advantage   293–295, 325

five forces (Porter)   274, 370–371

frugal innovation/engineering   280

futures thinking   273–275

G

gap analysis   277–278

General Enterprise Tendency (GET) test   341

generic business models   318–321, 396

growth share matrix   394–398

H

Herrmann Brain Dominance Instrument (HBDI)   233, 352

I

incubators   243–244, 354–355, 360, 389

innovation   58–77
  business model (*see* business model innovation)
  company size and industry   75–77 structure
    definition   59–61
    departments or functions   351–352, 354
    diffusion   73, 367–368
    incremental   60, 74, 132, 165, 219, 231
    intensity   70–72
    radical/disruptive   35, 60–63, 67, 70–72, 74, 75, 116, 165, 207, 219, 375, 383, 404

risk   72–74, 177, 204, 264

team (*see* venture team)

units or divisions   353

Institute of Corporate Responsibility and Sustainability (ICRS)   197

internal politics   345–346

intrapreneur/intrapreneurship   35, 118, 338–344, 354

J

joint venture, *see* partnerships

K

key
  activities   211, 313, 315, 317
  performance indicators (KPIs)   295
  risk indicators   213

Kirton Adapter-Innovator (KAI) test   232

knowledge
  networks   239–240
  tacit   95, 248, 249
  transfer   125, 128, 386, 389

L

leader/leadership   144–165
  Behavior Questionnaire (Sashin)   161
  entrepreneurial   126, 162–165, 422–425
  paradigms   161–162
  personal attributes   146–147
  role   145–146
  style   102, 155–160, 165
  style questionnaire   171–172
  team   423 (*see also* contingency theory)

Lean Canvas   317–318

lean start-up   292–294, 322, 327

learning organization   43–45, 97–98, 151, 153, 182, 248–249, 310

life cycle (product, market or industry)   46, 77, 116, 218, 277, 304, 328, 367–369, 411, 426

M

market
  development   366–367, 369–372
  life-cycle (*see* life cycle)
  multi-sided   323
  niche   77, 319–321, 324, 369
  paradigm shift   63, 66–67, 70, 261, 265, 266, 268, 289, 303, 427
  penetration   303, 366, 367, 369, 427

research   62, 262, 277–278, 292, 294, 301, 303, 327, 328
  segment/segmentation   304, 313, 319, 320
  size   297, 303–304
  testing   301–302

marketing
  mix   313, 318, 371
  plan   313, 317
  strategy   60, 260, 294, 302, 394, 396

mental models, *see* dominant logic

metrics, *see* performance metrics

mind maps   275, 277

minimum viable product (MVP)   293–297, 299–300, 313, 317, 327

mission/vision statement   149, 309–311, 427

motivation   123–126, 151, 153, 159, 343, 423

multi-sided markets, *see* markets

Myers-Briggs Type Indicator (MBTI)   349

N

network effects   368, 370

network structures   128–129

New Venture Creation Framework   313–315

niche, *see* market niche

Non-metric mapping   278

O

operations plan   313, 330

organizational
  architecture   35–36, 41–47, 59, 87, 144, 184, 351, 397, 411, 418, 431–432
  culture (*see* culture)
  learning (*see* learning organization)
  structures   35, 94–95, 113–120, 127–128, 130, 188, 411–412
  values (and beliefs)   87, 105, 129, 145, 147–149, 152, 179, 194, 309, 330, 418, 423

Organizational Cultural Assessment Instrument (OCAI)   102–104

P

partnerships (including strategic alliances and joint ventures)   35, 118, 132–136, 211, 239, 299, 315, 317, 338, 360, 361, 367, 371–372, 383–384, 389, 421, 426, 428

Author Index

Quotes Index